Two year
olds of 2013

29TH EDITION

Two year olds of 2013

29TH EDITION

STEVE TAPLIN

Foreword by Ed Dunlop

FRONT COVER: Toronado beats Dundonnell in the
Champagne Stakes on St Leger day, Doncaster
© Racing Post/Edward Whitaker.

BACK COVER: The author with Ed Dunlop at Tattersalls
© Thoroughbred Photography Ltd.

Published in 2013 by Raceform
High Street, Compton, Newbury, Berkshire, RG20 6NL

A catalogue record for this book is available from the British Library.

ISBN 978-1-908216-79-3

Designed by Fiona Pike

Printed and bound in the UK by CPI Group (UK) Ltd, Croydon, CR0 4YY

Contents

Foreword

For a trainer not necessarily associated with two-year-old racing I'm very well accustomed to Steve appearing at my yard each spring to discuss our new crop of juveniles. Indeed, our association goes back to when I first took over the license at Gainsborough Stables in Newmarket.

Understandably, racing fans are keen to get their hands on this book as early in the season as possible, but trainers need the time to properly assess their two-year-olds. So a publication date in May is a necessary compromise. I'm hoping that sometime soon I'll be assessing a two-year-old that will become my first Derby winner!

Anyone who has previously owned a copy of *Two-Year-Olds* won't need me to explain how valuable the information is. Without it, you will search in vain for reliable information on unraced two-year-olds.

Steve's commitment towards ensuring the book is as factually correct as possible means the reader can rely on the information it contains. Whether a trainer's assessment of a horse in early April remains unchanged throughout the season is another matter! But if past performances are anything to go by the one thing you can be sure of is that the winners from the book will continue to flow throughout the year.

I warmly recommend *Two-Year-Olds of 2013* both as a means of assessing this season's two-year-old races and as a work of reference.

Ed Dunlop
March 2013

Introduction

This year sees the 29th edition of *Two-Year-Olds*, which aims to pinpoint the best of the current crop of juvenile racehorses in England and Ireland.

I was so pleased that Ed Dunlop agreed to endorse my book through his foreword this year because I've been turning up at his Newmarket yard each spring ever since his first full Flat Season in 1995. It is always a pleasure to see him. His expertise as a trainer is exemplified year-in year-out with many big race wins and particularly through the exploits of his superstar fillies Ouija Board and Snow Fairy, along with his current stable star, the admirably genuine Red Cadeaux. All three have all been highly successful on the global stage, as well as in England.

My racing partnership managed yet another winner in 2012 when the Mick Channon-trained Waseem Faris won for us at York. What a great day that was. We have two horses with Mick this year so if you'd like a share in a racehorse without breaking the bank please get in touch.

Those trainers who are either new to the book this year or haven't been in for a while are Toby Coles, Robert Cowell, Tony Coyle, Ed de Giles, Robert Eddery, Paul Fitzsimons, Paul Green, Michael Grassick, Jo Hughes, Olly Stevens and Kristin Stubbs. In common with last year's edition you'll find comments from no less than 85 trainers and I do appreciate the help of each and every one of them.

Each year there are a few amusing names among the two-year-olds and one or two odd facts that the trainer's pass on to me. If you look through the trainer comments you'll come across one two-year-old with no eyebrows and another with just one grey leg! Elvis fans should take a keen interest in Jamie Osborne's "Thewandaofu" (you'll need to think about it) and another name with a musical theme is Peter Chapple-Hyam's "Hay Chewed"!

The two-year-olds are listed under their trainers and naturally my aim is to choose horses most likely to be winners. There are several horses to follow lists, such as the sections 'Fifty To Follow' and 'Star Two-Year-Olds'. These are always useful for those who want to follow a select number of horses. Last year my "Bloodstock Experts" section was once again a very good source of winners. Of the 74 selections that actually ran, 32 of them won. In the 'Bargain Buys' section there were 24 individual winners, with those at the odds of 50-1, 28-1 and 20-1 being particularly rewarding.

In the main body of the book you'll notice a 'star rating' for each of the two-year-olds. Those with three stars or more warrant particular inspection. Please note there are no star ratings for those two-year-olds without any comments from the trainer. I think to give them a rating just based on the pedigree is too speculative.

The following is a rough guide to my description of the ability of family members mentioned in the pedigree assessment of every two-year-old, based upon professional ratings. Please note that these descriptions are standard throughout the book in the vast majority of cases, but there are instances where I rely upon my own judgement of each horse's rating.

Below 60 = moderate
60 - 69 = modest
70 - 79 = fair
80 - 89 = quite useful
90 - 99 = fairly useful
100 - 107 = useful
108 - 112 = very useful
113 - 117 = smart
118 - 122 = very smart
123 - 127 = high-class
128 – 134 = top-class
135 and above = outstanding

To make it easier to find a specific horse the book is comprehensively indexed. So you'll find an index of the horses, their dams and their sires.

The book is divided into the following sections:

- Fifty To Follow.
- Ten to Follow in Ireland.
- Star Two-Year-Olds. This system gives an instant appraisal of the regard in which a horse is held. Those horses awarded the maximum of five stars are listed here.
- Bloodstock Experts Mark Your Card. Bloodstock agents and stud managers suggest potentially smart two-year-olds bought or raised by them.
- Bargain Buys. A list of relatively cheaply bought two-year-olds the trainers feel will turn out to be good deals.
- Two-Year-Olds of 2013. The main section of the book, with each two-year-old listed under the trainer. Trainers' comments (when given) are in italics after the pedigree assessments. Readers should bear in mind that all the trainers' comments come from my interviews, which took part in late March and early April.
- Stallion Reference, detailing the racing and stud careers of sires with two-year-old representatives in the book.

- Stallion Index.
- Racing Trends. An analysis of some juvenile events that regularly highlight the stars of the future. It includes a list of three-year-olds to follow this season.
- Index of Two-Year-Olds.
- Index of Dams.

Inevitably there are some unnamed horses in the book, but please access my website **www. stevetaplin.co.uk** throughout the season for updates on those horses named after the book was published.

I'd like to thank my friend Hilda Marshall, the racing and stud secretaries and of course the trainers for all their help in making the book worthwhile.

Researched and compiled
by Steve Taplin BA (Hons).

Fifty to Follow

The trainers have spoken highly about this choice selection of two-year-olds.

AMBIANCE

b.c. Camacho – Thawrah (Green Desert). "A lovely colt, he's an early sort and I'm hoping he'll be the type for Royal Ascot. He looked a 2-y-o type at the sales and he's exactly that. Whether it was five or six furlongs, it wouldn't matter to him and he's in the top group of our 2-y-o's". **Mick Channon.**

ARAB DAWN

gr.c. Dalakhani – Victoire Celebre (Stravinsky). "He seems to find everything quite easy, he's quite mature, 'together' and strong, so he may be running in July if he goes the right way. He has speed, he's a lovely mover and is a quality horse that doesn't look expensive at the moment". **Hughie Morrison.**

AROD (IRE)

b.c. Teofilo – My Personal Space (Rahy). "He's going to take a bit of time but he does everything really nice. One for seven furlongs around August-time and he's one I like a lot. He goes really well, does everything just right and he's a fantastic mover". **Peter Chapple-Hyam.**

AYERS ROCK (IRE)

b.c. Bushranger – Red Fuschia (Polish Precedent). "We've done well with the ones we've bought with Peter Doyle. This colt is in full work and the sire has lots of 2-y-o's so he seems sure to do really well in terms of number of winners. This colt is from a good family and he looks a proper 2-y-o. A good mover, he's straightforward and he'll be out fairly soon". **Marcus Tregoning.**

BANAADEER (IRE)

ch.c. Tamayuz – Loose Julie (Cape Cross). "One of the nicest colts we've got, he's very nice, a good-mover, not overly-sharp but with a good temperament. We like him a lot". **Richard Hannon.**

BELLETRISTE (FR)

gr.f. Literato – Mulled Wine (Night Shift). "A smashing filly with a wonderful temperament and I think the sire is doing quite well from limited opportunities. She's small and sharp, quick enough for six furlongs and she's laid-back. I really like her". **Sylvester Kirk.**

BOLD LASS (IRE)

b.f. Sea The Stars – My Branch (Distant Relative). "A nice filly and we'd like to think that she'd be a bit more precocious than some of the Sea The Stars 2-y-o's. She goes nicely, she's very straightforward and hopefully she'll be one we could start off at six furlongs around June time. She's a nice model". **David Lanigan.**

BOY AT THE BAR

ch.c. Dutch Art – Lipsia (Dubai Destination). "He's not the biggest, but most of the good Dutch Art 2-y-o's seem to be that way. He does everything right, has a lovely attitude and contrary to what I normally do I've given him a piece of work before his second birthday...He'll win over five furlongs, he's hopefully my Norfolk Stakes horse and he does go well. I really like him a lot". **Peter Chapple-Hyam.**

CARTHAGE (IRE)

b.c. Mastercraftsman – Pitrizzia (Lando). "This is a really nice colt. He's pleased us in every way, he moves really nicely and he has the right attitude. Although he hasn't done any work yet I wouldn't mind buying a share myself!" **Richard Hannon.**

CHARLES MOLSON

b.c. Monsieur Bond – Arculinge (Paris House). "This colt is from a family we've had a lot of success with, although this particular dam hasn't really starred yet. He's a very strong colt, a great mover, seems to have endless energy and is hard to handle ... I would imagine he'd be in action in May or June. He'll be an out-and-out sprinter". **Henry Candy.**

CHRISELLIAM (IRE)

b.f. Iffraaj – Danielli (Danehill). "A 2-y-o through-and-through, she's got loads of speed and is a nice filly. We won't be hanging about with her, she's tough enough to take it and she's built like a colt". **Charles Hills.**

CRITIQUE (IRE)

b.f. Art Connoisseur – Madame Boulangere (Royal Applause). "A very nice filly, we have the half-brother Barracuda Boy who I was quite keen on at this point last year. She should be sharper than he was and considering he's a track record holder over five furlongs at Haydock Park I'd be pretty hopeful for this filly. They are different models because he's a bull of a horse and she's quite fine and light but she's done some good work, flown out of the stalls and she may start her career in April". **Tom Dascombe.**

DEEDS NOT WORDS (IRE)

b.c. Royal Applause – Wars (Green Desert). "A very nice, very sharp 2-y-o. He was bought for the job and hopefully he'll go out there and do it. He's a sprinting type and I think he's up there in the top bracket of our two-year-olds". **Mick Channon.**

DESERT RANGER (IRE)

b.c. Bushranger – Maleha (Cape Cross). "A beautiful, big colt from the first crop of Bushranger that everyone seemed to go mad for at the Sales. He's a lovely, long-striding horse that shows plenty and although he won't start at five furlongs I might be tempted to run him over six because he goes so well. Definitely very nice". **James Tate.**

DOUBLE CZECH (IRE)

b.c. Bushranger – Night Of Joy (King's Best). "He's got plenty of speed, looks all over a 2-y-o and is ready to go. He was bought to run in the six furlong races at Goodwood and hopefully we'll see him there in May". **Amanda Perrett.**

ELEUSIS

b.f. Elnadim – Demeter (Diesis). "She's very nice, doing a bit of growing at the moment, but she looks like being a summer 2-y-o over six/seven furlongs, like her sister. A 2-y-o type

but with the scope to do well next year as well". **Chris Wall.**

ERTIJAAL (IRE)

b.c. Oasis Dream – Shabiba (Seeking The Gold). "He's a nice horse and a half-brother to one we had last year called Odooj. This one is bigger than Odooj already, he goes well and he could easily make a 2-y-o in May ... he's quite a strong horse and he wants to please. A five/six furlong 2-y-o". **William Haggas.**

EXTORTIONIST (IRE)

b.c. Dandy Man – Dream Date (Oasis Dream). "We're quite excited about this horse, he'll start in mid-April over five furlongs and he might get an easy six later on but no further than that. A muscular colt, he's built like a quarter horse and I wouldn't want to run him on a downhill track because he's such a heavy-topped horse. We'll point him towards the Coventry at Royal Ascot and hope he proves good enough to take his place". **Olly Stevens.**

FRESH AND FRESH

b.c. Medicean – Red Blossom (Green Desert). "A real nice 2-y-o by a stallion I love. I've had a bit of luck with Medicean's and this colt is from a good Cheveley Park family. He's doing everything right at the moment and I think he could be earlier than some by the sire as they can take a bit of time. He's very athletic, has a great attitude and I see him being a 2-y-o in June/July. We'll start him off at six furlongs because I think he'll have lots of speed. One of the most likeable of my 2-y-o's, he's very racey". **Ed Walker.**

GOLDEN SPEAR

ch.c. Kyllachy – Penmayne (Inchinor). "A colt with a great attitude, he's full of energy and a real speed horse. A five/six furlong 2-y-o". **Noel Quinlan.**

GULLAND ROCK

b.c. Exceed And Excel – Sacre Coeur (Compton Place). "He's a cracker, he's strong, does everything right, will be a 2-y-o and he'll be very good. I love him". **Willie Muir.**

HARDY BLACK (IRE)

b.c. Pastoral Pursuits – Wondrous Story (Royal

Academy). "A colt with a lot of quality, he does things very easily, he's got quite a bit of scope and doesn't have the physique of an early 2-y-o but he's taking what I can throw at him and doing it nicely. A very nice horse, he'd be my pick of the bunch at the moment. He cost quite a bit for a Pastoral Pursuits but the dam has already bred a good horse, this colt is exceptionally good-looking and his work so far would appear to be in line with that". **Jamie Osborne.**

HUMOUR (IRE)

b.c. Invincible Spirit – Hucking Hot (Desert Prince). "He's a good-looking horse with a good action and he'll be a 2-y-o from June onwards. I quite like what I've seen so far and he looks a six furlong type". **Roger Varian.**

HURRICANE HARRY

b.c. Royal Applause – Stormy Weather (Nashwan). "A strong colt, quite typical of the sire and I like him. He's got a touch of quality and he'll start off in six or seven furlong maidens from early June time. A nice mover, he's just a nice, solid colt". **William Knight.**

KAAB (IRE)

b.c. Kheleyf – Ms Victoria (Fasliyev). "I like this colt, he's a typical Kheleyf in that he's a little bit bouncy and active. There's plenty of speed, he's got size and scope and he looks tough enough at the moment. It wouldn't surprise me if he was early, so he's definitely one for the book". **Ed Dunlop.**

KIYOSHI

b.f. Dubawi – Mocca (Sri Pekan). "A lovely filly, Jamie Spencer has been down to ride her a couple of times for the owner and he thinks she's quite smart. A big, strong filly that'll make a 2-y-o, she's got plenty of 'poke' and she goes well. One to watch out for". **Charles Hills.**

KNOCKROON

b.c. Royal Applause – Spring Touch (Elusive Quality). "I'm really pleased with him, he's grown a lot and he should be out in May. From the little bits we've done with him he's got plenty of boot and he's a really nice stamp

of a horse and an exciting prospect". **Andrew Balding.**

MEETING WATERS

ch.f. Aqlaam – Paradise Isle (Bahamian Bounty). "She's got a lot of speed and she's a nice filly. The dam was a dual listed winner over six and this is a nice mover, so she's definitely a 2-y-o". **William Haggas.**

MISTER MAYDAY (IRE)

b.c. Kheleyf – Soxy Doxy (Hawk Wing). "This colt really is a 'quirky Kheleyf' but you can forgive them their quirks if they've got an engine – and this horse definitely has one. He'll be a sprinter, despite the fact that the dam stayed, I like what he's done so far and he could be quite special". **George Baker.**

MONTAIGNE

b.c. Exceed And Excel – Autumn Pearl (Orpen). "He's quite forward and we trained his half-brother Pabusar to win as a 2-y-o last year. This is a horse we'll be looking to get on with and he's done a bit of work and showed up well. As yet he hasn't shown any of the temperament issues his brother Pabusar had, the family is all speed and he's quite a relaxed horse, so we like him". **Ralph Beckett.**

MOUNT LOGAN (IRE)

ch.c. New Approach – Vistaria (Distant View). "He's really nice – I like him a lot. I've got two colts by New Approach that I like very much. This is a horse that doesn't look particularly precocious but he has a very easy way of going and seems to have natural talent, even though he hasn't got the strength yet. He'll make a 2-y-o by mid-season over seven furlongs". **Luca Cumani.**

NATHR (USA)

b.br.c. Dixie Union – Sweet Rider (Seeking The Gold). "A lovely horse. He's a typical 2-y-o, very natural and we'll be getting on with him. He'll have loads of speed". **Charles Hills.**

NIGHT SONG

b.f. Oasis Dream – All For Laura (Cadeaux Genereux). "A racey, attractive filly and a good mover. She could be out in May, she's nice, well-balanced and light on her feet. I'll nominate her as one of my most promising types, but remember it's been a cold spring so she's only cantered". **John Gosden.**

PARTY RULER (IRE)

b.c. Holy Roman Emperor – Calypso Dancer (Celtic Swing). "A nice horse, I'm really fond of the sire and this is a winner waiting to happen. He's probably not a true five furlong horse but he's very forward-going so we may just get away with nicking one. He'll end up needing seven I'm sure, he's a medium-sized horse, well put-together, straightforward and has a good attitude. I like him and he may have been relatively cheap". **Tom Dascombe.**

RED VELOUR

ch.f. Pivotal – Regal Velvet (Halling). "She's a nice filly and she should be racing by the back-end of July. A good mover, she's got a bit of quality and what I've seen so far makes me feel quite positive about her. I've got the 3-y-o Regal Silk who could be listed class, but this one is much nicer than her and in a different league". **Jeremy Noseda.**

SPEEDY APPROACH

ch.c. New Approach – Height Of Vanity (Erhaab). "He's a classy horse to look at, he gets up Warren Hill very easily and I like him. A very easy mover, he has plenty of scope and looks quite like his sire. He'll probably want seven furlongs this year and all the riders like him". **Michael Bell.**

STEVENTON STAR

b.c. Pastoral Pursuits – Premiere Dance (Loup Solitaire). "This colt goes very well, he'll be sharp and early and he's a really likeable 2-y-o. Will be winning over five or six furlongs (hopefully both) early on". **Richard Hannon.**

SUNSET SHORE

b.f. Oasis Dream – Summer Night (Nashwan). "The dam is a half-sister to the fastest filly I've ever trained called Starlit Sands who was second in the Queen Mary and won the Prix d'Arenburg. She was by Oasis Dream, like this filly. She's a similar type, small, stocky and enormously strong". **Sir Mark Prescott.**

SUPER KID

b.c. Acclamation – Galapagar (Miswaki). "This colt is a real sharp 2-y-o type who will be ready to run early May, barring hold-ups. He's precocious and will be fine to start over five furlongs before stepping up to six". **Saeed bin Suroor.**

SWAN LAKES (IRE)

gr.f. Dalakhani – Rock Salt (Selkirk). "Probably the most attractive filly we've got here. Even though she's by Dalakhani there's not a lot backward about her and she's very forward in everything she does. A nice-actioned filly with a lot of quality, she'll want seven furlongs to start with". **David Simcock.**

TERHAAB

b.f. Elusive Quality – Star Of Paris (Dayjur). "A good, strong filly that moves very well. She looks like a colt, goes nicely and will hopefully be racing in May. She looks strong and quick, so she might be sharp enough for five furlongs to begin with". **John Gosden.**

TOOFI (FR)

b.c. Henrythenavigator – Silver Bark (Royal Applause). "He's a good-moving horse, quite mature and he could be racing by the end of May or early June. A nice type, I quite like him and he goes well. A horse with a fast ground action". **Roger Varian.**

WAR SPIRIT

b.c. Exceed And Excel – Alybgood (Alydeed). "One of the nicest 2-y-o's we've got...He showed up very early, we gave him one piece of work and he looked exceptional. Hopefully that will continue and you'll see him out soon". **Richard Hannon.**

WEISSE SOCKEN (IRE)

b.f. Acclamation – Playful (Piccolo). "She'll have had her first race before the book comes out because she's showing up well and she's forward and sharp. I trained her mother and she was the just same. Very professional, she just gets on with her job". **Ralph Beckett.**

WHAT ABOUT CARLO (FR)

b.c. Creachadoir – Boccatenera (Artan). "A lovely horse, he's big, rangy and won't be out early but he could be really nice. I think he'll win as a 2-y-o, he'll not be out before August/September 2-y-o but he's got plenty of pace and does everything so easily". **Eve Johnson Houghton.**

WIND FIRE (USA)

b.f. Distorted Humor – A P Dream (A P Indy). "A very nice filly, she'll be reasonably early and is showing plenty. I expect her to rank highly, she's strong, athletic and very well put-together. The type to start at five or six furlongs but she'll progress and stay further as the year goes on". **David Brown.**

ZAWIYAH

b.f. Invincible Spirit – Marika (Marju). "A very nice filly, I like her a lot and she's quite forward. She should be out in June over six furlongs, she's quite likeable, quite precocious and well-developed". **Luca Cumani.**

ZESHOV (IRE)

b.c. Acclamation – Fathoming (Gulch). "One of the 2-y-o's I've done a bit of work with, he's definitely a 2-y-o type and he'll definitely win races, I just need to decide whether to wait for six furlongs or start him at five. He goes nicely and has a good temperament but he's not a typical five furlong horse". **Jeremy Noseda.**

UNNAMED

b.f. New Approach – Rouge Noir (Saint Ballado). "A nice filly, I loved her at the sales and she's going well. She's a good mover, very straightforward and sound with a good temperament. She just needs to mature physically a bit more because she lacks a bit of strength at the moment, but I'm hoping to be racing her from the mid-summer onwards. She's one we like a lot". **Marco Botti.**

UNNAMED

b.f. Giant's Causeway – Swan Nebula (Seeking The Gold). "Quite classy, she's a good-sized filly with a good way of going. She's not going to be early but she has quality, finds everything very easy and never gets tired. A filly I have a lot of time for". **David Simcock.**

Ten to Follow in Ireland

BUSH PILOT (IRE)
br.c. Bushranger – Dame Noir (Alzao). "He's a colt I like a lot. I can see him running by the end of May because he's very forward. A nice horse for six and seven furlongs". **Dermot Weld.**

GLORY BOY (IRE)
br.c. Myboycharlie – Spring Glory (Dr Fong). "He had his first run at Leopardstown and he was a shade unlucky not to win. He'll be out again in mid-May and he's one to watch out for I'd say". **Dermot Weld.**

HOMERIC HYMN (FR)
b.f. Acclamation – Mary Arnold (Hernando). "A nice Acclamation filly, she's a good mover and I'm happy with her. She'll be racing by late May/early June, she's going nicely and six/seven furlongs will suit her. Possibly the classiest of my 2-y-o's at this stage". **Jessica Harrington.**

MY TITANIA (IRE)
b.f. Sea The Stars – Fairy Of The Night (Danehill). "A very nice, very well-made, strong and short-coupled filly. A 2-y-o type to look at, she's done everything right and although we won't be rushing her she's likely to be out in late June or early July. We like her a lot". **John Oxx.**

PIT STOP (IRE)
b.c. Iffraaj – Journey's End (In The Wings). "A beautiful horse, he's big, tall, good-looking and well-balanced. He goes really well and we like him a lot. You'd like him, he does everything well, he's showing me plenty of pace and would probably start off at six furlongs but would be better over seven". **Michael Halford.**

RED BANDANA (IRE)
ch.f. Raven's Pass – Mowazana (Galileo). "She's my star I think. She's out of a Galileo mare and she'll want six/seven furlongs this year. I like her a lot, she goes very well and she's a fine, big strong filly". **Kevin Prendergast.**

ROUSAYAN (IRE)
b.c. Invincible Spirit – Rose Quartz (Lammtarra). "A precocious horse and typical of the sire who gets a lot of good-looking 2-y-o types and this colt is no exception. He's a very nice colt and might be one of the first of ours to run. Six furlongs in early June could be his starting point". **John Oxx.**

SAAKHEN (IRE)
b.c. Invincible Spirit – Upperville (Selkirk). "He ran well on his debut at the Curragh and was perhaps unlucky not to win. He's come out of the race well and he looks a nice horse. He's not big, but he's a nice, quality colt for five and six furlongs". **Kevin Prendergast.**

THIRD DIMENSION
b.c. Dubawi – Round The Cape (Cape Cross). "A lovely colt, we like him a lot and he's ready to run now but he's a May foal so we'll wait a bit. He's precocious and he might start at five furlongs but he'll go seven later on and he has some good entries". **Ger Lyons.**

UNNAMED
b.f. Sea The Stars – Blas Ceoil (Mr Greeley). "A good-moving filly, she's developing well and she'll come to hand quick enough, so she'll be racing in May over six or seven furlongs I should think". **Tommy Stack.**

Star Two-year-olds

The stars placed along the side of each two-year-old in the main section of the book give the reader an instant appraisal of the regard in which they are held. The highest rating a horse can attain is five stars.

Bear in mind that some of the "Five Star" horses will be at their peak as three-year-olds, so keep an eye on them next year as well.

The five-star two-year-olds of 2013 are listed below for quick reference.

BUNKER	**Richard Hannon**
CABLE BAY	**Charles Hills**
CONNECTICUT	**Luca Cumani**
FIG ROLL	**Richard Hannon**
HYDROGEN	**Peter Chapple-Hyam**
JOYEUSE	**Sir Henry Cecil**
LIGHTNING SPEAR	**Ralph Beckett**
MARAKOUSH	**John Oxx**
NIGHT SONG	**John Gosden**
SAAYERR	**William Haggas**
ZAWIYAH	**Luca Cumani**

The Bloodstock Experts Mark your Card

Last year this section had 32 individual winners of 46 races, a very similar result to the previous two years. No less than 12 of the experts managed to find two winners apiece – Peter Doyle, Charlie Gordon-Watson, Harry Herbert, Luke Lillingston, David McGreavy, Johnny McKeever, Robin O'Ryan, David Redvers, Ed Sackville, Robin Sharp, Amanda Skiffington and Larry Stratton.

Of those, David Redvers managed to get onto the podium in third place, thanks mainly to the triple winner and listed-placed Liber. The silver medal goes to Amanda Skiffington – her two winners both managed to win three races and her faith in the Group 2 Champagne Stakes winner Toronado was certainly proved justified. You almost won it Amanda (especially as you could have chosen Havana Gold as well) but the Gold goes to Ed Sackville whose two winners included Sky Lantern, winner of the Group 1 Moyglare Stud Stakes.

Thank you to all the experts who have had a go at selecting potential winners once again. Remember that most of the two-year-olds selected here can be found in the main section of the book listed under their trainers and highlighted by the symbol ♠

JAMES DELAHOOKE

SEA HERE
ch.c. *Sea The Stars – Look Here*. First foal of the Oaks winner Look Here by Sea The Stars. He was small as a foal but grew into an elegant, classy colt. The trainer reports he has all his dam's attitude. I hope he also shares her ability. Trained by **Ralph Beckett.**

UNNAMED
br.c. *Monsun – Miracle Seeker*. First foal of the Lingfield Oaks Trial winner. This colt was trashed by all the vets at Newmarket yearling sales – with the honourable exception of Mathilde Texier. So far she is proved right – he has yet to take a lame step. Bred to stay, he is unlikely to be seen before the autumn". **Clive Cox.**

ALASTAIR DONALD

CHRISELLIAM (IRE)
b.f. *Iffraaj – Danielli*. A lovely, scopey filly that has turned into a cracker. Her half-sister Janicellaine is doing well in the USA and is now black-type and the mare has bred two winners from two runners. She'll be a June 2-y-o and is doing everything well. **Charles Hills.**

DER MEISTER (IRE)
b.c. *Mastercraftsman – Agnetha*. He was in three pieces at the sales but we thought he was a real bargain, as we felt he would fill into a very good-looking horse. He'll take time, but it's a tough German family and he'll be an autumn 2-y-o, hopefully with a good 3-y-o future. **Andrew Balding.**

FULL MOON FEVER (IRE)
b.f. *Azamour – Hasaiyda*. A huge bargain, this is a beautiful filly and a full sister to Glorious Protector – a horse we have big hopes for. She will be backward, so she won't be out until around October time. **Ed Walker.**

GLORIOUS EMPIRE (IRE)
br.c. *Holy Roman Emperor – Humble And Proud*. A big, scopey, imposing son of a stallion that often throws them on the small side, he has the strength for his size and does everything very nicely with loads of class. It'll be October before he gets to races, over seven furlongs plus. **Ed Walker.**

INVINCIBLE FRESH
b.c. *Footstepsinthesand – Princess Serena*. A half-brother to Puissance De Lune the current Melbourne Cup favourite, so we expect we could sell him for a large profit on his 80,000 Gns purchase price already! He's very classy, the most athletic mover and has huge presence. He'll take time, so don't expect to see him before September, but hopefully he will be worth the wait. **Ed Walker.**

MOUTAI

b.c. Royal Applause – Naizak. A very strong but athletic colt, we felt he was the best Royal Applause all year and that he would make 100k and we wouldn't get him, so we were very surprised and delighted he only made 55K. He is very straightforward, doing everything well and will hopefully be ready before August. **Ed Walker.**

NATIVE FALLS

ch.c. Elnadim – Sagrada. It's a speedy family, the half-brother Sunny Sing won a Group 1 in Hong Kong and was fourth in the Gimcrack and the mare has produced two black-type horses from four runners. I'm a fan of the sire and this is a compact 2-y-o type that will be ready early in the season over five and six furlongs. The family has a great temperament. **Alan Swinbank.**

UNNAMED

b.f. Bahamian Bounty – Loveleaves. A tall, rangy filly, but from a very fast family that's already produced Lovelace and six winners from seven foals. She does everything very easily and should be ready late May over six furlongs. **Ed Walker.**

PETER DOYLE

ASTRONEREUS

ch.c. Sea The Stars – Marie Rheinberg. A smashing horse with plenty of scope. Purchased at Newmarket for £175K. **Amanda Perrett.**

KAISERWURDE

f. Dubawi – Kapitol. A really attractive filly with a decent pedigree. **Andre Fabre.**

LADY EMMUSKA

b.f. Sir Percy – Medicea Sidera. A lovely filly and particularly sharp-looking. Bought at Goffs for James Stafford and Thurloe Thoroughbreds. **Richard Hannon.**

WINDSHEAR

b.c. Hurricane Run – Portal. Developing into a lovely horse and with a future. Bought at Deauville for €95. Richard Hannon.

ROSS DOYLE

BUNKER

b.c. Hurricane Run – Endure. We bought him at Tattersalls for 50K and he is by a stallion we like a lot in Hurricane Run. A very mature horse, he just carries himself like a real professional and he looks to have the scope to hopefully compete in the really good races later in the year. **Richard Hannon.**

FIG ROLL

b.f. Bahamian Bounty – Cake. We arranged the mating for this filly on behalf of her owner breeder, we are big fans of the stallion as he is consistent with the individuals he gets and on the racetrack they are very solid. We bought her dam Cake as a yearling for £13,000 from Acclamation's first crop and she was very fast, winning a Listed race over 5 furlongs for team Hannon as a two year old. Fig Roll is bred to be quick and physically looks like she will be early, so hopefully she might make into a Royal Ascot filly. **Richard Hannon.**

TOORMORE

b.c. Arakan – Danetime Out. We bought this fella at Doncaster and he was a well-grown, mature type of yearling by a stallion that has been very good to Team Doyle, Hannon and connections in recent years with Dick Turpin and Trumpet Major. He has a lovely way of going and looks to have a bit of class as well, so it's fingers crossed he can live up to the previous two I mentioned by the stallion. **Richard Hannon.**

WAR SPIRIT

b.c. Exceed And Excel – Alybgood. We bought him at Goffs for €75,000 and the minute we saw him we hoped we'd be able to buy him. He's a very imposing horse, strong and carries himself like a real natural. By a very good stallion out of a black type mare, hopefully he could be a decent middle season type. **Richard Hannon.**

WILL EDMEADES

CAPE SUMMIT

ch.c. Tamayuz – Peace Summit (Cape Cross). This colt looked a real pro at the sales – every time he left his box, there was a willingness about him – he walked really well and was totally unfussed. By Tamayuz, who has started so well, he is also from a quick family. The trainer likes him, but I gather he has grown quite a bit so he may need a bit of time. **Ed Dunlop.**

CAY DANCER

gr.f. Danehill Dancer – White Cay (Dalakhani). Not very big, but very racy, this filly was bred here at Fair Winter Farm under a foal share agreement, which I dissolved with one bid at Tattersalls. This daughter of Danehill Dancer is the mare's first living foal, so we have sent her to Richard Hannon to get her a good start. The champion jockey had a feel of her last week at Everleigh, so she will be out soon. **Richard Hannon.**

CRYSTAL NYMPH

ch.f. Rock Of Gibraltar – Flower Of Kent (Diesis). Another very nice filly, she was bought for Bunny Roberts at Tattersalls, who has sent her to Richard Hannon. By Rock Of Gibraltar out of a Diesis mare, who won as a two year old, she should be effective over 6-7f. She also appeared to go well in a gallop last week. **Richard Hannon.**

PRIMITORIO

b.c. Oratorio – Primissima (Second Set). A strong, good-looking son of Oratorio bought at Doncaster for Thurloe Thoroughbreds. This colt is from a fast family that includes the Prestige Stakes winner Gracefully (subsequently the dam of Giofra) whom we also bought for Thurloe. Thought to be fairly forward. **Ralph Beckett.**

TOM GOFF
BOY AT THE BAR

ch.c. Dutch Art – Lipsia. This looked a pretty sharp horse at the Doncaster Premier Sale. He was consigned by Tony and Roger O'Callaghan's Tally-Ho Stud from whom we have been lucky to buy some good ones. He had quality at the sales and Peter Chapple-Hyam and I thought he had something of his old man so we had a go. I don't think we planned to go to £38,000 but that's what it took to buy him and I think Pete is happy with him so far. He has a very good way of going so we're very hopeful he may make up into a precocious type like his sire. **Peter Chapple-Hyam.**

CRADLE OF LIFE

ch.f. Notnowcato – Pursuit of Life. This is a filly purchased on behalf of Andrew Black's Chasemore Farm at Tattersalls for 55,000gns. She is a lovely, classy filly bred by Franca Vittadini and consigned by Ted Voute; the mare has produced some very classy performers so far including an Italian 1,000 Guineas winner by Iffraaj. Mr Black liked the pedigree and there's definitely something about her. It's too early now to say whether she has an engine or not but she's in great hands and I'm very hopeful at this stage. Fingers crossed. **Ed Dunlop.**

NOBLE METAL

gr.c. With Approval – Grain Only. Peter Chapple-Hyam asked me to take another look at this colt as he has the half-brother Caravan Rolls On. I liked him but he we had to give Kirsten Rausing's Staffordstown Stud 40,000gns for him at Tattersalls, which was more than we imagined. It's so far so good with him I think. I've watched him up Warren Hill a few times and he does everything nice and easy and seems to move very well. **Peter Chapple-Hyam.**

WESTERN HYMN

b.c. High Chaparral – Blue Rhapsody. This is a classy colt by High Chaparral, which we bought for 50,000gns at Tattersalls from Newsells Park Stud who always present their yearlings very well. He is closely related to Fantasia and Blue Duster so will hopefully have a bit of toe for a horse by a top middle distance performer. It's very early days but John Gosden seems happy enough so let's hope he's lucky for owner Robin Geffen. **John Gosden.**

UNNAMED

b.c. Yeats – Aitch. I fell in love with him and bought this colt on spec from Luke Barry's Manister House Stud, Ireland. He was just a really classy young staying horse at the sales. I fought with myself but then bid 60,000gns for him at Tattersalls. He is going to John Gosden which is great and has had plenty of time which he deserves being by the great four-time Gold Cup winner. A Derby entry, he is a long-term prospect but he moves well and I like him a lot. **John Gosden.**

ANGUS GOLD
BANAADEER (IRE)
ch.c. *Tamayuz – Loose Julie.* We bought this colt as a foal and he is one of the best by Tamayuz I have ever seen. He has very much gone the right way since we bought him, is blessed with a wonderful temperament and the Hannon's like what they have seen of him so far. **Richard Hannon.**

ETAAB (USA)
b.f. *Street Cry – Ethaara.* This is the second foal of a stakes winning Green Desert mare who herself was a half sister to two stakes winners, from the Bahri family. Like all the family she is not very big but she looks tough and hardy and I would be disappointed if she doesn't show plenty as a two year old. **William Haggas.**

MIHANY (IRE)
b.c. *Teofilo – Love Excelling.* This horse was a very expensive yearling but he is a beautiful horse by Teofilo and a half brother to a very good two year old of last year who I am sure will be a Group class horse this year. He looks to have done very well in the intervening months and, although he obviously won't be early, I hope he will show some class later in the year. **John Gosden.**

MUNFALLET (IRE)
b.c. *Royal Applause – Princess Mood.* This was an expensive Royal Applause horse from Newmarket. They have not been able to do much with them due to the appalling weather, but the Hannon's seem to like what they have seen of him so far.

TAGHREEB (IRE)
b.c. *Dubawi – Ghaneema.* This is a very good-looking Dubawi colt out of a young mare who cost a lot of money as a yearling but got injured. I am sure he won't be early, but again he looks to have a bit of class and could be one for later in the year. **Brian Meehan.**

TERHAAB(USA)
b.f. *Elusive Quality – Star of Paris.* This is a full sister to Elusive City who John Gosden liked very much as yearling in America. He says that so far she looks a natural athlete and certainly looks as if she should make a two year old. **John Gosden.**

CHARLIE GORDON-WATSON
RAPID ADVANCE
b.c. *Medicean – Snow Gretel.* Medicean X Snow Gretel (Green Desert). He was bought at Tattersalls Book 2 for 100,000 Gns for a long-standing client in Saeed Suhail. Newsells Park sold him and they consistently breed good horses and I enjoy buying from them. He is showing all the right signs. **Roger Varian.**

SHERIFF'S STAR (IRE)
gr.c. *Lawman – Silver Bandana.* Bought at Tattersalls Book 2 for 50,000 Gns for Saeed Suhail, he is such a good-looking horse and I really liked him. Lawman is a stallion that just gets better and better. Ballylinch is a good farm and they breed plenty of good horses, this is just a really nice horse and we were really lucky to get him at the price. **Roger Varian.**

UNNAMED
b.c. *Invincible Spirit – Carrig Girl.* Originally bought for 38,000 Gns from Highclere Stud at Tattersalls Book 2, we resold him at the Craven Breeze-Up sale this week for 300,000 Gns. He is going to **Richard Hannon** and despite being a May foal shows a lot of talent.

UNNAMED
b.c. *Exceed And Excel – Gower Song.* He was bought at Tattersalls Book 1 for 200,000 Gns for long standing client HRH Sultan Ahmad Shah. His pedigree goes back to an old Juddmonte family and he is a horse we are excited about. The sire is all the rage at the moment. **Roger Varian.**

TREVOR HARRIS
MUSICORA
b.f. *Acclamation – Belladera.* A lovely looking filly who is a full sister to Little Scotland, a dual winner and Listed placed. She cost 115,000 euros at the Arqana August sale and should

be out around mid-season. In training with **Richard Hannon.**

SWISS KISS

br.f. Dansili – Swiss Lake. The dam has so far produced quite precocious winners, her five so far of racing age all won at two during May/ June and all achieved a Timeform rating of at least 108. This one is a big, strong filly and may take a little longer. She is a half to Swiss Diva, dual Group 3 winner; Swiss Spirit, Group 3 winner and Swiss Dream, triple Listed winner. **John Gosden.**

TOUCH THE SKY

br.c. Sea The Stars – Love Divine. The dam won the Oaks and her second foal, Sixties Icon, won the St Leger. Her progeny are usually late two year olds but this one could be a little earlier. He is also a half brother to Native Ruler, twice Group 2 placed. A good-looking, elegant colt, his debut will be awaited with great interest. **Sir Henry Cecil.**

TWILIGHT SKY

b.f. Authorized – La Sky. This filly is a half sister to the Oaks winner Love Divine, the listed winner Dark Promise and the listed winner and Group placed Floreeda. The last progeny from her dam, she is athletic and her trainer likes her. She will, like the rest of her family, not be seen out until the latter part of the season. **Roger Varian.**

HARRY HERBERT

CONSTANTINE

b.c. Holy Roman Emperor – Whatami. This colt is owned by the Royal Ascot Racing Club and he looks to be very precocious. He is a son of Holy Roman Emperor and is the most charming colt who is already in fast work. He goes very nicely and should be ready to make an impact from the end of April or early May. **Richard Hannon.**

EXCHEQUER

ch.c. Exceed And Excel – Tara's Force. A beautiful son of Exceed And Excel who stands over plenty of ground, at the moment we've given him a break from training for three weeks or so as he is going through another growth phase, but he should be strong

enough to be making a debut later in the Summer. If looks and movement are anything to go by then he could be a really exciting prospect. He one of those horses on the move that simply floats over the ground. **Richard Hannon.**

HUMOUR

b.c. Invincible Spirit – Hucking Hot. I love this colt and think that he will be an early season starter for us. He is by Invincible Spirit and is finding it all very easy so far. He has really developed since being broken and, despite being precocious, he has enough scope to suggest that he will continue to develop and improve as the season progresses. Roger likes him a lot and thinks that he could be out by the end of May or early June, so maybe he is one for the Royal meeting! **Roger Varian.**

ORIEL

b.f. Fastnet Rock – Labisa. This filly is a daughter of top Australian sire Fastnet Rock and she looks to be very precocious. She was a bit spicy early on but she has now settled in well to her regime at Herridge. I suspect that she will be on the track in early May provided that we get some warmer weather as her coat is still wintry. She goes very well. **Richard Hannon.**

SATELLITE

b.c. Danehill Dancer – Perihelion. This a cracking son of Danehill Dancer out of a Galileo mare and he looks to be a very athletic horse who could be making his debut in July. He has always found it all pretty easy and he was one of Malcolm Bastard's picks of our new crop and he is often spot on! Malcolm breaks most of our yearlings and is a renowned judge who picked out Telescope from last year's crop. **Sir Henry Cecil.**

STAMPEDE

b.c. High Chaparral – Summerhill Parkes. This colt is a real corker and is part of a syndicate that races the two horses here for a couple of years before they transfer down to Australia to race at four and five. He is very athletic and carries himself like a good horse. It's early days but we love him and he looks the type to be starting in late summer. **Sir Michael Stoute.**

LUKE LILLINGSTON

ASTRAL ROSE
b.f. Pastoral Pursuits – Rosapenna (Spectrum).
I have enjoyed buying some horses for the
Ian Wood stable over the past few years, all
bar one of which has one won. His licence
has now been taken over by Paul Fitzsimons
who has expressed himself pleased with this
filly who sounds like she will be early and
has some talent. She should be interesting in
auction races. **Paul Fitzsimons.**

CRITIQUE (IRE)
b.f. Art Connoisseur – Madame Boulangere.
Her year older half brother, Barracuda
Boy, had been bought by Ed Sackville and
Tom Dascombe in 2011 and he proved a
progressive 2-y-o sprinter last year. They
returned to buy the year younger half-sister
who really shone at Fairyhouse and the owner
has sent us encouraging noises. Having
bought the sire as a yearling it would be a
special thrill if she could live up to current
hopes. **Tom Dascombe.**

PIGEON PIE
b.f. Bahamian Bounty – Pixie Ring. Having
founded the Hot To Trot Racing club with Sam
Hoskins in 2012 and had four wins in our first
year we are hoping to build on that with a
few sharp 2-y-o's. This filly sounds as if she has
come to hand early and we hope will get the
ball rolling for us this year. The trainer is giving
us early encouragement. **Mark Johnston.**

UNNAMED
ch.c. Mastercraftsman – Wait It Out. We
bought this lovely colt at Tattersalls Book 1.
James Delahooke, who works for the breeders
Car Colston Hall (also breeders of Reckless
Abandon), was extremely complimentary
about this colt at the time. He will run in
the colours of Michael Tabor, having been
approved by Demi O' Byrne. Let's hope we are
not all wrong! **Michael Bell.**

DAVID MCGREAVY

HATCH HALL
b.c. Sleeping Indian – Speech. He impressed
me as a foal and looked an athlete as a
yearling. Has gone into training with a very
good trainer in Ireland. **J Murphy.**

IRONDALE EXPRESS
b.f. Myboycharlie – Olindera. A real sprinting
type who looks fast. **Tony Coyle.**

UNNAMED
b.f. Piccolo – Fizzy Treat. A sweet filly who has
thrived in her training and has been pleasing
with her attitude. **Tony Coyle.**

JOHNNY MCKEEVER
The following four all look to be ready made
two year olds!

EXTREMITY (IRE)
ch.c. Exceed And Excel – Chanterelle. A son of
this great sire bought for **Hugo Palmer** who
says he is progressing really well.

MOCACHA (IRE)
b.c. Camacho – Mama Angela. Bought at
Doncaster for £24,000, owned by the Options
O syndicate and trained by **William Haggas.**

WINDFAST (IRE)
b.c. Exceed And Excel – Fair Sailing. A very
strong sprinting sort typical of his sire, owned
by the Sangster family's Trelawny syndicate.
Brian Meehan.

UNNAMED
b.f. Oasis Dream – Dame Alicia. An amazing
bargain I thought when I got her for only
€38,000 at Goffs Orby from the great Kilcarn
Stud. She was bought for one of my all time
luckiest clients Steve Parkin and will be trained
by **Ralph Beckett**.

KIRSTEN RAUSING

BARYE
b.c. Archipenko – Oblige. A very good-looking
colt in the mould of his first-season sire. The
dam won twice at 2 and was a close fifth in
the Group 1 Fillies Mile; she has hitherto been
unlucky at stud but her only runner Herrbuga
(by Hernando) won at 2 in France. Like many
of his sire's produce, this colt is described as a
"particularly good mover" and should make
his mark at 2. Sold by Staffordstown at Goffs
Orby Sales, he was purchased for €57,000 by
Blandford Bloodstock. **David Simcock.**

HARDSTONE (USA)
b.c. Birdstone – Songerie. Foaled in Kentucky but a fourth-generation Lanwades-bred and sold by Staffordstown at Goffs Orby Sales for €52,000. His sire was a triple Grade 1 winner in the US (including at 2 yrs) and sired two Champions and Classic winners from his first crop. This colt's dam won the Group 3 Prix des Reservoirs at 2 in Deauville and had a best Timeform rating of 118. The colt is a "hardy" type and has the look of a tough performer. **T. Carmody, Ireland.**

NOBLE METAL
gr.c. With Approval – Grain Only. A half-brother to the very useful but somewhat unlucky Caravan Rolls On (also with this colt's trainer) and the good two-year-old of 2011 Gabrial's Star. Bred to go 10f at 3 yrs, this colt is sufficiently forward to make his mark this year. Sold by Staffordstown, the colt was bought by Blandford Bloodstock for 40,000 Gns at October Sales Book Two. **Peter Chapple-Hyam.**

SUNSET SHORE
b.f. Oasis Dream – Summer Night. A third-generation homebred Lanwades produce, this filly is a half-sister to Black Type winning fillies Songerie, Souvenance, Soft Morning and Sourire; she is also a three-parts sister to the 5 furlong Group 3 winner (at 2) Starlit Sands and the 2012 Listed winner Chigun. Small but sturdy, this filly looks a sprinty type and it is hoped she can further add to her illustrious family's reputation. **Sir Mark Prescott, Bt.**

UNNAMED
b.c. Archipenko – Diablerette. A well-balanced, good-moving and quite forward colt, he is an interesting representative of his first-crop sire. His dam won from only two starts and was rated 90 at 2 years; she is a close relative of the European champion sprinter Polish Patriot and a half-sister to the Group One winner Lady Jane Digby and the Group 3 winner Gateman. The colt was sold by Staffordstown and bought for 42,000 Gns by Johnny McKeever at the October Sales Book Two. **Brian Meehan.**

UNNAMED
ch.c. Sir Percy – Hermanita. A really good-looking colt and a good walker, this second-generation Lanwades-bred colt was sold as a foal (from St Simon Stud) for 34,000 Gns. His dam won at 3 years and the second dam, Subjective, won at 2 in this country and was then a Stakes winner of 4 races in the USA; her dam in turn, Welsh Garden, was champion two-year-old filly in Ireland in 1975. This colt is a forward type who can remind us all that his sire was an unbeaten champion two-year-old. **James Tate.**

UNNAMED
b.c. Selkirk – Starlit Sands. First foal of a Group winner over 5f at 2 (Prix d'Arenberg), also second in Group 2 Queen Mary Stakes at Royal Ascot. This colt looks a real professional and it's worth noting that his sire produced plenty of good sprinters and classy two-year-olds as well as 15 individual Group One winners. The colt, a third-generation Lanwades-bred, was sold by Staffordstown to Rabbah Bloodstock for 70,000 Gns at the October Sales Book Two. **Ed Walker.**

BRUCE RAYMOND
CANNOCK CHASE
b.c. Lemon Drop Kid – Lynnwood Chase. A full-brother to Pisco Sour, he's a well-furnished, quality racehorse and he should do well later in season. **Sir Michael Stoute.**

DREAMING BEAUTY
b.f. Oasis Dream – Independence. A half-sister to Singersongwriter, she's very attractive, has a great pedigree and a lot of class. Will do well the second half of the season. **Jeremy Noseda.**

UNNAMED
b.c. New Approach – Bush Cat. A good horse by a great stallion, he will prove himself a racehorse later in the season. **Clive Brittain.**

UNNAMED
b.f. Cape Cross – Deveron. A very athletic filly, she's is already showing some talent although she will be better from mid-season onwards. **James Tate.**

DAVID REDVERS

GREEN DOOR

b.c. Camacho – Inourhearts (Pips Pride). Trained by Olly Stevens at Robins Farm, who have got off to a flyer in their first season training. Named after the great Shakin' Stevens' hit (or Sheikh and Stevens as the owner-trainer partnership have been refereed to!) **Olly Stevens.**

KIYOSHI

b.f. Dubawi – Mocca (Sri Pekan). Looks a sharp, precocious filly who could be our first 2yo runner this year. **Charlie Hills.**

RACE HUNTER

b.br.f. Dixie Union filly – Shriek. One of our Keeneland purchases. A strong looking filly who has always pleased us since the sale. She looks a 2-y-o and an exciting prospect. **David Barron.**

THE BEASTUNLEASHED

gr.c. Mastercraftsman – Prairie Moon (Halling). A strong colt by an exciting first season sire in Mastercraftsman, he's a definite 2-y-o. Trained by the man who handled Frederick Engles for us to win the Group 2 July Stakes and the listed Windsor Castle Stakes as a 2-y-o. **David Brown.**

CHRIS RICHARDSON

DUTCH COURAGE

b.f. Dutch Art – Poldhu. By the dual Group 1 winning sire Dutch Art, this filly was purchased to be an early two year-old and hopefully she will prove to be just that, being from the family of Champion two-year-old Hoh Magic. **Richard Fahey.**

RED VELOUR

ch.f. Pivotal – Regal Velvet. A strong daughter of resident stallion Pivotal, she's a full sister to Regal Silk who showed promise when placed on her debut at Newmarket. **Jeremy Noseda.**

ROYAL SEAL

b.f. Dansili – Queens Best. An eye-catching individual with a positive attitude, just like her dam who, having broken her maiden at two years, progressed in Group company at three and four. **Sir Michael Stoute.**

ED SACKVILLE

FINE 'N DANDY

ch.c. Dandy Man – Pearly Brooks. I regard Tom Dascombe as one of the best two-year-old trainers in the country. I know Tom likes this colt, so that's good enough for me. **Tom Dascombe.**

OUTLAWED

b.c. Kyllachy – Regent's Park (Green Desert). I loved this colt at the sales and was thrilled to buy him. I thought he oozed class. Time will tell! **Ed Walker.**

STEVENTON STAR

b.c. Pastoral Pursuits – Premiere Dance. A really athletic colt with a good outlook. He is from a speedy family and looks a two-year-old type. **Richard Hannon.**

ROBIN SHARP

BUREDYMA

ch.f. Dutch Art – Petong's Pet. Bred by a local entrepreneur Colin Murfitt. We prepared her for the Doncaster Premier and she was second highest priced filly. She's a beautiful filly and a great mover – she has it all. **William Haggas.**

EXCEED AND EXCEED

b.c. Exceed And Excel – Gandini. A bay colt I was very fond of, we bred him and two good judges have gone on to buy him. Gay O'Callaghan bought him as a foal and Peter Doyle bought him as a yearling. He will be sharp and early with a touch of class. **Richard Hannon.**

SAKHRA

b.c. Nayef – Noble Desert. Also bred by Colin Murfitt one of the best moving colts I have seen for a very long time he will not be early but looked to have a touch of class. **Kevin Prendergast.**

SIR PAUL DEAN

b.c. Byron – Hunters Fortune. Bred by very successful breeders Greenland Park who have boarded their mares with us for many years. A smashing colt who looked very early to me and was bought by a top judge in **Mark Johnston.**

AMANDA SKIFFINGTON
AVOCETTE
b.f. Pivotal – Ailette. Bought at Deauville for €140,000, she has always been a lovely sort. He won't be early, but should be worth waiting for. Malcolm Bastard, who broke her in, was always very keen on her and it seems the Hannon team are too. **Richard Hannon**

BLACK CAESAR
b.c. Bushranger – Evictress. I can't resist adding this colt. I loved a lot of the Bushrangers last year but I thought this was the best moving one that I saw. **Richard Hannon**

MAGNUS MAXIMUS
b.c. Holy Roman Emperor – Chanrossa. Probably to my eye, the best looking yearling I bought last year. He was my favourite when I saw them all ridden out before Christmas at Malcolm's. He is a lovely, deep colt and looks classy. **Richard Hannon.**

STORM RIDER
b.c. Fastnet Rock – On The Nile. I thought he was the image of his grandsire, Danehill, when I saw him before the sales at Barronstown and never thought I would be able to afford him – a nice surprise. He's a great mover and has a lovely temperament. **Richard Hannon.**

UNNAMED
b.c. Royal Applause – Rolexa. By a stallion I have been very lucky with, so I hope this will be no exception. He looked "a proper horse" with plenty of scope and I would not expect him to be out too early, but hopefully he will be around when the good races are being run. **Richard Hannon.**

PETER STANLEY
NIGHT SONG
b.f. Oasis Dream – All For Laura (Cadeaux Genereux). A sharp filly and a full sister to the Cheery Hinton winner Misheer. **John Gosden.**

UNNAMED
b.c. Oasis Dream – Enticing (Pivotal). Home-bred at New England for Mr & Mrs Jackson, Lael Stables. A lovely 2-y-o type. **William Haggas.**

UNNAMED
b.c. Dubawi – Ivory Gala. An impressive breezer, he was sold for 180,000 Gns at the Craven Breeze-Up. **Peter Stanley.**

UNNAMED
b.f. Danehill Dancer – Superstar Leo. A good-looking full-sister to the potentially top-class Sentaril. Home-bred for Mr & Mrs Jackson, Lael Stables. **William Haggas.**

LARRY STRATTON
BLOCKADE
b.f. Kheleyf – Barracade. A racy and classy filly pinhooked by Hannah Botterill and me. She was undersold at the Doncaster Premier Sale where the tail-end of the second day was decidedly a market for buyers, not sellers. She's sharp and should be speedy. **James Tate.**

INDIRA
ch.f. Sleeping Indian – Forever Loved. I helped foal this filly who was bred by my partner Louise Parry and her brother Peter Steele Mortimer, and always liked her so I bought her. She's a half-sister to a very decent horse in Rhythm Stick who won four in a row, so it made sense to send her to the guy who did such a good job with him. **John Berry.**

INJUN SANDS
b.c. Halling – Serriera. An outstanding looking colt bred by Louise and sold as a foal to a good judge in Brendan Holland. She has the looks and the pedigree to be a classic contender, but could be a decent 2-y-o on the way there. **Jane Chapple-Hyam.**

PINK DANCE
ch.f. Dutch Art – Dance Away. A foal pinhook with Tom Whelan, she's not very big but very strong and a wonderful mover. The pedigree looks weak at first glance, but the dam has bred two smart 2-y-o's and this filly has legitimate claims to be a contender in major 2-y-o filly contests. **Peter Chapple-Hyam.**

UNNAMED
b.f. Byron – Ennobling. Bred by me, she's a half-sister to Cometh, who was trained by Nick

to win twice for me at two and has since won several more in Qatar. She is bigger and more athletic than her sister and it's a mating I was very excited about, so I am hoping she could have a touch of class. **Nick Littmoden.**

ANTHONY STROUD
QUEENIE'S HOME
b.f. Shamardal – Nolas Lolly. A filly out of a mare who was Group 3 placed for Marco Botti, bought at the BBAG yearling sale in Germany. She has been pleasing her trainer in her work and looks a precocious type. **James Given.**

UNFORGIVING MINUTE
b.c. Cape Cross – Ada River. A lovely colt bought at Tattersalls Book One. He's the first foal of a black type mare who has impressed in everything he has done so far and should be ready for a late spring/summer campaign. **Clive Cox.**

UNNAMED
ch.f. Exceed And Excel – Amazon Beauty. A good-looking filly who came from the Tattersalls December Yearling Sale and looks to have a touch of class in her early work. **Richard Hannon.**

PAUL THORMAN
LILBOURNE LASS
ch.f. Pastoral Pursuits – Talampaya. We thought she was typical of what the Hannon's buy so well. She was inexpensive, very correct, strong and precocious. I'd be surprised if she didn't have a level of ability. **Richard Hannon.**

PIAZON
br.c. Striking Ambition – Colonel's Daughter. We sold him at Doncaster Premier. He wasn't a typical yearling for that sale in that he had size and scope, but he was very mature in his mind and the mare is exceptional. She seems to be one of those that can breed good horses to any stallion. This colt was like the sire Striking Ambition in that he was 'on the leg' a bit, but we thought he could still make an early 2-y-o". **Michael Bell.**

YAJAMILA
b.f. Royal Applause – Yatir. Sara and I sold this filly at Doncaster and we both really liked her. She's strong, easy moving, has a good temperament and is probably precocious. **James Tate.**

UNNAMED
b.c. Invincible Spirit – Lovely Thought (Dubai Destination). We sold him at the Doncaster Premier Sale and he's to be resold at the Doncaster Breeze-Up. Sara and I both liked him. Every time he did something he seemed to do it better next time. He's one to keep an eye on.

Trainers' Bargain Buys

When interviewing trainers in the Spring the last question I usually ask is: "Which of the two-year-olds do you think will prove to be your bargain buy at the yearling sales, for 25,000gns or less?" The horses listed below are their recommendations. I have cheated a bit with a couple of horses that cost a thousand pounds more than that! You'll also notice that one trainer asked me to enter two selections.

The highlights from the Bargain Buys last year were Baddilini (2 wins at 3-1 & 12-1), Starbotton (28-1), Yorkshireman (20-1), Ingleby Royale (11-1), Girl At The Sands (10-1 & 5-1), Keep The Secret (12-1) and the star of the show Pasaka Boy (50-1 & 7-1) – well done Jon Portman!

SLEEPING VENUS	12,000 Gns	George Baker
RIZAL PARK	€12,000	Andrew Balding
NEVERODDOREVEN	7,000 Gns	Ralph Beckett
PIAZON	25,000 Gns	Michael Bell
SUNNINGDALE ROSE	£20,000	Michael Bell
LIGHTNING SHOWER	19,000 Gns	Marco Botti
CAPTAIN MIDNIGHT	£12,000	David Brown
WHITE RUSSIAN	5,000 Gns	Henry Candy
CHESTURO	20,000 Gns	Mick Channon
HAY CHEWED	€18,000	Peter Chapple-Hyam
SKANDER	£16,000	Denis Coakley
ORTON PARK	£19,000	Toby Coles
B.F. NAAQOOS – SAFQA	£22,000	Tom Dascombe
HELLO BEAUTIFUL	£10,000	Ann Duffield
ROXANNA	£18,000	Ed Dunlop
RURAL AFFAIR	5,500 Gns	Harry Dunlop
B.F. KODIAC – INTER MADERA	£12,000	James Given
STATS MINISTER	2,000 Gns	William Haggas
LIGEIA	2,000 Gns	Richard Hannon
PORT MERRION	€11,000	Jessica Harrington
DANDEENA	£25,000	Ron Harris
GOWN	10,000 Gns	Charles Hills
B.C. ROYAL APPLAUSE – SPARKLING EYES	25,000 Gns	William Jarvis
B.C. TAGULA – THELMA LOUISE	£15,000	Eve Johnson-Houghton
SIMMA	12,500 Gns	Sylvester Kirk
B.F. DUKE OF MARMALADE – CRINOLETTE	18,000 Gns	William Knight
DISKO	£6,000	Dan Kubler
MISS MOUSEY	€5,000	Ger Lyons
INCITING INCIDENT	£14,000	Ed McMahon
SEAHAM	£20,000	Rod Millman
MY MY MY DILIZA	4,200 Gns	Stan Moore
SOUTHERN CROSS	22,000 Gns	Hughie Morrison
CHILLY IN RIO	£10,000	Willie Muir
B.F. CLODOVIL – SWEET TIMES	16,000 Gns	Jamie Osborne
B.F. ROYAL APPLAUSE – MISS OTIS	8,000 Gns	Hugo Palmer
SUMMERLING	7,000 Gns	Jon Portman
THE ORGAN GRINDER	€26,000	Kevin Prendergast
PAY THE GREEK	£8,000	Noel Quinlan

PHOENIX ANGEL	15,000 Gns	**Derek Shaw**
ANYA'S ANGEL	£14,000	**David Simcock**
B.F. ROYAL APPLAUSE – STARRY SKY	13,500 Gns	**Tommy Stack**
HOKU	£14,000	**Olly Stevens**
BLOCKADE	£12,000	**James Tate**
BETWEEN WICKETS	£26,000	**Marcus Tregoning**
HIGH ACCOLADE	£26,000	**Roger Varian**
QUAINTRELLE	10,000 Gns	**Ed Vaughan**
B.F. BAHAMIAN BOUNTY – LOVELEAVES	24,000 Gns	**Ed Walker**
JOHARA	22,000 Gns	**Chris Wall**

Two year olds of 2013

ERIC ALSTON

1. BLITHE SPIRIT ★★★

b.f. Byron – Damalis (Mukaddamah). March 15. Fifth foal. Half-sister to the modest 5f winner Dalarossie (by Kyllachy) and to the moderate 1m winner Saving Grace (by Lend A Hand). The dam, a useful sprint winner of 7 races from 2 to 5 yrs, is a half-sister to 4 winners. The second dam, Art Age (by Artaius), is an unraced half-sister to 9 winners. (Liam & Tony Ferguson). "She's small and won't get further than five furlongs. A nice filly, she's sharp but due to her size she'll probably need to be at her best in the first half of the season". This filly won at Ripon in mid-April.

2. MIGUELA MCGUIRE ★★

b.f. Sir Percy – Miss McGuire (Averti). March 14. Third foal. 6,000Y. Sue Alston. Half-sister to the fair 2-y-o 7f winner Feelthedifference (by Iceman) and to the hurdles winner Miss Exhibitionist (by Trade Fair). The dam, a fair 3-y-o 1m winner, is a half-sister to 3 winners including the dam of the dual Group 3 winner Side Glance. The second dam, Friend For Life (by Lahib), is a placed half-sister to 2 winners and to the placed dam of the Australian Group 1 winner Markham. (Red Rose Partnership). "She's doing well and she'll be racing by the end of April. Not over-big, she's well forward but although she'll start off at five furlongs I imagine she'll be better over six or seven later on. She moves nicely and she'll go on any ground".

3. SPRING WILLOW (IRE) ★★

b.c. Camacho – Twinberry (Tagula). April 11. Fourth foal. £26,000Y. Doncaster Premier. Peter & Ross Doyle. Half-brother to a minor winner in Italy at 3 yrs by Namid. The dam is an unplaced half-sister to 4 winners including the listed-placed Soviet Bureau. The second dam, Redwood Hut (by Habitat), is an unraced half-sister to 6 winners including the German Group 3 winner and sire Red Regent. (J W Stephenson). "I was very disappointed with him on his debut, but he was drawn one and the stalls were in the middle, so he found himself isolated. He's a lot better than that and I have a feeling he'll be better over six furlongs than five. I have his 4-y-o half-brother and he's a very heavy horse, whereas this colt is much more a 2-y-o type".

ALAN BAILEY

4. CRESTA RISE ★★

br.f. Authorized – Cresta Gold (Halling). March 7. Half-sister to Ingot Of Gold (by Dubawi), unplaced in one start at 2 yrs in 2012 and to the quite useful 7f (at 2 yrs) and dual 1m winner Rhagori (by Exceed And Excel). The dam, a useful 11f and 12f winner, was listed-placed and is a half-sister to the Group 3 Lingfield Classic Trial and Group 3 Dee Stakes winner African Dream and the listed-placed winners Fenella's Link and Lone Wolfe. The second dam, Fleet Hill (by Warrshan), winner of the listed Superlative Stakes and third in the Group 3 Rockfel Stakes, is a half-sister to 6 winners including the useful listed 6f Sandy Lane Stakes winner Lee Artiste. "A lovely-moving filly that'll want a bit of time, I trained the dam who was useful and she seems to have bred a lovely filly here. She shows a lot even now, even though I'm not thinking of running her until late summer".

5. MIMI LUKE (USA) ★★★

b.f. U S Ranger – Hard As Nails (Holy Bull). March 9. Sixth foal. £30,000Y. Doncaster Premier. Alan Bailey. Half-sister to four winners in the USA by Exchange Rate, Judge T C, Artie Schiller and War Chant. The dam, a 3-y-o winner in the USA, is a half-sister to 10 winners including three stakes winners in the USA. The second dam, Durability (by Affirmed), won in the USA and is a sister to one stakes winner and a half-sister to the stakes winners and US Grade 1 placed Out of The East and Painted Wagon. "A very nice filly, she won't be long in winning and of all the 2-y-o's she'll be my first of the season I should think. Hopefully I'll get her to Chester for the May meeting".

6. SAFFIRE SONG ★★★

ch.f. Firebreak – Saffwah (King's Best). April 10. Fourth foal. The dam, placed second over

6f at 2 yrs on her only start, is a half-sister to 3 winners. The second dam, Saafeya (by Sadler's Wells), a very useful dual listed 10f winner of 6 races, was second in the Group 2 Prix du Conseil de Paris and is a half-sister to one winner. *"I think she'll be ready to run in May and I'm looking forward to her. Probably a six furlong type to begin with, she's a well-made filly, a beautiful mover with a great temperament and she's built like a sprinter with a great backside on her".*

7. TRINITY LORRAINE (IRE) ★★★

b.f. Dark Angel – Known Class (Known Fact). March 5. Eleventh foal. £15,000Y. Doncaster Premier. Alan Bailey. Half-sister to the fair dual 7f winner Royal Applord (by Royal Applause), to 3 winners in the USA including the 2-y-o winner and stakes-placed Tocha (by Indian Charlie), a minor winner abroad by Monsieur Bond and the useful jumps winner C'Est Ca (by Groom Dancer). The dam is a placed half-sister to 2 minor winners. The second dam, Club Class (by Roberto), was third in the Group 3 Cheshire Oaks and subsequently won 4 races in the USA and is a full or half-sister to 9 winners. *"She's very nice. I bought two at Doncaster and whereas she was the smallest then she's now the bigger of the two. You could almost see her growing and filling out every day since she got broke in, she's developed so well. I'll wait until the end of May or early June with her and I think she'll be a seven furlong 2-y-o to start with".*

GEORGE BAKER

8. DER BLAUE REITER (IRE) ★★★★

ch.c. Art Connoisseur – Kafayef (Secreto). May 6. Fourteenth foal. €20,000Y. Tattersalls Ireland September. Sackville/Donald. Half-brother to the fairly useful 12f to 2m winner of 4 races Blimey O'Riley (by Kalanisi), to the Italian winner at 2 and 3 yrs and listed-placed Persian Filly (by Persian Bold and herself the dam of two listed winners), the French 2-y-o winner and listed-placed Ascot Dream (by Pennekamp), the fairly useful 2-y-o 7f winner Almaviva (by Grand Lodge), the fair 12f and hurdles winner Non Dom (by Hawk Wing), the modest 6f winner Gardrum (by Lycius), a winner abroad by Bertolini and a winner over hurdles by Spinning World. The dam is an unplaced half-sister to 10 winners including 3 stakes winners. The second dam, Sham Street (by Sham), a minor winner of 4 races in the USA, is a sister to the Italian Group 3 winner Stramusc and a half-sister to the dam of the Group 1 July Cup winner and champion sprinter Sakhee's Secret. *"A relatively cheap horse but he's right at the top of the pecking order of my 2-y-o's. He goes very nicely and I would hope to run him in late April. He's speedy and five furlongs will suit him fine. Ideally we'd like him to win well and go to Ascot with him. He's strong, compact and a typical sprinter".*

9. FIFTY SHADES OF GREY (IRE) ★★★

gr.c. Verglas – Vasilia (Dansili). January 24. Third foal. 50,000Y. Tattersalls October Book 1. George Baker. Brother to the useful 2-y-o 5f winner and Group 2 7f Superlative Stakes third Silverheels and half-brother to the fairly useful 2012 2-y-o 5f winner and listed-placed Lasilia (by Acclamation). The dam is an unraced half-sister to 7 winners including the Group 1 6f Cheveley Park Stakes and dual Group 2 winner Airwave. The second dam, Kangra Valley (by Indian Ridge), a moderate 2-y-o 5f winner, is a half-sister to 7 minor winners. (Team Fifty). *"Owned by a syndicate which includes the author of "Fifty Shades". He'll be racing in May over a stiff five/six furlongs, he's strong, compact and a proper 2-y-o".*

10. LAURELITA (IRE) ★★

b.f. High Chaparral – Chervil (Dansili). March 9. Fourth foal. 39,000Y. Tattersalls October Book 2. Angie Loder. Half-sister to the fair 2012 2-y-o 5f and 6f winner Mandy Layla (by Excellent Art). The dam, a quite useful 6f winner, is closely related to the US Grade 1 0f Yellow Ribbon Stakes winner Light Jig and a half-sister to 9 winners including the French 2-y-o listed 1m winner and dual Group 3 second Battle Dore. The second dam, Nashmeel (by Blushing Groom), won the Group 2 1m Prix d'Astarte, was second in the Prix Jacques le Marois, the Yellow Ribbon Invitational and the Matriarch Stakes and is a half-sister to 9 winners. (Mr & Mrs T Pittam & Partners). *"She's going to take a bit of time, she's tall, scopey and beautifully put-together. I need to wait for her to come to me but I suspect she'll be a seven furlong filly to start with".*

11. LOVING YOUR WORKS ★★★

b.c. Royal Applause – Time Crystal (Sadler's Wells). January 29. Sixth foal. 44,000Y. Tattersalls October Book 2. Angie Loder. Half-brother to the useful 1m (at 2 yrs) and listed 11f winner Sparkling Portrait (by Excellent Art), to the fairly useful 9f (at 2 yrs) and dual 1m winner Start Right (by Footstepsinthesand) and the moderate 11f winner Sparring Partner (by Rock Of Gibraltar). The dam, a 12f winner, is a half-sister to 6 winners. The second dam, State Crystal (by High Estate), a very useful winner of the Group 3 12f Lancashire Oaks and placed in the Yorkshire Oaks and the Prix Vermeille, is a half-sister to 6 winners including the Group 1 Fillies' Mile winner Crystal Music, the Group 3 winners Dubai Success and Solar Crystal and the Irish Derby third Tchaikovsky. (The Traditionalists). *"I really like him, we think plenty of him but we won't over cook him because he'll be treated as next year's horse really. We'll start him off in mid-summer and he's probably the best-looking 2-y-o we've got".*

12. MISTER MAYDAY (IRE) ★★★★

b.c. Kheleyf – Soxy Doxy (Hawk Wing). April 21. Second foal. £26,000Y. Doncaster Premier. Angie Loder. The dam, a moderate 12f placed maiden, is a half-sister to 4 winners including the listed King Charles II Stakes and subsequent US Grade 3 winner and Grade 2 placed Millennium Dragon. The second dam, Feather Bride (by Groom Dancer), won once at 3 yrs in France and is a half-sister to 5 winners. (Miss E Asprey, Mr T Kane, Mr S Thomas). *"I hate all these generalisations with stallions but this colt really is a 'quirky Kheleyf'. You can forgive them their quirks if they've got an engine and this horse definitely has one. He'll be a sprinter, despite the fact that the dam stayed, I like what he's done so far and he could be quite special".*

13. REDLORRYELLOWLORRY (IRE) ★★

b.c. Bushranger – Bronze Baby (Silver Charm). April 5. Second foal. 28,000Y. Tattersalls October Book 2. Angie Loder. The dam is an unplaced half-sister 3 winners including the

Group 3 Irish 1,000 Guineas Trial and Group 3 C L Weld Park Stakes winner and triple Group 1 placed Arch Swing. The second dam, Gold Pattern (by Slew O'Gold), a minor US winner of 4 races, is a half-sister to 2 stakes winners in the USA. *"A very straightforward, workmanlike horse that just gets on with his job. He's never going to catch the eye but he's a willing worker, he'll start his career in early May over six furlongs and he'll keep on improving".*

14. SLEEPING VENUS (IRE) ★★★

ch.f. Excellent Art – Sun Moon And Stars (Galileo). February 22. First foal. 12,000Y. Tattersalls October Book 2. George Baker. The dam is an unraced half-sister to 3 winners. The second dam, Darkling (by Grand Lodge), placed twice over middle-distance in Ireland, is a half-sister to 6 winners including the St Leger and Coronation Cup winner Scorpion, the US Grade 2 and Grade 3 winner Memories and the listed winners Danish Rhapsody and Garuda. (Equi ex Incertis Partners). *"She was a cheap purchase but she's really pleased me because from being weak and gangly she's really thrived. She looks really well now but I'm wondering if she's a bit weaker than she actually looks, because there's quite a bit of stamina in her pedigree – we'll just have to see".* TRAINERS' BARGAIN BUY

15. UNNAMED ★★

b.f. Kheleyf – Mistle Thrush (Storm Bird). April 15. Tenth foal. 10,000Y. Tattersalls October Book 2. Not sold. Half-sister to the smart Group 2 14.6f Park Hill Stakes winner Mistle Song (by Nashwan), to the fairly useful 6f (at 2 yrs) to 16.5f and hurdles winner Wise Owl (by Danehill) and the modest 10f winner Estimate (by Mark Of Esteem) and a minor winner in Italy by Fantastic Light. The dam, a fairly useful 10f winner, is a half-sister to 9 winners in Japan. The second dam, Head Of Victory (by Mr Prospector), is a placed half-sister to 3 winners including the Cheveley Park Stakes second Line Of Thunder (dam of the Belmont Stakes and Kentucky Derby winner Thunder Gulch). *"A very uncomplicated, straightforward filly who impresses me in her work. She'll be ready to go in early May over five furlongs, she shows speed, travels nicely and I like her".*

ANDREW BALDING

16. BELFILO (IRE) ★★★

ch.c. Teofilo – Belsay (Belmez). April 27. Twelfth foal. 100,000Y. Tattersalls October Book 2. Hugo Merry. Half-brother to the 6f, 7f (at 2 yrs) and Group 3 Craven Stakes winner and Group 2 second Killybegs (by Orpen), to the fairly useful Irish 1m (at 2 yrs) and 7.5f winner Pyrenees (by Rock Of Gibraltar), the fairly useful Irish 2-y-o 6f winner Lady's Mantle (by Sri Pekan), the quite useful Irish 7f winner Dreamalittledream (by Danehill Dancer), the fair 5f winner Red Senor (by Teofilo), the fair Irish 7f winner Dreamalittledream (by Danehill Dancer), the fair 6f (at 2 yrs) and 1m winner Tsaroxy (by Xaar) and minor winners abroad by Xaar and Cape Cross. The dam ran unplaced twice and is a half-sister to 4 winners including the Group 3 7f Nell Gwyn Stakes winner and 1,000 Guineas third Crystal Gazing. The second dam, Crystal Bright (by Bold Lad, Ire), won once in the USA and is a half-sister to 4 minor winners. (Mrs F H Hay). *"A nice, big, rangy horse that's going to take a bit of time, but he moves nicely and he should make up into a nice type towards the end of the season".*

17. BORN IN BOMBAY ★★

b.c. Shamardal – Pearl Dance (Nureyev). May 28. Half-brother to the 2012 French 2-y-o 1m winner and dual listed-placed Sparkling Beam (by Nayef), to the smart 2-y-o Group 1 Prix Marcel Boussac third Rainbow Springs and the useful 2-y-o dual 7f winner and Group 2 1m Royal Lodge Stakes fourth Ridge Dance (both by Selkirk). The dam, a useful 2-y-o 6f winner and third in the Group 1 Moyglare Stud Stakes, is a half-sister to the German listed winner and Group 1 German Derby fourth Ocean Sea and the US winner and Grade 3 third Dixie Splash. The second dam, Ocean Jewel (by Alleged), is an unraced half-sister to 6 minor winners. (Mr G Strawbridge). *"A late foal, he's not arrived yet but I've seen him and he's a smashing horse for the mid-season onwards".*

18. CAPE VICTORIA ★★★

b.f. Mount Nelson – Victoria Montoya (High Chaparral). March 5. First foal. The dam, a fairly useful dual 14f winner, was third in the Group 3 14f Lillie Langtry Stakes and is a half-sister to numerous winners including the very smart Group 2 1m Oettingen-Rennen and Group 3 8.5f Diomed Stakes winner Passing Glance, the smart Group 3 7f Prix de Palais-Royal and European Free Handicap winner Hidden Meadow, the smart listed 11f winner Scorned and the useful 6f (at 2 yrs) and listed 1m winner Kingsclere. The second dam, Spurned (by Robellino), a fairly useful 2-y-o 7f winner, later stayed 10f. (Kingsclere Racing Club). *"A home-bred of ours, the dam got better with age but this filly is a much sleeker version and I would hope she'd be out in mid-summer. Her mother was enormous but she's just a medium-sized, nice type of filly".*

19. COLLABORATION ★★★★

b.c. Halling – Red Shareef (Marju). February 25. Eighth foal. 57,000Y. Tattersalls October Book 2. A Balding. Brother to the quite useful 1m winner Spoke To Carlo and half-brother to the smart 6f and 1m winner of 10 races here, in the UAE and USA and listed placed Caesar Beware (by Daggers Drawn), to the fair 5f and 6f winner Radio City, the modest dual 6f winner Twice Red, the modest dual 7f winner Orangeleg (all by Intikhab), the modest dual 6f winner (including at 2 yrs) Gainshare and the minor French 1m winner Zylig (both by Lend A Hand). The dam won 3 races at 2 and 3 yrs in Italy and is a half-sister to 6 winners. The second dam, Dash Of Red (by Red Sunset), won the listed Silver Flash Stakes in Ireland at 2 yrs and is a half-sister to 7 winners. (Another Bottle Racing). *"He's a lovely horse, a good mover and one for seven furlongs in late June".*

20. COMANCHERO (IRE) ★★★

b.c. Camacho – Trempjane (Lujain). March 16. Fourth foal. 45,000Y. Tattersalls October Book 2. G Howson. Half-brother to the fair 2-y-o 6f and 7f winner Banner Road (by Dark Angel) and to the moderate triple 10f winner Market Place (by Bahamian Bounty). The dam, a fair 2-y-o 6f winner, is a half-sister to 3 winners including the 5.8f (at 2 yrs here) and subsequent four-time US Graded stakes winner Katdogawn. The second dam, Trempkate (by Trempolino), a French 2-y-o 9f winner, is a half-sister to 7 winners including the Group winners King Jock and Perfect Touch. (Kennet Valley Thoroughbreds VII). *"These owners seem to come up with a nice horse every year from the couple they buy. This one is the same, he looks very nice, he's grown a bit since he came in, he moves nicely and I would have thought he'd start off at six furlongs at the end of May or beginning of June".*

21. DARTING ★★

b.f. *Shamardal – Dararita (Halo)*. April 30. Eleventh foal. Half-sister to the Group 2 Goodwood Cup and Group 2 Prix Kergorlay winner Darasim (by Kahyasi), to the fairly useful 11f winner Minimise Risk (by Galileo), the quite useful 12f and 13.4f winner Darariyna (by Shirley Heights), the Irish 7f winner Darabela (by Desert King), the fair Irish 12f winner Daruliyya (by Highest Honor), the minor Irish 13f winner Darabanka (by In The Wings) and the moderate 2m winner Daraiym (by Peintre Celebre). The dam, a winner in France over 12.5f at 3 yrs, is a half-sister to 9 winners including the triple Group 1 winner Da Re Mi, the Hong Kong Group 1 winner Diaghilev, the Group 2 12.5f Prix Maurice de Nieuil winner Darazari and the Derby third Rewilding. The second dam, Darara (by Top Ville), won the Group 1 12f Prix Vermeille and is a half-sister to 11 winners including the Prix du Jockey Club winner and high-class sire Darshaan. (Birdcage/Lady Lloyd-Webber). *"She's been generously leased by Highclere in aid of the Basingstoke Hospital cancer unit. She's a little weak and immature still but she's a nice filly with a lot of quality. It's a lovely pedigree but we won't see her out for some time yet".*

22. DER MEISTER (IRE) ★★★★ ♠

b.c. *Mastercraftsman – Agnetha (Big Shuffle)*. April 8. Eighth foal. 20,000Y. Tattersalls October Book 2. Sackville/Donald. Half-brother to the quite useful Irish 1m and 9f winner Anaverna (by Galileo), to the quite useful Irish 7f winner Scarlet O'Hara (by Sadler's Wells), the fair Irish 5f winner April (by Rock Of Gibraltar), the fair 11f winner Starstruck (by Galileo) and the fair UAE 7f winner Pure Bluff (by Indian Ridge). The dam was a smart winner of the listed Silver

Flash Stakes (at 2 yrs) and the Group 3 5f King George Stakes at 3 yrs. She is a sister to the smart German Group 2 sprint winner Areion and to the Irish listed winner Anna Frid and a half-sister to 5 winners. The second dam, Aerleona (by Caerleon), a German 2-y-o 6f winner, is a half-sister to 5 winners including the Fillies' Mile winner Nepula. (James, Michaelson/Greenwood 1). *"Al Donald normally buys us one yearling a year and he has a very good track record with horses like Kalahari Gold and Simenon. This was his choice for this year and I think he's a really nice horse. He's big and still a bit on the weak side, but he has the scope to make a nice horse in time".*

23. END OF LINE ★★

b.c. *Pastoral Pursuits – Just Devine (Montjeu)*. March 2. Third foal. 50,000Y. Tattersalls October Book 2. David Redvers. Half-brother to the quite useful dual 6f winner Magic Secret (by Trade Fair). The dam, a modest 10f placed maiden, is a half-sister to 4 winners including the Group 3 Prix du Lys winner Airmail Special. The second dam, Shirley Blue (by Shirley Heights), placed once at 3 yrs in France, is a half-sister to 9 winners. (Qatar Racing Ltd). *"A nice horse but he's much more like the damsire Montjeu than Pastoral Pursuits. So we won't be in a hurry with him but he's a nice type".*

24. FIELD OF FAME ★★★

b.c. *Champs Elysees – Aswaaq (Peintre Celebre)*. February 8. First foal. 20,000Y. Tattersalls October Book 2. Not sold. The dam ran twice unplaced and is a half-sister to 4 winners including the 2-y-o listed 7f and 3-y-o Group 3 Fred Darling Stakes winner Muthabara. The second dam, Hureya (by Woodman), a quite useful 3-y-o 1m winner, is a half-sister to 3 winners including the Group 3 Greenham Stakes winner Muqbil. (Thurloe Thoroughbreds 31). *"He's done very well since he came in and I'm really pleased with the way he's done physically. I'd like to think we'd run him over six furlongs to get him started but he'd be more of a seven furlong type".*

25. FROM FROST ★★★

b.c. *Nayef – Salutare (Sadler's Wells)*. April 20.

Half-brother to the French 11f winner Send For Me (by Dalakhani) and to the French 7f winner Nomadic Kiss (by Medicean). The dam won twice over 15f and is a half-sister to numerous winners including the Group 1 2m Prix Royal-Oak winner Montare. The second dam, Contare (by Shirley Heights), won over 7f at 2 yrs and two listed events over 1m and 9f in France. (Mr G Strawbridge). *"A nice horse, he's in pre-training at the moment but he's a lot more forward-looking than most Nayef's and he should make a 2-y-o by July or August".*

26. GRACE AND FAVOUR ★★★

b.f. Montjeu – Gryada (Shirley Heights). May 3. Sister to the multiple Group 1 winner from 10f (at 2 yrs) to 2m 4f (Ascot Gold Cup) Fame And Glory and to the fair Irish 10f winner Yummy Mummy, closely related to the fairly useful 10f and 12f winner Rain Forest (by Sadler's Wells) and a minor winner in Germany by Galileo and half-sister to the smart 10.2f and 12f winner Grampian, to the fair 2-y-o 1m all-weather winner Gryskirk (both by Selkirk), the useful 10f and 12.3f winner Guaranda and the quite useful 11f winner Graham Island (both by Acatenango). The dam, a fairly useful 2-y-o 7f and 8.3f winner and third in the Group 3 1m Premio Dormello, is a full or half-sister to 4 middle-distance winners. The second dam, Grimpola (by Windwurf), won over 6f and 1m in Germany including the Group 2 German 1,000 Guineas and stayed 12f. (N Jones). *"A full-sister to Fame and Glory, she has loads of quality and is probably more precocious than you'd imagine looking at the pedigree. So hopefully we'll be able to start her off in a seven furlong maiden in mid-summer".*

27. GREY GEM (IRE) ★★★

gr.c. Danehill Dancer – Tiffany Diamond (Sadler's Wells). January 28. First foal. 46,000foal. Tattersalls December. Hursley Bloodstock. The dam, a useful 10f winner and second in the Group 3 Blue Wind Stakes, is a half-sister to one winner. The second dam, Niyla (by Darshaan), is an unraced half-sister to 6 winners. (J C Smith). *"The stud manager, David Bowe, picked him out as a foal and he's got a very good record with the ones he's pinhooked, so that bodes well. They were due to sell him until he got a minor injury so they*

withdrew and it's a good job because he goes nicely and looks like a nice type. He'll be a seven furlong type for June onwards".

28. HIGHLAND ACCLAIM (IRE) ★★★

b.c. Acclamation – Emma's Star (Darshaan). February 2. Ninth foal. 80,000Y. Tattersalls October Book 1. Not sold. Brother to the modest 7f and 1m winner of 4 races The Happy Hammer and half-brother to the Group 3 6f Chipchase Stakes winner of 8 races and Group 1 Haydock Sprint Cup third Genki (by Shinko Forest), the useful 2-y-o 6f winner and listed 7f second Za Za Zoom, the fairly useful 5f to 1m winner Highland Colori (both by Le Vie Dei Colori) and the quite useful 5f and 6f winner of 5 races Hazelrigg (by Namid). The dam, a winner over 8.5f in Italy at 3 yrs, is a half-sister to 4 other winners in Italy. The second dam, Notte Chiara (by Artaius), won the listed Premio Minerva and is a half-sister to 8 winners. (Mr E M Sutherland). *"One of our more precocious horses, he's a half-brother to Highland Colori who won four races for us last year. He looks a 2-y-o type and he's certainly forward-going enough. One for six furlongs in mid-May".*

29. ICONIC ARTIST (USA) ★★★

b.br.c. Arch – Seeking Silence (Seeking The Gold). March 11. Third foal. $375,000Y. Keeneland September. David Redvers. Half-brother to a minor 3-y-o winner in the USA by Hennessy. The dam was placed at 3 yrs and is a half-sister to 6 winners including the Grade 1 Frizette Stakes winner Confessional. The second dam, Whisper Who Dares (by Green Dancer), was a minor US 4-y-o winner and a half-sister to the Filly Triple Crown winner Chris Evert. (Qatar Racing Ltd). *"A big horse, he was expensive and he looks like his price tag suggests. It's a bit early to say how long he'll take to get ready, but he's probably a seven furlong type in July".*

30. IMPULSIVE MOMENT (IRE) ★★★★

ch.c. Galileo – Luas Line (Danehill). January 30. Fourth foal. €150,000Y. Goffs Orby. Badgers Bloodstock. Brother to Ballyglasheen, last of three over 7f on his only start at 2 yrs in 2012. The dam won the US Grade 1 Garden City Breeders Cup Stakes and was third in the

Irish 1,000 Guineas and is a half-sister to 4 winners. The second dam, Streetcar (by In The Wings), was placed fourth once over 8.5f at 2 yrs and is a half-sister to 9 winners including the Group 3 May Hill Stakes winner Intimate Guest and the dam of the Group/Grade 1 winners Prince Arch and Kingsfort. (Brook Farm Bloodstock). *"A Galileo with masses of quality, I'm very pleased with the way he's done since he came in. He hasn't half done well physically and he's making up into a quality horse. He's bred to be decent and he looks that way at the moment".*

31. JOHNNY RAE ★★★

b.c. Shirocco – Lady Brora (Dashing Blade). February 22. First foal. The dam, a fair 1m winner, is a half-sister to 2 winners. The second dam, Tweed Mill (by Selkirk), a quite useful 3-y-o 8.5f winner, is a half-sister to 5 winners. (Kingsclere Racing Club). *"A colt with the Monsun – Dashing Blade nick. He's a nice, forward-going colt and he should make a 2-y-o by mid-summer".*

32. KNOCKROON ★★★★

b.c. Royal Applause – Spring Touch (Elusive Quality). April 15. Second foal. €80,000Y. Goffs Orby. Andrew Balding. The dam is an unplaced daughter of the Group 2 Prix de Sandringham and US Grade 2 and Grade 3 winner Spring Star (by Danehill), herself a half-sister to 11 winners. (D E Brownlow). *"I'm really pleased with him, he's grown a lot and he should be out in May. From the little bits we've done with him he's got plenty of boot and he's a really nice stamp of a horse and an exciting prospect".*

33. KOKOVOKO (IRE) ★★

br.c. Trans Island – Khazaria (Sinndar). March 15. Third foal. €17,500Y. Tattersalls Ireland September. Andrew Balding. The dam is an unplaced half-sister to 2 winners including the Group 1 Grand Prix de Paris winner Khalkevi. The second dam, Khalisa (by Persian Bold), won 3 races in France including the Group 3 Prix Chloe and the Group 3 Prix Cleopatre and is a half-sister to 4 winners. (Mrs T Miller). *"A smashing horse, he's very Selkirk-looking and so we wouldn't be in a hurry with him but we're very pleased with him so far".*

34. LIBECCIO (FR) ★★

b.c. Shirocco – Francais (Mark Of Esteem). March 22. Sixth foal. 40,000Y. Tattersalls October Book 1. Andrew Balding. Half-brother to the French 2-y-o dual 1m winner and triple listed-placed Finding Neverland (by Green Desert). The dam ran once unplaced and is a half-sister to 7 winners including the Group 3 7f Tetrarch Stakes winner and Irish 2,000 Guineas second France. The second dam, Hyperspectra (by Rainbow Quest), a fairly useful 10.2f winner, is a half-sister to 5 winners including the dual Group 3 winner Poet. (Mick & Janice Mariscotti). *"A tall horse with a big raking stride on him, he looks an athlete but is one for the latter part of the season".*

35. MAN OF HARLECH ★★★

b.c. Dansili – Ffestiniog (Efisio). April 14. Half-brother to the quite useful 2012 2-y-o 5f winner New Fforest (by Oasis Dream), to the Group 3 1m Solonaway Stakes winner of 4 races Border Patrol (by Selkirk), the smart sprint winner of 11 races (including the Group 3 Prix de Meautry) Eisteddfod (by Cadeaux Genereux), the useful 2-y-o 5f to 7f winner Brecon Beacon (by Spectrum), the useful dual 7f (at 2 yrs) and UAE Group 3 1m winner Boston Lodge (by Grand Lodge), the fairly useful 2-y-o 6f winner Harlech Castle (by Royal Applause), the quite useful 5f and 6f winner Oceans Apart (by Desert Prince) and the quite useful 2-y-o dual 7f winner Tredegar (by Inchinor). The dam, a fairly useful 2-y-o listed 7.3f and 3-y-o 1m winner, is a half-sister to several winners. The second dam, Penny Fan (by Nomination), was placed once over 5f at 3 yrs, is closely related to the listed 5f Scarborough Stakes winner Rivers Rhapsody and a half-sister to the Group 3 5f Prix d'Arenburg winner Regal Scintilla. (Elite Racing Club). *"A lovely big horse, his half-brother New Fforest performed well for us last year but this a totally different type and he'll require a bit of patience. He's got quality though and I'm sure he'll be a nice horse, but he'll need time and at least seven furlongs this season".*

36. MERRY ME (IRE) ★★★

b.f. Invincible Spirit – Thought Is Free (by Cadeaux Genereux). April 9. Second foal. Half-sister to the modest 2012 7f placed 2-y-o

Elusive Thought (by Elusive City). The dam, a fairly useful listed 6f placed 2-y-o, is a half-sister to 5 winners including the fairly useful 5f and 6f winner and dual listed-placed Day By Day. The second dam, Dayville (by Dayjur), a quite useful triple 6f winner, is a half-sister to 4 winners including the Grade 1 Yellow Ribbon Handicap winner Spanish Fern. (Mrs F H Hay). *"The dam was quite a fast, precocious 2-y-o and this filly looks the same. She's not very big but she's speedy and when she comes in her coat we'll crack on with her".*

37. MICRAS ★★★
b.f. *Medicean – Purple Heather (Rahy).* February 20. Sixth foal. Half-sister to the fairly useful 7f (at 2 yrs) and 1m winner The Coires (by Green Desert) and to the fair 1m winner Gelder (by Grand Lodge). The dam, a fairly useful 10f winner, is a half-sister to the quite useful 12f winner Magnetic Pole. The second dam, Clear Attraction (by Lear Fan), is a once-raced half-sister to the outstanding broodmare Height Of Fashion (the dam of Nashwan, Nayef and Unfuwain). (The Queen). *"We have the 3-y-o half-brother by Tiger Hill who probably wants two miles but this filly looks like she's got a bit more speed and quality. She'll make a 2-y-o a bit later on".*

38. MIME DANCE ★★★★
b.c. *Notnowcato – Encore My Love (Royal Applause).* January 22. Sixth living foal. 32,000Y. Tattersalls October Book 2. Andrew Balding. Half-brother to the quite useful 2-y-o 5f and 6f winner Prospect Place and to the modest dual 1m winner Love Nest (both by Compton Place). The dam, a modest 6f placed 2-y-o, is a half-sister to 6 winners including the 2-y-o Group 1 Racing Post Trophy winner Be My Chief. The second dam, Lady Be Mine (by Sir Ivor), a minor 3-y-o 1m winner, is a half-sister to 6 winners including Mixed Applause (dam of both the Group 1 St James's Palace Stakes winner Shavian and the Group 1 Ascot Gold Cup winner Paean). (D E Brownlow). *"A very forward-going colt, he's likely to be one of my earlier 2-y-o types, starting off at six furlongs. It's quite encouraging because he'll probably end up staying seven furlongs and yet he's already showing a bit of speed. A nice enough horse".*

39. MUIR LODGE ★★★
ch.c. *Exceed And Excel – Miss Chaussini (Rossini).* April 18. Fourth foal. 130,000Y. Tattersalls October Book 1. Stephen Hillen. Half-sister to the fair 2012 2-y-o 7f winner Coincidentally (by Acclamation), to the quite useful 2-y-o dual 7f winner Strictly Silver (by Dalakhani) and the winner Chaussini (by Dubawi). The dam, a fair Irish 3-y-o 7f winner, is a half-sister to 9 winners. The second dam, Chaussons Roses (by Lyphard), is an unraced sister to the French dual Group 3 winner Tenue De Soiree and a half-sister to 5 winners including the triple Group 1 winner (including the French 1,000 Guineas Baiser Vole and the dual Group 2 winner Squill. (Mrs F H Hay). *"One of my earlier types, although he still hasn't come in his coat because of the cold weather. He's strong, he's been upsides a couple of times and he's got a bit of speed. He goes nicely and I'd be disappointed if he wasn't winning races this year".*

40. NABATEAN (IRE) ★★★
b.c. *Rock Of Gibraltar – Landinium (Lando).* April 18. Half-brother to the quite useful 1m winner Hallings Comet (by Halling). The dam, a useful winner of the listed 10f Premio Baggio, was Group 3 placed twice and is a half-sister to a minor winner in France. The second dam, Hollywood Girl (by Cagliostro), was a German 7f to 9.5f winner. (Lord Blyth). *"He was a little bit late in, but he's a really nice type, very straight forward and we had his half-brother who won last year. A very nice horse, he'll be a better 3-y-o but he'll certainly be running, and hopefully winning, this year from mid-season onwards".*

41. OBSTINATE (IRE) ★★
b.c. *Fastnet Rock – Sangita (Royal Academy).* April 5. Sixth foal. €260,000Y. Goffs Orby. Stephen Hillen. Closely related to the fairly useful listed 6f winner What's Up Pussycat and to a minor winner abroad (both by Danehill Dancer). The dam, a poor 4-y-o 2m winner, is a half-sister to 7 winners including the dam of the German Group 1 winner Scalo. The second dam, Saquiace (by Sagace), a listed-placed winner of 4 races, is a half-sister to 5 winners. (Mrs F H Hay). *"He's been on the grow since he came in and he*

needs to mature physically before we can do anything fast with him. It's too soon to judge him, really".

42. ON DEMAND ★★★

ch.f. Teofilo – Mimisel (Selkirk). April 19. Third foal. 28,000Y. Tattersalls October Book 2. Andrew Balding. Half-sister to the fair 2012 2-y-o 5f winner Keep The Dream (by Oasis Dream). The dam, a quite useful 2-y-o 7f winner, was listed-placed and is a half-sister to 2 winners. The second dam, Milly-M (by Cadeaux Genereux), is an unraced half-sister to 5 winners including the useful 6f winner and listed 6f placed Millybaa. (Sky Sports News). *"She's a nice, big filly and has been leased to Sky Sports News as part of the Racing For Change initiative. A mid-summer type 2-y-o and she's nice enough".*

43. PEARL SPECTRE (USA) ★★★★

ch.c. Street Cry – Dark Sky (Storm Cat). March 9. First foal. $600,000Y. Keeneland September. Blandford Bloodstock. The dam, a minor winner of 2 races at 3 yrs in the USA, is a half-sister to 5 winners including the Group 1 Prix de Diane and Group 1 Prix du Moulin winner Nebraska Tornado. The second dam, Media Nox (by Lycius), won the Group 3 Prix du Bois and is a half-sister to 6 winners including the Grade 2 winner Bonash. (Pearl Bloodstock Ltd). *"A fabulous looking horse, we haven't done anything fast with him yet but he's strong and looks like having the speed for six furlongs by the end of May. As his price tag would suggest he's a very nice colt. He's big, strong and has plenty of bone and presence".*

44. POOL HOUSE ★★★

b.c. Sakhee's Secret – Gitane (Grand Lodge). January 21. Sixth foal. £22,000Y. Doncaster Premier. Andrew Balding. Half-brother to the French winner of 3 races and 1m listed-placed Mega Back (by Zamindar). The dam, a minor French 11f winner, is a half-sister to 8 winners. The second dam, Grenouillere (by Alysheba), is a placed half-sister to 4 winners including the Group 1 Prix de la Salamandre winner Oczy Czarnie. (D E Brownlow). *"He looks a runner, he's forward going and might have the speed to start at five furlongs. One of the earlier types".*

45. RESTRAINT ★★★

b.c. Kheleyf – Inhibition (Nayef). February 17. First foal. The dam, a fairly useful 12f winner, is a half-sister to numerous winners including the very smart Group 2 1m Oettingen-Rennen and Group 3 8.5f Diomed Stakes winner Passing Glance, the smart Group 3 7f Prix de Palais-Royal and European Free Handicap winner Hidden Meadow and the smart listed winners Scorned and Kingsclere. The second dam, Spurned (by Robellino), a fairly useful 2-y-o 7f winner, later stayed 10f. (Kingsclere Racing Club). *"A nice colt from a family we've had a lot of luck with. He'll be fine, he won't be early because he's more like his mother than Kheleyf, but he'll make a 2-y-o by the latter part of the summer".*

46. RIZAL PARK (IRE) ★★★

b.g. Amadeus Wolf – Imelda (Manila). March 31. Eleventh foal. €12,000Y. Goffs Orby. A Balding. Half-brother to the quite useful 5f winner of 11 races Haajes (by Indian Ridge), to the quite useful 2-y-o 6f winner and subsequent US winner and Grade 3 placed Rapadash (by Boundary), the fair 1m and 9f winner of 4 races Todlea and the fair 6f (at 2 yrs) and 7f winner Foxtrot Alpha (both by Desert Prince). The dam ran once unplaced at 2 yrs and is a half-sister to 6 winners including the high-class Group 2 Prix du Rond-Point and Group 2 Prix d'Astarte winner Shaanxi. The second dam, Rich And Riotous (by Empery), won once over 1m in France and is a half-sister to 6 winners. (M & V Slade/ KTS). *"He looks a bargain. We had him gelded straight after the sale and he's done very well physically. He looks racey enough and as soon as the six furlong races start he should be ready to go. A good type".* TRAINERS' BARGAIN BUY

47. ROSKILLY (IRE) ★★★

ch.c. Hurricane Run – Party Feet (Noverre). February 10. Second foal. 50,000Y. Tattersalls October Book 1. Andrew Balding. Half-brother to the 2012 Irish 2-y-o 1m winner Love And Cherish (by Excellent Art). The dam is an unraced half-sister to the Group 2 Sun Chariot Stakes and Group 3 Matron Stakes winner of 4 races Independence (herself dam of the dual Group 1 winner Mount Nelson and the Group

2 winner Monitor Closely). The second dam, Yukon Hope (by Forty Niner), was a fair 6f and 1m placed maiden. (Mick & Janice Mariscotti). *"He looks more precocious than you'd imagine for a Hurricane Run and he'd certainly have enough speed for seven furlongs anyway".*

48. SCOTLAND (GER) ★★★

b.c. *Monsun – Sqillo (Bachelor Duke)*. April 1. First foal. €200,000Y. Goffs Orby. Hugo Merry. The dam was placed at 3 yrs in Germany and is a half-sister to 9 winners including the dam of the multiple Group 1 winner and sire Shirocco. The second dam, Sedulous (by Tap On Wood), a very useful winner from 5f to 1m at 2 yrs in Ireland including the Group 3 Killavullen Stakes, subsequently won in the USA and is a sister to the listed Tyros Stakes winner Tapolite and a half-sister to 3 winners. (Mrs F H Hay). *"A lovely horse. It's always encouraging when a horse that's going to stay a mile and a half shows a little bit of speed early on. He's certainly got ability".*

49. SECRET HINT ★★★

b.f. *Oasis Dream – Teeky (Daylami)*. January 29. First foal. The dam, a quite useful 12f winner, is a half-sister to numerous winners including the very smart Group 2 7f Challenge Stakes winner Sleeping Indian, the Group 2 12f Grand Prix de Chantilly winner Aiken, the useful listed 1m winner Nationalism and the useful 10f winner and Group 3 10f Prix de la Nonette third Felicity. The second dam, Las Flores (by Sadler's Wells), a useful 10f winner, was second in the Lingfield Oaks Trial and third in the Italian Oaks. She is a full or half-sister to numerous winners including the useful Irish 6f and 10f winner Dancing Goddess. (Mr G Strawbridge). *"She's still in pre-training, but she's very forward-going and looks a 2-y-o type, so she'll be in soon and we'll take it from there".*

50. SPECTATOR ★★★

br.c. *Passing Glance – Averami (Averti)*. March 5. Brother to the very smart Group 3 1m and Group 3 9f winner and Group 1 placed Side Glance and to the fair 7f (at 2 yrs) and 1m winner Advertise and half-brother to the quite useful 9f and 11f winner Rawaki (by Phoenix Reach) and the fair 12f winner Tagliatelle (by

Tagula). The dam, a moderate 7f winner, is a sister to 2 winners. The second dam, Friend For Life (by Lahib), was unplaced. (Kingsclere Racing Club). *"A full brother to Side Glance, he's a really nice type of horse, one for seven furlongs in July and I couldn't be happier with him".*

51. STYBBA ★★★★

b.f. *Medicean – Time Saved (Green Desert)*. April 30. Eighth foal. 240,000Y. Tattersalls October Book 1. David Redvers. Sister to the useful listed 6f winner Jira and half-sister to the smart 7f (at 2 yrs) and Group 2 12f King Edward VII Stakes winner Plea Bargain (by Machiavellian), the very useful Group 3 10f Winter Hill Stakes winner Lay Time (by Galileo), the useful 2-y-o 7f winner and Group 3 1m Prix des Chenes second Dubai Time (by Dubai Destination) and the quite useful 6f (at 2 yrs) and 1m winner Emirates Sports (by King's Best). The dam, a fairly useful 10f winner, is a sister to the useful 1m winner Illusion and a half-sister to 5 winners including Zinaad and Time Allowed (both winners of the Group 2 12f Jockey Club Stakes) and the dams of the Group winners Anton Chekhov, First Charter, Plea Bargain and Time Away. The second dam, Time Charter (by Saritamer), was an exceptional filly and winner of the Oaks, the King George VI and Queen Elizabeth Diamond Stakes, the Champion Stakes, Coronation Cup, Prix Foy and Sun Chariot Stakes. (Qatar Racing Ltd). *"We had this filly's half-sister Lay Time last year and she won a Group 3 for us. This filly is just like Lay Time was at the same age, she's got a bit of quality in her and she'll make up into a nice filly. Because of the cold spring we've had to suffer it's more difficult than normal to make predictions, but I would think she'd end up a miler".*

52. TELEGRAPH ★★★★

b.c. *Bushranger – Vampire Queen (General Monash)*. February 4. Sixth foal. 65,000Y. Tattersalls October Book 1. John Warren. Half-brother to the modest 2013 3-y-o 7f winner Tilstarr (by Shamardal), to the minor Italian winner of 5 races at 3 to 5 yrs Passi De Sanza (by Bertolini) and the modest Irish 10f winner Vampire Blues (by Azamour). The dam, a modest 3-y-o 6f winner, is a sister to the winner and dual Group 2 placed Bram Stoker and a half-sister to 4 winners. The second dam, Taniokey (by Grundy), won at 3 yrs and is a half-sister to 5 winners including Kittyhawk (Group 3 Lowther Stakes). (Highclere Thoroughbred Racing – Alcove). *"Certainly one of the more forward two-year-olds, he's strong and every inch a two-year-old type. He'll start at five furlongs".*

53. TRADING PROFIT ★★★

br.c. Kheleyf – Avessia (Averti). March 2. Sixth foal. 38,000Y. Tattersalls October Book 2. Andrew Balding. Closely related to Lucky Green (by Green Desert), unplaced in one start at 2 yrs in 2012 and to the quite useful 5f winner Avertor (by Oasis Dream). The dam, placed fourth once over 6f from two starts, is a sister to 2 winners including the smart dual 6f listed winner (including at 2 yrs) and sire Avonbridge and a half-sister to the Group 1 5f Prix de l'Abbaye winner Patavellian. The second dam, Alessia (by Caerleon), a quite useful 2-y-o 7f winner, is a sister to the Group 2 14.6f Park Hill Stakes winner Casey and a half-sister to 4 winners. (Another Bottle Racing). *"He's a nice type and he'll make a 2-y-o alright. From the same family as Avonbridge and Patavellian, he's a little bit 'up behind' still but he's got a good attitude and is a typical colt who would take plenty of work and respond to it".*

54. VECHEKA (IRE) ★★★

b.c. Lawman – Lidanski (Soviet Star). April 24. Fourth foal. 75,000Y. Tattersalls October Book 1. Andrew Balding. Brother to the listed 10f winner of 3 races Mustaheel and half-brother to the Group 1 5f Prix de l'Abbaye and Group 2 5f Prix du Gros-Chene winner Wizz Kid (by Whipper). The dam, a fairly useful Irish 7f winner, was listed-placed and is a half-sister to 5 winners including the listed winner Yaa Wayl. The second dam, Lidanna (by Nicholas), a dual Group 3 winner in Ireland over 5f and 6f, is a half-sister to 5 winners. (Mick & Janice Mariscotti). *"He's a half-brother to the Abbaye winner Wizz Kid and I'm sure he'll be a sprinting type too, but he's got very open knees and he's still 'up behind' so physically he's not there yet. He'll be a fast horse one day".*

55. WILLIE BRENNAN ★★★

b.c. Bushranger – Miss Assertive (Zafonic). April 21. Fourth foal. 46,000Y. Tattersalls October Book 2. McKeever Bloodstock. Half-brother to the useful 6f (at 2 yrs), listed 7f and subsequent US stakes winner Meydan Princess (by Choisir) and to the quite useful 6f winner of 3 races Summerinthecity (by Indian Ridge). The dam, a quite useful 2-y-o 6f winner, was listed-placed twice and is a half-sister to the useful 1m (including at 2 yrs) to 10f winner and subsequent US Grade 3 winner Ascertain. The second dam, Self Assured (by Ahonoora), a fairly useful 7f winner at 2 yrs, was second in the Group 3 1m May Hill Stakes and is a half-sister to 6 winners. (Dr P Brown). *"He looks an early 2-y-o type but his knees are open so we've backed off him. Hopefully he'll come good in early June and I should think he'll be a sprinter".*

56. WITH A TWIST ★★★

b.f. Excellent Art – Bint Zamayem (Rainbow Quest). April 23. Fourth foal. 22,000Y. Tattersalls October Book 2. G Howson. Closely related to the unplaced 2012 2-y-o Foie Gras (by Kyllachy) and to the useful 7f (at 2 yrs) to 9f winner of 9 races (including a 1m listed event) Mia's Boy (by Pivotal) and half-brother to the useful Irish 6f (at 2 yrs) and 7f winner and Group 3 Debutante Stakes third Sweet Deimos (by Green Desert), the quite useful 7.6f winner Queenie (by Indian Ridge), the fair 2-y-o 1m winner Rumbalara (by Intikhab) and the modest 10f winner Mayhem Freddie (by Haafhd). The dam, a fairly useful 10f winner, was listed-placed over 10f and is a half-sister to the Group 3 Prix Chloe winner Rouquette and the US stakes winner Moody's Cat. The second dam, Zamayem (by Sadler's Wells), is an unraced half-sister to 4 winners. *"I'm pretty pleased with her, she's got slightly open knees but when she comes together physically she'll have enough speed for six furlongs. We're probably looking at mid-June for her".*

57. UNNAMED ★★★

b.br.c. Arch – Doryphar (Lyphard). April 3. Second foal. £50,000 2-y-o. Kempton Breeze-Up. A Balding. Half-brother to the minor US winner at 2 and 3 yrs Majorca Sun (by Songandaprayer). The dam, a minor winner at 3 and 4 yrs in the USA, is a half-sister to the US stakes winner Ruthian (dam of the US Grade 1 winner Rutherienne). The second dam, Adoryphar (by Lyphard), a winner of 4 races in France (at 2 yrs) and the USA and third in the Grade 2 La Prevoyante Invitational Handicap, is a half-sister to 5 winners including the US Grade 3 winner Adcat. *"He breezed well at the sale and I liked the look of him and I'm very pleased with him. He should be one we can crack on with, but he won't just be a 2-y-o because he does have scope".*

58. UNNAMED ★★★

b.c. Jeremy – Double Vie (Tagula). April 24. Third foal. 20,000Y. Tattersalls October Book 2. Andrew Balding. Half-brother to the fairly useful 5f, 6f (both at 2 yrs) and 7f winner Big Note (by Amadeus Wolf). The dam, a listed 1m winner at 3 yrs in France, is a half-sister to 3 minor winners. The second dam, The Good Life (by Rainbow Quest), won once at 3 yrs in France and is a half-sister to 3 minor winners. (Mr N Botica & Mrs W Gorell). *"He's a half-brother to Big Note, a horse we had a bit of luck with last year and he's a big horse. The fact that Jeremy has done so well hurdling over the winter will give this colt some residual value! He's grand, a good mover and a nice type".*

59. UNNAMED ★★★

ch.c. Firebreak – Manderina (Mind Games). April 28. Ninth foal. €21,000Y. Tattersalls Ireland September. Andrew Balding. Half-sister to the fairly useful 2-y-o triple 5f winner and listed-placed Last Bid (by Vital Equine), to the fair 2-y-o 5f winner Foxy Games (by Foxhound), the moderate 11f and 12f winner Indian Scout (by Indesatchel) and a minor winner abroad by Foxhound. The dam is an unplaced half-sister to several winners including the useful winner over 5f (twice) and 6f and very useful broodmare Amber Mill. The second dam, Millaine (by Formidable), a half-sister to 7 winners including the Italian dual Group 1 winner Svelt, was placed once and stayed 12f. *"He had a couple of issues early on but he's coming good now and he'll be very much a 2-y-o type once we get some work into him".*

60. UNNAMED ★★★★

b.c. Rock Of Gibraltar – Portentous (Selkirk). April 30. Second foal. 70,000Y. Tattersalls October Book 1. Andrew Balding. The dam is an unraced sister to the Group 1 Nassau Stakes and dual Group 2 winner Favourable Terms and a half-sister to 3 winners including the listed winner Modern History. The second dam, Fatefully (by Private Account), a smart winner of 4 races including two listed events, is a half-sister to 6 winners including the US Grade 2 winner Points Of Grace. (Mr N Botica & Mrs W Gorell). *"A middle-distance type for next year, but he's got a bit of quality and I'm very happy with him. He's tall but very athletic and I'm sure that once we step him up a gear he'll come good. We like him".*

DAVID BARRON
61. AMOUR NOIR (IRE)

b.br.c. Footstepsinthesand – Announcing Peace (Danehill). February 19. Ninth foal. €150,000Y. Goffs Orby. David Redvers. Half-brother to the modest 2012 1m and 10f placed 2-y-o Jullundar (by Refuse To Bend), to the smart winner of 6 races from 6f (at 2 yrs) to 12f (dual listed) and Group 3 placed Crosspeace, the fairly useful 2-y-o dual 7f winner So Sweet (both by Cape Cross), the Irish 2-y-o 1m winner Desert Eagle (by Hawk Wing), the fair 1m winner Tatbeeq (by Invincible Spirit), the Italian 5f (at 2 yrs) and 7.5f winner Carburatore (by College Chapel) and the minor Irish 2-y-o 1m winner Desert Eagle (by Hawk Wing). The dam is an unplaced full or half-sister to 5 minor winners. The second dam, Remoosh (by Glint Of Gold), is an unplaced half-sister to 5 winners including Nomination (Group 2 Richmond Stakes). (Qatar Racing Ltd).

62. PREMIUM PRESSURE (USA)

b.br.c. War Front – Judy's Magic (Wavering Monarch). April 24. Ninth foal. $330,000Y. Keeneland September. David Redvers. Half-brother to 5 winners including the US winner and Grade 1 Go For Wand Handicap second She's Got The Beat (by Sultry Song). The dam, a minor US 2-y-o winner, is a sister to a stakes winner and a half-sister to 8 winners. The second dam, Mary Roland (by Relaunch), a minor US 3-y-o winner, is a half-sister to 8 winners. (Qatar Racing Ltd).

63. RACE HUNTER (USA) ♠

b.br.f. Dixie Union – Shriek (Street Cry). February 28. Second foal. $160,000Y. Keeneland September. David Redvers. The dam, a US stakes-placed winner, is a half-sister to 4 winners including the US Grade 2 San Luis Rey Handicap winner Stanley Park and the stakes winner and Grade 3 placed Turf Melody. The second dam, Tricky Bird (by Storm Bird), is an unplaced half-sister to 8 winners. (Qatar Racing Ltd).

64. VIVA VERGLAS

gr.c. Verglas – Yellow Trumpet (Petong). March 26. Seventh foal. £55,000Y. Doncaster Premier. Harrowgate Bloodstock. Brother to the quite useful 2-y-o 7f winner Right Divine and to the fair 10f winner Silverglas and half-brother to the useful dual 5f (including at 2 yrs) and subsequent Hong Kong winner and listed-placed City Of Tribes (by Invincible Spirit), the quite useful 2-y-o 5f winner Canary Island (by Groom Dancer) and the fair 1m (at 2 yrs) and 10f winner Golden Aria (by Rakti). The dam, a fair 2-y-o 5f winner, is a sister to 3 winners including the listed 5.2f St Hugh's Stakes winner Petula and a half-sister to 5 winners including the very useful Group 3 Ballycorus Stakes winner Naahy. The second dam, Daffodil Fields (by Try My Best), placed 6 times in Ireland, is a half-sister to 3 winners. (R C Miquel).

RALPH BECKETT

65. BOLD JACK DONAHUE (IRE) ★★★

b.br.c. Bushranger – Mother's Hope (Idris). April 14. Seventh foal. 30,000Y. Tattersalls October Book 2. McCalmont Bloodstock. Half-brother to the Italian triple listed 1m winner at 2 and 3 yrs Collesano (by Pearl Of Love) and two minor winners in Italy by Bluebird and Rakti. The dam, a winner on the flat and over hurdles in Italy, is a half-sister to 6 winners. The second dam, Mothers Blessing (by Wolver Hollow), was a placed half-sister to 6 winners. (The Outlaws). *"He might not take too long. It's a very tough family, they take plenty of racing and he looks the same – as if he'll take plenty of work. He's not a robust horse and he still needs to fill his frame but he has a good temperament. We felt he was underdone at the sales, but he's done well for work and I think*

he'll strengthen through the spring and appear on the track as a six furlong 2-y-o".

66. CRYSTAL LAKE (IRE) ★★★

gr.c. Verglas – Entail (Riverman). April 16. Ninth foal. £20,000Y. Doncaster Premier. Jamie McCalmont. Half-brother to the useful 2-y-o 6f and subsequent US winner Let Us Prey (by Hawk Wing), to the fair 2-y-o 6f winner Entailment (by Kris), the French winner of 15 races (including over 10f at 2 yrs) Grandretour (by Grand Lodge), the fair 1m winner Echo Dancer (by Danehill Dancer) and the moderate 5f winner Gothic Chick (by Araafa). The dam, a fairly useful winner of 3 races from 7f to 1m at 4 yrs, is a half-sister to 5 winners including the multiple US Grade 1 winner Ventura. The second dam, Estala (by Be My Guest), won once at 2 yrs in France, was listed-placed three times and is a half-sister to 5 winners including the Group 3 winners Vortex, Prove and Danefair (dam of the Group 3 winner Trade Fair). (The Pickford Hill Partnership). *"He's had a touch of sore shins but we'll be getting on with him again shortly. I think he'll need a bit of cut in the ground, he looks to have a good attitude and six or seven furlongs should be his trip this year. He's not particularly robust, he's more of an angular sort of horse, but he's not big or backward so he shouldn't take long to come to hand. I quite like him".*

67. DARK REALITY (IRE) ★★

b.f. Intikhab – Sunny Slope (Mujtahid). March 2. Seventh foal. 48,000Y. Tattersalls October Book 2. David Redvers. Half-sister to the Irish 2-y-o 7f and subsequent US Grade 2 winner Indigo River (by Kodiac), to the quite useful 7f, 1m (including at 2 yrs) and 11f winner of 6 races Lake Pontchartrain (by Invincible Spirit), the modest 6f (at 2 yrs) and 1m winner of 4 races Royal Holiday (by Captain Rio) and a minor winner in the USA by Xaar. The dam, a modest 1m and 9f winner, is a half-sister to 2 minor winners. The second dam, Scottish Eyes (by Green Dancer), is an unraced half-sister to 4 winners. (Qatar Racing Ltd). *"I really liked her at the yearling sales and I hoped that she'd get sent here. She's not precocious, she has a big frame and she's done a lot of growing just lately, so we haven't done much with her. The poor weather this spring hasn't helped her and I would think she'll be one for seven furlongs in August or September. She's more of a 3-y-o type and Intikhab's tend to get better for work and time".*

68. DINNERATMIDNIGHT ★★★

b.c. Kyllachy – The Terrier (Foxhound). February 27. Fourth foal. £35,000Y. Doncaster Premier. Global Equine Group. Half-brother to the useful 2012 triple 2-y-o 5f winner Dutch Masterpiece (by Dutch Art) and to the modest 6f and 7f winner Beachwood Bay (by Tobougg). The dam, a fair 2-y-o 5f winner, is a half-sister to 3 winners. The second dam, Branston Gem (by So Factual), placed over 5f at 2 yrs, is a half-sister to 3 winners including the dual listed winner Falcon Hill. (Mr N Patsalides & Mr M Patel). *"He's a forward 2-y-o and he's done a couple of pieces of work. I expect he'll appear sometime in May, he shows a bit and he's a strong sort of horse that should have the speed for five furlongs. He has a good way about him, he gets on with his work and is a likeable sort".*

69. DUDLEY QUEEN (IRE) ★★

ch.f. Excellent Art – Royal Bounty (Generous). April 1. Tenth foal. £50,000Y. Doncaster Premier. David Redvers. Half-sister to Harvest Queen (by Spinning World), a Group 3 placed winner of two listed events over 1m, to the quite useful dual 1m winner (including at 2 yrs), Knave Of Clubs (by Red Clubs), the quite useful dual 6f winner Generous Gesture, the quite useful Irish dual 1m winner Fred Fenster (both by Fasliyev) and the fair dual 7f winner Coconut Queen (by Alhaarth). The dam, a quite useful 2-y-o 7.5f winner, is a half-sister to 3 minor winners here and abroad. The second dam, Queen Helen (by Troy), a winner from 7f (at 2 yrs) to 14f including the listed Hyperion Stakes, was fourth in the Group 2 10f Sun Chariot Stakes. She is a half-sister to 6 winners including the Group 1 Prix du Cadran winner Sought Out (herself dam of the Derby winner North Light) and the dams of Gamut (Group 1 Grand Prix de Saint-Cloud) and the Group 2 winners Multicoloured and Bonny Scot. (Qatar Racing Ltd). *"She's had a problem and isn't in training at the moment. She's back at the stud for a short spell but it's a good pedigree, she*

grew quite a lot when she was here and she'll make a 2-y-o in the second half of the season".

70. EVITA PERON ★★★★

ch.f. Pivotal – Entente Cordiale (Ela-Mana-Mou). February 4. Seventh foal. 110,000Y. Tattersalls October Book 1. Not sold. Half-sister to the dual Group 1 King's Stand Stakes and Group 2 Prix du Gros-Chene winner Equiano (by Acclamation), the French winner of 6 races from 6f to 1m Orife (by Marchand De Sable), the modest 1m winner Elvira Delight (by Desert Style) and a winner in Spain by Key Of Luck. The dam was placed once at 4 yrs and is a half-sister to 3 winners. The second dam, Mirmande (by Kris), is an unplaced sister to one winner and a half-sister to the listed winner Sir Simon and the Group 2 Sun Chariot Stakes second Dartrey. (Newsells Park Stud Ltd). *"She's a lovely filly and if she's as tough as her half-brother Equiano then we'll have some sport. She's not huge like some Pivotal's can be, so she should make a 2-y-o but it'll be in the second half of the year. A six furlong type, she has a good way about her and she's got plenty of size and scope. I like her very much".*

71. FREE REIN ★★★

b.f. Dansili – Sant Elena (Efisio). April 8. Half-sister to the 2012 2-y-o Group 1 Prix Morny and Group 1 Middle Park Stakes winner Reckless Abandon (by Exchange Rate) and to the modest 9f winner Jumbo Prado (by El Prado). The dam, a quite useful dual 6f winner (including at 2 yrs), was subsequently listed-placed in Canada and is a half-sister to the 2-y-o 6.5f and 7f and subsequent US Grade 1 9f and 10f winner Ticker Tape. The second dam, Argent Du Bois (by Silver Hawk), was placed five times at 2 and 3 yrs in France, stayed 1m and is a half-sister to 7 winners including the 2-y-o Group 1 Racing Post Trophy winner Crowded House and the French listed winner and Group 3 placed On Reflection. (The Eclipse Partnership). *"She has a lovely pedigree, she's neat and her good half-brother from last year wasn't big either. A strong 2-y-o, she's quite woolly so she needs the sun on her back before we do anything with her. I like her and she's an honest sort of filly".*

72. FULL DAY ★★★

ch.f. Champs Elysees – Capistrano Day (Diesis).
April 30. Eighth foal. 35,000Y. Tattersalls
October Book 1. Not sold. Half-sister to the
useful 6f (at 2 yrs) to 1m winner and Group
3 Supreme Stakes second Sabbeeh (by Red
Ransom), to the fairly useful 2-y-o 6f winner
and Group 3 Nell Gwyn Stakes second Dream
Day, the quite useful 2-y-o 7f winner Ellaal
(both by Oasis Dream), the fair 7f and 1m
winner of 4 races Green Agenda (by Anabaa)
and a winner in Greece (by Green Desert).
The dam, a smart listed 7f winner, was third
in the Group 3 Fred Darling Stakes, fourth in
the 1,000 Guineas and is a full or half-sister
to 5 winners. The second dam, Alcando (by
Alzao), a smart 5f (at 2 yrs) to 10f winner here,
subsequently won the Grade 1 9f Beverly Hills
Handicap in the USA and is a half-sister to 5
winners. (R Barnett). *"It's a contrasting pedigree
because the sire got a mile and a half well but
there's speed and precocity on the dam's side.
A filly who gets on with her work and enjoys it,
I would think we'd be looking at seven furlong
maidens for her in July. I like her".*

73. GOT TO DANCE ★★★★

b.f. Selkirk – Mullein (Oasis Dream). February
20. First foal. The dam, a useful listed 6f
winner of 5 races, is a half-sister to numerous
winners including the Group 2 Goodwood
Cup and dual Group 3 winner of 10 races
Illustrious Blue. The second dam, Gipsy Moth
(by Efisio), a quite useful dual 5f winner at
2 yrs, subsequently won a listed event in
Germany and is a half-sister to 4 winners
including the useful listed 1m winner and
Group 2 Falmouth Stakes second Heavenly
Whisper. (Landmark Racing). *"She's a nice filly
and she's already showing up quite well for a
2-y-o filly by Selkirk. She's strong and a good-
sized filly, especially for a first foal and she's
already getting on with it. I would think she'd
be appearing around June or July and as the
ground came all alike to her dam I'm hoping
that won't be a factor. She's a good-moving filly
even though some Selkirk's can hit the ground
hard. She'll make a 2-y-o alright".*

74. HONOR BOUND ★★★

b.f. Authorized – Honorine (Mark Of Esteem).
April 24. Fourth foal. Half-sister to the quite
useful 2012 9f placed 2-y-o Elidor (by Cape
Cross) and to the Group 1 12f Irish Derby and
US Grade 1 Secretariat Stakes winner Treasure
Beach (by Galileo). The dam, a quite useful
1m and 10f winner of 3 races, is a half-sister
to the Group 2 Hardwicke Stakes and Group 3
Earl Of Sefton Stakes winner and triple Group
1 placed Indian Creek. The second dam, Blue
Water (by Bering), won 5 races in France
including the listed 12f Prix des Tourelles, was
third in the Group 3 10.5f Prix de Flore and is
a half-sister to 3 winners including the French
winner and Group 3 placed Norton Sound.
(Ashley House Stud). *"A half-sister to Treasure
Beach, you'd think she'd need time with her
pedigree and she'll be having a break shortly
for some spring grass. A tall, good-moving filly
for later in the year, she's very well-balanced
and doesn't look as backward as some of the
Authorized horses we've had".*

75. LIGHTNING SPEAR ★★★★★

ch.c. Pivotal – Atlantic Destiny (Royal
Academy). April 5. Sixth foal. 260,000Y.
Tattersalls October Book 1. David Redvers.
Half-brother to the listed 10f winner Ocean
War (by Dalakhani), to the fairly useful 10f
winner and 2-y-o 7f listed-placed Seaway
(by Dr Fong), the fairly useful 2-y-o 6f winner
Atlantic Light (by Linamix) and the French 3-y-
o dual winner and listed-placed First Destiny
(by Lawman). The dam, a useful winner of 7
races from 5f to 7f including the listed Sirenia
Stakes and a stakes event in the USA, is a half-
sister to 5 winners including the Group 2 Royal
Whip Stakes winner Make No Mistake. The
second dam, Respectfully (by The Minstrel),
is an unplaced full or half-sister to 6 winners.
(Qatar Racing Ltd). *"A lovely, really athletic and
good-moving horse. The dam did well as 2-y-o
and this colt should make a 2-y-o as well. It'll
be the second half of the year before he's ready
because he's quite a tall horse and there's
quite a lot of daylight under him still, but I was
delighted when they sent him to me".*

76. LUGAR DE VENTO ★★★

ch.c. Compton Place – Belle Des Airs (Dr Fong).
March 12. First foal. 35,000Y. Tattersalls
October Book 2. Neil Gilchrist. The dam, a
quite useful 6f (at 2 yrs) and 7f winner, is a
half-sister to 2 winners. The second dam, Belle

Reine (by King Of Kings), is an unraced half-sister to 4 winners. (Mrs H I Slade). *"I trained his mother who was a tough filly and like her I think he'll get seven furlongs by the end of the season. He should be appearing around July time and he's a good, hard-knocking sort of horse, the type for an auction race and hopefully he'll progress into a good fun horse".*

77. LUNAR SPIRIT ★★★

b.f. Invincible Spirit – Kitty O'Shea (Sadler's Wells). May 4. Fifth foal. Half-sister to the smart Irish 2-y-o 7f winner and Group 1 Moyglare Stud Stakes third Kissable, to the quite useful 2-y-o 7f winner and listed placed Kingdom Of Munster (both by Danehill Dancer) and the fair 10f and hurdles winner Counsel (by Dansili). The dam ran twice and won both races over 1m (including at 2 yrs and a listed event at 3 yrs). She is a sister to the Group 1 Racing Post Trophy and Group 1 St Leger winner Brian Boru and a half-sister to the Group winners Sea Moon and Moon Search to the dam of the Derby winner Workforce. The second dam, Eva Luna (by Alleged), won the Group 3 14.6f Park Hill Stakes and is a half-sister to 5 winners including the US listed winner Rougeur (herself dam of the US Grade 1 winner Flute). (Mr & Mrs David Aykroyd). *"I train her 3-y-o half-brother who hasn't run yet. She's a lot more precocious than him because he's huge and she's a much neater filly. So she'll make a 2-y-o and I'll start doing some fast work with her in early May".*

78. MAN OF LAW (USA) ★★★

b.c. Proud Citizen – Spring Tale (Stravinsky). February 28. First foal. 23,000Y. Tattersalls October Book 2. McCalmont Bloodstock. The dam, a quite useful 2-y-o 6f winner, was listed-placed and is a half-sister to 3 winners here and abroad. The second dam, Sadler's Profile (by Royal Academy), is an unraced half-sister to 5 winners including the dam of the Group 1 Cheveley Park Stakes winner Carry On Katie. (Anagram Partnership). *"He comes from a very speedy family on the dam's side so he should make a 2-y-o. He's quite a long horse and most Proud Citizen's get a mile so I would think he'll get six or seven furlongs later on. He's not far off doing some fast work".*

79. MERCURY MAGIC ★★★

b.c. Oratorio – Lochridge (Indian Ridge). March 12. Brother to the fair 2-y-o 6f winner Echo Ridge and half-brother to the fairly useful 2012 2-y-o 6f winner and Group 2 fourth City Girl (by Elusive City). The dam, a smart listed 6f winner of 5 races, is a half-sister to 3 winners including the useful listed 5f winner Loch Verdi. The second dam, Lochsong (by Song), a champion sprinter and winner of the Prix de l'Abbaye (twice), the Kings Stand Stakes and the Nunthorpe Stakes, is a half-sister to the Nunthorpe Stakes winner Lochangel. (J C Smith). *"This is the third one out of the mare I've trained and as an individual he's the nicest. He's a very strong, robust horse and he'll be doing fast work soon and we'll progress from there. He should follow in the footsteps of Echo Ridge and City Girl who were both 2-y-o winners".*

80. MONTAIGNE ★★★★

b.c. Exceed And Excel – Autumn Pearl (Orpen). January 26. Half-brother to the useful 2-y-o 6f winner and listed-placed Pabusar (by Oasis Dream), to the fairly useful dual 6f winner (including at 2 yrs) and listed-placed Fillionaire (by Kyllachy) and the modest dual 6f winner Thaliwarru (by Barathea). The dam, a winner of 3 races over 5f and 6f at 2 and 3 yrs, was second in the Group 2 Temple Stakes and is a half-sister to 2 winners abroad. The second dam, Cyclone Flyer (by College Chapel), won once at 3 yrs and is a half-sister to 8 winners including the Group 2 King's Stand Stakes winner Bolshoi. (Mr K Watts). *"He's quite forward and we trained his half-brother Pabusar to win as a 2-y-o last year. This is a horse we'll be looking to get on with and he's done a bit of work and showed up well. As yet he hasn't shown any of the temperament issues his brother Pabusar had, the family is all speed and he's quite a relaxed horse, so we like him".* Montaigne won on his debut in mid-April.

81. NEVERODDOREVEN ★★★

b.f. Intikhab – Esteraad (Cadeaux Genereux). March 1. 7,000Y. Tattersalls October Book 2. McCalmont Bloodstock. Sister to the fair 2-y-o dual 7f winner Caitlin and half-sister to the fair 2-y-o 7f winner and subsequent US Grade 2 placed Press Baron (by King's Best), the fair 1m to 14f winner of 6 races Noora (by Bahhare), the modest 6f winner Cassie's Choice and the modest Irish 12f winner Kokoro (both by Fath). The dam, a fairly useful 2-y-o 6f winner, is a half-sister to the 2-y-o 7f winner and useful Group 3 Musidora Stakes third Vagabond Chanteuse. The second dam, Eclipsing (by Baillamont), a fairly useful winner of three races over 1m, is out of the French 6f to 9.2f winner (including a listed event) Exgravity (by Explodent). (McDonagh, Murphy & Nixon). *"A neat, tough filly, she has lucky owners and I've had a lot of fun with the progeny of Intikhab. She has a solid temperament and she's done well physically since we bought her. An obvious 2-y-o type".* Incidentally, the name is a palindrome (it reads the same back to front). TRAINERS' BARGAIN BUY

82. PRIMITORIO ★★★★ ♠

b.c. Oratorio – Primissima (Second Set). March 24. Third foal. £50,000Y. Doncaster Premier. Will Edmeades. Half-brother to the useful 2012 2-y-o 5f winner and Group 3 6f Albany Stakes third Premier Steps (by Footstepsinthesand). The dam won at 3 yrs in Germany and is a half-sister to 5 winners there. The second dam, Princess Taufan (by Taufan), won the listed National Stakes and was third in the Group 2 Lowther Stakes and is a half-sister to the dam of the stakes winners Gracefully and Lady Grace. (Thurloe Thoroughbreds). *"A forward colt, he's done plenty of work and he's shown a bit already, so he is forward, like his sister Premier Steps was in fact. He's showing enough speed for five furlongs".*

83. RAGING BOB (IRE) ★★★

br.c. Big Bad Bob – Lanasara (Generous). April 18. €24,000Y. Tattersalls Ireland September. F Barberini. Half-brother to the fair 7f (at 2 yrs) and 2m winner Saida Lanasera (by Fasliyev), to the modest 1m and 9f winner of 4 races Spavento (by Verglas) and two minor winners in France and Italy by Anabaa and Zamindar. The dam is an unraced half-sister to 9 winners including the Italian Group 3 winner Revere and the dam of the 2-y-o Group 2 winner Red Duke. The second dam, Bint Pasha (by Affirmed), won the Group 1 12f Yorkshire Oaks, the Group 1 12f Prix Vermeille and

the Group 2 10f Pretty Polly Stakes. (A.W.A Partnership). *"His sire's statistics are terrific and apparently his stock come in all shapes and sizes but this is his first commercial crop of 2-y-o's. This colt is tall and lean but he should make a 2-y-o because most of the sire's stock do. We should have a bit of sport with him".*

84. RAVENOUS ★★★

b.c. Raven's Pass – Supereva (Sadler's Wells). February 6. Fourth foal. Half-brother to the fair 1m winner Carousel (by Pivotal) and to the fair 1m winner Royal Superlative (by King's Best). The dam, an Italian winner of 5 races, is a half-sister to several winners. The second dam, Final Farewell (by Proud Truth), ran once unplaced and is a half-sister to 3 winners and to the dam of Danehill. *"He hasn't been here long but I like the look of him. He has a good temperament, a good way about him and he's quite a neat horse, light on his feet. His brother was a good-looking horse who would have done well in the show ring but his horse looks a bit hardier, wiry and tougher. He looks like the right sort of horse to go to war with this year".*

85. REGARDEZ ★★★

b.f. Champs Elysees – Look So (Efisio). May 3. Half-sister to the fairly useful 6f (at 2 yrs) and 7f winner and listed-placed Compton (by Compton Place). The dam, a quite useful 7f and 1m winner of 4 races, is a half-sister to numerous winners including the Oaks winner Look Here. The second dam, Last Look (by Rainbow Quest), is an unraced half-sister to two minor winners. (J H Richmond-Watson). *"I've trained quite a few from the family and I think this filly will make a 2-y-o. Her dam had physical issues which stopped her from running as a 2-y-o but this filly would be a bit more athletic than her and more like her half-brother Compton. She's quite similar to him in many ways, but she's a late foal and although we've done a bit with her already she'll probably have a break now. But she's shown enough to say she'll have some sort of campaign as a 2-y-o".*

86. SEA HERE ★★★★ ♠

ch.c. Sea The Stars – Look Here (Hernando). April 2. First foal. The dam, a 7f (at 2 yrs) and Group 1 Epsom Oaks winner, is a half-sister to numerous winners. The second dam, Last Look (by Rainbow Quest), is an unraced half-sister to two minor winners. (J H Richmond-Watson). *"This colt is very similar to his mother – he has the same attitude and the same way about him. It would be fair to say he was a small yearling, but he's done well with work and he has a bit more size and scope about him now. It'll be some time before I do any fast work with him but he should appear around September time over seven furlongs or a mile. He has a lovely attitude and everything that was good about his mother shines through in him. It's great to have him about the place".*

87. TEA LEAF ★★★

b.f. Bushranger – Boston Ivy (Mark Of Esteem). April 19. 19,000Y. Tattersalls October Book 2. McCalmont Bloodstock. Half-sister to the very useful 2-y-o dual 5f winner and Group 2 6f Gimcrack Stakes second Master Noverre (by Noverre), to the quite useful Irish dual 7f winner Miss Faustina (by Antonius Pius) and the quite useful Irish 10f, 12f and hurdles winner Sportsmaster (by Ad Valorem). The dam is an unraced half-sister to 6 winners including the French listed winner and Group 3 placed Ivy League. The second dam, Hedera (by Woodman), a listed-placed 2-y-o winner, is a half-sister to 6 winners. (McCalmont and Drew). *"Quite a forward sort of filly, she had a touch of sore shins and we backed off her but we'll be getting on with her soon and she shouldn't take long to come to hand. We'll start her off at five furlongs".*

88. WEISSE SOCKEN (IRE) ★★★★

b.f. Acclamation – Playful (Piccolo). April 20. Second foal. £42,000Y. Doncaster Premier. R Frisby. The dam, a fairly useful 2-y-o dual 5f winner, was listed-placed and is a half-sister to 4 winners. The second dam, Autumn Affair (by Lugana Beach), a fairly useful 2-y-o 6f winner, was third in the Group 3 Fred Darling Stakes. (Mrs E Kennedy). *"She'll have had her first race before the book comes out because she's showing up well and she's forward and sharp. I trained her mother and she was the just the same. Very professional, she just gets on with her job".*

89. WILDE INSPIRATION (IRE) ★★★

ch.c. Dandy Man – Wishing Chair (Giant's Causeway). April 17. Second foal. 29,000Y. Tattersalls October Book 2. McCalmont Bloodstock. Half-brother to the fair 2012 2-y-o dual 5f winner Done Dreaming (by Diamond Green). The dam is an unraced half-sister to 7 winners including the US stakes winner and Grade 3 placed Dawn Princess. The second dam, Fighting Countess (by Ringside), a US stakes winner of 5 races, is a half-sister to 3 stakes winners including the US dual Grade 1 winner Countess Diana. (Mrs E Kennedy). *"As a specimen there's a lot of his damsire Giant's Causeway about him, which is not a bad thing because he's a very good broodmare sire. A very athletic sort of horse, he looks to have a good way about him and it's so far so good with him. I should be able to get on with him sometime in May and he'll be racing around June/July time. A good sort of horse with plenty of bone about him, he should make a 2-y-o and I like him".*

90. WIGGINS ★★★

b.c. High Chaparral – Al Ihsas (Danehill). April 14. Eighth foal. 75,000Y. Tattersalls October Book 1. McCalmont Bloodstock. Half-brother to the minor US winner of 4 races El Medwar (by Elusive Quality). The dam, a useful 3-y-o dual 7f winner and second in the Group 3 5f Queen Mary Stakes, is a full or half-sister to 7 winners including Windsor Palace (Group 3 Mooresbridge Stakes) and the listed winner Anna Karenina. The second dam, Simaat (by Mr Prospector), a fair 1m winner, is a half-sister to 2 winners. (Cheyne Walkers II). *"For a High Chaparral he's pretty precocious and I would think he'll be running sometime in May. The dam hasn't been successful but she was a good filly herself and very precocious. So we'll get on with him and hopefully he might be one for an early six furlong maiden. He gives the impression that he won't need a lot of fast work and that he gets himself ready".*

91. UNNAMED ★★★

ch.f. Galileo – Castara Beach (Danehill). February 4. Eighth foal. 200,000Y. Tattersalls October Book 1. Not sold. Half-sister to the modest 2012 7f placed 2-y-o Excellent Mariner (by Henrythenavigator), to the very smart 6f (at 2 yrs) and Group 3 1m Solonaway Stakes winner, Group 1 Dewhurst Stakes fourth and subsequent Hong Kong Group 3 9f winner Steinbeck (by Footstepsinthesand), the fairly useful 2-y-o 7.5f winner and Italian listed-placed Varenka (by Fasliyev) and the fair 2-y-o 7f winner Corsicanrun (by Medicean). The dam, placed fourth once over 7f at 2 yrs, is a sister to the useful Group 3 7f Criterion Stakes winner Hill Hopper (herself dam of the dual Group 1 winner Nannina) and a half-sister to 5 winners including the Australian Grade 1 winner Water Boatman. The second dam, Sea Harrier (by Grundy), ran twice unplaced and is a half-sister to 5 winners including the Group 2 12f King Edward VII Stakes winner Sea Anchor. (Mrs John Magnier). *"A filly with a wonderful pedigree, there's nothing really precocious about her but she's quite neat and we'll give her the chance to show us whether she's forward or not and take it from there. She's athletic and well-balanced, so she should figure at some point later in the year, probably over seven furlongs. She's a sweet filly with a good attitude".*

92. UNNAMED ★★★ ♠
b.f. Oasis Dream – Dame Alicia (Sadler's Wells). February 23. Sixth foal. €38,000Y. Goffs Orby. McKeever Bloodstock. Half-sister to the fair 2-y-o 6f winner Flip Flop (by Footstepsinthesand) and to the fair Irish 12f winner Lady Alicia (by Hawk Wing). The dam, fourth in the Group 3 7f C L Weld Park Stakes at 2 yrs, won over 9f at 3 yrs and is a half-sister to the Irish Group 2 1m and US Grade 2 9f winner Century City. The second dam, Alywow (by Alysheba), a champion filly in Canada, won 7 races including the Grade 3 8.5f Nijana Stakes, was second in the Grade 1 Rothmans International and the Grade 1 Flower Bowl Invitational and is a half-sister to 6 winners. *"A strong, forward-going filly who should appear in mid-summer".*

MICHAEL BELL
93. AL KHAWANEEJ STAR (USA) ★★★
b.br.c. Arch – Frolic Away (Pentelicus). February 17. Fifth foal. $110,000Y. Saratoga August. Blandford Bloodstock. Half-brother to 2 minor winners in the USA by Forestry and Tiznow. The dam is an unplaced half-sister to 9 winners including the US multiple Graded stakes winner Smok'n Frolic and two other stakes winners. The second dam, Cherokyfrolicflash (by Green Dancer), a stakes-placed winner of 4 races, is a sister to the Grade 3 stakes winner Fabulous Frolic and a half-sister to the Grade 3 winner and smart broodmare Lindsay Frolic. (A Al Shaikh). *"He's showing a bit of promise. Realistically he's going to want a minimum of seven furlongs but he gets up Warren Hill nicely and we like what we see so far".*

94. ALMAX ★★★
b.c. Rock Of Gibraltar – Inya Lake (Whittingham). March 31. Tenth foal. 50,000Y. Tattersalls October Book 1. Kern/Lillingston. Half-brother to the useful Group 3 6f Prix de Meautry, listed Cammidge Trophy and 6f Ayr Gold Cup winner Jimmy Styles (by Inchinor), to the quite useful 5f (at 2 yrs) and 6f winner of 4 races Oneladyowner, the fair 2-y-o dual 5f winner Lake Hero (by Arkadian Hero), the modest triple 5f winner Special Gold (by Josr Algarhoud) and a winner in Spain by Trade Fair. The dam, a useful 2-y-o winner of 4 races over 5f including the Group 3 Molecomb Stakes, subsequently won a listed 5f event at 3 yrs and is a half-sister to 4 winners. The second dam, Special One (by Aragon), a modest 2-y-o 5f winner, is a half-sister to 8 winners. (Karmaa Racing Ltd). *"He was bought to be a sharp 2-y-o type but it's taking a bit of time for the penny to drop. His dam won the Molecomb, she's bred a decent winner in Jimmy Styles and the sire gets loads of winners. So I'm just giving him the chance to get his act together at the moment. I think he'll need six furlongs".*

95. BORN TO REIGN ★★★
b.c. Sir Percy – Oat Cuisine (Mujahid). February 11. First foal. The dam, a quite useful 1m to 10f winner of 5 races, is a half-sister to the fairly useful 2-y-o listed 5f winner Pyman's Theory and to the Irish 2-y-o listed 6f Flame Of Tara Stakes winner Forthefirstime. The second dam, Gazebo (by Cadeaux Genereux), a modest 6f placed 2-y-o, is a half-sister to the US sprint winner of 13 races and listed-placed Hardball, to the listed-placed winner Injaaz and to the winner Corndavon (herself dam of the Group 2 July Stakes winner Nevisian Lad). (Mrs G Rowland-Clark). *"He's only just come*

in so I don't know much about him. I trained the dam who didn't do a lot as a 2-y-o but improved dramatically as she got older. A fine stamp of a horse, he should be an autumn 2-y-o".

96. CHATHAM HOUSE RULE ★★★
gr.c. Authorized – Cozy Maria (Cozzene). February 5. Sixth foal. 70,000Y. Tattersalls October Book 1. Tony Nerses. Half-brother to the 2-y-o Group 2 5f Flying Childers Stakes and Group 3 5f Molecomb Stakes winner of 6 races Zebedee (by Invincible Spirit). The dam, a useful 10f winner, was listed-placed twice and is a half-sister to 7 winners. The second dam, Mariamme (by Verbatim), won twice at 3 yrs in the USA and is a half-sister to 7 winners including the Grade 1 Breeders Cup Turf winner Miss Alleged. (Saleh Al Homaizi & Imad Al Sagar). "He's a half-brother to the fast 2-y-o Zebedee so it's strange pedigree really, but he's a good looking horse who gets up the gallop very easily. Obviously being by Authorized we haven't done a lot with him, but I like him, he's very athletic, has a good attitude and I think he was well-bought. A nice colt – although funnily enough he has no eyelashes!"

97. EXCEEDING POWER ★★★
b.c. Exceed And Excel – Extreme Beauty (Rahy). February 20. Fifth foal. 80,000Y. Tattersalls October Book 1. Blandford Bloodstock. Half-brother to the quite useful 2-y-o 6f winner Extreme Warrior (by Dubawi) and to the fair dual 1m winner Little Black Book (by Shamardal). The dam, a quite useful 6f (at 2 yrs) and 7f winner, was third in the Group 2 6f Cherry Hinton Stakes is a half-sister to 7 winners including the US Grade 1 Pacific Classic winner Go Between. The second dam, Mediation (by Caerleon), won the listed Irish 1,000 Guineas Trial and was Group 3 placed here and in the USA. (Dr A Ridha). "A strong colt, he's nice and he'll be quite a sharp 2-y-o type although he does have a sore shin at present. That will delay us bit but he's a 2-y-o type both to look at and on pedigree".

98. FIERY SUNSET ★★
b.f. Galileo – Five Fields (Chester House). March 23. Fourth foal. Half-sister to the fair 2-y-o 7f winner Upcountry (by Oasis Dream).

The dam, a fair 10f winner, is a half-sister to numerous winners including the US Grade 1 11f United Nations Handicap winner Senure, the useful French 6f (at 2 yrs) and 1m winner Speak In Passing and the French listed 1m winner Dexterity. The second dam, Diese (by Diesis), winner of the Group 3 10.5f Prix Corrida and a listed event over 10f in France, is a half-sister to numerous good winners including the champion European 2-y-o Xaar, winner of the Group 1 Dewhurst Stakes and the Group 1 Prix de la Salamandre and the Group 3 1m Prix Quincey winner Masterclass. (The Queen). "She's a filly with plenty of scope and a very nice, easy mover. She's just gone back to Sandringham to fill out and mature, but she's a quality filly for later on".

99. FINN CLASS ★★★★
b.c. Exceed And Excel – Finnmark (Halling). February 26. Fourth foal. Half-brother to the fair 1m to 14f winner Cape Safari (by Cape Cross). The dam is an unraced half-sister to 8 winners including the very smart Group 2 15f Prix Hubert de Chaudenay winner Affadavit, the French listed 12f winner Nalani, the 10f and 12f listed winner Altamura and the Italian listed winner Tea Garden. The second dam, Narwala (by Darshaan), won the Group 3 12f Princess Royal Stakes and was second in the Grade 2 12f Long Island Handicap. (S Ali). "The mare has been a bit disappointing but the sire is very good. This colt looks like being an early 2-y-o, he's in work and the girl who rides him really likes him, so I'm hopeful he'll be quite nice".

100. FUTOON ★★★
b.f. Royal Applause – Cefira (Distant View). March 14. Fifth foal. 52,000Y. Tattersalls October Book 1. A & A. Half-sister to the quite useful dual 5f winner (including at 2 yrs) Sirenuse (by Exceed And Excel) and to the fair 2-y-o 5f and 6f winner Forty Proof (by Invincible Spirit). The dam, a modest 3-y-o 6f winner, is a half-sister to 4 winners including Abou Zouz (Group 2 Gimcrack Stakes). The second dam, Bold Jessie (by Never So Bold), an Irish 2-y-o listed winner, is a half-sister to 5 winners including the Group 2 winners Prince Sabo and Millyant. (A Al Shaikh). "She's a nice, sharp filly who I imagine would be one of our

earlier 2-y-o's. She gets up the gallop nicely, she was bought to be a 2-y-o type and I think she will be. She looks quick, so she'll probably be alright to start over five furlongs".

101. GALIZZI (USA) ★★★

b.c. Dansili – Dancing Abbie (Theatrical). March 28. Second foal. The dam, a 9f winner here and a listed 9f winner in Norway and was third in the Group 2 11f Italian Oaks. The second dam, Sicy d'Alsace (by Sicyos), won the Grade 1 9f Del Mar Oaks. (Marwan Al Maktoum). *"This could be a nice horse in time but he's just ticking over at the moment. I trained the dam and she didn't do a lot at two, we're taking our time with him but he will be a nice, big, quality horse one day".*

102. GENDA AGENDA ★★★

b.f. Holy Roman Emperor – Friendlier (Zafonic). March 18. Sixth foal. Sister to the fairly useful 7f (at 2 yrs) and 1m winner Unex El Greco and half-sister to the fair 2012 2-y-o 1m debut winner Madame Defarge (by Motivator), the fairly useful 7f (at 2 yrs) and 1m winner Foolin Myself (by Montjeu) and the fair 2-y-o 1m and subsequent UAE 7f winner Comradeship (by Dubawi). The dam is an unraced half-sister to 3 winners including the top-class filly User Friendly, winner of the Oaks, the St Leger, the Irish Oaks and the Yorkshire Oaks and second in the Prix de l'Arc de Triomphe. The second dam, Rostova (by Blakeney), a fairly useful winner of 4 races from 12f to 14f, is a half-sister to 7 winners including the very successful Italian filly Judd. (W J Gredley). *"I like her - and we also train her very promising 3-y-o half-sister Madame Defarge. This filly has a sweet temperament and she looks like being fine over six or seven furlongs. A nice filly".*

103. GOOD HOPE ★★★

b.f. Cape Cross – Fairy Godmother (Fairy King). February 13. Sister to the fairly useful 10f winner Caraboss and half-sister to the smart triple 10f winner and Group 3 placed Kingdom Of Fife (by Kingmambo) and to the useful dual 1m winner (including at 2 yrs) and Group 3 1m Autumn Stakes third Four Winds (by Red Ransom). The dam, a

listed 10f winner, is a half-sister to several winners including the Group 2 12f Jockey Club Stakes winner Blueprint. The second dam, Highbrow (by Shirley Heights), a very useful 2-y-o 1m winner, was second in the Group 2 12f Ribblesdale Stakes, is closely related to the good middle-distance colt Milford and a half-sister to the Princess of Wales's Stakes winner Height of Fashion – herself the dam of Nashwan, Nayef and Unfuwain. (The Queen). *"A nice, easy-moving filly. Given her pedigree and her foaling date you'd expect her to be a late summer/autumn 2-y-o".*

104. GREY STREET ★★

gr.c. Aqlaam – Good Enough (Mukaddamah). April 1. Eighth foal. 22,000Y. Tattersalls October Book 2. Charlie Gordon-Watson. Closely related to the useful 7f (at 2 yrs) and listed 6f winner of 6 races Oasis Dancer (by Oasis Dream) and half-brother to the fair 2012 2-y-o 5f winner Grey Street (by Royal Applause), the very useful 1m winner of 4 races and subsequent Scandinavian listed winner Smart Enough (by Cadeaux Genereux), the fair 2-y-o 1m winner Bright Enough (by Fantastic Light) and the Japanese winner of 11 races Night School (by Machiavellian). The dam won once at 3 yrs in the USA and was third in the Group 1 Prix Saint-Alary and is a half-sister to 5 winners including the Group 3 Molecomb Stakes winner Classic Ruler. The second dam, Viceroy Princess (by Godswalk), a modest 2-y-o 7f seller winner, is a half-sister to 7 winners. (R N Frosell). *"He's just taking a bit of time to come to hand and he's a nice, big, scopey horse that looks like an autumn 2-y-o".*

105. HALLA HALLA ★★★

b.f. Invincible Spirit – Galistic (Galileo). February 18. Second foal. 30,000Y. Tattersalls October Book 2. Rabbah Bloodstock. The dam, a useful 10f, 12f and listed 14f winner in Ireland at 3 and 4 yrs, is a half-sister to one winner. The second dam, Mockery (by Nashwan), won 2 minor races at 3 yrs in France and is a half-sister to 3 other minor winners. (S Ali). *"She was well-bought I think, by a very good sire and out of a listed winning mare. She'll be a summer 2-y-o".*

106. INVOKE (IRE) ★★★

b.f. Kodiac – Tides (Bahamian Bounty). January 25. Fifth foal. £36,000Y. Doncaster Premier. John Warren. Sister to the modest 2012 2-y-o triple 6f winner Marmot Bay and to the useful 2-y-o dual 5f winner Hestian. The dam is an unplaced half-sister to 5 winners including the listed winner Amazing Bay. The second dam, Petriece (by Mummy's Pet), won at 3 yrs and is a half-sister to 5 winners including the dam of the Group 1 winning sprinters Lochsong and Lochangel. (Highclere Thoroughbred Racing – Herbert Jones). *"A full sister to two 2-y-o winners and on looks she should be a 2-y-o as well. It's a fast family, she's a January foal and we'll be kicking on with her when the weather improves. She's a little bit hot so we've been working on keeping her settled, but she'll be racing by the summer".*

107. MANTOU ★★★★

ch.c. Teofilo – Shadow Roll (Mark Of Esteem). May 9. Seventh foal. Half-brother to the quite useful 2-y-o 6f winner (on her only start) Undertone (by Noverre) and to the fair 1m to 10f winner of 5 races Carragold (by Diktat). The dam, a fair 2-y-o 7f listed-placed maiden, is a half-sister to 2 winners and to the listed-placed Shadowless. The second dam, Warning Shadows (by Cadeaux Genereux), won the Group 2 10f Sun Chariot Stakes and was second in the Irish 1,000 Guineas. (Marwan Al Maktoum). *"A very nice, classy horse that moves well and for a May foal with a heavy lad on his back he gets up Warren Hill quite easily. I'll keep my eye on him until late May and then start to do a bit more with him to see if he could be a summer 2-y-o".*

108. MISSISSIPPI QUEEN (USA) ★★★

b.f. Artie Schiller – Siempre Asi (Silver Hawk). April 3. Eleventh foal. 87,000Y. Tattersalls October Book 1. Kern/Lillingston. Closely related to the US Grade 1 Spinster Stakes winner Asi Siempre and to a minor 3-y-o winner in France (both by El Prado) and half-sister to 2 other minor winners in France by Bahri and Distant View. The dam is an unraced half-sister to the Group 3 Norfolk Stakes winner Magic Mirror, the listed winners Sun Worship and Treasure Trove and to the dam of the Group 2 Sandown Mile winner

Almushtarak. The second dam, Turkish Treasure (by Sir Ivor), won the Group 3 Cherry Hinton Stakes. (Mr Chris Wright). *"A nice filly on pedigree but she's in a pre-training yard at the moment. They like her there, but we're not rushing her and she's one for the mid to late summer".*

109. PIAZON ★★★★ ♠

br.c. Striking Ambition – Colonel's Daughter (Colonel Collins). April 9. Sixth foal. £25,000Y. Doncaster Premier. R Frisby. Closely related to the useful 6f winner of 7 races (including at 2 yrs) Colonel Mak (by Makbul) and half-brother to the smart 2-y-o Group 2 July Stakes and listed Windsor Castle Stakes winner Frederick Engels (by Iceman) and the modest 2-y-o dual 5f winner Dotty's Daughter (by Forzando). The dam was placed 3 times over 5f at 2 yrs and is a half-sister to 3 winners including the US Grade 3 winner Shuffling Kid. The second dam, Clashfern (by Smackover), was an unraced half-sister to 2 winners. (R P B Michaelson). *"Although he's by a relatively unfashionable stallion he looks to go well and he wasn't that expensive. The mare has bred good horses to Makbul and Iceman, and this colt looks smart as well. A sprinting type and one of our early birds".* TRAINERS' BARGAIN BUY

110. ROCK OF LEON ★★★

b.c. Rock Of Gibraltar – Leonica (Lion Cavern). February 18. Fourth living foal. 50,000Y. Tattersalls October Book 2. John Warren. Half-brother to the useful 6f (at 2 yrs) and 7f winner and listed placed winner Rodrigo de Torres (by Bahamian Bounty) and to the fair 2-y-o 5f winner Old Master Expert (by Royal Applause). The dam, a fairly useful 1m winner, is a half-sister to 5 minor winners including the listed Prix de Saint-Cyr winner South Rock. The second dam, South Shore (by Caerleon), a useful winner of 4 races at up to 12f, is a half-sister to 4 winners including the Lockinge Stakes winner Soviet Line. (Mr Malcolm Caine). *"A fine, big, stamp of a horse, he's an easy mover and has great depth to him. I like him and I trained his dam who would have been a stakes filly but she hurt her pelvis. I've been lucky with the family and I like this colt".*

111. SING BEAM ★★★
ch.f. *Shamardal – Basanti (Galileo).* March
1. Second foal. Half-sister to the unplaced
2012 2-y-o Man From Seville (by Duke Of
Marmalade). The dam, a fair 10f winner, is a
half-sister to 5 winners including the Group 3
5f Prix du Bois winner Ozone Layer, the very
useful dual 1m winner (including at 2 yrs)
and Group 2 Dante Stakes third Musalsal and
the French 10f and 10.5f winner and Group 3
third Amusing Time. The second dam, Ozone
Friendly (by Green Forest), a useful 2-y-o
winner of the Group 1 5.5f Prix Robert Papin
and fourth in the Group 1 6f Prix Morny, is a
half-sister to 5 winners including the US 2-y-o
stakes winner Storm Flight. (Lady Bamford).
*"She's a strong filly and I'd be disappointed
if she doesn't have the boot for six furlongs.
Should be a June/July runner".*

112. SPEEDY APPROACH ★★★★
ch.c. *New Approach – Height Of Vanity
(Erhaab).* April 1. Half-brother to the fair
2012 2-y-o 6f winner Danat Al Atheer (by
Shamardal) and to the quite useful UAE 1m
winner Blue Sea (by Singspiel). The dam is
an unplaced half-sister to numerous winners
including the French listed 9f and subsequent
US Grade 1 10f and Grade 1 11f winner
Lahudood. The second dam, Rahayeb (by
Arazi), a fair 12.3f winner, is a full or half-sister
to 4 winners. (Jaber Abdullah). *"He's a classy
horse to look at, he gets up Warren Hill very
easily and I like him. A very easy mover, he
has plenty of scope and looks quite like his sire.
He'll probably want seven furlongs this year
and all the riders like him".*

113. SPIRITOFTHEUNION ★★★
b.f. *Authorized – Kahlua Kiss (Mister Baileys).*
March 17. Second foal. 50,000Y. Tattersalls
October Book 1. Michael Bell. Half-sister to the
2012 Italian 2-y-o 6f winner, on his only start,
Windhoek (by Cape Cross). The dam, a fairly
useful 7f (at 2 yrs) and 10f winner of 4 races,
was listed-placed twice and is a half-sister to
the 2-y-o winner and dual Group 3 placed
Mister Genepi. The second dam, Ring Queen
(by Fairy King), is an unraced half-sister to 8
winners including the US dual Group 1 winner
Special Ring. (A Al Shaikh). *"A nice, powerful
filly and an easy mover, she'll take a bit more*

*time and we like her. The type to start at seven
furlongs".*

114. SUNNINGDALE ROSE (IRE) ★★★★
b.f. *Art Connoisseur – Eloquent Rose (Elnadim).*
February 16. Second foal. £20,000Y. Doncaster
Festival. Stephen Hillen. Half-sister to the quite
useful 6f and 7f winner Dutch Rose (by Dutch
Art). The dam, a quite useful 2-y-o dual 5f
winner, is a half-sister to 4 winners. The second
dam, Quintellina (by Robellino), was a quite
useful 2-y-o 7f winner. (Mrs Susan Roy). *"I like
her a lot. Both the sire and the dam were very
precocious and she's doing what it says on the
tin at the moment. She'll be running very soon
and she's speedy".* TRAINERS' BARGAIN BUY

115. TAUTIRA (USA) ★★★
b.br.f. *Kheleyf – Ballantrae (Diktat).* February
12. First dam. The dam, a quite useful 2-y-o
dual 7f winner, is a sister to the useful 2-y-o
7f winner and Group 3 7f Vintage Stakes
third Fox and half-sister to numerous winners
including the very useful Group 1 Cheveley
Park Stakes third Badminton, the useful Group
3 Nell Gwyn Stakes second Cala and the useful
Group 2 Vintage Stakes third Fox. The second
dam, Badawi (by Diesis), was a useful 1m and
9f winner of 4 races. (Marwan Al Maktoum). *"A
strong, sharp filly and one of our earlier types,
she definitely looks like a 2-y-o and she might
be running before the book is printed".*

116. THATCHEREEN (IRE) ★★★
b.f. *Mastercraftsman – Roof Fiddle (Cat Thief).*
March 5. First foal. €54,000Y. Goffs Orby. R
Frisby. The dam, a fairly useful 2-y-o 5f winner,
was listed-placed twice and is a half-sister to
2 winners. The second dam, Woodmaven (by
Woodman), was placed once at 3 yrs in the
USA and is a half-sister to 2 winners including
the dual Group 3 winner and 1,000 Guineas
second Arch Swing. (Mr T Redman & Mr P
Phillips). *"I've got two by the sire and I like
them both. This is a well-made filly with a bit
of quality and I would imagine she'd be a six/
seven furlong filly. She wants to please and she
moves well".*

117. WADI ALAMARDI ★★★
ch.c. *Lucky Story – Thicket (Wolfhound).* March
2. Eleventh foal. £30,000Y. Doncaster Premier.

R Frisby. Half-brother to the French 2-y-o listed 5f winner and US Grade 3 placed Dijarvo (by Iceman), to the quite useful dual 6f winner Basilica (by Zafeen), the modest 5f (including at 2 yrs) and 6f winner of 7 races Diminuto (by Iron Mask), the modest 5f winner Baileys Applause (by Royal Applause) and the moderate dual 6f winner Seductive Witch (by Zamindar). The dam, a fairly useful 2-y-o 5f winner, is a half-sister to 5 winners. The second dam, Sharpthorne (by Sharpen Up), a fairly useful dual 6f winner (including at 2 yrs), was listed-placed and is a half-sister to 9 winners. (A Al Shaikh). *"He's going to be relatively early. The dam had a good race record and she's bred a few decent winners without going to any particularly exciting sires. I've been lucky with the sire Lucky Story and this is a nice sharp colt that should have the speed for six furlongs".*

118. UNNAMED ★★
b.f. Nayef – Bedara (Barathea). April 10. Ninth foal. 33,000Y. Tattersalls October Book 2. Michael Bell. Half-sister to the useful 1m and 10f winner of 4 races and listed-placed Mutajarred (by Alhaarth), to the fairly useful 7f (at 2 yrs) and 1m and subsequent US stakes-placed winner Arm Candy (by Nashwan), the quite useful 2-y-o 1m winner Mozafin (by Zafonic), subsequently a winner in Austria at 3 yrs and the poor 2m 1f winner Lady Mandy (by Teofilo). The dam, a quite useful 10.5f winner, was listed-placed and is a half-sister to 5 minor winners here and abroad. The second dam, Cutting Reef (by Kris), a staying winner of 2 races in France including a listed event at Maisons-Laffitte, is a half-sister to 7 winners. *"Not in the yard at the moment, she's a nice filly and still for sale! Realistically she'll be seen to best effect over seven furlongs or a mile, and possibly beyond, so we're taking our time with her".*

119. UNNAMED ★★★
b.c. Fastnet Rock – Bowstring (Sadler's Wells). April 8. Fifth foal. 82,000Y. Tattersalls October Book 1. Kern/Lillingston. The dam, a fairly useful 9.7f winner, was third in the Group 2 Park Hill Stakes and is a half-sister to 7 winners including Cantilever (Group 3 12f Prix de Royaumont). The second dam, Cantanta (by Top Ville), won over 2m at 3 yrs and is a sister

to the Irish Oaks winner Princess Pati and a half-sister to 8 winners including the Group 2 Great Voltigeur Stakes winner Seymour Hicks. (Mr K J P Gundlach). *"A colt that's just beginning to get his act together, he's a fine, big stamp of a horse that cost quite a bit of money and he'll be an autumn 2-y-o. I like him".*

120. UNNAMED ★★★
ch.f. Manduro – Cape Marien (Cape Cross). March 15. First foal. 48,000Y. Tattersalls October Book 2. Rabbah Bloodstock. The dam, a fair 12f and 14f winner, is a half-sister to 5 winners including the Group 1 12f Prix de l'Arc de Triomphe and dual German Group 1 winner Marienbard. The second dam, Marienbad (by Darshaan), a French 1m winner at both 2 and 3 yrs, is a half-sister to 6 winners including the French and Italian listed winner Kentucky Coffee. (S Ali). *"She's not one of our earlier types but she's a good, strong, well-made filly and just getting her act together now. She's not slow, despite her staying pedigree, and in fact she's very strong and very forward in her coat. Nevertheless she's going to want a trip. She's nice".*

121. UNNAMED ★★★
b.f. Acclamation – Have Faith (Machiavellian). February 25. Fifth foal. 130,000Y. Tattersalls October Book 1. Tony Nerses. Half-sister to the quite useful 7f and 1m winner and listed-placed Faithful One (by Dubawi) and to a winner in Qatar by Cape Cross. The dam, a quite useful 2-y-o 7f winner, is a sister to the useful UAE winner of 7 races and Group 3 third Opportunist and a half-sister to the Group 1 Nassau Stakes and Group 2 1m Matron Stakes winner Favourable Terms and the French listed winner Modern History. The second dam, Fatefully (by Private Account), a smart winner of 4 races at 3 yrs including two listed events over 1m, is a half-sister to 6 winners including the Canadian Grade 2 winner Points Of Grace. (Saleh Al Homaizi & Imad Al Sagar). *"Quite sharp and an easy mover, the sire gets a stack of 2-y-o's and I think she'll be another".*

122. UNNAMED ★★★
b.c. Art Connoisseur – Narmeen (Royal

Applause). March 4. First foal. £42,000Y. Doncaster Premier. Tony Nerses. The dam, a modest 7f placed 2-y-o, is a half-sister to 2 winners. The second dam, Protectorate (by Hector Protector), a fairly useful 5f (at 2 yrs) and 6f winner, is a half-sister to 3 winners. (Saleh Al Homaizi & Imad Al Sagar). *"He could be alright, I loved him at the sales because he was an absolute dead ringer for his sire. Just doing easy canters at the moment, he's been a particular victim of the cold weather this spring but I think he will be a 2-y-o. He's really muscled up and done well in the past month so we're about to turn the screws because he should be doing more at this stage".*

123. UNNAMED ★★★★ ♠

ch.c. Mastercraftsman – Wait It Out (Swain). February 21. Third foal. 58,000Y. Tattersalls October Book 1. Kern/Lillingston. Half-brother to Hold On Tight (by Hernando), placed third over 1m on her only start at 2 yrs in 2012. The dam, a US stakes winner of 3 races and listed-placed, is a half-sister to 5 winners including a minor stakes winner. The second dam, As Long As Ittakes (by Sky Classic), is an unraced half-sister to 7 winners. (Mr M Tabor). *"A nice, big, quality horse and a very good mover, he's very clean limbed and I'm hoping he'll be an above average 2-y-o in the second half of the season".*

JOHN BEST

124. FRENCH ACCENT ★★

ch.f. Elnadim – Saralea (Sillery). April 4. Seventh foal. £18,000Y. Doncaster Premier. John Best. Half-sister to the US stakes winner Hasay (by Lomitas), to a minor winner in the USA by Giant's Causeway and three minor winners in France by Encosta De Lago, Fasliyev and Cozzene. The dam, a French 2-y-o listed 1m winner, was Group 3 placed and is a half-sister to 7 winners including 3 stakes winners. The second dam, Solidarite (by Far North), won in France and is a half-sister to 3 winners. *"She's coming along quite nicely, I haven't done lot with her but I should think she'll be out by June. A very sensible, laid-back filly and I'd be surprised if she doesn't turn out to be quite nice".*

125. IN SEINE ★★

b.c. Champs Elysees – Fancy Rose (Joyeux Danseur). April 13. Fourth foal. 26,000Y. Tattersalls October Book 2. Not sold. Half-brother to the 2012 6f placed 2-y-o, from two starts, Two Pancakes (by Compton Place). The dam, a minor winner at 5 yrs in the USA, is a half-sister to 6 winners including the Group 3 7f Horris Hill Stakes and dual 3-y-o 1m winner Dijeer and the US stakes winner and Group 3 placed Sharp Writer. The second dam, Sharp Minister (by Deputy Minister), is an unplaced sister to the multiple US Grade 2 winner Flag Down. *"He's coming along OK, he's quite flashy, he'll be earlier than my other Champs Elysees 2-y-o and I can imagine him starting off in late May/early June".*

126. MR WICKFIELD ★★

b.c. Champs Elysees – First Approval (Royal Applause). March 13. Fourth foal. 13,000Y. Tattersalls October Book 2. J R Best. Half-brother to the fair 2012 2-y-o 7f and 1m winner Jodies Jem (by Kheleyf). The dam, a fair 6f winner, is a half-sister to 6 winners including the high-class 7f to 11f winner Hawksley Hill, winner of the Arcadia Handicap, El Rincon Handicap and San Francisco Mile (all US Grade 2 events) and the dam of the Group 1 Prix de l'Abbaye winner Benbaun. The second dam, Gaijin (by Caerleon), a useful 2-y-o 6f winner, is a full or half-sister to 5 winners including Thousla Rock (Group 3 Premio Umbria). *"One of my favourite 2-y-o's but he is going to take time. He's big, scopey, very sensible and one for seven furlongs I should imagine".*

127. TRIPLE O SEVEN (IRE) ★★★

b.c. Kodiac – Triple Zero (Raise A Grand). February 10. Fourth foal. £26,000Y. Doncaster Premier. Helen Williams. Brother to the moderate 2012 2-y-o 5f winner Stripped Bear and half-brother to the modest 2011 2-y-o 7f winner Galilee Chapel (by Baltic King). The dam, the modest dual 1m (including at 2 yrs) and 6f winner, is a half-sister to the very useful Irish 7f winner and subsequent US Grade 2 third Good Day Too. The second dam, Locorotondo (by Broken Hearted), a fair 10f to 11f winner of 5 races, is a half-sister to 6 winners. (Lingfield Park Owners Group). *"One of my earlier types, I got him from Tally Ho Stud with whom we've been very successful in the past through Kingsgate Native and Mullionmilesanhour. He's got a great attitude, he's a real chunk of a horse and a proper 2-y-o. He'll be running in early to mid-May, probably over six furlongs, and he's very laid-back for a Kodiac".*

128. YANKEE RED ★★★

b.c. *Pastoral Pursuits – Miriam (Forzando).* April 27. Twelfth foal. £12,000Y. Doncaster Premier. John Best. Half-brother to the fairly useful triple 6f winner Para Siemple (by Mujahid), to the quite useful 5f to 7f winner of 13 races Ivory Lace (by Atraf), the fair 5f (including at 2 yrs) and 6f winner of 6 races Park Star (by Gothenberg), the modest 5f and 6f winner of 10 races Viewforth, the modest 2-y-o 6f winner Miriam's Song (by Royal Applause), the fair 5f winner of 3 races United Passion (both by Emarati) and a 2-y-o winner in Italy by Distant Relative. The dam, a modest dual 5f winner, is a half-sister to 7 winners. The second dam, Song Of Hope (by Chief Singer), a useful 2-y-o 5f winner, was second in the listed Firth of Clyde Stakes and is a half-sister to 10 winners. *"Likely to be out early, he's quite sharp, stocky and strong. He knows his job and he'll probably start off in a race over five furlongs in France early in May".*

129. UNNAMED ★★

b.c. *Bahri – Band Of Colour (Spectrum).* February 15. Half-brother to the moderate 6f and 7f winner Wadnagin (by Princely Heir). The dam, unplaced in one start, is a daughter of the Group 3 5f Prix d'Arenburg winner Regal Scintilla, herself a half-sister to the listed 5f Scarborough Stakes winner and smart broodmare Rivers Rhapsody. *"He's a bit weak at the moment but he moves really well and from what he's doing on the gallops I'm very excited about him. He'll take a bit of time to come to hand, hopefully towards the end of May. He'll start at six furlongs and then we'll see how he goes after that. He'll improve as the year goes on. I'm looking for an owner for him".*

130. UNNAMED ★★

b.f. *Amadeus Wolf – Pilda (Princely Heir).* April 16. Second foal. €5,000Y. Goffs Open. Not sold. The dam is an unraced sister to the Hong Kong and Italian listed 1m winner Romancero

and a half-sister to 4 winners. The second dam, Batilde (by Victory Piper), was placed four times in Italy at 3 yrs and is a half-sister to 7 winners including an Italian listed winner. *"She's a big, strong filly and we're taking it steady with her because the breeder says the dam's side are usually a bit 'buzzy'. She's a similar type to a good filly we had called Hucking Hot. Big and scopey, she'll take a bit of time but she's going in the right direction. She's for sale if anyone is interested".*

131. UNNAMED ★★★

br.c. *Myboycharlie – Retainage (Polish Numbers).* April 28. Third foal. £3,000Y. Ascot December. Not sold. Half-brother to the 2012 7f placed 2-y-o Sabre Rock (by Dubawi) and to the fair 2-y-o 7f winner Charles Fosterkane (by Three Wonders). The dam won 2 races at 3 and 4 yrs in the USA and is a half-sister to 3 minor US winners. The second dam, Seventeen Below (by Smarten), a minor winner of 2 races in the USA at 3 and 4 yrs, is a half-sister to 2 winners. *"A half-brother to Charles Fosterkane who won for us and also to Sabre Rock who looks like being a nice 3-y-o for us. This colt is a bit weak and leggy but he's showing plenty on the gallops. One for six/ seven furlongs, he has a good attitude and he's heading in the right direction. He's similar to Sabre Rock but a bit smaller so he should be a bit speedier. I think the sire Myboycharlie will do very well this year".*

132. UNNAMED ★★

b.c. *Baltic King – Zafaraya (Ashkalani).* February 6. Sixth foal. 14,000Y. Tattersalls October Book 2. J R Best. Half-brother to the quite useful 7f and 1m winner of 4 races If By Chance (by Danetime) and to the modest 1m winner The Educator (by Chineur). The dam, placed fourth twice in Ireland over 7f and 10f, is a half-sister to 4 winners. The second dam, Zafzala (by Kahyasi), a winner over 6f at 2 yrs and the listed 12f Ballyroan Stakes at 3 yrs, was placed in the Group 2 10f Pretty Polly Stakes and the Group 2 12.5f Prix de Royallieu and is a half-sister to 3 winners. (The Golf Partnership). *"Big and strong, but a bit backward mentally. I don't know how soon he'll be out but I do like him. He's got size and scope".*

JAMES BETHELL

133. BRAIDLEY ★★
b.c. Dylan Thomas – All Our Hope (Gulch).
February 21. Tenth foal. 11,000Y. Tattersalls
October Book 2. J D W Bethell. Half-brother
to the listed winner and dual Group 2 placed
Saphira's Fire (by Cape Cross). The dam, a
winner at 3 yrs and third in the Sun Chariot
Stakes, is a half-sister to 7 winners. The second
dam, Knoosh (by Storm Bird), won three listed
events and was fourth in the Oaks and is a
half-sister to 3 winners. *"He's very 'together'
and certainly looks like a 2-y-o type, but the sire
doesn't seem to get 2-y-o's so I'm erring on the
side of caution. We've had such a bad winter and
spring that I've done very little with my 2-y-o's
and I don't know that much about them as yet".*

134. KIRKMAN (IRE) ★★
ch.g. Virtual – Validate (Alhaarth). April 23.
Fourth foal. 30,000Y. Tattersalls October
Book 2. J D W Bethell. Closely related to the
quite useful 2-y-o 5f winner Little Lion Man
(by Kyllachy) and to the fair 2-y-o 7f winner
Personal Touch (by Pivotal). The dam is an
unraced half-sister to 4 winners including the
fairly useful dual 6f winner (including at 2 yrs)
and listed-placed Enact. The second dam,
Constitute (by Gone West), a quite useful 1m
winner, is a half-sister to 5 winners including
the dual listed winner and Group 3 10f Select
Stakes second Battle Chant. *"He was quite
a big yearling and he's grown a lot since. I
would have thought you'd be looking at July
or August for him this year, but he's a nice, big
type for seven furlongs and he moves well".*

135. PENHILL ★★★
b.c. Mount Nelson – Serrenia (High Chaparral).
March 16. Second foal. 24,000Y. Tattersalls
October Book 2. J D W Bethell. The dam is an
unraced half-sister to 9 winners including the
French listed winner and subsequent Grade
1 Hollywood Derby second Fast And Furious
and the US Grade 2 12f winner Herboriste. The
second dam, Helvellyn (by Gone West), a quite
useful 8.3f winner, is a half-sister to 6 winners.
*"He's a lovely horse and I'm very pleased with
him but he's one for later on. A seriously good
mover, he's a big boy, 16.3 hands, has a great
temperament and I hope he'll be ready for July
or August over seven furlongs to a mile".*

JIM BOLGER

136. AERIALIST (IRE)
ch.c. Sea The Stars – Maoineach (Congaree).
January 31. First foal. €400,000Y. Goffs Orby.
Bobby O'Ryan. The dam won the Group 3 6f
Round Tower Stakes (at 2 yrs) and the Group
3 7f Leopardstown 1,000 Guineas Trial and is a
half-sister to 2 winners including the US listed
winner and Group 2 placed Tiz Now Tiz Then.
The second dam, Trepidation (by Seeking The
Gold), is an unraced half-sister to 3 winners.
(Mrs J S Bolger).

137. ANSWERED
b.c. Authorized – Dublino (Lear Fan). February
27. Fourth living foal. 50,000foal. Tattersalls
December. John Ferguson. Half-brother to
the fair 2012 7f and 1m placed 2-y-o Woody
Bay (by New Approach). The dam, a French
2-y-o 1m winner, subsequently won the Grade
1 Del Mar Oaks and was Grade 1 placed
several times and is a half-sister to 6 winners.
The second dam, Tuscoga (by Theatrical),
was unplaced in 2 starts and is a sister to the
Grade 1 Matriarch Stakes winner Duda and a
half-sister to 5 winners. (Sheikh Mohammed).

138. BRU MOR (IRE)
ch.f. Intense Focus – Aeraiocht (Tenby). April
14. Half-sister to the fairly useful 2-y-o triple
7f winner Bunsen Burner (by Lil's Boy), to the
quite useful Irish 2-y-o 7f winner Chennai (by
Mozart) and the fair Irish 7f winner Webcast
(by Verglas). The dam, a dual Irish 2-y-o 7f
winner, is a half-sister to one winner. The
second dam, Direct Lady (by Fools Holme),
a winner of three races at 3 yrs over 11f and
12f and also three races over hurdles, is a
half-sister to the Group 1 Heinz "57" Phoenix
Stakes winner Eva Luna and the Group 3
Futurity Stakes winner Cois Na Tine. (Mrs J S
Bolger).

139. CONGRESSMAN (IRE)
ch.c. New Approach – Miss Marvellous (Diesis).
March 16. Third foal. 110,000Y. Tattersalls
October Book 1. Roger Varian. The dam, a
fair 10f winner, is a half-sister to 6 winners
including the multiple winner and dual US
Grade 2 placed Najecam (herself dam of the
champion US 2-y-o colt Action This Day) and
the listed-placed Lady Ilsley (dam of the UAE

Group 2 winner Lord Admiral). The second dam, Sue Warner (by Forli), is an unraced half-sister to 5 winners including the Group 2 Prix Maurice de Gheest winner Beaudelaire. (Sheikh Mohammed).

140. CRAIC AGUS SPRAOI (IRE)
b.f. *Intense Focus – Halla Siamsa (Montjeu).* May 9. Second foal. €300,000Y. Goffs Orby. BBA (Ire). Half-sister to the 2-y-o Group 1 7f Dewhurst Stakes winner Parish Hall (by Teofilo). The dam, a quite useful Irish 10f winner, is a half-sister to the Group 2 Irish Derby Trial winner Light Heavy. The second dam, Siamsa (by Quest For Fame), a fair Irish 9f and 11f winner, is a half-sister to 4 winners. (Mrs J S Bolger).

141. EVASON
b.c. *Galileo – Soneva (Cherokee Run).* March 21. First foal. €300,000Y. Arqana Deauville August. Neuilly Bloodstock. The dam won three Group 3 events over 1m in France (including at 2 yrs) and the UAE and is a half-sister to several winners including the triple US sprint stakes winner Coronado Rose. The second dam, Lakabi (by Nureyev), is an unraced sister to the US stakes winners and Grade 3 placed European Rose and Hessonite. (Claudia Jungo).

142. FOCUS ON VENICE
b.c. *Intense Focus – Marina Of Venice (Galileo).* February 1. First foal. The dam, a fairly useful 2-y-o 7f winner, is a half-sister to numerous winners including the useful listed winner Dawnus. The second dam, the French 1m winner Dame's Violet (by Groom Dancer), is a full or half-sister to 6 winners including the Group 2 Princess Of Wales's Stakes winner Wagon Master. This colt made a winning debut at Leopardstown in mid-April.

143. FRENCH APPLAUSE (FR)
b.c. *New Approach – Marion (Doyoun).* April 15. €105,000Y. Goffs November. J Bolger. Half-brother to the 2-y-o 7f winner and Group 2 Criterium de Saint-Cloud second Fauvelia (by Polish Precedent) and to the French 1m winner and listed-placed Liberty Chery (by Statue Of Liberty) and the minor French 2-y-o 6.5f winner Bunger (by Holy Roman Emperor).

The dam, a minor French dual winner at 3 yrs, is a half-sister to 4 winners. The second dam, Saxon Maid (by Sadler's Wells), a winner of two listed events and second in two Group 3 races, is a half-sister to 6 winners. (Mrs J S Bolger).

144. INTENSE DEBATE (IRE)
b.f. *Intense Focus – Bronntanas (Spectrum).* May 5. Second foal. Half-sister to the modest 1m winner Beart (by Invincible Spirit). The dam, a quite useful Irish 2-y-o 7f winner, is a half-sister to one winner. The second dam, Scarpetta (by Seattle Dancer), a fair 7f to 10f placed maiden, is closely related to the Irish listed middle-distance winner Classic Sport and a half-sister to the very smart Group 2 1m Berlin Brandenburg Trophy and Group 2 Hong Kong International Mile winner Docksider. (Mrs J S Bolger).

145. INTENSICAL (IRE)
b.c. *Intense Focus – Christinas Letter (Galileo).* February 19. Third foal. €55,000Y. Tattersalls Ireland September. J T Gorman. Half-brother to the 2012 2-y-o Group 3 6f Round Tower Stakes winner and Group 1 placed Leitir Mor (by Holy Roman Emperor). The dam is an unraced half-sister to 4 winners. The second dam, Danemarque (by Danehill), ran unplaced in Australia and is a half-sister to 7 winners including the listed winners Lady Shipley and Ellie Ardensky and to the dams of the Australian triple Group 1 winner Serenade Rose and the dual Group 3 winner Brave Act. (Mrs J S Bolger).

146. IONSAI NUA (IRE)
b.f. *New Approach – Toirneach (Thunder Gulch).* January 25. First foal. €80,000Y. Goffs Orby. Peter & Ross Doyle. The dam, a fairly useful Irish 7f (at 2 yrs) and 10f winner, is a half-sister to 2 minor winners in the USA. The second dam, Wandering Pine (by Country Pine), won at 3 yrs in the USA and is a half-sister to 4 winners including the listed winner and high-class broodmare Drina (the dam of 3 Group winners including the dual US Grade 1 winner Spain). (Mrs J S Bolger).

147. NOVEL APPROACH (IRE)
b.f. *New Approach – Altarejos (Vettori).*

February 9. Closely related to the fairly useful 2-y-o 7f winner and 3-y-o listed 10f third Cleofila (by Teofilo) and half-sister to the moderate 12f winner Global Recovery (by El Corredor). The dam is an unraced half-sister to 7 winners including the US dual Grade 1 winner Angara and the French Group 2 winner Actrice. The second dam, Ange Bleu (by Alleged), is a placed half-sister to 10 winners including the dual Grade 1 winner Arcangues. (Mrs J S Bolger).

148. PRINTHA (IRE)

ch.f. *New Approach – Scarpetta (Seattle Dancer)*. April 25. Half-sister to the 1m and 11f winner Ceannline (by Lil's Boy), to the Irish 2-y-o 7f winner Brontannas (by Spectrum) and the 7f and 11f winner Maidin Moch – all quite useful. The dam, a fair 7f to 10f placed maiden, is closely related to the Irish listed middle-distance winner Classic Sport and a half-sister to the very smart Group 2 1m Berlin Brandenburg Trophy and Group 2 Hong Kong International Mile winner Docksider. The second dam, Pump (by Forli), is an unraced daughter of the US 8.3f stakes winner Espadrille (by Damascus), herself a half-sister to Thatch, to the US Grade 1 winner King Pellinore and the dam of Nureyev. (Mrs J S Bolger).

149. PRUDENT APPROACH (IRE)

b.f. *New Approach – Hymn Of The Dawn (Phone Trick)*. May 1. Sixth foal. €775,000Y. Goffs Orby. Peter & Ross Doyle. Sister to the 2012 2-y-o Group 1 7f National Stakes and Group 2 6f Coventry Stakes winner Dawn Approach and half-brother to the fair 5f (at 2 yrs) to 7f winner Comadoir (by Medicis). The dam, placed fourth once at 2 yrs, is a half-sister to 3 winners including the Grade 1 third Galantas. The second dam, Colonial Debut (by Pleasant Colony), was placed in the USA and is a half-sister to 6 winners. (Mr Paddy Spain).

150. SUNDARA (IRE)

b.c. *Galileo – Saoire (Pivotal)*. April 25. Fifth foal. €390,000Y. Goffs Orby. Not sold. Half-brother to the useful 1m (at 2 yrs) and listed 7f winner Requisition (by Invincible Spirit) and to the fair 2-y-o 6f winner Pink Diva (by Giant's Causeway). The dam, winner of the Irish 1,000

Guineas and third in the Group 1 Moyglare Stud Stakes, is a half-sister to 6 winners. The second dam, Polish Descent (by Danehill), is an unraced half-sister to 4 winners. (Mrs M Joyce).

151. THEOPHILUS (IRE)

b.c. *Teofilo – Simonetta (Lil's Boy)*. April 22. Second foal. Half-brother to New Regalia (by New Approach), unplaced in two starts at 2 yrs in 2012. The dam, a fairly useful Irish 2-y-o 1m winner, was listed-placed and is a half-sister to numerous winners including the Group 3 12f Noblesse Stakes winner Danelissima. The second dam, by Zavaleta (Kahyasi), a useful dual listed 7f winner, is a half-sister to numerous winners including the 2-y-o Group 1 1m Gran Criterium winner Sholokov and the 2-y-o listed 7f winner Affianced (herself dam of the Irish Derby winner Soldier Of Fortune). (Mrs J S Bolger).

152. UNNAMED

b.c. *Intense Focus – Solas Na Greine (Galileo)*. May 3. Second foal. Half-brother to the fairly useful 2012 2-y-o 1m listed-placed Rehn's Nest (by Authorized). The dam, a fairly useful Irish 2-y-o 7f winner, is a half-sister to 2 winners including the fairly useful Irish 1m to 11f winner Coolcullen Times. The second dam, Key To Coolcullen (by Royal Academy), is an unraced half-sister to numerous winners including the Group 1 6f Phoenix Stakes winner Eva Luna and the Group 3 1m Futurity Stakes winner Cois Na Tine. (Mrs J S Bolger).

MARCO BOTTI

153. ABSOLUTE (IRE) ★★

b.c. *Danehill Dancer – Beyond Belief (Sadler's Wells)*. January 30. Third foal. €75,000Y. Goffs Orby. John Warren. The dam is an unraced half-sister to 5 winners including the listed Leopardstown 2,000 Guineas Trial winner and Irish 2,000 Guineas second Adjareli and to the placed Adjalisa (the dam of 2 stakes winners). The second dam, Adjriyna (by Top Ville), a French listed 8.5f winner, is a half-sister to 5 winners. (Highclere Thoroughbred Racing – Brunel). *"A nice, scopey horse, he's quite backward at the moment and still in pre-training so I wouldn't expect him to be racing until the back-end of the season".*

154. ALEXANOR (IRE) ★★★
b.c. Pivotal – Butterfly Cove (Storm Cat). May
1. Third foal. 45,000Y. Tattersalls October
Book 1. Alberto Panetta. Half-brother to the
Group 1 Moyglare Stud Stakes, Prix Marcel
Boussac (both at 2 yrs), Irish 1,000 Guineas
and Pretty Polly Stakes winner Misty For Me
and to the useful 7f (at 2 yrs) and listed 9f
winner and dual Group 3 placed Twirl (both by
Galileo). The dam is an unraced sister to the
Irish 1,000 Guineas Trial winner Kamarinskaya
and a half-sister to the champion 2-y-o colt
Fasliyev. The second dam, Mr P's Princess (by
Mr Prospector), is an unraced half-sister to the
US Grade 1 winners Menifee and Desert Wine.
(Op Centre). *"I thought he was quite cheap
for a horse with his pedigree, we're taking our
time with him and he's only cantering at the
moment. He does everything nicely but he's a
scopey horse for seven furlongs plus later in the
season".*

155. AL ZAMAN THAMAN (FR) ★★★
b.c. Nayef – Angie Eria (Galileo). February 5.
The dam is an unraced half-sister to 6 winners
including the US Grade 1 9f and Grade 1
12f winner Super Quercus (by Hero's Honor)
and the French listed winner Theos Quercus
(by Johann Quatz). The second dam, Ginger
Candy (by Hilal), a winner of 3 races in France
at 2 and 3 yrs, was listed-placed twice. (Jaber
Abdullah). *"He's a nice colt and for a Nayef he
looks quite compact, mature and precocious.
I'm really pleased with him and he's coming
along nicely, so he'll be an interesting horse for
the mid-summer onwards".*

156. DRAGOON GUARD ★★★
b.c. Jeremy – Elouges (Dalakhani). March 10.
Third foal. 33,000Y. Tattersalls October Book
3. Mark Crossman. The dam was placed twice
at 3 yrs in France and is a half-sister to 8
winners including Mons (Group 2 Royal Lodge
Stakes). The second dam, Morina (by Lyphard),
won over 11f in France and is a half-sister to
10 winners. *"He looks an early type because
physically he's already strong and we can kick
on with him. He should be out in May, he's very
straightforward and has a lovely attitude".*

157. FINALITY ★★★
b.c. Henrythenavigator – Dear Daughter

(Polish Precedent). January 26. The dam, a
useful listed-placed 1m winner, is a half-sister
to 2 winners. The second dam, Darayna (by
Shernazar), a listed-placed winner of 2 races
over 7f and 1m at 3 yrs, is a half-sister to 3
winners. (Mr Philip Newton). *"A good mover, I
like his attitude and he's in full work. He's doing
everything easily and considering he only came
in during January he's actually catching the
others up. A compact, precocious type, he's
levelled out so it looks like he isn't going to
grow much more".*

158. LIGHTNING SHOWER (USA) ★★★
b.c. Mr Greeley – Lightning Show (Storm Cat).
April 15. Fifth foal. 19,000Y. Tattersalls October
Book 2. Marco Botti. Half-brother to the fair
6f (including at 2 yrs) to 1m winner of 5 races
Whispered Times (by More Than Ready) and
to the minor US 3-y-o winner Shotgun Willy
(by Unbridled's Song). The dam is an unplaced
sister to the US Grade 1 winner Tactical Cat.
The second dam, Terre Haute (by Caro), a US
stakes winner and Grade 3 placed twice, is a
half-sister to 7 winners. (Mr J Allison). *"A good-
looking horse that wasn't expensive at the sale
and for what he cost I think he was a bargain.
He'll want seven furlongs in mid-summer to
begin with".* TRAINERS' BARGAIN BUY

159. MEANING OF LIFE (IRE) ★★★★
b.c. Exceed And Excel – Emirates Hills
(Dubawi). March 23. First foal. €44,000Y.
Tattersalls Ireland September. Alduino Botti.
The dam, a fair 2-y-o 6f winner, is a half-sister
to 2 winners including the useful listed 1m
winner Handassa. The second dam, Starstone
(by Diktat), is an unraced half-sister to the
Group 1 July Cup winner Pastoral Pursuits and
the Group 1 Haydock Park Sprint Cup winner
Goodricke. *"He could be an early type because
he looks like he'll be ready for fast work soon.
He's shown speed so we'll start to push him
soon and hopefully get him out in May. We
like him, he's good-looking, compact and
straightforward".*

160. NAADIRR (IRE) ★★★
b.c. Oasis Dream – Beach Bunny (High
Chaparral). February 7. First foal. 425,000Y.
Tattersalls October Book 1. Marco Botti. The
dam won 3 races including the listed Dance

Design Stakes and was second in the Group 1 Pretty Polly Stakes and is a half-sister to one winner. The second dam, Miss Hawai (by Peintre Celebre), is an unraced half-sister to 4 winners including the French dual listed winner Mer de Corail. (Sheikh Mohammed Bin Khalifa Al Maktoum). *"A very expensive yearling, I loved him at the sales because he was nice and compact and out of a very good mare. He has a very flashy head with a white face, I'm happy with him s far, he's a good mover and I'm just bringing him along nicely. Being by Oasis Dream I should think he'll be starting at six furlongs although his breeding suggests he'll be more of a miler. A good-looking horse, he's quite strong and a good size – especially for a first foal".*

161. SAYED YOUMZAIN ★★★

b.c. Dalakhani – Silver Touch (Dansili). April 10. The dam won the Group 3 7f Criterion Stakes and was third in the Group 1 Maurice de Gheest and is a half-sister to 2 winners. The second dam, Sanpala (by Sanglamore), is an unplaced half-sister to 10 winners including four stakes winners and the dam of the US multiple Grade 1 winner Ventura. (Jaber Abdullah). *"A big, scopey horse, he's moving well, has a good temperament and he's quite laid-back. I'm taking my time with him because we won't see him until seven furlongs in mid-season".*

162. YEAR OF GLORY ★★★

b.c. Kheleyf – Baila Salsa (Barathea). €27,000Y. SGA September, Italy. McKeever Bloodstock. Half-brother to the Italian 2-y-o winner of 3 races Kagera (by Halling). The dam won the Group 3 Carlo Chiesa and is a half-sister to 5 winners including the listed winner Step Dancer (herself dam of the Group 3 Diomed Stakes winner Fununalter). The second dam, Salsa Sound (by Law Society), won 8 races in Italy including a listed event (twice) and is a half-sister to 6 winners. *"He came from the Italian sales, he's quite straightforward and I like him a lot. I don't think he'll be a very early type, I would guess he'd want seven furlongs plus from the mid-summer onwards, but I love his attitude, he's a good mover and does everything easily. The lads all love him – he's that sort of horse".*

163. UNNAMED ★★★

ch.f. Shamardal – Fragrancy (Singspiel). February 15. Second foal. 52,000Y. Tattersalls October Book 2. Marco Botti. Half-sister to the fairly useful 2012 2-y-o 6f winner and Group 1 Fillies' Mile fourth Masarah (by Cape Cross). The dam, a useful 1m (including at 2 yrs) and 10f winner, was listed-placed and is a half-sister to 4 winners. The second dam, Zibet (by Kris), a fairly useful 7f winner, is a half-sister to 8 winners including the dam of the dual Group 1 winner Hibaayeb. *"A filly I liked a lot at the sales, she's going nicely. I don't think she'll be a sprinter, she's medium-sized and one for the middle of the season. I like her".*

164. UNNAMED ★★★★

b.f. New Approach – Rouge Noir (Saint Ballado). March 8. Sixth foal. €160,000Y. Goffs Orby. Blandford Bloodstock. Half-sister to the useful 2-y-o listed 5f winner Light The Fire (by Invincible Spirit), to the useful 2-y-o 7f winner and listed placed Cadley Road (by Elusive City) and two minor winners in Italy and France by Kheleyf and Hold That Tiger. The dam, a minor winner at 3 yrs in the USA, is a half-sister to 5 winners in Japan. The second dam, Ardana (by Danehill), won the Group 3 Premio Bagutta and is a half-sister to 5 winners. (Sheikh Mohammed Bin Khalifa Al Maktoum). *"A nice filly, I loved her at the sales and she's going well. She's a good mover, very straightforward and sound with a good temperament. She just needs to mature physically a bit more because she lacks a bit of strength at the moment, but I'm hoping to be racing her from the mid-summer onwards. She's one we like a lot".*

165. UNNAMED ★★★

b.f. Amadeus Wolf – Ryninch (Dr Devious). March 22. Third foal. €6,500foal. Goffs November. Aran Bloodstock. The dam, a fair 6f to 1m placed maiden in Ireland, is a half-sister to 3 minor winners. The second dam, Bella Pulchella (by Lomond), is an unraced half-sister to 3 winners including the Group 1 Moyglare Stud Stakes winner Gayle Gal. *"She's showing plenty of speed and she's not the biggest so we can start very soon. One of our early types".*

CLIVE BRITTAIN

166. CADEAUX POWER

b.f. Major Cadeaux – Right Answer (Lujain). February 22. Third foal. 20,000Y. Tattersalls October Book 1. Rabbah Bloodstock. Half-sister to the very useful 2-y-o 5f and 6f winner and dual listed-placed Galtymore Lad (by Indesatchel). The dam, a fairly useful 2-y-o 5f winner, was third in the listed St Hugh's Stakes and is a half-sister to 4 winners. The second dam, Quiz Show (by Primo Dominie), a quite useful 7f winner, is a half-sister to 4 winners including the high-class sprinter Mind Games, winner of the Group 2 Temple Stakes (twice), the Norfolk Stakes and the Palace House Stakes.

167. RIZEENA (IRE)

b.f. Iffraaj – Serena's Storm (Statue Of Liberty). March 24. Second foal. 50,000Y. Tattersalls October Book 2. Rabbah Bloodstock. Half-sister to the unplaced 2012 2-y-o Marble Silver (by Notnowcato). The dam, a quite useful 2-y-o 7f winner, is a half-sister to 2 winners. The second dam, Princess Serena (by Unbridled's Song), a minor US 4-y-o winner, is a half-sister to 4 winners including the US Grade 2 American Turf Stakes winner Doubles Partner. (Sheikh R D Al Maktoum).

168. UNNAMED ♠

b.c. New Approach – Bush Cat (Kingmambo). February 28. Sixth foal. 70,000Y. Tattersalls October Book 1. Blandford Bloodstock. Half-brother to the quite useful 2-y-o 1m winner and subsequent US Grade 3 placed Meer Kat (by Red Ransom), to the quite useful 2-y-o 7f winner Blue Tiger's Eye (by Motivator) and the moderate dual 1m seller winner Ask Dan (by Refuse To Bend). The dam, a quite useful 2-y-o 7f winner, is a half-sister to 6 winners. The second dam, Arbusha (by Danzig), won a listed 1m stakes in Germany, was third in the Group 3 Royal Whip Stakes and is a sister to the Group 2 6f Goldene Peitsche winner Nicholas and a half-sister to 9 winners including the dam of the dual Group 1 winner Strategic Choice. (Saeed Manana).

169. UNNAMED

b.f. Cape Cross – Fann (Diesis). February 15. Third foal. 80,000Y. Tattersalls October Book

1. G Howson. Half-sister to the 2012 2-y-o 1m debut winner Muhtaris and to the German listed 1m winner and Group 3 8.5f second Black Arrow (both by Teofilo). The dam, a useful 9f winner, was listed-placed and is a half-sister to 4 winners. The second dam, Forest Storm (by Woodman), is an unraced half-sister to 4 winners including the Group 1 Hollywood Turf Cup Handicap winner Storm Trooper and the dual Group 3 winner Marillette.

170. UNNAMED

b.c. Dandy Man – Miss Demure (Shy Groom). April 16. Fifteenth foal. £22,000Y. Doncaster Premier. Rabbah Bloodstock. Half-brother to 9 winners including the useful Irish 2-y-o 6f winner and listed-placed Miracle Match (by Oratorio), the useful 6f and US stakes winner and Group 1 Cheveley Park Stakes third Royal Shyness (by Royal Academy), the fairly useful 2-y-o 6f winner and Group 3 Coventry Stakes third Missel (by Storm Bird), the fairly useful 10f to 2m winner of 9 races Steamroller Stanly (by Shirley Heights), the quite useful 7f winner Dangerous Fortune (by Barathea) and four minor winners in Japan and the USA by Danzig, Storm Bird, Siphon and Private Terms. The dam won the Group 2 6f Lowther Stakes and is a half-sister to one winner. The second dam, Larosterna (by Busted), ran once unplaced and is a full or half-sister to 6 winners. (S Ali).

171. UNNAMED

b.f. Major Cadeaux – Quiz Show (Primo Dominie). March 4. Tenth foal. 22,000Y. Tattersalls October Book 1. Rabbah Bloodstock. Half-sister to the fairly useful 2-y-o 5f winner and listed-placed Right Answer (by Lujain), to the Scandinavian winner and listed-placed Better Built (by Xaar), the quite useful 5f (including at 2 yrs) and 6f winner Excellent Show (by Excellent Art), the quite useful 2-y-o dual 5f winner Bold Bidder (by Indesatchel) and the Irish 2-y-o 5f winner, on her only start, Twenty Questions (by Kyllachy). The dam, a quite useful 7f winner, is a half-sister to 4 winners including the high-class sprinter Mind Games, winner of the Group 2 Temple Stakes (twice), the Norfolk Stakes and the Palace House Stakes. The second dam,

Aryaf (by Vice Regent), is an unplaced half-sister to 6 winners. (Saeed Manana).

172. UNNAMED

b.c. *Dubawi – Scotch Bonnet (Montjeu)*. April 14. Third foal. 70,000Y. Tattersalls October Book 2. Rabbah Bloodstock. Half-brother to Mindy (by Zamindar), unplaced in one start at 2 yrs in 2012. The dam won twice over 11f and 14f in France is a half-sister to 4 winners including the 10f winner and Group 1 Irish Oaks third Sister Bella and the dam of the Grade 2 Las Palmas Handicap winner Beautyandthebeast. The second dam, Valley Of Hope (by Riverman), is an unraced half-sister to 5 winners including Vacarme (the Mill Reef Stakes and Richmond Stakes) and Vin de France (Prix Jacques le Marois). (Saeed Manana).

173. UNNAMED

gr.c. *Clodovil – Shambodia (Petardia)*. March 24. Sixth foal. 80,000Y. Tattersalls October Book 2. Rabbah Bloodstock. Half-brother to the fairly useful triple 7f winner (including at 2 yrs) Bettalatethannever (by Titus Livius) and to the fair 6f (at 2 yrs) to 1m winner of 6 races Master Of Dance (by Noverre). The dam is an unraced half-sister to 5 winners. The second dam, Lucky Fountain (by Lafontaine), is an unraced sister to the Group 2 Geoffrey Freer Stakes winner Shambo and a half-sister to 4 winners. (Saeed Manana).

174. UNNAMED

b.c. *New Approach – Shimna (Mr Prospector)*. April 18. Ninth foal. 85,000Y. Tattersalls October Book 2. Blandford Bloodstock. Half-brother to the useful 1m (at 2 yrs) and 10f winner and Group 3 Derby Trial second Hazeymm (by Marju), to the useful 2-y-o 7f and subsequent US winner Santa Fe (by Green Desert), the fairly useful dual 10f winner and listed-placed Black Eagle (by Cape Cross), the fairly useful 1m (at 2 yrs) and dual 10f winner Sahrati (by In The Wings) and a winner over hurdles by Shamardal. The dam, placed fourth over 10f in Ireland on her only outing, is a half-sister to the St Leger and Gran Premio del Jockey Club winner Shantou. The second dam, Shaima (by Shareef Dancer), a very useful 7.3f

(at 2 yrs) and 9f listed winner here, later won the Grade 2 12f Long Island Handicap and is a half-sister to 6 winners including the Prix Saint Alary winner Rosefinch. (Saeed Manana).

175. UNNAMED

b.f. *Royal Applause – Tarbiyah (Singspiel)*. March 1. Fifth foal. 25,000Y. Tattersalls October Book 2. Rabbah Bloodstock. Half-brother to the quite useful dual 1m winner (including at 2 yrs) Mukhber (by Anabaa) and to the quite useful 2-y-o 7f winner Mabaany (by Exceed And Excel). The dam, fairly useful 1m winner on her only start, is a half-sister to 3 winners including the 1,000 Guineas winner Lahan. The second dam, Amanah (by Mr Prospector), a useful 1m winner, is a sister to one winner and a half-sister to 5 winners. (Saeed Manana).

176. UNNAMED

b.f. *Invincible Spirit – Wing Stealth (Hawk Wing)*. March 26. Second foal. 50,000Y. Tattersalls October Book 2. Rabbah Bloodstock. The dam, a fair 7f (at 2 yrs) and 12f placed maiden, is a half-sister to 4 winners. The second dam, Starlight Smile (by Green Dancer), is an unraced half-sister to 4 winners including the multiple Irish listed winner Seasonal Pickup and the dam of the Irish Derby winner Grey Swallow. (Saeed Manana).

DAVID BROWN

177. CAPTAIN MIDNIGHT (IRE) ★★★★

b.c. *Bushranger – Beverley Macca (Piccolo)*. March 5. Fourth foal. £12,000Y. Doncaster Premier. David Brown. Half-brother to the fair 2-y-o dual 5f winner Little Big Boy (by Danehill Dancer). The dam, a fair 5f winner of 4 races including at 2 yrs, is a half-sister to 6 winners including the 2-y-o Group 1 Cheveley Park Stakes and dual Group 2 winner Airwave. The second dam, Kangra Valley (by Indian Ridge), a moderate 2-y-o 5f winner, is a half-sister to 7 minor winners. (D A West). *"A very nice horse, he's in the top group of my 2-y-o's and he'll be running in April. Very precocious, he's done everything right from day one and I think he's above average. The indications are that five furlongs will be just right for him and I think he could go places".* TRAINERS' BARGAIN BUY

178. HARD DIVORCE (USA) ★★

b.c. Hard Spun – Divorce Settlement (Stormin Fever). January 28. Second foal. £210,000Y. Keeneland September. David Redvers. The dam, unplaced in one start, is a half-sister to 7 winners including Prenup (Grade 1 Jerome Handicap) and the Graded stakes winners Cat's At Home, Giant Wrecker and Honor The Hero. The second dam, Homewrecker (by Buckaroo), is a placed half-sister to 3 stakes winners. (Qatar Racing Ltd). *"A lovely big horse, he's a bit backward and will want a bit of time. He's fine but he'll want seven furlongs later in the year".*

179. ILLUMINATING DREAM (IRE) ★★

b.f. High Chaparral – Massada (Most Welcome). April 30. Tenth foal. €50,000Y. Goffs Orby. David Redvers. Half-sister to the multiple listed winner Les Fazzani, to the minor French and German 3-y-o winner Marangu (both by Intikhab), the German listed winner and Group 3 6f placed Miss Lips, the minor German winner Moody Blues (both by Big Shuffle) and a minor 2-y-o winner in Spain by King Charlemagne. The dam, a listed-placed 7f and 1m winner at 2 yrs in Germany, is a half-sister to 3 minor winners. The second dam, Maracuja (by Riverman), won over 1m at 2 yrs in France and is a half-sister to 3 minor winners. (Qatar Racing Ltd). *"A lovely filly that'll need a bit of time. Probably one for seven furlongs to a mile from mid-season onwards".*

180. SIR JACK LAYDEN ★★★★

b.c. Sir Percy – Barawin (Hawk Wing). March 2. First foal. 40,000Y. Tattersalls October Book 2. D H Brown. The dam, a quite useful 2-y-o 1m winner, is a half-sister to one winner. The second dam, Cosabawn (by Barathea), is an unplaced half-sister to 7 winners. (Mr D Brown, Mr R Hull, Mr C Watson). *"A very nice colt and at the moment he ticks all the boxes. A lovely mover, he's just a nice size and it looks like he'll be above average. He'll start at six furlongs in May and he has the scope to improve as the season goes on. He's named after a very influential and much loved mayor of Rotherham who helped sort out the miner's strike and was an ex-miner himself".*

181. THEBEASTUNLEASHED (FR) ★★★ ♠

gr.c. Mastercraftsman – Prairie Moon (Halling). January 26. Third foal. €120,000Y. Arqana Deauville August. David Redvers. The dam is an unraced half-sister to two winners and to the listed-placed Shadowless. The second dam, Warning Shadows (by Cadeaux Genereux), won the Group 2 10f Sun Chariot Stakes and was second in the Irish 1,000 Guineas. (Qatar Racing Ltd). *"A lovely, strong, good-moving colt. One for the mid-season onwards, he's doing everything asked of him at the moment".*

182. WIND FIRE (USA) ★★★★

b.f. Distorted Humor – A P Dream (A P Indy). March 5. Third foal. $95,000Y. Keeneland September. David Redvers. The dam, a minor winner at 3 yrs in the USA, is a sister to two stakes winners including Majestic Warrior (Grade 1 Hopeful Stakes). The second dam, Dream Supreme (by Seeking The Gold), won the Grade 1 Ballerina Handicap and the Grade 1 Test Stakes. (Qatar Racing Ltd). *"A very nice filly, she'll be reasonably early and is showing plenty. I expect her to rank highly, she's strong, athletic and very well put-together. The type to start at five or six furlongs but she'll progress and stay further as the year goes on".*

183. UNNAMED ★★★

b.f. Green Desert – Record Time (Clantime). March 16. Eighth foal. Closely related to the 2012 5f placed 2-y-o Fidget and to the smart dual Group 3 5f winner Moorhouse Lad (both by Bertolini) and half-sister to the useful 5f (including at 2 yrs) and 6f winner of 5 races Off The Record (by Desert Style) and the modest 2-y-o 5f winner Pro Tempore (by Fraam). The dam, a fair 5f winner at 3 and 4 yrs, is a sister to the listed winning sprinter Lago Di Varano and a half-sister to 3 winners. The second dam, On The Record (by Record Token), a fair dual sprint winner at 2 and 4 yrs, is a half-sister to 3 winners. (Peter Onslow). *"She only arrived here quite late and won't be ready until the second half of the season. The pedigree has 'sprinting' written all over it".*

HENRY CANDY
184. BOROUGH BELLE ★★★

ch.f. Bertolini – Sheesha (Shadeed). April 27. Eleventh foal. £4,000 2-y-o. Doncaster January. H Candy. Half-sister to the quite useful 5f (at 2 yrs) and 6f winner of 4 races Seamus Shindig, to the fair 2-y-o 6f winner Shielaligh, the fair 7f winner Shebeen (all by Aragon) and the quite useful 6f and 7f winner Shangani (by Ishiguru). The dam, unplaced in one start, is a half-sister to 8 winners including the smart 12f King George V Handicap winner and St Leger third Samraan and the useful 6f (at 2 yrs) and 7f winner Star Talent. The second dam, Sedra (by Nebbiolo), a smart winner of 6 races from 6f (at 2 yrs) to 10f including the listed Ebbisham Handicap, was second in the Group 2 Sun Chariot Stakes and is a half-sister to 6 winners. (Mr J Porteous/Mr H Candy). *"We've had most of them out of this dam and they've nearly all won including Seamus Shindig who's just retired aged 10! So she's been a good mare. This filly is a tough little thing, not very big like the rest of them and she's high spirited. She came to us unbroken at the very end of January so she's going to take a while to catch up. I should think she'll be in action around June time though and she looks sharp. A five/six furlong 2-y-o".*

185. CHARLES MOLSON ★★★★

b.c. Monsieur Bond – Arculinge (Paris House). March 30. £28,000Y. Doncaster Premier. Not sold. Half-brother to Wrightington (by Dutch Art), unplaced in two starts at 2 yrs in 2012, to the fair 6f winner Byton (by Byron) and the fair dual 5f winner (including at 2 yrs) Normandy Maid (by American Post). The dam, a moderate 6f and 7f placed maiden, is a half-sister to 5 winners including the smart listed 5f winner Corrybrough and the fairly useful 5f to 6f winners Kingscross and Artie, and to the dam of the dual Group 3 winner Amour Propre. The second dam, Calamanco (by Clantime), a fair 5f winner at 3 and 4 yrs, is a sister to the sprint winner Cape Merino (herself dam of the Group 1 Golden Jubilee Stakes winner Cape Of Good Hope). (Simon Broke & Partners). *"This colt is from a family we've had a lot of success with, although this particular dam hasn't really starred yet. He's a very strong colt, a great mover, seems to have endless energy and is hard to handle. He got a touch of sore shins, so that put him back a while, but I would imagine he'd be in action in May or June. He'll be an out-and-out sprinter".*

186. CORNISH PATH ★★★

b.f. Champs Elysees – Quintrell (Royal Applause). March 30. Fourth foal. 4,000Y. Tattersalls October Book 3. H Candy. The dam, a fair dual 7f winner at 3 yrs, is a half-sister to 8 minor winners. The second dam, Peryllis (by Warning), a modest 6f (at 2 yrs) to 10.2f placed maiden, is a half-sister to 6 winners including the French listed 11.5f winner Honest Word and the very useful sprinter Cragside. (Mrs D Blackburn/Mr H Candy). *"We trained the dam to win as a 3-y-o with give in the ground. I bought this filly from Major Wyatt, she wasn't expensive but I just liked her very much when I was at the stud in the summer. She's a good-moving filly, not very tall but very strong and very tough. I've got two by this sire and they both look alright. I think this filly will probably cope with six furlongs, she may stay seven, but she doesn't look a stayer by any manner of means".*

187. COSETTE (IRE) ★★★

b.f. Champs Elysees – Luanas Pearl (Bahri). April 2. First foal. 22,000Y. Tattersalls October Book 2. H Candy. The dam is an unraced half-sister to 7 winners including the Chester Vase, September Stakes and Winter Derby winner (all Group 3 events) Hattan and the Group 3 Jockey Club Cup and listed Aston Park Stakes winner Tastahil. The second dam, Luana (by Shaadi), a useful triple 6f winner (including at 2 yrs), was listed-placed and is a half-sister to 5 winners including the high-class middle-distance horses and Group 1 winners Warrsan and Luso and the Group winners Cloud Castle and Needle Gun, and to the dams of the Group 3 winners Blue Monday, Nideeb, Queen's Best and Laaheb. (Mr P A Deal/Mr H Candy). *"A very nice filly from one of my favourite families in the stud book. We had Rugged Cross out of this family last year. This filly was very small and slight at the sales and I only bought her because of the way she moved. She's doing really well now and I'm very pleased with her, but she'll definitely want a trip. Hopefully start off at seven furlongs around July time".*

188. FAURE ISLAND ★★★

b.c. Myboycharlie – Free Offer (Generous). February 3. Second foal. Half-brother to Cape

Peron (by Beat Hollow), placed third over 6f on his only start at 2 yrs in 2012. The dam was a quite useful 7f (at 2 yrs) and dual 10f winner. The second dam, Proserpine (by Robellino), a fairly useful 2-y-o 1m winner, is a half-sister to several winners including the 1m and 10f winner and subsequent US Grade 1 14f placed Chelsea Barracks. (Lord Cadogan). *"A huge horse, he's very strong but because of his size he's going to take a bit of time. He looks OK and I should think he'll be a sprinter like his sire, but that won't be until towards the back-end of the season".*

189. GREENSIDE ★★★

b.c. Dubawi – Katrina (Ela-Mana-Mou). April 10. Seventh foal. 38,000Y. Tattersalls October Book 2. H Candy. Half-brother to the quite useful 12f winner Sri Lipis (by Cadeaux Genereux) and to the moderate 14f winner Kritzia (by Daylami). The dam is an unraced half-sister to the Group 3 12 St Simon Stakes and listed 12f Galtres Stakes winner Kithanga (herself dam of the St Leger and Great Voltigeur winner Milan). The second dam, Kalata (by Assert), was unplaced on her only start and is a half-sister to 7 winners including the Italian Group 3 winner Karkisiya and the dams of the Derby winner Kahyasi and the Yorkshire Oaks winner Key Change. (T Barr). *"Bred to want a trip, he's a very nice horse, a nice mover and he's going to be a big, strong boy. We probably won't see him until July time and he does remind you of his sire in terms of his colour and shape. I don't think he'll need a mile and a half like his two winning siblings and he should be capable of winning over seven furlongs this year".*

190. JETHOU ISLAND ★★★

ch.f. Virtual – Lihou Island (Beveled). April 3. Sixth foal. 7,500Y. Tattersalls December. Not sold. Closely related to the useful 7f (including at 2 yrs) and 6f winner of 6 races Horseradish (by Kyllachy) and half-sister to the unplaced 2012 2-y-o Hot Mustard (by Pastoral Pursuits). The dam, a quite useful 2-y-o 6f winner, is a half-sister to 6 winners. The second dam, Foreign Mistress (by Darshaan), was placed 12 times in Italy and is a half-sister to 3 winners. (Mrs F E Veasey). *"This is a nice filly, we're only just getting her going but she's making huge*

physical progress. She's very scopey and a very good mover, so she looks like being OK. It's hard to assess what trip she wants because she's done so little, but to look at her I would guess she'd want seven furlongs".*

191. LACOCK ★★★

b.c. Compton Place – Puya (Kris). April 19. Half-brother to the fair 2012 6f placed 2-y-o Herbalist (by Haafhd) and to the fair 2-y-o 7f winner Pandorea (by Diktat). The dam, a quite useful dual 7f winner, is a half-sister to several winners including the multiple Group 3 6f winner Gorse. The second dam, Pervenche (by Latest Model), is an unplaced half-sister to the smart 2-y-o Cut Throat. (Girsonfield Ltd). *"A typical sprinter, he's very strong and a nice mover. He seems to like give in the ground, which is true of most of the family and I can see him running in June".*

192. MARYDALE ★★★

ch.f. Aqlaam – Mary Goodnight (King's Best). February 10. First foal. 50,000Y. Tattersalls October Book 2. Dunchurch Lodge Stud. The dam, a quite useful 10f winner, is a half-sister to 2 winners including Namibian (Group 3 Gordon Stakes and Group 3 Queens Vase). The second dam, Disco Volante (by Sadler's Wells), a useful 1m winner, was listed-placed and is a half-sister to 3 winners including the Group 1 St James's Palace Stakes second Valentino. (Major M G Wyatt). *"We like her and thought she'd be an early type when we bought her, but she's grown a lot so it'll take a while before we get her out. A lovely, big, scopey filly and a nice mover. She should have the speed for six furlongs I think".*

193. MIND ★★★

b.c. Zamindar – Danae (Dansili). April 11. First foal. The dam, a fairly useful 7f winner at 3 yrs, is a several winners including the multiple Group 3 6f winner Gorse. The second dam, Pervenche (by Latest Model), is an unplaced half-sister to the smart 2-y-o Cut Throat. (Girsonfield Ltd). *"A compact, very good-moving horse, he looks like making a 2-y-o and we like him a lot".*

194. RAPUNZAL ★★

b.f. Mount Nelson – Cinnas Ransom (Red

Ransom). March 2. First foal. 3,500Y. Tattersalls October Book 3. H Candy. The dam is an unraced half-sister to 7 winners including the Group 3 5f Prix de Saint-Georges winner Black Rock Desert and the Japanese stakes winner Toyo Seattle. The second dam, City Dance (by Seattle Slew), a listed stakes winner in the USA and second in the Grade 2 7f Comely Stakes, is a sister to the dual Grade 1 winner Slew City Slew and a half-sister to the stakes winner and Grade 1 Ballerina Stakes third Dream Touch. (The Port & Brandy Syndicate). *"A nice, big, scopey filly and a lovely mover. She'll be very nice in time and I should think she'll want seven furlongs to start with".*

195. ROSITA ★★★

b.f. Firebreak – Muskat Rose (One Cool Cat). February 24. £1,800Y. Ascot December. Not sold. Second foal. Half-sister to the modest 2012 dual 7f placed 2-y-o Muskat Link (by Rail Link). The dam is an unraced half-sister to numerous winners including the fairly useful Sonning Rose, New Jersey and Vienna's Boy (all three listed-placed). The second dam, Shinkoh Rose (by Warning), placed over 9f at 3 yrs in Ireland, is a half-sister to one winner. (The Muskat Rose Syndicate). *"She could easily be our first 2-y-o runner. She's small, compact, very lively and wants to get on with it. She really enjoys her work and she'll be racing in May".*

196. VEILED INTRIGUE ★★★

b.f. Pastoral Pursuits – Verbal Intrigue (Dahar). May 12. Tenth foal. Half-sister to the fairly useful 2012 2-y-o dual 7f winner Code Of Honor (by Zafeen), to the US Grade 2 winner Monkey Puzzle (by Country Pine), the very useful listed 7f winner and Group 3 Jersey Stakes second Codemaster (by Choisir), the fair 10f and hurdles winner Sainglend (by Galileo), four minor winners in the USA by Dr Caton, Bates Motel, Saint Ballado and Pleasant Tap and a winner in Spain by Bahri. The dam, a minor US 3-y-o winner, is a half-sister to 6 winners including the US Grade 1 placed Verbasle (herself dam of the US Grade 1 winner High Fly and the dual UAE Group 3 winner Estimraar). The second dam, Verbality (by Verbatim), a stakes winner and Grade 2 placed in the USA, is a half-sister to

2 winners. (Mr D B Clark/Mr J J Byrne). *"The last foal out of the dam who has been a good mare and we've had both Code Of Honor and Codemaster out of her. This filly is very small and rather immature but she's an exceptionally good mover. She'll make a 2-y-o around June time, probably over six furlongs".*

197. WARRENDALE ★★★

b.f. Three Valleys – Swynford Pleasure (Reprimand). March 9. Fifth foal. £16,000Y. Doncaster Festival. Henry Candy. Half-sister to the 2012 2-y-o 7f winner Bee Brave (by Rail Link), to the fair 7f winner Saskia's Dream (by Oasis Dream) and the modest 1m and 10f winner Petsas Pleasure (by Observatory). The dam, a modest 1m to 10f winner of 6 races, is a half-sister to 6 winners including the Group 3 9f Prix de Conde winner Rashbag and the smart 7f listed winner Suggestive. The second dam, Pleasuring (by Good Times), is a sprint placed half-sister to 5 winners including the Group 3 1,000 Guineas Trial winner Rose Of Montreaux and the Group 3 Princess Elizabeth Stakes winner Bay Street (herself the dam of 5 stakes winners). (Mrs D Blackburn/Lady Morrison/H Candy/A L Smith-Maxwell). *"I like this filly, she goes really well and I can see her running in May. She's a lovely, long-striding 2-y-o so she doesn't have a sprinter's action, but six furlongs will be fine I should think".*

198. WHITE RUSSIAN ★★★★

ch.f. Sir Percy – Danse Russe (Pivotal). March 7. Second foal. 5,000Y. Tattersalls October Book 3. H Candy. The dam is an unraced half-sister to 3 winners. The second dam, Danse Classique (by Night Shift), a listed-placed winner in Ireland, is a half-sister to 5 winners including the triple Group 1 winner Petrushka. (Six Too Many). *"She's grown enormously since we bought her, so she's a big, strong, scopey filly now and an outstanding mover. We like her a lot and I should think she'll be racing around July time".* TRAINERS' BARGAIN BUY

199. UNNAMED ★★★

ch.c. Nayef – Emily Blake (Lend A Hand). March 29. Second foal. Half-brother to the modest 2012 2-y-o 6f winner Gallena (by Galileo). The dam won the Group 3 7f Athasi Stakes and the Group 3 1m Equestrian Stakes (both at the Curragh). The second dam, Kirri (by Lycius), was unplaced in one start and is a half-sister to 2 minor winners. (Mr & Mrs R Scott). *"A big 2-y-o, as you might expect for a Nayef, he's very athletic and full of energy but he'll take time and is one for the second half of the year. A nice horse, he'll want seven furlongs to start off with".*

SIR HENRY CECIL

200. AIRFIELD ★★★

b.f. Dansili – Emplane (Irish River). January 31. Sister to the smart 1m (at 2 yrs) and Group 3 10.4f Musidora Stakes and subsequent US Grade 2 1m winner Aviate, to the 2-y-o Group 3 7f Prix la Rochette winner and Group 1 placed Early March and the very useful 2-y-o dual 7f winner Wingwalker and half-sister to the fairly useful French 10f winner Itinerary (by Dr Fong), the quite useful 7f winner Painted Sky (by Rainbow Quest) and the minor French 11f winner Coach Lane (by Barathea). The dam, a useful 3-y-o 1m winner, is a sister to the useful 2-y-o 1m winner Boatman and a half-sister to the quite useful 2-y-o 7f winner Palisade. The second dam, Peplum (by Nijinsky), a useful winner of the listed 11.3f Cheshire Oaks, is a half-sister to the top class filly Al Bahathri, winner of the 1,000 Guineas and the Coronation Stakes. (Khalid Abdulla). *"This filly has an early foaling date and she's a nice mover, but she'll need time and is one for the later in the season". Sir Henry pointed out to me that most of his 2-y-o's arrived quite late in the yard this year".*

201. BOUYANT ★★★

b.br.f. Oasis Dream – Passage Of Time (Dansili). February 15. Second foal. The dam, winner of the Group 1 10f Criterium de Saint-Cloud (at 2 yrs) and the Group 3 10.3f Musidora Stakes, is a sister to 2 winners including the 6f (at 2 yrs) and Group 2 12f King Edward VI Stakes winner Father Time and a half-sister to several winners including the Group 1 Falmouth Stakes winner Timepiece. The second dam, Clepsydra (by Sadler's Wells), a quite useful 12f winner, is a half-sister to numerous winners including the useful listed 10.5f winner Double Crossed. (Khalid Abdulla). *"A nice filly from a good family, her*

sire produces speedy horses but this filly needs a bit more time".

202. BUTTON DOWN ★★★

b.f. Oasis Dream – Modesta (Sadler's Wells). April 1. Fifth foal. Half-sister to the very useful 10f winner and Group 3 Chester Vase second Model Pupil (by Sinndar) and to the fairly useful 7f (at 2 yrs) and 1m winner Intense (by Dansili). The dam, a useful 11.5f and listed 14f winner, is closely related to the Oaks, Fillies Mile, Musidora Stakes and May Hill Stakes winner Reams of Verse and to the smart 2-y-o 1m winner and Group-placed High Walden and a half-sister to the high-class Group 1 10f Coral Eclipse Stakes and Group 1 10f Phoenix Champion Stakes winner Elmaamul. The second dam, Modena (by Roberto), is an unraced half-sister to the smart 2-y-o 7f winner and Queen Elizabeth II Stakes third Zaizafon – herself the dam of Zafonic. (Khalid Abdulla). *"A good-moving filly from a family I know well".*

203. DORSET CREAM ★★★

b.f. Dansili – Blend (Zafonic). March 23. The dam, a modest 10f and 12f placed maiden (from three starts), is a half-sister to the Group 3 7f Prestige Stakes winner Sense Of Joy, the multiple Group 3 middle-distance winner and French Derby fourth Day Flight and the very useful 2-y-o 7f winner Bionic (herself dam of the Group 3 Earl Of Sefton Stakes winner and multiple Group 1 second Phoenix Tower). The second dam, Bonash (by Rainbow Quest), a very useful filly, won 4 races in France from 1m to 12f including the Prix d'Aumale, the Prix Vanteaux and the Prix de Malleret and is a full or half-sister to 4 winners. (Khalid Abdulla). *"A big filly by a top-class sire, she's very likeable".*

204. EQUITABLE ★★★

b.c. Dansili – Honest Quality (Elusive Quality). January 13. The dam, a useful 2-y-o listed 7f winner, is a half-sister to numerous winners including the US Grade 1 7f Forego Stakes winner First Defence and the French listed 1m winner Phantom Rose. The second dam, Honest Lady (by Seattle Slew), winner of the Grade 1 Santa Monica Handicap, is a half-sister to the US triple Grade 1 winner Empire

Maker and the Grade 1 Arlington Million winner Chester House. (Khalid Abdulla). *"He was late in and is only just about to start cantering, but he has plenty of spirit".*

205. FAIR SHARE ★★★

b.c. Rail Link – Quota (Rainbow Quest). March 18. Closely related to the quite useful 12f and 14f winner Acquisition (by Dansili) and half-brother to the useful 2-y-o listed 7f winner Protectress (by Hector Protector), to the useful 12f to 14f winner and listed-placed Market Forces (by Lomitas), the quite useful 7f (at 2 yrs) and 1m winner Amount (by Salse) and the French 12f and hurdles winner Share Option (by Polish Precedent). The dam, a useful 10f winner, is a sister to 4 winners including the top-class Group 1 1m Racing Post Trophy winner and St Leger second Armiger and the useful 2-y-o 1m and 8.5f winner and Group 1 Racing Post Trophy fourth Besiege. The second dam, Armeria (by Northern Dancer), a fair 10f winner at Windsor, is a half-sister to the Park Hill Stakes winner I Want To Be and is out of a half-sister to the dams of Media Starguest, Glint of Gold, Diamond Shoal and Ensconce. (Khalid Abdulla). *"A colt by the Arc winner Rail Link, he's nice and a good mover".*

206. HOOP OF COLOUR (USA) ★★

b.f. Distorted Humor – Surya (Unbridled). April 19. Half-sister the US Grade 1 9f Spinster Stakes winner Aruna (by Mr Greeley), to the French 2-y-o 10f winner Loverdose (by Giant's Causeway) and the fair 2-y-o 7f winner (on her only start) Spy Eye (by Tale Of The Cat). The dam won the Grade 2 Dahlia Handicap in the USA and is a half-sister to numerous winners. The second dam, Wild Planet (by Nureyev), won at 2 yrs here and the listed Prix Coronation in France, was third in the Group 3 Prestige Stakes and is a half-sister to 6 winners. (Niarchos Family). *"Going through a growing phase at present, it's too early to comment on her ability".*

207. JOYEUSE ★★★★★

b.f. Oasis Dream – Kind (Danehill). April 10. Fifth foal. Sister to Morpheus (unplaced in one start at 2 yrs in 2102) and half-sister to the outstanding multiple Group 1 winner Frankel (Dewhurst Stakes, 2,000 Guineas, Juddmonte International, Sussex Stakes, Queen Anne Stakes etc), to the smart Group 3 12f Gordon Stakes winner Noble Mission (both by Galileo) and the very useful Group 3 11.5f Derby Trial winner Bullet Train (by Sadler's Wells). The dam, a dual listed winner over 5f and 6f, was Group 3 placed and is a half-sister to the Arlington Million and Tattersalls Rogers Gold Cup winner Powerscourt (by Sadler's Wells) and to the smart 14f winner of 3 races Brimming. The second dam, Rainbow Lake (by Rainbow Quest), a smart winner of 3 races including the Group 3 12f Lancashire Oaks and the listed 10f Ballymacoll Stud Stakes, is a half-sister to several winners including the useful middle-distance winner Vertex. (Khalid Abdulla). *"A nice filly and a very good mover, she'll make a 2-y-o and I like her".*

208. LAKE ALFRED (USA) ★★★

gr.c. Mizzen Mast – Brief Look (Sadler's Wells). February 5. First foal. The dam, a quite useful dual 12f winner, is half-sister to one winner. The second dam, Half Glance (by Danehill), won 3 races including the 2-y-o Group 3 1m May Hill Stakes and is a half-sister to the Irish Derby, St Leger and Turf Classic placed Tycoon. (Khalid Abdulla). *"A well-developed colt, he moves nicely but won't make an early 2-y-o".*

209. METEOROID (USA) ★★★★

b.br.c. Dynaformer – Enthused (Seeking The Gold). March 23. Eighth foal. Half-brother to the quite useful 2012 2-y-o 1m winner Flow (by Medaglia D'Oro), to the very useful 2-y-o Group 3 6f Round Tower Stakes winner and Group 2 6f Criterium de Maisons-Laffitte second Norman Invasion (by War Chant), the useful 1m winner and subsequent US Grade 3 turf 8.5f second Ea (by Dynaformer) and the quite useful 2-y-o dual 6f winner Erytheis (by Theatrical). The dam won the Group 2 6f Lowther Stakes and the Group 3 6f Princess Margaret Stakes and is a half-sister to the listed 12f Prix Vulcain winner From Beyond. The second dam, Magic Of Life (by Seattle Slew), won the Group 1 1m Coronation Stakes and the Group 2 Mill Reef Stakes and is a half-sister to 4 winners. (Niarchos Family). *"This colt is a nice individual and a good mover".*

210. MORNING WATCH (IRE) ★★★
b.c. Azamour – Lady Of Kildare (Mujadil).
March 26. Seventh foal. 62,000Y. Tattersalls
October Book 2. Sackville/Donald. Brother to
the quite useful dual 1m winner Katherine Lee
and half-brother to the quite useful Irish 2-y-o
6f winner El Soprano (by Noverre). The dam,
a fairly useful 2-y-o listed 6f winner, is a half-
sister to one winner. The second dam, Dancing
Sunset (by Red Sunset), a smart winner of the
Group 3 10f Royal Whip Stakes, is a full or
half-sister to 5 winners including the US stakes
winner Truly. (Lord De La Warr). *"A likeable filly
that moves well".*

211. NICTATE (IRE) ★★★
br.f. Teofilo – Woodmaven (Woodman). March
31. Seventh foal. 240,000Y. Tattersalls October
Book 1. Course Investment Co. Half-sister
to the fairly useful dual 7f winner (here and
in the USA) Sylvestris (by Arch), to the fairly
useful 2-y-o 5f winner and dual listed-placed
Roof Fiddle (by Cat Thief) and the fair 2-y-o
6f winner Trumpet Voluntary (by Red Clubs).
The dam, placed once at 3 yrs in the USA, is
a half-sister to 2 winners including the dual
Group 3 winner and 1,000 Guineas second
Arch Swing. The second dam, Gold Pattern (by
Slew O'Gold), a minor US winner of 4 races, is
a half-sister to 7 winners. (Niarchos Family). *"A
filly that's grown a lot and will take time".*

212. PERIL ★★★
ch.c. Pivotal – Portodora (Kingmambo). April
22. Second foal. The dam, a quite useful dual
7f winner, is a half-sister to one winner. The
second dam, High Walden (by El Gran Senor),
a smart 2-y-o 1m winner, was Group-placed
and is closely related to the Oaks, Fillies Mile,
Musidora Stakes and May Hill Stakes winner
Reams of Verse and a half-sister to the Group
1 10f Coral Eclipse Stakes and Group 1 10f
Phoenix Champion Stakes winner Elmaamul
(by Diesis). (Khalid Abdulla). *"A nice colt, but
he's quite a big 2-y-o and will take time".*

213. POSSET ★★★
b.f. Oasis Dream – Midsummer (Kingmambo).
April 27. Sixth foal. Sister to the high-class
racemare Midday, winner of six Group 1 races
(Breeders Cup Filly & Mare Turf, Prix Vermeille,
Yorkshire Oaks and Nassau Stakes (three

times) and to the fair 10f winner Popular and
half-sister to the 2012 2-y-o 1m and 2013
Group 3 7f Nell Gwyn Stakes winner Hot Snap
(by Pivotal) and the useful 10f and 12f winner
Midsummer Sun (by Monsun). The dam, a
quite useful 11f winner and listed-placed
over 12f, is a half-sister to numerous winners
including the Oaks and Fillies Mile winner
Reams of Verse and the Eclipse Stakes and
Phoenix Champion Stakes winner Elmaamul.
The second dam, Modena (by Roberto), is
an unraced half-sister to the smart 2-y-o 7f
winner and Queen Elizabeth II Stakes third
Zaizafon - herself the dam of Zafonic. (Khalid
Abdulla). *"This filly's half-sister Hot Snap has
recently won the Nell Gwyn Stakes, carrying
on the family tradition of winning good class
races. She's not over-big so she should make a
2-y-o and she moves nicely".*

214. PROPHET'S THUMB (IRE) ★★★
b.c. Fastnet Rock – Holly Blue (Bluebird).
April 6. Ninth foal. €70,000Y. Goffs Orby. BBA
(Ire). Closely related to the Irish 2-y-o and
subsequent South African triple Group 2
winner Gibraltar Blue, to the quite useful 10f
and 11f winner Pilgrims Rest (both by Rock Of
Gibraltar) and the fairly useful 2012 Irish 2-y-o
5f winner Scream Blue Murder (by Oratorio)
and half-brother to 3 minor winners including
one over jumps by Dr Fong. The dam, a
useful listed 1m winner, is a half-sister to 6
minor winners. The second dam, Nettle (by
Kris), a useful listed 7f winner, is a half-sister
to 5 winners. (P Hickman). *"I think the sire
breeds them big and this 2-y-o certainly fits
that description, but he's a nice mover and a
likeable colt".*

215. PUSHKAR ★★★★
*b.f. Danehill Dancer – Mail The Desert (Desert
Prince).* April 25. Seventh foal. 140,000Y.
Tattersalls October Book 1. C de Moubray.
Half-sister to the 2-y-o winner in Russia, Mail
Princess, to the fair 1m winner Al Muthanaa
(both by Pivotal) and the modest 1m winner
of 5 races Postman (by Dr Fong). The dam,
winner of the Group 1 7f Moyglare Stud
Stakes and third in the Coronation Stakes, is a
half-sister to 2 winners. The second dam, Mail
Boat (by Formidable), is an unraced half-sister
to 4 winners including the Group 3 Chester

Vase winner and St Leger third Dry Dock. (Lady Bamford). *"A very nice filly, she's a good mover and has plenty of scope but I think she will make a 2-y-o".*

216. RINGS OF SATURN (IRE) ★★★★

b.c. Galileo – Hveger (Danehill). January 31. Third foal. 450,000Y. Tattersalls October Book 1. Stephen Hillen. Half-brother to the Australian 3-y-o winner and dual Group 1 second Valdemoro (by Encosta De Lago). The dam won once in Australia and was Group 1 placed and is a sister to the multiple Group 1 winner Elvstroem and a half-sister to the Group 1 Queen Anne Stakes and dual Australian Group 1 winner Hardasun. The second dam, Circles Of Gold (by Marscay), won the Group 1 AJC Oaks in Australia and is a half-sister to 5 winners including the Australian Group 2 winner Gold Wells. (P Hickman). *"He's big and will take time, but he was an early foal and he's a very nice colt".*

217. RIVER GLASS (IRE) ★★★

gr.c. Verglas – Spartan Girl (Ela-Mana-Mou). March 28. Eighth foal. £24,000Y. Doncaster Premier. Angie Loder. Half-brother to the quite useful 10f winner of 3 races Northside Prince and to a bumpers winner (both by Desert Prince). The dam won over 10f at 3 yrs from three starts and is a half-sister to 5 winners including the Breeders Cup Turf, King George VI and St Leger winner Conduit. The second dam, Well Head (by Sadler's Wells), is an unraced half-sister to 6 winners including the dual Group 1 winner Spectrum and the dam of the champion filly Petrushka. (W H Ponsonby). *"A good mover, he's a strong, well-made colt but he's a very big colt and his pedigree suggests he won't be early".*

218. ROBOTIC ★★★

*b.c. Oasis Dream – Bionic (Zafonic).*February 9. Half-brother to Demonic (by Dansili), placed fourth over 1m from one start at 2 yrs in 2012, to the Group 3 9f Earl Of Sefton Stakes winner Phoenix Tower (by Chester House), the quite useful 2-y-o 7f winner Winter Bloom (by Aptitude) and the quite useful 2-y-o 5f winner Krynica (by Danzig). The dam, a very useful 2-y-o 7f winner, is a half-sister to the Group 3 7f Prestige Stakes winner Sense Of

Joy (by Dansili) and the multiple Group 3 middle-distance winner and French Derby fourth Day Flight. The second dam, Bonash (by Rainbow Quest), a very useful filly, won 4 races in France from 1m to 12f including the Prix d'Aumale, the Prix Vanteaux and the Prix de Malleret and is a full or half-sister to 4 winners. (Khalid Abdulla). *"A nice colt and a good mover".*

219. SATELLITE (IRE) ★★★★

b.c. Danehill Dancer – Perihelion (Galileo). April 25. Second foal. €115,000Y. Goffs Orby. John Warren. The dam, a useful Irish 14.7f winner and second in the Group 2 Park Hill Stakes, is a half-sister to 5 winners. The second dam, Medicosma (by The Minstrel), a quite useful 12f and 2m winner, is a half-sister to 5 winners including the Park Hill Stakes winner Eva Luna (herself dam of the dual Group 1 winner Brian Boru) and the dam of the US Grade 1 winner Flute. (Highclere Thoroughbred Racing – Distinction). *"A very nice colt, he's active and should make a 2-y-o".*

220. SUNRISE STAR ★★★

b.f. Shamardal – Tudor Court (Cape Cross). March 30. Second foal. 57,000Y. Tattersalls October Book 2. C de Moubray. The dam won two races at 3 yrs in France and was listed-placed twice in Germany and is a half-sister to 7 winners including the Group 1 7f Lockinge Stakes winner Fly To The Stars and the listed winner Fallen Star (dam of the Group 1 Coronation Stakes winner Fallen For You). The second dam, Rise And Fall (by Mill Reef), is an unplaced full or half-sister to 7 winners including the listed winners Special Leave, Spring To Action and Laughter. (Lady Bamford). *"A nice filly that should make a 2-y-o".*

221. TOUCH THE SKY ★★★ ♠

br.c. Sea The Stars – Love Divine (Diesis). April 1. Ninth foal. 200,000Y. Tattersalls October Book 1. Not sold. Closely related to the useful 10f winner and Group 2 12f Jockey Club Stakes second Native Ruler and half-brother to the Group 1 St Leger, Group 2 Jockey Club Cup and Group 3 Gordon Stakes winner Sixties Icon (by Galileo) and the fair 9.5f winner Kissing (by Grand Lodge). The dam, winner of the Group 1 12f Oaks and the listed Lupe

Stakes, is a half-sister to 6 winners including the listed 12f winner Floreeda and the listed 1m winner Dark Promise. The second dam, La Sky (by Law Society), a useful 10f winner and second in the Lancashire Oaks, is closely related to the Champion Stakes winner Legal Case and a half-sister to 4 winners. (Lordship Stud). *"A strong, tough colt that moves nicely. He's obviously not bred to be early and is more of a 3-y-o type".*

222. VENEZIA (IRE) ★★★★

gr.c. *Galileo – St Roch (Danehill).* April 20. Fourth foal. €235,000Y. Goffs Orby. BBA (Ire). Brother to the quite useful Irish 2-y-o 1m winner Last Crusade. The dam is an unraced sister to the Irish listed winner, Irish 1,000 Guineas third and subsequent US Grade 1 winner Luas Line and a half-sister to 4 winners including the Group 2 Lonsdale Cup third Lost In The Moment. The second dam, Streetcar (by In The Wings), is a placed half-sister to 9 winners including Intimate Guest (Group 3 May Hill Stakes). (P Hickman). *"A sensible colt, a nice mover and likeable, he's well furnished but needs time".*

223. UNNAMED ★★★★

b.f. *Invincible Spirit – Entre Nous (Sadler's Wells).* April 3. Second foal. 150,000Y. Tattersalls October Book 1. Rob Speers. The dam is an unplaced sister to the useful listed 12f winner Scriptwriter and a half-sister to 7 winners including the smart Group 2 Grand Prix de Deauville winner Courteous. The second dam, Dayanata (by Shirley Heights), is an unraced sister to the French Derby winner and high-class sire Darshaan and a half-sister to 11 winners including the Prix Vermeille winner Darara (herself dam of four Group 1 winners) and the Prix de Royallieu winner Dalara (dam of the Group 1 Coronation Cup winner Daliapour). (Mr V I Araci). *"This is a nice filly. The family breeds 3-y-o types but she has plenty of potential and scope. Should make a 2-y-o later on".*

224. UNNAMED ★★

b.f. *Galileo – Jessica's Dream (Desert Style).* April 22. Eighth foal. 400,000Y. Tattersalls October Book 1. Rob Speers. Closely related to a minor winner in Germany by Montjeu

and half-brother to the useful 2012 2-y-o Group 3 7f Somerville Tattersall Stakes winner Havana Gold (by Teofilo), to the fair 5f winner of 8 races (including at 2 yrs) Rocker (by Rock Of Gibraltar) and a winner in Hong Kong by Royal Applause. The dam, a very smart sprinter, won the Group 3 Ballyogan Stakes and the Group 3 Premio Omenoni and is a half-sister to the listed winner and dual Group 1 placed Majors Cast. The second dam, Ziffany (by Taufan), a 2-y-o 7f seller winner, is a half-sister to one winner abroad. (Mr V I Araci). *"A well-bred colt but he's going to take time".*

225. UNNAMED ★★

b.c. *Invincible Spirit – Red Feather (Marju).* February 19. Fourth foal. €250,000Y. Goffs Orby. John Warren. Half-brother to the 2012 2-y-o 6f winner and Group 3 7f Silver Flash Stakes third Roseraie (by Lawman) and to the very useful listed 6f and listed 7f winner and dual Group 3 placed Rose Bonheur (by Danehill Dancer). The dam, a Group 3 1m winner in Ireland, was second in the Group 1 Moyglare Stud Stakes and is a half-sister to the smart dual 10f winner and dual Group 3 12f placed Frankies Dream. The second dam, Galyph (by Lyphard), a modest Irish 10f winner at 4 yrs, is a half-sister to 2 minor winners. (Highclere Thoroughbred Racing – Harbinger). *"A nice colt, but slightly immature in his hocks and he's back at the stud to give him time".*

MICK CHANNON

226. AMAHORO ★★★

b.f. *Sixties Icon – Evanesce (Lujan).* April 25. Fifth foal. Sister to the fair 2012 2-y-o dual 7f winner Yorkshire Icon and half-sister to the modest 2-y-o dual 5f seller winner Selinda (by Piccolo) and the fair 6f winner (including at 2 yrs) to 2m and jumps winner Alfraamsay (by Fraam). The dam, a fair 2-y-o 6f winner, is a half-sister to one winner. The second dam, Search Party (Rainbow Quest), a fair 8.3f and 10f placed maiden, is a half-sister to the 6f (at 2 yrs) and subsequent Grade 1 10f Santa Barbara Handicap winner Bequest and to the useful 2-y-o 7f winner Fitzcarraldo. (Gill & Dave Hedley). *"A very nice filly for the second half of the season. She had a little setback so she needs to catch up but she's going the right way and she'll be one of our nicer fillies I think".*

227. AMBIANCE ★★★★

b.c. Camacho – Thawrah (Green Desert). February 19. Third living foal. £70,000Y. Doncaster Premier. Gill Richardson. Half-brother to the quite useful 6f (at 2 yrs) and 5f winner Heeraat (by Dark Angel) and to the minor German winner at 4 and 5 yrs Dance Every Dance (by Chineur). The dam is an unraced half-sister to 6 winners including the Group 1 Golden Jubilee Stakes winner Malhub. The second dam, Arjuzah (by Ahonoora), a useful winner of the listed 7f Sceptre Stakes, was third in the Group 2 7f Challenge Stakes and is a half-sister to 2 winners including the Irish listed winner Ormsby. (Prince A A Faisal). *"A lovely colt, he's an early sort and I'm hoping he'll be the type for Royal Ascot. He looked a 2-y-o type at the sales and he's exactly that. Whether it was five or six furlongs, it wouldn't matter to him and he's in the top group of our 2-y-o's".*

228. ARANTES ★★

b.c. Sixties Icon – Black Opal (Machiavellian). March 21. Fourth foal. The dam, placed four times in France at 2 and 3 yrs, is a daughter of the French listed winner Gold Field (by Unfuwain), herself a half-sister to 4 winners. *"Named after Pele – there were no bigger Sixties Icon's than him! He's a nice horse but he's big and he needs plenty of time".*

229. BRIDIE FFRENCH ★★

b.f. Bahamian Bounty – Wansdyke Lass (Josr Algharoud). April 8. £2,000Y. Ascot December. Not sold. Half-sister to the quite useful 2012 2-y-o dual 6f winner and listed-placed Cruck Realta (by Sixties Icon) and to the fair 7f (at 2 yrs) and dual 6f winner Universal Circus (by Imperial Dancer). The dam, a modest 10f seller winner, is a half-sister to 2 minor winners. The second dam, Silannka (by Slip Anchor), a moderate 12f and 13f winner, is a half-sister to numerous winners. (Steve and Ann Fisher). *"She's quite nice, but she's a biggish filly and one for the middle of the season onwards".*

230. CALETTA BAY ★★★★

b.f. Rock Of Gibraltar – Cartimandua (Medicean). March 11. Second foal. 52,000Y. Tattersalls October Book 1. Gill Richardson. The dam, a dual listed 6f winner and third in the Group 3 Ballyogan Stakes, is a half-sister to 3 winners including the useful 5f winner of 5 races (including at 2 yrs) Terentia. The second dam, Agrippina (by Timeless Times), a useful 2-y-o listed 7f winner, is a half-sister to 2 winners. (Miss Emily Asprey & Chris Wright). *"A very nice filly indeed, she does everything like a professional and we'll get her out in May to see if she's good enough to go for one of the nicer races. She's a good sized filly with a good attitude and I think a fair bit of her".*

231. CHARACTERISE ★★★

ch.c. Winker Watson – Artistic License (Chevalier). January 4. First foal. The dam, a quite useful 5f (at 2 yrs) and 6f winner of 6 races, is a half-sister to the fair 5f (including at 2 yrs) and 6f winner of 12 races Brandywell Boy and the modest 2-y-o 5f winner Ruby Alexander. The second dam, Alexander Eliott (by Night Shift), an Irish maiden, was placed at up to 10f and is a half-sister to one winner. (Wood Street Syndicate). *"A nice horse, he's only just getting going but he seems to be coming quite quickly now. He'll be racing in May and he's a nice, big strong colt".*

232. CHESTURO (IRE) ★★★

ch.f. Manduro – Joyfullness (Dixieland Band). April 28. Eighth foal. 20,000Y. Tattersalls October Book 2. Gill Richardson. Half-sister to the Italian 2-y-o winner and listed-placed Flying Teapot (by King Charlemagne), to the quite useful Irish 1m winner Song In My Heart (by Spartacus), the fair 7f winner of 3 races Khajaaly (by Kheleyf), the fair 2-y-o 1m winner Sir Trevor (by Refuse To Bend) and the modest 6f and 7f winner Contented (by Orpen). The dam is an unraced half-sister to 11 winners including the dam of the Group 2 Royal Lodge Stakes winner Mons. The second dam, Arewehavingfunyet (by Sham), won the Grade 1 Oak Leaf Stakes and is a half-sister to 6 winners. (Jaber Abdullah). *"She was a very nice yearling and I remember when we bought her she looked a 2-y-o then. I thought she might be our next Flashy Wings. She goes very well, I'm not saying she is a Flashy Wings, I'm just saying that despite being a Manduro she will be a 2-y-o. She's quite forward so we'll have a look at her in May and see what happens".*
TRAINERS' BARGAIN BUY

233. CHINA IN MY HANDS ★★

gr.f. Dark Angel – Cheap Thrills (Bertolini). February 6. The dam, a fair 6f and 7f winner, is a half-sister to numerous winners including the useful 2-y-o dual 5f winner and Group 2 5f King George Stakes second Group Therapy, the smart 2-y-o dual Group 3 5f winner Bungle Inthejungle and the fairly useful listed 6f winner of 4 races Waveband. The second dam, Licence To Thrill (by Wolfhound), a quite useful dual 5f winner, is a half-sister to 4 winners including the useful 2-y-o 5f winner Master Of Passion. (Chris Wright). *"She came in late and she's quite backward so I can't tell you a lot more about her at the moment".*

234. CRAZEE DIAMOND ★★★★

b.f. Rock Of Gibraltar – Final Dynasty (Komaite). March 6. First foal. £44,000Y. Doncaster Premier. Gill Richardson. The dam, a useful 5f winner at 2 and 3 yrs, was listed-placed twice and is a sister to the 2-y-o Group 3 5f Cornwallis Stakes winner Castelletto and a half-sister to 8 winners including the useful 6f winner (including at 2 yrs) Lake Garda. The second dam, Malcesine (by Auction Ring), a 1m seller winner at 4 yrs, is a half-sister to 5 winners including the Wokingham Handicap winner Red Rosein. (Nick and Olga Dhandsa & John and Zoe Webster). *"This is a very nice filly and she's just starting to go the right way. She was going to be early but she threw a splint and I had to give her some time, but that could have been a blessing. She's going very nicely now and I think she'll be alright. She's a definite 2-y-o and we'll find out in May if she's good enough to go to one of the better meetings".*

235. DANGEROUS FLOWER (USA) ★★★

b.f. Grand Slam – Miss Sea Oats (Langfuhr). February 7. First foal. $85,000Y. Keeneland September. David Redvers. The dam, placed at 3 yrs, is a half-sister to 6 winners including the US Grade 1 winners Shackleford and Lady Joanne and the US triple Grade 3 winner Baghdaria. The second dam, Oatsee (by Unbridled), was a stakes-placed dual winner at 3 yrs in the USA. (Qatar Racing Ltd). *"A lovely filly, she's very good-looking, a good mover and I like her a lot. She's big and still growing, so I can't say much more about her because we haven't been able to get on with her yet".*

236. DEEDS NOT WORDS (IRE) ★★★★

b.c. Royal Applause – Wars (Green Desert). February 3. Sixth foal. 60,000Y. Tattersalls October Book 2. Gill Richardson. Half-brother to the quite useful 6f (at 2 yrs) and 1m winner Heroes, to the Irish 2-y-o 7f winner Redrightreturning (both by Diktat) and the fair 7f winner Usk Poppy (by Mark Of Esteem). The dam is an unplaced sister to the very smart 7f and 1m performer Gabr and a half-sister to 4 winners including the smart middle-distance horse Kutta. The second dam, Ardassine (by Ahonoora), a 12f winner in Ireland, was fourth in the Group 3 Irish 1,000 Guineas Trial and is a half-sister to 7 winners. (George Materna). *"A very nice, very sharp 2-y-o. He was bought for the job and hopefully he'll go out there and do it. He's a sprinting type and I think he's up there in the top bracket of our two-year-olds".*

237. DIFFIDENT ★★★

ch.f. New Approach – Shy Appeal (Barathea). January 17. First foal. 10,000foal. Tattersalls December. Not sold. The dam was a modest 7f placed 2-y-o in Ireland. The second dam, Special Cause (by Fasliyev), won once over 7f at 3 yrs in France and is a half-sister to 6 winners including the dam of Zafeen (Group 1 St James's Palace Stakes). *"A sharp filly that goes well, she's up there with our better fillies I think".*

238. FINFLASH ★★★

b.br.c. Jeremy – Sinegronto (Kheleyf). March 19. First foal. 20,000Y. Tattersalls October Book 2. Gill Richardson. The dam is an unraced half-sister to 4 winners including the 2-y-o Group 3 Cornwallis Stakes winner and Group 2 Diadem Stakes third Show Me The Money. The second dam, Snappy Dresser (by Nishapour), a listed-placed winner of one race at 2 yrs in Ireland, is a half-sister to 5 minor winners. (Insignia). *"A very nice colt, he's got a big backside on him and he's built to be an early 2-y-o, but he had a small setback and missed a couple of pieces of work. Nevertheless I think he's quite sharp, we'll see in the next two or three weeks but I think he'll be OK".*

239. GOOD MORNING LADY ★★★

b.f. Compton Place – Baldemosa (Lead On Time). February 28. Eleventh foal. 10,000Y.

Tattersalls October Book 2. Gill Richardson. Half-sister to the very useful 7f winner of 4 races here and in the UAE Sirocco Breeze (by Green Desert), to the fairly useful 5f and 6f winner of 4 races Show Flower (by Shamardal), the 5f and 6f winner of 15 races (including when useful at 2 yrs) Caustic Wit (by Cadeaux Genereux), the modest 8.5f winner Seldemosa (by Selkirk) and a winner in Greece by Diktat. The dam won over 1m in France at 3 yrs and is a half-sister to 4 winners including the Group 1 5.5f Prix Robert Papin winner Balbonella (herself dam of the top-class sprinter and sire Anabaa, the French 1,000 Guineas winner Always Loyal and the sire Key Of Luck) and the French listed 12f winner Bamwhite. The second dam, Bamieres (by Riverman), was placed fourth twice in France. (Jaber Abdullah). *"She's a very nice filly and she just needs some sun on her back, like a lot of the fillies. She's not quite ready to go yet, so I'll let her tell me when".*

240. HEARTSTRINGS ★★★
b.br.f. Invincible Spirit – Strings (Unfuwain). April 8. Sixth foal. 70,000Y. Tattersalls October Book 2. Gill Richardson. Half-brother to the fairly useful 2-y-o 1m winner State Opera (by Shamardal), to the quite useful dual 7f (at 2 yrs) and dual 10f winner Bahamian Flight (by Bahamian Bounty) and a winner abroad by Exceed And Excel. The dam is an unraced half-sister to 6 winners including the French 2,000 Guineas winner Victory Note. The second dam, Three Piece (by Jaazeiro), an Irish placed 2-y-o, is a half-sister to 8 winners including Orchestration (Group 2 Coronation Stakes) and Welsh Term (Group 2 Prix d'Harcourt). (Mrs Ann Black). *"Very nice, she goes really well and just needs to get rid of her winter coat before I do any more with her. I think she could be sharp".*

241. HEDY ★★★
ch.f. Winker Watson – Jollyhockeysticks (Fantastic Light). April 10. Second foal. Half-sister to the modest 2012 7f and 1m placed 2-y-o Barefoot Sandy (by Sixties Icon). The dam, placed over 1m from four runs as a 2-y-o and a modest 3-y-o 1m winner, was also disqualified from first place in another

1m event. She is a half-sister to 5 winners including Pic Up Sticks (a fairly useful listed-placed winner of 9 races at up to 7f). The second dam, Between The Sticks (by Pharly), a listed-placed dual 5f winner at 2 yrs, is a half-sister to 4 winners. (Living Legend Racing Partnership 1). *"When she comes in her coat there'll be a massive improvement in her. An easy filly in everything she does, she's got a big backside on her now, she's definitely alright and five or six furlongs won't be a problem to her".*

242. HESKA ★★
b.c. Rock Of Gibraltar – Sweet Sioux (Halling). April 15. Third foal. 38,000Y. Tattersalls October Book 2. Gill Richardson. Half-brother to Standing Bear (by Excellent Art), placed fourth once over 6f from four starts at 2 yrs in 2012. The dam is an unplaced half-sister to 5 winners and to the dam of the Group 3 Sirenia Stakes winner Satchem. The second dam, Mohican Girl (by Dancing Brave), a dual listed 10f winner and third in the Group 2 Nassau Stakes, is a half-sister to 6 winners including the good fillies Untold, Sally Brown (both winners of the Yorkshire Oaks) and Shoot Clear (Waterford Candelabra Stakes winner). (Box 41). *"A lovely, big horse but he's backward and hasn't come in his coat. I can't tell you much more about him because I haven't been able to get after him yet".*

243. HOME STRETCH ★★★
b.c. Holy Roman Emperor – Sharp Mode (Diesis). March 17. Fifth foal. Half-brother to the quite useful 2012 2-y-o 7f winner Amralah (by Teofilo) and to the modest 2-y-o 5f winner Midget (by Invincible Spirit). The dam is an unraced half-sister to 2 minor winners. The second dam, A La Mode (by Known Fact), placed at 2 yrs and subsequently a minor winner at 5 yrs in the USA, is a sister to the US Grade 3 winner Modernise and a half-sister to 9 winners including the Group 1 winners Elmaamul and Reams Of Verse and the Group winners Manifest, Modernise and Modern Day. (Prince A A Faisal). *"A nice home-bred of Prince Faisal's, he goes well and he's definitely a 2-y-o. He should be racing in May, I think he could be very nice but it's too early to say really".*

244. HOY HOY (IRE) ★★★

b.c. Iffraaj – Luxie (Acclamation). April
2. First foal. €130,000Y. Goffs Orby. Gill
Richardson. The dam, a fair Irish 7f and 1m
winner, is a half-sister to 4 winners including
the dual listed 6f winner and Group 3
placed Mister Manannan and the 2-y-o 5f
and 5.7f winner and dual Group 3 placed
Shermeen. The second dam, Cover Girl (by
Common Grounds), a fair 2-y-o 6f and 7f and
subsequent Scandinavian listed winner, is a
half-sister to 3 winners. (Sheikh Mohammed
Bin Khalifa Al Maktoum). *"A very nice colt, he
just threw a splint which has held us up and
he's growing now as well, so we might not see
him until mid-summer. But I'm very pleased
with him and he's a very good-looking horse".*

245. ISABELLA BIRD ★★★

*b.f. Invincible Spirit – Meetyouthere (Sadler's
Wells).* February 12. Second foal. 75,000foal.
Tattersalls December. Gill Richardson. The
dam, a minor 12f winner in France, is a sister
to the very useful dual 12f winner and Group
2 placed Rostropovich and to the Group 2
Prix de Royallieu winner Moon Queen, closely
related to the useful Group 3 1m Premio
Dormello winner Barafamy and a half-sister to
the US Grade 2 and Grade 3 winner Innuendo.
The second dam, Infamy (by Shirley Heights),
a very smart 10f to 12f filly, won the Grade
1 Rothmans International, the Group 2 Sun
Chariot Stakes and the Group 3 Gordon
Richards Stakes and is a half-sister to 3
winners. (Jon & Julia Aisbitt). *"She's a very nice
filly, but more of a six/seven furlong type and
quite a big filly that needs a bit of time".*

246. JALLOTA ★★★

b.c. Rock Of Gibraltar – Lady Lahar (Fraam).
March 15. Seventh foal. 100,000Y. Tattersalls
October Book 1. Gill Richardson. Half-brother
to the fairly useful listed 1m (at 2 yrs) and 10f
winner Classic Legend, to the useful 12f and
14f winner I Have A Dream (both by Galileo),
the fairly useful 10f winner and listed-placed
Popmurphy (by Montjeu), the fairly useful 7f
(at 2 yrs), 1m and hurdles winner of 7 races
Kilburn (by Grand Lodge) and the quite useful
7f (at 2 yrs) to 9f winner of 6 races Syrian (by
Hawk Wing). The dam, a useful 2-y-o Group
3 7f Futurity Stakes and 3-y-o 8.3f winner,

was third in the Group 2 Cherry Hinton Stakes
and the Group 2 Falmouth Stakes and is a
half-sister to 4 winners. The second dam,
Brigadier's Bird (by Mujadil), is an unraced
half-sister to 3 winners. (Nick and Olga
Dhandsa & John and Zoe Webster). *"A lovely
big horse, but he's more of a seven furlong/
mile 2-y-o for the second half of the season.
He goes well and does everything nicely, but he
won't be early".*

247. JAYWALKER (IRE) ★★

b.c. Footstepsinthesand – Nipping (Night Shift).
March 14. Fifth foal. 16,000Y. Tattersalls
October Book 2. Gill Richardson. Half-brother
to the minor French 3-y-o winner Constant
Lover (by King's Best). The dam, a winner
of 3 races including the Group 3 5f Prix du
Petit Couvert, is a half-sister to 6 winners
including the Group 2 5.5f Prix Robert Papin
winner Zipping and the Group 3 5f Prix du
Bois winner Zelding (herself the dam of two
stakes winners). The second dam, Zelda (by
Caerleon), won once over 6.5f in France at
3 yrs and is a half-sister to the Breeders Cup
Mile and William Hill Sprint Championship
winner Last Tycoon, the Group winners
Astronef and The Perfect Life and the dams of
the Group 1 winners Immortal Verse, Tie Black
and Valentine Waltz. (Insignia). *"Quite a nice
horse, he's got a touch of sore shins so that's
holding us up. I haven't rushed him and he's
one for a bit later on".*

248. KANZ ★★★★

ch.f. Kyllachy – Frambroise (Diesis). February 24.
Fourth foal. 13,000Y. Tattersalls October Book
2. Hugo Merry. Half-sister to the modest 7f
winner Yarra River (by Aussie Rules). The dam,
a minor French 3-y-o winner, subsequently
won the USA and is a half-sister to 6 winners
including the fairly useful listed 1m Masaka
Stakes winner Jazz Jam. The second dam,
Applaud (by Rahy), a smart 2-y-o winner of
the Group 2 6f Cherry Hinton Stakes, is a full
or half-sister to 6 winners including the listed
winner Sauterne. *"Quite a nice filly, she goes
nicely and she's a 2-y-o alright".*

249. KAIULANI ★★★★

*b.f. Danehill Dancer – Royal Shyness (Royal
Academy).* April 27. Eighth foal. €100,000Y.

Goffs Orby. Gill Richardson. Half-sister to the useful 2012 2-y-o 5f winner Jillnextdoor (by Henrythenavigator), to the useful 7f and 1m winner and listed-placed Commander Cave (by Tale Of The Cat), the quite useful dual 1m winner Van Rooney (by Van Nistelrooy) and the fair 7f to 10f winner of 6 races Shy Glance (by Red Ransom). The dam, a useful 2-y-o 6f winner, was third in the Group 1 6f Cheveley Park Stakes and subsequently won a listed stakes race in the USA and is a half-sister to 8 winners. The second dam, Miss Demure (by Shy Groom), won the Group 2 6f Lowther Stakes. *"A very nice filly, she shows us plenty and she's in the top bracket of our 2-y-o's. I think she could be very nice, so you'll have to put her in the book".*

250. KEEP CLOSE ★★

b.f. *Cape Cross – Kelucia (Grand Lodge)*. March 21. Fourth foal. 35,000Y. Tattersalls October Book 2. Gill Richardson. Half-sister to the moderate 2012 2-y-o 9f winner Corton Lad (by Refuse To Bend) and to the modest dual 6f winner Monel (by Cadeaux Genereux). The dam, a useful 2-y-o dual 1m winner and third in the Group 2 7f Rockfel Stakes, is a half-sister to 3 winners. The second dam, Karachi (by Zino), a listed-placed winner of 6 races in Spain, is a half-sister to 7 other minor winners. (Jaber Abdullah). *"She's one for the second half of the season, she's sweet and hasn't grown much but she's fine".*

251. KICKBOXER (IRE) ★★★

gr.c. *Clodovil – Ajig Dancer (Niniski)*. April 7. Eighth foal. €26,000Y. Tattersalls Ireland November. Gill Richardson. Half-brother to the very useful 2-y-o 5f and German Group 2 6f winner Ajigolo (by Piccolo), to the fairly useful 2-y-o 5f winner and Group 2 Norfolk Stakes fourth Silver Guest (by Lujain) and the fairly useful 2-y-o dual 5f winner and listed-placed Indiannie Star (by Fraam). The dam, a quite useful 7f winner of 4 races, is a half-sister to 2 winners. The second dam, Gloire (by Thatching), is an unraced sister to the smart sprinter Puissance, winner of the Group 3 Greenlands Stakes. *"Quite a nice colt, he's had a little setback. It's nothing serious but he was going nicely and I thought he was alright. He'll come pretty quick when he's ready*

and although he's on the back burner for now I do like him".*

252. LAZZAZZ (IRE) ★★★

b.c. *Teofilo – Queen Of Lyons (Dubai Destination)*. February 12. First foal. €170,000Y. Goffs Orby. Gill Richardson. The dam ran twice unplaced and is a half-sister to 4 winners including Benbaun (Group 1 Prix de l'Abbaye). The second dam, Escape To Victory (by Salse), won twice at 2 yrs in Italy and is a half-sister to 6 winners including the US triple Grade 2 winner Hawksley Hill. (Sheikh Mohammed Bin Khalifa Al Maktoum). *"A nice, strong, good-looking horse, he probably needs seven furlongs already but he does everything right".*

253. LINCOLN (IRE) ★★★

b.c. *Clodovil – Gilt Linked (Compton Place)*. February 8. Third foal. 25,000Y. Tattersalls December. Gill Richardson. The dam, a quite useful 2-y-o 5f winner, is a half-sister to 5 winners including the Group 2 John Of Gaunt Stakes winner and dual Group 3 placed (including at 2 yrs) Pastoral Player. The second dam, Copy-Cat (by Lion Cavern), is an unplaced half-sister to 7 winners including the very useful Group 3 5f King George Stakes winner Averti. *"He does everything in a professional way, he's really nice and I like him a lot, but he's grown so he's having some time off. He's a big colt now but apart from that he's pretty straightforward".*

254. LUNARIAN (IRE) ★★★

ch.f. *Bahamian Bounty – One Giant Leap (Pivotal)*. March 14. Third foal. 40,000Y. Tattersalls October Book 2. R Frisby. Half-sister to the 2012 French placed 2-y-o Lookbeforeyouleap (by Teofilo) and to the quite useful 3-y-o dual 5f winner Morocco Moon (by Rock Of Gibraltar). The dam, a modest 7f winner, is a half-sister to 8 winners including the useful 2-y-o Group 3 7f C L Weld Park Stakes winner Rag Top and the dam of the 2-y-o listed winner Elhamri. The second dam, Petite Epaulette (by Night Shift), a fair 5f winner at 2 yrs, is a full or half-sister to 3 winners. (Mrs Ann Black). *"A big, tall filly for the second half of the season. She's nice but she needs some sun on her back".*

255. MAWZOONA ★★★★
b.f. Authorized – Umniya (Bluebird). February 16. Fifth foal. £48,000Y. Doncaster Premier. Gill Richardson. The dam, a quite useful 2-y-o 6f winner, was fourth in the Group 1 Moyglare Stud Stakes and third in the Group 3 Premio Dormello and is a half-sister to 5 winners including the dual listed 6f winner Lady Links (herself dam of the dual listed winner Selinka). The second dam, Sparky's Song (by Electric), a moderate 10.2f and 12f winner, is a half-sister to 3 winners including the very smart Group 1 6.5f winner Bold Edge and the listed winner and Group 2 5f Temple Stakes second Brave Edge. (Sheikh Mohammed Bin Khalifa Al Maktoum). "We trained the dam who was pretty good and this filly is very nice. She goes well and is probably a six furlong type for May. We'll see what happens to her in the next few weeks, but I think she could be quite good".

256. MEMORY STYX ★★★
b.f. Clodovil – Quickstyx (Night Shift). April 27. Sixth foal. £14,000Y. Doncaster Premier. Gill Richardson. Half-sister to Collingbourneducis, a modest fourth over 7f from 3 starts at 2 yrs in 2012, to the fairly useful 6f winner of 4 races (including at 2 yrs) Hairspray (both by Bahamian Bounty), the quite useful 6f (at 2 yrs) and 1m winner Watneya (by Dubawi), the modest 2-y-o 7.5f and subsequent Swedish winner Blusher (by Fraam) and a hurdles winner by Singspiel. The dam, a fair 1m winner, is a half-sister to 5 winners including the smart 12f listed winner and US dual Grade 1 placed Red Fort and the useful 12f listed winner Red Carnation. The second dam, Red Bouquet (by Reference Point), won 3 minor races from 12f to 13f at 4 yrs in Germany and is a half-sister to 4 winners including the Group 3 7f Prestige Stakes winner Red Camellia (herself dam of the Group 1 Fillies' Mile winner Red Bloom). "A smashing filly, she was second on her first start, she's not very big but does everything professionally. I love her, she's a sweet filly and he'll go five or six furlongs no problem".

257. NANCY FROM NAIROBI ★★★
b.f. Sixties Icon – Madame Hoi (Hawk Wing). March 4. First foal. The dam, a fair 6f winner, was placed over 1m at 2 yrs and is a half-sister to the fairly useful 2-y-o Group 1 6f Phoenix Stakes second Amadeus Mozart. The second dam, Lindesburg (by Doyoun), was placed 3 times over 6f including at 2 yrs and is a half-sister to 6 winners including the very smart triple Group 2 1m winner Gothenburg. (Norman Court Stud). "She's a lovely big filly and so was Nancy, from what I can gather from the owner! One for seven furlongs later in the year".

258. NARBOROUGH ★★★
b.c. Winker Watson – Solmorin (Fraam). April 25. Sixth foal. Half-brother to the modest 6f (at 2 yrs) and 5f winner Majestic Rose (by Imperial Dancer), to the fairly useful dual 5f winner (including at 2 yrs) Lucky Leigh, the modest 2-y-o 6f winner Saxonette (both by Piccolo) and the modest dual 1m winner (including at 2 yrs) Alfredtheordinary (by Hunting Lion). The dam is an unplaced half-sister to 2 winners. (Mrs Jane Maxted). "Quite a nice, strong colt, he's had a run and he should win as a 2-y-o".

259. RIVERBOAT SPRINGS (IRE) ★★★
b.c. Bushranger – Mashie (Selkirk). March 15. Third foal. 55,000Y. Tattersalls October Book 2. Gill Richardson. Half-brother to Four Iron (by Oasis Dream), a minor winner of 5 races in Australia at 4 and 5 yrs. The dam is an unraced half-sister to 11 winners including the US Grade 1 10f Yellow Ribbon Stakes winner Light Jig and the French listed winners Battle Dore and Lynton. The second dam, Nashmeel (by Blushing Groom), a very smart winner of three races over 1m including the Group 2 Prix d'Astarte and second in the Prix Jacques le Marois (to Miesque), the Yellow Ribbon Invitational and the Matriarch Stakes, is a half-sister to 9 winners. (C Wright & The Hon Mrs J M Corbett). "He seems quite sharp, we'll get on with him reasonably early and see what happens. He's OK and a sprinting type".

260. ROSE GLORIA (IRE) ★★★
ch.f. Haatef – Western Sky (Barathea). April 30. Fourth foal. 32,000Y. Tattersalls October Book 1. Gill Richardson. Half-sister to the German dual Group 3 1m winner (including at 2 yrs) and Group 1 11f German Oaks second Djumama (by Aussie Rules) and to a winner in Cyprus by Namid. The dam, placed fourth

once over 6f at 3 yrs from two starts, is a sister to the Group 3 Greenham Stakes winner and triple Group 1 placed Barathea Guest and a half-sister to 5 winners. The second dam, Western Heights (by Shirley Heights), is an unraced half-sister to 6 winners including the listed Galtres Stakes winner Startino. (Jaber Abdullah). *"She's a real character, looks to have some speed and wants to get on with it, but she needs some sunshine because she has a coat like a teddy bear. She's alright and she goes well".*

261. ROSSO CORSA ★★★★

b.c. *Footstepsinthesand – Lady Scarlett (Woodman).* March 24. Seventh foal. 80,000Y. Tattersalls October Book 2. Gill Richardson. Half-brother to the quite useful 2-y-o 1m winner Whistleinthewind (by Oratorio), to the quite useful 5f and 6f winner of 7 races and listed-placed Sunrise Safari (by Mozart), the quite useful 10f winner Val O'Hara (by Ad Valorem), the modest 5f and 7f winner Polemica (by Rock Of Gibraltar) and a winner over hurdles by High Chaparral. The dam is an unraced half-sister to 5 winners including the listed Sha Tin Trophy winner and Irish Derby third Desert Fox and the US Grade 3 winners Poolesta and Home Of The Free and to the unplaced dam of the US Grade 1 winner Grand Couturier. The second dam, Radiant (by Foolish Pleasure), won once at 3 yrs and is a half-sister to the triple Grade 1 winner Gold And Ivory and to the dams of the Group/ Graded stakes winners Heart Of Darkness, Anees, Elusive Quality and Rossini. (Box 41). *"A very nice colt, he'll win at five furlongs but he'll be better at six. He'll be one of our best colts I should think".*

262. ROUGH COURTE ★★★

b.f. *Clodovil – Straight Sets (Pivotal).* March 10. Second foal. 15,000Y. Tattersalls October Book 3. Gill Richardson. The dam, a fair 4-y-o 7f winner, is a half-sister to 4 winners including the very smart Group 3 10.3f Huxley Stakes and 2-y-o listed 7f winner Championship Point. The second dam, Flying Squaw (by Be My Chief), winner of the Group 2 6f Moet and Chandon Rennen at 2 yrs, is a half-sister to 7 winners. *"She isn't very big but she doesn't half go. One of our early fillies".*

263. SARTORI ★★★★

b.c. *Elnadim – Little Caroline (Great Commotion).* April 12. Fourth foal. 20,000Y. Tattersalls October Book 2. Gill Richardson. Half-brother to the unplaced 2012 2-y-o Baker's Pursuit (by Pastoral Pursuits) and to the fair 5f (including at 2 yrs) and 6f winner of 8 races Pick A Little (by Piccolo). The dam, a minor winner at 4 yrs in the USA, is a half-sister to 6 winners. The second dam, Pooka (by Dominion), is a placed half-sister to 9 winners. (Box 41). *"He goes well and he'll be in the top bracket for early in the season. A nice colt, he looks sharp and seems to know the business, a sprinting type 2-y-o".*

264. SCARGILL ★★★

br.c. *Sixties Icon – Rose Cheval (Johannesburg).* February 2. First foal. The dam, a fair 7f (at 2 yrs) to 9f placed maiden, is a half-sister to 2 winners in North America. The second dam, La Samanna (by Trempolino), won 2 minor races at 3 and 4 yrs in the USA and is a half-sister to 5 winners. (Bargate). *"He was disappointing on his second start but he's better than that. He'll win a race alright".*

265. SENORITA GUEST (IRE) ★★★

b.f. *Kheleyf – Atishoo (Revoque).* April 13. Fifth foal. €110,000Y. Goffs Orby. Gill Richardson. Half-sister to the fair 2012 2-y-o 5f winner Kodatish (by Kodiac), to the fairly useful 6f, 7f (both at 2 yrs) and 10f winner and listed-placed Sonoran Sands (by Footstepsinthesand) and the modest 6f winner Point At Issue (by One Cool Cat). The dam, a modest Irish 1m placed maiden, is a half-sister to 3 winners including the listed winner and Group 2 Pretty Polly Stakes second Snippets. The second dam, Sniffle (by Shernazar), is an unplaced half-sister to 5 winners including the Grade 1 12f Hollywood Turf Cup and Group 3 1m Beresford Stakes winner Frenchpark and the Group 1 Prix Vermeille winner Pearly Shells. (John Guest Racing). *"Very nice, she's just starting to do some nice work but she's hanging onto her coat so she looks backward, but she goes alright and she'll win".*

266. SHADOWS OFTHENIGHT ★★

b.f. *Fastnet Rock – Madaen (Nureyev).* May 11. Seventh foal. €70,000Y. Goffs Orby. Gill

Richardson. Half-sister to the 7f (at 2 yrs) to 2m winner and dual Group 3 placed Baan (by Diesis), to the fair 9f and subsequent minor US 4-y-o winner Magical Cat (by Giant's Causeway) and a minor winner abroad by Gulch. The dam is an unraced half-sister to 7 winners in the USA including the Grade 2 placed Simon Pure. The second dam, Life's Magic (by Cox's Ridge), won five Grade 1 events in the USA and is a half-sister to 3 winners. (C Wright & The Hon Mrs J M Corbett). *"She's a very nice filly but she was a late foal so she's one for later in the season".*

267. SHIMBA HILLS ★★★
b.c. Sixties Icon – Search Party (Rainbow Quest). May 8. Half-brother to the quite useful 2-y-o triple 6f winner Bateleur (by Fraam), to the fair 2-y-o 6f winner Evanesce (by Lujain) and the modest 10f, 14f and hurdles winner Foster's Road (by Imperial Dancer). The dam, a fair 8.3f and 10f placed maiden, is a half-sister to the 6f (at 2 yrs) and subsequent Grade 1 10f Santa Barbara Handicap winner Bequest and to the useful 2-y-o 7f winner Fitzcarraldo. The second dam, Quest (by The Minstrel), won 3 races from 9f to 10f at 3 yrs, was third in the Group 3 Queen Mary Stakes, is a sister to the Group 1 Grand Criterium winner Treizieme and a half-sister to the Group 2 Yorkshire Cup winner Eastern Mystic. (Dave & Gill Hedley). *"A very nice colt, he's going through a plain stage at the minute and growing. He was a late foal, but he goes well".*

268. SLEEPY JOE ★★★
b.c. Jeremy – Rocking (Oasis Dream). April 2. Second foal. Half-brother to the fairly useful 2012 2-y-o 5f winner and listed-placed Boston Rocker (by Acclamation). The dam, a quite useful 2-y-o 5f winner, is a half-sister to 10 winners including the very smart Group 2 5f Flying Childers Stakes and Weatherbys Super Sprint winner Superstar Leo (herself dam of the dual Group 3 winner Enticing). The second dam, Council Rock (by General Assembly), a fair 9f and 10f placed 3-y-o, is a half-sister to 9 winners including the Group 3 Prestige Stakes winner Glatisant (dam of the 2,000 Guineas winner Footstepsinthesand) and the listed Virginia Stakes winner Gai Bulga. *"Just like our*

other Jeremy colt, he's a 2-y-o type that goes well and he'll definitely win his race".

269. TANOJIN ★★★★
ch.f. Thousand Words – Indiannie Moon (Fraam). April 22. Third foal. €25,000Y. Tattersalls Ireland September. Gill Richardson. Half-sister to the 2012 1m placed 2-y-o, from two starts, Audacia (by Sixties Icon) and to a winner in the Czech Republic by Clodovil. The dam ran once unplaced and is a sister to the winner and listed-placed Indiannie Star and a half-sister to the German 2-y-o Group 2 6f winner Ajigolo and the listed-placed winner Silver Guest. The second dam, Ajig Dancer (by Niniski), a quite useful 7f winner of 4 races, is a half-sister to 2 winners. (Nick and Olga Dhandsa & John and Zoe Webster). *"A smashing filly, she's big and flashy – like Tonto's horse! She's lovely but she's on the back burner for now because she's such a big filly. But she's well-made and I think she'll be a real good filly in time. I like her a lot and she'd be my outside tip".*

270. THE SMART ONE (IRE) ★★★
b.c. Exceed And Excel – Bareilly (Lyphard). April 3. Half-brother to the useful 6f (at 2 yrs) and 8.3f winner and listed-placed La Mottie, to the minor Italian 9f winner King's Star (both by King's Best), the 2-y-o Group 2 6f Richmond Stakes winner Revenue, the quite useful 6f (at 2 yrs) and 5f winner Zahour Al Yasmeen and the 8.5f seller and hurdles winner General (all by Cadeaux Genereux). The dam is an unraced three-parts sister to the Group 3 1m Prix de la Grotte winner Baya and the Italian Group 2 winner Narrative. The second dam, Barger (by Riverman), won the Group 3 9f Prix Vanteaux and is a sister to the outstanding racemare Triptych out of the Group 1 Prix Ganay winner Trillion. (Jaber Abdullah). *"He's sharp, he goes well and he'll be running in April. He's not very big but he wants to get on with it".*

271. TINGA (IRE) ★★★★
ch.f. Galileo – Tingling (Storm Cat). February 8. Second foal. The dam, a quite useful 7f and 1m placed 2-y-o in Ireland, is a half-sister to 3 winners including the Canadian Grade 3 winner Rosberg. The second dam, Bosra

Sham (by Woodman), an outstanding filly and winner of three Group 1 events, is a sister to the multiple Group 1 winner Hector Protector and a half-sister to the French 2,000 Guineas winner Shanghai and the dam of the Group/Grade 1 winners Ciro and Internallyflawless. (Nurlan Bizakov). *"A very nice filly with a lot of quality about her. You won't see her until after Ascot I wouldn't have thought, but she'll definitely be a 2-y-o".*

272. UNNAMED ★★★

b.f. Royal Applause – Arctic Song (Charnwood Forest). February 20. Fifth foal. 42,000Y. Tattersalls October Book 2. Rabbah Bloodstock. Half-sister to the very useful 6f winner (at 2 yrs) and listed placed Hartley (by Lucky Story) and to the quite useful Irish dual 10f and hurdles winner Peacock's Pride (by Groom Dancer). The dam is an unraced half-sister to 3 winners including the triple listed winner and Group 2 6f Gimcrack Stakes second Andronikos. The second dam, Arctic Air (by Polar Falcon), a quite useful 2-y-o 7f winner, is a sister to the useful listed 7f winner Arctic Char and a half-sister to 6 winners including the Group 2 winners Barrow Creek and Last Resort and the dam of the Group 2 winner Trans Island. (Saeed Manana). *"Quite a big filly, she's nice and she could come any time, but the fillies are a bit behind at the moment because of the poor spring we've had. She'll be alright".*

273. UNNAMED ★★★

b.f. Sixties Icon – Brigadiers Bird (Mujadil). February 14. Eleventh foal. Half-sister to the 2-y-o Group 3 7f Futurity Stakes winner and Group 2 1m Falmouth Stakes winner Lady Lahar, to the fairly useful 5f winner of 7 races, including at 2 yrs, Captain Carey, the moderate 12f winner Lord Lahar (all by Fraam), the fairly useful 2-y-o 5f winner and dual Group 3 placed Miss Lahar (by Clodovil) and the quite useful 1m 2-y-o winner Sri Pekan Two (by Montjeu). The dam is an unraced half-sister to 3 winners. The second dam, Brigadiers Nurse (by Brigadier Gerard), is an unraced half-sister to 4 minor winners. (Barry Walters Catering). *"She was late coming in, she goes nice and she's a big filly that'll be a really nice later in the year".*

274. UNNAMED ★★★

b.f. Sixties Icon – Cibenze (Owington). March 9. Seventh foal. 10,000Y. Tattersalls December. Not sold. Half-sister to the fair 6f (including at 2 yrs) to 1m winner of 5 races My Best Bet (by Best Of The Bests), to the fair 2-y-o 6f winner Gee Bee Em (by Piccolo), the modest 11f to 2m winner of 4 races Josh You Are and a winner in Greece (both by Josr Algarhoud). The dam, a modest maiden, was placed six times from 5f to 1m at 2 and 3 yrs and is a half-sister to 4 winners. The second dam, Maria Cappuccini (by Siberian Express), a quite useful 2-y-o 5f winner, is a half-sister to 8 winners including the dual Group 3 winner Marina Park. *"A lovely big filly for later in the year. I like her, she's a little bit nervous but she's fine and she'll be OK".*

275. UNNAMED ★★★

b.c. Sixties Icon – Elegant Dance (Statoblest). April 28. Half-brother to the modest 2-y-o dual 6f winner Country Waltz (by Pastoral Pursuits) and to the quite useful 2-y-o dual 6f winner Mazzola (by Bertolini). The dam, a modest 4-y-o 6f winner, is a half-sister to several winners. The second dam, Furry Dance (by Nureyev), is an unplaced half-sister to the useful winner and listed-placed Florid. *"A nice, strong colt for later in the year. He's a very nice horse and the dam does produce 2-y-o winners. He's a lovely looking colt, a big horse with a lot of scope and quality".*

276. UNNAMED ★★★

ch.c. Compton Place – Kindallachan (Magic Ring). April 7. First foal. £16,000Y. Doncaster Premier. Gill Richardson. The dam, a moderate dual 6f winner, is a half-sister to 5 winners. The second dam, Moore Stylish (by Moorestyle), won over hurdles and is a half-sister to 8 winners including the dam of the US dual Grade 1 winner Donna Viola. *"He's a smasher. A very nice colt, I haven't done a lot with him but he shows already that he could be a real nice 2-y-o".*

277. UNNAMED ★★★

b.c. Sixties Icon – La Gifted (Fraam). First foal. £5,500Y. Ascot December. Not sold. The dam, a fair 7f winner of 6 races at 3 yrs, is a half-sister to the Irish 1,000 Guineas and US Grade

1 9f winner Samitar and to the 2-y-o Group 3 Albany Stakes winner Nijoom Dubai. The second dam, Aileen's Gift (by Rainbow Quest), is an unraced half-sister to 5 winners including the fairly useful listed-placed Roker Park and the dam of the Group 2 Gimcrack Stakes winner Shameel. *"A nice colt from a very good family, he rapped a joint and got held up for a while but he'll be alright. We'll get on with him and he'll make a 2-y-o".*

278. UNNAMED ★★★

b.c. Royal Applause – Pure Speculation (Salse). April 27. Fifth foal. 38,000Y. Tattersalls October Book 2. Gill Richardson. Closely related to the fairly useful dual 5f winner Doughnut (by Acclamation) and half-brother to the fair dual 6f winner (including at 2 yrs) Dressed In Lace (by Dark Angel). The dam, a 7f winner at 2 yrs, is a half-sister to 6 minor winners here and abroad. The second dam, Just Speculation (by Ahonoora), won once at 2 yrs in Ireland and was third in the Group 3 Killavullan Stakes and is a half-sister to the Ascot Gold Cup second Tyrone Bridge. *"He's a very nice colt, I still own him at the moment but he goes alright. He won't be real early but he won't be far away and he might be out by the end of May. A nice Royal Applause".*

279. UNNAMED ★★★

ch.c. Assertive – Princess Almora (Pivotal). May 5. Fifth foal. £4,000Y. Doncaster November. Gill Richardson. Half-brother to the modest 6f winner Almora Guru (by Ishiguru). The dam, a fair triple 6f winner at 3 yrs, is a half-sister to 8 winners including the Group 3 Park Hill Stakes placed Rada's Daughter. The second dam, Drama School (by Young Generation), is an unplaced half-sister to 3 winners. *"He's quite a nice horse, he didn't cost much but he goes alright and he's definitely a 2-y-o".*

280. UNNAMED ★★★

b.f. Captain Gerrard – Reeli Silli (Dansili). March 30. Fourth foal. £2,400Y. Doncaster November. Brian Robe. Half-sister to the fair 2012 5f to 7f placed maiden Marchwood (by Assertive). The dam is an unraced half-sister to 3 winners. The second dam, Real Emotion (by El Prado), won twice at 3 yrs in Italy and is a half-sister to 4 winners. (Brian Robe). *"She goes well, she was cheap and might not be a superstar, but she's OK and definitely a 2-y-o, so we'll get on with her".*

JANE CHAPPLE-HYAM

281. INJUN SANDS ★★★ ♠

b.c. Halling – Serriera (Highest Honor). February 13. Fifth foal. 25,000foal. Tattersalls December. Grove Stud. Half-brother to the fair 6f and 7f winner of 4 races Batgirl (by Mark Of Esteem). The dam, placed twice at 2 and 3 yrs in France, is a half-sister to 3 winners including the multiple French listed winner Sarrasin. The second dam, Sevilliana (by General Holme), was placed three times in France and is a half-sister to 11 winners including Sillery (Group 1 Prix Jean Prat). (Mrs M D Morriss). *"He's not exactly bred to be a 2-y-o type, but he's nice and I think he'll be racing by July".*

282. UNNAMED ★★

b.c. Rock Of Gibraltar – Hannah Frank (High Chaparral). March 22. First foal. 10,000Y. Tattersalls December. Not sold. The dam is an unraced half-sister to 4 winners including the US Grade 1 Garden City Stakes and Group 3 Irish 2,000 Guineas Trial winner Alexander Tango. The second dam, House In Wood (by Woodman), is an unraced half-sister to 4 winners including Housamix (Group 2 Prix Niel). (Norcroft Park Stud). *"A home-bred, he's on the small side but he's tough and should make a 2-y-o".*

PETER CHAPPLE-HYAM

283. AROD (IRE) ★★★★

b.c. Teofilo – My Personal Space (Rahy). April 21. Sixth foal. £170,000Y. Goffs Orby. David Redvers. The dam, a fair 2-y-o 6f winner, is a half-sister to 7 winners including the Group 3 7f Darley Stakes winner Far Lane and to the dam of the US Grade 2 winner Dark Islander. The second dam, Pattimech (by Nureyev), a winner at up to 7f in the USA, is a sister to the triple US Grade 1 winner Annoconnor and a half-sister to 9 winners including the Group 1 2m Grand Prix de Paris and the Grade 1 Melbourne Cup winner At Talaq. (Qatar Racing Ltd). *"He's going to take a bit of time but he does everything really nice. One for seven* furlongs around August-time and he's one I like a lot. He goes really well, does everything just right and he's a fantastic mover".

284. BOY AT THE BAR ★★★★ ♠

ch.c. Dutch Art – Lipsia (Dubai Destination). April 30. Second foal. £38,000Y. Doncaster Premier. Blandford Bloodstock. The dam is an unplaced half-sister to 7 winners including the listed winner Lagudin. The second dam, Liaison (by Blushing Groom), a French 4-y-o listed winner, is a half-sister to 5 winners. *"He's not the biggest, but most of the good Dutch Art 2-y-o's seem to be that way. He does everything right, has a lovely attitude and contrary to what I normally do I've given him a piece of work before his second birthday. He was a late April foal so I'll probably wait until the end of May before I run him. He'll win over five furlongs, he's hopefully my Norfolk Stakes horse and he does go well. I really like him a lot".*

285. DIRECT TIMES (IRE) ★★★

b.c. Acclamation – Elegant Times (Dansili). February 8. Fourth foal. 20,000Y. Tattersalls October Book 1. Not sold. Half-brother to Timeless Appeal (by Kheleyf), unplaced in one start at 2 yrs in 2012, to the fairly useful 2-y-o 5f winner Tioman Legend (by Kyllachy) and the fair 6f winner Al Janadeirya (by Oasis Dream). The dam, a modest 6f winner, is a half-sister to 6 winners including the Group 2 7f Hungerford Stakes and Group 3 6f Bentinck Stakes winner Welsh Emperor, the very useful listed 5f winner Majestic Times and the useful 6f and 7f winner and Group 3 6f third Brave Prospector. The second dam, Simply Times (by Dodge), ran twice unplaced at 2 yrs and is a half-sister to 5 winners including the US 2-y-o stakes winner Bucky's Baby. (Mr Allan Belshaw). *"He's a homebred and went to the sales but was bought back. He was tiny at the sale but since he's been in here he's grown unbelievably. It's a fast family and I think when he strengthens up a bit more he should be a six furlong type. A very quiet, placid horse, hopefully around June time he should be stepping out. I haven't done much with him yet but everything he has done has been good".*

286. ETERNITYS GATE ★★★★

b.c. Dutch Art – Regency Rose (Danehill). February 28. Third foal. 190,000Y. Tattersalls October Book 1. John Warren. Half-brother to the useful 2-y-o Group 3 6.3f Anglesey Stakes winner Regional Counsel and to the fair 1m winner Regal Salute (both by Medicean). The dam is an unraced sister to the Group 1 6f Cheveley Park Stakes winner Regal Rose and to the Japanese 10f stakes winner Generalist and a half-sister to 8 winners. The second dam, Ruthless Rose (by Conquistador Cielo), ran twice unplaced and is a half-sister to 9 winners including the high-class miler Shaadi. (Mrs Fitri Hay). *"He cost plenty, he goes very well and being by Dutch Art he's not that big, but he's big enough. He should be out in May and he could win over five furlongs but he'll be better at six. It's a pretty good family, it's a fast family – and he looks fast. More than useful".*

287. FEMALE STRATEGY (IRE) ★★★

b.f. Holy Roman Emperor – Strategy (Machiavellian). March 4. Fifth foal. £40,000Y. Doncaster Premier. Blandford Bloodstock. Closely related to the US Grade 3 winner and Grade 1 placed Justaroundmidnight (by Danehill Dancer) and half-sister to the useful Irish 2-y-o 5f winner and Group 3 6f Anglesey Stakes third Boris Grigoriev (by Excellent Air). The dam, a quite useful 10f and 11f winner, is a half-sister to 2 winners. The second dam, Island Story (by Shirley Heights), a quite useful 10f winner, is a half-sister to 6 winners. (Mrs Fitri Hay). *"She goes along quite nicely but she's grown a lot and got quite big for a Holy Roman. So she's going to take a bit of time, but I think when she does come she'll be sharp. I'd guess that would be over six furlongs around June time. She's strong, she moves nicely and does everything just right".*

288. HAY CHEWED (IRE) ★★★★

b.f. Camacho – Titian Saga (Titus Livius). April 8. Second foal. €18,000Y. Goffs Sportsman's. Grove Stud. Half-sister to the fair triple 5f winner Imperial Legend (by Mujadil). The dam, a fair 2-y-o 6f winner, is a half-sister to 7 winners. The second dam, Nordic Living (by Nordico), is an unplaced half-sister to one winner. (Mr John C Davies). *"She is very sharp indeed. She goes really well, five furlongs won't* be a problem to her and if everything goes right she should be out in May. She'll be alright at six furlongs too, but she's got quite strong, has a big back-end on her and really does look like a sprinter". TRAINERS' BARGAIN BUY

289. HYDROGEN ★★★★★
b.c. Galileo – Funsie (Saumarez). March 12. Seventh foal. 2,500,000Y. Tattersalls October Book 1. David Redvers. Closely related to the Epsom Derby, Juddmonte International Stakes and Racing Post Trophy winner Authorized and to the quite useful Irish 2-y-o 1m winner Sirgarfieldsobers (both by Montjeu) and half-brother to the fairly useful 10f and 12f winner Empowered (by Fasliyev). The dam is an unraced half-sister to 9 winners including the Group 3 10.5f Prix Cleopatre winner Brooklyn's Dance (herself the dam of six stakes winners) and the dam of the Group 1 winner Okawango. The second dam, Valle Dansante (by Lyphard), won once in France and is a full or half-sister to 12 winners including the French 2,000 Guineas winner and sire Green Dancer. (Qatar Racing Ltd). *"I can hardly put him as my Bargain Buy can I?! He's just a beautiful horse, does everything perfectly and he's a good size without being too big. He moves really well and he's probably earlier than you'd think, so it's a matter of sitting on my hands and waiting. He's strong enough and he's got the ability to go now, but I'll wait until July or August over seven furlongs. He's a very exciting horse and in a perfect world he'll go for a maiden, the Washington Singer at Newbury and the Racing Post Trophy".*

290. INCHILA ★★★
b.f. Dylan Thomas – Inchiri (Sadler's Wells). April 6. 19,000Y. Tattersalls October Book 2. Not sold. Closely related to the fair 7f (at 2 yrs) to 9f winner of 6 races Saharia (by Oratorio) and half-sister to the fairly useful 12f and 13f winner Inchwood (by Dubai Destination), the quite useful dual 10f winner Hawk's Eye (by Hawk Wing), the quite useful dual 7f (at 2 yrs) and 1m winner Celtic Step (by Selkirk) and the minor French 13f winner Petit A Petit (by Holy Roman Emperor). The dam, a very useful 12f listed winner, is a half-sister to 3 winners. The second dam, Inchyre (by Shirley Heights), a useful 1m winner, is a half-sister

to 7 winners including the very smart and tough triple Group 3 7f winner and sire Inchinor. *"She moves really well and she's a good size but being by Dylan Thomas she's going to take time and is more of a 3-y-o type. She's certainly got an engine, so I'd say seven furlongs around July or August will be her starting point. I like her – she goes well".*

291. KATAWI ★★★★
b.f. Dubawi – Purring (Mountain Cat). May 7. Seventh foal. Half-sister to the Group 3 7f Prix du Calvados winner and Group 2 May Hill Stakes second Purr Along (by Mount Nelson), to the fairly useful 9f and subsequent US winner and dual listed-placed Lady Francesca (by Montjeu), the quite useful 10f and 12f winner of 8 races Jeer (by Selkirk), the fair 12f and 14f winner of 4 races Cat O' Nine Tails (by Motivator) and the modest dual 12f winner Kittens (by Marju). The dam, a quite useful 7f winner, is a half-sister to the Group 2 1m Falmouth Stakes and Group 3 1m Prix de Sandringham winner Ronda (herself dam of a Group 3 winner) and to the smart 1m (at 2 yrs) and listed 2m winner Silver Gilt. The second dam, Memory's Gold (by Java Gold), a modest 3-y-o 7.6f winner, is a half-sister to 5 winners including the useful middle-distance filly and German Group 3 winner Fields Of Spring. (Moyns Park Estate & Stud). *"She's coming to hand really well now. She's a perfect size, not too big, very laid-back and I like her a lot. More of a seven furlong filly around June or July and she does everything really well".*

292. KEY TO VICTORY (USA) ★★★
ch.c. English Channel – Treysta (Belong To Me). April 8. Seventh foal. $27,000Y. Keeneland September. Not sold. Half-brother to the useful 7f (at 2 yrs) and 1m winner Bridgefield (by Speightstown) and to a minor US winner by Crowd Pleaser. The dam, a minor winner at 2 yrs, is a half-sister to 3 winners including the US Grade 1 winner and sire Hard Spun. The second dam, Turkish Tryst (by Turkoman), was a stakes winner and Grade 2 placed in the USA. *"I thought he was going to be very sharp but he's grown a lot. He's doing very well now though, coming along nicely and he'll be a six furlong type in May or June. He moves well and I like him".*

293. KICKING THE CAN (IRE) ★★
gr.c. Aussie Rules – Silk Meadow (Barathea).
April 2. Second foal. £15,000Y. Doncaster
Premier. Paul Hancock. Half-brother to the
modest 2012 9f placed 2-y-o Borodino (by
Strategic Prince). The dam is an unplaced
sister to the Irish listed 1m winner Hymn Of
Love and a half-sister to 5 winners. The second
dam, Perils Of Joy (by Rainbow Quest), a
3-y-o 1m winner in Ireland, is a half-sister to 5
winners including the Italian Group 3 winner
Sweetened Offer. (Paul Hancock). *"He's only
just arrived and he seems to go nicely but he'll
probably want time and seven furlongs".*

294. NOBLE METAL ★★★ ♠
gr.c. With Approval – Grain Only
(Machiavellian). March 16. Fourth foal.
40,000Y. Tattersalls October Book 2. Blandford
Bloodstock. Half-brother to Granule, unplaced
in one start at 2 yrs in 2012, to the fairly useful
10f to 13f winner of 5 races Caravan Rolls
On and the quite useful 2-y-o 1m winner
Gabrial's Star (all by Hernando). The dam is an
unraced half-sister to 3 winners abroad. The
second dam, All Grain (by Polish Precedent),
a useful 12.6f winner, was third in the Group
3 Lancashire Oaks and is a sister to the Irish
Oaks and Yorkshire Oaks winner Pure Grain
and a half-sister to 7 winners. (Miss K Rausing).
*"A half-brother to a middle-distance horse we
have, Caravan Rolls On, so where he finds his
pace from I don't know! He's a lot sharper than
'Caravan' and he goes really well. Probably a
seven furlong type 2-y-o to start with, he's a
good size and getting stronger again now after
going through a weak phase. I'd say he'd want
fast ground and he goes as well as anything".*

295. PINK DANCE ★★★ ♠
ch.f. Dutch Art – Dance Away (Pivotal). April
19. Sixth foal. 60,000Y. Tattersalls October
Book 2. Stephen Hillen. Closely related to the
fair 2012 2-y-o 6f winner Medici Dancer and
to the useful 2-y-o 5f and 6f winner Foghorn
Leghorn (both by Medicean) and half-sister
to the modest 5f winner Azif (by Where Or
When). The dam, a fairly useful 2-y-o 5f
winner, is a half-sister to 2 winners. The second
dam, Dance On (by Caerleon), a fairly useful
2-y-o dual 5f winner, was listed-placed and is
a half-sister to 6 winners. (Mrs Fitri Hay). *"She's

small but she tries her hardest and we'll try
and get her out in May. Probably a six furlong
type, she wouldn't set the world alight but she
moves well, doesn't do anything wrong and
she's a nice filly".*

296. SEMARAL (IRE) ★★
b.f. High Chaparral – Semaphore (Zamindar).
April 15. Half-sister to the useful 2012 2-y-o
7f winner and Group 3 7f Oh So Sharp Stakes
third Annie's Fortune (by Montjeu). The dam
is an unraced half-sister to 2 winners. The
second dam, Blue Duster (by Danzig), winner
of the Group 1 6f Cheveley Park Stakes, the
Group 3 6f Princess Margaret Stakes and the
Group 3 5f Queen Mary Stakes, is a sister to
the smart Group 1 6f Middle Park Stakes and
Group 2 7f Challenge Stakes winner Zieten
and a half-sister to 9 winners. (Moyns Park
Estate & Stud). *"She's more of a 3-y-o but she's
a decent size, she moves very well and goes
very well too, but she'll take a lot of time. She
does everything just right and I do like her a
lot, but she's probably one of those that'll have
the odd run towards the back-end. One day
she'll definitely be OK".*

297. SONG OF ROWLAND (IRE) ★★★★
b.c. Holy Roman Emperor – Makarova
(Sadler's Wells). February 27. Eighth foal.
£50,000Y. Doncaster Premier. Hugo Merry.
Closely related to the fairly useful Irish 7f
winner Picture Perfect and the hurdles winner
Johnny Owen (both by Danehill Dancer). The
dam is an unraced sister to French Ballerina,
a winner of three listed events in Ireland
from 1m to 2m and a half-sister to 5 winners
including the Group 1 Fillies Mile winner
and Group 1 Irish Oaks second Sunspangled.
The second dam, Filia Ardross (by Ardross), a
very smart filly, won three Group 2 events in
Germany and the Group 3 10f Select Stakes at
Goodwood. (Mrs Fitri Hay). *"He's a good size
for a Holy Roman colt and very mature. Like
all of them he's cheeky and tough as nails. He
goes very well, does everything perfect and
he'll win over five furlongs but be better at six.
He'll be out in May time, I like him a lot and he
could be pretty good".*

298. STEELE RANGER ★★★★
b.c. Bushranger – Tatora (Selkirk). February

19. Eighth foal. 70,000Y. Tattersalls October Book 1. Not sold. Half-brother to the Group 2 Betfair Lennox Stakes and Group 3 Jersey Stakes winner Tariq, to the quite useful 7f winner of 5 races including at 2 yrs Tariq Too (both by Kyllachy) and the French 2-y-o winner Duniatty (by Green Desert). The dam is an unraced half-sister to 3 winners and to the placed dam of the Group 2 Flying Childers Stakes winner Wi Dud. The second dam, Tatouma (by The Minstrel), won twice at 2 yrs and is a half-sister to 4 winners. (Mr Khalifa Dasmal & Mrs Clodagh McStay). *"A half-brother to a good horse I had, Tariq, he goes along nicely and all being well he'll be a May 2-y-o but he definitely wants six furlongs. He wouldn't win over five and he'll probably get better when he gets seven. The Bushranger's I've seen all look like 2-y-o's so I think you'll know your fate pretty soon, but this horse does do things right, he's a good-size and a good mover".*

299. STUBBORN LOVE ★★★

ch.f. New Approach – Blue Rocket (Rock Of Gibraltar). February 5. Second foal. 100,000Y. Tattersalls October Book 1. Not sold. Half-sister to Everlasting Light (by Authorized), unplaced in one start at 2 yrs in 2012. The dam, a fairly useful dual 6f winner (including at 2 yrs), was third in the Group 3 Nell Gwyn Stakes, is a half-sister to 5 winners including the smart Group 3 5f Cornwallis Stakes and dual 6f listed winner Halmahera. The second dam, Champagne Girl (by Robellino), a modest 2-y-o 5f winner, is a half-sister to 5 winners including the useful sprinter Deep Finesse and to the placed dam of the dual Group 1 winner Dick Turpin. (Mr J Barton). *"She arrived here unbroken in January so she was just a bit behind the others but she's catching up quickly now. She's grown a hell of a lot and she needed to because she wasn't the biggest. She's just starting to do well now and show plenty. She comes up the canter really good, I think she'll be a six furlong type and I'll try and get her out in May with a view to seeing where we go from there".*

300. VOICE OF A LEADER (IRE) ★★★★

b.c. Danehill Dancer – Thewaytosanjose (Fasliyev). January 10. First foal. 210,000Y. Tattersalls October Book 1. Stephen Hillen. The dam, a moderate 1m (at 2 yrs) and 9f winner, is a half-sister to 4 winners. The second dam, Soltura (by Sadler's Wells), is an unraced half-sister to 9 winners including the US Grade 2 winner Sword Dance. (Mrs Fitri Hay & Mr John Magnier). *"A big, strong colt and a great mover. I'm not sure about the pedigree on the dam's side but this colt shows plenty. He's one for seven furlongs plus, but I don't seem to be able to get Danehill Dancer right, everyone else seem to have good ones but all the ones I've had have been slow. This colt could be different, he goes very well and he should be out around August time".*

301. UNNAMED ★★★

b.f. Dubawi – Everlasting Love (Pursuit Of Love). March 23. Half-sister to the French winners and listed-placed Samsa (by Zafonic) and Lasting Applause (by Royal Applause), to the quite useful 12f winner Daliance (by Dalakhani) and the fair 10f and 11f winner Honorable Love (by Highest Honor). The dam, a useful 2-y-o 7f winner and third in the Group 3 May Hill Stakes, is a half-sister to 3 winners. The second dam, Now And Forever (by Kris), is an unraced half-sister to 8 winners including the Group 3 Curragh Cup winner Witness Box. (A W Black). *"Not the biggest filly in the world, but she's always trying to please and she's got very strong recently. She's about to start moving along and she'll kick off at six furlongs, hopefully in May, but she'll be better at seven. Goes nicely and does everything right".*

302. UNNAMED ★★★

b.f. Shamardal – Gimasha (by Cadeaux Genereux). February 4. Fourth foal. Half-sister to Hasbah (by Cape Cross), placed fourth once from 2 starts at 2 yrs in 2012 and to the fairly useful 2-y-o 6f winner and 3-y-o listed-placed Samminder (by Red Ransom). The dam, a useful 5f and 6f winner of 5 races, is a half-sister to 5 winners including the very useful triple 1m and hurdles winner Atlantic Rhapsody and the useful French winner of 3 races and Group 3 Prix Thomas Bryon third Gaitero. The second dam, First Waltz (by Green Dancer), winner of the Group 1 6f Prix Morny and second in the Cheveley Park

Stakes, is a half-sister to the dam of the Prix Lupin second Angel Falls. (Mr Ziad A Galadari). *"Probably not as precocious as the rest of them but she's improving all the time. It may sound stupid, but I think when she does come she'll be fast, so she'll be five or six furlongs, but I don't see that happening until July time. I do like her, she goes along well, shows a good attitude and just needs to strengthen".*

303. UNNAMED ★★★

b.f. *Pivotal – Heavenly Bay (Rahy).* April 9. Sixth foal. £60,000Y. Doncaster Premier. Blandford Bloodstock. The dam, a fairly useful 12f winner, was listed-placed twice and is a half-sister to 3 winners. The second dam, Bevel (by Mr Prospector), a French 1m winner, is out of a half-sister to Ajdal, Formidable and the dam of Arazi. (Mrs Fitri Hay). *"Doing everything right, she's very slight for a Pivotal and she'll be a six furlong type. Not over-big, but just a decent size, she'll be out in May with a view to seeing where we stand. She does go very well".*

304. UNNAMED ★★★★

b.br.f. *Cape Cross – Maramba (Rainbow Quest).* April 22. Sister to the useful 7f (at 2 yrs) and listed 10f winner Cape Amber (by Cape Cross) and half-sister to the very useful 2-y-o 5f, 6f listed and 6.5f Watership Down Stud Sales Race winner and Group 3 placed Nyramba (by Night Shift) and the fair 12f winner Warneford (by Dansili). The dam, a fairly useful 3-y-o 1m winner, is a half-sister to 7 winners. The second dam, Gayane (by Nureyev), a very smart winner of the 6f Sandy Lane Stakes and the 7f Oak Tree Stakes, was second in the Group 1 July Cup and is a half-sister to 7 winners including the Group 2 10f Sun Chariot Stakes winner Ristna and the Group 3 Beeswing Stakes winner Shahid. (Five Horses Ltd). *"A sister to a listed winning filly I had called Cape Amber, she's very similar to her and I see her having the same sort of plan. So we'll look for a seven furlong maiden for her in August on quick ground. The sister didn't run again that year but hopefully we'll get another run into this filly. She goes very well and she's one of the nicest 2-y-o fillies I've got".*

305. UNNAMED ★★★

b.c. *Winker Watson – Nedwa (In The Wings).*

January 16. Fourth foal. 22,000Y. Doncaster Premier. Blandford Bloodstock. The dam is an unraced half-sister to 5 winners including the French listed winner Mary Boleyn. The second dam, Bint Kaldoun (by Kaldoun), a quite useful 7f (at 2 yrs) to 12f placed maiden, is a sister to the German listed sprint winner Shy Lady (herself dam of the St James's Palace Stakes winner Zafeen) and a half-sister to 6 winners. *"He's quite mature but he's big and just taking a bit of time. He's always moved well though and he's definitely a six furlong 2-y-o, possibly in May or maybe June. It surprises me how well he goes, so I'm very pleased with him. He's strong and has a big backside – nothing like his sire at all who was small, chestnut and narrow"!*

306. UNNAMED ★★★

ch.c. *Exceed And Excel – Waafiah (Anabaa).* April 10. Half-brother to the 2012 7f placed 2-y-o Arbeel (by Royal Applause), to the useful 6f (at 2 yrs) and 7f winner and listed-placed Telwaar (by Haafhd), the fairly useful triple 1m winner Jaser and the modest 6f and subsequent UAE 7f winner Ragad (both by Alhaarth). The dam, second over 7f at 3 yrs on her only start, is a half-sister to several winners including the very useful 1m and hurdles winner Atlantic Rhapsody. The second dam, First Waltz (by Green Dancer), winner of the Group 1 6f Prix Morny and second in the Cheveley Park Stakes, is a half-sister to the dam of the Prix Lupin second Angel Falls. (Mr Ziad A Galadari). *"He's very laid-back for a chestnut Exceed And Excel – they're normally quite hot. He goes up the canter really well but he'll want a bit of time and seven furlongs. He does go along nicely and he's a good size now having been a bit small when he came in. There's nothing wrong with him at all".*

ROGER CHARLTON
307. AMBER ISLE (USA) ★★★

b.f. *First Defence – Family (Danzig).* February 28. Sister to the 2012 2-y-o Group 3 7f Acomb Stakes winner, Group 2 7f Champagne Stakes second and Grade 1 Breeders Cup Juvenile Turf fourth Dundonnell. The dam is an unraced sister to the top-class sprinter and sire Danehill, the US Grade 2 9f winner Eagle Eyed, the very smart Group 3 Criterion Stakes winner Shibboleth, the US Grade 3 winner Harpia and the listed 7f winner Euphonic. The second dam, Razyana (by His Majesty), was placed over 7f at 2 yrs and 10f at 3 yrs. (Khalid Abdulla). *"She looks quite forward, she isn't as big or as strong as her brother Dundonnell, but she's a nice filly that should make a 2-y-o".*

308. ASPIRANT ★★★

b.c. Rail Link – Affluent (Oasis Dream). February 6. First foal. The dam, a quite useful dual 5f winner (including at 2 yrs), is closely related to 2 winners including the useful 2-y-o 6f winner and Group 3 7f placed Cantabria and a half-sister to numerous winners including the useful 2-y-o 5f and listed 6f winner Deportivo and the useful 2-y-o listed 5f winner Irish Vale. The second dam, Valencia (by Kenmare), placed over 1m at 2 yrs on her only start, is a half-sister to numerous winners including the dual US Grade 1 winner Wandesta, the Group 2 12f winner De Quest and the smart 10f to 15f winner Turners Hill. (Khalid Abdulla). *"He's a deep, strong horse and despite being by the Arc winner Rail Link he actually looks precocious. The pedigree is a bit of a mixture, but hopefully he'll make a 2-y-o".*

309. BE SEEING YOU ★★★

ch.c. Medicean – Oshiponga (Barathea). March 1. Ninth foal. Half-brother to the fair 2012 triple 6f placed 2-y-o Caramack (by Danehill Dancer), to the 2-y-o Group 2 7f Superlative Stakes and US Grade 3 7f winner Hatta Fort (by Cape Cross), to the fair 1m to 13f winner of 5 races Ostentation (by Dubawi) and the modest 9f winner Teide Lady (by Nashwan). The dam, a fair 9f winner, is a half-sister to 8 winners including the Grade 1 E P Taylor Stakes winner Miss Keller, the Group 3 Select Stakes second Sir George Turner and the Group 2 May Hill Stakes second Kotsi. The second dam, Ingozi (by Warning), a fairly useful winner over 7f and 1m at 3 yrs including a listed event, is a half-sister to 7 winners including the very smart and tough triple Group 3 7f winner Inchinor. (Mrs M Stewart). *"I trained the dam and this is a big, strong colt. I'm pleased with him but he hasn't been here that long".*

310. CANOVA (IRE) ★★★

ch.c. Art Connoisseur – Rain Dancer (Sadler's Wells). March 28. Ninth foal. 45,000Y. Tattersalls October Book 2. John Warren. Half-brother to the unplaced 2012 Irish 2-y-o Fulminata (by Holy Roman Emperor), to the fairly useful Irish 2-y-o listed 1m winner Boca Dancer (by Indian Ridge), to the French 12f winner Rainboy (by Darshaan) and the flat and hurdles winner Dice (by Kalanisi). The dam is an unraced full or half-sister to 4 minor winners. The second dam, Final Farewell (by Proud Truth), ran once unplaced and is a half-sister to the dam of the Group 1 Haydock Park Sprint Cup winner and top-class sire Danehill. (Royal Ascot Racing Club). *"He's recently had a bit of a setback but he's a good mover and you would hope that he'd make a 2-y-o around June/July. He's got plenty of scope".*

311. CHAUVELIN ★★★

b.c. Sir Percy – Enforce (Kalanisi). May 6. Third foal. 28,000Y. Tattersalls December. Not sold. Brother to the quite useful 2012 2-y-o 1m winner Van Percy. The dam, a smart listed 1m winner, was in third in the Group 3 8.5f Princess Elizabeth Stakes and is a half-sister to 4 winners. The second dam, Kinetic Force (by Holy Bull), was placed over 6f at 2 yrs in France and is a half-sister to 7 winners including the US Grade 1 7f winner Mizzen Mast. (Sir Simon de Zoete & Partners). *"He's a neat, strong horse who looks quite precocious, but he was quite a late foal. Probably one for July onwards over six/seven furlongs".*

312. CONTINENTAL DRIFT (USA) ★★★

b.br.f. Smart Strike – Intercontinental (Danehill). February 25. Fourth foal. Half-sister to the fair triple 9f winner So Wise (by Elusive Quality). The dam, winner of Grade 1 Matriarch Stakes and the Grade 1 Filly & Mare Turf, is a sister to the triple Group/Grade 1 winners Banks Hill and Champs Elysees, the dual Group 1 winner Cacique and the Group 2 winner and high-class sire Dansili and closely related to the Grade 1 Matriarch Stakes and Grade 1 Beverly D Stakes winner Heat Haze. The second dam, Hasili (by Kahyasi), won over 5f at 2 yrs and stayed a mile. (Khalid Abdulla). *"A very well-bred filly, she's not over-big but she's athletic and should be a 2-y-o".*

313. DARK LEOPARD ★★★

b.c. Dubawi – Clouded Leopard (Danehill).
February 26. Half-brother to the 1m (at 2 yrs) and 6f winner Tiger Cub (by Tiger Hill). The dam, placed once over 7f at 2 yrs, is a half-sister to numerous winners including the Breeders Cup Juvenile Turf winner Pounced. The second dam, Golden Cat (by Storm Cat), won over 1m at 3 yrs in Ireland and was listed-placed and is a half-sister to 9 winners including the Irish listed winners and subsequent US winner Eurostorm and Bowmore. (Lady Rothschild). *"He looks a typical Dubawi, very strong, deep and smallish. You'd hope he could start off in mid-summer over six furlongs".*

314. FRANGIPANNI (IRE) ★★

b.br.f. Dansili – Frizzante (Efisio). April 19. Half-sister to the quite useful 6f (at 2 yrs) and 7f winner of 4 races Greensward (by Green Desert) and to the fair 6f winner Pin Cushion (by Pivotal). The dam won 7 races including the Group 1 July Cup and is a half-sister to 4 winners including the Stewards Cup winner Zidane and the dual 6f listed winner Firenze. The second dam, Juliet Bravo (by Glow), a modest 2-y-o 5f winner, is a half-sister to the very smart filly Donna Viola, a winner of 11 races here and abroad including the Grade 1 Yellow Ribbon Handicap, the Grade 1 Gamely Handicap and the Group 2 Prix de l'Opera. (Lady Rothschild). *"She's like her mother at this stage in that she's small and not obviously precocious, but she's an attractive filly. The dam didn't run until she was three, so it's hard to say when this filly is likely to run – maybe the family needs a bit of time".*

315. HIKING (USA) ★★★

b.f. First Defence – Trekking (Gone West). March 23. Sixth foal. Half-sister to Top Trail (by Exchange Rate), unplaced in one start at 2 yrs in 2012 and to the quite useful 10f winner Deck Walk (by Mizzen Mast). The dam, a quite useful 10f winner, is a half-sister to 4 winners including the smart dual listed 7f winner Tantina (herself dam of the Group winners Bated Breath and Cityscape). The second dam, Didina (by Nashwan), a winner over 6f at 2 yrs here, subsequently won the Grade 2 8.5f Dahlia Handicap in the USA and

is a sister to one winner and a half-sister to 4 winners including the French listed 10f winner Espionage. (Khalid Abdulla). *"Quite a nice filly, she looks as if she ought to be a 2-y-o by mid-season, probably over seven furlongs".*

316. HOODED ★★

b.c. Empire Maker – Yashmak (Danzig). March 4. Half-brother to the quite useful 7f to 10f and subsequent Australian 7f winner Sound Of Nature (by Chester House) and to the useful 3-y-o 1m winner (on her only start) Eyes Only (by Distant View). The dam, winner of the Grade 1 10f Flower Bowl Invitational Handicap and the Group 2 12f Ribblesdale Stakes, is a sister to the Great Voltigeur Stakes winner Dushyantor and a half-sister to the Epsom Derby and Irish Derby winner Commander in Chief, the champion 2-y-o and miler Warning and the Irish Derby second Deploy. The second dam, Slightly Dangerous (by Roberto), a very smart filly and winner of the 7.3f Fred Darling Stakes, was second in the Oaks to Time Charter and is a half-sister to the dams of the Arc winner and top class sire Rainbow Quest and the Dewhurst Stakes dead-heater Scenic. (Khalid Abdulla). *"A big, strong, attractive colt that moves well. He's very much one for the second half of the year and more of a 3-y-o type".*

317. KIDDING APART (USA) ★★★

ch.c. Lemon Drop Kid – Oceans Apart (Desert Prince). March 18. Third foal. Half-brother to the moderate 2012 5f to 1m placed 2-y-o Panama Cat (by Tale Of The Cat). The dam, a quite useful 5f and 6f winner, is a half-sister to numerous winners including the smart sprint winner of 11 races (including the Group 3 Prix de Meautry) Eisteddfod, the Group 3 1m Solonaway Stakes winner of 4 races Border Patrol, the useful 2-y-o 5f to 7f winner Brecon Beacon and the useful dual 7f (at 2 yrs) and UAE Group 3 1m winner Boston Lodge. The second dam, Ffestiniog (by Efisio), a fairly useful 2-y-o listed 7.3f and 3-y-o 1m winner, is a half-sister to several winners. (Elite Racing Club). *"He's a forward-going, good-moving, quite powerful horse. You wouldn't expect him to be precocious so he's one for the second half of the year and likely to develop into a better 3-y-o".*

318. LAUGHARNE ★★★

b.c. Authorized – Corsican Sunset (Thunder Gulch). March 3. Half-brother to the quite useful 12f and hurdles winner Clowance House (by Galileo). The dam, a useful 10f winner, was placed in the Group 3 12f Premio Maria Inciza and in several listed races and is a half-sister to the useful winner and triple Group 3 placed Si Seductor. The second dam, Miss Evans (by Nijinsky), won in France and was second in the listed 10f Prix Charles Laffitte and is a half-sister to Mamselle Bebette, a winner of five Grade 3 stakes events in the USA. (Seasons Holidays). *"He's a good-moving, attractive horse and never going to be over-big so he could be a seven furlong 2-y-o in the second half of the year".*

319. LILYFIRE (USA) ★★★★

b.f. First Defence – Didina (Nashwan). March 27. Eighth foal. Half-sister to the smart dual listed 7f winner Tantina (by Distant View), to the quite useful 10f winner Trekking (by Gone West) and the quite useful 2-y-o 1m winner Auction Room (by Auction House). The dam, a winner over 6f at 2 yrs here, subsequently won the Grade 2 8.5f Dahlia Handicap in the USA and is a sister to one winner and a half-sister to 4 winners including the listed winners Espionage and Star Cluster. The second dam, Didicoy (by Danzig), a useful winner of 3 races over 6f, is closely related to the Group 3 1m Prix Quincey winner Masterclass and a half-sister to the champion 2-y-o Xaar. (Khalid Abdulla). *"She's an attractive filly with a nice temperament and does everything asked of her. We should see her out from the middle of the summer onwards over seven furlongs".*

320. MAJOR JACK ★★★

b.c. Kheleyf – Azeema (by Averti). April 7. Third foal. Half-brother to Liberty Jack (by Sakhee) (unplaced in one start at 2 yrs in 2012) and to the fairly useful 2-y-o 1m winner Trader Jack (by Trade Fair). The dam, a fair 3-y-o 7f winner, is a half-sister to 2 winners including the Group 2 12f Jockey Club Stakes winner Al Kazeem. The second dam, Kazeem (by Darshaan), is an unplaced sister to the winner and subsequent US Grade 2 winner Treasurer and a half-sister to 6 minor winners. (Mr D J Deer). *"Quite a nice horse, he's not been here*

long but he's an attractive horse that moves well. He'll make a 2-y-o in the second half of the year".*

321. OBSERVATIONAL ★★★

ch.c. Galileo – Party (Cadeaux Genereux). February 7. Second foal. £200,000Y. Tattersalls October Book 1. Seasons Holidays. Closely related to the quite useful multiple 12f winner Party Line (by Montjeu). The dam won the 2-y-o listed 7f Radley Stakes and is a half-sister to 2 winners. The second dam, Forty Belles (by Forty Niner), was placed 6 times in France and is a half-sister to 8 winners including the French Group 3 winner In Clover. (Seasons Holidays). *"A nice-looking horse, with a pedigree like his you wouldn't expect him to appear before the second half of the year. I don't know a lot about him yet but he seems OK".*

322. OLD GUARD ★★

b.c. Notnowcato – Dolma (Marchand de Sable). February 22. Half-brother to the quite useful 2012 2-y-o 5f winner Don Marco (by Choisir) and to the very useful triple listed 1m winner Thistle Bird (by Selkirk). The dam won 6 races over 6f and 7f (including at 2 yrs), notably three listed events at 3 yrs. The second dam, Young Manila (by Manila), was listed placed over 10f and is a half-sister to Fabulous Hostess, a winner of three Group 3 events from 11f to 13f. (Lady Rothschild). *"A big, rangy horse, he's a nice mover but very much one for the end of the season and next year".*

323. PAGEANT BELLE ★★★

ch.f. Bahamian Bounty – Procession (Zafonic). March 9. Eighth foal. 21,000Y. Tattersalls October Book 2. Axom. Closely related to the moderate 1m and 10f winner Ricci De Mare (by Cadeaux Genereux) and half-sister to the moderate 2012 2-y-o 5f and 9f winner Lucy Bee (by Haafhd), the fairly useful 2-y-o 5f winner Katell (by Statue Of Liberty), the fair 2-y-o 6f winner Predict (by Oasis Dream), and 2 winners abroad by Dansili and Rock Of Gibraltar. The dam, a fair 7f (at 2 yrs) to 10f placed maiden, is a half-sister to 6 winners including the listed Masaka Stakes winner Jazz Jam. The second dam, Applaud (by Rahy), a smart 2-y-o winner of the Group 2

6f Cherry Hinton Stakes, is a full or half-sister to 6 winners. (Axom XLV). *"A very good mover and I'm hoping she'll be out in the second half of May, probably over six furlongs. A filly with good quarters, she's quite well developed".*

324. SCARLET PLUM ★★★

b.f. *Pivotal – Scarlet Runner (Night Shift).* January 2. First living foal. The dam, a very useful Group 3 Princess Margaret Stakes (at 2 yrs) and Group 3 7f Nell Gwyn Stakes winner, is a half-sister to 2 winners. The second dam, Sweet Pea (by Persian Bold), a quite useful 1m winner of 4 races, is a half-sister to numerous winners including the listed 6f winner Star Tulip. (Mr N Jones). *"A nice, big, strong Pivotal filly for the second half of the year".*

325. SKI BLAST ★★★

ch.c. *Three Valleys – Chasing Stars (Observatory).* February 16. First foal. The dam, a French listed 1m winner of 4 races, is a half-sister to the useful 1m and 11f winner and Group 3 Chester Vase third Risk Taker. The second dam, Post Modern (by Nureyev), is an unraced sister to the Oaks and the Fillies Mile winner Reams of Verse and a half-sister to 10 winners including Elmaamul (Coral Eclipse Stakes and Phoenix Champion Stakes) and the Group winners Manifest, Modernise and Modern Day and the dam of the high-class middle-distance filly Midday. (Khalid Abdulla). *"He looks quite precocious and we'll get him going now to see if he can run at the end of May or early June, over six furlongs".*

326. SLEEP WALK ★★★

gr.f. *Oasis Dream – Scuffle (Daylami).* February 28. First foal. The dam, a useful triple 1m winner, was listed-placed and is a half-sister to the high-class Group 1 9f Dubai Duty Free and triple Group 3 winner Cityscape and to the very smart Group 2 5f Temple Stakes and multiple Group 1 placed Bated Breath. The second dam, Tantina (by Distant View), a smart winner of 4 races including two listed events over 7f, was Group 3 placed and is a half-sister to 2 winners. (Khalid Abdulla). *"She's had a little setback recently but she looks more precocious than her dam, which isn't surprising being by Oasis Dream. She's strong, powerful and seems quite a nice filly".*

327. STARS ABOVE ME ★★★

b.f. *Exceed And Excel – Kalinova (Red Ransom).* April 22. Second foal. Half-sister to the poor 2012 1m and 9f placed 2-y-o Kingsville (by Royal Applause). The dam is an unraced half-sister to the Group 1 Fillies Mile, Falmouth Stakes, Sussex Stakes and Matron Stakes winner Soviet Song and to the useful 5f (at 2 yrs) and triple 6f winner Baralinka. The second dam, Kalinka (by Soviet Star), a quite useful 2-y-o 7f winner, is a half-sister to 2 winners. (Elite Racing Club). *"She looks quite sharp and precocious. One for six furlongs on fast ground from May onwards".*

328. STOMP ★★★★

b.c. *Nayef – Strut (Danehill Dancer).* March 3. Third foal. Half-brother to the Group 3 6f Bengough Stakes and dual listed 6f winner Mince (by Medicean). The dam, a 2-y-o listed 5.2f winner, was Group 3 placed twice and is a half-sister to 3 winners including the US Grade 3 6.5f third Vaunt. The second dam, Boast (by Most Welcome), a useful 5f and 6f winner, is a half-sister to 6 winners including the fairly useful 2-y-o 5f and 4-y-o 1m winner Great Bear. (Lady Rothschild). *"Like his half-sister Mince he has a nice temperament and he's laid-back. He's a strong horse and he ought to be a 2-y-o in the second half of the year".*

DENIS COAKLEY

329. CASTAGNA GIRL ★★★

ch.f. *Major Cadeaux – Ewenny (Warrshan).* March 14. Tenth foal. 7,000Y. Tattersalls October Book 2. Denis Coakley. Half-sister to the fairly useful 6f and 7f winner Johnny The Fish (by Most Welcome), to the fairly useful 7f and 1m winner Fast Or Free (by Notnowcato), the quite useful triple 6f winner Elusive Prince (by Storming Home), the fair 6f winner of 4 races (including at 2 yrs) Bazguy (by Josr Algarhoud), the moderate 7.5f seller winner Hymns And Arias (by Mtoto) and a hurdles winner by Reset. The dam, a fair 2-y-o 5f winner, is a half-sister to 5 winners. The second dam, Laleston (by Junius), won two races at 2 and 3 yrs. (Finders Keepers Partnership). *"Quite big and rangy, she probably won't be out until July, we like her and we'll probably start her off at six furlongs".*

330. KING CALYPSO ★★
ch.c. Sir Percy – Rosa De Mi Corazon
(Cozzene). April 24. Third foal. 5,000Y.
Tattersalls October Book 2. Denis Coakley. The
dam, a fair 6f and 7f winner, is a half-sister to
2 winners including the fairly useful 2-y-o dual
7f winner and subsequent German dual listed
placed Flor Y Nata. The second dam, Rose
Of Zollern (by Seattle Dancer), won 9 races
including the German 1,000 Guineas and a
stakes event in the USA and is a half-sister to
3 winners. (Count Calypso Racing). "A lengthy
colt, he'll take a bit of time and won't be out
until the second half of the year over seven
furlongs. He wasn't expensive but he goes well".

331. KUALA QUEEN (IRE) ★★★
b.f. Kodiac – See Nuala (Kyllachy). April 19.
Third foal. £8,500Y. Doncaster Premier. Denis
Coakley. The dam, a modest 6f winner, is a
half-sister to 4 winners including the Group 2
winner Aspectoflove. The second dam, Rose
Vibert (by Caerleon), is an unraced full or half-
sister to 6 winners. (Keeper's 12). "She's going
nicely and hopefully she'll be racing in early
May. A 2-y-o type even though she's a fairly
late foal, she's quite strong and she'll be ready
to go soon".

332. MON CIGAR (IRE) ★★★
b.c. Bushranger – Practicallyperfect (King
Charlemagne). April 24. Second foal. £26,000Y.
Doncaster Premier. Lofti Raissi. Half-brother
to the modest 2102 2-y-o 7f winner Beau
Select (by Lucky Story). The dam, a fair 7f
at 2 yrs and 1m winner, is a half-sister to 2
winners including the dam of the Group 1
Golden Jubilee Stakes winner Art Connoisseur.
The second dam, Morningsurprice (by Future
Storm), is an unraced half-sister to 5 winners
including the dam of the dual Group 1 winner
Balanchine. (Mr L Raissi). "A fairly late foal, he's
quite backward and won't be running until the
second half of the season, probably over seven
furlongs".

333. MONSIEUR BLANC (IRE) ★★★
ch.c. Kheleyf – Sley (Lomitas). January 10. First
foal. £10,000Y. Doncaster Premier. Longways
Stables. The dam is an unplaced sister to the
listed Oaks Trial winner Santa Sophia and
a half-sister to several winners. The second

dam, Samara (by Polish Patriot), a winner of
two listed events over 1m and 8.5f, was third
in the Group 3 Park Stakes and is a half-sister
to 8 winners including the German Group 2
winner Soto-Grande. (Mr L Raissi). "An early
foal, he should be out in early May. He goes
alright, he's a good, strong, 2-y-o type and he's
working well so we should be able to pick up a
race with him".

334. PRINCESS HANANE (IRE) ★★★
gr.f. Clodovil – Golden Ora (Nordance). January
10. Third foal. £15,000Y. Doncaster Premier.
Lofti Raissi. Half-sister to the unplaced 2012
2-y-o Mujadora (by Mujadil) and to a minor
winner in Russia by Titus Livius. The dam won
6 minor races at 3 to 5 yrs in Italy and is a half-
sister to 3 winners including the dual Group 3
winner and Grade 1 placed Golden Titus. The
second dam, Oraplata (by Silver Hawk), was
placed at 4 yrs in the USA and is a half-sister
to 9 winners including the Grade 1 Blue Grass
Stakes winner Taylor's Special. (Mr L Raissi). "A
nice filly that goes well, hopefully she'll start off
at the end of May over six furlongs. She moves
well, she's not over-big but big enough and
we're happy with her".

335. SKANDER ★★★
b.c. Archipenko – Midnight Allure (Aragon).
February 17. £16,000Y. Doncaster Premier.
Lofti Raissi. Half-brother to the quite useful
1m, 9f and jumps winner Country Escape (by
Zafonic), to the quite useful 2-y-o 5f winner
Midnight Tycoon (by Marju) to the fair 7f
winner Sand Owl (by Dubawi), the fair 2-y-o
5f winner Twilight Allure (by Shamardal) and
a winner over hurdles by Dr Fong. The dam, a
quite useful dual 1m winner, is a sister to the
smart Group 3 Flying Five and listed 5f winner
Midnight Escape. The second dam, Executive
Lady (by Night Shift), was placed 3 times at up
to 7f. (Mr L Raissi). "A good-looking horse and
a good mover, he'll run towards the end of May
over six furlongs and he wants good ground".
TRAINERS' BARGAIN BUY

PAUL COLE
336. CAFETIERE
b.f. Iffraaj – Coffee Cream (Common Grounds).
March 14. Seventh foal. Half-sister to the fair
2012 2-y-o 6f winner French Press, to the

2-y-o Group 3 Prix du Bois winner and Group 2 Prix Robert Papin second Percolator (both by Kheleyf), the moderate 7f winner Carte Noire (by Revoque) and the moderate 6f and 7f winner of 6 races Mocha Java (by Bertolini). The dam was a quite useful 7f (at 2 yrs) and 1m winner. The second dam, Sugar Town (by Tate Gallery), a modest 7f (at 2 yrs) and 10f winner, is a half-sister to 3 winners including the listed winner La Vie En Primrose and the dam of the 2,000 Guineas second Even Top. (A H Robinson).

337. CAPE ARROW

b.c. Cape Cross – Aiming (Highest Honor). May 6. Fifth foal. 48,000Y. Tattersalls October Book 2. Oliver Cole. Half-brother to the useful 6f (at 2 yrs) to 9f winner of 5 races and listed-placed Easy Option (by Danehill Dancer), to the quite useful 2-y-o 7f winner La Adelita (by Anabaa) and the fair 2-y-o 7f winner Conducting (by Oratorio). The dam was placed over 7f (at 2 yrs) and 1m and is a half-sister to 5 winners including the very smart dual listed 5f winner Watching. The second dam, Sweeping (by Indian King), a useful 2-y-o 6f winner, is a half-sister to 10 winners. (C Shiacolas).

338. COMPLICIT (IRE)

b.c. Captain Rio – Molomo (Barathea). May 4. Seventh foal. 21,000Y. Tattersalls October Book 2. Oliver Cole. Half-brother to the Group 3 7f Jersey Stakes winner and dual Group 1 third Rainfall (by Oasis Dream) and to the quite useful 2-y-o 7f winner Onida (by Noverre). The dam, an Irish 12f winner and second in both the Group 2 10f Pretty Polly Stakes and the Group 2 10f Royal Whip Stakes, is a sister to the Irish 1m and 9f winner and listed-placed Pepperwood and a half-sister to 3 winners. The second dam, Nishan (by Nashwan), is a placed half-sister to 3 winners including the Group 3 Prix de Sandringham winner and good broodmare Orford Ness.

339. DASHED (IRE)

ch.c. Iffraaj – Up On Points (Royal Academy). March 20. Sixth foal. 20,000Y. Tattersalls October Book 2. P Cole. Half-brother to the fair dual 6f winner (including at 2 yrs) Buckie Massa (by Best Of The Bests), to the 2-y-o 5f winners Key Lago (by Kheleyf) and Stand And

Fight (by Invincible Spirit) and the fair 2-y-o 7f winner Zafantage (by Zafonic). The dam, a useful 2-y-o 7f winner, is a half-sister to 4 winners abroad. The second dam, Champagne 'n Roses (by Chief Singer), won once at 4 yrs and is a half-sister to 3 winners including the Group 3 Nell Gwyn Stakes winner Thrilling Day.

340. FORT BERKLEY (IRE)

b.c. Fastnet Rock – Verbania (In The Wings). April 5. Seventh foal. 35,000Y. Tattersalls October Book 2. P Cole. Half-brother to the quite useful 2-y-o 7f winner Kalahaag (by Iffraaj), to the quite useful 11f winner Tiger Cliff (by Tiger Hill), the fair 12f winner Summerlea (by Alhaarth) and a 2-y-o winner abroad by Bertolini. The dam, an Irish 10f winner, is a half-sister to the useful 2-y-o 5.5f winner Pescara and to the useful French listed 10.8f winner Mistra (herself dam of the Group 1 Prix Saint-Alary winner Marotta). The second dam, Mackla (by Caerleon), won the Group 3 1m Prix d'Aumale and is a half-sister to 6 winners.

341. GRECIAN (IRE)

gr.c. Dark Angel – Law Review (Case Law). May 3. Ninth foal. €50,000Y. Goffs Orby. Stephen Hillen. Brother to the promising 2012 2-y-o 6f winner Integrity and half-brother to the useful 6f (at 2 yrs) and 9f winner Layazaal (by Mujadil), to the fairly useful 5f (at 2 yrs) and 6f winner of 5 races Falasteen, the quite useful 2-y-o 5f and 6f winner Latin Review and the quite useful 6f to 1m winner of 7 races Opus Maximus (all by Titus Livius). The dam was placed once over 1m and is a half-sister to 10 winners including the Group 1 July Cup winner and sire Lake Coniston. The second dam, Persian Polly (by Persian Bold), a useful Irish 2-y-o 7f winner, was third in the Group 3 Park Stakes and is a half-sister to 2 winners. (Mrs F H Hay).

342. POLISH BALLET

b.c. Iffraaj – Madam Ninette (Mark Of Esteem). March 1. Seventh foal. 48,000Y. Tattersalls October Book 2. Hugo Merry. Half-brother to the quite useful 2012 2-y-o 6f winner Blessington (by Kheleyf), to the useful dual 5f (at 2 yrs) and 3-y-o listed 5f winner Excelette (by Exceed And Excel) and the modest 9f to 12f winner of 4 races Waahej (by Haafhd). The dam is an unraced half-sister to 9 winners including the very smart King's Stand Stakes and Temple Stakes winner Bolshoi and the useful sprinters Mariinsky, Great Chaddington and Tod. The second dam, Mainly Dry (by The Brianstan), is an unraced half-sister to 4 winners. (Mrs F H Hay).

TOBY COLES

343. LA GRASSETTA (GER) ★★

b.f. Nayef – La Reine Noir (Rainbow Quest). February 12. First foal. The dam is an unraced half-sister to 4 winners including the Group 1 Prix de l'Opera and dual Group 3 winner Lady Marian (by Nayef) and the German Group 3 winner Lucidor. The second dam, La Felicita (by Shareef Dancer), a listed-placed winner in Germany, is a half-sister to 4 winners. (Far Yard Racing Club). *"She was born with one eye, so she takes a bit longer to learn than the others. She hasn't shown me much yet but I do get the feeling that there's something there. She's not particularly big, so I wouldn't right her off as a 2-y-o".*

344. MOONSPRING ★★

gr.f. Aussie Rules – Unintentional (Dr Devious). March 23. Fourth foal. 9,000Y. Tattersalls October Book 2. Tobias Coles Racing. Half-sister to the moderate 6f winner Mushy Peas (by Bahri) and to a minor 4-y-o winner in Canada by Refuse To Bend. The dam, placed once in a 9f seller at 2 yrs, is a half-sister to 4 winners including the Group 2 Prix Hocquart winner Coroner. The second dam, Tamnia (by Green Desert), a useful 2-y-o winner of the listed 7f Milcars Star Stakes, was second in the Group 1 7f Moyglare Stud Stakes and is a half-sister to 7 winners including the very useful Group 2 13.3f Geoffrey Freer Stakes winner Azzilfi and the very useful Group 3 15f Coppa d'Oro di Milano winner Khamaseen. (Paul Foster & Friends). *"She had a small setback at the start of the year but she's coming sound now. She did one piece of work and showed me enough in it to tell me we'll have to take our time. She'll make a 2-y-o and she'll be OK although I'm not saying she'll be a world beater".*

345. ORTON PARK (IRE) ★★★★

b.f. Moss Vale – Notley Park (Wolfhound). March 18. £19,000Y. Doncaster Premier. McKeever Bloodstock. Sister to the fair 2012 2-y-o dual 5f winner Tharawal Lady and half-sister to the useful 6f winner of 11 races Knot In Wood (by Shinko Forest), to the quite useful dual 6f winner Namwahjobo (by Namid), the fair 5f winner of 4 races (including at 2 yrs) Alugat (by Tagula), the fair 6f winner Mandelieu (by Acclamation) and the modest 7f winner Mulan Princess (by Mukaddamah). The dam, placed three times over 7f at 3yrs, is a half-sister to 5 winners including the US Grade 3 winner Prince Bobby B and the listed 5f Scarborough Stakes winner Notley. The second dam, Riviere Bleue (by Riverman), won over 11f and is a half-sister to the US Grade 2 and Group 3 Child Stakes winner Star Pastures. (The Orton Park Partnership). *"She'll have started her career before your book is published and she has a very good turn of foot. Not particularly small, she showed a bit of speed early on and she's very professional. I think she's likely to win early in the season and then progress into the mid-summer".* This filly won on her debut in April. TRAINERS' BARGAIN BUY

346. RESIST ★★★

b.f. Rock Of Gibraltar – Cecily (Oasis Dream). March 2. First foal. The dam, quite useful 5f (at 2 yrs) and 6f winner, is a half-sister to 5 winners including the Group 3 6f Firth Of Clyde Stakes winner and Group 2 Rockfel Stakes second Violette, the useful 2-y-o 5f and 6f winner and Group 3 placed Virginia Hall and the listed 6f (at 2 yrs) and Group 3 7f Nell Gwyn Stakes winner Silca's Gift. The second dam, Odette (by Pursuit Of Love), a fair 3-y-o 5f and 5.7f winner, is a half-sister to 4 winners including the useful 6f (at 2 yrs) and 7f winner and Group 2 5f Flying Childers Stakes fourth Caballero. (Mr C G Rowles-Nicholson). *"She's quite small and she has the same sort of attitude as her dam's half-sister Violette – I was at Sir Mark Prescott's when she was trained there. She's a little bit lazy and doesn't pay much attention until you ask her to do that little bit of faster work. With all the bad weather we've had I haven't able to do much of that because she hasn't lost her coat at all. She will be a 2-y-o and I would have thought she'd be out in late April or early May.*

347. UNNAMED ★★

b.f. *Lemon Drop Kid – Nafisah (Lahib)*. March 22. Seventh foal. 130,000Y. Tattersalls October Book 1. Andrew Balding. Closely related to the useful UAE Group 3 1m winner of 5 races Snaafy (by Kingmambo) and half-sister to a hurdles winner by Elusive Quality and a minor winner in the USA by Distorted Humor. The dam, a very useful 7f (at 2 yrs), 9f and listed 10f winner, was second in the Group 2 Ribblesdale Stakes and is a half-sister to 8 winners including the Irish 12f listed and hurdles winner Mutakarrim. The second dam, Alyakkh (by Sadler's Wells), a fair 3-y-o 1m winner, is a full or half-sister to 7 winners including the Champion Stakes and 2,000 Guineas winner Haafhd. (Qatar Racing Ltd). *"A very expensive filly, I'm very lucky to get her. She's not particularly forward and is more of a backward type, but saying that I would hope to be able to run her in August/September time, rather than late in the year. She's grown in the last month and blossomed a fair bit, but she still has some developing to do so I won't be pressing on with her for a while yet".*

348. UNNAMED ★★

ch.c. *Hernando – Ryella (Cozzene)*. February 18. Third foal. 29,000Y. Tattersalls October Book 2. McKeever Bloodstock. Half-brother to a winner in Russia by Awesome Again. The dam, a minor 3-y-o winner in Canada, is a half-sister to 6 winners including the dual Grade 3 winner Raylene. The second dam, Petite Princess (by Dayjur), a dual 2-y-o winner in Ireland and Group 3 placed, is a half-sister to 5 winners including the dual Group 1 winner Ad Valorem. *"A smart colt, he's big but at the same time he's very 'together'. He showed plenty during the early stages of his training but we backed off him because of the weather and because he is so big. So I've had to slow down with him even though he could have easily gone faster".*

ROBERT COWELL

349. SPEED HAWK (USA) ★★★★

b.br.c. *Henny Hughes – Cosmic Wing (Halo)*. March 23. Tenth foal. $55,000Y. Keeneland

September. F Barberini. Brother to a winner in Japan and half-brother to 4 minor winners. The dam, a stakes-placed winner of 2 races in the USA, is a half-sister to the US stakes winner and Grade 3 placed Charlie Tango and to the dam of the US Grade 2 winner Tizaqueena. The second dam, Ziggy's Act (by Danzig), won the Grade 3 Pucker Up Stakes in the USA. (K A Dasmal). *"He's lovely, the sharpest of my 2-y-o's and already doing some quite snazzy pieces of work. He'll be a five/six furlong 2-y-o from May onwards and he looks like a dragster with his big and burly behind. He's got speed written all over him and he'll be aimed at Royal Ascot if he proves good enough".*

350. UNNAMED ★★★

b.c. *Kyllachy – Fondled (Selkirk)*. February 11. Second foal. 42,000Y. Tattersalls December. Global Equine Group. The dam, a quite useful dual 1m winner, is a half-sister to 4 winners including the fairly useful 7f to 9f winner Tartan Gunna. The second dam, Embraced (by Pursuit Of Love), a useful listed 1m winner, is a half-sister to 6 winners on the flat including the Group 2 Summer Mile winner Cesare and the Group 3 12f Prix la Force winner and French Derby second Nowhere To Exit and to the Grade 2 winning hurdler Trenchant. *"He's a strong, stocky individual. We bought him with his 2-y-o career in mind and the sire is a very good source of 2-y-o's. He did his second piece of work this morning and he's going the right way. I wouldn't say he'd be a five furlong speedster but he's got the body to be a 2-y-o and he'll make his mark this year from the mid-season onwards".*

351. UNNAMED ★★

ch.c. *Teofilo – Neat Shilling (Bob Back)*. April 23. Eighth foal. 68,000Y. Tattersalls December. Global Equine Group. Brother to the 2012 7f and 1m placed 2-y-o Nickels And Dimes and half-brother to the listed winner and UAE Group 2 placed Kalahari Gold (by Trans Island), to the quite useful 7f (at 2 yrs) to 10f and hurdles winner of 8 races Mr Jack Daniells, the fair 6f (at 2 yrs) to 1 winner of 5 races Tidy (both by Mujadil) and the moderate 5f winner Staceymac (by Elnadim). The dam is an unraced sister to the Irish 7f (at 2 yrs) and 10f winner and Group 3 placed Fill The Bill and a half-sister to 6 winners including the US Grade 3 winner Riddlesdown. The second dam, Neat Dish (by Stalwart), won once over 6f at 2 yrs in Ireland, was second in the Group 3 Railway Stakes and is a half-sister to 9 winners including the US stakes winner and Grade 1 placed Western Winter. *"A lovely horse, he's only cantering at the moment and he'll be one for the mid to back-end of the season. He doesn't look backward because he's all there, but we're going to give him time because he's got more size than my other 2-y-o's".*

352. UNNAMED ★★★
ch.f. Langfuhr – Tres Chaud (French Deputy). January 17. Fifth foal. $33,000Y. Fasig-Tipton Kentucky Fall. F Barberini. Half-sister to 2 minor winners in North America by D'Wildcat and Unbridled's Image. The dam won two minor races at 4 yrs in the USA and is a half-sister to 3 other minor winners. The second dam, Improper Princess (by Wild Again), a US winner of 5 races, was stakes-placed and is a half-sister to 7 winners. (Mr T W Morley & Partners). *"She was bought with the hope that she might prove good enough to go to Royal Ascot. She's doing some work at the moment, she looks forward and is a nice, attractive, early filly that almost looks like a colt. She should be out before the end of May".*

TONY COYLE
353. BARBARA ELIZABETH ★★
b.f. Sir Percy – Fair View (Dashing Blade). April 15. Third foal. £2,200Y. Doncaster August. Tony Coyle. Half-sister to the unplaced 2012 2-y-o Halling's Wish (by Halling). The dam won in Germany and is a half-sister to 3 winners. The second dam, Fairy Tango (by Acatenango), won at 3 yrs in Germany and is a half-sister to 7 winners there. (M A O'Donnell). *"Not overly big, but she's a lovely filly and as tough as old boots. I got her cheap because I think she was in the wrong sale but she'll be ready to go as soon as the seven furlong races start".*

354. IRONDALE EXPRESS ★★ ♠
b.f. Myboycharlie – Olindera (Lomitas). March 22. Fourth foal. £6,000Y. Doncaster Festival. Not sold. Half-sister to a winner in Switzerland by Big Shuffle. The dam won at 2 yrs in

Germany and is a half-sister to 4 winners there. The second dam, Olinderry (by Try My Best), won 10 races in the USA and was listed-placed and is a half-sister to 8 winners. (W P Flynn). *"A six/seven furlong filly, she was a bit awkward to break but we'll kick on with her now and she'll be running in May".*

355. LILY RULES ★★★★
br.f. Aussie Rules – Causeway Charm (Giant's Causeway). February 23. Second foal. 8,500Y. Tattersalls October Book 3. PGF Stud. The dam is an unplaced half-sister to 5 winners the US and German listed winner Can Chan. The second dam, Candy Charm (by Capote), is an unraced half-sister to 6 winners. (C E Whiteley). *"Sharp and early, she's a nice filly that's ready to go. She'll be winning as a 2-y-o alright, she's a five furlong 2-y-o with plenty of boot".*

356. NEVADA BLUE ★★★★
ch.c. Pastoral Pursuits – Nevada Princess (Desert Prince). March 5. Third foal. £25,000Y. Doncaster Festival. Tony Coyle. The dam, a minor 3-y-o winner in France, is a half-sister to 8 winners including the smart 2-y-o Group 2 1m Royal Lodge Stakes winner Atlantis Prince and the dam of the Group 2 Richmond Stakes winner Prolific. The second dam, Zoom Lens (by Caerleon), placed once over 7f at 2 yrs, is a half-sister to 4 winners. *"A lovely horse, he goes really well and is the nicest we have. A smashing, strong colt, he's entered in the Sales races, we haven't rushed him but he'll be ready by the middle to end of May. Six furlongs is his trip, but the sire can get them a bit hot so we've took our time with him. We could run tomorrow if we wanted to, but we've left him alone. He was third highest price at the sale – he stood out and we wanted him!"*

357. UNNAMED ★★ ♠
b.f. Piccolo – Fizzy Treat (Efisio). March 6. Seventh foal. 20,000Y. Tattersalls October Book 3. Tony Coyle. Half-sister to the 2-y-o 6f winner (on his only start) Richmond Fontaine (by Pastoral Pursuits), to the fair 9f to 12f winner of 9 races Formidable Guest (by Dilshaan) and a winner in Greece by Kyllachy. The dam, a fair 5f and 6f winner at 4 yrs, is a sister to the useful 2-y-o 5f and 6f winner and

Group 3 placed Hoh Chi Min and a half-sister to 7 winners including the listed 7f winner Cragganmore and the dam of the Group 3 Molecomb Stakes winner Inya Lake. The second dam, Special Guest (by Be My Guest), a modest 2-y-o 7f winner, is a half-sister to 3 minor winners. *"A bit slow to come to hand, she kept growing on us and I don't think she'll be out until June, over five/six furlongs. She's a big filly and she'll tell us when she's ready".*

LUCA CUMANI

358. BACK TO BUXTED (IRE) ★★★

b.c. Aqlaam – Incoming Call (Red Ransom). March 19. Third foal. 72,000Y. Tattersalls October Book 2. Charlie Gordon-Watson. Half-brother to Missed Call (by Authorized), unplaced in one start at 2 yrs in 2012. The dam, placed third over 7f at 3 yrs on her only start, is a half-sister to 4 winners including the French Group 3 10.5f winner Dance Dress (herself dam of the US Grade 2 winner Costume). The second dam, Private Line (by Private Account), a useful 7f (at 2 yrs) and listed 1m winner, is a half-sister to 8 winners including the 2-y-o listed 1m winner and Group 1 placed Most Precious (the dam of four stakes winners including the French 1,000 Guineas winner Matiara). (Buxted Partnership). *"A very likeable colt, he's strong, well put-together and should be out around July time. We don't know much about the sire but I presume this will be a six/seven furlong 2-y-o".*

359. BRACKEN ★★

gr.c. Dubawi – Belle Reine (King Of Kings). March 11. Fifth living foal. 100,000Y. Tattersalls October Book 1. John Warren. Half-brother to the fair 2012 6f placed 2-y-o Secret Beau (by Sakhee's Secret), to the fairly useful 5f and 6f winner Ishbelle (by Invincible Spirit), the fairly useful 1m (including at 2 yrs) to 12f winner Layline (by King's Best) and the quite useful 6f (at 2 yrs) and 7f winner Belle Des Airs (by Dr Fong). The dam is a half-sister to the very useful 1m winner of 4 races and subsequent Scandinavian listed winner Smart Enough and to the useful listed 6f winner Oasis Dancer. The second dam, Good Enough (by Mukaddamah), won once at 3 yrs in the USA and was third in the Group 1 Prix Saint-Alary and is a half-sister to 5 winners including

the Group 3 Molecomb Stakes winner Classic Ruler. (Sheikh Mohammed Obaid Al Maktoum). *"He's a big horse so not necessarily a 2-y-o, but he could possibly be running from August onwards. Much more of a 3-y-o type really".*

360. COMEDY KING (IRE) ★★★★

b.br.c. Dansili – Comic (Be My Chief). April 18. Ninth foal. 90,000Y. Tattersalls October Book 1. John Warren. Brother to the useful 1m, listed 11f and US Grade 3 winner Laughing and half-brother to Viva Pataca (by Marju), a winner of 5 races here at 2 yrs from 7f to 9f including a listed event prior to winning the Grade 1 Queen Elizabeth II Cup in Hong Kong (twice) and £5.9 million, to the quite useful 10f to 14f and hurdles winner Comedy Act (by Motivator) and the moderate 15f and hurdles winner Circus Clown (by Vettori). The dam, a quite useful 10f and 11.5f winner, is a half-sister to 4 winners including the 2-y-o Group 3 Solario Stakes and multiple US Grade 2 winner Brave Act. The second dam, Circus Act (by Shirley Heights), is an unraced sister to the listed 10f Lupe Stakes winner Lady Shipley and a half-sister to 6 winners including the listed 10f Upavon Stakes winner Ellie Ardensky and the dam of the Australian triple Group 1 winner Serenade Rose. (Sheikh Mohammed Obaid Al Maktoum). *"A nice horse, he's well put-together and he moves well. He's fairly forward too, especially for a Dansili and for one of my 2-y-o's! He could be one to start off around July time over seven furlongs".*

361. CONNECTICUT ★★★★★

b.c. New Approach – Craigmill (Slip Anchor). February 4. 110,000Y. Tattersalls October Book 1. Charlie Gordon-Watson. Half-brother to the smart 1m winner and listed-placed Castleton, the fairly useful dual 10f winner Craigstown (both by Cape Cross), the German listed winner and Group 3 placed Fleurie Domaine (by Unfuwain), the fairly useful 12f and 2m winner Astyanax (by Hector Protector), the quite useful 2-y-o 1m winner Stirling Castle (by Dubai Destination), the quite useful 10.5f winner Heather Mix (by Linamix), the quite useful 9.5f winner Oscillator (by Pivotal), the fair 1m and 10f winner Certral (by Iffraaj), the modest 6f and 7f winner Represent (by Exceed

And Excel) and the German 2-y-o winner Global Champion (by Elnadim). The dam, a fair 2-y-o 7f winner, is a half-sister to 6 winners including the Group 3 Park Hill Stakes winner Coigach and the Park Hill Stakes second and smart broodmare Applecross. The second dam, Rynechra (by Blakeney), was a useful 12f winner and a half-sister to 6 winners. (Sheikh Mohammed Obaid Al Maktoum). *"I like him. He looked to be a like a backward horse at the sales but he's actually much more forward than that. He's developing really nicely and quickly, so I wouldn't be surprised if he was out by August, probably over seven furlongs. A five star horse – but whether that'll be this year as well as next I couldn't say at this point!"*

362. CROSS COUNTRY (IRE) ★★

b.c. Cape Cross – Altruiste (Diesis). April 20. Sixth foal. €320,000Y. Goffs Orby. John Warren. Brother to the quite useful 10f, 15f and hurdles winner Maxim Gorky and half-brother to the listed 12f winner Alpine Snow (by Verglas). The dam is an unraced half-sister to the 2,000 Guineas winner King's Best, to the Arc winner Urban Sea (the dam Galileo, Sea The Stars, Black Sam Bellamy and the US Grade 1 My Typhoon) and the Group 3 winner Allez Les Trois (dam of the French Derby winner Anabaa Blue). The second dam, Allegretta (by Lombard), a useful 2-y-o 1m and 9f winner and second in the Lingfield Oaks Trial, is a sister to the German St Leger winner Anno. (Sheikh Mohammed Obaid Al Maktoum). *"He was a nice yearling, he's very well-bred on the female side and he's nice but I can't say anything more than that. He won't be early and it's a bit too soon for me to say how good he's likely to be".*

363. DON'T ★★★

b.f. Invincible Spirit – Frigid (Indian Ridge). May 12. Third foal. Half-sister to the fair 2-y-o 5f winner Impassive (by Choisir). The dam ran once unplaced and is a half-sister to several winners including the Canadian Grade 2 winner Forte Dei Marmi and the very useful 12f and listed 14f winner Savarain. The second dam, Frangy (by Sadler's Wells), a fair dual 12f winner, is a full or half-sister to 8 winners including the German 1m to 9.5f winner of

7 races and listed-placed Flying Heights. (Fittocks Stud Ltd). *"Possibly the best named filly in the yard! She's nice – and probably the nicest the mare has had so far. Being an Invincible Spirit she should run and do well as a 2-y-o, even though the family tends to get better with age. I wouldn't be surprised if she was to start off at six furlongs in July. She was a late foal but that doesn't seem to affect her because she's quite a well-grown sort".*

364. JOYS OF SPRING (IRE) ★★★★

b.f. Invincible Spirit – Sonachan (Darshaan). March 13. Fifth foal. 320,000Y. Tattersalls October Book 1. Charlie Gordon-Watson. Half-sister to the Group 3 7f Sweet Solera Stakes winner Albabilia (by King's Best) and to the quite useful 2-y-o 1m and subsequent US winner Brainy Benny (by Barathea). The dam, a minor Irish 14f winner, is a half-sister to the listed 1m Brownstown Stud Stakes and US stakes winner Inchacooley. The second dam, Blue Cashmere (by Secreto), is an unraced half-sister to 10 winners including the US Grade 2 placed Receiver and Phone Bird. (Sheikh Mohammed Obaid Al Maktoum). *"A really nice filly, but she's more of a Darshaan than an Invincible Spirit, so she's got a lot of scope. I think she'll be nice one day and we'll hopefully get her out over seven furlongs or a mile towards the back-end".*

365. KINSHASA ★★★★

b.c. Pivotal – Kibara (Sadler's Wells). April 26. Fourth foal. 85,000Y. Tattersalls October Book 2. Not sold. Half-brother to the fair 2012 2-y-o 1m winner Kikonga (by Danehill Dancer) and to the quite useful 12f winner Kiwayu (by Medicean). The dam, a fair 11f winner, is a sister to 4 winners including the St Leger and Great Voltigeur Stakes winner Milan and half-sister to the Irish 2-y-o 7f winner and Group 2 Great Voltigeur Stakes third Go For Gold. The second dam, Kithanga (by Darshaan), was a smart winner of 3 races including the Group 3 12f St Simon Stakes and the listed 12f Galtres Stakes. (Fittocks Stud Ltd). *"Really nice, he's doing very well but Pivotal's are not renowned for being 2-y-o's and the female line is the same. It would be good if he could win as a 2-y-o and progress as a 3-y-o. An even better specimen than the dam's 2-y-o of last year*

Kikonga, he'll be worth waiting for, even if we have to wait until next year".

366. LAWYER (IRE) ★★★★

b.c. *Acclamation – Charaig (Rainbow Quest).* March 27. Third foal. 110,000Y. Tattersalls October Book 1. Charlie Gordon-Watson. Half-brother to the fair 2012 2-y-o 7f winner Empiricist (by Holy Roman Emperor). The dam ran once unplaced and is a half-sister to 2 minor winners. The second dam, Chesnut Bird (by Storm Bird), a dual listed 10f winner, is a half-sister to 4 winners including the French Group 3 winner and Group 2 placed Caesarion. (Sheikh Mohammed Obaid Al Maktoum). *"He's very nice, a typical Acclamation, well put-together and strong, so he could be one of the earlier 2-y-o's from the yard. I can see him being out in June/July but he has Rainbow Quest as a damsire so he won't necessarily be a six furlong horse, even if we start him at that trip".*

367. LA FAISAN BLANCHE (USA) ★★★

gr.f. *Exchange Rate – Tjinouska (Cozzene).* Half-sister to the fairly useful 2-y-o 7f and 1m winner and subsequent US Grade 2 placed In The Slips (by More Than Ready), to the fair 10f winner Straits Of Hormuz (by War Chant) and the fair 2-y-o 7f winner Delta Diva (by Victory Gallop). The dam, a quite useful 12f winner, is a half-sister to several winners including the useful 2-y-o 6f winner and Group 1 Moyglare Stud Stakes third Pearl Dance. The second dam, Ocean Jewel (by Alleged), was unraced. (Mr C Wright). *"She's only just arrived but I saw her about two months ago when she was in pre-training and she looked nice. The sire is doing very well in Europe so I should think this filly is worth putting in the book".*

368. LUNASEA (IRE) ★★★

b.c. *Sea The Stars – Musical Treat (Royal Academy).* April 11. Eighth living foal. 500,000Y. Tattersalls October Book 1. McCalmont Bloodstock. Half-brother to the Prix Marcel Boussac, 1,000 Guineas and Irish 1,000 Guineas winner Finsceal Beo (by Mr Greeley), to the Group 2 German 2,000 Guineas winner Frozen Power (by Oasis Dream), the fairly useful 2-y-o 6f winner and listed-placed Zabeel Park (by Medicean),

the quite useful 7f winner and listed placed Musical Bar (by Barathea) and a 3-y-o winner abroad by Red Ransom. The dam, a useful 3-y-o 7f winner and listed-placed twice, subsequently won in the USA and is a half-sister to 6 winners. The second dam, Mountain Ash (by Dominion), won 10 races here and in Italy including the Group 3 Premio Royal Mares and is a half-sister to 7 winners. (Jon S Kelly). *"Very nice, but he's a very scopey horse and wouldn't be an early type at all. He's the type to have one or two runs at the back-end and have a 3-y-o career. He's big but he's well put-together and you can see he's going to develop and progress with time. He'll be a very nice 3-y-o".*

369. MADAME CLOUSEAU (IRE) ★★★

b.f. *Galileo – Healing Music (Bering).* March 24. 145,000foal. Tattersalls December. Jamie McCalmont. Sister to the useful Irish 2-y-o 1m winner and Epsom Derby second At First Sight and closely related to the quite useful 11f winner Kuda Huraa (by Montjeu). The dam, a French listed-placed 2-y-o winner, is a half-sister to 8 winners including the US Grade 2 winner Herboriste and the French listed winner and subsequent Grade 1 Hollywood Derby second Fast And Furious. The second dam, Helvellyn (by Gone West), a quite useful 8.3f winner, is a half-sister to 6 winners. (Jon S Kelly). *"A nice filly, not necessarily a 2-y-o type and we're unlikely to see her until the autumn".*

370. MIZZOU (IRE) ★★★

b.c. *Galileo – Moments Of Joy (Darshaan).* March 28. Fifth foal. 275,000Y. Tattersalls October Book 1. McCalmont Bloodstock. Brother to the Irish 2-y-o 7f winner and Group 3 Give Thanks Stakes third Eternal Beauty and closely related to the 12f winner and dual Group 3 12f third Unity (by Sadler's Wells). The dam, a smart 12f and listed 14f winner, is a half-sister to 4 winners. The second dam, My Emma (by Marju), a smart winner of the Group 1 12f Prix Vermeille, is a half-sister to 6 winners including the Group 1 St Leger and Group 1 Ascot Gold Cup winner Classic Cliché. (Jon S Kelly). *"The pedigree indicates he'll be more of a 3-y-o type than 2-y-o and he's quite a scopey, lengthy horse that covers a lot of ground. He carries himself well and he's a nice colt that could be anything, but we won't see him out until later in the season".*

371. MOUNT LOGAN (IRE) ★★★★

ch.c. New Approach – Vistaria (Distant View). April 30. Second foal. €135,000Y. Goffs Orby. Charlie Gordon-Watson. The dam ran once unplaced and is a sister to the top-class Group 1 1m Queen Elizabeth II Stakes and Group 1 9.3f Prix d'Ispahan winner Observatory and a half-sister to 7 winners including High Praise (Group 2 Prix de Malleret) and the dam of the Group 3 Gordon Stakes winner Rebel Soldier. The second dam, Stellaria (by Roberto), won from 5f to 8.5f including the listed 6f Rose Bowl Stakes and is a half-sister to 8 winners. (Sheikh Mohammed Obaid Al Maktoum). *"He's really nice – I like him a lot. I've got two colts by New Approach that I like very much. This is a horse that doesn't look particularly precocious but he has a very easy way of going and seems to have natural talent, even though he hasn't got the strength yet. He'll make a 2-y-o by mid-season over seven furlongs".*

372. PATTERNED ★★

b.f. Dansili – Paisley (Pivotal). April 2. First foal. The dam, a fair 10f winner, is a half-brother to the quite useful 2-y-o 1m winner and listed-placed Poplin. The second dam, Pongee (by Barathea), a very useful Group 2 12f Lancashire Oaks winner, is closely related to the smart listed 12f and listed 14f winner Lion Sands and to the very useful 10f (at 2 yrs) and 11f winner and listed-placed Pukka and a half-sister to 2 winners. (Fittocks Stud Ltd). *"She's a nice filly, but it's a mile and a half family so she'll take a bit of time I suspect. It would be nice if she could win a race as a 2-y-o but if she does it'll be in the autumn".*

373. PICK POCKET ★★★

b.c. Dansili – Quelle Vitesse (Sadler's Wells). February 18. First foal. 320,000Y. Tattersalls October Book 1. McCalmont Bloodstock. The dam, a minor French 3-y-o winner, is a sister to the 2-y-o Group 2 7f Debutante Stakes winner Silk And Scarlet (herself the dam of two stakes winners including the UAE Group 1 winner Master Of Hounds) and a half-sister to 2 winners including the Group 3 6f Prix de Seine-et-Oise winner Danger Over. The second

dam, Danilova (by Lyphard), is an unraced half-sister to the high-class middle-distance colt Sanglamore - winner of the French Derby and the 9.3f Prix d'Ispahan – and the very useful listed 10f winner Opera Score. (Jon S Kelly). *"A well put-together horse, but he doesn't strike me as being a particularly early sort and the dam being by Sadler's Wells doesn't indicate precocity. One that will be campaigned with his 3-y-o career in mind, but he might well do something towards the end of this season".*

374. POSTPONED ★★★★

b.c. Dubawi – Ever Rigg (Dubai Destination). April 4. Second foal. 360,000Y. Tattersalls October Book 1. Charlie Gordon-Watson. Half-brother to the fair 2012 7f and 1m placed 2-y-o Neamour (by Oasis Dream). The dam, a fair 12f winner, is a half-sister 3 winners including the Irish 2-y-o 7f winner and listed placed Pietra Dura (herself dam of the US Grade 3 winner and Grade 1 second Turning Top). The second dam, Bianca Nera (by Salse), a smart 2-y-o winner of the Group 1 7f Moyglare Stud Stakes and the Group 2 6f Lowther Stakes, is half-sister to 4 winners including the very useful Group 1 Moyglare Stud Stakes second Hotelgenie Dot Com (herself dam of the dual Group 1 winner Simply Perfect). (Sheikh Mohammed Obaid Al Maktoum). *"He's a nice colt and he could be earlier than the other Dubawi's we've got. He should be strong enough to make a July type 2-y-o, probably starting at seven furlongs".*

375. ROSEBURG (IRE) ★★

ch.c. Tamayuz – Raydaniya (In The Wings). February 16. Sixth living foal. €48,000Y. Goffs Orby. Charlie Gordon-Watson. Half-brother to the listed 12f winner Raydiya (by Marju) and to the quite useful 10f, 12f and 14f winner O Ma Lad (by Redback). The dam was placed over 12f in Ireland and is a half-sister to 5 winners including the useful listed 12f winner Rafayda. The second dam, Rayseka (by Dancing Brave), won the Group 3 Royal Whip Stakes and was second in the Group 1 Irish St Leger and is a half-sister to 5 winners. (Sheikh Mohammed Obaid Al Maktoum). *"The female line is from one of the Aga Khan's families which indicates improvement with time and distance. We don't know much about the sire, so we'll have to feel our way a bit, but perhaps he'll make a 2-y-o in the second half of the season".*

376. TAP YOUR TOES (IRE) ★★★★

b.c. Danehill Dancer – Sharplaw Star (Xaar). March 30. Third foal. 160,000Y. Tattersalls October Book 1. McCalmont Bloodstock. Half-brother to Meeting In Paris (by Dutch Art), placed third over 6f from 2 starts at 2 yrs in 2012. The dam, a fairly useful 2-y-o dual 5f winner, was third in the Group 3 5f Queen Mary Stakes and is a half-sister to 2 winners. The second dam, Hamsah (by Green Desert), a quite useful 2-y-o dual 5f winner, was listed-placed and is a half-sister to the Irish 2,000 Guineas winner Wassl and to the dam of the Queen Mary Stakes winner On Tiptoes. (Jon S Kelly). *"He's quite precocious and strong, so I expect he'll make a 2-y-o from July onwards over seven furlongs. There is speed in his family, but he strikes me as being more of a seven furlong type than six".*

377. TRIPLE CHIEF (IRE) ★★

b.br.c. High Chaparral – Trebles (Kenmare). April 30. Tenth foal. 52,000Y. Tattersalls October Book 2. John Warren. Half-brother to two winners abroad by Titus Livius including the German Group 2 and dual Group 3 winner Sehrezad. The dam, a minor French 3-y-o winner, is a half-sister to 5 winners. The second dam, Doubles (by Damister), a listed-placed winner of 6 races in France, is a half-sister to 6 winners. (Mr S A Stuckey). *"A nice colt but he'll take time because he's a slight horse that needs to develop and strengthen. He should be racing over seven furlongs or a mile from August/ September onwards, then we'll look forward to his 3-y-o career".*

378. WISTAR ★★★

b.c. Dubawi – Vallota (Polish Precedent). April 20. Sixth foal. 260,000Y. Tattersalls October Book 1. John Warren. Half-brother to the Group 3 5f and listed 5f winner Ialysios (by So Factual). The dam is an unraced half-sister to 5 winners including the useful 6f (at 2 yrs) and 7f listed winner Epagris. The second dam, Trikymia (by Final Straw), was placed third over 5f at 2 yrs on her only outing and

is a half-sister to 9 winners including the Irish Derby winner Tyrnavos, the champion 2-y-o Tromos, the Coronation Stakes winner Tolmi and the Middle Park Stakes winner Tachypous. (Sheikh Mohammed Obaid Al Maktoum). *"A very nice, good-looking horse. He's big for a Dubawi, but he's well put-together and he'll make a 2-y-o from the mid-season onwards. He won't be a sprinter like his half-brother Ialysios, he's got more scope and will be at least a miler later on".*

379. ZAWIYAH ★★★★★

b.f. Invincible Spirit – Marika (Marju). April 2. Eighth foal. 90,000Y. Tattersalls October Book 1. Stuart Stuckey. Closely related to the French dual listed 6f winner Sabratah (by Oasis Dream) and half-sister to the quite useful 7f (including at 2 yrs) and 1m winner Folly Lodge (by Grand Lodge) and the minor Italian winner of 2 races at 3 and 4 yrs La Sibilla (by Fantastic Light). The dam, a useful 6f listed and 1m winner, is a half-sister to 8 winners including the Group 3 7.3f Fred Darling Stakes winner and Group 2 10f Nassau Stakes third Sueboog (herself dam of the Group 1 Prix d'Ispahan winner Best Of The Bests). The second dam, Nordica (by Northfields), a useful 6f and 1m winner, is a half-sister to 2 winners. (Mr S A Stuckey). *"A very nice filly, I like her a lot and she's quite forward. She should be out in June over six furlongs, she's quite likeable, quite precocious and well-developed".*

380. UNNAMED ★★★

ch.f. Smart Strike – Queen Of The Night (Sadler's Wells). March 14. The dam was placed over 10f on her only start and is a half-sister to Falbrav (a winner of eight Group/ Grade 1 races from 1m to 12f). The second dam, Gift Of The Night (by Slewpy), won over 7.5f in France at 2 yrs. (Mrs S Magnier). *"She's well-developed, very good-looking and strong. Obviously she's from a family I like, being out of a sister to Falbrav. She's quite big, still growing and developing, so I'd say she'll start at seven furlongs from July onwards".*

KEITH DALGLEISH

381. ROBYNELLE ★★★

b.f. Royal Applause – Chicita Banana (Danehill Dancer). February 25. First foal. £15,000Y.

Doncaster Premier. Not sold. The dam, a fair 2-y-o 5f winner, is a half-sister to 3 winners including the Group 2 Dante Stakes and Group 1 Criterium International third Bonfire and the Group 2 Windsor Forest Stakes and Group 3 Musidora Stakes winner Joviality. The second dam, Night Frolic (by Night Shift), a modest 1m winner, is a half-sister to 5 winners including the US Grade 3 Cardinal Handicap winner Miss Caerleona (herself dam of the Group winners Karen's Caper and Miss Coronado). (Mac Asphalt Ltd). *"She ran well on her debut and she'll come on a lot for it. She's probably capable of winning in the next few weeks over five furlongs but I think she'll be better when she steps up to six. She's quite athletic-looking and has a bit of length to her"*.

382. WEE FRANKIE (IRE) ★★

ch.c. Heliostatic – Kimono (Machiavellian). April 19. Ninth foal. £20,000Y. Doncaster Premier. O'Ryan/Dalgleish. Half-brother to the French and US listed winner Breviesca (by Peintre Celebre), to the quite useful 1m to 9f winner of 5 races Kinsya (by Mister Baileys), the fair Irish 10f winner Karma (by Fraam) and the moderate 1m winner Height Of Spirits (by Unfuwain). The dam ran twice unplaced and is a half-sister to 4 winners including the German listed winner Kiswahili. The second dam, Kiliniski (by Niniski), won the Group 3 Lingfield Oaks Trial and was second in the Group 1 Yorkshire Oaks and is a half-sister to 5 winners. (Lamont Racing). *"Quite a tall colt, he has a good attitude and he goes well considering he's more of a back-end 2-y-o over seven furlongs. Shows natural ability"*.

383. UNNAMED ★★

b.c. Archipenko – Flylowflylong (Danetime). April 30. Third foal. Half-brother to Secret Advice (by Sakhee's Secret), placed fourth once over 6f from two starts at 2 yrs in 2012 and to the quite useful 2-y-o 7f winner and 1m listed placed Sound Advice (by Echo Of Light). The dam, a fair 6f (at 2 yrs), 7f and 1m winner, is a sister to the fair 5f to 1m winner of 10 races Goodbye Cash. The second dam, Jellybean (by Petardia), a modest 2-y-o 9f winner, is a half-sister to 2 winners. (GLS Partnership). *"A nice horse, he's really come on during the last month but he has a bit of*

growing to do and we won't see him out before the autumn over seven furlongs. I trained the half-brother Sound Advice who won on his 2-y-o debut over seven furlongs but this is a different type both on looks and attitude. This colt is very straightforward"*.

384. UNNAMED ★★★

b.c. Iffraaj – Monarchy (Common Grounds). May 6. Tenth foal. £30,000Y. Doncaster Premier. O'Ryan/Dalgleish. Half-brother to the 2012 Irish 5f placed 2-y-o Red Queen (by Red Clubs), to the useful 2-y-o 5f winner and Group 2 5f Norfolk Stakes second Art Advisor, the modest 6f to 9f winner of 9 races Pipers Piping (both by Noverre), the modest 2-y-o 1m winner Queen's Gift (by Alzao), the minor Italian 3-y-o winner Mr Positano (by Foxhound) and a winner in Poland by Brave Act. The dam is an unplaced full or half-sister to 4 winners. The second dam, Royal Rumpus (by Prince Tenderfoot), is an unplaced half-sister to 6 winners including the Group 1 St James's Palace Stakes winner Second Set. (Weldspec Glasgow Ltd). *"I like him, he's grown quite a lot since I've had him so it'll be late summer before he's ready. He's going well now and I can only see him getting better. He'll probably start off at six furlongs and then we'll step him up to seven"*.

TOM DASCOMBE

385. AMADAFFAIR ★★

b.f. Amadeus Wolf – Italian Affair (Fumo Di Londra). March 30. Fifth foal. £3,000Y. Doncaster Festival. Not sold. Half-sister to the fair 6f and subsequent Norwegian Group 3 7f winner Chicken Momo (by Pyrus). The dam, a moderate dual 6f winner, including at 2 yrs, is out of the placed Sergentti (by Common Grounds), herself a half-sister to 2 minor winners. (The MHS 2013 Partnership). *"Sharp and early, this filly wasn't bought at the sales and was leased to us for one of our partnerships. I'd say she'll probably win a little race somewhere and she's hopefully one we'll be able to race a few times and have some fun with"*.

386. BETTY THE THIEF (IRE) ★★★

b.f. Teofilo – Siphon Melody (Siphon). March 24. Fourth foal. 20,000Y. Tattersalls October

Book 1. Sackville/Donald. Half-sister to the quite useful 1m and 10f winner Shamdarley (by Shamardal). The dam, a minor winner of 4 races at 3 and 4 yrs in the USA, is a half-sister to 10 winners including the US Grade 2 winner Talloires. The second dam, Logiciel (by Known Fact), a listed-placed winner of 4 races at 3 yrs in France, is a half-sister to 7 winners including the listed winner Frenetique (the dam of 3 stakes winners including the Grade 1 Gran Criterium winner Will Dancer). (Mr David Ward). *"A big filly, I thought she'd take time but actually she's coped with everything we've given her and had no problems, so we're just going to increase her work now and look towards getting her out in May. She's a tall, fine filly, so I'd say there's more to come".*

BOUNTY HUNTER ★★★★

387. b.c. Bahamian Bounty – Lindesberg (Doyoun). March 15. Ninth foal. €42,000Y. Tattersalls Ireland September. Sackville/Donald. Half-brother to the fairly useful 2-y-o Group 1 6f Phoenix Stakes second Amadeus Mozart (by Mozart), to the fair 6f winner and listed placed Madame Hoi (by Hawk Wing), the Irish 7f winner Dolce Voche (by Intikhab) and two winners abroad by Grand Lodge and Librettist. The dam was placed 3 times over 6f including at 2 yrs and is a half-sister to 6 winners including the very smart triple Group 2 1m winner Gothenburg. The second dam, Be Discreet (by Junius), won 5 races in France at up to 7f and is a half-sister to 9 winners including 3 stakes winners. "One we like a lot, he's a powerful colt that looks like he's ready to go, so he'll have a run over five furlongs in April. He'll probably want a bit further but if he continues to muscle-up he'll probably get quicker as well. So it's a job to know whether he's going to be a five furlong horse or a six furlong horse. I think he's above average and we're looking forward to running him".

388. CONCOCT (IRE) ★★★

b.f. Aqlaam – Jinskys Gift (Cadeaux Genereux). January 28. Fourth foal. €18,000Y. Goffs Sportsman's. Sackville/Donald. Half-sister to the fair 14f winner Sharp Relief (by Galileo). The dam is an unraced half-sister to 8 winners including the triple listed 7f winner Modeeroch, the 2-y-o 8.5f winner and Group

1 1m Gran Criterium third Chinese Whisper and the useful Irish 2-y-o 6f winner and Group 1 6f Cheveley Park Stakes third Danaskaya. The second dam, Majinskaya (by Marignan), winner of the listed 12f Prix des Tuileries, is a half-sister to 6 winners including the dam of the Group 1 5f Prix de l'Abbaye winner Kistena. (De La Warr Racing). *"To be honest she was a cheap filly because she looks nice and she goes well. She'll start at the end of April if there's a fillies' maiden about then and five or six furlongs will be fine for her".*

389. CRITIQUE (IRE) ★★★★ ♠

b.f. Art Connoisseur – Madame Boulangere (Royal Applause). February 18. Seventh foal. €43,000Y. Tattersalls Ireland September. Sackville/Donald. Half-sister to the quite useful 2012 2-y-o dual 5f winner Barracuda Boy (by Bahamian Bounty), to the fairly useful 2-y-o dual 7f winner Lamh Albasser (by Mr Greeley) and the quite useful Irish 10f and 12f winner of 5 races Jazz Girl (by Johar). The dam, a useful dual 6f winner (including at 2 yrs), was listed-placed and is a half-sister to one winner. The second dam, Jazz (by Sharrood), a fair 7f (at 2 yrs) and 10f placed maiden, is a half-sister to 12 winners including the US Grade 2 winner Sign Of Hope and the Group 2 placed Finian's Rainbow and Carmot. (Laurence Bellman & Lyn Rutherford). "A very nice filly, we have the half-brother Barracuda Boy who I was quite keen on at this point last year. She should be sharper than he was and considering he's a track record holder over five furlongs at Haydock Park I'd be pretty hopeful for this filly. They are different models because he's a bull of a horse and she's quite fine and light but she's done some good work, flown out of the stalls and she may start her career in April".

390. DRIFTER ★★★

b.c. Footstepsinthesand – Bright Bank (Sadler's Wells). March 24. Fifth foal. €85,000Y. Goffs Orby. Sackville/Donald. Half-brother to Capella's Song (by Oratorio), placed third over 7f and 1m on her only two starts at 2 yrs in 2012 and to the fairly useful 2-y-o 7f winner and Group 3 Derrinstown Stud 1,000 Guineas Trial second Devotion (by Dylan Thomas). The dam is an unraced half-sister to 7 winners including the very useful listed 6f and 7f winner and dual Group 1 placed My Branch (herself the dam of the Group 1 Sprint Cup winner Tante Rose). The second dam, Pay The Bank (by High Top), a quite useful 2-y-o 1m winner, stayed 10f and is a half-sister to 4 winners. (L Bellman, D Lowe & K Trowbridge). *"For a tall horse it was surprising just how forward he was early doors. I thought he'd be one of our first runners until he got a dose of ringworm which set him back. I think the sire's stock tend to need six furlongs anyway, so we'll see how we go on but he might be out in May. He's gone a bit leggy now, but he's still a nice horse".*

391. FINE 'N DANDY (IRE) ★★★★ ♠
ch.c. Dandy Man – Pearly Brooks (Efisio). February 28. Seventh foal. £30,000Y. Doncaster Premier. Sackville/Donald. Half-brother to the fair dual 1m winner, including at 2 yrs, Classic Voice (by Oratorio) and to a hurdles winner by High Chaparral. The dam, a fair 3-y-o 6f winner, is a sister to 4 winners including the Group 1 Phoenix Stakes winner Pips Pride and a half-sister to 4 winners. The second dam, Elkie Brooks (by Relkino), is a placed half-sister to one winner. (The United Rocks). *"He's sharp and an out-and-out 2-y-o, but with plenty of substance about him and he would have run in the first week in April but for the soft ground. He's by the first season sire Dandy Man and because we like him we bought another at the breeze-up sale. He'll probably improve for his first run".*

392. GABBLE ★★
ch.f. Compton Place – Royal Manor (King's Best). February 20. First foal. The dam, a modest 7f winner, is a half-sister 3 winners. The second dam, She's Classy (by Boundary), a winner of 2 races at 2 yrs in the USA including a stakes event, was Grade 1 placed twice and is a half-sister to 5 minor winners. (Owen Promotions Ltd). *"Bred by Michael, she's a first foal and reasonably small, but we'll be getting on with her and it would be nice for the dam to start off with a winner. We'll be trying our best to place her to win in the first half of the season".*

393. HICKSTER ★★
b.c. Intense Focus – Surrender To Me (Royal Anthem). April 19. Fourth foal. €10,000Y. Tattersalls Ireland September. Sackville/Donald. Half-brother to Royal Beauty (by Redback), unplaced in two starts at 2 yrs in 2012 and to the modest dual 6f winner Fifth In Line (by Kodiac). The dam is an unraced half-sister to 5 winners including the Italian listed winner Six Hitter. The second dam, Granny Kelly (by Irish River), was placed once over 7f at 2 yrs in Ireland and is a half-sister to 4 minor winners. (Edwards, Hughes, Jenkins, Roberts). *"We got him for relatively little money, he's ready to bash on with, he's an early 2-y-o, has a good attitude and tries hard. He's not the best but he certainly looks like he has a race in him. A 2-y-o by this sire Intense Focus sold quite well at the breeze-ups and if we'd taken this colt there we'd have probably got more than we bought him for".*

394. HIGH LOVE (IRE) ★★
b.f. High Chaparral – All Embracing (Night Shift). March 14. Sixth foal. €33,000Y. Tattersalls Ireland September. Sackville/Donald. Half-sister to Free Days (by Tamayuz), unplaced in one start at 2 yrs in Ireland in 2012 and to the French 3-y-o 7f winner Cricqueboeuf (by Cape Cross). The dam, a quite useful 7f winner, is a half-sister to 5 winners including the very smart 6f and 7f (at 2 yrs) and Group 2 10f Prix Guillaume d'Ornano winner Highdown and the Group 2 12f King Edward VII Stakes second Elshadi. The second dam, Rispoto (by Mtoto), a modest 12f winner, is a half-sister to 7 winners including the Group 3 10f Royal Whip Stakes winner Jahafil. (Laurence Bellman & David Lowe). *"A big filly, we bought her knowing she'd need plenty of time. A seven furlong filly for the second half of the season, her dam's been disappointing so far but she's a good model – a real fine looking horse".*

395. HOWZ THE FAMILY (IRE) ★★★
b.c. Myboycharlie – Lady Raj (El Prado). March 28. First foal. €62,000Y. Arqana Deauville October. Sackville/Donald. The dam, a dual listed stakes winner in the USA, was Grade 3 placed twice over 9f and is a half-sister to 9 winners. The second dam, Perfect Raj (by Rajab), won 3 minor races in the USA and is a half-sister to 6 winners including the US Grade

3 winner Perfect Poppy and to the placed dam of the US Grade 1 Breeders Cup Juvenile Fillies' winner Brave Raj. (Ham N Eggers). *"He would appear to be a nice colt, we bought him in France and although we don't know how successful the sire is going to be this colt has every chance of being a speedy 2-y-o. He looks like he'll sharpen up a bit and we'll start him at five furlongs but he'll probably want six".*

396. IZBUSHKA (IRE) ★★★

b.c. Bushranger – Zaynaba (Traditionally). March 3. First foal. £40,000Y. Doncaster Premier. Sackville/Donald. The dam is an unraced half-sister to 4 winners including the listed winner and Group 3 placed Zanughan. The second dam, Zanara (by Kahyasi), an Irish 12f winner, is a half-sister to 6 winners. (The Slurry Tavern Partnership). *"At the sales the Bushranger yearlings looked as if they'd be sharp and early, but our two are quite big lads, so they're not that forward. But both have good attitudes, plenty of bone and size. This colt is likely to be racing over six furlongs in May and he's a nice type".*

397. LADY RED OAK ★★★

ch.f. Medicean – Nuit Sans Fin (Lead On Time). May 5. Ninth living foal. €20,000Y. Goffs Orby. Not sold. Half-sister to Navajo Nights (by Sleeping Indian), placed fourth once over 6f at 2 yrs in 2012, to the French listed 1m winner Matin De Tempete (by Cardoun), the fairly useful 2-y-o 6f winner Amour Sans Fin (by Kendor), a minor winner in Spain and a winner over jumps in France by Ocean Of Wisdom. The dam is an unplaced half-sister to 9 winners including the listed winner Take On Time and the dam of the Group 1 Preis von Europa winner Jukebox Jury. The second dam, Feerie Boreale (by Irish River), a French 2-y-o winner and third in the Group 1 Prix Marcel Boussac, is a half-sister to 6 winners including the Group 1 Grand Prix de Paris winner Soleil Noir. (Mr D R Passant). *"A really nice filly, she was a May foal and physically she's a still a little bit weak but mentally I could have run her in March. A filly that loves her work, she's light and tall but she's also compact so she just needs her body to catch up with her mental attitude. I guess she'll have a spin over five furlongs in May but she'll get better as she progresses.*

398. LARSEN BAY (IRE) ★★

b.br.c. Kodiac – Teem (Xaar). April 22. Second foal. €20,000Y. Tattersalls Ireland September. Sackville/Donald. The dam won over 11f at 4 yrs in Germany and is a half-sister to 2 winners. The second dam, Deluge (by Rainbow Quest), is an unraced sister to the winner and Group 2 Prix de Pomone second Tuning and a half-sister to 5 winners. (The Connolly Partnership). *"He's just started working and he's been sold to a new owner, which is always great. A sharp, five/six furlong 2-y-o type, he's tall and narrow so we'll have to wait and see how he develops over the season".*

399. MAI WHI (IRE) ★★★

b.f. Whipper – May (Montjeu). March 17. Third living foal. €27,000Y. Arqana Deauville August. Sackville/Donald. The dam is an unraced half-sister to 11 winners including the Irish 1,000 Guineas winner Classic Park (herself dam of the Epsom Derby second Walk In The Park) and the US Grade 2 winner Rumpipumpy. The second dam, Wanton (by Kris), a useful 2-y-o 5f winner and third in the Group 2 Flying Childers Stakes, is a half-sister to 8 winners including the listed 5f St Hugh's Stakes winner and Group 2 5f Prix du Gros-Chene second Easy Option (herself dam of the dual Group 1 winner Court Masterpiece). (The Whipper Partnership). *"We bought her in France and she's a French-bred, so if she's any good we'll aim her towards Deauville in August. She's not over-big but very straightforward, enjoys her work and she's sort of light-boned. Whipper's tend to like a bit of cut in the ground but looking at her you'd say she wants it quick, so there's that sort of conundrum to answer, but she skips along and she's not an out-and-out 2-y-o. The pedigree suggests there'll be enough stamina for her to get a mile, so we'll take our time".*

400. MIMBLEBERRY ★★★

b.f. Winker Watson – Baldovina (Tale Of The Cat). February 12. Third foal. Half-sister to the 2012 Group 2 5f Queen Mary Stakes winner Ceiling Kitty (by Red Clubs) and to the fair 2-y-o triple 5f winner Van Go Go (by Dutch Art). The dam is a placed half-sister to the Japanese dual Group 3 winner One Carat. The second dam, Baldwina (by Pistolet Bleu), won the Group 3 Prix Penelope and is a half-sister to 5 winners. (Mr Andrew Black). *"I think it's fair to say that this time last year we gave this filly's half-sister Ceiling Kitty a glowing report. This Winker Watson filly is the best model that we've had out of the dam because she has plenty of size and scope, but so far she isn't showing early speed like Ceiling Kitty did. So I'd say she may not prove to be a Group 2 winner like her half-sister, but nevertheless she's a nice filly that's bound to win races. She'll be racing in late April/early May"*

401. PARTY RULER (IRE) ★★★★

b.c. Holy Roman Emperor – Calypso Dancer (Celtic Swing). March 12. Fourth foal. £36,000Y. Doncaster Premier. Sackville/Donald. Half-brother to the fairly useful 2-y-o 5f winner and listed placed City Dancer (by Elusive City), to the quite useful 7f (at 2 yrs) and 1m winner Come On Safari (by Antonius Pius) and the quite useful 9f winner Calypso Magic (by Aussie Rules). The dam won once over 5f at 3 yrs in France and is a half-sister to one winner. The second dam, Calypso Grant (by Danehill), winner of the listed 1m Masaka Stakes, is a sister to the listed 10f winner and Group 2 Sun Chariot Stakes third Poppy Carew and the Group 3 Winter Hill Stakes winner Leporello a half-sister to 7 winners. (Attenborough, Bellman, Ingram, Lowe). *"A nice horse, I'm really fond of the sire and this is a winner waiting to happen. He's probably not a true five furlong horse but he's very forward-going so we may just get away with nicking one. He'll end up needing seven I'm sure, he's a medium-sized horse, well put-together, straightforward and has a good attitude. I like him and he may have been relatively cheap".*

402. PASSIONATE AFFAIR (IRE) ★★

b.c. Broken Vow – Charmgoer (Nureyev). May 4. Ninth foal. €16,000Y. Tattersalls Ireland September. Sackville/Donald. Half-brother to the French 2-y-o listed 1m winner of 7 races Beringoer, to the modest 1m to 10f winner Tres Froide (both by Bering), the French 11f and 12f winner Aloeil (by Medicean), the French 1m and 12f winner Numerologue (by Numerous) and a minor French winner by Poliglote. The dam, a minor winner at 4 yrs in France, is a half-sister to 9 winners

including the US Grade 1 winners Dare And Go and Go Deputy and the good broodmare Wakigoer (the dam of three Group 3 winners). The second dam, Partygoer (by Secretariat), a minor US 3-y-o winner, is a half-sister to 7 winners including the US Graded stakes winners Virilify and Agacerie and the dam of the Grade 1 winner Quiet American. (The Passionate Partnership). *"He had a setback which will keep him out for the first half of the season, but he's a big horse and a May foal anyway, so having to wait a while is no real problem".*

403. QUANTUM DOT (IRE) ★★★★

ch.c. Exceed And Excel – Jeed (Mujtahid). April 28. Eighth foal. 60,000Y. Tattersalls October Book 1. Sackville/Donald. Half-brother to the modest 2012 6f placed 2-y-o Sakhib (by Haatef), to the very useful 2-y-o listed 6f winner and Group 3 6f Princess Margaret Stakes second Nidhaal (by Observatory), the fairly useful 12f winner of 5 races on the Flat and dual hurdles winner Maslak (by In The Wings), the fair 9f winner Riqaab (by Peintre Celebre) and a minor 3-y-o winner abroad by Green Desert. The dam, a quite useful 2-y-o 6f winner, is a half-sister to 2 winners. The second dam, Secretary Bird (by Kris), is an unraced half-sister to the classic winners Assert (French and Irish Derby), Bikala (French Derby) and Eurobird (Irish St Leger). (Mrs Yvonne Fleet). *"He looks racey and sharp and the owner is very keen to go to Chester in May so beforehand he'll either run in a maiden or have a racecourse gallop. Definitely a 2-y-o type".*

404. QUATUOR (IRE) ★★★

b.f. Kodiac – Infinitely (Fantastic Light). March 7. First foal. €20,000Y. Arqana Deauville October. Sackville/Donald. The dam is an unraced half-sister to one minor winner. The second dam, Maybe Forever (by Zafonic), won the Group 3 Prix de Saint-Georges and is a half-sister to the dual Group 1 winner Court Masterpiece. (Edwards, Hughes, Jenkins, Roberts). *"She's French-bred so she isn't eligible for any of our 2-y-o races that have bonuses. Instead we'll aim her at what you would assume will be our weaker maidens and if she's successful we'll then be looking at races in France. She's probably the smallest 2-y-o we've got, but at this stage of the year she's probably the quickest. Whether that continues we'll have to wait and see".*

405. ROCKSEE (IRE) ★★★

ch.f. *Rock Of Gibraltar – Sightseer (Distant View).* February 15. Second foal. €32,000Y. Tattersalls Ireland September. Sackville/ Donald. Half-sister to the minor Italian 3-y-o winner Spongy Bob (by Heliostatic). The dam, a minor winner at 3 yrs in the USA, is a sister to the US Grade 2 winner and Grade 1 placed Dr Brendler and a half-sister to 6 winners including the listed stakes winner Polish Vision. The second dam, Lady Of Vision (by Vision), a 2-y-o 7f winner, is a half-sister to 9 winners including the French Group 2 winner Lucky Dream. (Deva Racing Classic Partnership). *"So far she's been forwards and backwards, ready to go one week and then a bit weak the next. We'll take our time with her but you wouldn't know if she'd be racing in April or June. There's no panic with her, she's not over-big but she's a solid, strong, 2-y-o type and at some point we'll be able to kick on with her".*

406. SECRET ROMANCE ★★

ch.f. *Sakhee's Secret – Our Little Secret (Rossini).* April 10. Fourth foal. Half-sister to Pearl Bridge (by Avonbridge), placed third over 5f on his only start at 2 yrs in 2012 and to the smart listed 5f winner Pearl Secret (by Compton Place). The dam, a useful listed 5f winner of 6 races, is a half-sister to 3 winners. The second dam, Sports Post Lady (by M Double M), a fair 5f winner of 4 races, is a half-sister to 5 winners including the useful sprinter Palacegate Episode (a winner of 11 races here and abroad including a Group 3 race in Italy and numerous listed events). (Hot to Trot Racing Club). *"She came into the yard late, looking backward in her coat. She still looks a bit weak and she needs a bit of sun on her back, but she does have a nice pedigree. We'll go steady with her because although she's got everything you'd want she's still got some catching up to do".*

407. SHELLEY'S CHOICE ★★★

b.f. *Lawman – Fantastic Opinion (Fantastic Light).* January 27. First foal. €28,000Y.

Goffs Orby. Sackville/Donald. The dam is an unplaced half-sister to 7 winners including the useful 3-y-o 7f winner Meiosis and the useful 7f and 1m winner Excellento. The second dam, Golden Opinion (by Slew O'Gold), won the Group 1 Coronation Stakes and the Group 3 Prix du Rond Point, was second in the July Cup and third in the French 1,000 Guineas and is a half-sister to 7 winners. (OPBMS Ltd). *"She'll start her career in April and this is the first horse these owners have had, so I hope she gets them enthusiastic and interested. She's small and strong and has shown enough to suggest she'll win a normal maiden, so the early part of the season is her time".*

408. STEPPING OUT (IRE) ★★★★

b.f. *Tagula – Teodora (Fairy King).* March 14. Ninth foal. Doncaster Premier. £30,000Y. Sackville/Donald. Sister to the useful 5f winner of 7 races (including 3 times at 2 yrs) and listed-placed Duchess Dora and to the quite useful dual 7f winner (including at 2 yrs) Fadhb Ar Bith and half-sister to the fair 5f and 6f winner Lady Kildare (by Bachelor Duke), the fair 2-y-o 7f winner Feeling Wonderful, the useful 2-y-o dual 7f winner Prince Of Love (both by Fruits Of Love), the fair 2-y-o dual 6f winner Benato The Great (by Acclamation) and the modest 7f winner Dora's Sister (by Dark Angel). The dam, a fairly useful 2-y-o 6f winner, was fourth in the Group 3 6f Princess Margaret Stakes and is a half-sister to 6 winners. The second dam, Pinta (by Ahonoora), won over 5f in Ireland and a listed event in Italy over 7.5f and is a half-sister to 6 winners. (Attenborough, Bellman, Ingram, Lowe). *"She's one that we really like. She's probably going to want six furlongs but I quite like running them over five first time out, just to sharpen them up a bit. She had a bout of ringworm in February, but now she looks just about the best horse in the yard physically – in terms of her coat and everything. We'll be considering her for a nice maiden, give her a good education and go on from there".*

409. THATABOY (IRE) ★★★★

b.c. *Green Desert – Hawas (Mujtahid).* March 1. Eleventh foal. €50,000Y. Goffs Orby. Sackville/Donald. Brother to the French winner and German listed-placed Green Dandy, closely related to the quite useful Irish dual 5f and subsequent German listed winner La Sylvia (by Oasis Dream) and half-brother to the 2-y-o listed 7f Prix Herod winner and smart hurdler Power Elite (by Linamix), the fair 6f (at 2 yrs) and 7f winner and listed-placed She's My Dandy (by Holy Roman Emperor), the fair 1m, 2m and hurdles winner Nans Best (by Rock Of Gibraltar) and the fair 7f (at 2 yrs) and 10f winner Reaction (by Alhaarth). The dam, a 1m winner at 3 yrs in Ireland, is a sister to the listed winner Mutakarrim and a half-sister to 7 winners including the listed winner Nafisah. The second dam, Alyakkh (by Sadler's Wells), a fair 3-y-o 1m winner, is a full or half-sister to 7 winners including the Champion Stakes and 2,000 Guineas winner Haafhd and the Group 2 Challenge Stakes winner Munir. (David Lowe & Laurence Bellman). *"He's only been doing half-speeds on the gallops so far, but he is a bloody nice horse. Probably the heaviest 2-y-o we've got, he's very thick-set and looks like a 3-y-o already. There's no rush with him, but he'll probably run in early May and if he proves he's good enough we'll aim him at Royal Ascot".*

410. THE CHARACTER (IRE) ★★★★

b.c. Bushranger – Operissimo (Singspiel). January 29. Third foal. 60,000Y. Tattersalls October Book 1. Sackville/Donald. Half-brother to the fairly useful 2-y-o 6f winner and Group 3 1m Prix Thomas Bryon second Silver Grey (by Chineur) and to the minor French 2-y-o winner Allegrissimo (by Redback). The dam is an unraced sister to the 2-y-o Group 3 1m Prix Thomas Bryon winner and Group 2 10f UAE Derby second Songlark and a half-sister to 5 winners including the Dubai Group 3 and Irish listed 1m winner Blatant and the useful 2-y-o 7f winner Shawanni (herself the dam of four stakes winners including the Group 1 2-y-o winner Sky Lantern). The second dam, Negligent (by Ahonoora), a champion 2-y-o filly, won the 7f Rockfel Stakes at 2 yrs and was third in the 1,000 Guineas and is a full or half-sister to 5 winners including the Queen Alexandra Stakes winner Ala Hounak. (Aykroyd & Sons Ltd). *"Just like my other Bushranger colt he's not as forward as I expected him to be, but he's a big horse and just a bit weak at present. That's not*

a criticism of him – it just means we'll give him a bit of time. He's very much one we'd expect to have next year and beyond, but first of all you'd be surprised if he couldn't add to the dam's good record as a producer of 2-y-o winners".

411. THE KID ★★★★

b.c. High Chaparral – Shine Like A Star (Fantastic Light). May 3. Third foal. 70,000Y. Tattersalls October Book 2. Sackville/Donald. Half-brother to the useful 2012 2-y-o 6f and 7f winner and Group 2 May Hill Stakes third Light Up My Life (by Zamindar) and to the quite useful 2-y-o 6f winner Money Never Sleeps (by Kyllachy). The dam is an unplaced half-sister to 4 winners including the Group 1 Coronation Stakes winner Fallen For You, the listed 1m winner Fallen Idol and the useful 2-y-o 1m winner and Group 2 12f Lancashire Oaks second Fallen In Love. The second dam, Fallen Star (by Brief Truce), a listed 7f winner and Group 3 placed twice, is a half-sister to 7 winners including the Group 1 7f Lockinge Stakes winner Fly To The Stars. (Mr David Ward). *"He's a bit of a lad and very full of himself so you'd love to get some work into him, but he's by High Chaparral and he needs a bit of time. A good-looking horse, a good model and a good size and shape, I actually didn't think we'd be able to afford him at the sales and I'll be amazed if he doesn't win as a 2-y-o. If he's any good we'll be thinking of the Chesham Stakes for him but he hasn't done more than a canter yet. We'll try and get a run into him before the end of May and he's one we like".*

412. WHALEWEIGH STATION ★★★★

b.c. Zamindar – Looby Loo (Kyllachy). January 30. First foal. The dam, placed once over 5f at 2 yrs, is a half-sister to half-sister to the 2-y-o Group 1 Middle Park Stakes and Group 1 Prix Morny winner Dutch Art and to the Group 2 Blandford Stakes winner Up. The second dam, Halland Park Lass (by Spectrum), ran 3 times unplaced and is a half-sister to 4 winners including the Scandinavian Group 3 winner King Quantas. (Mr A Black). *"A first foal, he may not be over-big but he's certainly not small. He's got a bit of character about him and we wouldn't be rushing him. We'll aim him for a maiden in May or June and hope he proves good enough for some black-type races after that. He'll certainly make a 2-y-o, but he's more than likely to make a 3-y-o as well. We'll be hoping to get the mare off to a good start with this colt".*

413. UNNAMED ★★★

b.c. Royal Applause – Aegean Shadow (Sakhee). March 11. First foal. 40,000Y. Tattersalls October Book 2. Sackville/Donald. The dam, a fair 6f and 7f winner of 3 races at 3 and 4 yrs, is a half-sister to 4 winners including the useful 2-y-o 6f listed winner of 3 races and Group 2 7f Vintage Stakes third Corporal Maddox. The second dam, Noble View (by Distant View), placed fourth over 5f and 6f at 2 yrs, is a half-sister to 5 winners including the French 1,000 Guineas winner Houseproud. *"He's not been sold yet but he'll be ready to race in May, so we could end up owning him ourselves. He's a bit of a boy but he's a nice horse. He hasn't galloped yet but he has done some good canters and I'm sure he'll soon be ready for faster work with the rest of them. He's quite big and was bought with the view that he'd be a quality horse and be campaigned with his 3-y-o career in mind, but we can always reconsider that option".*

414. UNNAMED ★★

b.f. Haatef – Cafe Creme (Catrail). January 10. Sixth foal. €20,000Y. Tattersalls Ireland September. Ed Sackville. Half-sister to the fairly useful 2-y-o 7f winner Parisian Art (by Clodovil), to the fair 7f (at 2 yrs) and 1m winner Ice Cool Lady (by Verglas), the fair 2-y-o 6f winner Café Express (by Bertolini) and the modest 11f and 12f winner Red Expresso (by Intikhab). The dam is an unraced half-sister to 6 winners including the 2-y-o Group 1 6f Cheveley Park Stakes winner Seazun and the 2-y-o 7f winner and listed-placed Mahogany. The second dam, Sunset Cafe (by Red Sunset), a minor Irish 12f winner, is a sister to the Group 3 Prix Foy winner Beeshi and a half-sister to 8 winners including the listed winner Chaumiere and the dam of the high-class 10f colt Insatiable. (The MHS 2013 Partnership). *"It's not easy to work out how early she'll be, or what trip she'll want really. She's big and scopey and yet she's coping with everything perfectly well, so I'm tempted to give a bit of*

work and see whether she copes with that. Physically she's a good size and shape and you'd think she'd want six furlongs minimum, but they can surprise you.

415. UNNAMED ★★★

b.c. Invincible Spirit – Chica Roca (Woodman). March 24. Sixth foal. Goffs Orby. €95,000Y. Not sold. Brother to the modest 7f (at 2 yrs) and dual 6f winner Qubuh (by Invincible Spirit) and half-brother to the fair Irish 6f (at 2 yrs) and 7f winner Chibcha (by High Chaparral). The dam, placed twice at 2 yrs in France, is a half-sister to 5 winners including the Group 2 Criterium de Maisons-Laffitte winner and useful broodmare Zinziberine. The second dam, Amenixa (by Linamix), a 4-y-o 10f winner, is a sister to the dual Group 1 Prix Royal-Oak winner Amilynx and the listed winner Amie De Mix and a half-sister to the Group 2 Criterium de Maisons-Laffitte winner Amiwain. *"The 4-y-o out of this mare, Menelik, is possibly the most disappointing horse I've ever trained, but I'm sticking with the dam because this is a gorgeous-looking horse by a good sire. Menelik has all the speed in the world at home and this colt is a nicer-looking, bigger and stronger horse. I haven't done much with him yet, we haven't sold him and he'll be brought on slowly. Possibly a second half of the season 2-y-o".*

416. UNNAMED ★★

b.c. Dandy Man – Chimay (Kris Kin). February 27. First foal. £20,000 2-y-o. Kempton Breeze-Up. Sackville/Donald. The dam is an unplaced half-sister to 2 winners. The second dam, Desert Order (by Desert King), is an unraced half-sister to 5 winners including the Group 1 National Stakes winner Beckett. *"I felt he breezed well at the sales and he fell into the right price bracket for the owner. Other than that I can't comment because we've only just got him".*

417. UNNAMED ★★★★

gr.c. Invincible Spirit – Exclusive Approval (With Approval). April 11. Eighth foal. 85,000Y. Tattersalls October Book 2. Sackville/Donald. Brother to the quite useful 10f winner Gobooll and half-brother to the very useful 6f and 10.5f winner and listed-placed In The Light (by

Inchinor), the quite useful 1m, 10f and hurdles winner Thumbs Up (by Intikhab), the fair 1m winner Exclusive Dancer (by Notnowcato), the French 1m to 10f winner of 5 races By Appointment (by Mojave Moon) and a hurdles winner by Alhaarth. The dam, a minor US 3-y-o winner, is a sister to the stakes winner Be Elusive and a half-sister to 8 winners including the US stakes winner Vignette (herself dam of the St Leger winner Lucarno). The second dam, Be Exclusive (by Be My Guest), won 5 races in France and the USA including the Group 3 Prix Chloe and is a half-sister to 2 winners. *"This is a horse we like a lot. The dam has bred loads of winners, none of them exceptional, but this is a fine-looking horse. He's a beautiful colour, he floats along, does everything easily and although he hasn't got an owner yet I'd be surprised if he isn't one the better quality 2-y-o's we've got. We'll start him at six furlongs".*

418. UNNAMED ★★

b.f. Royal Applause – Fabine (Danehill Dancer). March 6. Second foal. £32,000Y. Doncaster Premier. Sackville/Donald. The dam won at 3 yrs and is a half-sister to 3 winners including the very useful 2-y-o Group 2 5.5f Prix Robert Papin winner Never A Doubt (herself the dam of a listed winner). The second dam, Waypoint (Cadeaux Genereux), a fairly useful 6f and 7f winner, is a half-sister to the Group 2 Diadem Stakes winner and high-class sire Acclamation. *"She looked like being really sharp and early but she went a bit weak and a little bit backward. She's grown but she hasn't really filled out with it, so she's gone a bit light. But she's done plenty of work so she's bought herself a bit of time and she'll start off at six furlongs in May. I'm sure she'll get better as the season progresses, she's bigger than the earlier 2-y-o types we have, so she'll develop as she goes on".*

419. UNNAMED ★★★

b.f. Dubawi – Logic (Slip Anchor). March 30. Ninth foal. 48,000Y. Tattersalls October Book 1. Sackville/Donald. Half-sister to the 1m and 10f winner Everybody Knows (by King's Best), to the 1m to 14f winner Rationale (by Singspiel), the 6f (at 2 yrs) to 9f winner of 7

races Logsdail (by Polish Precedent), the 12f and hurdles winner Joseph Lister (by Nayef) – all four quite useful, the fair 9f and hurdles winner Royal Rationale (by Desert Prince) and the fair 2-y-o 6f winner Ecologically Right (by Entrepreneur). The dam, a useful 1m placed 2-y-o, is a half-sister to 4 winners including the listed Oaks Trial winner and Group 2 Park Hill Stakes third Port Helene. The second dam, Docklands (by On Your Mark), a listed-placed winner of 3 races at 4 yrs, is a half-sister to 11 winners including the 1,000 Guineas winner Night Off. *"She's a half-sister to a lot of reasonably well-rated winners and Dubawi is a really good sire, so if she proves to be any good you'd be looking at some good quality races in the summer. The pedigree doesn't scream 'early type' at you so there's no panic with her. We bought her from Highclere, who produce and sell a lot of decent horses, so I'm amazed we haven't sold her yet. She's got everything going for her".*

420. UNNAMED ★★★

b.f. Compton Place – Queen Bodicea (Revoque). April 14. Fifth foal. €67,000Y. Arqana Deauville October. Sackville/Donald. Half-sister to the Group 2 July Stakes winner Classic Blade (by Daggers Drawn) and to the winner and Group 3 Prix de Saint-Georges second Captain Dunne (by Captain Rio). The dam is an unplaced sister to the Italian listed winner Meanya and a half-sister to the fairly useful winner of 8 races at around 7f Santisima Trinidad. The second dam, Brazilia (by Forzando), a modest 6f placed 2-y-o, is a half-sister to 4 winners including the Group 2 5f Kings Stand Stakes winner Dominica. (N & S Mather, Owen Promotions & I Flanagan). *"Her half-brother Classic Blade won a Group 2 for me and he knew the time of day from the moment he was born. This filly she doesn't even know she's born yet! She's laid-back but has a fighting spirit and she just needs the penny to drop. A little bit weak still, she goes nicely and she's certainly one that we like. I'm sure that given another month and a bit more time she'll be alright. Being French-bred we could always aim her at some black-type over there later on if she's good enough".*

421. UNNAMED ★★

b.c. Exceed And Excel – Quinzey's Best (King's Best). February 8. Second foal. £30,000 2-y-o. Kempton Breeze-Up. Sackville/Donald. The dam is an unplaced half-sister to the useful 2-y-o 5f and subsequent US Grade 3 1m Senorita Stakes winner Mrs Kipling (by Exceed And Excel). The second dam, Quinzey (by Carnegie), is an unraced half-sister to 2 winners. (Deva Racing Partnership). *"A nice, big horse that breezed well at the sales but he's only been here a few days so we don't know anything else about him yet".*

422. UNNAMED ★★

ch.c. Compton Place – Raphaela (Octagonal). February 18. Seventh foal. £44,000Y. Doncaster Premier. Sackville/Donald. Half-brother to the quite useful 1m and 10f winner Gold Rules, to a minor French winner of 3 races Radieuse (both by Gold Away) and a winner in Italy by Stormy River. The dam won once over 11f in France and is a half-sister to 6 winners. The second dam, Redden Queen (by Bering), won twice at 3 yrs in France and is a half-sister to 5 winners. (Mr Laurence Bellman). *"He's a big colt and yet when we bought him we were thinking he'd be a proper early 2-y-o. But he's grown so much that he's now probably the biggest 2-y-o we've got, so we're just sitting on him now and letting him develop. He looks really well and he's still fat but that's not a bad thing and the owner is very patient so we'll just see how we go with him".*

423. UNNAMED ★★★★

b.f. Naaqoos – Safqa (Singspiel). February 2. Second foal. £22,000Y. Doncaster Festival. Manor House Stables. Half-sister to the French listed 1m winner Gaazaal (by Iffraaj). The dam, a quite useful 1m winner, is a half-sister to 3 winners including the fairly useful 10f and 2m 2f Chester Cup winner Daraahem. The second dam, Shamah (by Unfuwain), a winner at 3 yrs, is a half-sister to 6 winners. (Mr A W Black). *"I like her a lot. When I went to the sale she was the last lot in the ring but she was the only horse I liked, so we waited around a long time to buy her! The dam obviously has the ability to produce a nice horse and this filly is a 2-y-o to look at, she's done a bit of work and went really well. She'll tell us when she's ready for* another piece of work and I wouldn't be in a panic if that wasn't until mid-May". TRAINERS' BARGAIN BUY

ED DE GILES

424. HOSTILE FIRE (IRE) ★★

b.c. Iffraaj – Royal Esteem (Mark Of Esteem). April 12. Third foal. €24,000Y. Tattersalls Ireland September. Kevin Ross. Half-brother to a 2-y-o winner in Russia by Ramonti. The dam, a dual winner at 3 yrs in the USA, is a half-sister to one winner abroad. The second dam, Inchacooley (by Rhoman Rule), an Irish and US listed winner of 6 races at 3 to 8 yrs, is a half-sister to one winner. (Mr A Mortazavi). *"He was quite big at the sales and he's still bigger than the rest of my 2-y-o's, but he isn't huge and he'll make a 2-y-o. Nevertheless he'll improve with time. He's a nice mover, very sensible and he takes his work. One for the mid-summer onwards, probably starting off at six furlongs before going seven".*

425. KOPENHAGEN (IRE) ★★★

ch.c. Captain Rio – Quizzical Lady (Mind Games). April 10. Sixth foal. €23,000Y. Tattersalls Ireland September. Kevin Ross. Half-brother to a fair 6f and 7f winner Winning Impact (by Pyrus) and to a 2-y-o winner in Spain by City On A Hill. The dam, a modest 2-y-o 5f winner, is a half-sister to 6 winners. The second dam, Salacious (by Sallust), a useful Irish 7f (at 2 yrs) and 9f winner, is a half-sister to 8 winners. (Mr A Mortazavi). *"A bonny little thing, he'll be an early type and I like him a lot. He has a great attitude, he's sensible enough and as he's on the small side we'll look to getting him out sooner rather than later. A five furlong 2-y-o".*

426. ZUGZWANG (IRE) ★★★

b.c. Kodiac – Kris's Bank (Inchinor). April 30. Second foal. €20,000Y. Tattersalls Ireland September. Kevin Ross. Half-brother to a minor Italian 3-y-o winner by Le Vie Dei Colori. The dam won 9 minor races in Italy and is a half-sister to 5 winners including the Group 3 Darley Stakes winner and dual Group 1 third Enforcer. The second dam, Tarneem (by Zilzal), The second dam, Tarneem (by Zilzal), a quite useful 3-y-o 1m winner, is a half-sister to 4 minor winners abroad. (Mr S Treacher).

"Not over-big but all there, he has a great attitude and he's a good mover. An early type, he'll be out in late April/early May and I'm very pleased with him. The name is a chess move, by the way!"

ANN DUFFIELD

427. BOY RANGER (IRE) ★★
b.g. Bushranger – Nonsense (Soviet Star). March 7. Fourth foal. £13,000Y. Doncaster Premier. Ann Duffield. Half-brother to Strange Angel (by Dark Angel) placed fourth in a 5f seller at 2 yrs in 2012. The dam is an unraced half-sister to 4 winners including Prince Arthur (Group 1 Italian 2,000 Guineas). The second dam, Daniela Samuel (by No Robbery), won 6 races in Italy at 3 and 4 yrs and is a half-sister to 4 minor winners in the USA. *"I hope he'll win as a 2-y-o, but I've just gelded him – so the jury's out at the moment".*

428. FOCUSOFOURTHOUGHTS (IRE) ★★★
b.c. Intense Focus – Inourthoughts (Desert Style). April 25. Second foal. €11,000Y. Tattersalls Ireland September. Ann Duffield. Half-brother to the moderate 2012 dual 5f placed 2-y-o Grand Jipeck (by Soviet Star). The dam, a quite useful Irish 2-y-o 5f winner, is a half-sister to 2 minor winners. The second dam, Inourhearts (by Pips Pride), a useful listed 5f winner of 4 races, is a half-sister to 2 winners. (Eshwin Racing). *"Quite capable of winning, he's genuine and tough but he's just started to grow so we'll have to wait a bit. He's got a good attitude, he looks like a proper little sprinter, everything's in the right place and I like him".*

429. GARFUNKEL (IRE) ★★★
b.c. Excellent Art – Intricate Dance (Aptitude). March 12. Second foal. 12,000Y. Tattersalls October Book 2. Ann Duffield. Half-brother to a 2-y-o winner in Poland by Le Vie Dei Colori. The dam ran twice unplaced and is a half-sister to 3 winners including the very useful listed 7f (at 2 yrs) and listed 1m winner Short Dance and to the placed dam of the Group 2 and triple Group 3 winner Lolly For Dolly. The second dam, Clog Dance (by Pursuit Of Love), a useful maiden, was second in the Group 3 7f Rockfel Stakes and the listed 10f Pretty Polly Stakes and is a half-sister to 6 winners

including the smart 14f Ebor Handicap winner Tuning. (Morecool Racing). *"I like him, he goes well, has a good attitude and is a nice, big, strong horse that wants a bit of time. He's one for the middle of the season, he's really good-looking and is probably a seven furlong type".*

430. GREENBURY (IRE) ★★★
b.g. Jeremy – Truly Genuine (Hernando). February 22. Fourth foal. £10,000Y. Doncaster November. Ann Duffield. Half-brother to the quite useful Irish 2-y-o 6f winner Truly Genius (by Iffraaj). The dam ran once unplaced and is a half-sister to 4 winners including the French listed 1m winner and Group 3 Prix de Psyche third Antique. The second dam, Truly Generous (by Generous), won the listed Prix Petite Etoile and is closely related to the Group 3 10.5f Prix de Royaumont winner Truly Special (herself dam of the Group 2 winners Wareed and Truly A Dream) and a half-sister to 7 winners including the Group 2 13.5f Grand Prix de Deauville winner Modhish and the Group 2 12.5f Prix de Royallieu winner Russian Snows. (David Barker). *"We've been very lucky with the sire because we've managed to win with them all. He's a nice sort, the type to start by the end of May all being well. Just a nice sized 2-y-o, his pedigree says he'll get he'll get further than five furlongs but he has got pace".*

431. HELLO BEAUTIFUL (IRE) ★★★
ch.f. Captain Rio – Tekhania (Dalakhani). March 23. Second foal. £10,000Y. Doncaster Premier. Ann Duffield. Half-sister to the unplaced 2012 2-y-o High Hill Beauty (by Papal Bull). The dam is an unraced half-sister to 2 winners including the Hong Kong Group 2 winner Wade Giles. The second dam, Tekindia (by Indian Ridge), a minor French 3-y-o winner, is a half-sister to 6 winners. (Nick Allenby). *"A very nice filly, she'll start her career in April, she's going very well and doing everything right. I really like her".* TRAINERS' BARGAIN BUY

432. IN VINO VERITAS (IRE) ★★
b.c. Art Connoisseur – Robin (Slip Anchor). January 25. €14,000Y. Tattersalls Ireland November. Ann Duffield. Half-brother to the fairly useful 2-y-o 1m and subsequent

Hong Kong winner London Express (by King Charlemagne), to the Japanese winner of 8 races Loulan Cape (by Cape Cross), the modest triple 2m winner Waterford Star (by Oratorio) and the moderate 10f winner Ifit (by Inchinor). The dam is an unraced half-sister to 7 winners including the Group 2 Geoffrey Freer Stakes winner Top Class. The second dam, Cassina (by Habitat), a fairly useful 3-y-o 6f winner, is a half-sister to 2 winners. (James Kay). *"We're only cantering him because he's a great, big horse that'll want time. So we're not in any hurry with him, but he's a lovely mover with a good attitude".*

433. LADY JAMESWAY (IRE) ★★★

b.f. Acclamation – Baltic Dip (Benny The Dip). March 4. Third foal. 25,000Y. Tattersalls October Book 2. Ann Duffield. Half-sister to Rosie Hall (by Lion Heart), unplaced in one start at 2 yrs in 2012. The dam, a fairly useful 2-y-o 6f winner, is a half-sister to 5 winners including the 5.3f (at 2 yrs) and US winner and Grade 2 placed Pina Colada and to the unraced Mrs Marsh (dam of the multiple Group 1 winner Canford Cliffs). The second dam, Drei (by Lyphard), placed fourth over 1m at 3 yrs on her only outing, is a half-sister to 3 winners. (James Pak). *"A very nice filly with bags of ability, but she's growing very rapidly and needs time, so she's one for the mid-to-late season".*

434. MASTER CLOCKMAKER (IRE) ★★★★

gr.c. Mastercraftsman – Mairead Annie (Elusive Quality). March 31. Second foal. 40,000Y. Tattersalls October Book 2. Ann Duffield. Half-brother to the Italian winner of 3 races Grey Arrow (by Verglas). The dam, a minor winner at 3 yrs in the USA, is a half-sister to 6 winners. The second dam, Quarrel Over Halo (by Halo), won 2 minor races at 3 yrs in the USA and is a half-sister to 9 winners including Suvi (Grade 2 Del Mar Oaks). (Mr & Mrs Thompson). *"A very nice, quality colt, he does everything right but he's just a giant of a horse. He'll need time, so he's one for the second half of the season".*

435. MUSPELHEIM ★★★

b.c. Firebreak – Ticcatoo (Dolphin Street). March 25. Sixth foal. £7,500Y. Doncaster November. Ann Duffield. Half-brother to

the fairly useful 5f and 6f winner of 7 races Ishetoo (by Ishiguru), to the quite useful 5f and 6f winner of 4 races Mottley Crew (by Mujahid), the modest 5f (including at 2 yrs) and 6f winner of 8 races Weet A Surprise (by Bertolini) and the moderate 6f winner Charlietoo (by King Charlemagne). The dam was a modest 2-y-o 5f winner. The second dam, Accountancy Jewel (by Pennine Walk), a modest 2-y-o 7f winner, is a half-sister to the dam of the Group 1 July Cup winner Lake Coniston. (Grange Park Racing). *"He'll start his career in mid-April, he only does just enough – whatever you ask for there's always a bit more, so we don't really know what he's got left in the tank. We like him and he's capable of winning".*

436. PATISSERIE ★★★

b.f. Myboycharlie – Khafayif (Swain). March 26. Fifth foal. €20,000Y. Tattersalls Ireland September. Ann Duffield. Half-sister to the modest 2-y-o 6f winner Transcentral (by Kheleyf) and to the moderate 7f winner See The Storm (by Statue Of Liberty). The dam, a modest 7f placed 3-y-o, is a half-sister to 5 winners. The second dam, Copper Play (by Fast Play), a stakes-placed winner of 5 winners from 2 to 4 yrs in the USA, is a half-sister to 10 winners including four stakes winners. (Derek & Sandra Shewring). *"She was ready to run early but she's had a growth spurt and gone backwards on us. She's a nice filly though, doing everything right and she'll run soon. Probably a five/six furlong 2-y-o".*

437. PETITE MADAME (IRE) ★★

b.f. Champs Elysees – Seeking The Fun (Alhaarth). March 28. Second foal. €8,500Y. Tattersalls Ireland September. Ann Duffield. The dam, a minor winner at 3 yrs in France, is a half-sister to the Group 3 Prix Exbury winner Polytechnicien. The second dam, Golden Party (by Seeking The Gold), is a placed half-sister to 10 winners including the US Grade 1 winners Dare And Go and Go Deputy. (Nick Saint). *"She's growing like mad so we've backed off her a bit, but she's full of herself and hasn't put a foot wrong. A nice filly, but we haven't put a gun to her head at all".*

438. TRICKSOME ★★

b.f. Jeremy – Travel Tricks (Presidium). April

21. Seventh foal. €14,000Y. Tattersalls Ireland September. Ann Duffield. Half-sister to the quite useful dual 6f winner (including at 2 yrs) and dual listed-placed Antica (by Raise A Grand) and to the fair dual 5f winner Fly By Magic (by Indian Rocket). The dam is an unraced half-sister to 3 minor winners. The second dam, Travel Magic (by Henbit), a quite useful 7f winner, is a half-sister to 7 winners including the listed winners Jazz Ballet and Cutting Reef. *"A nice filly, she was small when we bought her but she's grown a lot, has a good attitude and is a real 'terrier' type".*

439. UNNAMED ★★★

b.c. Whipper – Hedera (Woodman). March 24. Eleventh foal. €17,000Y. Goffs Orby. Ann Duffield. Half-brother to Shagwa, placed fourth once over 6f from two starts at 2 yrs in 2012, to the fairly useful 1m (at 2 yrs) and 10f winner Deia Sunrise (both by Clodovil), the French listed 12f winner and Group 3 second Ivy League (by Doyoun), the fairly useful 12f winner Heisse (by Darshaan), the fairly useful triple 10f winner here and in the UAE Hunters Glen (by Bahri), the fairly useful Irish 9f winner Syann and a jumps winner in Ireland (both by Daylami). The dam, a quite useful 2-y-o 7f winner, is a half-sister to 6 winners. The second dam, Ivrea (by Sadler's Wells), a very useful 2-y-o 7f winner, was placed in the Group 2 12f Ribblesdale Stakes and the Group 3 10.5f Musidora Stakes at 3 yrs, is a sister to the useful 2-y-o 6f winner Iviza (also placed in the Musidora and Ribblesdale) and a half-sister to the very useful Irish 1m (at 2 yrs) and Group 1 12f Italian Oaks winner Ivyanna. (James Kay). *"A very nice colt, he's doing everything right and I like him. He won't run early, he's more of a mid-to-late season 2-y-o".*

440. UNNAMED ★★

b.g. Lucky Story – Toboggan Lady (Tobougg). January 29. First foal. £8,000Y. Doncaster Premier. Ann Duffield. The dam, a moderate 12f and 2m 2f winner, is a half-sister to one winner abroad. The second dam, Northbend (by Shirley Heights), was placed at 3 yrs in France and is a half-sister to 3 winners. (David McMahon). *"He's doing nicely, he has more speed than his dam, who I trained and he's not a bad sort. I think he'll be OK".*

ED DUNLOP

441. ANIPA ★★★

ch.f. Sea The Stars – Anna Amalia (In The Wings). March 18. Fifth foal. Half-sister to the 7f (at 2 yrs), Grade 1 10f Flower Bowl International and Group 3 9.5f winner Ave (by Danehill Dancer), to the useful 2-y-o 7f winner and Group 3 7f Solario Stakes third Dubai Phantom (by Dubawi) and the fair 9f winner Ampleforth (by Pivotal). The dam won once at 3 yrs in France and is a half-sister to 5 winners including the smart French 2-y-o Group 3 1m Prix d'Aumale winner and smart broodmare Anna Palariva. The second dam, Anna Of Saxony (by Ela-Mana-Mou), a very useful winner of the Group 2 14.6f Park Hill Stakes, is a half-sister to 10 winners including the Group 2 winners Annaba and Pozarica. (Mr Nurlan Bizakov). *"A beautifully-bred filly, she's not the biggest but we saw from his sales yearlings that Sea The Stars has bred a lot of different-sized horses. She's very athletic, moves well and could be relatively early as a result of her size".*

442. AURORA BOREALIS (IRE) ★★★

b.f. Montjeu – Elaflaak (Gulch). April 15. Seventh foal. The dam, a useful listed 5f winner, is a half-sister to the US triple Grade 3 9f winner Indescribable. The second dam, Catnip (by Flying Paster), a US 12f winner, is a half-sister to the Belmont Stakes winner Editor's Note. (Sir Robert Ogden). *"A good-looking filly and a good mover, she appears to have a good temperament for a Montjeu. Very much one for the second half of the season, she's a big, attractive filly that's having a break at the moment but she'll be back in fairly soon".*

443. BIG BONED (USA) ★★★

b.f. Street Sense – Lizzy Cool (Saint Ballado). April 24. Seventh foal. $95,000Y. Keeneland September. David Redvers. Half-sister to the US stakes winner and Grade 2 second Cool Bullet (by Red Bullet) and to the US winner and Grade 3 placed Casper's Touch (by Touch Gold). The dam, a US stakes winner, is a half-sister to 8 winners including the Irish listed 9f winner Sense Of Honour. The second dam, Well Supported (by Key To The Mint), is an unplaced half-sister to several winners out of the US dual Grade 1 winner Windy's Daughter.

(Qatar Racing Ltd). *"A nice filly, she looks very racey and I like her. The first one I've trained for Qatar Racing, she looks to move well and she's got size and scope. I wouldn't be surprised if she was a six furlong filly and maybe more. She looks to have some speed".*

444. CAPE SUMMIT ★★★★ ♠

ch.c. Tamayuz – Peace Summit (Cape Cross). February 5. First foal. 60,000Y. Tattersalls October Book 2. Will Edmeades. The dam is an unraced half-sister to 4 winners including the useful 2-y-o 7f winner Grosvenor Square and to the unraced dam of the Group 1 winner King's Apostle. The second dam, Embassy (by Cadeaux Genereux), a champion 2-y-o filly and winner of the Cheveley Park Stakes, is a half-sister to 6 winners including the Group 2 Pretty Polly Stakes winner Tarfshi. (Thurloe Thoroughbreds XXXI). *"For a first foal this an amazingly mature, good-looking, powerful 2-y-o. You'd look at him and say he was a 3-y-o. I liked him at the sales but wasn't able to afford him, so we were lucky enough to be sent him by his owners Thurloe. He goes well, he's sound and hasn't had any problems. Probably one for six furlongs plus and I'm happy with him so far".*

445. CRADLE OF LIFE (IRE) ★★★★ ♠

ch.f. Notnowcato – Pursuit Of Life (Pursuit Of Love). March 14. Fifth foal. 55,000Y. Tattersalls October Book 2. Blandford Bloodstock. Half-sister to the Italian Group 3 winners Gimmy (by Lomitas and also Group 1 third) and Stay Alive (by Iffraaj) and to two minor winners in Italy by Diktat and Cape Cross. The dam, a winner of 4 races in Italy at 2 and 3 yrs and listed-placed 3 times, is a half-sister to 5 winners including the French dual Group 3 winner Di Moi Oui. The second dam, Biosphere (by Pharly), a listed-placed winner in Italy, is a sister to the triple listed winner Scribano. (A W Black). *"She's athletic and moves well, but after we got her going she just grew and went a little bit weak, so I sent her back to the farm for some spring grass. We always liked her and although she won't be early, as you'd expect from her sire, she is a nice filly".*

446. FIALKA ★★

b.f. Cape Cross – First (Highest Honor). March 27. Sixth foal. Closely related to the smart listed 1m and listed 10f winner and dual Group 3 third Perfect Stride and to the fairly useful 2-y-o 6f winner Among Equals (both by Oasis Dream) and half-sister to the French 2-y-o listed 6f winner Law Lord (by Diktat) and the French 10f winner Next (by In The Wings). The dam, a listed 1m winner at 3 yrs in France, is a half-sister to 12 winners including the smart Group 3 winners Bluebook and Myself. The second dam, Pushy (by Sharpen Up), a very useful 2-y-o winner of 4 races including the Group 2 Queen Mary Stakes, is a half-sister to 10 winners including the high-class 2-y-o Precocious and the Group 1 Japan Cup winner Jupiter Island. (Mr Nurlan Bizakov). *"A very well-bred filly, but she's 'up behind' a present and she won't be early. Much more of a 3-y-o type".*

447. FREDDIE KILROY ★★★

b.c. Pastoral Pursuits – Pretty Davis (Trempolino). April 12. Eighth foal. 26,000Y. Tattersalls October Book 2. R Frisby. Half-brother to the quite useful 1m (at 2 yrs) to 15f winner and smart jumper Fait Le Jojo (by Pistolet Bleu), to the fair 12f to 2m and hurdles winner Timing (by Alhaarth) and a minor 2-y-o winner in Italy by Pennekamp. The dam, a French 3-y-o winner, was third in the listed 6f Prix Yacowlef at 2 yrs and is a half-sister to 5 winners including the Italian listed winner Giselle Penn. The second dam, Garconniere (by Gay Mecene), ran unplaced twice in France and is a half-sister to 9 winners including the Group 1 Gran Criterium winner Grease and the dual Group 3 winner Godot. (Mr C R Kilroy). *"He was meant to be by earliest 2-y-o but he had a slight setback. He shows plenty of speed but won't be back in training until May".*

448. KAAB (IRE) ★★★★

b.c. Kheleyf – Ms Victoria (Fasliyev). March 18. First foal. 42,000Y. Tattersalls October Book 2. Shadwell Estate Co. The dam was a quite useful Irish 5f and 6f winner at 3 yrs. The second dam, Musical Refrain (by Dancing Dissident), is a placed half-sister to 5 winners including the Group 2 Duke Of York

Stakes winner Monsieur Bond. (Hamdan Al Maktoum). *"I like this colt, he's a typical Kheleyf in that he's a little bit bouncy and active. There's plenty of speed, he's got size and scope and he looks tough enough at the moment. It wouldn't surprise me if he was early, so he's definitely one for the book".*

449. KINEMA (IRE) ★★★★
b.c. Galileo – Bon Nuit (Night Shift). April 10. Second foal. €250,000Y. Goffs Orby. Marc Keller. Half-brother to the fair 2013 3-y-o 7f debut winner Whispering Lady (by Pivotal). The dam, a smart 6f (at 2 yrs) and 1m listed winner, is a half-sister to 4 winners including the useful 6f (at 2 yrs) to 10f winner and listed-placed In A Silent Way. The second dam, Pray (by Priolo), is an unraced half-sister to 4 winners including the Grade 2 San Bernadino Handicap and Group 3 7f Supreme Stakes winner Anshan. (Mr M Keller). *"An attractive, good-moving colt, he's not a backward Galileo and he's bound to be a six/seven furlong 2-y-o. He might even make Royal Ascot, we like him and he goes well".*

450. LIFEJACKET (IRE) ★★★
ch.c. Notnowcato – My American Beauty (Wolfhound). April 21. Sixth foal. 10,000Y. Tattersalls October Book 3. Ed Dunlop. Half-brother to the modest 2012 Irish 7f placed 2-y-o Miller Beach (by Sakhee's Secret), to the quite useful dual 5f winner of 4 races Beauty Pageant (by Bahamian Bounty), the moderate 5f winner Marie's Fantasy (by Whipper) and a minor winner abroad by Domedriver. The dam, a fairly useful 5f and 6f winner of 7 races from 2 to 5 yrs, is a half-sister to 2 winners including the US dual Grade 3 winner Desert Lady. The second dam, Hooray Lady (by Ahonoora), a fairly useful listed-placed winner of 6 races at around 1m, is a half-sister to 7 winners. (Miltil Consortium). *"I haven't got this colt yet but apparently he's nice and at pre-training he goes well, so I'd give him a mention".*

451. MAGHAANEM (IRE) ★★★
b.c. Acclamation – Shishangaan (Mujadil). March 21. Second foal. £130,000Y. Doncaster Premier. Ed Dunlop. Half-brother to

Youtalktoomuch (by Thousand Words), placed fourth once over 7f at 2 yrs in 2012 in Ireland. The dam won at 2 yrs in Italy and was listed-placed twice and is a half-sister to one winner. The second dam, Irish Flower (by Zieten), a listed-placed winner of 4 races in France, is a half-sister to 9 winners. (Hamdan Al Maktoum). *"I particularly liked this horse at the Sales but that said he's not as precocious as I'd hoped he be. I think Acclamations tend to take a bit more time than people imagine. He seems fine, he won't be that early, but we're happy with him".*

452. MIYACHIKU ★★★
b.c. Pivotal – First Bloom (Fusaichi Pegasus). February 19. Third foal. The dam, a modest 7f placed 2-y-o, is a half-sister to 9 winners including the very smart colt Diffident, winner of the Group 3 6f Diadem Stakes, the Group 3 6f Prix de Ris-Orangis and the listed 7f European Free Handicap and to the dams of 4 stakes winners. The second dam, Shy Princess (by Irish River), a smart French 2-y-o 7f winner and second in the Group 1 Prix Morny, won over 6f as a 3-y-o and is a half-sister to 7 winners including the Breeders Cup Mile winner and Eclipse Stakes second Opening Verse and the US Grade 3 winner So She Sleeps. (Mrs S M Roy). *"He looked like being early but not surprisingly for a Pivotal he's grown and done well. He's found life very easy with what he's doing, he's a bit of a cheeky boy but we don't mind that. One for the second half of the season I'd say, but we like him".*

453. MUSALAHA (IRE) ★★
b.f. Nayef – Gilded (Redback). March 30. Second living foal. 80,000Y. Tattersalls October Book 1. Shadwell Estate Co. The dam, a winner of 5 races including the Group 2 5f Queen Mary Stakes, is a half-sister to 2 winners. The second dam, Tumbleweed Pearl (by Aragon), a fairly useful 5.7f (at 2 yrs) and 6f winner of 3 races, is a half-sister to 6 winners including the Group 3 Horris Hill Stakes, Ballycorus Stakes and Prix de la Porte Maillot winner Tumbledown Ridge. (Hamdan Al Maktoum). *"A good-moving filly with a bit of a strange pedigree being by Nayef out of a Queen Mary winner. Quite light-framed, I would expect her to make a 2-y-o sometime from mid-to-late*

season. She doesn't seem to have inherited the speed of her dam".

454. OASIS FANTASY (IRE) ★★★

br.c. Oasis Dream – Cara Fantasy (Sadler's Wells). April 16. Sixth foal. Half-brother to the very smart 2-y-o Group 3 7f Acomb Stakes and Group 3 1m Craven Stakes winner and Group 1 Racing Post Trophy second Elusive Pimpernel (by Elusive Quality), to the smart 1m (at 2 yrs), Group 3 10f Strensall Stakes and listed 9f winner Palavicini (by Giant's Causeway), the fair 10f and 12f winner Miss Topsy Turvy (by Mr Greeley) and the moderate 2-y-o 10f winner Better Be Mine (by Big Bad Bob). The dam, a quite useful dual 12f winner, is closely related to the Group 2 winner Lucky Guest and a half-sister to numerous winners. (Windflower Overseas Holdings Inc & J L Dunlop). *"He's only recently arrived here but he's fitted in very well. A good-looking horse and very athletic, he seems to go nicely so far".*

455. REHANAAT (USA) ★★

b.f. Daaher – Sultana (Storm Cat). Half-sister to the smart 7f (at 2 yrs), UAE Group 1m and listed 1m winner Derbaas (by Seeking The Gold) and to the quite useful 1m winner Jaleela (by Kingmambo). The dam is an unraced sister to the high-class Group 1 7f Prix de la Salamandre and Group 1 1m Sussex Stakes winner Aljabr. The second dam, Sierra Madre (by Baillamont), a very smart winner of the Group 1 1m Prix Marcel Boussac and the Group 1 12f Prix Vermeille, is a half-sister to several minor winners. (Hamdan Al Maktoum). *"She's still in Dubai so I can't comment on her. The sire is a son of Awesome Again, he won the Cigar Mile in the USA and he's bred the US dual Grade 2 winner Gypsy Robin".*

456. ROXANNA ★★★

b.f. Myboycharlie – Anagram (Efisio). April 1. First foal. £18,000Y. Doncaster Premier. Ed Dunlop. The dam, a modest 6f and 7f placed maiden, is a half-sister to 4 winners including the listed-placed Sienna Storm. The second dam, Saint Ann (by Geiger Counter), placed fourth once at 2 yrs, is a half-sister to 5 winners. (PLP Partnership). *"She was bought cheaply and yet by the end of the year everyone wanted to buy the sire's yearlings.*

A good-bodied filly, it's a not a phenomenal pedigree – no disrespect to the breeder – but being by Myboycharlie out of an Efisio mare suggests speed. She grew a lot but she's done well and she's now back to where we bought her. A good-looking filly, I like her and she goes OK".* TRAINERS' BARGAIN BUY

457. SHUSHU SUGARTOWN (IRE) ★★★★

b.f. Invincible Spirit – Landela (Alhaarth). March 30. Fifth foal. €50,000Y. Goffs Orby. McKeever Bloodstock. Half-sister to the French 2-y-o 7f winner and listed-placed Impendor (by Holy Roman Emperor), to the quite useful 2-y-o 1m and subsequent US winner Get A Grip (by Royal Applause) and the quite useful 1m and 9f winner Trumpington Street (by Noverre). The dam, placed fourth on both her starts over 7f and 1m at 4 yrs, is a half-sister to 6 winners including the Group 1 Grand Prix de Paris and Group 2 Prix Foy winner Zambezi Sun and the Group 2 Prix Guillaume d'Ornano winner Kalabar. The second dam, Imbabala (by Zafonic), won at 3 yrs in France and is a half-sister to 6 winners including the French Group 3 winner Short Pause, the French 1m listed winner Cheyenne Dream and the dam of the Group 1 winner Continent. (Mr N Martin). *"A fastish 2-y-o with a slight knee action, she'll be a six furlong filly I would have thought. She wouldn't want the ground too firm, looks tough, looks to show some speed and she'll be relatively early".*

458. TAQNEEN (IRE) ★★★★

b.c. Cape Cross – Badee'a (Marju). April 6. Sixth foal. 240,000Y. Tattersalls October Book 1. Shadwell Estate Co. Half-brother to the smart winner of four listed races over 7f and 1m winner Dunelight (by Desert Sun), to the very useful dual 7f and subsequent UAE winner Leahurst (by Verglas) and the fair 2-y-o 6f winner Writingonthewall (by Danetime). The dam is an unraced sister to the Group 3 Prix Quincey winner Mahboob and a half-sister to 4 winners. The second dam, Miss Gris (by Hail The Pirates), won the Group 1 Italian 1,000 Guineas and the Group 1 Italian Oaks and is a half-sister to two US stakes winners. (Hamdan Al Maktoum). *"This is a nice horse. He's grown quite a lot recently and being by Cape Cross he'll be one for the second half of the season. A good-looking horse with no physical problems whatsoever – we like him".*

459. ZAAWIA (IRE) ★★
ch.f. Elnadim – Nidhaal (Observatory).
March 21. Fourth foal. Half-sister to the fair 2012 2-y-o 6f winner Sharaarah, to the quite useful 2-y-o 5f and 6f winner Sadafiya (both by Oasis Dream) and the useful 2-y-o 5f winner and dual Group 2 placed Burwaaz (by Exceed And Excel). The dam, a very useful 2-y-o listed 6f winner and second in the Group 3 6f Princess Margaret Stakes, is a half-sister to 2 winners. The second dam, Jeed (by Mujtahid), a quite useful 2-y-o 6f winner, is a half-sister to 2 winners. (Hamdan Al Maktoum). *"A strange one, because I thought she'd be early but she's probably not going to be and she's back at the farm having a break now. I've trained them all out of the dam and she's bred to be fast, but the jury's out at present".*

460. UNNAMED ★★★★
b.br.c. Henrythenavigator – Archstone (Arch).
February 2. First foal. $47,000foal. Keeneland November. Not sold. The dam, a winner of 3 races in the USA at 3 and 4 yrs, was stakes-placed and is a half-sister to 7 winners. The second dam, Aliata (by Mr Prospector), won twice at 2 yrs and is a half-sister to the Group 3 winners Brogan and War Of Words and of the useful sire Topsider. *"A big horse, I like him and he's a beautiful mover. The stallion's doing well and this will be a second half of the season 2-y-o due to his size. Nice".*

461. UNNAMED ★★★★
gr.f. Galileo – Hotelgenie Dot Com (Selkirk).
March 18. Ninth foal. 210,000Y. Tattersalls October Book 1. Hugo Lascelles. Closely related to Enaitch (by New Approach), placed third over 1m on her only start at 2 yrs in 2012 and half-sister to the Group 1 Fillies' Mile and Group 1 Falmouth Stakes winner Simply Perfect (by Danehill) and the minor Irish 12f winner Allied Answer (by Danehill Dancer). The dam, a 7f winner at 2 yrs, was second in the Group 1 7f Moyglare Stud Stakes and third in the Group 1 Fillies' Mile and is a half-sister to 4 winners including the Moyglare Stud Stakes and the Group 2 6f Lowther Stakes winner Bianca Nera. The second dam, Birch

Creek (by Carwhite), was placed five times including when third in the Group 3 1m Premio Royal Mares and is a half-sister to 7 winners including the useful Group 3 winning sprinter Great Deeds. (St Albans Bloodstock). *"A half-sister to a Group 1 winner, she's a nice filly that looks very racy. Very athletic, she does everything easily and she should be in the book. Nice".*

462. UNNAMED ★★★
b.c. Dalakhani – Jamboretta (Danehill). April 1. Second foal. 90,000Y. Tattersalls October Book 2. Charlie Gordon-Watson. The dam, a quite useful 9f winner, is a half-sister to 2 winners including the very useful listed winner and Group 3 second Excusez Moi. The second dam, Jiving (by Generous), a fair 6f placed 2-y-o, is a half-sister to 7 winners including the outstanding broodmare Hasili (dam of the Group 1 winners Banks Hill, Cacique, Champs Elysees, Heat Haze and Intercontinental and the Group 2 winner and leading sire Dansili) and the listed winner Arrive (dam of the Group 1 Pretty Polly Stakes winner Promising Lead) and to the unraced dam of the US Grade 1 winner Leroidesanimaux. (Mr R G Arculli & Mr Robert Ng). *"This is a nice colt, I like him but he's by Dalakhani so he'll need some time. A big horse that goes OK "*

463. UNNAMED ★★★
b.f. Galileo – La Sylvia (Oasis Dream). February 10. First foal. 570,000Y. Tattersalls October Book 1. Badgers Bloodstock. The dam, a quite useful Irish dual 5f and subsequent German listed winner, is a half-sister to 5 winners including the 2-y-o listed 7f Prix Herod winner and smart hurdler Power Elite. The second dam, Hawas (by Mujtahid), a 1m winner at 3 yrs in Ireland, is a sister to the listed winner Mutakarrim and a half-sister to 7 winners including the listed winner Nafisah. (Mrs G A Rupert). *"Not a big, backward Galileo, she's athletic, moves well and hasn't had any problems so far. We haven't done much with her yet but she'll probably be a 2-y-o, especially as she's out of an Oasis Dream mare".*

464. UNNAMED ★★★
b.c. Oratorio – Lucy Cavendish (Elusive Quality). April 3. Second foal. 100,000Y.

Tattersalls October Book 2. Charlie Gordon-Watson. The dam is an unraced half-sister to 7 winners including the 2-y-o Group 3 1m Prix des Reservoirs winner and Group 1 Prix Saint-Alary third Summertime Legacy (herself dam of the French Group 1 winners Wavering and Mandaean). The second dam, Zawaahy (by El Gran Senor), a fairly useful 1m winner, was placed at up to 11.5f and is closely related to the Derby winner Golden Fleece. (Mr R G Arculli & Mr Robert Ng). *"I like him but he's a big horse and more of a back-end of the season 2-y-o. A good-looking horse and a very good mover".*

465. UNNAMED ★★★
ch.f. Galileo – Mubkera (Nashwan). February 5. Seventh foal. 150,000Y. Tattersalls October Book 1. Badgers Bloodstock. Closely related to the fair 12f winner First Battalion (by Sadler's Wells) and half-sister to the very smart Group 3 9f Strensall Stakes and Group 3 11f Dubai Duty Free Arc Trial winner Green Destiny (by Green Desert), the useful 1m (at 2 yrs) and 10f winner Aqwaal (by Red Ransom) and the minor 12f and hurdles winner Manjam (by Almutawakel). The dam, a quite useful 1m winner (at 2 yrs) and listed placed over 10f and 11.5f, is a half-sister to 4 winners. The second dam, Na Ayim (by Shirley Heights), a modest 2-y-o 6f winner, is a half-sister to 5 winners out of a half-sister to the dams of Rainbow Quest, Warning and Commander In Chief. (Mrs G A Rupert). *"I trained the dam and a couple of her offspring so I know the family very well. I liked her at the Sales, she's very racey and athletic. Having a break at the moment, I see her as a seven furlong plus 2-y-o".*

466. UNNAMED ★★★
b.c. Sakhee's Secret – Sinduda (Anabaa). March 31. Third foal. 75,000Y. Tattersalls December. Charlie Gordon-Watson. Half-brother to the quite useful 2012 2-y-o 7f winner Banovallum (by Invincible Spirit). The dam, a French 3-y-o 1m winner, is a half-sister to 8 winners including the very useful 2-y-o 5f and 6f winner and Cornwallis Stakes second Deadly Nightshade, the useful Irish 7f and 10f winner Hamad and the quite useful 6f winner Dodo (herself the dam of 2 stakes winners). The

second dam, Dead Certain (by Absalom), a very smart winner of the Group 1 6f Cheveley Park Stakes, the Queen Mary Stakes, the Lowther Stakes (all at 2 yrs) and the Group 2 6.5f Prix Maurice de Gheest, is a half-sister to 7 winners. (Mr R G Arculli & Mr Robert Ng). *"He had a slight problem but he's over that now and he's a strong, scopey horse. I like him but he won't be an early 2-y-o although his pedigree suggests he will run this year".*

HARRY DUNLOP
467. CADMIUM ★★★
b.f. Major Cadeaux – Miss Mirasol (Sheikh Albadou). April 17. 6,500Y. Tattersalls October Book 2. McKeever Bloodstock. Half-sister to the unplaced 2012 2-y-o (in two starts) Dalhousie Lassie (by Indesatchel), to the quite useful 10f to 12f and hurdles winner Dark Prospect (by Nayef), the fair 2-y-o 7f winner Cool Valentine (by One Cool Cat) and the fair 2-y-o 6f and 7f winner Blodwen Abbey (by Firebreak). The dam, a 2-y-o listed 6f winner, is a half-sister to 6 winners including the fairly useful 2-y-o dual 5f winner Let's Be Fair and the fairly useful 5f (at 2 yrs) and 6f winner Labrett. The second dam, Play The Game (by Mummy's Game), a fair 2-y-o 5f winner, is a half-sister to 6 winners including the Italian Group 1 winner Svelt, the Italian Group 3 winner and Group 1 placed Smageta and the dam of the Italian Group 1 winner Shulich. (Susan Abbott Racing). *"She wasn't expensive, I think she'll be relatively forward and she's doing some upsides cantering work now. I like her, she's from a nice, female family and I think we'll be starting her off at six furlongs. She's beginning to look like a sharper sort now".*

468. CINNAMON SPICE ★★★
b.br.c. High Chaparral – Hot And Spicy (Grand Lodge). February 9. Fourth foal. 21,000Y. Tattersalls October Book 2. Harry Dunlop. Half-brother to the useful 2012 2-y-o 7f winner and Group 2 7f Vintage Stakes third Luhaif (by Cape Cross). The dam, placed third over 7f at 2 yrs in Ireland, is a half-sister to 3 winners including the Group 1 11f Italian Oaks winner Zanzibar (herself dam of the US Grade 2 winner Spice Route) and the listed winner New Guinea. The second dam, Isle Of Spice (by Diesis), a fair 3-y-o 9.7f winner, is a

half-sister to 5 winners including the minor US 2-y-o stakes winner Crown Silver. (Be Hopeful (2)). *"A horse we like very much, but he'll take some time and he's had a break in the paddocks recently. Seven furlongs should do for him to start with"*.

469. EARLY MORNING (IRE) ★★★★

gr.c. *New Approach – Summer's Eve (Singspiel).* April 15. First foal. 36,000Y. Tattersalls October Book 2. Not sold. The dam, a fairly useful 9f winner, was third in the Group 3 Prix Chloe and in the listed Lingfield Oaks Trial and is a half-sister to 9 winners including the triple Group 1 winner Silver Patriarch and the Group 1 Ascot Gold Cup winner Papineau. The second dam, Early Rising (by Grey Dawn II), a minor winner at 3 yrs in the USA, is a half-sister to 6 winners including the Group 3 winner and smart broodmare Clare Bridge. (Early Risers). *"A big, grey horse, he hasn't been here long but he goes nicely. He'll take some time and he's probably a seven furlong type, but he's by the right sire in New Approach, I like him and he goes OK"*.

470. GAMGOOM ★★★

b.c. *Exceed And Excel – Danidh Dubai (Noverre).* March 19. Second foal. The dam, a fairly useful 2-y-o 6f winner, was third in the Group 3 Albany Stakes and is a half-sister to the 2-y-o winner and Group 3 6f Princess Margaret Stakes second Full Mandate. The second dam, Dani Ridge (by Indian Ridge), a quite useful triple 6f winner, is a sister to the Group 3 Diomed Stakes winner Blomberg and a half-sister to 2 winners. (J Abdullah). *"He's done very well physically, having looked quite backward when he arrived. The dam was a useful 2-y-o and at the moment I'm happy with what I'm seeing. A big, rangy horse, he's probably a seven furlong 2-y-o"*.

471. GENEROUS HEART ★★★

ch.f. *Sakhee's Secret – Lonely Heart (Midyan).* February 25. Half-sister to the smart Group 3 7f Tetrarch Stakes winner Leitrim House (by Cadeaux Genereux), to the fairly useful 7f and 1m winner of 5 races Ace Of Hearts (by Magic Ring), the fairly useful 2-y-o 5f winner Place In My Heart (by Compton Place), the fair 2-y-o 7f winner Missed A Beat (by Mister Baileys)

and the fair 7f winner Golden Heart (by Salse). The dam, a useful dual 10f winner, was listed-placed and is a half-sister to 4 winners out of the quite useful 7f to 10f winner Take Heart (by Electric), herself a half-sister to 3 minor winners. (Harry Dunlop Racing Partnership). *"She's a filly we've leased from Whitsbury Stud. A lovely mover and light on her feet, she'll probably want decent ground and I think she'll be a sprinter from July onwards"*.

472. HAVANA GIRL (IRE) ★★★

ch.f. *Teofilo – Future Flight (Polar Falcon).* February 26. Seventh foal. 40,000Y. Tattersalls October Book 1. Crimbourne Stud. Half-sister to the Italian 3-y-o winner and listed 7f placed Gothic Dance (by Dalakhani) and to the fair dual 1m winner Flying Silks (by Barathea). The dam, a 6f winner at 3 yrs, is a half-sister to 5 winners including the Group 1 Haydock Park Sprint Cup winner Tante Rose and the Sweet Solera Stakes winner Bay Tree. The second dam, My Branch (by Distant Relative), a winner of two listed races over 6f (at 2 yrs) and 7f, was placed in the Cheveley Park Stakes and the Irish 1,000 Guineas and is a half-sister to 6 winners. (Sir Eric Parker & Mary Anne Parker). *"She's done very well recently and I should imagine she'll be out in June or July over seven furlongs. What we're seeing at the moment we like"*.

473. JANET'S LEGACY ★★★

b.f. *Bahamian Bounty – Spunger (Fraam).* January 15. Third foal. £13,000Y. Doncaster Premier. Harry Dunlop. Half-sister to the modest 2012 5f to 7f placed 2-y-o Annie Gogh (by Dutch Art) and to the modest 2-y-o 6f and 9f winner Guava (by Kyllachy). The dam, a modest 1m and 10f winner, is a half-sister to 3 winners including useful 2-y-o 7f winner and Group 3 7f Acomb Stakes second Gweebarra. The second dam, Complimentary Pass (by Danehill), a quite useful 1m placed maiden, is a half-sister to 5 minor winners. (The Spungers). *"She's got some speed in the pedigree but the mother did stay, so she's probably going to be a seven furlong filly. At the moment she's going OK"*.

474. LACERTA ★★★

b.c. *Astronomer Royal – Rubber (Namid).* April

4. Second foal. 35,000Y. Tattersalls October Book 1. D Farrington. Brother to Elastomer, placed fourth once over 5f at 2 yrs in Ireland in 2012. The dam, placed four times here over 5f and 6f and subsequently a listed stakes winner in the USA, is a half-sister to 3 winners. The second dam, Bold Fashion (by Nashwan), a minor French 10.5f winner, is a sister to one winner and a half-sister to 11 winners including the French and US Group 2 winner Spring Star. (S F Bloodstock). *"A big, strong colt, he's a lovely mover and we've done well with the sire. I think he could be an interesting horse over seven furlongs and a mile".*

475. MACNAMARA ★★★

ch.f. Dylan Thomas – Portrait Of A Lady (Peintre Celebre). April 12. 18,000Y. Tattersalls October Book 2. Not sold. Half-sister to the 2012 2-y-o 7f winner and Group 1 10f Criterium de Saint-Cloud third Miss You Too, to the useful Irish 2-y-o 7f winner and Group 3 7f Killavullan Stakes second Vitruvian Man (both by Montjeu) and the modest 6f winner Marshall Art (by Lawman). The dam was a fairly useful listed-placed 12f winner of 3 races and a half-sister to 3 winners. The second dam, Starlight Smile (Green Dancer), is an unraced half-sister to 4 winners including the dam of the Irish Derby winner Grey Swallow. (Sir Eric Parker & Mary Anne Parker). *"A rangy chestnut filly, she goes quite well and hopefully she'll be one to follow later on".*

476. RURAL AFFAIR ★★★

b.f. Pastoral Pursuits – Torcross (Vettori). February 19. Fourth living foal. 5,500Y. Tattersalls October Book 3. Harry Dunlop. Half-sister to the fair 10f, 12f and hurdles winner Bagber (by Diktat). The dam, a useful 2-y-o 7f winner, is a half-sister to the very useful 6f (at 2 yrs), Group 3 7.5f Concorde Stakes and dual listed winner Sheppard's Watch. The second dam, Sheppard's Cross (by Soviet Star), a quite useful 7f winner of 3 races, is a half-sister to 5 winners including the Irish listed sprint winner Clean Cut. *"I trained her half-brother Bagber who was a big horse, but this filly is very much a 2-y-o type, she's done some work and I like her. I don't think she's a five furlong type, so I can see her starting off in a six furlong maiden".* TRAINERS' BARGAIN BUY

477. SPACE WALKER (IRE) ★★★★

b.c. Astronomer Royal – Hot Property (Thunder Gulch). February 23. Second foal. €25,000Y. Arqana Deauville August (private sale). Brother to the 2012 French 1m placed 2-y-o Seven Seas. The dam, a winner of 3 minor races in the USA, is a half-sister to 6 winners including the US Grade 2 winner New Economy. The second dam, Sunyata (by Proud Truth), is an unraced half-sister to 8 winners including the US Grade 3 winner Wings Of Grace (herself dam of the US Grade 1 winners Soaring Softly and Plenty Of Grace). *"A horse I really like, he's changed enormously over the last couple of months. He'll probably race in England at least to start with, but there's always the option of him going over to France because of the French premiums. A seven furlong type 2-y-o that could be interesting later in the season".*

478. SPANISH ARTIST ★★★

gr.c. Archipenko – Alicante (Pivotal). February 2. First foal. 17,000Y. Tattersalls October Book 3. Not sold. The dam, a fair dual 11f winner, is a half-sister to 3 winners. The second dam, Alba Stella (by Nashwan), a fairly useful dual 12f winner, is a half-sister to 7 winners including the high-class dual Champion Stakes winner Alborada, the triple German Group 1 winner Albanova and the dam of the Epsom Derby second Dragon Dancer. (Bluehills Racing Ltd). *"A bonny little horse that's doing all the time. He was bred by the owners, I would imagine he might be a six furlong horse to start with, but I can see him progressing to seven. He's going OK".*

479. STAR ANISE (FR) ★★★

b.f. Astronomer Royal – Sasicha (Montjeu). February 5. First foal. €17,000Y. Arqana Deauville August. Sackville/Donald. The dam is an unplaced half-sister to 5 winners including the triple Group 3 winner Carribean Sunset. The second dam, Bonheur (by Royal Academy), a fairly useful Irish 3-y-o 6f winner, is a half-sister to 7 winners including the Group 1 German 2,000 Guineas winner Quebrada and to the placed dam of the Group 1 German Oaks winner Silvester Lady. (The Astronomers 2). *"A filly we bought on the back of the useful 2-y-o we had last year, Sir Patrick Moore, for the same owners. She'll hopefully be racing here in England and then end up going over to France to race for their premiums. She was a filly who showed a lot of speed initially, but she's grown and changed since then. My feeling now is that she'll be a six/seven furlong 2-y-o and her action suggests she might appreciate softer ground".*

TIM EASTERBY

480. BOUNTY GIRL (IRE)
b.f. Bushranger – Josphiel (Okawango). January 25. First foal. €20,000Y. Goffs Sportsman's. Tim Easterby. The dam, a moderate dual 6f placed maiden, is a half-sister to 7 winners including the listed winner and Group 1 Cheveley Park Stakes third Good Girl. The second dam, Indian Honey (by Indian King), is an unraced half-sister to 7 winners. (P C J Bourke).

481. DANZIG IN THE DARK (IRE)
b.f. Mastercraftsman – Cape Jasmine (Danehill). April 9. Third foal. £20,000Y. Doncaster Premier. Tim Easterby. Half-sister to Chorister Choir (by Choisir), unplaced in two starts at 2 yrs in 2012. The dam is an unplaced half-sister to 5 winners including the smart 7f (at 2 yrs) and Group 3 1m Desmond Stakes winner Haami and the dam of the Group 2 winner Akmal. The second dam, Oumaldaaya (by Swain), a very useful filly, won over 7f at 2yrs and the Group 2 10f Premio Lydia Tesio and listed 10f Lupe Stakes at 3 yrs. She is a half-sister to 6 winners including the Derby winner Erhaab. (Mr & Mrs J D Cotton).

482. DUTCH BREEZE
ch.c. Dutch Art – Oasis Breeze (Oasis Dream). March 21. First foal. £62,000Y. Doncaster Premier. Tim Easterby. The dam, a quite useful 2-y-o 5f and 6f winner, is a half-sister to 7 winners including the US stakes winner Stormy Forever. The second dam, Forever Fine (by Sunshine Forever), a US stakes-placed winner at 2 yrs, is a half-sister to 7 winners. (Mr & Mrs J D Cotton).

483. SOUL BROTHER (IRE)
b.c. Captain Rio – Goodwood March (Foxhound). February 15. Fourth foal. £38,000Y. Doncaster Premier. Tim Easterby. Brother to the fairly useful 2012 2-y-o 5f and listed 6f winner Body And Soul and half-

brother to the fairly useful Irish 1m winner Strada Colorato (by Le Vie Dei Colori) and the Italian 2-y-o winner Stella Senza Cielo (by Elusive City). The dam, a moderate 6f winner at 3 yrs, is a half-sister to 5 winners including the useful 7f to 10f winner and listed placed Nice Tune and the fairly useful 7f winner and dual listed placed Play That Tune. The second dam, Military Tune (by Nashwan), is an unraced half-sister to the smart Group 1 10f Prix Saint-Alary winner Muncie, to the smart Group 1 15.5f Prix Royal-Oak winner Mersey and the dam of the US Grade 1 winner Subtle Power. (C H Stevens).

484. STORYLINE (IRE)
b.f. Kodiac – Petite Histoire (Desert Story). April 25. Third foal. £15,000Y. Doncaster Premier. Tim Easterby. The dam, a fairly useful triple 5f winner, was third in the listed Marble Hill Stakes and is a half-sister to 4 winners including the Group 3 5f Molecomb Stakes Whitbarrow. The dam, Danccini (by Dancing Dissident), a minor Irish 2-y-o 5f winner, is a half-sister to 4 winners. (Miss Y M G Jacques).

ROBERT EDDERY

485. DONNCHA ★★★
br.c. Captain Marvelous – Seasonal Style (Generous). March 29. Ninth foal. €14,500Y. Tattersalls Ireland September. Robert Eddery. Half-brother to the fairly useful Irish and US 6f to 1m winner Perfect Casting (by Diesis), to the fairly useful Irish triple 12f winner Rich Sense (by Mt Livermore), the quite useful 10f winner Tropical Chic (by Thunder Gulch), to the Spanish 2-y-o winner Sergei, the fair Irish 2-y-o 7f and subsequent German winner Hard Warrior (both by Gulch) and the fair 2-y-o 6f winner Greatest Dancer (by Iffraaj). The dam, a fairly useful Irish 9f and 10f winner, subsequently won in the USA and is a half-sister to 3 winners. The second dam, Just Society (by Devil's Bag), won over 5f and 6f at 3 yrs in Ireland and is a half-sister to 3 winners. *"He'll probably end up getting a mile and I'd put him down as one of my nicest 2-y-o's. He's in the Sales race in Ireland, so I don't want to do too much too early with him. A good-looking, strong horse that will make a 2-y-o in the second half of the season. I own him and I'm keeping him as well!".*

486. OLYMNIA ★★★

b.f. Teofilo – Diotima (High Estate). February 23. Ninth foal. €34,000Y. Arqana Deauville August. Robert Eddery. Closely related to the 11f winner and listed-placed Melisos (by Galileo) and half-sister to 6 winners including the French middle-distance winners Diango (by Spinning World) and Alfreda (by Unfuwain). The dam, a winner of 3 races at 2 to 4 yrs and listed-placed three times, is a half-sister to 3 winners. The second dam, Rentina (by Adonijah), is a placed half-sister to 7 winners including Upend (Group 3 St Simon Stakes). (EDF Roofing Supplies Midlands Ltd). *"A big, tall, rangy filly, I've only just started cantering her but she's a lovely mover and has a great attitude. She'll be out around August or September time. A nice, progressive filly, she was bought in France so if she's any good she'll be sent to race over there. I like her a lot".*

487. RED OASIS ★★★

b.c. Captain Gerrard – Sahara Silk (Desert Style). February 19. Fourth foal. £11,000Y. Doncaster Festival. Robert Eddery. Half-brother to the modest 2012 5f and 6f placed 2-y-o Whistling Buddy (by Piccolo). The dam, a fair winner of 10 races over 5f and 6f, is a half-sister to one winner. The second dam, Buddy And Soda (by Imperial Frontier), is a half-sister to 9 winners. (Danethorpe Racing Partnership). *"He'll be racing by the end of April. He's a very strong little colt, I think he'll be a fast ground horse and although he might need his first run I'm sure he'll win races. Definitely a sprinting type, he's matured and is ready now".*

488. SHREWD BOB (IRE) ★★★

b.c. Whipper – Cheyenne Spirit (Indian Ridge). January 22. €20,000Y. Tattersalls Ireland September. Robert Eddery. Brother to the French 3-y-o 1m winner Spirit Danon and half-brother to the useful 2-y-o dual 6f winner and subsequent US stakes winner Alinga, the modest 12f winner Regal Warrior (both by King's Theatre) and the modest 9f winner Shoooz (by Soviet Star). The dam, a useful winner of 7 races including a listed event over 6f, is a half-sister to 5 winners including the dam of the Group 3 winner Ashdown Express. The second dam, Bazaar Promise (by Native Bazaar), is an unplaced sister to the very useful sprinter Crofthall. (Mr E Phillips). *"Quite a tall horse, he's big and rangy, he's only just started working but he does show up really well. He's in the Sales race in Ireland because he was bought at that sale and I hope to get him out around June time. He's quite speedily bred and he should be quick enough for six furlongs".*

DAVID ELSWORTH

489. DASHING PRINCE ★★★

b.c. Nayef – Dashiba (Dashing Blade). February 4. Half-brother to the quite useful 2012 2-y-o 1m winner Dashing Star (by Teofilo), to the dual Group 2 Lancashire Oaks winner of 7 races Barshiba (by Barathea), the useful 2-y-o listed 1m winner Doctor Dash, the fair 2-y-o 1m winner Dashing Doc (both by Dr Fong) and the modest dual 10f winner Westhaven (by Alhaarth). The dam, a useful 9f and 10f winner, is a half-sister to several winners including the fairly useful 10f and 12f winner Smart Blade. The second dam, Alsiba (by Northfields), a modest winner of one race at 4 yrs, was a staying half-sister to several winners and to the dam of the Irish St Leger winner Oscar Schindler. (J C Smith). *"A big, strong horse. Like his siblings he'll be a back-end 2-y-o and I expect him to show me something then, so he won't be early but he's a quality 2-y-o".*

490. JUSTICE DAY ★★★★

b.c. Acclamation – Rock Exhibition (Rock Of Gibraltar). March 17. First foal. £42,000 2-y-o. Kempton Breeze-Up. D Elsworth. The dam, a fair Irish 1m winner, is a half-sister to 4 winners. The second dam, Finity (by Diesis), a useful 2-y-o 7f winner, was third in the Group 3 7f C L Weld Park Stakes and is a half-sister to 4 winners including Cavalryman (Group 1 Grand Prix de Paris). *Bought at the Breeze Up sale, he won on his debut at Newbury in mid-April.*

491. PRAIRIE PRIZE ★★★

b.c. High Chaparral – Premier Prize (Selkirk). March 1. Sixth foal. Half-brother to the useful 2012 2-y-o 1m winner and Group 3 1m Prix des Reservoirs second Cocktail Queen (by Motivator) and to the fair 7f and 1m winner Hidden Fire (by Alhaarth). The dam, a useful

7f (at 2 yrs) and listed 10f winner, was third in the Group 2 Sandown Mile and is a half-sister to 7 winners including the Group 2 15f Prix Kergorlay winner Gold Medallist. The second dam, Spot Prize (by Seattle Dancer), a useful filly, won over 5f at 2 yrs and was fourth in the Oaks. (J C Smith). *"A three-parts brother to Western Prize, a decent horse Ralph Beckett trained by High Chaparral out of Spot Prize. This is a princely-looking horse – he's got a lot of style, he's not backward-looking and he'll be a second half of the season 2-y-o".*

492. WATER DANCER (IRE) ★★★

ch.c. Ad Valorem – River Patrol (Rousillon). April 15. Thirteenth foal. 30,000Y. Tattersalls December. D Elsworth. Half-brother to 8 winners including the Group 3 Earl Of Sefton Stakes and Group 3 Sovereign Stakes winner and multiple Group 1 placed Norse Dancer, the quite useful Irish 9f winner Romie's Kastett (both by Halling), the German winner and listed-placed Rhapsody In Blue (by Winged Love), the fair 10f winner Regal Patrol (by Red Ransom), the German 12f, 14f and jumps winner Reginaldinho (by Galileo) and the modest 10f winner Incarnation (by Samum). The dam, a fairly useful 10.2f winner, is a half-sister to 3 winners including the smart middle-distance stayer Dry Dock and to the dams of the Group/Grade 1 winners Mail The Desert and Good Faith. The second dam, Boathouse (by Habitat), a smart winner of 2 races, was third in the Sun Chariot Stakes and is a half-sister to 8 winners including the Oaks winner Bireme and the Coronation Cup winner Buoy. (J C Smith). *"A very well-balanced horse that's improved rapidly since I got him here from the sales. We'll start him off at six or seven furlongs in mid-season but I'd say a mile would be his optimum trip later on".*

493. UNNAMED ★★

ch.f. Compton Place – Phoenix Rising (Dr Fong). March 6. First foal. £18,000foal. Tattersalls December. D Elsworth. The dam is an unraced half-sister to 9 winners including the very useful 2-y-o 5f and 6f winner and Cornwallis Stakes second Deadly Nightshade. The second dam, Dead Certain (by Absalom), a very smart winner of the Group 1 6f Cheveley Park Stakes and the Group 2 6.5f

Prix Maurice de Gheest, is a half-sister to 7 winners and to the placed dam of the Group 2 Gimcrack Stakes winner Bannister. (Al Hodge and D Elsworth). *"She's a filly from one of my old families and that's the reason I bought her. She looks quite forward so she'll be a 2-y-o alright, but I haven't got going with her yet so I couldn't say how early she'll be".*

JAMES EUSTACE

494. DANCING ANGEL ★★

ch.f. Norse Dancer – Indian Angel (Indian Ridge). February 14. The dam is an unraced half-sister to 3 winners. The second dam, Lochangel (by Night Shift), a very smart winner of the Group 1 5f Nunthorpe Stakes, is a half-sister to the champion sprinter Lochsong. (J C Smith). *"She's an amazing filly in that she had quite a serious problem with her foot as a yearling, but she's got over it and now she's a very nice-looking filly. She's got a crest like a colt and yet seems very amenable and isn't an aggressive filly at all. She's levelled out and very strongly made, so I certainly wouldn't rule out a 2-y-o career for her, but she's only just being ridden away after her foot problems".*

495. GREEN MUSIC ★★★

b.f. Oratorio – Loch Verdi (Green Desert). March 13. Second foal. Half-sister to the 2012 2-y-o 6f winner, on her only start, Gift Of Music (by Cadeaux Genereux). The dam, a useful listed 5f winner of 4 races, is a half-sister to several winners including the smart listed 6f winner of 5 races Lochridge. The second dam, Lochsong (by Song), a champion sprinter and winner of the Prix de l'Abbaye (twice), the Kings Stand Stakes and the Nunthorpe Stakes, is a half-sister to the Nunthorpe Stakes winner Lochangel. (J C Smith). *"A half-sister to Gift Of Music who won her only start right at the back-end as a 2-y-o. I think Green Music is physically more forward at this stage than she was – I hesitate slightly in saying that because it's Lochsong's family and they do improve with age. She's cantering up Warren Hill and she's not struggling, she's compact, very strong and built like a sprinter. Hopefully she's taking after the dam's side and she has a great attitude, just like Gift Of Music. The way she's built I would be looking at five/six furlongs and then we'll see where we go. I like her, particularly because of her attitude".*

496. MAJOR CRISPIES ★★★

b.c. Pastoral Pursuits – Nellie Melba (Hurricane Sky). April 23. Fifth foal. 26,000Y. Tattersalls October Book 2. James Eustace. Closely related to the quite useful 5f (including at 2 yrs) and 6f winner of 8 races Bosun Breese (by Bahamian Bounty) and half-brother to the 2-y-o 5f winner and 5f listed-placed Dam Beautiful (by Sleeping Indian). The dam, a fair 7f and 1m winner of 3 races, is a half-sister to 4 other minor winners. The second dam, Persuasion (by Batshoof), won 2 races over 10f and 12f and is a half-sister to 2 winners. (Mr Guy Carstairs). *"He's coming along nicely, he's a 2-y-o type and a half-brother to two 2-y-o winners. I'd expect him to be ready relatively early, maybe at the end of April or early May. Physically he's doing well and I'm pleased with how he gets up Warren Hill".*

497. NIMBLE KIMBLE ★★★

ch.f. Kirkwall – Lovely Lyca (Night Shift). March 6. Tenth living foal. 6,500Y. Tattersalls October Book 3. James Eustace. Half-sister to the fair 2-y-o 1m winner Brooksby (by Diktat), to the quite useful 2-y-o 6f winner and listed-placed Jeanmaire (by Dansili), the quite useful 3-y-o 1m winner Polish Off (by Polish Precedent), the fair 3-y-o 7.5f winner Lyca Ballerina (by Marju), the fair 6f winner Island Rhapsody (by Bahamian Bounty), the modest 7f and 1m winner Sophia Gardens (by Barathea) and a minor winner abroad by Zafonic. The dam, a fair 1m and 11.8f winner, is a sister to the listed 1m winner Barboukh (herself dam of the Group 3 10f Prix Exbury winner Barbola) and a half-sister to 6 winners. The second dam, Turban (by Glint Of Gold), a fair 10f and 11.7f winner, is a half-sister to the top-class middle-distance colt Old Vic and the dual Group 3 12f winner Splash Of Colour. (Mr Ian Rushby). *"I think she's quite sharp and I think the sire can get a 2-y-o alright - I've had a couple of nice winners by him. I like this filly and the dam has a decent record having had seven winners, including two as two-year-olds".*

498. POSTAL ORDER ★★★

b.f. Medicean – Postage Stampe (Singspiel).

February 2. Third foal. Half-sister to Poste Restante (by Halling), unplaced in two starts at 2 yrs in 2012 and to the fair 1m winner Fulney (by Dr Fong). The dam, a quite useful 7f (at 2 yrs) and 10f winner, is a half-sister to numerous winners. The second dam, Jaljuli (by Jalmood), a useful 2-y-o 5f and 6f winner, was third in the Group 1 Cheveley Park Stakes. (Major M G Wyatt). *"A very nicely-made filly, she's got a bit of size and scope but she's quite strong with it. So I think she'll be a mid-summer 2-y-o and she just might have a bit of class".*

RICHARD FAHEY

499. ABBEY VILLAGE (IRE)

ch.c. Aqlaam – Balladonia (Primo Dominie). March 18. Eighth foal. 80,000Y. Tattersalls October Book 1. Highfield Farm. Half-brother to the quite useful 2012 2-y-o 7f winner Related (by Kheleyf), to the very smart 2-y-o Group 1 7f Prix Jean-Luc Lagardere winner of 5 races Wootton Bassett (by Iffraaj), the fairly useful 5f (at 2 yrs) to 1m winner of 7 races and listed-placed Mister Hardy, the quite useful 6f winner Pretty Primo (both by Kyllachy), the fairly useful 2-y-o 6f to 1m and subsequent Hong Kong winner Zaal (by Alhaarth), the quite useful 6f winner of 4 races (including at 2 yrs) Mister Laurel (by Diktat) and the unplaced dam of the dual listed winner Katla. The dam, a useful 9f winner, was listed-placed twice over 10f and is a half-sister to 5 winners. The second dam, Susquehanna Days (by Chief's Crown), a fair 1m and 8.2f winner, is a half-sister to 6 winners including the Group 3 Gilltown Stud Stakes winner and good broodmare Clare Bridge.

500. BAHAMIAN C

b.c. Bahamian Bounty – Amandian (Indian Ridge). April 17. Seventh foal. 36,000Y. Tattersalls October Book 2. Robin O'Ryan. Half-brother to the quite useful Irish 2-y-o 7f winner Graceful Star (by Soviet Star), to the fair 2-y-o 6f winner Sunniva Duke (by Bachelor Duke), the modest 5f and 6f winner Tamarind Hill (by Shamardal) and a 4-y-o winner abroad by Librettist. The dam, an Irish 3-y-o 6f winner, is a half-sister to 9 winners including the very useful Group 3 1m Desmond Stakes winner Swift Gulliver and the useful 6f (at 2 yrs) and subsequent US stakes winner Abderian. The second dam, Aminata (by Glenstal), a useful winner of the Group 3 5f Curragh Stakes, is a half-sister to 4 winners.

501. BANDOLIER

b.c. *Bahamian Bounty – Todber (Cape Cross)*. April 25. First foal. The dam, a modest 5f and 6f winner of 3 races, is a half-sister to 2 winners. The second dam, Dominica (by Alhaarth), winner of the Group 2 5f Kings Stand Stakes and the Group 3 Cornwallis Stakes, is a half-sister to 3 winners including the listed-placed sprinter Bowness.

502. BAY STREET BELLE

ch.f. *Bahamian Bounty – Donna Anna (Be My Chief)*. March 15. Seventh foal. 25,000Y. Tattersalls October Book 3. Bobby O'Ryan. Half-sister to the quite useful 2012 2-y-o 5f to 7f winner Jamesbo's Girl (by Refuse To Bend), to the useful 5f (including at 2 yrs) to 7f winner of 8 races Northern Fling (by Mujadil) and the moderate 1m winner Desert Chieftain (by Green Desert). The dam is an unplaced sister to the US dual Grade 1 winner Donna Viola and a half-sister to 4 winners including the dam of the Group 1 July Cup winner Frizzante. The second dam, Countess Olivia (by Prince Tenderfoot), a fair 7f (at 2 yrs) and 10f winner, is a half-sister to 8 minor winners.

503. BRUNI HEINKE (IRE)

ch.f. *Dutch Art – Penchant (Kyllachy)*. April 3. Second foal. £75,000Y. Doncaster Premier. Highfield Farm. Sister to the very useful 2012 2-y-o listed 6f winner and Group 3 5f Cornwallis second Garswood. The dam is an unraced half-sister to 4 winners including the Group 3 7f Nell Gwyn Stakes winner and dual Group 1 placed Infallible. The second dam, Irresistible (by Cadeaux Genereux), a fairly useful 5f (at 2 yrs) and listed 6f winner, was Group 3 placed and is a half-sister to 2 winners.

504. CANYARI (IRE)

b.c. *Dandy Man – Morna's Fan (Lear Fan)*. March 4. Fourth foal. £50,000Y. Doncaster Premier. Robin O'Ryan. Half-brother to the useful 6f, 7f (both at 2 yrs) and listed 1m

winner Barack (by Pyrus) and to the fair 1m to 10f and hurdles winner Fly To Dubai (by Fly To The Stars). The dam is an unraced half-sister to 4 winners. The second dam, Morna's Moment (by Lear Fan), is a placed half-sister to 8 winners including two US Grade 3 winners.

505. CHATALONG (IRE)

b.f. *Invincible Spirit – Chatline (One Cool Cat)*. March 6. First foal. The dam, a quite useful Irish 3-y-o 6f winner, is a half-sister to 4 winners including the smart listed 6f winner and Group 3 second Mugharreb. The second dam, Marling (by Lomond), a high-class winner of the Cheveley Park Stakes, the Irish 1,000 Guineas, the Coronation Stakes and the Sussex Stakes is a half-sister to 7 winners including the Irish 2,000 Guineas and Prix de l'Abbaye second Caerwent.

506. DRINKS FOR LOSERS (IRE)

b.c. *Mastercraftsman – Heart's Desire (Royal Applause)*. March 27. Sixth foal. €32,000Y. Goffs Orby. Robin O'Ryan. Half-brother to the quite useful 2012 2-y-o dual 6f winner (both his starts) Unsinkable (by Verglas), to the Irish 2-y-o listed 6f winner Heart Of Fire (by Mujadil), the fairly useful Irish 1m (at 2 yrs) and 14f winner Knight Eagle (by Night Shift) and the modest 2-y-o 7f winner Hearts And Minds (by Clodovil). The dam, a fair 7f and 1m placed maiden, is a half-sister to 5 winners including the French listed winner and Group 3 placed Bashful. The second dam, Touch And Love (by Green Desert), a 2-y-o winner in France, was second in the Group 2 Prix du Gros-Chene and is a half-sister to 8 winners.

507. DUTCH COURAGE ♠

b.f. *Dutch Art – Poldhu (Cape Cross)*. March 19. Second foal. 100,000Y. Tattersalls October Book 2. Cheveley Park Stud. Half-sister to the fair 2012 2-y-o 6f Maid A Million (by Kyllachy). The dam is an unraced half-sister to the Group 1 Falmouth Stakes winner Rajeem. The second dam, Magic Sister (by Cadeaux Genereux), a modest 3-y-o 7f placed maiden, is a sister to the very smart 2-y-o Group 1 6f Prix Morny and Group 3 5f Molecomb Stakes winner Hoh Magic and a half-sister to 5 winners. (Cheveley Park Stud).

508. EASTERN IMPACT (IRE)
b.c. Bahamian Bounty – Kate The Great (Xaar).
February 27. First foal. £25,000Y. Doncaster
Premier. Robin O'Ryan. The dam, a quite useful
2-y-o 5f winner, is a half-sister to 3 winners.
The second dam, Ros The Boss (by Danehill), a
quite useful 7f and 1m winner, is a half-sister
to 8 winners including the Irish 2-y-o listed 9f
winner and Group 1 second Yehudi.

509. ECCLESTON
b.c. Acclamation – Miss Meggy (Pivotal).
March 28. Third foal. £10,000Y. Doncaster
November. Robin O'Ryan. Half-brother to the
quite useful 2012 2-y-o 7f and 1m winner and
subsequent German 7f listed placed Charlie
Em (by Kheleyf). The dam won a listed 5f
event at 2 yrs and a class 4 handicap over 7f
at 4 yrs. The second dam, Selkirk Rose (by Pips
Pride), a fair 5f (at 2 yrs) and 6f winner, is a
half-sister to 5 minor winners.

510. FLYCATCHER (IRE)
gr.f. Medicean – Night Haven (Night Shift).
February 22. Ninth foal. 45,000Y. Tattersalls
October Book 2. Robin O'Ryan. Half-sister
to the useful 2-y-o 7f and listed 10f winner
and US dual Grade 2 placed Rosa Grace (by
Lomitas), the fairly useful 5f and 6f winner
and listed-placed Secret Night (by Dansili),
the fair 6f (at 2 yrs) and 10f winner Eastern
Destiny (by Dubai Destination), the moderate
5f winner of 5 races, including at 2 yrs, Duke
Of Rainford (by Bahamian Bounty) and a
winner in Denmark by Observatory. The dam,
a fairly useful 5f (at 2 yrs) and 6f winner and 6f
listed-placed, is a sister to 3 winners including
the French 2-y-o listed 5f winner Shoalhaven.
The second dam, Noble Haven (by Indian
King), won once at 2 yrs and is a half-sister to
6 winners.

511. FOXY CLARETS (IRE)
ch.c. Camacho – Muscari (Indian Ridge).
February 26. Second foal. £18,000Y. Doncaster
Premier. Robin O'Ryan. Half-brother to the
quite useful 2-y-o 5f winner Major Muscari
(by Exceed And Excel). The dam, a modest 1m
winner, is a half-sister to 4 winners. The second
dam, Desert Serenade (by Green Desert),
ran twice unplaced and is a sister to the top
class sprinter Sheikh Albadou, winner of the

Keeneland Nunthorpe Stakes, the Breeders
Cup Sprint, the Haydock Park Sprint Cup and
the Kings Stand Stakes and a half-sister to 6
winners.

512. HESKIN (IRE)
b.f. Acclamation – Carpet Lady (Night Shift).
March 19. Ninth foal. €105,000Y. Goffs Orby.
Highfield Farm. Sister to the useful 2-y-o listed
5f winner of 4 races and Group 3 Cornwallis
Stakes third Cake and half-sister to the quite
useful 5f and 6f winner of 5 races Tagula
Night, the quite useful 7f and 1m winner
Suited And Booted (both by Tagula), the
modest 2-y-o 6f winner Wachiwi (by Namid),
and the German 6f winner Nadal (by Shinko
Forest). The dam, a fair dual 6f placed 2-y-o, is
a half-sister to 5 winners including the Hong
Kong stakes winner Classic Fountain. The
second dam, Lucky Fountain (by Lafontaine),
is an unraced sister to the Group 2 Geoffrey
Freer Stakes winner Shambo.

513. INNOCENT TOUCH (IRE)
br.c. Intense Focus – Guajira (Mtoto).
April 21. Fourth foal. 55,000Y. Tattersalls
October Book 2. Robin O'Ryan. Half-brother
to the very useful dual 5f (at 2 yrs) and 1m
winner and Group 1 Sussex Stakes third
Gabrial (by Dark Angel). The dam, a minor
French 11f winner of 3 races, is a half-sister to
9 winners including Jaunatxo and Iron Deputy
(both US Grade 2 winners) and the dam of
the German Group 2 winner Shamalgan. The
second dam, Femme de Fer (by Iron Duke),
won twice in France and is a half-sister to 3
winners.

514. JAN VAN HOOF (IRE)
b.c. Dutch Art – Cosenza (Bahri). February 14.
Second foal. 80,000Y. Tattersalls October Book
2. Robin O'Ryan. Half-brother to the fair dual
9f winner Zain Princess (by Hawk Wing). The
dam, placed fourth once over 5f from three
starts at 2 yrs, is a half-sister to 3 winners
including the listed winner Longhunter. The
second dam, Dawnus (by Night Shift), a useful
listed 10f winner, is a half-sister to 4 winners.

515. KALAHARI KINGDOM
*b.c. Footstepsinthesand – Visite Royale
(Danehill Dancer).* February 1. First foal.

€50,000foal. Goffs November. Norman Steel. The dam, a fair 9f winner, is a half-sister to 2 winners. The second dam, Fantasy Royale (by Pleasant Colony), a fairly useful 1m winner, was listed-placed over 14f and is a half-sister to 6 winners including the US Graded stakes winners Dance Master and Naninja.

516. KHALICE
b.f. *Bahamian Bounty – Siena Gold (Key Of Luck)*. March 15. Third living foal. £13,000Y. Doncaster Festival. Robin O'Ryan. The dam, a useful winner of the 2-y-o 5f Weatherbys Supersprint, is a half-sister to 8 winners including the very useful 2-y-o 6f winner and Group 1 Cheveley Park Stakes second Crazee Mental (herself dam of the multiple Group 2 winner Premio Loco). The second dam, Corn Futures (by Nomination), a fair 2-y-o 6f winner, is a half-sister to 7 winners including the dam of the March Stakes and Glorious Stakes winner Midnight Legend.

517. KINDANYCE (IRE)
b.f. *Bushranger – Rublevka Star (Elusive Quality)*. March 7. First foal. €26,000Y. Goffs February. Bobby O'Ryan. The dam, a moderate 2-y-o 5f winner, is a half-sister to 3 winners including the South African stakes-placed winner Distance Done. The second dam, Al Desima (by Emperor Jones), a fairly useful 2-y-o 7f winner, subsequently won in the USA, was third in the Grade 1 Yellow Ribbon Stakes and is a half-sister to 9 winners.

518. LONGTON
b.c. *Myboycharlie – Lauren Louise (Tagula)*. March 26. Fourth foal. 135,000Y. Tattersalls October Book 2. Highfield Farm. Half-brother to the 2012 2-y-o Group 2 6f Gimcrack Stakes winner Blaine (by Avonbridge) and to the very useful 2-y-o listed 6f winner Bogart (by Bahamian Bounty). The dam, a moderate 6f winner at 4 yrs, is a half-sister to 4 winners. The second dam, Movie Star (by Barathea), ran once unplaced and is a full or half-sister to 3 winners including the French listed winner Kilometre Neuf.

519. MCCARTHY MOR (IRE)
b.c. *Bushranger – Alexander Anapolis (Spectrum)*. March 16. Sixth foal. €62,000Y.

Goffs Orby. Robin O'Ryan. Closely related to the fairly useful dual 6f winner Film Maker and to the quite useful dual 5f (including at 2 yrs) to 7f winner of 6 races Cut The Cackle (both by Danetime) and half-brother to the quite useful dual 6f winner Jessie's Spirit (by Clodovil) and the fair 6f winner Vanilla Loan (by Invincible Spirit). The dam, a quite useful 12f winner, is a full or half-sister to 3 winners. The second dam, Pirouette (by Sadler's Wells), winner of the listed 7f Athasi Stakes and the listed 7f Boland Stakes in Ireland and Group 3 placed, is a half-sister to 8 winners including the Irish listed 6f Greenlands Stakes winner and very useful sire Ballad Rock.

520. MENDELITA
ch.f. *Archipenko – Dame de Noche (Lion Cavern)*. February 1. Half-sister to the quite useful 7f (at 2 yrs) and 9f winner Nemushka (by Sakhee). The dam, a useful 5f to 1m winner of 4 races, is a sister to the Japanese 7f stakes winner Dublin Lion. The second dam, Goodnight Kiss (by Night Shift), was placed 7 times including a second in the Irish 1,000 Guineas and is a half-sister to 3 winners.

521. NEIGHBOTHER
b.c. *Invincible Spirit – Aravonian (Night Shift)*. February 20. Sixth foal. €120,000Y. Goffs Orby. Norman Steel. Brother to the dual 5f (at 2 yrs) and Group 3 6f Ballyogan Stakes winner Age Of Chivalry and to the fair 2-y-o 5f winner The Cuckoo and half-brother to the smart Irish 2-y-o 7f winner, Group 3 7f Somerville Tattersall Stakes second and subsequent US Grade 1 second Sebastian Flyte (by Observatory). The dam won once over 1m at 3 yrs. The second dam, Age Of Reality (by Alleged), is a placed full or half-sister to 8 winners including the Group 2 Royal Whip Stakes winner Chancellor.

522. NEW STREET (IRE)
gr.c. *Acclamation – New Deal (Rainbow Quest)*. April 13. Fifth foal. £105,000Y. Doncaster Premier. Highfield Farm. Brother to the fairly useful 2012 2-y-o 5f winner New Pearl and to the useful 6f (at 2 yrs) and 12f winner Alrasm. The dam, a minor 3-y-o 1m winner in France, is a half-sister to 6 winners including the Group 2 Lowther Stakes third Dunloskin. The

second dam, Dalinda (by Nureyev), a winner at 4 yrs in France, is a half-sister to 4 winners.

523. OVERDRIVE

b.f. Sakhee's Secret – La Fija (Dixieland Band). March 2. Ninth foal. £6,000Y. Doncaster Festival. Robin O'Ryan. Half-sister to the quite useful 2-y-o 6f winner Archived (by Millkom), to the fair 1m winner Fajita (by Lahib) and the modest 2-y-o 6f winner Time For You (by Vettori). The dam, placed fourth once over 7f at 3 yrs from 3 starts, is a half-sister to 6 winners, including in Japan. The second dam, Turkstand (by Turkoman), won at 2 yrs in the USA and was second in the Grade 1 Oak Leaf Stakes and is a half-sister to 7 winners including the US Grade 2 winner Captain Valid.

524. PARBOLD (IRE)

b.c. Dandy Man – Gala Style (Elnadim). April 16. Sixth foal. 42,000Y. Tattersalls October Book 1. Highfield Farm. Half-brother to the 2012 2-y-o winner Majestic Moon and to the very useful 5f, 6f and listed 7f winner and dual Group 3 placed Majestic Myles (both by Majestic Missile) and to the quite useful 7f winner Oonagh (by Arakan). The dam is an unraced half-sister to 2 minor winners. The second dam, Style N' Elegance (by Alysheba), is a placed half-sister to 11 winners including the Group 2 Premio Legnano winner Easy To Copy (herself the dam of 3 stakes winners) and the Irish 1,000 Guineas winner Trusted Partner (dam of the high-class filly Dress To Thrill). The second dam, Talking Picture (by Speak John), a champion American 2-y-o filly, won at up to 7f.

525. PENIAPHOBIA (IRE)

b.c. Dandy Man – Umlani (Great Commotion). April 8. Sixth foal. £20,000Y. Doncaster Premier. Hugo Merry. Half-brother to the fairly useful 2-y-o 5f winner and Group 3 5f Molecomb Stakes third Safari Sunset (by Fayruz). The dam is an unraced half-sister to 3 minor winners. The second dam, Travel Magic (by Henbit), a quite useful 7f winner, is a half-sister to 7 winners.

526. PICCADILLY JIM (IRE)

gr.c. Royal Applause – Silver Dip (Gulch).

February 16. Third foal. 28,000Y. Tattersalls October Book 2. Robin O'Ryan. Closely related to the moderate 2-y-o 6f winner Bellechance (by Acclamation). The dam, a quite useful triple 7f winner (including at 2 yrs), is a half-sister to one winner. The second dam, Silver Bandana (by Silver Buck), a US stakes winner of 6 races at 3 to 5 yrs and Grade 3 placed twice, is a half-sister to 5 winners.

527. RUFFORD (IRE)

b.c. Invincible Spirit – Speedy Sonata (Stravinsky). February 19. Fourth foal. £50,000Y. Doncaster Premier. Highfield Farm. Half-brother to the fairly useful 2-y-o 6f winner Yesnabay (by Grand Slam). The dam won 6 races from 2 to 4 yrs in the USA and was stakes-placed and is a half-sister to 5 winners. The second dam, Sandshell (by Silver Hawk), is a placed sister to the Prix de Diane winner Lady In Silver and a half-sister to 8 winners.

528. SANDIVA (IRE)

ch.f. Footstepsinthesand – Miss Corinne (Mark Of Esteem). February 21. Fifth foal. £18,000Y. Doncaster Premier. O'Ryan/Middleham. Half-sister to the promising 2012 2-y-o 7f winner Wentworth (by Acclamation), to the modest 2-y-o 6f and 7f winner Captain Loui (by Verglas), the Spanish 2-y-o winner Irish Cliff (by Marju) and a winner in the Czech Republic by Denon. The dam won 6 races in Italy from 3 to 5 yrs and is a half-sister to 4 minor winners here and abroad. The second dam, Percy's Girl (by Blakeney), a useful 10f and 10.3f winner, is a sister to the Group 3 September Stakes winner Percy's Lass (herself dam of the Derby winner Sir Percy) and a half-sister to 5 winners including the very smart Grade 1 E P Taylor Stakes and Group 2 Sun Chariot Stakes winner Braiswick.

529. SHORE PATROL (IRE)

br.c. Footstepsinthesand – Fatwa (Lahib). April 10. Seventh foal. €100,000Y. Goffs Orby. Norman Steel. Half-brother to the quite useful 2-y-o 5f winner Raedah (by Elusive Quality), to the modest dual 10f and subsequent French winner Chant de Guerre (by War Chant) and the modest Irish 12f winner Dearest (by Arch). The dam, a fairly useful 3-y-o 6f winner, was second in the Group 3 7f Fred Darling Stakes and is a full or half-sister to 6 winners including the useful 6f (at 2 yrs) and 1m winner Hirasah. The second dam, Mayaasa (by Lyphard), a fair 10f winner, is a half-sister to 7 winners including Maroof (Group 1 Queen Elizabeth II Stakes).

530. SKYE'S THE LIMIT
ch.c. Pastoral Pursuits – Sound Of Sleat (Primo Dominie). March 3. Eighth foal. 32,000Y. Tattersalls October Book 2. Robin O'Ryan. Half-brother to the quite useful 2-y-o 7f winner Kinloch Castle (by Kyllachy), to the fair 2-y-o dual 5f winner Mahiki (by Compton Place) and to a minor winner in Italy by Dr Fong. The dam is an unraced half-sister to 7 winners including the Group 3 Prix de la Jonchere winner Soft Currency, the listed winner Fawzi and the 2-y-o winner of three races over 6f and useful broodmare Choire Mhor. The second dam, Little Loch Broom (by Reform), is a placed half-sister to 7 winners and the dams of the Group winners Ozone Friendly, Ardkinglass, Wiorno and Reprimand.

531. SPICEUPYOURLIFE
b.f. Sakhee's Secret – Tiger Spice (Royal Applause). March 4. Second foal. 27,000Y. Tattersalls October Book 2. Not sold. Half-sister to the 2012 2-y-o 7f winner, from two starts, Azrur (by Sir Percy). The dam, a modest 2-y-o 9f winner, is a half-sister to 4 winners including the dam of the Group 3 Oak Tree Stakes winner Summer Fete and to the unplaced dam of the US Grade 2 and Grade 3 winner Up In Time. The second dam, Up And About (by Barathea), a fair 14.8f winner, is a half-sister to 9 winners including the listed winner and Group 1 placed Musicanna and the dam of the champion European 3-y-o sprinter Overdose.

532. SUPPLICANT
b.c. Kyllachy – Pious (Bishop Of Cashel). March 10. Eighth foal. 65,000Y. Tattersalls October Book 1. Oliver St Lawrence. Brother to the smart 7f and listed 1m winner of 5 races Penitent and half-brother to the fair 2012 2-y-o 5f winner My Boy Bill (by Dutch Art), the fairly useful 2-y-o 7f winner Blithe, the quite useful 5f winner of 7 races Solemn,

the quite useful 7f winner Anoint, the fair 7f winner Divine Call (all by Pivotal) and the modest 9f winner Christingle (by Iceman). The dam, a fair dual 6f winner (including at 2 yrs), is a half-sister to 5 winners. The second dam, La Cabrilla (by Carwhite), a fairly useful 2-y-o 5f and 6f winner, was third in the Group 3 Princess Margaret Stakes and is a half-sister to 6 winners including the Group 1 Nunthorpe Stakes winner Ya Malak and the listed winner Dominio (dam of the Group 2 King's Stand Stakes winner Dominica). (Cheveley Park Stud).

533. THE GRUMPY GNOME
b.c. Dandy Man – Certain Charm (Thunder Gulch). April 25. Eighth foal. 28,000Y. Tattersalls October Book 2. Robin O'Ryan. Half-brother to the useful 7f winner and listed-placed Sanserif, to the minor winner abroad Baveno (both by Fasliyev), the fair 12f winner Onatha (by Dansili), the fair Irish 2-y-o 6f winner Nerys (by Namid) and the moderate 6f (at 2 yrs) and 7f winner Regal Acclaim (by Acclamation). The dam was placed over 1m and 10f and is a half-sister to 2 minor winners. The second dam, Style n'Elegance (by Alysheba), is a placed half-sister to 11 winners including the Irish 1,000 Guineas winner Trusted Partner (herself dam of the US Grade 1 winner Dress To Thrill) and to the Group 3 winner and good broodmare Easy To Copy.

534. WESTERN SANDS (IRE)
ch.f. Footstepsinthesand – West One (Gone West). February 20. Seventh foal. 10,000foal. Tattersalls December. Not sold. Half-sister to the fairly useful 2-y-o listed 1m winner Zenella (by Kyllachy), to the modest 7f and 9f winner of 7 races Hoh Wotanite (by Stravinsky) and to the Italian winner of 7 races from 2 to 6 yrs West Act (by Act One). The dam ran twice unplaced and is closely related to the US stakes-placed winner Go Baby Go and a half-sister to a winner in Italy. The second dam, Bequest (by Sharpen Up), a very useful 2-y-o 6f winner here, subsequently won the Grade 1 10f Santa Barbara Handicap and is a half-sister to 4 winners.

535. WITHERNSEA (IRE)
b.c. Dark Angel – Charlene Lacy (Pips Pride). April 10. Eleventh foal. 38,000Y. Tattersalls

THE LAST STALLION
SON OF DANZIG

A Group 1 performer from one of the most prolific lines of Classic and Group 1 performers

A standout individual, like his sire:
"The best yearling I have ever seen"
-Marcus Tregoning

A high-class potential cut short by injury, like his sire: *'Mawatheeq looks sure to be winning at the highest level in the next season'*
-Timeform of 2009

A dominant bay sire, like Danzig and his best stallion son, Danehill

LIKE SIRE, LIKE SON

Salute the
RED ARMY

**THE CHEVELEY PARK STUD
STALLION ROSTER**

DUTCH ART
European Champion 1st Crop Sire 2011.
The Leading UK-Based 2nd Crop Sire 2012.
2012 yearlings made up to 190,000gns.

KYLLACHY
Gr.1 sire of over 100 individual winners
for the third successive year in 2012.
2012 yearlings made up to 150,000gns.

MAYSON
Gr.1 July Cup winner by INVINCIBLE SPIRIT;
also 2nd (nk) in the Gr.1 Prix de l'Abbaye.
STANDS HIS FIRST SEASON IN 2013

MEDICEAN
Gr.1 sire of SIYOUMA, CAPPONI and BAYRIR
in 2012 and of 9 individual Gr.1 winners in all.
2012 yearlings made up to €320,000.

PIVOTAL
Multiple Champion Sire of
21 individual Gr.1 winners to date.
2012 yearlings made up to 485,000gns.

VIRTUAL
Gr.1 winning miler by PIVOTAL,
who is a three parts brother to ICEMAN.
HIS FIRST CROP ARE 2YOS IN 2013

MAYSON

Cheveley Park Stud
Duchess Drive, Newmarket, Suffolk CB8 9DD
Tel: (01638) 730316 Fax: (01638) 730868
enquiries@cheveleypark.co.uk
www.cheveleypark.co.uk

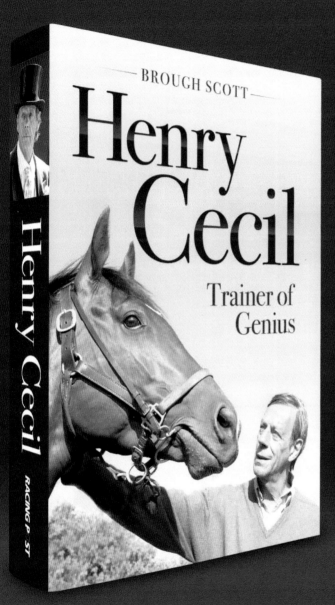

October Book 2. Robin O'Ryan. Brother to the quite useful 2012 2-y-o 7f winner Regal Dan and half-brother to the very useful 2-y-o listed 5f winner of 6 races Star Rover, to the fairly useful 2-y-o dual 5f winner and listed-placed Jamesway (both by Camacho), the minor Italian 2-y-o winner Bod Common Pride (by Bad As I Wanna Be) and the modest 4-y-o 8.6f winner Tetcott (Definite Article). The dam won once over 5f at 2 yrs and is a half-sister to 4 winners. The second dam, Friendly Song (by Song), is a placed sister to the winner of 7 races and sire Fayruz.

PAUL FITZSIMONS

536. ASTRAL ROSE ★★★ ♠

b.f. Pastoral Pursuits – Rosapenna (Spectrum). May 10. Fourth foal. 11,000Y. Tattersalls October Book 3. Kern/Lillingston. The dam, a fair 6f winner of 4 races, is a half-sister to 6 winners. The second dam, Blaine (by Lyphard's Wish), is a placed half-sister to 7 winners including Alligatrix (dam of the dual Group 1 winner Croco Rouge and the top-class broodmare Alidiva). (Messrs Lambourne, Forbes & Losse). *"She'll have started her career before your book is out. A strong, compact and a very good moving filly, she's working well and I expect her to show up well early on. A filly that carries herself really well, she'll start at five furlongs but I can see her getting six a bit later on".*

537. CLAPPERBOARD ★★★

b.f. Royal Applause – Roseum (Lahib). March 23. Seventh foal. 19,000Y. Tattersalls October Book 2. Sackville/Donald. Half-sister to the useful 2-y-o dual 6f winner and Group 2 6f Mill Reef Stakes third Dubai Builder (by Tobougg), to the fair 5f winner of 4 races and subsequent German winner Glasshoughton (by Dansili), the fair 7f and 1m winner Bosambo (by King's Best), the moderate 11f winner Bramante (by Peintre Celebre) and a minor winner in Germany by Primo Valentino. The dam, a useful 5f and 6f winner of 5 races, is a half-sister to 4 winners. The second dam, Rose Barton (by Pas de Seul), is an unraced half-sister to 9 winners. (Raymond Tooth). *"A very nice filly, she looks like she's got a bit of growing to do but even at this stage she's going very well. She'll start off in late April and*

she's a forward, sharp-minded type of 2-y-o that I expect will win over five furlongs. I'd say she's probably a bit slighter than my Pastoral Pursuits filly, but once we get more work into her she'll be even nicer as the weeks go on".

538. UNNAMED ★★

ch.c. Dutch Art – Photographie (Trempolino). March 8. Ninth foal. 42,000Y. Tattersalls October Book 2. Sackville/Donald. Brother to the fair 1m (at 2 yrs) and 12f winner Little Dutch Girl and half-brother to the 2m and hurdles winner Downing Street (by Sadler's Wells), the fair 12f and 14f winner Duty Free (by Rock Of Gibraltar) and a winner in Greece by Fasliyev. The dam is an unplaced sister to the Group 1 Prix Marcel Boussac winner Juvenia and a half-sister to 7 winners including the dual French Group 3 winner In Extremis and the dams of the Group winners Millemix (in France) and Bullish Luck (in Japan). The second dam, Vintage (by Foolish Pleasure), won 3 minor races at 3 yrs in the USA. *"A big horse, he looks more like a 3-y-o type but I'm hoping to get a run into him around September. I haven't sold him yet but he's a good-looking individual and a nice long-term prospect".*

JAMES GIVEN

539. BAILEYS FOREVER ★★★

ch.f. Mount Nelson – Forever Fine (Sunshine Forever). March 23. Twelfth foal. 12,000Y. Tattersalls October Book 3. James Given Racing. Half-sister to the moderate 2012 2-y-o 5f winner Faffa (by Araafa), to the minor US stakes winner Stormy Forever (by Storm Boot), the useful 1m (at 2 yrs) and 10f winner Familiar Territory (by Cape Cross), the quite useful 2-y-o 5f and 6f winner Oasis Breeze (by Oasis Dream), the fair 5f and 6f winner of 6 races including at 2 yrs Jack Smudge (by One Cool Cat) and the minor US and Mexican winners by Peaks And Valleys and Announce. The dam, a US stakes-placed winner at 2 yrs, is a half-sister to 7 winners. The second dam, She's Sofine (by Bold Hour), won 5 races in the USA and is a half-sister to 9 winners including the US Grade 1 winner Rest Your Case and the dam of the Grade 1 winners Bates Motel, Hatim and Optimistic Gal. (G R Bailey Ltd). *"I get the feeling that Mount Nelson's aren't precocious types, but the dam has bred a few 2-y-o winners and this filly is more forward than I expected her to be. I'm very pleased with her, she's taken everything in her stride and she looks very much a 2-y-o in the making. It's hard to imagine her being a sprinter but she's not very-big, she's well-proportioned and reasonably sharp".*

540. CHEEKY PETA'S ★★★

b.f. Compton Place – Cheeky Girl (College Chapel). March 18. Third living foal. £10,000Y. Doncaster Festival. P Swann. Half-sister to the modest 2012 French 2-y-o 1m winner Composed (by Sakhee's Secret) and to the fair 7f (at 2 yrs) and 9f winner Bountiful Girl (by Bahamian Bounty). The dam, a modest 12f winner of 4 races, is a half-sister to 9 winners including the dual listed winner Paradise Isle. The second dam, Merry Rous (by Rousillon), won once at 2 yrs and is a half-sister to 5 winners including the dual Group 3 winning sprinter Tina's Pet. (P Swann). *"She looks a 2-y-o type but the weather has been so bad that I've done less with my 2-y-o's at this stage than I have for years. This filly is quite forward though and we'll crack on with her now".*

541. MASTER DAN ★★★

b.c. Mastercraftsman – Danella (Platini). March 21. Eighth foal. 24,000Y. Tattersalls October Book 2. Anthony Stroud. Half-brother to the fair 9f to 2m winner Gabrial's King (by Hurricane Run), to the German 2-y-o winner and listed-placed Dajolie (by Auenadler) and two minor winners in France by Sholokov and Banyumanik. The dam, a minor winner at 2 yrs in Germany, is a half-sister to 8 winners including the German Group 2 winner Denaro and the German Group 3 winner Davidoff. The second dam, Dapprima (by Shareef Dancer), a listed winner in Germany and second in the Group 2 German 1,000 Guineas, is a half-sister to 8 winners. (Danethorpe Racing Partnership). *"I've been hearing good things about the sire and this colt only adds to that as far as I'm concerned. He's grown a lot and he's now quite tall, willowy and long. But he's maintained his balance throughout and hasn't gone weak on us. He's far from the finished article at the moment but I like him a great deal".*

542. MISS LAWLASS ★★★

b.f. Lawman – Corryvreckan (Night Shift). March 29. Sixth foal. £4,000Y. Doncaster Festival. Mr P Swann. Half-sister to the fair 2012 6f winner Entwined (by Elusive City), to the quite useful 2-y-o 5f winner Leftontheshelf (by Namid), the modest Irish 2-y-o 7f winner Dearg (by Intikhab) and the moderate 2m winner Mollyow (by Iceman). The dam, a fair Irish 7f and 1m placed maiden, is a half-sister to 9 winners including the very useful listed sprint winners Bufalino and Maledetto. The second dam, Croglin Water (by Monsanto), is an unplaced half-sister to the smart sprinter Governor General. (Danethorpe Racing Partnership). *"A butty 2-y-o type, she's strong with a big backside and big shoulders. She's just finishing a growth spurt and is ready to crack on with now. I would imagine she'd be a sprinting type".*

543. QUEENIE'S HOME ★★★★ ♠

b.f. Shamardal – Nolas Lolly (Lomitas). March 22. Second foal. €52,000Y. Baden-Baden. Anthony Stroud. The dam, a winner and Group 3 third in Germany, is a half-sister to the US Grade 2 and Grade 3 winner Preachinatthebar and to the French listed winner Royal Revival. The second dam, Holy Nola (by Silver Deputy), a stakes winner of 5 races in the USA, is a sister to the triple US Grade 3 winner Bare Necessities and a half-sister to 4 winners. (Danethorpe Racing Partnership). *"You could easily expect this filly to be a back-end type but not a bit of it, she's taking everything in her stride and I think she'll be out relatively early, considering her pedigree. She'll improve as she gets older and goes further but I think she'll be starting at six furlongs".*

544. SANDS LEGENDS ★★★

b.f. Avonbridge – T.G's Girl (Selkirk). January 28. Ninth foal. £5,000Y. Doncaster Festival. Mr P Swann. Half-sister to the fairly useful 2-y-o 5f winner Bridge It Jo (by Josr Algarhoud), to the quite useful dual 5f (at 2 yrs) and 6f winner Calypso King (by Agnes World), the fair 7f winner Selkie's Friend (by Elnadim) and the modest 6f winner of 4 races (including at 2 yrs) Magic Cross (by Bertolini). The dam is an unplaced half-sister o 9 winners here and abroad. The second dam, River's Rising (by Mendez), won at 3 yrs and is a half-sister to 3 winners. (Danethorpe Racing Partnership). *"She looks very much as you'd expect an early Avonbridge 2-y-o to look, she did some pleasing bits of work early on and I expect to be cracking on with her now".*

545. SHADES OF SILK ★★★

b.f. Bahamian Bounty – Terentia (Diktat). February 22. First foal. £34,000Y. Doncaster Festival. Peter Swann/Anthony Stroud. The dam, useful 5f winner of 5 races (including at 2 yrs), is a half-sister to 3 winners including the dual listed 6f winner and Group 3 Ballyogan Stakes third Cartimandua. The second dam, Agrippina (by Timeless Times), a useful 2-y-o listed 7f winner, is a half-sister to 2 winners. (Danethorpe Racing Partnership). *"She was the top lot at the second Doncaster sales. She's a very nice-framed horse that's just growing at the moment. The work she was doing earlier was encouraging and I expect she'll come back in time. I think she'll be a six/seven furlong type and she has a willing attitude".*

546. SWEET ANGELICA ★★

ch.f. Pastoral Pursuits – Glencal (Compton Place). March 12. Second foal. 7,000Y. Tattersalls October Book 3. James Given. The dam, a modest 6f and 7f winner of 3 races, is a half-sister to 2 winners including the useful listed 1m winner of 6 races Kasumi. The second dam, Raindrop (by Primo Dominie), placed fourth once over 7f, is a half-sister to 5 winners. (Danethorpe Racing Partnership). *"Bred to be speedy, she had a big backside on her when I bought her but she's grown a lot recently and she's looking a bit weak now. I suspect she'll fill back up and end up as an imposing, sprinting type".*

547. WILFUL MINX ★★

b.f. Le Havre – Miskina (Mark Of Esteem). April 29. Fourth foal. £3,200Y. Doncaster November. James Given. Half-sister to the fair 6f winner of 4 races Links Drive Lady (by Striking Ambition). The dam, a moderate 7f winner, is a half-sister to 5 winners. The second dam, Najmat Alshemaal (by Dancing Brave), a fairly useful 10f winner, was listed-placed twice, is a half-sister to 3 winners. (Stephanie Oliver).

"She grew, levelled off and was filling out but she's just going through another growth spurt. So she'll be quite a big filly when she's finished growing. One for seven furlongs I should think, but she's a very good-looking filly".

548. UNNAMED ★★★

b.f. Kodiac – Inter Madera (Toca Madera). March 15. £12,000 2-y-o. Kempton Breeze-Up. Anthony Stroud. Half-sister to the fairly useful Irish 2-y-o 7f winner Sandton City, the Irish 13f winner Tauranga (both by Daggers Drawn), the fairly useful 2-y-o 5f and 6f winner Sanbenito, the fair 7f winner Faithfulbond (both by Elbio), the Irish 7f winner on his only start Time In Madera (by Danetime) and the moderate Irish 11f winner Scottish Minstrel (by Houmayoun). The dam is an unraced half-sister to 6 winners out of the unraced Interj (by Salmon Leap), herself a half-sister to 5 winners. (Mr P Swann). *"She did a pretty fast time at the breeze up sales and she just looks like a 2-y-o type. She's strong and has obviously been brought forward for the sale, so now we're teaching her to do five furlongs and not two furlongs. She seems to be getting her head round that and she should be out fairly early".* TRAINERS' BARGAIN BUY

549. UNNAMED ★★★★

b.f. Galileo – Thermopylae (Tenby). January 27. Ninth foal. 140,000Y. Tattersalls October Book 1. Not sold. Half-sister to the Group 3 Give Thanks Stakes winner and Group 1 St Leger second Unsung Heroine (by High Chaparral), to the quite useful triple 7f and subsequent Australian winner Ghostmilk (by Golan), the modest 10f and hurdles winner Laconicos (by Foxhound) and the moderate 10f winner Spartan King (by King's Best). The dam is a placed full or half-sister to 9 winners including the Group 1 Gran Premio d'Italia winner Posidonas and to the dam of the Group 2 Italian 2,000 Guineas winner Spirit of Desert. The second dam, Tamassos (by Dance In Time), won at 3 yrs and is a half-sister to the Group 1 Juddmonte International winner Ile de Chypre. (Biddestone Stud & Robin Jones). *"I love her to bits, she's taken absolutely everything we've done with her in her stride. She's definitely going to want a trip but I like her very much. An early foal, she's very settled, she's done her growing and is very willing but not passive with it. Very much a longer-term project, but I think she'll run at two and run well".*

550. UNNAMED ★★★

b.f. *Teofilo – Wunders Dream (Averti).* April 9. Sixth foal. Sister to the modest 1m to 12f winner Spartilla and half-sister to the useful 2012 2-y-o 5f winner and listed-placed Fire Eyes (by Exceed And Excel) and a winner in Poland by Oasis Dream. The dam, a winner of 5 races at 2 yrs including the Group 2 5f Flying Childers Stakes and the Group 3 5f Molecomb Stakes, is a half-sister to 6 winners including the Irish Group 3 winner Grecian Dancer. The second dam, Pizzicato (by Statoblest), a modest 5f and 5.3f winner at 3 yrs, is a half-sister to 5 winners including the high-class Hong Kong horses Mensa and Firebolt. (Bolton Grange). *"She's just a bigger version of her mother who did so well for us. A smashing horse, she's came to us quite late but she's a strong, big filly. She's level-headed and takes things in her stride, so although it's early days for her I like what she's doing".*

GODOLPHIN

At the time of going to press the trainer of the following horses was undetermined

551. BEACHY HEAD (IRE)

b.c. *Shamardal – Chaquiras (Seeking The Gold).* March 27. Half-brother to the French 1m winner Chequers (by Pivotal). The dam is an unraced sister to the outstanding Dubai Millennium, winner of the Dubai World Cup, the Prix Jacques le Marois, the Prince Of Wales's Stakes and the Queen Elizabeth II Stakes (all Group 1 events) and a half-sister to the Group 2 10.5f Prix Greffuhle second Denver County. The second dam, Colorado Dancer (by Shareef Dancer), a very smart winner of the Group 2 13.5f Prix de Pomone and the Group 3 12f Prix de Minerve and Group 1 placed, is closely related to the Grade 1 Gamely Handicap winner Northern Aspen, to the Group 1 July Cup winner Hamas and the Group 1 Grand Prix de Paris winner Fort Wood and a half-sister to the Prix d'Astarte winner Elle Seule (herself dam of the Irish 1,000 Guineas winner Mehthaaf) and the

champion US 2-y-o colt Timber Country.

552. BURLANDO (IRE)

b.c. *Dubawi – Calando (Storm Cat).* April 11. Eighth foal. Half-brother to the useful 2-y-o listed 7f Chesham Stakes winner Champlain (by Seeking The Gold), to the quite useful 10f winner Ustura (by Nayef) and the modest 5f to 1m winner of 10 races Sovereignty (by King's Best). The dam won the Group 3 1m May Hill Stakes, was second in the Group 1 Fillies Mile and third in the French 1,00 Guineas and is a half-sister to 2 winners. The second dam, Diminuendo (by Diesis), won the Hoover Fillies Mile, Cherry Hinton Stakes (both at 2 yrs), Epsom Oaks, Irish Oaks (in a dead-heat), Yorkshire Oaks and Musidora Stakes.

553. CHORTLE ★★★★

b.f. *Dubawi – Portmanteau (Barathea).* February 6. Fourth foal. Sister to the Group 1 10f Premio Roma winner Hunter's Light and half-sister to the French dual 10f winner Linda Radlett (by Manduro). The dam, a quite useful dual 10f winner, is a half-sister to numerous winners including the smart Group 3 10f Sandown Classic Trial winner Courteous and the useful listed 12f winner Scriptwriter. The second dam, Dayanata (by Shirley Heights), is an unraced sister to the French Derby winner Darshaan and a half-sister to 11 winners including the Prix Vermeille winner Darara (herself dam of numerous winners) and the Prix de Royallieu winner Dalara. *"Although she is a full sister to Hunter's Light, who only had one 2-y-o start right at the back-end of that season, and from the family of Darshaan, she looks a bit more precocious at this stage. She's very willing, strong and is thriving at the moment, doing all that is asked of her with ease".*

554. CLEAN LIVING

b.c. *Sea The Stars – Virtuosity (Pivotal).* May 24. Third foal. 125,000Y. Tattersalls October Book 1. John Ferguson. Half-brother to Judgement (by Medicean), a minor winner in Qatar. The dam, a quite useful 10f winner, is a sister to the Group 1 1m Lockinge Stakes winner Virtual, closely related to the very smart 2-y-o Group 2 6f Coventry Stakes winner and Group 1 6f Middle Park Stakes third Iceman and a half-sister to 3 winners. The second dam, Virtuous (by Exit To Nowhere), a fairly useful 2-y-o 1m winner, was third in the listed 11.5f Oaks Trial and is a half-sister to 3 winners.

555. CRY JOY (USA)

b.c. Street Cry – Blushing Ogygian (Ogygian). May 5. Sixth foal. $400,000Y. Saratoga August. John Ferguson. Brother to the US Grade 1 Triple Bend Invitational Handicap and Grade 1 Bing Crosby Handicap winner Street Boss and half-brother to the US winner and dual Grade 2 placed Habiboo. The second dam, Fruhlingshochzeit (by Blushing Groom), a winner and stakes-placed in France, is a half-sister to the US dual Grade 2 winner Running Stag.

556. DAWN STRIKE

b.c. Dubawi – Lion Forest (Forestry). February 27. First foal. 260,000Y. Tattersalls October Book 1. John Ferguson. The dam is an unraced sister to the US Grade 1 Hollywood Starlet Stakes winner Diplomat Lady and half-sister to 8 winners including the US Grade 2 Comely Stakes winner Dream Play. The second dam, Playcaller (by Saratoga Six), a winner of 3 stakes races at 2 and 3 yrs in the USA, is a half-sister to 8 winners.

557. DESERT SKYWALKER (IRE) ★★★★

ch.c. Raven's Pass – Damiana (Thatching). February 18. Eighth foal. 140,000foal. Tattersalls December. John Ferguson. Half-brother to the 6f (at 2 yrs) and Group 2 7f Challenge Stakes winner Stimulation (by Choisir), to the fairly useful 7f to 10f winner Desert Cristal (by Desert King), the fair 7f to 9f winner Thatcherite (by Verglas) and the fair 7f winner Labisa (by High Chaparral). The dam was placed 5 times in France at 2 and 3 yrs and is a half-sister to 4 winners including the listed Prix Coronation winner and US Grade 2 placed Dirca. The second dam, Derena (by Crystal Palace), is an unraced half-sister to 4 winners. *"This is a beautifully well-made colt, well-grown, rangy with a strong, good-ground action. There is a lot to like about him and we will look forward to him debuting around August-time, over a mile".*

558. EARL OF MENTEITH (IRE)

b.c. Shamardal – Inchmahome (Galileo). March 17. Third foal. €72,000Y. Goffs February. John Ferguson. Half-brother to the fair 2m winner Wayne Manor (by Cape Cross). The dam, a modest 11f winner, is a half-sister to 7 winners including the triple Group 3 7f winner and sire Inchinor and the listed winners Ingozi and Incheni. The second dam, Inchmurrin (by Lomond), a very useful winner of three races at 2 yrs over 5f and three races at 3 yrs including the Group 2 Child Stakes, was second in the Group 1 1m Coronation Stakes and is a half-sister to 7 winners including the Mill Reef Stakes winner Welney and the dam of the Group 1 Coronation Stakes winner Balisada.

559. EMPIRIC ★★★★

b.c. New Approach – Speirbhean (Danehill). January 31. Sixth foal. Closely related to the champion 2-y-o colt and Group 1 Dewhurst Stakes and Group 1 National Stakes winner Teofilo, to the fairly useful Irish 10f winner Senora Galilei and the quite useful 7f winner Teo's Sister (all by Galileo). The dam, an Irish listed 1m winner, is a half-sister to numerous winners including the Irish listed 9f winner Graduated. The second dam, Saviour (by Majestic Light), won 3 races at 2 and 3 yrs and is a half-sister to 5 winners including the triple US Grade 1 winner Judge Angelucci and the US Grade 1 winners Peace and War. *"This is a big, good-looking three-parts brother to Teofilo, who didn't make his debut until July over seven furlongs and this horse's timeline will be quite similar. He's a nice type, with a lot to live up to".*

560. FEEDYAH (USA) ★★★★

f. Street Cry – Red Dune (Red Ransom). March 1. First foal. The dam, a useful 7f and 1m winner, was listed-placed over 7f and 1m and is a half-sister to several winners. The second dam, Desert Beauty (by Green Desert), a useful 7f and 1m winner, is a half-sister to the Yorkshire Oaks and Nassau Stakes winner Islington, to the smart stayer Election Day and the smart 10f performer Greek Dance. *"She has scope and stamina in her pedigree from Islington, New Morning etc, but she has plenty of girth and is showing some speed at the moment. She could well go through a weak stage in the next month, but if not she will be out earlier than imagined on paper".*

561. FIRE BLAZE (IRE) ★★★★

gr.f. Dubawi – Nahoodh (Clodovil). February 13. Second foal. The dam, winner of the Group 1 1m Falmouth Stakes and the Group 2 6f Lowther Stakes, was second in the Group 1 1m Matron Stakes and is a half-sister to one winner. The second dam, Mise (by Indian Ridge), is an unraced half-sister to 6 winners including the French Group 3 winner Not Just Swing and the French listed winner Minoa. *"Put up a gutsy performance to win her debut at Newmarket this week in a very strong wind. She'll be suited by a furlong further and will head to Royal Ascot if she proves she can step up in class".*

562. FRANCISTOWN (IRE)

b.c. Cape Cross – Dove (Sadler's Wells). February 11. First foal. The dam, a quite useful 10f winner, is a half-sister to 4 winners including the very smart Group 3 10f Winter Hill Stakes and Group 3 7f Champagne Lanson Vintage Stakes winner Naheef. The second dam, Golden Digger (by Mr Prospector), was placed fourth 3 times from 6f (at 2 yrs) to 1m and is a sister to the dam of the Irish Oaks winner Lailani and a half-sister to the high-class Group 2 10f Prince Of Wales's Stakes winner Faithful Son and the very smart Coventry Stakes and Prix Quincey winner Always Fair.

563. FRAZIER (IRE)

b.c. Teofilo – Innclassic (Stravinsky). March 3. Fifth foal. €95,000foal. Goffs November. John Ferguson. Half-brother to the fair Irish 2-y-o 9f winner Mahaazen (by Cape Cross) and to the minor Italian winner of 5 races at 2 and 3 yrs Pile Ou Face (by Exceed And Excel). The dam, a modest 6f winner, is a half-sister to 5 winners including the US dual Grade 1 winner Daytona. The second dam, Kyka (by Blushing John), is an unraced half-sister to 5 winners including the French 1,000 Guineas winner Madeleine's Dream and the US Grade 3 9f Bewitch Stakes winner Miss Lenora (herself dam of the triple Grade 3 winner Stylish).

564. GOLD TRAIL (IRE)

ch.c. Teofilo – Goldthroat (Zafonic). April 26. Eighth foal. €280,000Y. Goffs Orby. John Ferguson. Half-brother to the 2012 5f and 6f placed 2-y-o Gold Hunter (by Invincible Spirit), to the 2-y-o Group 1 Criterium International and dual Group 3 winner Zafisio (by Efisio), the fairly useful 1m and 9f winner of 4 races Harald Bluetooth (by Danetime) and the quite useful 9.5f (at 2 yrs) and 10f winner New Beginning (by Keltos). The dam, a fair 7f winner at 2 yrs, is a half-sister to 2 winners. The second dam, Winger (by In The Wings), a fair Irish 9f winner, is a half-sister to 6 winners.

565. KINGDOM'S CALL (USA) ★★★★

b.br.c. Smart Strike – Wile Cat (Storm Cat). March 4. Second foal. $500,000Y. Keeneland September. Richard O'Gorman. Half-brother to the 2-y-o Group 3 Sirenia Stakes winner Shumoos (by Distorted Humor). The dam is an unraced sister to the Grade 2 La Canada Stakes winner Cat Fighter and a half-sister to the Group 3 winner and sire Ishiguru. The second dam, Strategic Maneuver (by Cryptoclearance), winner of the Grade 1 6f Spinaway Stakes, the Grade 1 7f Matron Stakes and two Grade 2 events at 2 yrs in the USA, is a half-sister to 10 winners including the US stakes winners Ashford Castle and Missionary. *"A half-brother to Shumoos and from the family of sprinter Ishiguru, he is not showing that kind of promise of speed at the moment but is quite precocious and could debut over six or seven furlongs in July: will be suited by top of the ground, and has a lovely temperament".*

566. MAJEYDA (USA) ★★★★

f. Street Cry – Alzerra (Pivotal). January 15. The dam, a smart 2-y-o Group 3 5f Cornwallis Stakes and listed 5f winner, was second in the Group 2 Cherry Hinton Stakes and is a half-sister to numerous winners including the useful 2-y-o Group 3 7f third Matloob. The second dam, Belle Argentine (by Fijar Tango), a listed winner in France and third in the French 1,000 Guineas, is a half-sister to one winner. *"Her dam was a Group 3 winner at 2, and this is a strong, stocky two-year-old type who is showing speed and precocity at the moment to start in May over six furlongs".*

567. MOONTIME

b.c. Sea The Stars – Time On (Sadler's Wells).
April 13. First living foal. 125,000Y. Tattersalls
October Book 1. John Ferguson. The dam, a
Group 2 Prix de Malleret and listed Cheshire
Oaks winner, is a sister to one minor winner
and closely related to another by Montjeu.
The second dam, Time Away (by Darshaan),
won the Group 3 10.4f Musidora Stakes, was
third in the Group 1 Prix de Diane and the
Group 1 Nassau Stakes and is a half-sister to
6 winners including the 10f winner and Prix
de Diane second Time Ahead.

568. ORKNEY ISLAND

gr.c. Dubawi – Ronaldsay (Kirkwall). February
22. Second foal. £180,000Y. Doncaster Premier.
John Ferguson. Half-brother to the useful
2012 2-y-o 6f winner and Group 2 5f Norfolk
Stakes second Gale Force Ten (by Oasis
Dream). The dam, a very useful listed 11f
winner of 4 races, is a half-sister to 5 winners
including the dam of the US dual Grade 3
winner Pickle. The second dam, Crackling (by
Electric), a modest 9f and 12f winner, is a half-
sister to 4 winners including the Group 1 7f
Moyglare Stud Stakes winner Bianca Nera and
the dam of the Group 1 Fillies' Mile winner
Simply Perfect.

569. PANTOLONI

b.c. Dansili – Short Skirt (Diktat). April 13.
Second foal. Half-brother to the fairly useful
7f winner and listed-placed Minidress (by
Street Cry). The dam, a very useful winner of
4 races including the Group 3 10.4f Musidora
Stakes and the Group 3 12f St Simon Stakes,
was third in the Oaks and is a sister to the
listed-placed 1m winner Shorthand and a half-
sister to numerous winners including Little
Rock (Group 2 Princess Of Wales's Stakes) and
Whitewater Affair (Group 2 Prix de Pomone).
The second dam, Much Too Risky (by Bustino),
won twice at 2 yrs and is a half-sister to the
Group 1 winners Arctic Owl and Marooned.

570. PERSONAL OPINION

*ch.c. New Approach – Sentimental Value
(Diesis).* January 13. Fourth foal. 105,000foal.
Tattersalls December. John Ferguson. Half-
brother to the quite useful 9f and 10f winner
Oriental Cat (by Tiger Hill) and to the quite

useful dual 10f winner Barwell Bridge (by
Red Ransom) and the fair 9f, 10f and hurdles
winner Memorabilia (by Dansili). The dam,
a winner of 2 stakes events in the USA and
Grade 3 placed, is a half-sister to 6 winners
in Japan. The second dam, Stately Star (by
Deputy Minister), a stakes winner of 6 races in
the USA, is a half-sister to 9 winners.

571. PINZOLO

b.c. Monsun – Pongee (Barathea). March
12. Fifth foal. 400,000Y. Tattersalls October
Book 1. John Ferguson. Half-brother to the
quite useful 2-y-o 1m winner and listed-
placed Poplin (by Medicean) and to the fair
10f winner Paisley (by Pivotal). The dam,
a very useful Group 2 12f Lancashire Oaks
winner, is closely related to the smart listed
12f and listed 14f winner Lion Sands and to
the very useful 10f (at 2 yrs) and 11f winner
and listed-placed Pukka and a half-sister to
4 winners including the dam of the French
Group 3 winner Pacifique. The second dam,
Puce (by Darshaan), a very useful listed 12f
winner, is a half-sister to 10 winners including
the dam of the dual Oaks winner Alexandrova
and the Cheveley Park Stakes winner Magical
Romance.

572. SALTHOUSE (IRE)

b.c. New Approach – Firth of Lorne (Danehill).
February 3. Fourth foal. Half-brother to the
listed 1m and UAE Group 3 10f winner Falls
Of Lora (by Street Cry), to the French 1m
(at 2 yrs) and German listed 7f winner Etive,
the useful 1m winner Loch Linnhe (both
by Elusive Quality) and the fair dual 1m
winner (including at 2 yrs) Bint Almatar (by
Kingmambo). The dam, a French 2-y-o listed
1m winner and second in the French 1,000
Guineas, was Grade 2 placed in the USA is a
half-sister to 5 winners including the smart
2-y-o 6f winner and Group 3 placed Shmoose.
The second dam, Kerrera (by Diesis), a smart
winner of the Group 3 Cherry Hinton Stakes
and second in the 1,000 Guineas, is a half-
sister to the high-class 2-y-o Rock City.

573. SKY JOCKEY

ch.c. Dubawi – Danella (FR) (Highest Honor).
April 10. Sixth foal. 100,000foal. Tattersalls
December. John Ferguson. Half-brother to the

listed 1m Prix des Lilas winner Azabara (by Pivotal) to the quite useful 2-y-o 7f winner Kentish Dream (by Oasis Dream) and a winner in Greece by Dubai Destination. The dam, a French listed 3-y-o 7f winner, is a half-sister to 5 minor winners in France and Italy. The second dam, Dixianella (by Bering), won twice at 3 yrs in France and is a half-sister to 8 minor winners.

574. SNOW SQUALL

b.c. Dansili – Snow Ballerina (Sadler's Wells). March 23. Third foal. Half-brother to the fair 2-y-o 1m winner Equity Card (by Dubai Destination). The dam is an unplaced sister to the useful 1m and 10f winner and listed-placed Abhisheka and a half-sister to 4 winners including the Derby, King George and Arc winner Lammtarra. The second dam, Snow Bride (by Blushing Groom), was awarded the Oaks on the disqualification of Aliysa and won the Group 3 Musidora Stakes and the Group 3 Princess Royal Stakes.

575. SOLIDARITY ★★★★

b.c. Dubawi – Assabiyya (Cape Cross). March 11. First foal. The dam, a quite useful 10f winner, is a half-sister to several winners including the fairly useful 10f winner and listed placed Shared Dreams. The second dam, Coretta (by Caerleon), won the Grade 2 Long Island Handicap and the Grade 2 La Prevoyante Handicap and is a half-sister to the very useful 10f winner and listed-placed Trumpet Sound, the very useful 10.5f winner and listed placed Rosa Parks and the 2-y-o 9f listed winner Mikado. *"It looks like he should debut in July, probably over seven furlongs. He's a lovely mover, really grabs the ground and carries himself well"*.

576. SUDDEN WONDER (IRE) ★★★★

ch.c. New Approach – Dubai Surprise (King's Best). January 27. Fourth foal. 280,000Y. Tattersalls October Book 1. John Ferguson. Half-brother to the fairly useful dual 7f winner Born To Surprise (by Exceed And Excel), to the fairly useful 2-y-o 7f and 1m winner Star Surprise (by Dubawi) and the quite useful 6f (at 2 yrs), 10f and 11f winner Sand Skier (by Shamardal). The dam, a winner of 4 races here and in Italy including the Group 1 Premio

Lydia Tesio and the Group 3 Prestige Stakes, was second in the Group 1 Criterium de Saint-Cloud and is a half-sister to 3 winners. The second dam, Toujours Irish (by Irish River), is an unraced half-sister to 7 winners including the French multiple Group winner Athyka (herself dam of the US Grade 1 winner Atticus). *"A powerful, well-balanced colt, well-made with a good action, he could be out in July over seven furlongs"*.

577. TARRAFAL

b.c. Shamardal – Cape Verdi (Caerleon). April 19. Half-brother to the fairly useful 7f to 10f winner of 10 races Benandonner, to the quite useful 10f winner Nabucco (by Dansili) and the fair 7f winner Salsa Verdi (both by Giant's Causeway). The dam, a top-class winner of the 1,000 Guineas and the Lowther Stakes, is a half-sister to the useful French 12f winner L'Africain Bleu. The second dam, Afrique Bleu Azur (by Sagace), a French 11.5f winner, is a sister to the Breeders Cup Classic winner Arcangues and a half-sister to the French 1,000 Guineas second Agathe.

578. WEDDING RING (IRE) ★★★★

b.f. Oasis Dream – Cast In Gold (Elusive Quality). February 23. Second foal. 310,000Y. Tattersalls October Book 1. John Ferguson. Half-sister to the unplaced 2012 2-y-o Golden Causeway (by Giant's Causeway). The dam, a quite useful 2-y-o 7f winner, is a half-sister to 3 winners including Rule Of Law (Group 1 St Leger and Group 2 Great Voltigeur Stakes). The second dam, Crystal Crossing (by Royal Academy), winner of the listed 6f Doncaster Bloodstock Rose Bowl Stakes, is a sister to the very useful 2-y-o Group 3 7f Prestige Stakes winner and subsequent US Grade 2 placed Circle Of Gold and a half-sister to 4 winners. *"Her dam is a half-sister to the St Leger winner Rule of Law, but his stamina was an exception in the family and she looks like she could start over six furlongs, possibly in May"*.

579. WICKHAMBROOK

ch.c. Dubawi – Beautiful Filly (Oasis Dream). January 25. First foal. 210,000Y. Tattersalls October Book 1. John Ferguson. The dam, a fair 6f and 7f winner at 3 yrs, is a half-sister to one minor winner in the USA. The second dam, Royal Alchemist (by Royal Academy), was placed in the USA and is a half-sister to the Group 1 Sprint Cup winner Dowsing and the US Grade 1 winner Fire The Groom (dam of the dual Group 1 winning sprinter Stravinsky).

580. UNNAMED

b.c. Shamardal – Miracolia (Montjeu). April 10. Second living foal. 150,000Y. Tattersalls October Book 1. John Ferguson. Half-brother to the 2012 7f placed 2-y-o, from two starts, Omoor (by Tamayuz). The dam is an unraced sister to 2 winners including the UAE Group 3 winner Stagelight and a half-sister to 7 winners including the smart Group 2 12f Premio Ellington winner Ivan Luis, the listed 1m Masaka Stakes winner and 1,000 Guineas third Hathrah and the French/German listed winners Amathia and Zero Problemo. The second dam, Zivania (by Shernazar), a useful Irish winner of 4 races from 1m to 9.5f, is a half-sister to 7 winners including the Group 3 Prix Gontaut Biron winner Muroto.

581. UNNAMED

b.c. Dubawi – Miss Delila (Malibu Moon). February 9. Third foal. 320,000Y. Tattersalls October Book 1. John Ferguson. Half-brother to the quite useful 2-y-o 6f and 7f winner Lady Of The House (by Holy Roman Emperor) and to the fair 6f and 7f placed 2-y-o and subsequent German 3-y-o winner Marching On (by Rock Of Gibraltar). The dam is an unplaced half-sister to 4 winners including Sander Camillo (Group 2 Cherry Hinton Stakes and Group 3 Albany Stakes). The second dam, Staraway (by Star de Naskra), won 20 races in the USA including three listed stakes and is a half-sister to 5 winners.

582. UNNAMED

b.c. Street Cry – Serenading (A P Indy). January 25. First foal. $1,200,000Y. Saratoga August. John Ferguson. The dam, winner of Grade 2 Falls City Handicap in the USA and two listed events in Canada, is a sister to the minor US stakes winner Handpainted and a half-sister to 3 winners. The second dam, Daijin (by Deputy Minister), a US stakes winner and third in the Grade 1 Test Stakes, is a sister to the Grade 1 Belmont Stakes winner Touch Gold.

583. UNNAMED

b.c. Dubawi – Tender Is Thenight (Barathea). February 20. Ninth foal. 85,000foal. Tattersalls December. John Ferguson. Half-brother to the French 1,000 Guineas winner Tie Black (by Machiavellian), to the winner All Night Blues (by Night Shift), the modest 1m winner Zaarmit and the minor Irish 7f winner Midnight Folk (both by Xaar). The dam won once at 3 yrs in France and is a half-sister to 10 winners including the Breeders Cup Mile and William Hill Sprint Championship winner Last Tycoon, the Group 2 6f Premio Melton winner Astronef, the French winner Save Me The Waltz (herself dam of the Group 1 winners Sense Of Style and Valentine Waltz) and the listed winner Side Of Paradise (dam of the dual Group 1 winner Immortal Verse). The second dam, Mill Princess (by Mill Reef), won over 10f at 2 yrs in France and is a half-sister to the Irish Derby winner Irish Ball and the top-class broodmare Irish Bird (dam of the classic winners Assert, Bikala and Eurobird).

GODOLPHIN (SAEED BIN SUROOR)

584. ALMERZEM (USA)

br.c. Medaglia d'Oro – Tashawak (Night Shift). April 15. Half-brother to the quite useful 2012 2-y-o 7f winner Shebebi (by Mr Greeley), to the quite useful 7f and 1m winner Nadawat (by Kingmambo) and the fair 2-y-o 7f winner Afnoon (by Street Cry). The dam, a smart 6f (at 2 yrs) and Group 2 1m Falmouth Stakes winner, is a sister to the fair 6f (at 2 yrs) and 1m winner of 8 races Speedfit Free and a half-sister to the Irish 8.5f (at 2 yrs) and 10f winner and Group 1 1m Criterium International third Acropolis and the Group 2 12f Ribblesdale Stakes and Group 2 12.5f Prix de la Royallieu winner Fairy Queen. The second dam, Dedicated Lady (by Pennine Walk), a useful Irish 2-y-o 5f and 6f winner, is a half-sister to 5 winners including the German listed winner and Group 3 10.5f Prix de Flore third Silk Petal (herself dam of the listed Sandy Lane Stakes winner Star Tulip). (Hamdan Al Maktoum).

585. ARMY LEADER

b.c. New Approach – Mannington (Danehill). April 1. Half-brother to the Australian Group 1 12f winner Benicio (by More Than Ready) and to the Australian Group 2 1m and Group 3 7f winner Romneya (by Red Ransom). The dam was Group 1 placed twice over 6f in Australia and is a half-sister to the Australian Group 1 1m winner Bollinger.

586. BASEM ★★★★

b.c. Pivotal – Gonbarda (Lando). April 17. Fourth foal. Brother to the high-class 7f (at 2 yrs) and 1m winner and multiple 1m and 10f Group 1 placed Farhh and to the fairly useful 2-y-o 1m winner Welcome Gift. The dam, a German dual Group 1 12f winner, is a full or half-sister to numerous winners including Gonfilia, a winner of the Group 3 8.5f Princess Elizabeth Stakes and four listed events. The second dam, Gonfalon (by Slip Anchor), is a half-sister to several winners. *"A mature July/ August type for seven furlongs, he's a very good-looking colt with a positive attitude and is showing potential. At this stage we can dream that he has the same kind of talent as his brother".*

587. BE READY (IRE)

ch.c. New Approach – Call Later (Gone West). April 14. €43,000foal. Goffs November. John Ferguson. Half-brother to the modest 3-y-o dual 5f winner Trending (by Dark Angel). The dam is an unraced half-sister to 6 winners including the multiple US Grade 1 winner Ventura. The second dam, Estala (by Be My Guest), won over 1m at 2 yrs in France and was listed-placed and is a half-sister to 4 stakes winners.

588. BLUE ARMY

ch.c. New Approach – Evil Empire (Acatenango). January 8. Half-brother to the 1m (at 2 yrs) and listed 10f winner Empire Day (by Lomitas) and to the useful 11f and 12f winner Counterpunch (by Halling). The dam, a Group 3 12f winner in Germany, is a sister to the German triple listed winner El Tango and a half-sister to the German listed winner El Tiger.

589. DESERT SNOW ★★★

gr.f. Teofilo – Requesting (Rainbow Quest). March 9. Sister to the quite useful 2-y-o 1m winner Assizes and half-sister to the fairly useful 1m (at 2 yrs) to 11f winner and UAE Group 3 second Dr Faustus (by Sadler's

Wells), the fair 1m winner Call To Arms (by Shamardal), the fair 2-y-o 6f winner Desert Flora (by Green Desert) and the French 2m winner Marmoom Flower (by Cape Cross). The dam is an unraced half-sister to the very useful Irish listed 14f winner and Irish Oaks third Arrikala, to the useful Irish 12f listed winner Alouette (herself dam of the dual Champion Stakes winner Alborada and the triple German Group 1 winner Albanova), the Doncaster Cup winner Alleluia, the very smart Group 2 10f Nassau Stakes and Sun Chariot Stakes winner Last Second (dam of the French 2,000 Guineas winner Aussie Rules) and the placed dam of the Group 1 winners Yesterday and Quarter Moon. The second dam, Alruccaba (by Crystal Palace), a quite useful 2-y-o 6f winner, is a half-sister to 3 minor winners. "This is a lovely big, rangy filly who is bred to want a trip as a three-year-old. She is still a bit weak unsurprisingly but she catches the eye on the canter and is one for September-time".

590. ELJADDAAF (IRE)

b.c. Shamardal – Almansoora (Bahri). February 14. Fifth foal. Half-brother to Ostaad (by Marju), placed second over 1m on both his starts at 2 yrs in 2012 and to the quite useful 2-y-o 1m winner Dahaam (by Red Ransom). The dam, a quite useful 2-y-o 7f winner, is a half-sister to 4 winners including the fairly useful dual 1m winner Mosayter. The second dam, Bashayer (by Mr Prospector), a useful dual 1m winner, is a sister to the useful 1m and 10.4f winner Wijdan and the useful 10f listed winner Sarayir and a half-sister to numerous winners including Nashwan, Nayef and Unfuwain. (Hamdan Al Maktoum).

591. FAHEEM

b.c. Halling – White Star (Darshaan). March 6. Brother to the smart Group 2 10f Prix Eugene Adam and listed 10f winner Harland. The dam, a winner in France over 12f and third in the Group 2 12f Prix de Malleret, is a half-sister to numerous winners including the Group 2 Prix de Pomone winner Whitehaven and the dam of the Italian Oaks winner Valley Of Gold. The second dam, White Star Line (by Northern Dancer), won the Alabama Stakes, the Delaware Oaks and the Kentucky Oaks (all Grade 1 events) and is a half-sister to

7 winners including the Prix Morny winner Filiberto.

592. FINAL ATTACK (IRE)
b.c. Cape Cross – Northern Melody (Singspiel). March 14. Second foal. Half-brother to the quite useful 1m (at 2 yrs), 12f and 14f winner Rythmic (by Dubai Destination). The dam is an unraced sister to one winner and a half-sister to the Group 1 12f Prix du Jockey Club winner Anabaa Blue and the listed 10f winners Reunite and Measured Tempo. The second dam, Allez les Trois (by Riverman), a smart winner of 3 races in France including the Group 3 10.5f Prix de Flore, is a half-sister to 6 winners including the Prix de l'Arc de Triomphe winner Urban Sea and the 2,000 Guineas winner King's Best.

593. FLIGHT OFFICER
b.c. New Approach – Danuta (Sunday Silence). January 17. Half-brother to the US 2-y-o 7f and UAE 3-y-o listed 9f winner Devotee (by Elusive Quality) and to the quite useful dual 7f winner Discoverer (by Bernardini). The dam, a US 1m and UAE 1m and 9f winner, is a half-sister to numerous winners including the UAE listed 1m and listed 9f winner Folk. The second dam, Polish Style (by Danzig), was a French listed 6f winner.

594. FULLAAH (IRE) ★★★
b.f. Shamardal – Zahrat Dubai (Unfuwain). April 5. Sister to the useful 1m (at 2 yrs) and listed 10f winner Modeyra (by Shamardal) and half-sister to the quite useful 2-y-o 1m winner Shariki (by Spectrum). The dam won the Group 1 10f Nassau Stakes and the Group 10.4f Musidora Stakes winner Zahrat Dubai. The second dam, Walesiana (by Star Appeal), won the German 1,000 Guineas and is a half-sister to 8 winners. *"This is a full-sister to our very useful Modeyra. She is still quite long and narrow but is another to show promise, is straightforward and sensible and one to look forward to early autumn".*

595. HEAT STORM (IRE) ★★★
br.c. Lawman – Coconut Show (Linamix). April 3. Sixth foal. €230,000Y. Arqana Deauville August. John Ferguson. Half-brother to the

French and US listed winner and Grade 2 placed Thai Haku, to the listed winner and Group 3 placed Albaraah (both by Oasis Dream) and the 2012 French 2-y-o winner La Belliere (by Kheleyf). The dam, a minor French 3-y-o winner of 3 races, is a half-sister to 5 winners. The second dam, Vingt Et Une (by Sadler's Wells), a minor French 3-y-o winner, is a sister to the Group 1 10.5f Prix Lupin and US Grade 2 1m winner Johann Quatz and to the 10.5f to 13.5f listed winner Walter Willy and a half-sister to the top-class middle-distance colt Hernando, winner of the Group 1 Prix du Jockey Club and the Group 1 Prix Lupin. *"This is a nice type for the future and is really just going through the motions while he matures. There's no rush with him and his likely start will be late August/September over a mile".*

596. IHTIMAL (IRE) ★★★
b.f. Shamardal – Eastern Joy. February 11. First foal. The dam was placed fourth once over 10.5f in France and is a half-sister to numerous winners including the Group 1 10.5f Prix de Diane winner West Wind and the very useful listed 12f winner of 3 races Redbridge. The second dam, Red Slippers (by Nureyev), a very useful 7f (at 2 yrs) and Group 2 10f Sun Chariot Stakes winner, is a sister to the smart Derby third Romanov and closely related to the Oaks and Irish Derby winner Balanchine. *"A July/August type, she'll be well suited to start over seven furlongs. Her dam is a half-sister to the Prix de Diane winner West Wind and this filly has a lot to like about her, being light on her feet, attractive and well-balanced".*

597. ISTIMRAAR (IRE)
b.c. Dansili – Manayer (Sadler's Wells). April 2. Half-brother to the minor Irish 10f winner Seraakh (by Azamour). The dam is an unraced sister to one winner and a half-sister to 3 winners. The second dam, Dazzling Park (by Warning), a very smart winner of the Group 3 1m Matron Stakes and a listed 9f event, was placed in the Group 1 Irish Champion Stakes and the Irish 1,000 Guineas. She is a half-sister to 7 winners including the Derby, Champion Stakes, Dewhurst Stakes and National Stakes winner New Approach. (Hamdan Al Maktoum).

598. KING'S LAND ★★★

b.br.c. New Approach – Kazzia (Zinaad). January 23. Half-brother to the Group 1 12f Dubai Sheema Classic winner Eastern Anthem, to the 2-y-o Group 3 9f Prix de Conde winner Zeitoper (both by Singspiel) and the useful listed 10f winner Kailani (by Monsun). The dam won the 1,000 Guineas, Oaks and Flower Bowl Invitational and is a half-sister to the German listed winner Kimbajar (by Royal Abjar). The second dam, Khoruna (by Lagunas), won 2 minor races at 2 and 4 yrs in Germany and is a half-sister to one winner. "We were all obviously very sad to lose Kazzia, and would be delighted if this colt could do her well, like some of her other progeny have done. He is very much a back-end of the season type, very tall, but he has a great, powerful action and could be anything".

599. MEMORIAL DAY (IRE)

b.c. Cape Cross – Reunite (Kingmambo). March 2. Third foal. The dam, a very useful listed 10f winner, was second in the Group 3 10f Winter Hill Stakes and is a half-sister to 5 winners including the Group 1 12f Prix du Jockey Club winner Anabaa Blue and the listed 10f winner Measures Tempo. The second dam, Allez les Trois (by Riverman), a smart winner of 3 races in France including the Group 3 10.5f Prix de Flore, is a half-sister to 6 winners including the Prix de l'Arc de Triomphe winner Urban Sea and the 2,000 Guineas winner King's Best.

600. MOUNTAIN FIGHTER ★★★★

b.c. Dubawi – River Pearl (Turfkonig). March 16. Eighth foal. 95,000foal. Tattersalls December. John Ferguson. Half-brother to the French and German triple listed 1m winner Rubiano (by Sholokov)to the German winner and Group 3 placed River Melody (by Keos) and two minor winners in Germany by Zieten and Shirocco. The dam won 3 races at 3 and 4 yrs in Germany and is a half-sister to 3 winners. The second dam, Reduced (by Irish River), won once at 3 yrs in France and is a half-sister to 6 other minor winners. "A powerful son of Dubawi, this colt should debut over seven furlongs in mid-season: he is big, scopey and has a good action".

601. NIGHT PARTY (IRE) ★★★

b.f. Dansili – La Salina (Singspiel). February 13. Fourth foal. €210,000Y. Baden-Baden. John Ferguson. Sister to the German winner and listed-placed La Dawa and half-sister to a minor winner in Germany by Hernando. The dam is an unplaced half-sister to 9 winners notably Lomitas (four Group 1 wins in Germany). The second dam, La Colorada (by Surumu), was a German Group 3 winner. "She's not bred for speed, being from the family of Lomitas, but she is a neat little filly, with a sharp action and has a great temperament for racing, so at the moment we can imagine her debuting late June/July over six furlongs, if not seven".

602. REVOLUTION STREET (IRE)

b.c. Authorized – Wood Vine (Woodman). April 2. Half-brother to the Group 2 12f Ribblesdale Stakes winner Silkwood, to the fair dual 10f winner Vine Street (by Singspiel), the 2-y-o Group 2 6f Cherry Hinton Stakes winner and Group 2 6f Lowther Stakes third Silent Honor, the useful 1m winner Kavango (by Cape Cross) and the 10f seller winner Contemplation (both by Sunday Silence). The dam is an unraced daughter of the French 3-y-o 7f listed winner Massaraat (by Nureyev) – a sister to the great filly Miesque (winner of ten Group/Grade 1 races including the Breeders Cup Mile (twice), the 1,000 Guineas, the Prix Jacques le Marois (twice) and the Prix du Moulin).

603. ROSE AUTHOR

b.c. Authorized – Rosenreihe (Catcher In The Rye). May 3. Second foal. €55,000Y. Baden-Baden September. John Ferguson. The dam won the Group 1 German Oaks and is a half-sister to one winner. The second dam, Rosengeste (by Be My Guest), was a multiple listed winner in Germany.

604. SUPER KID ★★★★

b.c. Acclamation – Galapagar (Miswaki). March 26. Fifth foal. 100,000Y. Tattersalls October Book 2. John Ferguson. Half-brother to the fair 6f and hurdles winner Magic Jack (by Trade Fair) and to the modest 2-y-o 7f winner Inniscastle Boy (Sir Percy). The dam, a French 1m and 9f winner, is a half-sister to 4 other minor winners in the USA. The second dam, Runaway Fair Lady (by Runaway Groom), was a stakes winner of 5 races in the USA. *"This colt is a real sharp 2-y-o type who will be ready to run early May, barring hold-ups. He's precocious and will be fine to start over five furlongs before stepping up to six; probably lacks a bit of scope for the long-term".*

605. TABJEEL
b.c. Sakhee – Intishaar (Dubai Millennium). March 17. Fourth foal. Half-brother to the fair 2012 2-y-o 6f winner Bairam (by Haatef). The dam is an unraced half-sister to 2 winners. The second dam, Bint Shadayid (by Nashwan), a very useful winner of the Group 3 7f Prestige Stakes, was placed in the 1,000 Guineas and the Fillies Mile and is a half-sister to numerous winners including the smart listed 10f winner Imtiyaz. (Hamdan Al Maktoum).

606. THINK AHEAD
b.c. Shamardal – Moonshadow (Diesis). February 1. Third foal. 55,000foal. Tattersalls December. John Ferguson. Half-brother to the fair 1m (at 2 yrs) and dual 7f winner Four Better (by Holy Roman Emperor). The dam is a 12f placed sister to the Group 1 12f Oaks winner Love Divine (herself dam of the Group 1 St Leger winner Sixties Icon) and a half-sister to 5 winners including the useful listed 12f winner Floreeda. The second dam, La Sky (by Law Society), a useful 10f winner and second in the Lancashire Oaks, is closely related to the Champion Stakes winner Legal Case.

607. WINTER THUNDER ★★★
gr.c. New Approach – Summer Sonnet (Baillamont). April 15. Half-brother to the high-class Group 1 Criterium International and Group 1 Prix Lupin winner Act One (by In The Wings), to the very useful 2-y-o 7f winner and Group 1 Fillies Mile second Summer Symphony, the French 12f listed winner Summer Solstice (both by Caerleon), the French 7f (at 2 yrs) and UAE 1m winner and French 2,000 Guineas third Gharir (by Machiavellian) and the fairly useful 10f and 12f winner War Poet (by Singspiel). The dam won over 12f in France and is a half-sister to 2 winners including the Japanese stakes winner Ibuki Perceive. The second dam,

Noesis (by Persepolis), a minor winner of 2 races in France, is a half-sister to 5 winners including the Grade 2 Canadian Handicap winner Calista. *"As you can imagine, this is not a precocious type and would be unlikely to see a racecourse until September. He'll need a mile plus and at the moment just needs time to fill out his big frame, but has a lovely action and temperament".*

608. UNNAMED
ch.c. Pivotal – Local Spirit (Lion Cavern). January 31. Fourth foal. Half-brother to Wildcatching (by Exceed And Excel), unplaced in two starts at 2 yrs in 2012 and to the quite useful 7f (at 2 yrs) and 12f winner Al Saham (by Authorized). The dam, a useful 10f winner, was second in the Group 2 12f Lancashire Oaks and is a sister to the high-class Irish 1,000 Guineas, Coronation Stakes and Nassau Stakes winner Crimplene and a half-sister to 7 winners including the smart Group 3 12.3f Chester Vase winner Dutch Gold. The second dam, Crimson Conquest (by Diesis), a quite useful 2-y-o 6f winner, is a half-sister to the US stakes winner at around 1m Sword Blade.

JOHN GOSDEN
609. ALLEGRIA (IRE) ★★★
gr.f. Dalakhani – Drifting (by Sadler's Wells) February 2. Third foal. Half-sister to the quite useful 2-y-o 1m winner Devdas (by Dylan Thomas). The dam, a fair Irish 3-y-o 6f winner, is a half-sister to 2 winners including the fair 2-y-o 7f winner Glinting Desert (herself dam of the Group 1 Phoenix Stakes winner Alfred Nobel). The second dam, Dazzling Park (by Warning), a very smart winner of the Group 3 1m Matron Stakes and a listed 9f event, was placed in the Group 1 Irish Champion Stakes and the Irish 1,000 Guineas and is a half-sister to 7 winners including New Approach. *"A well-balanced filly, she's settled in perfectly well here and I'm happy with her. She's cantering along nicely and is a filly for later in the year towards the autumn over seven furlongs or a mile.*

610. ANGELIC AIR ★★★
b.f. Oasis Dream – Innocent Air (by Galileo). March 25. The dam won two listed events over 7f and 10f at 2 and 3 yrs and is a half-sister to 6 winners including the French listed and US

stakes winner and US Grade 1 placed Skipping and the dual Group 3 placed Minority. The second dam, Minskip (by The Minstrel), won once at 2 yrs and is a sister to the US Grade 2 winner Savinio and a half-sister to the Italian dual Group 1 winner St Hilarion and the dam of the dual Group 1 winner Muhtarram. (Khalid Abdulla). *"A nice type, she moves well, but there's some immaturity about her at this stage and we wouldn't see her until around August time. Her mother was obviously with us and she was a staying filly that did well at 3. I'd be happy with her but she's certainly not one to have out early".*

611. BEYOND SMART (USA) ★★★

b.c. *Smart Strike – Beyond The Waves (Ocean Crest)*. February 8. Half-brother to the US Grade 3 11f winner Emerald Beech (by Maria's Mon), to the French 2-y-o 7f winner and dual listed-placed Water View (by Petionville) and the fairly useful Irish 9f to 2m and hurdles winner Sir Ector (by Dynaformer). The dam, a listed 12f in France, was second in the Group 2 13f Prix Royallieu and is a half-sister to 7 winners including the US multiple listed stakes winner Seahawk Gold. The second dam, Excedent (by Exceller), is an unplaced half-sister to several winners. *"He's a well-balanced colt that moves well and hopefully he'll be coming out around July time. We're perfectly happy with him and he's a nice type at this stage".*

612. BILLY BLUE (IRE) ★★

b.c. *High Chaparral – Silk Dress (Gulch)*. April 12. Third foal. 28,000Y. Tattersalls October Book 2. Huntingdon/Norris. Half-brother to the modest 10f winner Top Frock (by Acclamation). The dam was a fairly useful 2-y-o Group 3 7f C L Weld Park Stakes placed maiden. The second dam, Zvezda (by Nureyev), is an unplaced full or half-sister to 5 winners including the 7f (at 2 yrs) and subsequent US stakes winner and Group 1 Dewhurst Stakes and US Grade 1 third Zentsov Street. *"Cantering along nicely, he's a big, leggy boy and very much the type to be running in September over a stiff seven furlongs or a mile. He's done everything right at this stage".*

613. BRIMFUL ★★★★

b.f. *Invincible Spirit – Alsharq (Machiavellian)*. April 11. Fifth foal. £115,000Y. Doncaster Premier. John Ferguson. Half-sister to the 2012 2-y-o listed 6f winner and Group 3 6f Princess Margaret Stakes second Sandreamer (by Oasis Dream), to the fair 7f (including at 2 yrs) and 1m winner Lolita Lebron (by Royal Applause), the fair triple 5f winner, including at 2 yrs, Commanche Raider (by Tale Of The Cat) and the fair 1m winner Eastern Breeze (by Red Ransom). The dam, a modest 7f winner, is a sister to one winner and a half-sister to 5 winners including the Group 2 7f Rockfel Stakes winner Sayedah. The second dam, Balaabel (by Sadler's Wells), a quite useful 1m winner, is a half-sister to 6 winners including the US Grade 2 7f winner Kayrawan and the good broodmare Sayedat Alhadh (dam of the Group winners Haatef and Walayef). *"A neat filly that goes well, the mother was pretty ordinary but I can see this filly being a six furlong 2-y-o, coming out in late May or early June. We're pretty happy with her".*

614. CORDIAL ★★

b.f. *Oasis Dream – Mirabilis (Lear Fan)*. March 15. The dam, a listed 7f winner in France, was third in the Group 1 7f Prix de la Foret and subsequently won a Grade 3 event in the USA over 1m at 4 yrs. She is a half-sister to the Group 1 1m Prix du Moulin and Group 1 10.5f Prix de Diane winner Nebraska Tornado and the Group 2 10f Prix Eugene Adam winner Burning Sun. The second dam, Media Nox (by Lycius), a useful 2-y-o winner of the Group 3 5f Prix du Bois, is a half-sister to the very useful Bonash, a winner of 4 races in France from 1m to 12f including the Prix d'Aumale, the Prix Vanteaux and the Prix de Malleret. (Khalid Abdulla). *"He goes fine and he's cantering at this stage, but he hasn't shown me a great deal just yet. He'll probably want seven furlongs this year".*

615. COURT ROOM ★★★

b.c. *Cape Cross – Reform Act (Lemon Drop Kid)*. April 23. Third foal. 85,000Y. Tattersalls October Book 2. John Ferguson. Brother to the fair 2012 2-y-o 1m winner Dolphin Village. The dam, a 1m (at 2 yrs), 10f and listed 12f winner in Ireland and third in the Grade 2 Long Island Handicap in the USA, is a half-sister to the US winner and dual Grade 1 placed Soul Search. The second dam, Solar Colony (by Pleasant Colony), won twice at 3 yrs and is a sister to the US Grade 1 winner Pleasant Stage and to the US Graded stakes winners Colonial Play (herself dam of the dual Grade 1 winner Marsh Side) and Stage Colony. *"The type to develop as the season goes on, he'll make a 2-y-o in the second half of the season over seven furlongs plus. A strong colt with size and scope, he goes fine".*

616. CRAFTY BUSINESS (IRE) ★★★

b.c. Bushranger – Champion Tipster (Pursuit Of Love). April 18. Fifth foal. 110,000Y. Tattersalls October Book 2. John Ferguson. Half-brother to the quite useful 2012 5f and 6f 2-y-o winner and listed-placed All On Red (by Red Clubs), to the quite useful 6f winner Shearman (by Elusive City) and the fair 5f to 1m winner Shadow Bay (by Deportivo). The dam is an unraced half-sister to 3 winners. The second dam, Halloa (by Wolfhound), a fairly useful listed-placed 2-y-o 6f winner, is a half-sister to 4 winners. *"A big colt that moves well, his knees are open so we have to give him a bit of time for that but he's a nice, straightforward colt. A 2-y-o for after Ascot, not before".*

617. CRITERIA ★★

b.f. Galileo – Aleagueoftheirown (Danehill Dancer). April 28. Second foal. 535,000Y. Tattersalls October Book 1. Cheveley Park Stakes. Sister to the useful 2012 Irish 2-y-o 7f winner and Group 3 third Kingston Jamaica. The dam, a useful Irish 9f winner, was listed-placed and is a half-sister to 2 winners. The second dam, Golden Coral (by Slew O'Gold), is an unplaced sister to the Group 1 Coronation Stakes and Group 3 Prix du Rond Point winner Golden Opinion and a half-sister to 7 winners. (Cheveley Park Stud). *"She's a nice-moving filly but she's going to take time due to immaturity".*

618. DANJEU (IRE) ★★★★

b.c. Montjeu – Wanna (Danehill Dancer). February 4. First foal. 725,000Y. Tattersalls October Book 1. Waratah Thoroughbreds. The dam, a quite useful Irish 12f winner, is a sister to the useful Irish listed 1m winner

Pirateer, closely related to the Group 1 6f Cheveley Park Stakes and Group 2 6f Cherry Hinton Stakes winner Wannabe Grand and a half-sister to the useful listed 12f Galtres Stakes winner and Group 3 second Wannabe Posh (by Grand Lodge), the useful 2-y-o dual 1m winner and listed placed Assaaf (by Night Shift) and the minor French 3-y-o dual winner Masseera (by Alzao). The second dam, Wannabe (by Shirley Heights), a quite useful 1m and 10f winner, is a half-sister to 3 winners including the very useful 5f and 6f winner and Group 1 Cheveley Park Stakes second Tanami (herself dam of the Group 2 Rockfel Stakes winner Cairns). *"He's a nice-moving horse and we're pleased with him at this stage, he's got a nice attitude and a good way of moving. One for seven furlongs around July time, he's a nice, medium-sized colt that would appreciate some cut in the ground".*

619. DOROTHY B (IRE) ★★★

b.f. Fastnet Rock – Slow Sand (Dixieland Band). March 9. Second foal. 130,000Y. Tattersalls October Book 2. Charles Liverton. Half-sister to the 2012 1m placed 2-y-o winner Northern Star (by Montjeu). The dam ran twice unplaced and is a half-sister to 4 winners including the French listed winner and Group 2 second Slow Pace. The second dam, Slow Down (by Seattle Slew), a winner in France and a listed winner in the USA, is a half-sister to 7 winners including the US dual Grade 3 winner Olmodavor. *"A nice type of filly, she's well-made, strong and likeable. I could see her running from the mid-season onwards. Fastnet Rock has carried all before him in Australia, so let's hope he adapts to our conditions".*

620. ENRAPTURED (IRE) ★★★★

b.f. Oasis Dream – Arty Crafty (Arch). February 7. First foal. 450,000Y. Tattersalls October Book 1. Hugo Lascelles. The dam, a modest 10f and 12f winner of 4 races, is a sister to the US Grade 1 11f winner Prince Arch and a half-sister to the Group 1 National Stakes winner Kingsfort. The second dam, Princess Kris (by Kris), a quite useful 3-y-o 1m winner, is half-sister to 8 winners including the Group 3 May Hill Stakes winner Intimate Guest and to the placed dam of the US Grade 1 winner Luas Line. *"A nice filly, she's active and a good* mover. The dam stayed, but this filly shows a nice level of exercise, she hasn't worked or anything but she could possibly be out in May over six furlongs".

621. EPIC VOYAGE ★★★

b.c. Empire Maker – Costume (Danehill). March 31. First foal. The dam, a 1m winner here and subsequently a US dual Grade 2 winner over 1m and 9f, is a half-sister to 2 winners. The second dam, Dance Dress (by Nureyev), a French Group 3 10.5f winner, is a half-sister to 3 winners. (Khalid Abdulla). "A nice type of colt, he's well-balanced and a good mover. We trained the dam and this is a likeable sort".

622. FASTNET RED ★★★

b.c. Fastnet Rock – Gyroscope (Spinning World). March 31. Second foal. Half-brother to the unplaced 2012 2-y-o Dizzy Contessa (by Medicean). The dam, a quite useful 1m and 10f winner, is a half-sister to the high-class Group 3 7f Supreme Stakes and Group 3 7f Criterion Stakes winner Arakan. The second dam, Far Across (by Common Grounds), is an unraced half-sister to 5 winners including the Group/Grade 3 winners Donkey Engine and Petit Poucet. (Cheveley Park Stud). "He's a nice, big, strong horse, he's done nothing wrong, he does his canters nicely and he goes well. He'll be a mid-season 2-y-o".

623. FINE TUNE (IRE) ★★★

b.c. Medicean – Phillippa (Galileo). April 20. Third foal. £58,000Y. Doncaster Premier. Blandford Bloodstock. Half-brother to the fair 2012 2-y-o 7f winner Starlight Symphony (by Oratorio) and to the fairly useful 10f and 12f winner and Group 3 13f second Naseem Alyasmeen (by Clodovil). The dam is an unraced half-sister to 4 winners including the listed Zetland Stakes winner Amir Zaman. The second dam, Kardashina (by Darshaan), won 3 races in France from 11f to 12.5f and is a full or half-sister to 6 winners including the listed winners Kart Star and Karmifira. "He's a nice horse, well-balanced and he has a good mind on him. The dam stayed, so I could see him leaning more towards seven furlongs or a mile. A strong and likeable colt".

624. GAY MARRIAGE (IRE) ★★★★

b.f. New Approach – Doctrine (Barathea). April 25. Sixth foal. 60,000Y. Tattersalls October Book 2. Blandford Bloodstock. Half-sister to Pop Art (by Excellent Art), a 6f winner on her only start at 2 yrs in 2012, to the fairly useful dual 6f winner (including at 2 yrs) Sunraider (by Namid), the fairly useful Irish dual 7f winner Always Be True (by Danehill Dancer) and the quite useful dual 7f winner Oblitereight (by Bertolini). The dam, a fairly useful 2-y-o 7f and 1m winner, is a half-sister to 6 winners. The second dam, Auspicious (by Shirley Heights), a fairly useful 10.2f winner, is a sister to the smart Group 2 11.9f Great Voltigeur Stakes winner Sacrament and a half-sister to 5 winners and to the unraced dam of the Group 1 winner Chorist. "She goes nicely and she's an attractive filly. I trained the mother and she looks a nice type, we're probably looking at seven furlongs for her, but she's a very likeable filly at this stage".

625. GM HOPKINS ★★★

b.c. Dubawi – Varsity (Lomitas). April 23. Second foal. €140,000Y. Arqana Deauville August (private sale). The dam, a useful 10f to 12f winner of 4 races in France and Ireland, was listed-placed three times and is a half-sister to 3 winners including the Italian listed 11f winner Renowing. The second dam, Renowned (by Darshaan), is an unraced sister to the top-class colt Mark of Esteem, winner of the 2,000 Guineas, Queen Elizabeth II Stakes and Tripleprint Celebration Mile. "He's fine. A nice, balanced Dubawi from the Deauville Sales, he's grown and moves well and looks the type for a stiff six furlongs. I'm happy with him. It's a tough sort of family – the mother ran 43 times!"

626. GOLD STRUCK ★★★

b.br.c. Raven's Pass – Love The Rain ((Rainbow Quest). March 1. Tenth foal. Half-brother to the very useful 7f (at 2 yrs) and 10f winner and Group 2 Dante Stakes second Raincoat, to the French 1m winner Precipitate (both by Barathea), the useful listed 12f winner Quenched and the French dual 13f winner Lifting Cloud (both by Dansili). The dam, a winner over 11f in France, is a sister to the very useful Prix d'Aumale, Prix Vanteaux and

Prix de Malleret winner Bonash and a half-sister to 3 winners including Media Nox (2-y-o Group 3 5f Prix du Bois winner and dam of the dual Group 1 winner Nebraska Tornado). The second dam, Sky Love (by Nijinsky), a fairly useful 10f winner, is a half-sister to the high-class Prix de la Cote Normande winner Raft. (Khalid Abdulla). *"He's a nice sort of horse, he's big, strong and he carries himself well. We had the mother and I like the way he goes at this stage, but I can see him being like his father and coming out at seven furlongs".*

627. GRANDEST ★★★

b.c. Dansili – Angara (Alzao). January 21. Half-brother to the fair 2012 1m placed 2-y-o Space Ship (by Galileo) and to the fair 7f winner The Mongoose (by Montjeu). The dam, winner of Grade 1 10f Beverly D Stakes and Grade 1 9f Diana Stakes in the USA, is a half-sister to numerous winners including the French Group 2 Prix Corrida winner Actrice. The second dam, Ange Bleu (by Alleged), was placed at 3 yrs in France and is a half-sister to 10 winners including the Group 3 Prix de Psyche winner and French 1,000 Guineas and French Oaks placed Agathe (herself dam of the Grade/Group 1 winners Artiste Royale and Aquarelliste), to the Breeders Cup Classic winner Arcangues and the dam of the 1,000 Guineas winner Cape Verdi. *"He's a well-balanced horse – we have the 3-y-o half-brother who was placed the other day. I can see this horse being more precocious than him, but he'll wait for the seven furlong races in late June or early July".*

628. HUNTERS CREEK (IRE) ★★

b.c. Cape Cross – Cinnamon Rose (Trempolino). March 14. Tenth foal. 80,000Y. Tattersalls October Book 1. Blandford Bloodstock. Half-brother to the Group 1 7f Moyglare Stud Stakes winner of 5 races Chelsea Rose (by Desert King), to the Irish 6f (at 2 yrs) and listed 1m and subsequent US winner and Grade 2 placed European (by Great Commotion), the quite useful 7f (at 2 yrs) and 12f winner Woodcutter (by Daylami), the Japanese 3-y-o winner Admire Golgo (by Fasliyev), the 2-y-o 7f winner Next Move (by Tiger Hill) and the minor French and Spanish winner of 4 races Ruente (by Persian Bold). The dam, an Irish 10f

winner, is a half-sister to 6 winners including the Group 2 Prix Eugene Adam winner River Warden and the US Grade 3 winner Sweettuc. The second dam, Sweet Simone (by Green Dancer), is a placed half-sister to 7 winners. *"A smallish colt that needs to strengthen up. He's very much one for the autumn over seven furlongs or a mile and this is something of a filly family".*

629. IF SO MINDED ★★★

ch.f. Shamardal – Crystal Maze (Gone West). January 21. Second foal. Half-sister to the 2012 French 2-y-o 1m winner and 3-y-o listed 11f winner Ocovango (by Monsun). The dam is an unraced half-sister to 3 winners including the fairly useful 2-y-o winners and listed-placed Treasury Devil and Crystany. The second dam, Crystal Music (by Nureyev), a smart winner of the Group 1 Fillies' Mile at 2 yrs, is closely related to the Group 3 12f John Porter Stakes winner Dubai Success and the smart 7f (at 2 yrs) and 10f winner Tchaikovsky and a half-sister to the Group 3 1m May Hill Stakes winner Solar Crystal and the Group 3 12f Lancashire Oaks winner State Crystal. *"This is a nice filly, she's a little bit highly strung, but she's an active filly and I'm hoping she'll go the right way. She'd want to start at seven furlongs and it's interesting to note that her half-brother looks very promising for Andre Fabre".*

630. IRISH TEARS ★★★

b.c. Compton Place – Deora De (Night Shift). March 17. First foal. 55,000Y. Tattersalls October Book 2. Blandford Bloodstock. The dam ran once unplaced and is a sister to the fairly useful 2-y-o 5f winner and subsequent US stakes winner Deal Breaker and a half-sister to the Group 2 6f Richmond Stakes winner Prolific. The second dam, Photo Flash (by Bahamian Bounty), a fair 1m winner, is a half-sister to 8 winners including the Group 2 Royal Lodge Stakes winner Atlantis Prince. *"A nice, handy colt, he's well-balanced, he carries himself well and I can see him running over six furlongs in early June. The mother wasn't much good but she was by Night Shift so hopefully that'll help. He goes well".*

631. JACQUELINE JOULIAC ★★★

b.f. Oasis Dream – Sugar Mill (Polar Falcon).

April 24. Sister to the quite useful dual 10f winner Dick Doughtywylie and half-sister to the Group 2 12f Lancashire Oaks winner Gertrude Bell (by Sinndar) and the modest 11f winner Gertrude Versed (by Manduro). The dam, a French 10f winner, was listed-placed twice. The second dam, Anastina (by Thatching), a fair 7f and 1m winner, is a half-sister to numerous winners. *"An attractive filly, she moves well and has a nice way about her. I can see her running over seven furlongs around July and she's a nice type".*

632. KINGMAN ★★★

b.c. Invincible Spirit – Zenda (Zamindar). February 26. Fifth foal. Half-brother to the quite useful 7f winner Panzanella (by Dansili). The dam won the French 1,000 Guineas, was second in the Coronation Stakes and the Grade 1 Queen Elizabeth II Challenge Cup at Keeneland and is a half-sister to the July Cup and Nunthorpe Stakes winner Oasis Dream and the very useful dual listed 1m winner Hopeful Light. The second dam, Hope (by Dancing Brave), is an unraced sister to the very smart filly Wemyss Bight, a winner of five races from 9f (at 2 yrs) to 12f including the Group 1 Irish Oaks and the Group 2 Prix de Malleret. (Khalid Abdulla). *"He moves well, he's a big, strapping colt and just about the nicest the mare's had so far. We need to come up with one for her and I'm happy with him at this stage, he's a nice type of horse".*

633. LONG CROSS ★★

b.c. Cape Cross – Majestic Roi (Street Cry). March 14. Second foal. Half-brother to the fair 2012 7f placed 2-y-o Majestic Jasmine (by New Approach). The dam won the Group 1 1m Sun Chariot Stakes and the Group 3 7f Fred Darling Stakes and is a half-sister to the very useful 7f (at 2 yrs) and 1m winner and Grade 2 Prix Guillaume d'Ornano third Black Spirit, the US Grade 3 placed Heza Gone West and the useful 2-y-o 7f winner and listed placed Hiddnah. The second dam, L'Extra Honor (by Hero's Honor), won a listed race in France over 10f and is a half-sister to 11 winners including the Group 2 Gallinule Stakes winner Montelimar. *"A big colt, he's going to be an autumn horse and more of a 3-y-o, but he's very likeable".*

634. MATALLEB (USA) ★★★

b.c. Elusive Quality – Our Rite Of Spring (Stravinsky). May 7. Fifth foal. $180,000Y. Keeneland September. Shadwell Estate Co. Half-brother to 2 minor winners in the USA by Empire Maker and Mineshaft. The dam, a stakes winner of 3 races in the USA, is a half-sister to 4 winners including the Grade 1 King's Bishop Stakes winner and sire Hard Spun. The second dam, Turkish Tryst (by Turkoman), a stakes winner in the USA, was Grade 2 placed. (Hamdan Al Maktoum). *"He's moving well and I'm pleased with him, he's a rangy colt with a good action and he'll start at seven furlongs".*

635. MAVERICK WAVE (USA) ★★★

ch.c. Elusive Quality – Misty Ocean (Stormy Atlantic). February 20. Second foal. $100,000Y. Saratoga August. John Ferguson. The dam won 4 races in the USA including the Grade 2 Honeymoon Handicap and is a half-sister to 7 winners including the US stakes winner and Grade 3 placed Gala Knockout. The second dam, Shocking Sport (by Lypheor), is a placed half-sister to 8 winners. *"A big, strong colt, he's nice with a good body on him, I probably wouldn't try and sprint him".*

636. MIHANY (IRE) ★★★★ ♠

b.c. Teofilo – Love Excelling (Polish Precedent). March 6. Sixth foal. 600,000Y. Tattersalls October Book 1. Shadwell Estate Co. Half-brother to the promising 2012 2-y-o 7f winner, from two starts, Race And Status (by Raven's Pass), to the smart Group 3 6f Anglesey Stakes and Group 3 1m Irish 2,000 Guineas Trial winner Dunboyne Express (by Shamardal), the fairly useful Irish dual 10f winner Angels Story (by Galileo) and a minor winner abroad by Rock Of Gibraltar. The dam ran once unplaced and is a half-sister to 7 winners including the high-class Group 1 12f Oaks and listed Lupe Stakes winner Love Divine (herself dam of the St Leger winner Sixties Icon) and the listed winners Dark Primise and Floreeda. The second dam, La Sky (by Law Society), a useful 10f winner and second in the Group 3 Lancashire Oaks, is closely related to the Champion Stakes winner Legal Case and a half-sister to 4 winners. (Hamdan Al Maktoum). *"A lovely, big, rangy horse, he moves well and has a good attitude.*

A tall colt, I'm happy with him and we'll see him around August or September time over seven furlongs. I like him".

637. MR SMITH ★★

gr.c. Galileo – Intrigued (Darshaan). February 11. Fourth foal. 280,000Y. Tattersalls October Book 1. Blandford Bloodstock. Brother to the listed 11f winner and Group 1 St Leger Stakes third Michelangelo and to the quite useful dual 12f winner No Heretic. The dam, a very useful 2-y-o 8.5f winner, was listed-placed twice and fourth in the Group 1 Prix Marcel Boussac and is a sister to the 7.5f (at 2 yrs) and listed 10f winner and US Grade 2 second Approach (dam of the Group 2 Irish Derby Trial winner Midas Touch) and a half-sister to the French 2,000 Guineas and US Grade 1 winner Aussie Rules. The second dam, Last Second (by Alzao), winner of the 10f Nassau Stakes and the 10f Sun Chariot Stakes, is a half-sister to 7 winners including the Moyglare Stud Stakes third Alouette (herself dam of the Group 1 winners Albanova and Alborada), the Group 2 Doncaster Cup winner Alleluia (dam of the Group 1 Prix Royal-Oak winner Allegretto) and to the placed dam of the Group 1 winners Yesterday and Quarter Moon. *"A likeable horse, his full-brother Michelangelo didn't run as a 2-y-o and although I can see this colt getting a run or two this year he won't a have a 2-y-o campaign as such. He strikes me as very much a staying horse".*

638. MUCH PROMISE ★★★

b.f. Invincible Spirit – Prowess (Peintre Celebre). February 19. Third foal. Half-sister to the quite useful 2012 2-y-o 7f winner Talent (by New Approach) and to the smart 7f and 1m winner and listed-placed Skilful (by Selkirk). The dam, a fairly useful 12f winner, was listed-placed and is a half-sister to the fairly useful 11.5f winner and listed placed Genoa and the useful 2-y-o 1m winner and listed-placed Clipper. The second dam, Yawl (by Rainbow Quest), winner of the Group 3 7f Rockfel Stakes, was second in the 10f Lupe Stakes and is a half-sister to 7 winners. *"I like her, she goes nicely and is just cantering at the moment but she's a nice type of filly with a good mind on her. I wouldn't rule out six furlongs for her as a starting point".*

639. NIGHT SONG ★★★★★ ♠

b.f. Oasis Dream – All For Laura (Cadeaux Genereux). April 30. Fourth foal. 280,000Y. Tattersalls October Book 1. John Gosden. Sister to the Group 2 6f Cherry Hinton Stakes winner and Group 1 Cheveley Park Stakes second Misheer and half-sister to the fair 2012 2-y-o 6f winner Hartwright and to the fair 5f winner Storm Lightning. The dam, a fairly useful 2-y-o 5f winner, was listed-placed and is a full or half-sister to 4 winners. The second dam, Lighthouse (by Warning), a fairly useful 3-y-o 8.3f winner, is a half-sister to 4 winners including the Group 1 Middle Park Stakes winner First Trump. *"A racey, attractive filly and a good mover. She could be out in May, she's nice, well-balanced and light on her feet. I'll nominate her as one of my most promising types, but remember it's been a cold spring so she's only cantered".*

640. OBSIDIAN ★★★

b.c. Street Cry – Latice (Inchinor). Brother to the 2-y-o listed 7f winner and Group 1 Racing Post Trophy third Fencing. The dam won the Group 1 Prix de Diane and is a half-sister to the Group 1 French Derby and Group 1 Prix Jean Prat winner Lawman and the Group 3 Prix du Palais-Royal winner and Group 1 second Satri. The second dam, Laramie (by Gulch), placed fourth once over 7f at 3 yrs in Ireland, is a half-sister to 2 minor winners. *"He's only just come in so he's only cantering but he's worth putting in the book. He seems a nice horse and is very much a mid-season type".*

641. OH STAR ★★★

b.f. Tale Of The Cat – Sleepytime (Royal Academy). February 18. Eleventh foal. $310,000Y. Keeneland September. Blandford Bloodstock. Half-sister to the Group 3 Winter Derby winner of 9 races Gentleman's Deal, to the Irish 2-y-o 7f winner and Group 3 Gallinule Stakes second Spanish Harlem (both by Danehill), the minor US stakes winner Dame Ellen (by Elusive Quality) and the fair 10f winner Lashyn (by Mr Greeley). The dam, a very smart filly and winner of the 1,000 Guineas and third in the Coronation Stakes and the Fillies' Mile, is a sister to the Group 1 1m Sussex Stakes winner Ali Royal and a half-sister to the dual Group 1 winner Taipan and the US Grade 2 winner Oonagh Maccool. The second dam, Alidiva (by Chief Singer), a useful winner of 3 races from 6f to 1m including a listed event, is a half-sister to 6 winners including the dual French Group 1 winner Croco Rouge. *"A lively, attractive filly with a good action, she shows a lot of spirit. One for seven furlongs in mid-season and she goes nicely".*

642. PENNY SIXPENCE (FR) ★★★★

b.f. Kheleyf – Zerky (Kingmambo). February 25. Second foal. €190,000Y. Arqana Deauville August. Hugo Lascelles. Sister to the 2012 French 2-y-o listed 5f winner Penny's Picnic. The dam, a modest 1m placed 2-y-o from 3 starts, is a sister to the triple Group 3 winner Penny's Gold and a half-sister to the dam of the Japanese Group 1 winner Curren Black Hill. *"A strong, very well-built filly that moves well, hopefully she'll be out in May".*

643. PRINCE OF STARS ★★★

b.c. Sea The Stars – Queen's Logic (Grand Lodge). April 15. Half-brother to the 2012 dual 1m placed 2-y-o Abu Nayef (by Nayef), to the Group 2 6f Lowther Stakes, Group 3 6f Princess Margaret Stakes (both at 2 yrs) and Group 2 6f Diadem Stakes winner Lady Of The Desert (by Rahy), the quite useful 2-y-o 1m and subsequent UAE 6f winner Go On Be A Tiger (by Machiavellian), the fair UAE 1m winner Enjoy Today (by Kingmambo) and the fair 9f winner Dunes Queen (by Elusive Quality). The dam, a champion 2-y-o filly and winner of the Group 1 6f Cheveley Park Stakes and the Group 2 6f Lowther Stakes, is a half-sister to the top-class multiple Group 1 winner Dylan Thomas. The second dam, Lagrion (by Diesis), was placed 5 times in Ireland and stayed 12f and is a full or half-sister to 3 winners. (Jaber Abdullah). *"A nice type, he's doing everything fine and he has a good attitude and a good action. I could see him starting off at seven furlongs or a mile. I was underbidder on the mother at Deauville".*

644. PSILOVEYOU ★★★

ch.f. Sea The Stars – Soinlovewithyou (Sadler's Wells). March 17. Second foal. The dam, a quite useful 2-y-o 7f winner, is a half-sister to

the multiple Group 1 10f to 12f winner Duke Of Marmalade and the US Group 3 placed Countess Lemonade. The second dam, Love Me True (by Kingmambo), an Irish 1m winner, was third in the Group 3 Killavullan Stakes and is a half-sister to the Grade 2 Sanford Stakes winner Bite The Bullet and the smart listed 10f winner Shuailaan. (Lady Bamford). *"Nicely-balanced, she's a little immature at this stage but she has a good attitude and moves well".*

645. SAARREM (USA) ★★★

b.c. Dynaformer – Effectual (Carson City). April 13. Third foal. $650,000Y. Keeneland September. Shadwell Estate Co. Half-brother to No La Hace (by Forestry), a minor winner of 4 races in the USA at 4 and 5 yrs. The dam won the Grade 3 Debutante Stakes at 2 yrs in the USA. The second dam, Hooklineandsinker (by Skywalker), is a placed half-sister to 7 winners including the US Grade 3 winner Meter Maid. (Hamdan Al Maktoum). *"He came from the Keeneland Sales and he's been here for some time. He moves well and he's a likeable colt".*

646. SACRED ACT ★★★

b.c. Oasis Dream – Stage Presence (Selkirk). March 4. Sixth foal. Half-brother to the Group 3 7f Sweet Solera Stakes winner and Group 1 Fillies' Mile third English Ballet (by Danehill Dancer) and to the quite useful 2-y-o 5f winner Spectacular Show (by Spectrum). The dam, a 7f and 1m 3-y-o winner, is a half-sister to 5 winners including the 6f (at 2 yrs) and Group 3 7f Ballycorus Stakes winner Rum Charger. The second dam, Park Charger (by Tirol), a useful winner over 1m and 10f at 3 yrs in Ireland, was listed-placed 4 times and is a half-sister to 9 winners. *"A nice type of colt with some scope about him and he moves well. He seems to take after the dam's side and will be a mid-season onwards type of 2-y-o".*

647. SEMBLANCE ★★★

b.f. Pivotal – Illusion (Anabaa). February 7. First foal. The dam, a fairly useful 1m winner, was listed-placed and is a half-sister to one winner. The second dam, Fantasize (by Groom Dancer), a useful 7f (at 2 yrs) and 1m listed winner, is a half-sister to the Group 3 6f Cherry Hinton Stakes winner and 1,000 Guineas third Dazzle and to the useful 2-y-o listed 7f winner

Hypnotize. (Cheveley Park Stud). *"One for July or August, she'd appreciate some cut in the ground and she goes fine".*

648. SHAHEEN ZAIN (IRE) ★★★
b.f. *Oasis Dream – Majestic Desert (Fraam).* February 17. Second foal. Half-sister to the fair 5f (at 2 yrs) and 6f winner of 4 races Grand Zafeen (by Zafeen) and to the quite useful UAE 2-y-o 6f winner Desert Of Dreams (by Exceed And Excel). The dam was a smart winner of the Group 3 Fred Darling Stakes and the Group 3 Oak Tree Stakes and was second in the Group 1 Cheveley Park Stakes. The second dam, Calcutta Queen (by Night Shift), was placed twice over 1m. *"A racey filly, she's neat and a nice type. We'll be heading towards June over six furlongs with her".*

649. STAR CHART (IRE) ★★★
b.f. *Dubawi – Star Express (Sadler's Wells).* March 26. Seventh foal. 200,000Y. Tattersalls October Book 1. Cheveley Park Stud. Sister to the quite useful 1m and 9f winner Dubai Sunshine and half-sister to the fair 7f winner Desert Shine (by Green Desert), the modest 5f winner Star Twilight and the moderate 6f winner Haedi (both by King's Best). The dam, a minor 12f winner in France, is a sister to the Group 3 7f Greenham Stakes winner and Irish 2,000 Guineas fourth Yalaietanee and a half-sister to 5 winners including the Group 3 5f Molecomb Stakes winner Sahara Star (herself dam of the Group 2 5f Flying Childers Stakes winner Land Of Dreams). The second dam, Vaigly Star (by Star Appeal), a smart sprint winner of 3 races, was second in the Group 1 July Cup and a half-sister to 6 winners including the high-class sprinter Vaigly Great. (Cheveley Park Stud). *"A strong filly with a good, sharp action, she should be out in mid-season or maybe a bit before, over six/seven furlongs".*

650. SWISS KISS ★★★★ ♠
br.f. *Dansili – Swiss Lake (Indian Ridge).* February 15. Sixth foal. Half-sister to the smart Group 3 6f Prix de Meautry and Group 3 5f Prix de Petit Couvert winner Swiss Diva (by Pivotal), to the smart 2-y-o 5f winner and triple Group 2 placed Swiss Franc (by Mr Greeley), the very useful 6f (at 2 yrs) and

Group 3 5f winner Swiss Spirit (by Invincible Spirit) and the quite useful 7f (at 2 yrs) and 6f winner Swiss Cross (by Cape Cross). The dam, a dual listed 5f winner (including at 2 yrs), is a half-sister to the useful 2-y-o dual 5f winner and listed placed Dubai Princess. The second dam, Blue Iris (by Petong), a useful winner of 5 races over 5f and 6f including the Weatherbys Super Sprint and the Redcar Two-Year-Old Trophy, is a half-sister to 9 winners. (Lordship Stud). *"A nice, big rangy filly, she has a good attitude and a good stride on her. Despite her size she could be out earlier than you'd think because she's quite active and handles things easily. A big, powerful filly with a big head".*

651. TAGHROODA ★★
b.f. *Sea The Stars – Ezima (Sadler's Wells).* January 27. The dam, a smart 1m, listed 10f and listed 12f winner, is a full or half-sister to 2 winners. The second dam, Ezilla (by Darshaan), is an unraced sister to the top-class broodmare Ebaziya, a triple listed winner from winner from 7f (at 2 yrs) to 12f in Ireland (herself dam of the Group 1 winners Edabiya, Ebadiyla and Enzeli) and a half-sister to 7 winners. *"She's just doing canters at this stage and is a back-end type, definitely more of a 3-y-o".*

652. TERHAAB (USA) ★★★★ ♠
b.f. *Elusive Quality – Star Of Paris (Dayjur).* February 6. Eighth foal. $330,000Y. Keeneland September. Shadwell Estate Co. Sister to the Group 1 Prix Morny winner and sire Elusive City and half-sister to 2 winners including the US stakes winner Parisian Affair (by Mr Greeley and herself the dam of a stakes winner). The dam is an unraced half-sister to 8 winners including Millions, winner of the Grade 3 Laurel Futurity. The second dam, Liturgism (by Native Charger), a stakes winner of 7 races in the USA, is a half-sister to the US Grade 1 winner Coup de Fusil. (Hamdan Al Maktoum). *"A good, strong filly that moves very well. She looks like a colt, goes nicely and will hopefully be racing in May. She looks strong and quick, so she might be sharp enough for five furlongs to begin with".*

653. THRONE ROOM ★★★★
b.c. *Oasis Dream – Magnificient Style (Silver*

Hawk). February 21. Half-brother to the King George VI and Queen Elizabeth Stakes and Eclipse winner Nathaniel, to the Group 1 Irish Oaks winner Great Heavens (both by Galileo), to the Group 1 Fillies' Mile winner Playful Act, the Group 3 11.5f Lingfield Derby Trial winner Percussionist, the 10f winner and Group 3 10f Prix de Psyche second Changing Skies (all by Sadler's Wells), the Group 2 1m Sun Chariot Stakes and Group 2 14.6f Park Hill Stakes winner Echoes In Eternity (by Spinning World), the US stakes winner and Grade 3 placed Stylelistick (by Storm Cat), the 1m (at 2 yrs) and listed 9f winner and Group 2 placed Petara Bay (by Peintre Celebre) and 2 minor winners by Montjeu and Danehill. The dam won the Group 3 10.5f Musidora Stakes and is a half-sister to the Grade 1 10f Charles H Strub Stakes winner Siberian Summer. The second dam, Mia Karina (by Icecapade), a minor 3-y-o winner in France, is a half-sister to the dam of the US Grade 1 Pegasus Handicap winner Silver Ending. *"A nice type of colt, he's well-balanced, medium-sized and moves well. It's a different style of breeding for the mare than previously. I'm happy with him and I can see him starting over seven furlongs. I'm pleased with him".*

654. TOO THE STARS (IRE) ★★★★

ch.f. *Sea The Stars – Finsceal Beo (Mr Greeley).* February 25. Second foal. €850,000foal. Goffs November. John McCormack. The dam, winner of the Prix Marcel Boussac, 1,000 Guineas and Irish 1,000 Guineas, is a half-sister to the smart German Group 2 1m winner Frozen Power and the fairly useful winners and listed-placed Musical Bar and Zabeel Park. The second dam, Musical Treat (by Royal Academy), a useful 3-y-o 7f winner and listed-placed twice, subsequently won four races at 4 yrs in Canada and the USA and is a half-sister to 6 winners. *"She's cantering nicely, she has a big frame on her which she needs to fill but she's got a nice attitude and she enjoys her exercise. She looks a promising filly".*

655. TORNESEL ★★★

b.c. *Teofilo – Bezant (Zamindar).* March 2. Fifth foal. 125,000Y. Tattersalls October Book 1. John Ferguson. Half-brother to Deposer (by Kheleyf), a 2-y-o 6f and subsequent Hong Kong winner and placed in the Group 3 Jersey Stakes, the Group 3 Diomed Stakes and a US Grade 1 event. The dam, placed once at 3 yrs over 1m, is a half-sister to 3 winners including the Group 2 Beresford Stakes third Sant Jordi. The second dam, Foresta Verde (by Green Forest), is a placed half-sister to 8 winners including the smart broodmare Tanouma. *"A nice, solid colt, I like him. He's a nice sort of 'trainer's horse', he gets on with the job and he'd be the sort for June or July over seven furlongs. A likeable colt".*

656. TRUST THE WIND ★★★

b.f. *Dansili – Hypnology (Gone West).* January 8. First foal. 195,000Y. Tattersalls October Book 1. Not sold. The dam is an unraced half-sister to 4 winners including the Group 3 Winter Derby winner Gentleman's Deal. The second dam, Sleepytime (by Royal Academy), won the 1,000 Guineas and is a sister to the Group 1 Sussex Stakes winner Ali Royal and a half-sister to the German and Italian Group 1 winner Taipan and to the US Grade 2 winner Oonagh Maccool. *"She's an active filly that can take a bit of a hold. She moves along well but at this stage she's just doing her canters and I wouldn't want to do any more right now. A nice type that could well be out in June".*

657. TWIN POINT ★★★

br.c. *Invincible Spirit – Gemini Joan (Montjeu).* January 20. First foal. 105,000Y. Tattersalls October Book 1. John Gosden. The dam is an unraced half-sister to the useful 6f (at 2 yrs) and listed 1m winner and Group 3 7f Nell Gwyn Stakes third Festivale and to the useful 6f (at 2 yrs) and 1m winner and Group 3 second Tell. The second dam, Cephalonie (Kris S), a French 12f winner, is a half-sister to 3 winners including the Japanese stakes winner Fifty Oner. *"He's a nice colt. Interestingly he's out of an unraced Montjeu mare but at this stage he seems to have a laid-back attitude. He showed a little temper early on but he's been good recently, so I'm happy with him. He's definitely a 2-y-o type, but the Invincible Spirit – Montjeu cross is quite a hot one in terms of temperament, so we'll have to see".*

658. VENTUROUS SPIRIT ★★★

b.f. *Invincible Spirit – Venturi (Danehill Dancer).* April 25. Sixth foal. 210,000Y. Tattersalls

October Book 1. John McCormack. Half-sister to Deficit (by Dalakhani), placed fourth once over 7f from three starts at 2 yrs in 2012, to the fairly useful 10f winner and dual listed fourth Stella Point, the quite useful 1m winner Call To Reason (both by Pivotal) and the quite useful Irish 1m and 11f winner and listed-placed Cilium (by War Chant). The dam, winner of the Group 3 7f C L Weld Park Stakes, was subsequently second in two US Grade 3 events and is a sister to the French listed winner and Group 1 Criterium de Saint-Cloud third Feels All Right. The second dam, Zagreb Flyer (by Old Vic), is an unraced half-sister to 8 winners including the listed winner and Group 1 Italian Oaks second Flying Girl. *"An active filly, she carries herself well and there's a nice balance and strength about her. Hopefully she'll come out in June".*

659. WESTERN HYMN ★★★★ ♣

b.c. High Chaparral – Blue Rhapsody (Cape Cross). March 8. Second foal. 50,000Y. Tattersalls October Book 2. Blandford Bloodstock. Half-brother to the fair 2012 2-y-o 1m winner Blue Nova (by Nayef). The dam, a fair 2-y-o 7f winner, is a half-sister to the very smart Group 3 7f Prestige Stakes (at 2 yrs) and Group 3 Nell Gwyn Stakes winner and dual Group 1 placed Fantasia and the Group 3 winner Pink Symphony. The second dam, Blue Symphony (by Darshaan), a fair 10f winner, is a half-sister to one winner out of the Group 1 6f Cheveley Park Stakes winner Blue Duster. *"A nice type of colt with a good action, he moves along well and does everything right. He has a nice attitude and I'm pleased with him. One for seven furlongs or a mile later on in the season".*

660. WESTWARD HOE ★★★

b.c. Oasis Dream – Disco Volante (Sadler's Wells). February 23. Sixth foal. Closely related to the smart 7f (at 2 yrs), Group 3 12f and Group 3 2m winner Namibian (by Cape Cross) and half-brother to the quite useful 10f winner Mary Goodnight (by King's Best) and the modest 1m winner Cinerama (by Machiavellian). The dam, a useful 1m winner, was listed-placed and is a half-sister to 3 winners including the Group 1 placed Valentino. The second dam, Divine Danse (by Kris), a smart sprinter and winner of 5 races

including the Group 2 Prix du Gros Chene and the Group 3 Prix du Ris-Orangis, is a half-sister to 5 winners including the high-class colt Pursuit of Love, winner of the Group 2 Prix Maurice de Gheest and second in the July Cup. *"A rangy colt, he moves nicely and I can see him racing from July onwards over seven furlongs".*

661. WING FOOT (USA) ★★★

ch.c. Giant's Causeway – Vignette (Diesis). Half-brother to the promising 2012 2-y-o 1m winner Flying Officer, to the Group 1 St Leger and dual Group 2 12f winner Lucarno, the 1m (at 2 yrs) and Group 2 12f Great Voltigeur Stakes winner Thought Worthy (all by Dynaformer) and to the 2-y-o 7f winner (on only start) Morning Charm (by North Light). The dam, a US stakes winner, is a half-sister to numerous winners. The second dam, Be Exclusive (by Be My Guest), won 5 races in France and the USA including the Group 3 Prix Chloe and is a half-sister to 2 winners. (Mr G Strawbridge). *"He's only just come in from America. He's a nice type of colt, he's good-looking and moves fine. He might come to hand earlier than his half-brothers".*

662. ZEPHYR ★★★

ch.c. Shirocco – Pelagia (Lycius). February 6. Fifth foal. 100,000Y. Tattersalls October Book 1. John Warren. Half-brother to the useful 6f (at 2 yrs) and 1m winner and Group 2 6f Richmond Stakes second Upper Hand (by Mark Of Esteem) subsequently a winner over 1m in Hong Kong as Royal Prince, to the fair 7f (at 2 yrs) and dual 1m winner Dutiful (by Dubawi) and the modest 14f winner Musically (by Singspiel). The dam is a 7f fourth-placed half-sister to 4 winners including the Group 1 1m Prix Marcel Boussac and Group 2 1m Prix d'Astarte winner Lady Of Chad and the Group 1 Prix Royal-Oak winner Alcazar. The second dam, Sahara Breeze (by Ela-Mana-Mou), a quite useful 7f and 1m placed maiden, is a half-sister to 5 winners including the Group 1 Fillies Mile winner Ivanka and the dam of the top-class stayer Yeats. *"A Shirocco colt that's just cantering away, he's a medium-sized colt and looks the type to get out by August over seven furlongs and make up into a staying horse next year".*

663. ZERFAAL ★★★
b.c. Dubawi – Dhelaal (Green Desert). April
9. Brother to the 2,000 Guineas and Prix
Jacques le Marois winner Makfi (by Dubawi).
The dam is an unraced half-sister to 7 winners
including the champion 2-y-o Alhaarth,
winner of the Dewhurst Stakes, the Laurent
Perrier Champagne Stakes, the Prix Dollar,
the Budweiser American Bowl International
Stakes and the Prix du Rond-Point and the
very useful 2-y-o Group 3 7f Prix du Calvados
winner Green Pola. The second dam, Irish
Valley (by Irish River), is an unplaced half-sister
to 10 winners, notably the Observer Gold
Cup, French 2,000 Guineas and 10.5f Prix
Lupin winner and good sire Green Dancer,
the US Grade 3 winner Ercolano and the US
Graded stakes winner Val Danseur. (Hamdan
Al Maktoum). "A neat colt that moves well and
has a good attitude. I'd hope to have him out
by mid-season, he's very likeable but as I say
he's very much on the neat side".

664. UNNAMED ★★★
b.f. Invincible Spirit – Crossmolina (Halling).
February 8. Third foal. 200,000Y. Tattersalls
October Book 1. Rabbah Bloodstock. Half-
sister to the 6f (at 2 yrs) and listed 1m winner
and Group 2 July Stakes second Neebras (by
Oasis Dream). The dam, a minor winner at 3
yrs in France, is a sister to the smart dual listed
10f winner Foodbroker Fancy (herself the dam
of two stakes winners) and a half-sister to the
listed winner Femme Fatale. The second dam,
Red Rita (by Kefaah), a fairly useful 4-y-o 6f
winner, was second in the Group 3 6f Cherry
Hinton Stakes and the Group 3 6f Princess
Margaret Stakes at 2 yrs and is a half-sister to
3 minor winners. "A nice type of filly, she moves
well and has a good attitude. One for the
middle of the season".

665. UNNAMED ★★★
b.f. Intikhab – Indolente (Diesis). April 20.
Fifth foal. 60,000Y. Tattersalls October Book 2.
Rabbah Bloodstock. Sister to the 2012 French
7f and 1m placed 2-y-o Filatelia and to the
fairly useful 10f and 11f winner and listed
11f second Expense Claim and half-sister
to the minor French 10f winner Issacar (by
Traditionally). The dam is an unraced half-
sister to 2 winners. The second dam, Tycoon's

Dolce (by Rainbows For Life), won the listed
Prix de Lieurey and was Group 3 placed three
times and is a half-sister to three listed winners
in France and Italy. "A neat filly, she goes well
and is a sharp type that could be out in May
over six furlongs".

666. UNNAMED ★★★
b.c. High Chaparral – Lure Of The Moon (Lure).
March 4. Fourth foal. 130,000Y. Tattersalls
October Book 1. Demi O'Byrne. Half-brother
to the useful Irish 2-y-o 6f winner and Group
2 7f Debutante Stakes third Elusive Galaxy, to
the quite useful Irish 6f winner Atacx and the
minor Italian winner of 7 races To Believe (all
by Elusive City). The dam, placed once at 3 yrs,
is a half-sister to 4 winners. The second dam,
Moonlit (by Bold Ruckus), a minor US 3-y-o
winner, is a half-sister to 5 winners. "A nice colt
and a good mover, he's very much one for July
onwards over seven furlongs. A nice type".

667. UNNAMED ★★★
b.c. Montjeu – Reina Blanca (Darshaan).
March 29. Half-brother to the quite useful
triple 7f winner (including at 2 yrs) Bellomi (by
Lemon Drop Kid) and to the French 5-y-o 12f
winner Notion (by Sadler's Wells). The dam, a
fairly useful Irish 1m winner, subsequently won
2 minor events in the USA and is a half-sister
to 5 winners including the useful 2-y-o 6f
winner and Group 3 Solario Stakes third Miss
Universe and the useful German 7f (at 2 yrs) to
11f winner Silver Sign. The second dam, Reine
d'Beaute (by Caerleon), a fairly useful 1m and
9f winner on her only starts, is a half-sister
to 8 winners including the Group 3 May Hill
Stakes winner Intimate Guest. (Mrs J Magnier).
"A well-balanced, neat, medium-sized colt, he'll
appreciate some give in the ground. A nice sort
of horse and very much an autumn 2-y-o".

668. UNNAMED ★★★★
b.c. Bushranger – Sassy Gal (King's Best).
January 23. First foal. 60,000Y. Tattersalls
October Book 2. Rabbah Bloodstock. The dam,
a quite useful 1m (at 2 yrs) and 7f winner, is
a half-sister to 7 winners including the very
useful 6f (at 2 yrs) to 10f winner and Group 3
placed Firebet, the useful 10f winner Dancing
Phantom and the UAE winner and Group 3
placed Seeking The Prize. The second dam,

Dancing Prize (by Sadler's Wells), a useful maiden and third in the listed Lingfield Oaks Trial, is a sister to 3 winners including the Group 1 Fillies Mile second and good broodmare Dance To The Top and a half-sister to 5 winners. *"A neat, sharp colt, hopefully he'll be out early enough because he looks speedy at this stage. I think Bushranger will be odds-on to be leading first season sire".*

669. UNNAMED ★★★

ch.f. *New Approach – Zam Zoom (Dalakhani).* February 14. Second foal. 52,000Y. Tattersalls October Book 2. G Howson. Half-sister to the quite useful 2012 2-y-o 9f winner Nichols Canyon (by Authorized). The dam is an unraced half-sister to Group 3 10f Winter Derby, listed 7f and listed 10f winner Nideeb. The second dam, Mantesera (by In The Wings), is an unraced sister to the Group 3 Nell Gwyn Stakes winner and Group 1 Yorkshire Oaks and Group 1 Prix Vermeille placed Cloud Castle (herself the dam of 2 stakes winners) and a half-sister to 5 winners including the high-class middle-distance horses and multiple Group 1 winners Warrsan and Luso and the Group 2 winner Needle Gun. *"A nice type of filly and we have her half-brother here too. She's likeable but she's going to take some time – probably from August onwards".*

MICHAEL GRASSICK
670. BLUEBERRY GAL (IRE) ★★★

b.f. *Bushranger – Mythie (Octagonal).* February 19. Fifth living foal. 42,000Y. Tattersalls December. Aidan O'Ryan. Half-sister to the Group 3 Nell Gwyn Stakes winner and Group 3 Musidora Stakes third Esentepe (by Oratorio), to the fairly useful 2-y-o 6f winner Versaki (by Verglas) and the quite useful 7f to 9f winner Yojimbo (by Aussie Rules). The dam, a minor French 3-y-o 1m winner, is a half-sister to 5 winners including the French listed winner Mytographie. The second dam, Mythologie (by Bering), won two races at 2 and 3 yrs in France and is a half-sister to 7 winners including Malaspina (Group 3 Prix Perth). (Joseph E Keeling & Partners). *"She'll be racing by mid-May, she's fairly sharp and we were only delayed because she got a bit of a cold after the December Sales. She shows*

plenty of speed and is a very sharp, compact five/six furlong type. A real sprinter with a good attitude".

671. TEXAS ROCK (IRE) ★★

b.c. *Rock Of Gibraltar – Vestavia (Alhaarth).* April 19. Third foal. €45,000foal. Goffs November. Not sold. The dam is an unraced half-sister to 6 winners including the Group 3 placed 2-y-o Rosabee. The second dam, Tilbrook (by Don't Forget Me), won over 1m at 3 yrs in Ireland and is a half-sister to 8 winners including the listed winner and Group 1 Phoenix Stakes second Maledetto. (Joseph E Keeling & Tadhg Geary). *"He's probably not going to be ready until September time, I haven't done any fast work with him but he's a very good-actioned horse for seven furlongs".*

PAUL GREEN
672. DE REPENTE ★★★

b.f. *Captain Rio – Suddenly (Puissance).* April 26. Ninth foal. €10,000Y. Tattersalls Ireland September. Jenson Bloodstock. Half-sister to the fairly useful 5f and 6f winner of 4 races (including at 2 yrs) Sudden Impact (by Modigliani), to the fairly useful 2-y-o 6f and 7f winner Sudden Dismissal (by Inchinor), the quite useful 1m winner Sudden Silence (by Kris), the quite useful 7f winner Imaginationrunwild (by Red Clubs) and the moderate 8.7f winner Cankara (by Daggers Drawn). The dam, a quite useful 2-y-o 7f winner, is a half-sister to 3 winners. The second dam, Sudden Hope (by Darshaan), is a placed half-sister to 5 winners including the Grade 1 E P Taylor Stakes winner Sudden Love. (Mike Nolan). *"A really nice prospect, she's a good-shaped filly with plenty of size and length about her. She's a lot like her half-sister Sudden Impact who was one of five decent winners out of the dam. This filly has a fantastic attitude, she's very laid back and to start her career she'll be aimed for a six furlong event at Haydock Park in May".*

673. PAPARIMA (IRE) ★★★

b.f. *Elnadim – Daily Double (Unfuwain).* April 3. €4,000Y. Tattersalls Ireland September. E Sciarrillo. Half-sister to the fair 2-y-o 5f winner Sharpener (by Invincible Spirit), to the fair 2-y-o 1m winner Our Boy Barrington (by

Catcher In The Rye), the fair 9f and 10f winner of 4 races from 3 to 5 yrs Princess Cocoa (by Desert Sun), the fair Irish 4-y-o dual 6f winner Lady Power (by Almutawakel) and the minor Italian winner of 3 races from 2 to 4 yrs Live To Run (by Intikhab). The dam is an unraced half-sister to 4 minor winners in France and Germany. The second dam, Double Line (by What A Guest), is a placed half-sister to 5 winners including the Group 3 winner and good broodmare Perlee. (Ged Barton & Gary Williams). *"A big, strong, strapping filly and a half-sister to five winners, she's very forward and should be running in April. She's leggy, scopey, travels well and shows plenty of speed".*

674. YNWA ★★★★

b.c. Myboycharlie – Sudden Impact (Modigliani). May 2. First foal. The dam, a fairly useful 5f and 6f winner of 4 races at 2 and 3 yrs, is a half-sister to 4 winners including the fairly useful 2-y-o 6f and 7f winner Sudden Dismissal. The second dam, Suddenly (by Puissance), a quite useful 2-y-o 7f winner, is a half-sister to 3 winners. (Gary Williams). *"A home-bred out of Sudden Impact who was one of two winners we've had of the Tattersalls Sales race in Ireland. This is a proper horse – he looks like a stallion now. He was quite a late foal so we won't see him until a bit later on and he's probably a six furlong type 2-y-o. The name stands for You'll Never Walk Alone!"*

675. UNNAMED ★★★

ch.f. Windsor Knot – Carpet Lover (Fayruz). February 27. Fifth foal. €9,500Y. Tattersalls Ireland September. Jenson Bloodstock. Sister to the quite useful triple 5f winner (including at 2 yrs) Beau Mistral. The dam ran once unplaced and is a half-sister to 4 winners including Misty Eyed (Group 3 5f Molecomb Stakes). The second dam, Bold As Love (by Lomond), is an unraced half-sister to 3 winners. (The Winsor Not Group Two). *"She's just like her sister Beau Mistral in every respect. She looks like her and she's built like her – very robust and a very hardy, early type. Hopefully she'll run at Chester's May meeting because her sister can certainly handle the bends there. There are two shares left if anyone is interested".*

676. UNNAMED ★★★

b.f. Myboycharlie – Jilly Why (Mujadil). May 10. First foal. The dam, a fair and tough winner of 9 races from 5f to 7f, is a half-sister to 3 winners. The second dam, Ruwy (by Soviet Star) won over 1m and is a half-sister to 6 winners. *"A late foal, she's a good specimen and very much in the mould of her dam. A good-looking filly, she should be out in mid-season, I'm looking forward to seeing her and I'm still looking for an owner".*

RAE GUEST

677. ARCHDUCHESS ★★★

b.f. Archipenko – Eminencia (Sadler's Wells). February 25. Fourth foal. Half-sister to Jan Jeffer (by Tamayuz), unplaced on her only start at 2 yrs in 2012. The dam is an unraced half-sister to 4 winners including the listed 14f winner Moments Of Joy. The second dam, My Emma (by Marju), a smart winner of the Group 1 Prix Vermeille and the Group 1 Yorkshire Oaks, is a half-sister to 5 winners including the Group 1 St Leger and Group 1 Ascot Gold Cup winner Classic Cliché. (Miss K Rausing). *"I'm very happy with her because she's the first one I've had from My Emma's family. She's a very nice filly, I think she'll need seven furlongs to a mile this year but she's one we like a lot. A lovely, well-balanced filly, she's strong and moves well".*

678. CAPE FACTOR (IRE) ★★

b.f. Oratorio – Crossanza (Cape Cross). March 28. Third foal. €10,000Y. Goffs Sportsman's. Rae Guest. Half-sister to the 2012 7f placed 2-y-o, from 2 starts, Hidden Belief (by Holy Roman Emperor) and to the quite useful 1m and 9f winner Benzanno (by Refuse To Bend). The dam is an unraced half-sister to two minor winners. The second dam, Alegranza (by Lake Coniston), a winner over 5f at 3 yrs, was listed-placed and is a full or half-sister to 7 winners including the listed winner Army Of Angels and the dam of the Group 1 Cheveley Park Stakes and Canadian Grade 1 6f winner Serious Attitude. (Derek Willis). *"The owner also part-owned one of our best fillies Serious Attitude with me and if you look at the pedigree she's at the bottom of it somewhere! So that was one attraction for us and she was cheap enough. A nice filly that's done very well since we bought her, but she does look more of a 3-y-o type".*

679. CHESS VALLEY ★★

b.f. Shamardal – Grecian Air (King's Best).
March 10. Third foal. 28,000Y. Tattersalls
October Book 1. Rae Guest. The dam is an
unraced half-sister to 4 winners. The second
dam, Greek Air (by Ela-Mana-Mou), Group
3 second over 1m at 2 yrs, won a listed 1m
event at 3 yrs and is a half-sister to 2 winners
including Grecian Urn (Group 2 Criterium
de Maisons-Laffitte). (The Boot Sarratt
Partnership). *"She's a nice, big filly but she'll
take some time. But she's by Shamardal and
she's showing enough speed to say she could
run as a 2-y-o but it won't be until the seven
furlongs/mile races".*

680. FIRST EXPERIENCE ★★★

b.f. Tamayuz – Lolla's Spirit (Montjeu). April 6.
Fourth foal. 9,000Y. Tattersalls December. Rae
Guest. Half-sister to Cherry Tiger (by Tiger
Hill), unplaced in one start at 2 yrs in 2012, to
the fairly useful 2-y-o 7f winner Loving Spirit
(by Azamour) and the modest dual 7f winner
Spark Of Genius (by Oratorio). The dam, a
modest 11f and 12f winner, is a half-sister to 6
winners including the very smart 6f (at 2 yrs)
and subsequent Hong Kong winner, Group 1
1m Racing Post Trophy third and Epsom Derby
fourth Housemaster. The second dam, Glenarff
(by Irish River), a winner over 1m in France, is
a half-sister to 4 winners. *"A filly that was very
cheap, she's done very well and grown a lot so
we're very pleased with her now. I hope she'll
be a 2-y-o because she's going that way, even
though she's out of a Montjeu mare. I think
she'll be sharp enough for six or seven furlongs
in mid-summer and despite her price tag
there's nothing wrong with her".*

681. GOD'S SPEED (IRE) ★★★

b.c. Oratorio – Guilia (Galileo). March 15. Third
foal. Half-brother to the modest 10f and 12f
winner Guiletta (by Dalakhani). The dam, a
useful 2-y-o 7f winner, was listed-placed over
10f and 13f and is a half-sister to 2 winners.
The second dam, Lesgor (by Irish River), won
over 10f in France, was third in the Group
3 10f Prix de Psyche and is a half-sister to 3
winners. (The Hornets). *"A really nice horse, we*

trained the dam who was fifth in the Oaks and
we've had both her previous foals including
God's Gift who wants two miles. This is a
different type of horse altogether. He's well-
made, he looks the part and although he won't
be early he'll be a nice 2-y-o towards the end
of the season, probably over a mile".*

682. KISS FROM A ROSE ★★★

ch.f. Compton Place – Dayrose (Daylami).
March 30. Fourth foal. 9,500Y. Tattersalls
October Book 2. Rae Guest. The dam, a quite
useful 10f and 11f winner, is a half-sister to 7
winners including the listed winner Rambling
Rose (herself dam of the triple Group 1 winner
and sire Notnowcato). The second dam, Blush
Rambler (by Blushing Groom), a 12f winner
in Ireland, is a half-sister to 5 winners. (Sakal,
Davies & Jennings). *"We bought her quite
reasonably I thought and she's by Compton
Place who I like a lot. Daylami is doing very
well as a broodmare sire and this filly has
done very well since we bought her. She's filled
out and I think she could be a 2-y-o from the
mid-summer onwards. We'll start her off at six
furlongs and take it from there".*

683. MISS BUCKSHOT (IRE) ★★★

ch.f. Tamayuz – Miss Bellbird (Danehill). March
6. Fifth foal. €36,000Y. Goffs Orby. Rae Guest.
Half-sister to the fair 10f winner Chatterer (by
Alhaarth). The dam is an unraced half-sister
to 8 winners including the Group 2 12f King
Edward VII Stakes winner Amfortas and the
Group 3 10.5f Prix de Royaumont winner
Legend Maker (herself dam of the 1,000
Guineas winner Virginia Water) and the dam
of the Group 2 Challenge Stakes winner Miss
Lucifer. The second dam, High Spirited (by
Shirley Heights), a quite useful winner of two
of her seven races over 14f and 2m at 3 yrs,
is a sister to the Premio Roma, Ribblesdale
Stakes and Park Hill Stakes winner High Hawk
(herself dam of the Breeders Cup Turf winner
In the Wings) and a half-sister to 8 winners
including the dams of the Derby winner High
Rise and the Rothmans International winner
Infamy. (Mr Tony Hirschfeld). *"She's a nice filly
and well-related. She's sharp and she looks
like being early enough to run in May or June.
Tamayuz has showed he can get fast horses
and she's out of a Danehill mare, so despite*

the middle-distance winners in her pedigree you'd hope there'd be some speed in there. A forward-going 2-y-o filly".

684. STRIKE A LIGHT ★★★
gr.f. Dutch Art – Bridal Path (Groom Dancer).
March 29. Fourth foal. 35,000Y. Tattersalls October Book 2. Rae Guest. Half-sister to the fair dual 7f winner Icy Blue (by Iceman). The dam, a fair 2-y-o dual 5f winner, is a sister to one winner and a half-sister to 8 winners including the smart Group 3 7f Horris Hill Stakes winner Cupid's Glory and the Group 3 Princess Elizabeth Stakes winner Clinical. The second dam, Doctor's Glory (by Elmaamul), a fairly useful 5.2f (at 2 yrs) and 6f winner, is a half-sister to 6 winners. *"A lovely filly, she's big but she goes well. She's a typical Dutch Art so you couldn't knock her and she's really nice. I like her a lot, she shows plenty now but because she's big she'll be one for the six/seven furlong races in mid-summer".*

685. STROLL ON (IRE) ★★★★
ch.f. Exceed And Excel – Violet (Mukaddamah).
February 14. Tenth foal. 45,000Y. Tattersalls October Book 2. Rae Guest. Half-sister to the dual 6f and subsequent US Grade 2 San Clemente Handicap winner and Grade 1 second Starlarks (by Mujahid), to the quite useful 1m to 9.3f winner of 5 races Boo (by Namaqualand), the modest 7f and 1m winner Kannon (by Kyllachy) and the moderate 9f winner Indigo Dancer (by Groom Dancer). The dam, a fair 6f and 8.5f winner, is a full or half-sister to 8 winners including the smart 10.4f John Smiths Handicap and triple Hong Kong listed stakes winner and Group 2 12f Gordon Stakes third Sobriety. The second dam, Scanno's Choice (by Pennine Walk), a modest middle-distance placed maiden in Ireland, is a half-sister to 6 winners including the US Grade 2 winner Dilmoun. (Mr Trevor Benton). *"Nice and sharp, she'll be an early 2-y-o. Exceed And Excel's always seem to have plenty of go about them and this filly should be racing in May. A lovely shape and size, she's a typical sprinter and one of my most forward-going 2-y-o's".*

686. UNNAMED ★★
b.f. Aqlaam – Fen Guest (Woodborough). April 11. Third foal. 44,000Y. Tattersalls October

Book 1. Not sold. Half-sister to the fair 2-y-o 7f winner Vinnie Jones (by Piccolo). The dam, a moderate 6f winner, is a half-sister to 5 winners including the listed winner of 4 races Ronaldsay and the dam of the US dual Grade 3 winner Pickle. The second dam, Crackling (by Electric), a modest 9f and 12f winner, is a half-sister to 4 winners including the Group 1 7f Moyglare Stud Stakes winner Bianca Nera and the dam of the Group 1 Fillies' Mile winner Simply Perfect. (Mr C J Murfitt). *"A lovely filly, she's grown a lot since she came in so she's going to take time. We trained the dam, it's a nice family and I should think this filly will get a mile in time. One of those that will just get the one run at the back-end because she'll be better next year".*

687. UNNAMED ★★
ch.g. Halling – Magdalene (Act One). April 3. Second foal. The dam, a modest 10f winner, is a half-sister to 7 winners including the French listed 7f winner and Group 2 third Thames and the listed 1m winner Three Wrens. The second dam, Three Terns (by Arctic Tern), won over 9f in France and is a half-sister to 3 winners including the Group 3 1m Prix des Reservoirs winner Three Angels. (Mrs Paula Smith). *"A home-bred, he's backward and he's been gelded. He'll want seven furlongs or a mile but he's doing very well and he'll be alright to run this year. He has a good action and a good attitude".*

688. UNNAMED ★★
b.f. Dubawi – Still Small Voice (Polish Precedent). February 22. Second foal. The dam is an unraced sister to 3 winners including Pure Grain (Group 1 12f Irish Oaks and Group 1 12f Yorkshire Oaks) and the dam of the Japanese Group 1 winner Fine Grain and a half-sister to 6 winners. The second dam, Mill Line (by Mill Reef), a fair 14.6f winner at 3 yrs, is a half-sister to 6 winners. (Laundry Cottage Stud). *"After we broke her in we sent her home because she's still weak. She'll be back in sometime in April but she'll take time".*

689. UNNAMED ★★★
b.f. High Chaparral – Twyla (AUS) (Danehill). April 15. Ninth foal. 150,000Y. Tattersalls October Book 1. Paul Moroney. Half-sister to

5 winners in Australia including the Group 3 winner Murjana (by Giant's Causeway). The dam, a minor winner at 3 yrs in Australia, is a half-sister to 6 winners including the Australian Group 1 winners Hurricane Sky and Umatilla and the dams of four Group 1 winners in Australia. The second dam, Dancing Show (by Nijinsky), was a minor winner at 4 yrs in the USA. (Mr John Cammileri). *"She's only just come in but she's a really nice stamp of filly. It's a great Australian pedigree and we wouldn't be looking to run her until the autumn. A really nice type and although she's unfurnished at the moment she's one you'd love to have".*

WILLIAM HAGGAS

690. ALSHADHIA (IRE) ★★

b.f. *Marju – Wijdan (Mr Prospector).* March 10. Sister to the Group 2 1m Premio Ribot winner Oriental Fashion and to the quite useful dual 10f winner Tanfidh and half-sister to the very useful listed 7f and subsequent US Grade 2 10f winner Makderah (by Danehill), the useful 1m and 10f winner Ezdiyaad (by Galileo), the useful 10f winner and listed-placed Fatanah (by Green Desert) and the fair 10f winner Mohafazaat (by Sadler's Wells). The dam, a useful 1m and 10.4f winner, is a sister to the 7f (at 2 yrs) and 1m listed winner Sarayir and a half-sister to the brilliant 2,000 Guineas, Derby, Eclipse and King George winner Nashwan and to the high-class middle distance colt Unfuwain. The second dam, Height of Fashion (by Bustino), a high-class winner of 5 races from 7f to 12f including the Group 2 Princess of Wales's Stakes, is a half-sister to the good middle-distance colt Milford. (Hamdan Al Maktoum). *"I had her full-sister, Shuhra, who wasn't genuine. This filly is much more genuine but not as good-looking! She looks workmanlike, whereas Shuhra was beautiful but didn't try. It's one of Sheikh Hamdan's favourite families, stemming as it does from Height Of Fashion. I wouldn't know too much about this filly yet, but I've got a few sharper ones".*

691. BELAHODOOD ★★★★

b.c. *New Approach – Broken Peace (Devil's Bag).* May 30. Eleventh foal. 60,000Y. Tattersalls October Book 1. Rabbah

Bloodstock. Half-brother to the French listed 1m winner Riverse Angle (by Spinning World), to the fair 1m winner Blitzed (by Fantastic Light), the modest dual 12f winner Stormy Day (by Rainbow Quest), the minor US stakes-placed winner of 8 races Tightlies, the minor US dual 3-y-o winner Global Threat (by Conquistador Cielo) and a winner in Hong Kong by Kyllachy. The dam won the listed 1m Prix de Bagatelle, was third in the Group 3 Prix Vanteaux and is a half-sister to 2 winners. The second dam, Bedside (by Le Fabuleux), won 7 minor races in the USA and is a half-sister to the stakes winner and Grade 2 placed Open Gate. (Sultan Ali). *"A nice horse, he wasn't an expensive yearling, relatively, but he's never put a foot wrong whilst we've had him. He's just a nice horse to have around. I can hardly believe he was a late May foal because he's a really nice, uncomplicated horse. He's having a break at the moment and he'll make a 2-y-o over seven furlongs in the second half of the season".*

692. BEST TAMAYUZ ★★★

ch.c. *Tamayuz – Pink Ivory (Sakhee).* March 5. The dam, a 3-y-o 1m winner on her only start, is a half-sister to 6 winners including the smart French 2-y-o Group 3 1m Prix d'Aumale winner and smart broodmare Anna Palariva and the dam of the US Grade 1 winner Ave. The second dam, Anna Of Saxony (by Ela-Mana-Mou), a very useful winner of the Group 3 14.6f Park Hill Stakes, is a half-sister to 10 winners including the Group 2 winners Annaba and Pozarica and to the dams of the Group 1 winners Anna Monda and Helmet. (J Abdullah). *"He's a nice, uncomplicated horse by a sire I quite like. He hasn't done a lot yet but he's a nice type and he's one we should see out around August time – maybe earlier".*

693. BILIMBI (IRE) ★★

b.c. *Duke Of Marmalade – Starship (Galileo).* March 19. Fourth foal. Closely related to the fairly useful 2-y-o 7f and 1m winner Pickled Pelican (by Dylan Thomas), to the smart 7f, 1m (both at 2 yrs) and Group 3 10f Gallinule Stakes winner Packing Tycoon and the fairly useful Irish 2-y-o 7f and 1m winner Alexander Pope (both by Danehill Dancer). The dam, a fair 7f (at 2 yrs) to 8.3f winner, is a half-sister to numerous winners including the very smart Group 2 5f Flying Childers Stakes and Weatherbys Super Sprint winner Superstar Leo. The second dam, Council Rock (by General Assembly), a fair 9f and 10f placed 3-y-o, is a half-sister to 6 winners including the Group 3 Prestige Stakes winner Glatisant and the listed Virginia Stakes winner Gai Bulga. (Scott/Magnier/Piggott). *"He's a backward horse and I have his full-brother Martian who was awful last year but has improved a lot. Bilimbi is much more forward than Martian was at this stage, so I'd be hopeful of him running later this season".*

694. BUREDYMA ★★★ ♠

ch.f. *Dutch Art – Petong's Pet (Petong).* March 11. Fifth foal. £110,000Y. Doncaster Premier. Tony Nerses. Sister to the fairly useful 5f and 6f winner of 10 races at 3 and 4 yrs Aubrietia and half-sister to the fair 2-y-o 6f winner Dormer Fleet (by Kyllachy). The dam is an unraced sister to the Group 2 Champagne Stakes and Group 3 Coventry Stakes winner Petardia and a half-sister to 3 winners. The second dam, What A Pet (by Mummy's Pet), a minor winner at 3 yrs in France, is a sister to the US Grade 3 winner and Group 1 placed Teacher's Pet. (Saleh Al Homaizi & Imad Al Sagar). *"She's a nice filly and her sister Aubrietia keeps on winning. She had a bit of a temperament at first, but she's settled down nicely and she's definitely a 2-y-o".*

695. DANEHILL REVIVAL ★★★

b.f. *Pivotal – Danehill Destiny (Danehill Dancer).* March 7. First foal. The dam, a useful dual 5f (at 2 yrs) and listed 6f winner, was third in two Group 3 events over 6f and 7f and is a half-sister to one winner. The second dam, Comeraincomeshine (by Night Shift), a modest 5.5f winner, is a half-sister to 5 winners including the high-class Group 1 1m Queen Elizabeth II Stakes winner Where Or When and the smart 10f and 12f winner and Group 1 St Leger fourth All The Way. (Cheveley Park Stud). *"She's a very attractive filly, not as precocious as her mother who won at the Craven meeting, but she'll be a mid-season 2-y-o. A medium-sized filly that should make a 2-y-o alright".*

696. DREAM SPIRIT (IRE) ★★

b.c. *Invincible Spirit – Dream Valley (Sadler's Wells).* February 24. Fourth foal. 38,000Y. Tattersalls October Book 2. W Haggas. Half-brother to the fair Irish 2-y-o 7f winner Rantavan Wood (by One Cool Cat). The dam is an unplaced half-sister to 4 winners including the Group 1 1m Coronation Stakes and Group 2 7f Rockfel Stakes winner Maid's Causeway. The second dam, Vallee des Reves (by Kingmambo), is an unraced half-sister to the Group 2 Prix du Muguet winner Vetheuil, the Group 3 Prix de l'Opera winner Verveine (herself dam of the Grade 1 winners Vallee Enchantee and Volga) and the dam of the Group 1 Grand Prix de Paris winner Vespone. (Roberts/Green/Savidge/Whittal-Williams). *"Bought by four farmers from Herefordshire. They're patient and like backward types, whereas this looks more forward than most of the ones they've had. A nice horse, he's big and needs time because he's 16 hands already, but he's a nice mover and shifts along well. He's out of a Sadler's Wells mare, so he'll be a ten furlong horse next year".*

697. EHTIFAAL (IRE) ★★★

b.c. *Teofilo – Kashoof (Green Desert).* January 29. The dam, a quite useful 2-y-o 5f winner, is a half-sister to one winner. The second dam, Khulood (by Storm Cat), a useful listed 7f (at 2 yrs) and Group 3 7f Nell Gwyn Stakes winner, is a half-sister to numerous winners including the Irish 1,000 Guineas winner Mehthaaf and the July Cup winner Elnadim. (Hamdan Al Maktoum). *"I've never seen him, he's in Dubai and they arrive here tomorrow, but they like him over there. In fact I have three in Dubai and they like them all".*

698. ERTIJAAL (IRE) ★★★★

b.c. *Oasis Dream – Shabiba (Seeking The Gold).* March 11. Third foal. Half-brother to the useful 2012 2-y-o 6f winner and listed-placed Odooj (by Pivotal). The dam, a useful 6f (at 2 yrs) and listed 1m winner, was third in the Group 3 7f Oak Tree Stakes and is a half-sister to the useful 2-y-o 6f winner and Group 3 placed Darajaat. The second dam, Misterah (by Alhaarth), a very useful listed 6f (at 2 yrs) and Group 3 7f Nell Gwyn Stakes winner, is sister to one winner and a half-sister to the useful 2-y-o 6f winner Muqtarb. (Hamdan Al Maktoum). *"He's a nice horse and a half-brother to one we had last year called Odooj. This one is bigger than Odooj already, he goes well and he could easily make a 2-y-o in May. He's a little bit slack of his patterns but he's quite a strong horse and he wants to please. A five/six furlong 2-y-o".*

699. ETAAB (USA) ★★★ ♠

b.f. Street Cry – Ethaara (Green Desert). January 27. Second foal. Half-sister to the fair 2012 7f placed 2-y-o Estiqaama (by Nayef). The dam, a useful listed 6f winner, is closely related to the very useful 2-y-o listed 7f Star Stakes winner and Group 3 7f Prestige Stakes second Mudaaraah and a half-sister to the useful 2-y-o listed 7f winner Sudoor. The second dam, Wissal (by Woodman), is an unraced sister to the high-class 2-y-o Group 2 7f Laurent Perrier Champagne Stakes Bahhare and a half-sister to the Group 1 1m St James's Palace Stakes and Group 1 1m Queen Elizabeth II Stakes winner Bahri. (Hamdan Al Maktoum). *"Another one that's arriving here from Dubai tomorrow and although I haven't seen her myself they like her a lot and say she's very nice. I have the 3-y-o Estiqaama who is quite nice and should win, but she isn't a good horse like this one is supposed to be".*

700. EXAMINER (IRE) ★★

ch.c. Excellent Art – Therry Girl (Lahib). April 30. Fifth foal. 25,000Y. Tattersalls October Book 2. W Haggas. Half-brother to two minor winners in Italy by Desert Prince and Celtic Swing. The dam won 6 races in Italy including over 7.5f at 2 yrs and is a half-sister to 2 minor winners there. The second dam, Selenia (by Danehill), won 2 minor races at 2 and 3 yrs in Italy and is a half-sister to 8 winners. (Mr & Mrs Ian Beard). *"He's grown a bit, we liked him when we were breaking him and getting him going but now he's looking like one for the second half of the season. A colt with a nice attitude".*

701. GHANY (IRE) ★★★

b.f. Lawman – Broken Spectre (Rainbow Quest). April 28. Ninth foal. 90,000Y. Tattersalls October Book 2. Shadwell Estate Co. Sister to the 2012 2-y-o Group 1 1m Gran Criterium

winner Law Enforcement and half-sister to a minor winner in Germany by Dansili. The dam, unplaced in two starts, is a sister to the top-class 2-y-o Group 1 1m Racing Post Trophy winner and St Leger second Armiger, the very useful 10.2f winner Migration and the useful 2-y-o 1m and 8.5f winner and Group 1 Racing Post Trophy fourth Besiege. The second dam, Armeria (by Northern Dancer), a fair 3-y-o 10f winner, is a half-sister to the Park Hill Stakes winner I Want To Be. (Hamdan Al Maktoum). *"She's grown on me a lot, she was late in but she's a nice, genuine filly and a good mover with big ears. I like her and she's one for seven furlongs or a mile. A nice filly".*

702. GOLD APPROACH ★★★★

ch.f. New Approach – Samira Gold (Gold Away). March 18. Second foal. Half-sister to Paris Gold (by Cape Cross), unplaced in one start at 2 yrs in 2012. The dam, a very useful dual listed 10f winner, was third in the Group 3 Princess Royal Stakes. The second dam, Capework (by El Gran Senor), is an unplaced full or half-sister to numerous winners. (J Abdullah). *"I like her and I think the mare is quite good because I've had both foals and the 3-y-o Paris Rose is useful. I think this filly is lovely".*

703. GRASS GREEN ★★★★

b.f. Dubawi – Grasshoppergreen (Barathea). March 2. Second foal. 85,000Y. Tattersalls October Book 1. William Haggas. The dam is an unraced half-sister to 4 winners including the Group 1 6f Cheveley Park Stakes and Group 1 1m Coronation Stakes winner Indian Ink. The second dam, Maid Of Killeen (by Darshaan), a fairly useful 9f winner, was listed-placed and is a half-sister to 6 winners. (R C Tooth). *"A small, sharp-actioned filly and she should be a 2-y-o in May or June. I just have a reservation about Dubawi's being that precocious, but if you looked at her in the box she looks all 2-y-o. Small, neat and quite set".*

704. HAIKBIDIAC (IRE) ★★★

b.c. Kodiac – Silk Fan (Unfuwain). March 16. Fourth foal. £32,000Y. Doncaster Premier. Rabbah Bloodstock. Half-brother to the quite useful 5f and 6f winner of 4 races (including at 2 yrs) Fanrouge (by Red Clubs), to the quite useful 12f and hurdles winner Eagle Rock (by High Chaparral) and the fair 12f winner Widezain (by Chineur). The dam, a fairly useful triple 7f winner (including at 2 yrs), is a half-sister to 3 winners. The second dam, Alikhlas (by Lahib), a fair 3-y-o 1m winner, is a half-sister to 4 winners including the listed winner and Group 2 Lancashire Oaks second Sahool and the dam of the multiple Group winner Maraahel. (Sheikh Juma Al Dalmook Maktoum). *"He's a 2-y-o type alright, despite being out of an Unfuwain mare. He's quite mature and ready to go and will be one of those in the batch I'm kicking on with, so hopefully he'll be ready to run in May over five furlongs".*

705. KAHEYLL ★★★

br.c. Pastoral Pursuits – Dansa Queen (Dansili). March 18. Third foal. 85,000Y. Tattersalls October Book 2. W Haggas. Half-brother to the modest 2012 dual 5f placed 2-y-o Rangooned (by Bahamian Bounty). The dam, a quite useful 7f and 1m winner of 3 races, is a half-sister to 4 winners including Halicardia (listed Lupe Stakes) and the dam of the Group 2 Duke Of York Stakes winner Tiddliwinks. The second dam, Pericardia (by Petong), is an unplaced half-sister to 4 winners including Prince Ferdinand, winner of the Group 3 7f Jersey Stakes. (Sheikh Ahmed Al Maktoum). *"He's a nice horse, he's had a slight setback so he's on the easy list for now but I liked him and he'll make a 2-y-o alright. A strong little horse that cost a fair bit, he's got a good way about him and he'll be out in June".*

706. KHAAWY (USA) ★★★

b.f. Arch – Jaleela (Kingmambo). February 20. Third foal. Half-sister to the fairly useful 1m winner Kahruman (by Mr Greeley). The dam, a quite useful 1m winner, is closely related to the very useful 7f (at 2 yrs) and subsequent UAE Group 2 1m winner Derbaas. The second dam, Sultana (by Storm Cat), is an unraced sister to the high-class Group 1 7f Prix de la Salamandre and Group 1 1m Sussex Stakes winner Aljabr. (Hamdan Al Maktoum). *"She arrives tomorrow from Dubai. I've got both the dam's previous foals, Kahruman is rated 100 and now racing in Dubai and the unraced 3-y-o isn't bad either. So hopefully this is a good*

mare for Sheikh Hamdan. I don't know much about this 2-y-o yet, but I like the pedigree".*

707. LADY IN BLUE (IRE) ★★

ch.f. Iffraaj – Compton Girl (Compton Place). February 4. Sixth foal. 20,000Y. Tattersalls October Book 2. W Haggas. Half-sister to the fair 5f (at 2 yrs) to 7f winner of 6 races Night Trade (by Trade Fair). The dam is an unraced half-sister to 5 winners including Repertory (13 wins including the Group 3 Prix Petit-Couvert three times). The second dam, Susie's Baby (by Balidar), is an unplaced half-sister to 6 winners including The Go-Between (Group 3 Cornwallis Stakes). (The Duchess Syndicate). *"She was bought as a replacement for Momalorka who did so well for us last year. This is a much nicer looking filly, but she'll probably be half as good! She's alright, I don't know any more than that, but she's well-made and will be a mid-season 2-y-o".*

708. LILLY JUNIOR ★★

br.f. Cape Cross – Sweet Lilly (Tobougg). February 15. First foal. The dam, a smart listed 1m and listed 10f winner of 6 races and second in the Group 3 Musidora Stakes, is a half-sister to the useful 9f and 10f winner of 7 races Ofaraby. The second dam, Maristax (by Reprimand), a fair 2-y-o 7f winner, is closely related to the useful 2-y-o listed 5f winner Four-Legged-Friend and a half-sister to 6 winners including the dual US Grade 3 winner Superstrike and the dam of the Group 1 winning sprinters Goodricke and Pastoral Pursuits. (J Abdullah). *"This is a small filly but she has a lovely way about her. She's not going to be that early and I see her being a back-end 2-y-o that'll come into her own as a 3-y-o".*

709. LYRA ★★★

b.f. Myboycharlie – Park Melody (Refuse To Bend). February 23. First foal. £70,000Y. Tattersalls October Book 1. John Warren. The dam, placed fourth over 10f and 12f, is a half-sister to 7 winners including the 6f (at 2 yrs) and Group 3 7f Ballycorus Stakes winner Rum Charger (herself dam of the US multiple Grade 1 winner Winchester) and the dam of the Sweet Solera Stakes winner English Ballet. The second dam, Park Charger (by Tirol), a useful winner over 1m and 10f at 3 yrs in Ireland, was listed-placed four times and is a half-sister to 9 winners. (Highclere Thoroughbred Racing – Conquest). *"A strong, well-made filly, he has a sharp action, a very attractive head and she'll be racing in May".*

710. MANGE ALL ★★★
b.g. Zamindar – Blancmange (Montjeu). April 5. First foal. The dam is an unraced half-sister to 2 winners. The second dam, Blue Dream (by Cadeaux Genereux), a useful 6f winner, was listed-placed and is a half-sister to 5 winners including the 1m (at 2 yrs) and 9.2f winner and listed-placed Equity Princess. (J B Haggas). *"He's a very solid, well-made horse. The dam was useful but had a fracture and we retired her. This is a bloody nice, solid horse that's a bit nervous and was gelded as a foal. He'll be a July 2-y-o with a bit of scope to improve as the season goes on".*

711. MEETING WATERS ★★★★
ch.f. Aqlaam – Paradise Isle (Bahamian Bounty). March 20. Third foal. 45,000Y. Tattersalls October Book 2. Jill Lamb. Half-sister to the fair 2012 2-y-o 5f winner Exotic Isle (by Exceed And Excel) and to the modest 2-y-o 5f winner Princess Banu (by Oasis Dream). The dam, a useful 5f (at 2 yrs) and 6f winner of 8 races including two listed events, was third in the Group 3 6f Summer Stakes and is a full or half-sister to 9 winners including the useful broodmare Clincher Club. The second dam, Merry Rous (by Rousillon), a moderate 2-y-o 6f winner, is a half-sister to 5 winners including the dual Group 3 winning sprinter Tina's Pet. (Mr L Sheridan). *"She's got a lot of speed and she's a nice filly. The dam was a dual listed winner over six and this is a nice mover, so she's definitely a 2-y-o".*

712. MITRAAD (IRE) ★★★
ch.c. Aqlaam – Badweia (Kingmambo). February 26. Second foal. The dam, a fair 6f and 7f winner, is a half-sister to 3 useful winners including the 7f to 9f winner of 7 races and listed-placed Haatheq. The second dam, Alshadiyah (by Danzig), a useful 2-y-o 6f winner, is a half-sister to 7 winners including the smart 7f (at 2 yrs) and 10f listed winner Imtiyaz and the very useful Bint Shadayid, winner of the Group 3 7f Prestige Stakes and

placed in the 1,000 Guineas and the Fillies Mile. (Hamdan Al Maktoum). *"More of a seven furlong type 2-y-o and he doesn't look anything like his father but he has a good way about him, he moves nicely and has a good outlook to life. Keen to please, he's a nice horse and one for the autumn".*

713. MOCACHA (IRE) ★★★★ ♠
b.c. Camacho – Mama Angela (Titius Livius). April 21. First foal. £24,000Y. Doncaster Premier. McKeever Bloodstock. The dam, an Irish 2-y-o 6.5f winner, is a half-sister to 5 winners including the useful Irish 2-y-o 6f winner and Group 3 Brownstown Stakes third Dixie Evans. The second dam, Kingpin Delight (by Emarati), is an unraced half-sister to 8 minor winners. (Options O Syndicate). *"A sharp colt, he's a well-made sort and although he's definitely got some speed he's got a bit of scope as well. He'll be a 2-y-o alright".*

714. MUTAKAYYEF (USA) ★★★★
ch.c. Sea The Stars – Infallible (Pivotal). May 5. Second foal. 260,000Y. Tattersalls October Book 1. Shadwell Estate Co. The dam, a very smart 7f (at 2 yrs) and Group 3 7f Nell Gwyn Stakes winner, was second in the Group 1 Coronation Stakes and the Group 1 Falmouth Stakes and is a full or half-sister to 3 winners. The second dam, Irresistible (by Cadeaux Genereux), was a fairly useful 5f (at 2 yrs) and listed 6f winner and is a half-sister to 2 winners. (Hamdan Al Maktoum). *"A well-bred, expensive, nice-moving colt and if he's got a change of speed he'll be a good horse. He's such a nice mover though and those types don't always quicken so he could just be a galloper, we'll have to wait and see. He was a May foal so he's backward at the moment but he does everything easily".*

715. NOTEBOOK ★★★
b.c. Invincible Spirit – Love Everlasting (Pursuit Of Love). March 23. Seventh foal. 110,000Y. Tattersalls October Book 1. John Warren. Half-brother to the quite useful 2012 2-y-o dual 7f winner Penny Rose (by Danehill Dancer), to the fairly useful 12f winner and listed Cheshire Oaks second Acquainted (by Shamardal) and the fair 2m winner Yours Ever (by Dansili). The dam, a very useful 2-y-o 7.5f and 3-y-o

listed 12f winner, is a half-sister to 6 winners including the smart Group 3 10f Scottish Classic winner Baron Ferdinand. The second dam, In Perpetuity (by Great Nephew), a fairly useful 10f winner, is a half-sister to 6 winners including the Derby winner Shirley Heights and to the placed Bempton (dam of the Group 2 winner Gull Nook and the Group 3 winners Mr Pintips and Banket). (Highclere Thoroughbred Racing – Brunel). *"He got a sore shin early on so we backed off him and he's having a break at the moment, but he's a very pretty, bonny horse. He moves well but I don't know much about him yet. I suspect he'll be a seven furlong type and one for later in the season".*

716. OXSANA ★★★
b.f. Dubawi – Turning Leaf (Last Tycoon). March 16. Ninth foal. 65,000Y. Tattersalls October Book 1. Rabbah Bloodstock. Half-sister to the quite useful 2012 2-y-o 6f winner Exceptionelle (by Exceed And Excel), to the German 3-y-o Group 3 1m and listed 11f winner Turning Light (by Fantastic Light and herself dam of the US stakes winner Surrey Star) and two minor winners in Italy by King's Best and Motivator. The dam, a German 2-y-o winner and third in the Group 2 German 1,000 Guineas, is a half-sister to 6 winners. The second dam, Tamacana (by Windwurf), a German listed winner of 3 races at 2 and 3 yrs, is a half-sister to 4 winners. (Sultan Ali). *"She's alright, she's small and has been having a break but there's nothing wrong with her except she'll need time. Most of the Dubawi's seem to be on the small side and this one will make a 2-y-o but not until later in the season".*

717. PENNY DROPS ★★★
b.f. Invincible Spirit – Penny Cross (Efisio). April 26. Sixth foal. 27,000Y. Tattersalls October Book 2. Not sold. Half-sister to Rosia Bay (by Rock Of Gibraltar), unplaced in two starts at 2 yrs in 2012 and to the very useful 2-y-o 7f winner and Group 3 1m Autumn Stakes second Prompter (by Motivator) and to the fair 10f to 14f winner of 4 races Quinsman (by Singspiel). The dam, a useful 7f to 8.5f winner of 3 races, was listed placed twice and is a half-sister to 7 winners including the Group 2 Celebration Mile winner Priors Lodge. The second dam, Addaya (by Persian Bold), ran

once unplaced and is a half-sister to 8 winners abroad. (Mr & Mrs G Middlebrook). *"She came in quite late so I don't really know much about her and she's still a bit green. But she's a nice type, the dam was useful and Invincible Spirit is a good stallion so she has a chance. A mid-season 2-y-o".*

718. PERFECT LIGHT (IRE) ★★★
ch.f. Galileo – Beauty Bright (Danehill). April 25. Fourth foal. 100,000Y. Tattersalls December. Jill Lamb. Sister to the quite useful 2012 2-y-o 1m winner Greek Goddess and to the quite useful 12f winner Highflying. The dam, an Irish 5f (at 2 yrs) and Group 3 6f winner, is a sister to one winner and a half-sister to 4 winners including the Group 3 6f second Marquesa. The second dam, Dietrich (by Storm Cat), won the Group 3 5f King George Stakes and Group 3 5f Ballyogan Stakes and is a half-sister to 2 winners. (Mrs L Sheridan). *"It's a lovely pedigree, she's a nice size and a nice mover and looks to have a good attitude. She's not a backward Galileo and she's out of a speedy mare, so she's got a chance".*

719. PRINCESS ROSE ★★★
b.f. Royal Applause – Mystical Spirit (Xaar). January 24. First foal. £32,000Y. Doncaster Premier. Amanda Skiffington. The dam, placed third over 1m at 2 yrs, is a half-sister to 4 winners including the very useful 2-y-o 5f winner and Group 2 6f Mill Reef Stakes second Mystical Land. The second dam, Samsung Spirit (by Statoblest), a fair dual 6f winner (including at 2 yrs), is a half-sister to 7 winners and to the placed dam of the Group 2 6f Mill Reef Stakes winner Indian Rocket. (Ian & Christine Beard). *"She has a plain head and a nasty temper but she's as tough as old boots and she's a 2-y-o that'll run in May".*

720. REDKIRK ★★
ch.c. Notnowcato – Flag (Selkirk). April 6. Eighth foal. 22,000Y. Tattersalls October Book 2. Jill Lamb. Half-brother to the quite useful 5f winner of 5 races (including at 2 yrs) Azygous (by Foxhound), to the quite useful 1m winner State Gathering (by Royal Applause), the modest 1m winner Ageebah (by Acclamation) and the modest triple 5f

winners Liberty Ship (by Statue Of Liberty) and Twosheetstothewind (by Bahamian Bounty). The dam is an unraced half-sister to 3 winners including the Italian listed winner Armenian Dancer. The second dam, Flower Arrangement (by Lomond), is an unraced half-sister to 5 winners including the Kentucky Derby second Bold Arrangement. (Scotney/Symonds/Fisher Partnership). *"We had a bit of luck with the sire last year and I think he's very underrated. The owners tend to have sharp ones every time and we've sold them all on, so we decided to get one that'll last! A nice, kind, backward horse".*

721. RESOLUTE ★★

b.g. Pivotal – Coy (Danehill). February 19. Sixth foal. 50,000Y. Tattersalls October Book 2. Amanda Skiffington. Brother to the modest 4-y-o UAE 6f winner Redden. The dam won over 6f (at 2 yrs) and the listed 1m Valiant Stakes and is a sister to one winner and a half-sister to 5 winners including the very useful dual listed winner Il Warrd. The second dam, Demure (by Machiavellian), is an unraced half-sister to 9 winners including the very smart colt Diffident, winner of the Group 3 6f Diadem Stakes and the Group 3 6f Prix de Ris-Orangis. (Cheveley Park Stud). *"I trained the full-brother Redden who was a bit disappointing. We gelded this horse because he got a bit sweaty as a yearling, but he's a strong, well-made horse. He's a Pivotal out of a Danehill mare so there's plenty of speed in the pedigree, but he doesn't look like an early 2-y-o".*

722. ROYAL MEZYAN (IRE) ★★★★

b.c. Royal Applause – Rice Mother (Indian Ridge). March 26. Fourth foal. €130,000Y. Goffs Orby. W Haggas. Half-brother to a minor 3-y-o winner in Italy by Refuse To Bend. The dam, a modest 10f winner, is a half-sister to 7 winners including the Group 3 6f Prix de Meautry winner Do The Honours and the 2-y-o listed 7f Chesham Stakes winner Seba. The second dam, Persian Secret (by Persian Heights), a fairly useful 2-y-o 6f winner here, subsequently won a listed race in France and is a half-sister to 8 winners including the dual Group 2 winning sprinter Cassandra Go (dam of the triple Group 1 winner Halfway To Heaven) and the Group 3 6f Coventry Stakes

winner and sire Verglas. (Sheikh Juma Al Dalmook Maktoum). *"I like him a lot. I loved him at the sales, Richard Hannon took us on and we outbid him for a lot of money. A very nice, uncomplicated 2-y-o, we've had a bit of luck with Royal Applause and hopefully this colt is a pretty nice 2-y-o. He reminded me a lot of Majestic Missile when he was at the sales and if nothing goes wrong I'll be aiming to get him out in May".*

723. SAAYERR ★★★★★

b.c. Acclamation – Adorn (Kyllachy). February 27. First foal. 90,000Y. Tattersalls October Book 2. Shadwell Estate Co. The dam, a useful 2-y-o 6f winner, was fourth in the Group 1 6f Cheveley Park Stakes and is closely related to the US 5f (minor stakes) to 8.5f winner Red Diadem and a half-sister to 3 winners. The dam, a moderate 7.6f fourth-placed maiden, is closely related to the Japanese sprint stakes winner Meiner Love and a half-sister to 4 winners. (Sheikh Ahmed Al Maktoum). *"A five star 2-y-o. He'll be early, in fact he wants to go now, but he'll want quick ground. A really nice horse and one we'll be aiming at Royal Ascot".*

724. SCRUTINY ★★★

b.c. Aqlaam – Aunty Mary (Common Grounds). March 23. Seventh foal. 85,000Y. Tattersalls October Book 1. John Warren. Closely related to the quite useful 7f winner Ertikaan (by Oasis Dream) and half-brother to the fairly useful 2012 2-y-o 6f winner and Group 3 Firth Of Clyde Stakes second Mary's Daughter, the quite useful 5f (at 2 yrs), 7f and hurdles winner King's Bastion (both by Royal Applause) and the quite useful 7f and 1m winner Pride Of Kings (by King's Best). The dam, a quite useful 2-y-o 5f winner, is a half-sister to 4 winners including the 1,000 Guineas, Irish 1,000 Guineas, Coronation Stakes, Matron Stakes and Sun Chariot Stakes winner Attraction. The second dam, Flirtation (by Pursuit Of Love), ran unplaced once and is a half-sister to 4 winners including the French listed 12f winner and Group 2 placed Carmita. (Highclere Thoroughbred Racing – Lake Coniston). *"Quite a willing, kind horse that should be a 2-y-o because there's quite a bit of strength about him. I would think he'd be a July type, he has a nice outlook on life and I quite like him".*

725. SIMSAAM (IRE) ★★

ch.g. Intikhab – Klang (Night Shift). March 11. Fifth foal. 52,000Y. Tattersalls October Book 2. William Haggas. Half-brother to the quite useful Irish 7f winner Yali (by Orpen). The dam is an unplaced half-sister to 8 winners including the Group 2 Derrinstown Stud Derby Trial Stakes winner Fracas. The second dam, Klarifi (by Habitat), won the listed 7f Ballycorus Stakes and is a full or half-sister to 7 winners including the dam of the Irish Oaks winner Wemyss Bight. (Sheikh Ahmed Al Maktoum). *"He's a gelding and he needed to be because he was tricky and didn't focus on the job in hand. He's a good sort physically, although a bit heavy, but not a bad-looking type at all".*

726. SPIRITUAL FLAME ★★★

b.f. Invincible Spirit – Secret Flame (Machiavellian). April 25. Fifth foal. Half-sister to the quite useful 1m winner Secret Quest (by Pivotal), to the fair 7f (at 2 yrs) to 9f winner Double Act (by Where Or When) and the fair 1m and 9f winner Cabal (by Kyllachy). The dam, a fair 9f winner, is a half-sister to 7 winners including the useful 2-y-o 6f winner and Group 3 third Obsessive (herself dam of the St James's Palace Stakes winner Excellent Art). The second dam, Secret Obsession (by Secretariat), a fairly useful 10f winner, is a half-sister to 7 winners including the Group 2 12f King Edward VII Stakes winner Beyton. (Cheveley Park Stud). *"I trained the mother who was OK and a winner, it's a nice pedigree and this filly has a bit of fire in her belly. She's neat she'll be a 2-y-o, possibly by June time, she's quite willing and prepared to get stuck in. Her mother was long and narrow and not too determined, but this filly is very strong and very much like her sire".*

727. STATS MINISTER ★★★

b.f. Champs Elysees – Sailing Days (Kris). February 19. Second foal. 2,000Y. Tattersalls October Book 3. Not sold. The dam, a modest 1m and 9f placed maiden, is a half-sister to 2 winners including the listed winner and Group 3 Geoffrey Freer Stakes third Land 'N Stars. The second dam, Uncharted Waters (by Celestial Storm), a moderate 10f and 12f winner, is a half-sister to 4 winners. (Mrs C A Cyzer). *"I like this filly, you must put her in the book. She's lovely – a nice, big, backward type that'll come into her own in the second half of the season. We like her and she's always been a nice mover. She's one of those that slipped through the net at the Sales, maybe because the market had gone a bit cold on the sire".* TRAINERS' BARGAIN BUY

728. SURVIVED ★★★

b.f. Kyllachy – Regina (Green Desert). February 28. Fourth foal. Half-sister to the quite useful 5f winner of 9 races from 2 to 5 yrs Six Wives (by Kingsalsa). The dam, a fairly useful 2-y-o dual 5f winner, is a half-sister to 3 winners including the fairly useful dual 1m winner Dubois. The second dam, Dazzle (by Gone West), a smart winner of the Group 3 6f Cherry Hinton Stakes and placed in both the Cheveley Park Stakes and the 1,000 Guineas, is a half-sister to the listed winners Fantasize and Hypnotize (herself dam of the Group 1 Cheveley Park Stakes winner Hooray) and to the placed dam of the Group 2 winner Danehurst. (Cheveley Park Stud). *"A very strong filly. I trained the dam's first foal, Six Wives, who won a claimer for us but was claimed by her present owners. She's still running and winning for them. This is a much nicer looking filly, she's well-made with a good backside and will be a May 2-y-o".*

729. TELMEYD ★★★

b.c. Dutch Art – Blithe (Pivotal). February 28. Second foal. 120,000Y. Tattersalls October Book 2. Shadwell Estate Co. The dam, a fairly useful 2-y-o 7f winner, is a half-sister to 5 winners including the Group 2 1m winner Penitent. The second dam, Pious (by Bishop Of Cashel), a fair dual 6f winner (including at 2 yrs), is a half-sister to 5 winners. (Sheikh Ahmed Al Maktoum). *"He's a nice horse. We trained the dam and she was very useful but fractured a sesamoid behind as a 2-y-o and she never ran again. I was very sorry that Cheveley Park decided to sell this colt and I became determined to try and find someone to buy him. He's one for the second half of the season and he'll be a very nice horse one day. Whether he's a stakes horse I don't know, but it's a family that get better with age".*

730. WRANGLER ★★★

b.c. High Chaparral – Tipsy Me (Selkirk). February 25. Third foal. 80,000Y. Tattersalls October Book 2. John Warren. Half-brother to the quite useful 2-y-o dual 7f winner Just Fabulous (by Sakhee). The dam, a modest 1m placed maiden, is a half-sister to 5 winners including the Group 2 12f King Edward VII Stakes winner Plea Bargain and the listed winners Lay Time and Jira. The second dam, Time Saved (by Green Desert), a fairly useful 10f winner, is a sister to the useful 1m winner and listed-placed Illusion and a half-sister to 5 winners including Zinaad and Time Allowed, both winners of the Group 2 12f Jockey Club Stakes and the dams of the Group winners Anton Chekhov, First Charter, Plea Bargain and Time Away. (Highclere Thoroughbred Racing – Ashes). *"A lovely horse. He's backward now and is likely to be a ten/twelve furlong 3-y-o. He was bought to go to Australia eventually and he's a good type for that. As a yearling he was quite narrow, tall and leggy, but he's done particularly well and he's a nice mover".*

731. YUFTEN ★★★

b.c. Invincible Spirit – Majestic Sakeena (King's Best). February 23. Fifth foal. Half-brother to the 2012 2-y-o 7f debut winner Lady Nouf (by Teofilo), to the very useful dual listed 10f winner Nouriya (by Danehill Dancer) and the quite useful 10f winner Zanotti (by Authorized). The dam is an unraced half-sister to the German listed sprint winner Shy Lady (herself dam of the St James's Palace Stakes winner Zafeen) and to the French listed winner Sweet Story. The second dam, Shy Danceuse (by Groom Dancer), a minor French 1m winner, is a half-sister to the very smart colt Diffident, winner of the Group 3 6f Diadem Stakes, the Group 3 6f Prix de Ris-Orangis and the listed 7f European Free Handicap. (Saleh Al Homaizi & Imad Al Sagar). *"A nice horse, we have the half-sister Lady Nouf who we like a lot. This colt has done well, he's not a beautiful horse, he's a workman, and he'll be a second half of the season 2-y-o with a bit of scope to him".*

732. UNNAMED ★★★★

b.f. Invincible Spirit – Applauded (Royal Applause). February 11. Second foal. 180,000Y. Tattersalls October Book 1. William Haggas. The dam, a quite useful 2-y-o 7f winner, is a half-sister to 3 winners including the Group 1 National Stakes winner Power and the Group 2 12f Ribblesdale Stakes winner Thakafaat. The second dam, Frappe (by Inchinor), a fairly useful 2-y-o 6f winner, is a half-sister to 3 winners including the 2,000 Guineas winner Footstepsinthesand. (St Albans Bloodstock). *"A sharp filly, definitely a 2-y-o and she should be out in May. She's not got the greatest action but she's quite strong and quite well-made".*

733. UNNAMED ★★

ch.c. Teofilo – Arctic Char (Polar Falcon). February 13. Fifth foal. 85,000Y. Tattersalls October Book 1. William Haggas. Half-brother to the useful 2-y-o 1m winner Alfathaa (by Nayef), to the fair 7f and 1m winner Boots And Spurs (by Oasis Dream) and the modest 5f winner Piste (by Falbrav). The dam, a useful listed 7f winner, is a half-sister to 7 winners including the Group 2 winners Barrow Creek and Last Resort and the dam of the Group 2 winner Trans Island. The second dam, Breadcrumb (by Final Straw), a very useful 6f and 7f winner, is a half-sister to 4 winners including the Group 2 Prix Maurice de Gheest winner College Chapel. (Mr A G Bloom). *"He's quite small and hasn't changed much since we bought him, which is quite disappointing, but he's by a stallion I like and we had his half-brother by Nayef, Alfathaa, who was very nearly a good horse. I'd expected this horse to change but the damsire Polar Falcon was small so I'm just hoping that it doesn't mean he'll be limited. Should be a 2-y-o".*

734. UNNAMED ★★

b.f. Cape Cross – Avila (Ajdal). February 26. Fifteenth living foal. 85,000Y. Tattersalls October Book 2. Blandford Bloodstock. Half-sister to the very smart Group 1 1m Racing Post Trophy and Group 2 10.4f Dante Stakes winner Dilshaan, to the fair staying winner of 6 races Aveiro (both by Darshaan), the smart 7f (at 2 yrs) and listed 10f winner and Group 1 1m Prix Marcel Boussac second Darrfonah (both by Singspiel), the quite useful 12f winner Calakanga (by Dalakhani), the modest 1m winner Al Joza (by Dubawi), the modest

10.5f winner Mama-San (by Doyoun) and three minor winners abroad by Lahib, Royal Applause and Shirley Heights. The dam, a fair 7f placed maiden, is a half-sister to the smart middle-distance colts Alleging, Monastery and Nomrood. The second dam, Sweet Habit (by Habitat), is an unraced half-sister to 5 winners including the Group 2 Pretty Polly Stakes winner Fleur Royale. (Saeed Manana). *"She's not very big but has a lot of quality. She's out in a field at the moment and she's one for the second half of the season".*

735. UNNAMED ★★

ch.c. Exceed And Excel – Crystal Moments (Haafhd). February 21. First foal. 52,000Y. Tattersalls October Book 3. Harrogate Bloodstock. The dam, a quite useful 5f, 6f (both at 2 yrs) and 7f winner, is a half-sister to 3 minor winners. The second dam, Celestial Choir (by Celestial Storm), a quite useful 7f to 12f winner of 9 races on the flat, also won 7 races over jumps and is a half-sister to 5 winners. (Mohammed Jaber). *"He topped the Book 3 sale but got spun by David Barron who bought him. The vets said he had a wind problem, so now we're just seeing how we get on with him and trying to sort out his wind. We're not convinced he does have a problem, so we're bashing on with him, he's had a bit of a break and we'll look at him again in time".*

736. UNNAMED ★★★

b.c. Sea The Stars – Dash To The Top (Montjeu). April 16. Third foal. 190,000Y. Tattersalls October Book 1. Jill Lamb. Half-brother to the Irish 2-y-o 6f winner and Group 3 Tetrarch Stakes second Dynasty (by Montjeu) and to the fairly useful 2-y-o 7f winner Deep South (by Red Ransom). The dam, a very useful 2-y-o listed 1m winner, was placed in the Group 1 Fillies' Mile and the Group 1 Yorkshire Oaks and is a half-sister to the listed 10.8f winner Dash To The Front. The second dam, Millennium Dash (by Nashwan), a fairly useful 10.2f winner, is a half-sister to 4 winners and to the unplaced dam of the Sun Chariot Stakes winner Kissogram. (Mr A G Bloom). *"He has a nice pedigree, so he has a chance. He threw a splint in December which knocked him out for a bit but he's back cantering now, but he's a 3-y-o in the making".*

737. UNNAMED ★★★ ♠

b.c. Oasis Dream – Enticing (Pivotal). April 5. Second foal. The dam, a very smart Group 3 5f Molecomb Stakes and Group 3 5f King George Stakes winner, is a sister to one winner and a half-sister to 2 winners including the useful listed 1m winner Sentaril. The second dam, Superstar Leo (by College Chapel), a very smart 2-y-o, won 5 races including the Group 2 5f Flying Childers Stakes and the Weatherbys Super Sprint and is a full or half-sister to numerous winners. (Lael Racing). *"He injured a knee when they were breaking him, he's OK now but he hasn't been with me long. I don't know enough about him yet but he should be a 2-y-o because he's a strong colt with a big backside".*

738. UNNAMED ★★★

b.f. Lawman – Lisieux Orchid (Sadler's Wells). March 20. Fifth foal. 30,000Y. Tattersalls October Book 2. Rabbah Bloodstock. Half-sister to I Say (by Oratorio), placed second over 1m on her only start at 2 yrs in 2012 and to the fair Irish 10f and 12f winner Notalossonya (by Cadeaux Genereux). The dam, a quite useful Irish 12f winner, is a half-sister to 5 winners including the Group 1 National Stakes third Force Of Will. The second dam, Clear Issue (by Riverman), won once over 7f in Ireland at 3 yrs and is a half-sister to 8 winners including the US Grade 1 winner Twilight Agenda and the dam of the Group 1 winners Media Puzzle, Refuse To Bend and Go And Go. (Sultan Ali). *"A half-sister to a 3-y-o we have called I Say, this filly is nice and has a bit of quality. She goes well and looks quicker than I Say, so she'll be a seven furlong 2-y-o".*

739. UNNAMED ★★

ch.f. Pivotal – Moon Dazzle (Kingmambo). March 17. Third living foal. 110,000Y. Tattersalls October Book 1. Not sold. Half-sister to the winner of 3 minor races abroad Jean Jeannie (by Giant's Causeway). The dam, a useful 1m and UAE 9f winner, was listed-placed and is a half-sister to 9 winners including the Group 2 German 2,000 Guineas winners Dupont and Pacino. The second dam, June Moon (by Sadler's Wells), is an unraced half-sister to 7 winners including the French

1,000 Guineas second Firth Of Lorne. (Mr B Kantor). *"A backward filly, not very big, but she'll need a bit of time. An August type 2-y-o".*

740. UNNAMED ★★★ ♠

b.f. *Danehill Dancer – Superstar Leo (College Chapel).* March 11. Sister to the useful 3-y-o 7f and listed 1m winner and Group 3 7f Jersey Stakes second Sentaril and half-sister to the fair 2012 6f placed 2-y-o Sky Garden (by Acclamation), the very smart Group 3 5f Molecomb Stakes and Group 3 5f King George Stakes winner Enticing, the fair 7f winner Map Of Heaven (both by Pivotal) and the quite useful dual 5f winner (including at 2 yrs) Speed Song (by Fasliyev). The dam, a very smart 2-y-o, won 5 races including the Group 2 5f Flying Childers Stakes and the Weatherbys Super Sprint and is a full or half-sister to numerous winners. The second dam, Council Rock (by General Assembly), a fair 9f and 10f placed 3-y-o, is a half-sister to 6 winners including the Group 3 Prestige Stakes winner Glatisant (dam of the 2,000 Guineas winner and sire Footstepsinthesand) and the listed Virginia Stakes winner Gai Bulga. (Lael Stable). *"A full sister to Sentaril, a listed winner we have big plans for this year. They're not dissimilar, but Sentaril never ran as a 2-y-o because she was immature. The dam obviously did very well as a 2-y-o, so I'll be having a look at her to see what we come up with. I suspect she'll need a bit of time".*

741. UNNAMED ★★

ch.c. *Champs Elysees – Zee Zee Gee (Galileo).* March 29. Second foal. 75,000Y. Tattersalls October Book 2. Anthony Stroud. Half-brother to the unplaced 2012 2-y-o Jazz On The Beach (by Footstepsinthesand). The dam is an unraced half-sister to 2 winners including the Group 1 Pretty Polly Stakes and Group 2 Middleton Stakes winner Izzi Top. The second dam, Zee Zee Top (by Zafonic), won the Group 1 Prix de l'Opera and was third in the Group 1 Nassau Stakes and is a half-sister to 6 winners including the Group 1 winners Kayf Tara and Opera House. (Mr B Kantor). *"A lovely mover, but he's backward at the moment and a 3-y-o type".*

MICHAEL HALFORD

742. AUSBURY BOSS (IRE) ★★★★

b.br.c. *Dalakhani – Nick's Nikita (Pivotal).* January 22. Second foal. The dam, a useful winner of 4 races in Ireland including the Group 3 12f Noblesse Stakes, was placed in four other Group 3 events and is a half-sister to 5 winners. The second dam, Elaine's Honor (by Chief's Crown), won twice at 2 and 3 yrs in France and is a half-sister to 7 winners including the US Grade 3 winner Savannah's Honor. (Mrs N Hartery). *"A lovely, well-balanced, good-bodied horse that's likely to wants seven furlongs, we like him and he goes well. One from mid-season onwards, he certainly looks like making a 2-y-o".*

743. BLEEDING HEARTS (IRE) ★★★

ch.c. *Peintre Celebre – Society Gal (Galileo).* January 24. First foal. €26,000Y. Goffs Orby. Michael Halford. The dam is an unraced half-sister to the US Grade 3 winner Good Mood. The second dam, Pillars Of Society (by Caerleon), a fairly useful Irish 10f winner, is a half-sister to 5 winners out of the Group 1 Prix Saint-Alary winner Grise Mine. (Gigginstown House Stud). *"He's been doing half-speeds, he's a good, sound-limbed, straightforward colt. He's well-balanced, will probably want seven furlongs and we'll see him sometime from June onwards".*

744. HAZLEDOC (IRE) ★★★

b.f. *Azamour – Grand Oir (Grand Slam).* April 2. Third foal. €54,000Y. Goffs Sportsman's. Aidan O'Ryan. The dam was placed three times in the USA and is a half-sister to 2 minor winners. The second dam, Kerry Gold (by Private Terms), placed twice in the USA, is a half-sister to 10 winners including the dual US Grade 1 winner Tranquility Lake (herself the dam of two US Grade 1 winners) and the US triple Grade 2 winner Benchmark. (Mr John Kennedy). *"She's been doing plenty and is one for the second half of the year over seven furlongs. Not over-big, but a well-made and correct filly".*

745. KERNOFF (IRE) ★★★

b.c. *Excellent Art – Daganya (Danehill Dancer).* March 21. Fifth foal. Half-brother to the fairly useful 1m to 11f winner of 5 races Akasaka (by

King's Best), to the fairly useful dual 12f winner Cape Of Good Grace (by Cape Cross) and the modest dual 6f winner Chasca (by Namid). The dam won 2 races including a listed 6f event in Ireland and was second in the Group 2 5f Flying Five. She is a sister to the listed 5f winner Snaefell and a half-sister to 3 winners including the quite useful 5f winner of 10 races Henry Hall. The second dam, Sovereign Grace (by Standaan), won over 5f in Ireland and is a half-sister 9 winners. (Mr J D Cague). *"He looks a real 2-y-o, he's a good-bodied, strong horse that we'll probably start off at six furlongs. He's more the shape of a sprinter than a staying horse".*

746. PIT STOP (IRE) ★★★★

b.c. Iffraaj – Journey's End (In The Wings). April 18. Fourth foal. €50,000Y. Goffs Orby. John Ferguson. Half-brother to a minor 3-y-o winner in Italy by Noverre. The dam ran twice unplaced and is a half-sister to 8 winners including the Irish listed winners Dashing Colours and Dash Of Red and the dam of the 2-y-o Group 2 winner Captain Marvelous. The second dam, Near The End (by Shirley Heights), is an unraced half-sister to 2 winners. (Sheikh Mohammed). *"A beautiful horse, he's big, tall, good-looking and well-balanced. He goes really well and we like him a lot. You'd like him, he does everything well, he's showing me plenty of pace and would probably start off at six furlongs but would be better over seven".*

747. POLITICAL POLICY (IRE) ★★

b.c. Bushranger – Alexander Express (Sri Pekan). March 30. Eighth foal. €38,000Y. Goffs Orby. Not sold. Half-brother to the Irish 2-y-o 7f winner, on only start, Andalacia, to the minor Italian 2-y-o winner Air Mail (both by Choisir) and 2 minor winners in Greece by Cape Cross and Indian Danehill. The dam, a fairly useful Irish 1m winner, was listed-placed and is a half-sister to 3 winners including the US Grade 1 placed Occhi Verdi. The second dam, Mali (by Storm Bird), won once at 3 yrs in France and is a half-sister to 4 winners. (Mr F Lynch). *"A nice, well-balanced colt with a good attitude. He's grown recently so we won't be in a hurry with him but he's doing everything well".*

748. WARBIRD ★★★★

b.c. Royal Applause – Air Biscuit (Galileo). January 30. Second foal. €95,000Y. Goffs Orby. John Ferguson. The dam, a quite useful 1m and 10f winner, is a half-sister to 6 winners including the Group 3 5f Prix du Bois and Group 3 5f Prix du Petit-Couvert winner Ziria. The second dam, Surprise Visitor (by Be My Guest), was placed once in France and is a half-sister to 9 winners including the dual German listed winner Mirage (herself dam of the Group 2 winner Swallow Flight) and the champion Scandinavian older horse Red Hero. (Sheikh Mohammed). *"He looks a nice colt, he's well-balanced, good-bodied and with a good action. I haven't done a lot with him but he seems to have the pace for six furlongs and we do like him. He's one of the more forward ones and he does go well".*

749. ZAINDERA (IRE) ★★★★

b.f. Acclamation – Zalaiyma (Rainbow Quest). February 9. Half-sister to the useful Irish 7f winner and listed-placed Zabarajad (by Invincible Spirit). The dam won twice in France over 1m and was listed-placed. The second dam, Zalaiyka (by Royal Academy), won the French 1,000 Guineas. (HH Aga Khan). *"She would be one of the more forward of the fillies we have. She could start off at six furlongs because she's strong and quite precocious. We like her and she's a lovely filly".*

750. UNNAMED ★★★

gr.f. Galileo – Alabastrine (Green Desert). April 28. Seventh foal. €340,000Y. Goffs Orby. Hugo Merry. Closely related to the useful Irish 7.5f (at 2 yrs) and 9f winner Hail Caesar (by Montjeu) and half-sister to the quite useful 2-y-o 7f winner Albaspina (by Selkirk). The dam, placed over 7f at 2 yrs, is a half-sister to 8 winners including the Nassau Stakes and Sun Chariot Stakes winner Last Second (dam of the French 2,000 Guineas winner Aussie Rules), the Doncaster Cup winner Alleluia (dam of the Prix Royal-Oak winner Allegretto), the Moyglare Stud Stakes third Alouette (dam of the dual Champion Stakes winner Alborada and the triple German Group 1 winner Albanova) and to the placed dam of the Group 1 winners Yesterday and Quarter Moon. The second dam, Alruccaba (by Crystal

Palace), a quite useful 2-y-o 6f winner, is out of a half-sister to the dams of Aliysa and Nishapour. (Mr M Enright). *"We haven't done much with her and she's having a break at the moment. She does everything well, she's a beautiful mover, well-balanced with a good attitude. One for the second half of the year".*

751. UNNAMED ★★
b.f. *Acclamation – Caherassdotcom (Compton Place)*. April 22. First foal. The dam, a fair 5f to 7f placed maiden, is a half-sister to 7 winners including the very useful 6f (at 2 yrs) and triple listed winner Dubai's Touch, the very useful 8.5f and 9f winner and Group 3 Diomed Stakes third Wannabe Around, the useful triple 6f winner (including at 2 yrs) and subsequent Abu Dhabi listed winner Grantley Adams and the useful 7.5f to 10f winner and French Group 3 1m third Nobelist. The second dam, Noble Peregrine (by Lomond), an Italian 10f winner, is closely related to the French 2-y-o listed 10f winner Noble Ballerina and a half-sister to 6 winners. (Mr N Hartery). *"She's gone home for a break because she was a bit backward. A nice filly, a good mover but she'll just take a bit of time".*

752. UNNAMED ★★★
b.f. *Clodovil – Serious Delight (Lomond)*. April 25. Tenth foal. Sister to the fairly useful dual 7f winner and listed-placed Maid In Heaven and half-sister to the fairly useful 6f (at 2 yrs) and 7f winner of 3 races Delphie Queen, the fair 5f and 6f winner Everygrainofsand (both by Desert Sun), the fairly useful 2-y-o 6f and 8.5f winner Wathiq (by Titus Livius), the Irish 5f to 7f winner of 4 races Foxhollow Lady (by Goldmark) and the modest Irish 1m winner Danick Of Time (by Iffraaj). The dam is an unraced half-sister to 8 winners including the dam of the Group 1 Haydock Park Sprint Cup winner Pipalong. The second dam, Grey Goddess (by Godswalk), won 5 races from 7f to 8.5f including two Group 3 events in Ireland and is a half-sister to 2 winners. (Mr N Hartery). *"She's been doing half-speeds, she's strong, looks a 2-y-o type, has a good attitude and has the look of a six furlong 2-y-o".*

753. UNNAMED ★★★
b.f. *Clodovil – Smoken Rosa (Smoke Glacken)*.

May 1. Third foal. Half-sister to the quite useful Irish 6f placed 2-y-o Lanett Lady (by Teufelsberg). The dam, placed 3 times in the USA, is a half-sister to 4 winners including Snowdrops (three Graded stakes wins). The second dam, Roses In The Snow (by Be My Guest), a useful 1m winner and listed-placed here, subsequently won in the USA and is a half-sister to 6 winners. (Mr John Dewberry). *"She looks quite forward and mature, she's done everything we've asked of her and I'd expect her to start over six furlongs around June time".*

RICHARD HANNON
754. A CHILDS DREAM ★★★★
b.f. *Intense Focus – Keriyka (Indian Ridge)*. February 21. Second foal. 55,000Y. Tattersalls October Book 2. Peter & Ross Doyle. Half-sister to the fairly useful 2012 2-y-o 6f winner Rocky Ground (by Acclamation). The dam, placed fourth over 7f in Ireland on her only start, is a half-sister to 2 winners. The second dam, Kermiyana (by Green Desert), won the listed Brownstown Stakes and is a half-sister to 3 winners. (Adam Victor). *"A very sharp filly, you'll be seeing her early doors I'd say. She's done one piece of work and done it very well. A good actioned 2-y-o".*

755. ACQUAINT (IRE) ★★★
gr.f. *Verglas – Azia (Desert Story)*. February 20. Fourth foal. 82,000Y. Tattersalls October Book 1. John Warren. Sister to the useful listed Ripon Champion 2-y-o Trophy winner Hold Your Colour and to the modest 11f to 14f and hurdles winner Taste The Wine. The dam, a 2-y-o 7f winner in Ireland, is out of the unraced Safdara (by Shahrastani), herself an unraced half-sister to 10 winners including the Group 2 Lockinge Stakes winner Safawan. (Highclere Thoroughbred Racing – Alcove). *"A nice filly that holds onto her weight, she's quite big, looks pretty sharp and seems to have a good attitude. Probably a six furlong type 2-y-o".*

756. ADAPTABILITY ★★
ch.f. *Mastercraftsman – Sierra (Dr Fong)*. February 26. Half-sister to the fairly useful 7f and 9f winner and listed-placed Mister Music (by Singspiel) and to the quite useful 6f and

7f winner Choral (by Oratorio). The dam, a moderate 7f and 1m winner, is a half-sister to several winners including the useful 2-y-o 7f winner Desert Warning. The second dam, Warning Belle (by Warning), is an unraced half-sister to 7 winners including the high-class Group 2 10f Prince of Wales's Stakes and Group 3 10f Brigadier Gerard Stakes winner Stagecraft and the Group 3 Strensall Stakes winner Mullins Bay and the listed winners Balalaika and Hyabella. (Longview Stud & Bloodstock Ltd). *"A nice big filly, it looks like she'll want seven furlongs or a mile and I wouldn't think you'd see her until later in the season".*

757. AFTER THE GOLDRUSH ★★★

b.c. Kyllachy – Fine Lady (Selkirk). April 20. Third foal. 85,000Y. Tattersalls October Book 1. Peter & Ross Doyle. Half-brother to the Italian 2-y-o winner Visionaria (by Byron). The dam is a placed half-sister to 3 winners including the useful performer at up to 1m Gypsy Passion. The second dam, Rua d'Oro (by El Gran Senor), won the listed Derrinstown Stud 1,000 Guineas Trial, was third in the Group 3 Matron Stakes and is a sister to the dual Irish listed winner Portico and a half-sister to 3 winners. (The Gold Rush Partnership). *"A real nice 2-y-o that goes really well. We're hoping he'll be a decent quality 2-y-o from the mid-season onwards".*

758. ALASKAN (IRE) ★★★

b.c. Kodiac – Olympia Theatre (Galileo). March 26. Third foal. £46,000Y. Doncaster Premier. Amanda Skiffington. Brother to the fair 2012 2-y-o 7f winner Mandeville. The dam is an unraced half-sister to 3 minor winners. The second dam, Opari (by Night Shift), a French 2-y-o 6f winner, is a half-sister to one winner. (Carmichael Humber). *"He's very sharp, so he's an early type that we like".*

759. ANJAAL ★★★

ch.c. Bahamian Bounty – Ballymore Celebre (Peintre Celebre). April 4. Sixth foal. 105,000Y. Tattersalls October Book 2. Peter & Ross Doyle. Half-brother to the fair 2m winner No Time To Lose (by Authorized), to the fair 10f and 12f winner Pintrada (by Tiger Hill) and the modest 10f winner Sweet Secret (by Singspiel). The

dam won twice at 3 yrs in France and is a half-sister to 10 winners including the Irish multiple Group 3 winner Nysaean. The second dam, Irish Arms (by Irish River), won once in France and is a half-sister to 9 winners including the US Grade 2 winner Morold. (Hamdan Al Maktoum). *"Quite tall, so he wouldn't be the sharpest, but he's a nice colt with a good action. One for seven furlongs in mid-season".*

760. ANTICIPATED (IRE) ★★★

b.c. Whipper – Foreplay (Lujain). April 13. Fourth foal. €30,000Y. Goffs Sportsman's. Peter & Ross Doyle. Brother to the French 2-y-o 5f winner Finisterien (by Whipper) and half-brother to the fair 5f winner Midnight Rider (by Red Ransom). The dam, a fair 6f (at 2 yrs) and 7f winner, is a half-sister to the smart listed 9f and listed 10f winner and Group 1 Prix Jean Prat third Rocamadour and to the Irish 2-y-o 5f winner and listed-placed Church Cross. The second dam, Watch Me (by Green Desert), a useful 6f winner and third in the Group 3 6f Cork And Orrery Stakes, is a half-sister to 3 winners here and abroad. (Woodcock, Bull, Ivory, Hannon). *"He'll be one for the auction races and I should think Windsor would be on the agenda. A nice enough colt".* This colt won on his debut at Windsor in mid-April.

761. ARRANGER (IRE) ★★★

b.br.f. Bushranger – El Morocco (El Prado). March 10. Second foal. £28,000Y. Doncaster Premier. Peter & Ross Doyle. Half-sister to the fair 2012 2-y-o 6f winner Cardmaster (by Red Clubs). The dam is an unraced half-sister to 2 winners including the Group 3 placed Smart Coco. The second dam, Djebel Amour (by Mt. Livermore), won 2 minor races at 3 yrs in the USA and is a half-sister to 4 winners including Almushahar (Group 2 Champagne Stakes). (Mrs Julie Wood). *"She worked yesterday, she seems a nice filly and fairly sharp".*

762. ART OFFICIAL (IRE) ★★★

b.c. Excellent Art – Dama'a (Green Desert). February 19. Fourth foal. £36,000Y. Doncaster Premier. Peter & Ross Doyle. Half-brother to the quite useful 2-y-o 7f winner Darkening (by Shamardal). The dam, a quite useful 6f winner at 3 yrs, is a half-sister to 2 winners including the useful 2-y-o 6f winner and Group 2 placed Himalya. The second dam, Lady Miletrian (by Barathea), a useful 1m winner and second in the listed Princess Elizabeth Stakes, is a sister to the listed winning 2-y-o Duty Paid and a half-sister to 3 winners. (Chris Giles, Potensis Ltd, J Palmer-Brown). *"A nice, big horse that goes well. He's a great mover and I'd say he'll want six furlongs".*

763. ASCENDING ANGEL (IRE) ★★★
b.f. Sea The Stars – Maskaya (Machiavellian). February 6. Sixth foal. €80,000Y. Goffs Orby. Peter & Ross Doyle. Half-sister to the Irish 2-y-o 7f winner and Group 1 Criterium de Saint-Cloud second Drumbeat (by Montjeu), to the fair 7.6f winner Red Blooded Woman (by Red Ransom) and a winner in Japan by Giant's Causeway. The dam, an Irish 2-y-o 5f winner, is a half-sister to 7 winners including the Irish triple listed winner and Group 2 placed Modeeroch and the Irish 2-y-o 6f winner and Group 1 6f Cheveley Park Stakes third Danaskaya. The second dam, Majinskaya (by Marignan), winner of the listed 12f Prix des Tuileries and second in the Group 3 Prix de Psyche, is a half-sister to 6 winners including the French 2-y-o 7f winner Mabrova (herself dam of the Group 1 5f Prix de l'Abbaye winner Kistena). (Mrs A Turner). *"A nice filly, a little fatty but very sweet. She has a bit more substance than a lot by the sire, we like her and she looks quite sharp but we won't be rushing her".*

764. AVOCETTE (FR) ★★★ ♠
b.f. Pivotal – Ailette (Second Set). March 31. Seventh foal. €140,000Y. Arqana Deauville August. Amanda Skiffington. Half-sister to the useful 2-y-o 7f and 1m winner and Group 3 Prix Thomas Bryon third Ameer (by Monsun), to the German 2-y-o 7.5f winner Asinara (by Big Shuffle) and the minor 3-y-o winner Lopez Lake (by Teofilo). The dam won once at 2 yrs in Germany and is a half-sister to 7 winners including the Group 1 German 2,000 Guineas winner Aviso and the dam of the Group 1 German Oaks winner Amarette. The second dam, Akasma (by Windwurf), won 3 races at 3 yrs in Germany, is a half-sister to 5 winners including the German Group 2 winner Ajano. (Carmichael/Simmons/Humber). *"She's a real*

nice filly, it's early days for her yet but she looks the part and we'd have quite high hopes for her".

765. BABY BUSH (IRE) ★★★
b.f. Holy Roman Emperor – Mainstream Opinion (Indian Ridge). March 3. Fourth foal. 36,000Y. Tattersalls October Book 2. Global Equine Group. Half-sister to the Italian winner of 6 races and listed-placed Different Opinion (by Noverre) and to the modest Irish 2-y-o winner Definite Opinion (by Kheleyf). The dam, a fair 1m winner, is a half-sister to 6 winners. The second dam, Insider's View (by Caerleon), won 3 races from 6f (at 2 yrs) to 1m and is a half-sister to 5 winners. (Malih Al Basti). *"A lovely filly, she'll need time though and she won't be ready until later on".*

766. BANAADEER (IRE) ★★★★ ♠
ch.c. Tamayuz – Loose Julie (Cape Cross). February 19. First foal. 90,000foal. Tattersalls December. Shadwell Estate Co. The dam is an unraced half-sister to several winners including the 2-y-o listed 6f Silver Flash Stakes winner Desert Sky and the 6f winner and listed placed Moonis. The second dam, Badrah (by Private Account), is a placed half-sister to 5 winners including the Group 3 Brigadier Gerard Stakes winner Husyan. (Hamdan Al Maktoum). *"One of the nicest colts we've got, he's very nice, a good-mover, not overly-sharp but with a good temperament. We like him a lot".*

767. BEAU NASH (IRE) ★★★
b.c. Dandy Man – Dathuil (Royal Academy). March 2. Eleventh foal. £25,000Y. Doncaster Premier. Peter & Ross Doyle. Half-brother to the fair 7f and 1m winner Precipitous (by Indian Ridge), to the fair 2-y-o 6f winner Ymlaen (by Desert Prince), the modest 10f and 12f winner Mr Napoleon (by Daylami), the Scandinavian 6f (at 2 yrs) to 10f winner Stinking Bishop (by Fantastic Light) and a hurdles winner by Key Of Luck. The dam, a fairly useful 1m winner, was subsequently Grade 3 placed in the USA and is a half-sister to 6 winners including the 2-y-o listed 6f winner and Group 1 placed Luminata. The second dam, Smaoineamh (by Tap On Wood), an Irish 6f winner at 2 yrs and useful at up to

14f, is a half-sister to the champion sprinter Double Form and the Lupe Stakes winner Scimitarra. (The Best Turned Out Partnership). *"A sharp and early 2-y-o, he wasn't expensive, he's a tough little horse and he could be one of our first winners".*

768. BIOGRAPHY ★★★

ch.c. Assertive – Dahshah (Mujtahid). March 23. Eighth foal. £26,000Y. Doncaster Premier. Peter & Ross Doyle. Brother to the unplaced 2012 2-y-o Cash Rich and half-brother to the fair 7f (at 2 yrs) and 1m winner of 5 races and listed-placed Eastern Gift (by Cadeaux Genereux), to the modest dual 5f winner (including at 2 yrs) Mini Bon Bon (by Kyllachy) and a winner in Spain by Cherokee Run. The dam, a fair 3-y-o 1m winner, is a half-sister to 6 winners including the Group 3 Horris Hill Stakes winner La-Faah. The second dam, Rawaabe (by Nureyev), a quite useful dual 5f winner, is a half-sister to 4 winners including the Gimcrack Stakes winner Doulab and the dam of the champion US 2-y-o filly Chilukki. (Mrs V Hubbard & Mrs J K Powell). *"A nice, big colt and very much like his grandsire Bold Edge. You wouldn't know how good he is until you get him to the races, he's that type of horse".*

769. BIRD OF LIGHT (IRE) ★★★

b.f. Elnadim – Lady Docker (Docksider). February 23. First foal. £26,000Y. Doncaster Premier. Sackville/Donald. The dam is an unplaced half-sister to 11 winners including the Group 2 5f Temple Stakes winner Tipsy Creek and the Group 3 7f Ballycorus Stakes winner Abunawwas. The second dam, Copper Creek (by Habitat), a fair 3-y-o 6f winner, is a sister to the US Grade 3 winner Placer Queen and a half-sister to 9 winners including the Group 3 Mulcahy Stakes winner My Sister. (Rockcliffe Stud). *"A nice, sharp little filly, she's one for the auction races and maybe the Supersprint if she proves good enough".*

770. BLACK CAESAR (IRE) ★★★ ♣

b.c. Bushranger – Evictress (Sharp Victor). April 20. Twelfth foal. €60,000Y. Goffs Orby. Amanda Skiffington. Half-brother to the Group 3 Concorde Stakes and Group 3 Brownstown Stakes winner Miss Sally (by

Danetime), to the fairly useful Irish 2-y-o 1m winner Majestic Eviction (by King's Theatre), the fair Irish 1m winner One Up One Down (by Chineur), the smart jumper Quazar (by Inzar) and a winner in Greece by Petardia. The dam was placed three times from 6f (at 2 yrs) to 1m in Ireland and is a half-sister to 8 minor winners. The second dam, Nurse Jo (by J O Tobin), ran twice unplaced in the USA and is a half-sister to the dual US Grade 1 winner Love Sign, the Irish and Italian Oaks winner Melodist and the US Grade 2 winner Fatih. (Carmichael/Humber). *"I like him, he's nice and he ought to win a race or two".*

771. BOLD SPIRIT ★★★

b.c. Invincible Spirit – Far Shores (Distant View). March 9. The dam is an unplaced sister to one winner and a half sister to numerous winners including the top-class sprinter and sire Danehill, the US Grade 2 9f winner Eagle Eyed, the very smart Group 3 Criterion Stakes winner Shibboleth and the listed 7f winner Euphonic. The second dam, Razyana (by His Majesty), was placed over 7f at 2 yrs and 10f at 3 yrs. (The Queen). *"A nice horse, I quite like him and he's a typical Invincible Spirit. He can be a little bit hot but he's quite a nice, well-made horse".*

772. BONNIE WEE LASSIE ★★★

b.f. Exceed And Excel – Scottish Exile (Ashkalani). January 31. Fourth foal. £9,000Y. Doncaster Premier. Peter & Ross Doyle. Half-sister to the smart 5f and 6f 2-y-o winner and multiple Group 3 second Bonnie Charlie (by Intikhab). The dam, a fair triple 5f winner, is a sister to the fairly useful 6f winner of 11 races and listed-placed Million Percent and a half-sister to 4 winners. The second dam, Royal Jade (by Last Tycoon), a fairly useful 7f winner, is a half-sister to 6 winners including the Group 3 5f King George Stakes winner Averti. (Major Shear). *"A cheap little filly, her half-brother Bonnie Charlie was small and she's a tough 2-y-o that'll win early".*

773. BROWN GLAZE (USA) ★★★

b.f. War Front – Easy To Cope (Copelan). March 5. Seventh foal. $150,000Y. Keeneland September. David Redvers. Half-sister to 4 winners including the stakes winners Lucky

Livi (by Mr Greeley) and Lottacosta (by Cat Thief). The dam, a minor winner of 2 races at 3 yrs in the USA, is a sister to the stakes winner Self Evident. The second dam, Apply Yourself (by Beat Inflation), a minor US winner at 2 and 3 yrs, is a half-sister to 4 winners. (Qatar Racing Ltd). *"She's quite heavy and we haven't done anything with her yet, but she has a good attitude. For a filly she's quite strong all through her neck and shoulders. A nice filly by a stallion they tell me is going to be top drawer".*

774. BROWN SUGAR (IRE) ★★★

b.c. Tamayuz – Lady Livius (Titus Livius). March 19. Third foal. £47,500Y. Goffs Orby. Sackville/Donald. Half-brother to the quite useful 2012 2-y-o 6f winner Elle Woods (by Lawman). The dam, a fairly useful 2-y-o 5f Weatherbys Supersprint winner of 3 races, is a half-sister to 5 winners including the Group 2 6f Mill Reef Stakes winner and Group 1 placed Galeota and the listed 13f winner Loulwa. The second dam, Refined (by Statoblest), a fairly useful dual 5f winner, is a half-sister to 6 winners including the very smart Group 3 7f Criterion Stakes winner Pipe Major. (De La Warr Racing). *"A nice little horse, he's grand and one for the middle of the season. We haven't done a lot with him yet but he appears to be fine and he's sound".*

775. BUNKER (IRE) ★★★★★ ♠

br.c. Hurricane Run – Endure (Green Desert). January 24. Fourth foal. 50,000Y. Tattersalls October Book 2. Peter & Ross Doyle. Half-brother to the quite useful 2-y-o 6f winner Atacama Crossing and to the fair 2-y-o 5f and 6f winner Beach Candy (both by Footstepsinthesand). The dam ran twice unplaced and is a half-sister to 6 winners including the Canadian Grade 3 winner Alexis and the Irish listed winner Freshwater Pearl. The second dam, Sister Golden Hair (by Glint Of Gold), a listed-placed winner at 2 yrs in Germany, is a half-sister to 2 winners. (Morecombe, Anderson, Hughes). *"A very nice colt – I really like him and he could be one for the Chesham at Royal Ascot. He has a little bit of a plain head but he's got a good action and is a horse we've always liked".*

776. CAMEO TIARA (IRE) ★★★

b.f. High Chaparral – Cuilaphuca (Danetime). February 6. Second foal. €16,000foal. Goffs November. Woodstock. The dam, a fairly useful Irish 6f and 7f winner, was listed-placed and is a half-sister to 6 winners including the listed winner and useful broodmare Soreze. The second dam, Run Bonnie (by Runnett), won over 6f in Ireland at 3 yrs and is a half-sister to 4 winners. (Mrs Julie Wood). *"A lovely big filly but she's backward and you won't see her until towards the back-end of the season. A lovely mover with a very nice way about her".*

777. CARTHAGE (IRE) ★★★★

b.c. Mastercraftsman – Pitrizzia (Lando). March 5. Third foal. €100,000Y. Goffs Orby. Peter & Ross Doyle. Half-brother to the modest 7f (at 2 yrs) and 1m winner Bitaphon (by Acclamation). The dam is an unraced half-sister to 3 winners including the Italian listed winner Prianca. The second dam, Palanca (by Inchinor), won the Group 3 Premio Primi Passi and is a half-sister to 3 minor winners. (M Pescod). *"This is a really nice colt. He's pleased us in every way, he moves really nicely and he has the right attitude. Although he hasn't done any work yet I wouldn't mind buying a share myself!"* This colt is one that Richard Hughes tells me he likes.

778. CAY DANCER ★★★ ♠

gr.f. Danehill Dancer – White Cay (Dalakhani). April 29. Second foal. 40,000Y. Tattersalls October Book 1. Will Edmeades. The dam, a minor winner of 2 races at 3 yrs in France, is a half-sister to 5 winners including the Group 1 1m Coronation Stakes winner Balisada. The second dam, Balnaha (by Lomond), a modest 3-y-o 1m winner, is a sister to Inchmurrin (a very useful winner of the Child Stakes and herself dam of the very smart and tough colt Inchinor) and a half-sister to 6 winners including the Mill Reef Stakes winner Welney. (R Barnett). *"A nice filly, she's a great mover but she'll need a bit of time I would say".*

779. CHAMPAGNE SYDNEY (IRE) ★★★★

ch.c. Iffraaj – Special Touch (Spinning World). April 5. Fourth foal. 17,000Y. Tattersalls October Book 2. Peter & Ross Doyle. Half-brother to the 2012 Italian placed 2-y-o

Special Reddy (by Red Clubs). The dam, a moderate Irish 12f placed maiden, is a half-sister to 5 winners including the Irish dual Group 3 placed Festival Princess. The second dam, Uliana (by Darshaan), an Irish 10f winner, is a half-sister to 8 winners including the German Group 1 10f winner Ransom O'War. (The Sydney Arms, Chelsea). *"A sharp little horse, he's a nice colt and could be one for the Supersprint. He didn't cost a lot of money but we'll get going early with him and he won't be long in winning – he's pretty clever".*

780. CHAMPIONSHIP (IRE) ★★★★
ch.c. Exceed And Excel – Aljafliyah (Halling). March 15. Fifth foal. €99,000foal. Goffs November. Woodstock. Brother to the fairly useful 2-y-o 5f and 6f winner The Only Boss and half-brother to the fairly useful 2-y-o dual 6f winner Waltz Darling (by Iffraaj). The dam is an unplaced half-sister to 5 winners including the US Grade 3 winner Sohgol. The second dam, Arruhan (by Mujtahid), a quite useful 5f (at 2 yrs) and 7f winner, is a half-sister to 5 winners including the smart listed 7f winner Royal Storm. (Mrs Julie Wood). *"A very nice colt that did a little bit yesterday. We might see him showing up at one of the nice Newbury meetings".*

781. CHIEF BARKER (IRE) ★★
b.c. Azamour – Millay (Polish Precedent). March 23. Sixth foal. 38,000Y. Tattersalls October Book 2. Not sold. Half-brother to the unplaced 2012 2-y-o Murjanah (by Tamayuz), to the fairly useful 2-y-o 6f winner Salford Art (by Sir Percy), the moderate 2m winner M'Lady Rousseur (by Selkirk) and a winner in Switzerland by Red Ransom. The dam, a minor winner at 3 yrs in France, is a half-sister to 6 winners including the listed winner Millstreet. The second dam, Mill Path (by Mill Reef), ran once unplaced and is a half-sister to 4 winners including the Irish Oaks winner Give Thanks. (Middleham Park Racing XXIII). *"I like him, but he's got 3-y-o written all over him so he might not run until towards the back-end. A lovely, big horse".*

782. CHUTNEY ★★★★
b.f. Exceed And Excel – Crackle (Anshan). May 3. Eighth foal. 50,000Y. Tattersalls October

Book 2. G Howson. Half-sister to the modest 2012 2-y-o 7f winner The Obvious Choice (by Royal Applause), to the US dual Grade 3 winner over 1m and 9f Pickle (by Piccolo and herself dam of the multiple listed winner Gusto), the useful 7f (at 2 yrs) and 10f winner and Group 3 Classic Trial third Auld Burns (by Pastoral Pursuits), the fair French 6f and 7f winner Pivock (by Pivotal) and a winner in Spain by Mujahid. The dam, a quite useful 5.7f (at 2 yrs) to 10f winner of 3 races, is a half-sister to 5 winners including the listed winner of 4 races Ronaldsay. The second dam, Crackling (by Electric), a modest 9f and 12f winner, is a half-sister to 4 winners including the Group 1 7f Moyglare Stud Stakes winner Bianca Nera and the dam of the Group 1 Fillies' Mile winner Simply Perfect. (R McCreery). *"A six furlong type 2-y-o, we haven't done much with her yet but she's a nice filly and one we like".*

783. CONFLICTING ★★★★
b.c. Kyllachy – Piper's Ash (Royal Academy). April 27. Fifth foal. €85,000Y. Goffs Orby. Hugo Merry. Half-brother to the fair 2012 2-y-o 5f winner Shrimper Roo (by Byron), to the modest 5f (including at 2 yrs) and 6f winner of 7 races Avonvalley (by Avonbridge) and the modest 9f (at 2 yrs) and 11f winner Diplomasi (by Iceman). The dam, a quite useful 2-y-o 5f winner, is a half-sister to 4 winners. The second dam, Merida (by Warning), a 1m winner in France and the USA, is a full or half-sister to 8 winners including the dual US Grade 2 1m winner Tychonic. (Mrs F H Hay). *"A nice colt that goes well, he was bought to be early and that's exactly what he's going to be. We'll get going early with him and he's shown a little bit even though he hasn't done any serious work yet. Showing up pretty well".*

784. CONSTANTINE ★★★ ♠
b.c. Holy Roman Emperor – Whatami (Daylami). March 26. First foal. 75,000Y. Tattersalls October Book 1. John Warren. The dam, a modest 12f placed maiden, is a sister to the 2-y-o listed Chesham Stakes winner Whazzat and a half-sister to 5 winners including the useful 7f (at 2 yrs), listed 1m and Italian Group 3 1m winner Whazzis. The second dam, Wosaita (by Generous), a

fair 12.3f placed maiden, is a half-sister to 10 winners including the very smart Group 1 10.5f Prix de Diane winner Rafha (herself the dam of four stakes winners including the Haydock Sprint Cup winner Invincible Spirit) and the Group 3 12f Blandford Stakes winner Chiang Mai (dam of the Group 1 Pretty Polly Stakes winner Chinese White). (The Royal Ascot Racing Club). *"A mid-season type 2-y-o, he's a good mover and a scopey type with a future".*

785. CORNCOCKLE ★★★

b.f. Invincible Spirit – Alovera (King's Best). March 28. Third foal. Closely related to the fair 2-y-o 5f winner Balm (by Oasis Dream) and half-sister to the fair 2012 7f placed 2-y-o Erodium (by Kyllachy). The dam, a fairly useful 2-y-o 6f winner, is a sister to the smart 6f (at 2 yrs) and listed 8.3f winner Army Of Angels and a half-sister to numerous winners including the useful 2-y-o 6f winner and Group 2 Lowther Stakes second Seraphina. The second dam, Angelic Sounds (by The Noble Player), a minor 2-y-o 5f winner, is a half-sister to 7 winners including the Group 1 Prix de la Foret winner Mount Abu. (Rockcliffe Stud). *"She goes nicely, she's not overly-big but she's a nice little filly and everything that this stud breeds seems to turn to gold. So it wouldn't surprise me if she was very useful".*

786. COULSTY (IRE) ★★★★

b.c. Kodiac – Hazium (In The Wings). March 22. Third foal. 57,000Y. Tattersalls October Book 2. Sackville/Donald. Half-brother to the fair 2012 2-y-o 6f and 7f winner Bonnie Lesley (by Iffraaj). The dam, a modest Irish 10f and 11f winner of 3 races, is a half-sister to 3 winners. The second dam, Safe Care (by Caerleon), is an unraced full or half-sister to 7 winners including the dual Group 3 winning sprinters Lugana Beach. (Lord Vestey). *"This is a nice, sharp horse. They wanted something to go to Royal Ascot so let's hope that's what they've got. He's done one piece of work which he did very nicely and he's improved since, so he's going the right way".*

787. CRYSTALIZED (IRE) ★★★

b.f. Rock Of Gibraltar – Magnificent Bell (Octagonal). May 18. Fifth foal. €38,000Y.

Tattersalls Ireland September. Peter & Ross Doyle. Half-sister to the fairly useful 10f to 2m and hurdles winner Inventor (by Alzao), to the quite useful 5f (at 2 yrs) to 10f winner Las Verglas Star (by Verglas) and a winner in Russia (by Celtic Swing). The dam is an unraced half-sister to 6 winners including the very useful 7.5f (at 2 yrs) and listed 10f winner Esyoueffcee (by Alzao). The second dam, Familiar (by Diesis), a fairly useful 3-y-o 1m winner, is a half-sister to 8 winners including the high-class Prix du Moulin winner and Epsom Oaks second All At Sea and the smart French dual Group 3 winner Over The Ocean. (Bull, Ivory, Woodcock, Hannon). *"She's nice, she's sharp and ready to run. Not a world-beater, but she'll win a maiden".*

788. CRYSTAL NYMPH (IRE) ★★★ ♠

ch.f. Rock Of Gibraltar – Flower Of Kent (Diesis). March 8. Third foal. 25,000Y. Tattersalls October Book 2. Will Edmeades. Half-sister to the fair 2012 6f and 7f placed 2-y-o Gravitational (by Rock Of Gibraltar). The dam, a fair 2-y-o 1m winner, is a half-sister to 2 winners. The second dam, Apple Of Kent (by Kris S), winner of the Grade 2 1m Shuvee Handicap, is a sister to one winner and a half-sister to 9 winners including the US dual Grade 2 winner True Flare (the dam of three graded stakes winners) and the Group/Grade 3 winners Set Alight, Capital Secret and War Zone. (Mrs E C Roberts). *"She was a bit late in but she's quite nice and probably one for the second half of the season".*

789. DIZZY MISS LIZZY (IRE) ★★★

gr.f. Verglas – Maramba (USA) (Hussonet). March 11. Second foal. Half-sister to the 2013 3-y-o 7f placed Wakeup Little Suzy (by Peintre Celebre). The dam, a fairly useful 2-y-o listed-placed 6f winner, is a half-sister to 3 winners. The second dam, Coco (by Storm Bird), a fairly useful listed-placed 1m winner of 2 races, is a half-sister to the US stakes winner and Grade 1 placed Last Romance. (P Newton). *"A nice, sharp little filly, she's not overly-big but she's eager to please and gets on with the job. We'll get going early with her".*

790. DJINNI ★★★

b.f. Invincible Spirit – La Persiana (Daylami).

April 24. Fifth foal. Half-sister to the 2012 7f placed 2-y-o Persepolis (by Dansili) and to the quite useful 7f (at 2 yrs) and 12f winner Qushchi (by Encosta De Lago). The dam, a very useful dual listed 10f winner, is a half-sister to 7 winners including the champion 2-y-o Grand Lodge (Group 1 7f Dewhurst Stakes and Group 1 1m St James's Palace Stakes winner) and the useful 1m listed winner Papabile. The second dam, La Papagena (by Habitat), is an unraced half-sister to 7 winners including the listed winners Lost Chord and Eagling. (Lady Howard de Walden). *"She had a touch of sore shins early on but she's fine again now. A nice, sharp filly that looks pretty speedy".*

791. DOVER THE MOON (IRE) ★★★

b.c. Bushranger – Gold Script (Script Ohio). April 13. Thirteenth foal. 100,000Y. Tattersalls October Book 1. John Warren. Half-brother to the quite useful 2012 2-y-o 6f winner Shahdaroba (by Haatef), to the Group 3 6f Railway Stakes winner and Group 1 7f Prix de la Salamandre second Honours List (by Danehill), the fairly useful dual 6f winner (including at 2 yrs) Cnocan Gold (by Danehill Dancer), the Italian 1m winner of 3 races and listed placed Zina La Belle (by Mark Of Esteem), the minor French 1m winner Ballpoint (by Oasis Dream) and the minor French winner of 5 races Supreme Talent (by Desert King). The dam, a French 5.5f (at 2 yrs) and listed 12f Prix de Thiberville winner of 5 races, is a half-sister to 5 winners. The second dam, Quiet Thoughts (by Thatching), won the Group 3 7f Athasi Stakes. (The Arts Club (London) Ltd). *"A big horse, but he's a good mover and not that backward considering his size".*

792. DOWNTON ★★★

b.c. Invincible Spirit – Jouet (Reprimand). March 18. Ninth foal. 115,000Y. Tattersalls October Book 1. Peter & Ross Doyle. Half-brother to the dual listed 6f winner Rising Shadow (by Efisio), to the quite useful 1m to 10f and hurdles winner Night Cru (by Night Shift), the quite useful 1m winner Chiefdom Prince (by Dansili) and the modest 6f winner Bonne (by Namid). The dam, a fair 7f placed 3-y-o, is a sister to the dual Group 3 winning

sprinter Deep Finesse and a half-sister to 5 winners and to the dams of the Group 1 Prix Jean Prat winner Dick Turpin and the Group 3 Cornwallis Stakes winner Halmahera. The second dam, Babycham Sparkle (by So Blessed), a quite useful 5f and 6f winner, is a half-sister to 6 winners and to the dams of the Group winners Premiere Cuvee, Monsieur Bond and River Falls. (Mrs Julie Wood). *"A typical Invincible Spirit, he's a nice, sharp 2-y-o. A good-moving horse with plenty of size about him".*

793. EMPEROR'S HOPE (IRE) ★★★

b.f. Holy Roman Emperor – Nadwah (Shadeed). Ninth foal. £17,000Y. Doncaster Premier. Peter & Ross Doyle. Sister to the unplaced 2012 2-y-o Amirah, closely related to the fair 6f winner Golden Taurus (by Danehill Dancer) and half-sister to the fairly useful French and UAE 6f to 1m winner Estihdaaf (by Distant View), to the modest 6f and 7f winner Dash Back (by Sahm) and the modest 1m winner Macanta (by Giant's Causeway). The dam, winner of the Group 3 5f Queen Mary Stakes and third in the Group 2 Lowther Stakes, is a sister to the Scandinavian Group 3 winner Musadif and is a half-sister to 6 winners. The second dam, Tadwin (by Never So Bold), was a very useful sprint winner of 3 races including the listed Hopeful Stakes and is a half-sister to 4 winners including the very smart sprinter Reesh and the dam of the smart sprinter Averti. (P A Byrne). *"A nice, sharp little filly. She's a bit of a cow but she's got ability and we'll get her out early doors and get on with her".*

794. ESTIDRAAJ (USA)

b.br.f. Medaglia d'Oro – Bsharpsonata (Pulpit). March 30. Second foal. $650,000Y. Saratoga August. Shadwell Estate Co. The dam, a winner of 7 races in the USA including the Grade 2 Forward Gal Stakes and Grade 2 Davona Dale Stakes, was Grade 1 placed twice and is a half-sister to the US Grade 2 winner Backtalk. The second dam, Apasioanta Sonata (by Affirmed), a listed stakes winner in the USA, is a half-sister to 3 winners. (Hamdan Al Maktoum).

795. EXCEED AND EXCEED ★★★ ♠

b.c. Exceed And Excel – Gandini (Night Shift). April 6. Seventh foal. £56,000Y. Doncaster

Premier. Peter & Ross Doyle. Brother to the modest 2012 2-y-o 7f winner Pippy and half-brother to the modest 2-y-o dual 5f and 3-y-o dual 6f winner Russian Bullet (by Royal Applause), to the Italian winner of 6 races and 5f listed-placed Powerful Speed (by Compton Place) and two minor winners in Italy and Spain by Diktat and Tagula. The dam, a minor winner at 3 yrs in Italy, is a full or half-sister to 8 winners. The second dam, Actress (by Arctic Tern), is a placed half-sister to 2 winners. (Mr A Al Mansoori). *"He's quite sharp and he'll be fairly early. A grand-looking 2-y-o".*

796. EXCHEQUER (IRE) ★★★★ ♠

ch.c. Exceed And Excel – Tara's Force (Acclamation). April 19. Second foal. €85,000Y. Goffs Orby. John Warren. The dam is an unraced half-sister to 4 winners including the 2-y-o Group 3 7f Somerville Tattersall Stakes winner and Group 3 Jersey Stakes third Ashram. The second dam, Tara's Girl (by Fayruz), a fairly useful 2-y-o dual 5f winner, was listed placed twice and fourth in the Queen Mary Stakes and is a full or half-sister to 5 winners. (Highclere Thoroughbred Racing – Lake Coniston). *"A really nice horse. He's a good-moving, big horse with a lot of scope and he could be anything. He wants a bit of time and that's exactly what he going to get. A nice colt".*

797. EXPERT (IRE) ★★★★

gr.c. Mastercraftsman – Raphimix (Linamix). March 12. Fourth foal. 26,000foal. Tattersalls December. Woodstock. Half-brother to the quite useful 12f winner Reflect (by Hurricane Run). The dam is an unraced half-sister to 2 minor winners in France. The second dam, Restifia (by Night Shift), a listed winner in France, is a half-sister to 3 winners. (Mrs Julie Wood). *"Quite an extravagant-moving horse that looks very much like his sire with his markings and everything. We like him, he's good-looking and a good mover. A little extravagant, but he'll learn to point his toe as he goes on".*

798. FIG ROLL ★★★★★ ♠

b.f. Bahamian Bounty – Cake (Acclamation). March 23. First foal. The dam, a useful 2-y-o listed 5f winner of 4 races, is a half-sister to

4 winners. The second dam, Carpet Lady (by Night Shift), a fair dual 6f placed 2-y-o, is a half-sister to 5 winners including the Hong Kong stakes winner Classic Fountain. (Mr D J Anderson). *"A sharp little filly. She's the first foal out of Cake and she's not dissimilar to her. A good mover, she might be our first winner".*

799. FILOSOFO (IRE) ★★

b.br.c. Teofilo – Think (Marchand de Sable). March 30. Fourth foal. 62,000Y. Tattersalls October Book 2. Peter & Ross Doyle. The dam, a French 2-y-o 6f winner, was third in the Group 3 Prix du Bois and is a half-sister to 8 minor winners. The second dam, Montagne Bleue (by Legend Of France), is a placed half-sister to 5 winners. (Mr P W Reglar). *"He's quite a nice horse but you won't see him out early. One that just needs a bit of time".*

800. GLEBE SPIRIT (IRE) ★★★★

b.c. Invincible Spirit – Starry Messenger (Galileo). April 24. Third foal. 190,000Y. Tattersalls October Book 1. Not sold. Half-brother to the fairly useful 2012 2-y-o 1m winner Starbright (by Duke Of Marmalade) and to the fair dual 1m winner (including at 2 yrs) The Giving Tree (by Rock Of Gibraltar). The dam, a fair 12f winner, is a half-sister to the US Grade 1 Gamely Handicap and multiple Grade 2 1m winner Tuscan Evening and to the dual listed winner Barbican. The second dam, The Faraway Tree (by Suave Dancer), a very useful 6f (at 2 yrs) and 14f winner, was second in the Group 2 Park Hill Stakes and is a half-sister to 12 winners including the high-class 9.3f Prix d'Ispahan winner Sasuru, the high-class Challenge Stakes and Jersey Stakes winner Sally Rous and the dam of the French 1,000 Guineas winner Rose Gypsy. (D J Barry). *"I like him a lot, he's a nice horse that wants a bit of time and six/seven furlongs. A real nice colt".*

801. GOLD TOP (IRE) ★★★

ch.f. Teofilo – Top Row (Observatory). February 6. Fourth foal. £34,000Y. Doncaster Premier. Peter & Ross Doyle. Half-sister to the modest 2012 6f placed 2-y-o Moss Top (by Moss Vale) and to the useful 2-y-o 6f winner and Group 2 5f Norfolk Stakes third Crown Dependency (by Acclamation). The dam is an unplaced half-sister to 9 winners including the useful 2-y-o

Group 3 7f C L Weld Park Stakes winner Rag Top and the dams of the listed winner Elhamri and the 2-y-o Goffs Million winner Lucky General. The second dam, Petite Epaulette (by Night Shift), a fair 5f winner at 2 yrs, is a full or half-sister to 3 winners including the Group 1 1m Gran Criterium second Line Dancer. (D Boocock). *"We thought she'd be sharp and early but she's done a piece of work which suggests she might need a bit more time. She'll not take long though".*

802. GREEN RUN ★★★

b.f. Compton Place – Gee Kel (Danehill Dancer). February 24. Third foal. 70,000Y. Tattersalls October Book 2. David Redvers. Half-sister to the useful 2012 2-y-o dual 6f winner Cour Valant (by Bahamian Bounty) and to the fair 10f and 12f winner Arley Hall (by Excellent Art). The dam, a useful 6f winner at 2 yrs in Ireland and second in the Group 3 6f Swordlestown Sprint Stakes, is a half-sister to 4 winners. The second dam, Shir Dar (by Lead On Time), won the US Grade 2 Palomar Handicap and is a half-sister to 9 winners. (Qatar Racing Ltd). *"I quite like her and she looks as though she's got a bit of speed".*

803. HEDGE END (IRE) ★★★

gr.f. Verglas – Trilemma (Slip Anchor). March 10. Fourth foal. 11,000Y. Tattersalls October Book 2. Peter & Ross Doyle. Half-sister to the useful listed 10f placed Mariner's Cross (by Dubawi) and to the hurdles winner In A Nutshell (by Xaar). The dam, a quite useful dual 2m winner, is a half-sister to 4 winners. The second dam, Thracian (by Green Desert), a fairly useful 2-y-o 6f and 7f winner, is a half-sister to 12 winners including the Group 2 12f Ribblesdale Stakes winner Third Watch, the Group 3 Prix Foy winner Richard of York, the Group 2 Premio Dormello winner Three Tails (herself dam of the high-class colts Tamure and Sea Wave), the Group 3 Fred Darling Stakes winner Maysoon and the dams of the Group winners Lend A Hand and Talented. (Grimes, Ivory, Bull, Hannon). *"She's like a little bullock and she'll be racing in April. One of the early types".*

804. HYMENAIOS (IRE) ★★★

ch.c. Danehill Dancer – Wedding Morn (Sadler's Wells). March 27. Seventh foal. 350,000foal. Tattersalls December. Blandford Bloodstock. Brother to the useful 2012 2-y-o Group 2 6f Railway Stakes winner Probably and to the fair 9f and 10f winner Canary Wharf. The dam is an unplaced half-sister to 2 winners including the dam of the US stakes winner and Grade 2 placed Cedar Mountain. The second dam, Wedding Bouquet (by Kings Lake), a useful 5f to 7f winner (including the Group 3 C L Park Stakes), was Group 1 placed in Ireland at 2 yrs and subsequently won the Grade 3 6.5f Monrovia Handicap in the USA and is closely related to the outstanding Derby, Irish Derby and King George winner Generous and a half-sister to the Oaks winner and good broodmare Imagine. (Sheikh Mohammed bin Khalifa Al Thani). *"A nice, big, strong horse with a lot of scope. He moves nicely, he was quite expensive but he looks to have all the attributes for a horse that cost so much. A good-moving horse with a good pedigree, but we haven't done anything with him yet".*

805. ICE SLICE (IRE) ★★★

b.c. Dark Angel – Ice Rock (Rock Of Gibraltar). January 25. Third foal. €9,000foal. Goffs November. Woodstock. The dam, placed twice at 3 yrs in France, is a half-sister to 3 listed winners. The second dam, Choc Ice (by Kahyasi), won the Grade 1 E P Taylor Stakes and was Group 1 placed twice in France and is a half-sister to 3 winners including the Canadian Grade 2 winner Royal Oath. (Mrs Julie Wood). *"By a very good stallion that seems to do well here, he's a nice colt but we haven't got going with him yet".*

806. JALLAL (IRE) ★★★★

b.c. Royal Applause – Peaceful Kingdom (King Of Kings). March 23. Third foal. 100,000Y. Tattersalls October Book 1. Mandore International. Half-brother to the fair 2012 2-y-o 7f winner Asgardella (by Duke Of Marmalade) and to the quite useful Irish 2-y-o 1m winner Righteous Man (by Mr Greeley). The dam is an unraced half-sister to 4 winners including the US Grade 1 Man O'War Stakes winner Magistretti. The second dam, Ms

Strike Zone (by Deputy Minister), won once in the USA and is a half-sister to 6 other minor winners. (Sheikh J B H bin Khalifa Al Thani). *"A really nice colt, he could be a Royal Ascot sort and although we haven't worked him yet he's very pleasing to look at. We like him a lot".*

807. JANA ★★★
ch.f. Compton Place – Hasten (Lear Fan). February 2. Eighth foal. 8,000Y. Doncaster Premier. Not sold. Sister to the quite useful 2012 2-y-o 7f winner Great Run and half-sister to the fair UAE 6f and 7f winner Myownway (by Dubawi), to the fair 1m winner Hasty Lady (by Dubai Destination), the modest 2-y-o 7f winner Gassal and a minor winner abroad by Johannesburg. The dam was placed twice in the USA and is a half-sister to 6 winners including the 2-y-o Group 3 Autumn Stakes winner and Group 1 Racing Post Trophy second Fantastic View. The second dam, Promptly (by Lead On Time), a quite useful 6f winner here, subsequently won a minor stakes event over 1m in the USA and is a half-sister to 7 winners. (Barry Bull). *"A sharp little filly, she'll be running early over five furlongs and hopefully she'll be winning early".*

808. JEREMOS (IRE) ★★★
b.c. Jeremy – Bon Ton Roulet (Hawk Wing). February 9. Second foal. 30,000Y. Tattersalls October Book 2. Amanda Skiffington. The dam, a moderate maiden, was placed fourth three times over 1m and is a half-sister to the 2-y-o Group 2 6f Lowther Stakes winner Infamous Angel. The second dam, Evangeline (by Sadler's Wells), is an unraced half-sister to 4 winners. (Mr G Moss). *"A big horse that'll take a bit of time but he's nice. He has a big action and we'll just take our time with him".*

809. KAMALAYA ★★★★
b.c. Teofilo – Saint Ann (Geiger Counter). March 31. Tenth foal. £52,000Y. Doncaster Premier. Peter & Ross Doyle. Half-brother to the fairly useful 2-y-o 1m winner and listed Predominate Stakes second Sienna Storm, to the modest 10f winner White Moss (both by Peintre Celebre), the quite useful 1m winner Heversham (by Octagonal), the fair 10f winner State Visit (by Dr Fong). The dam, placed fourth once at 2 yrs, is a half-sister to

5 winners. The second dam, Swan Princess (by So Blessed), won the Group 1 Phoenix Stakes and is a half-sister to 6 winners including Primo Dominie. (J Palmer-Brown, Potensis Ltd, Chris Giles). *"A really nice colt. Six or seven furlongs later in the year will be right for him, he's got a lot of scope, appears to be very sound and he's well worth his money at the moment. If he went to the breeze-ups he'd make an awful lot of money".*

810. KARRAAR ★★★
b.c. Dubawi – Maghya (Mujahid). February 10. Second foal. Half-brother to Rabdaan (by Sakhee), unplaced in one start at 2 yrs in 2012. The dam, a quite useful 1m winner of 3 races, is a half-sister to the French winner and listed-placed Argos Quercus. The second dam, Khaizarana (by Alhaarth), a quite useful listed-placed 7f winner, is a half-sister to several winners. (Hamdan Al Maktoum). *"A big, strong sort, he'll take a bit of time so you'll see him later on over seven furlongs".*

811. KINLOSS ★★★
ch.f. Kheleyf – Celtic Cross (Selkirk). February 6. Half-sister to the 7f and 1m winner Broad Cairn (by Green Desert), to the 9f and 10f winner Maclean (by Machiavellian) and the 10f, 14f and hurdles winner Fretwork (by Galileo) – all quite useful. The dam, a useful 1m winner, is a half-sister to 7 winners including the useful 2-y-o 7f winner Right Approach and the useful stayer Temple Way. The second dam, Abbey Strand (by Shadeed), a fair Irish 10f winner, is a half-sister to numerous winners including the very useful 2-y-o Group 3 1m Prix La Rochette winner Grand Chelem and the smart 2-y-o Group 3 1m winner Splendid Moment. (The Queen). *"Quite a nice filly, the family don't seem to make 2-y-o's, but this one is sharp and shows plenty".*

812. LADY CROSSMAR (IRE) ★★★
b.f. Duke Of Marmalade – Rekindled Cross (Cape Cross). February 23. First foal. 24,000Y. Tattersalls October Book 1. Not sold. The dam, placed once at 4 yrs in Italy, is a half-sister to 7 winners including the Australian Group 2 winner Rekindled Interest and the US Grade 3 winner Where We Left Off. The second dam,

Rekindled Affair (by Rainbow Quest), is an unraced half-sister to 4 winners and to the unraced smart broodmare Summer Trysting (the dam of two Group winners). (Middleham Racing VI). *"A nice, petite filly with a good action, she needs to grow a bit so we haven't done anything with her yet".*

813. LADY EMMUSKA ★★★ ♣

b.f. Sir Percy – Medicea Sidera (Medicean). January 28. First foal. €70,000Y. Goffs Orby. Peter & Ross Doyle. The dam, a fairly useful triple 7f winner, was listed-placed twice and is a half-sister to 2 winners. The second dam, Broughtons Motto (by Mtoto), a modest 5f (at 2 yrs) to 10f winner, is a half-sister to 4 winners. (Thurloe Thoroughbreds XXXI).

814. LAHUROOB ★★★

b.c. Kyllachy – Complimentary Pass (Danehill). March 26. Eighth foal. 110,000Y. Tattersalls October Book 2. Peter & Ross Doyle. Half-brother to the useful 2-y-o 7f winner and Group 3 7f Acomb Stakes second Gweebarra (by Lomitas), to the useful 7f (at 2 yrs) and 9f winner Mafaaz (by Medicean), the fair 14f and hurdles winner Priors Gold (by Sakhee) and the modest 1m and 10f winner Spunger (by Fraam). The dam, a quite useful 1m placed maiden, is a half-sister to 5 minor winners. The second dam, Capo Di Monte (by Final Straw), a smart 6f (at 2 yrs), dual 10f listed and subsequent Grade 3 11f winner in the USA, is a half-sister to 5 winners including the Group 1 12f Aral-Pokal winner Wind In Her Hair (herself dam of the Japan Cup winner Deep Impact). (Hamdan Al Maktoum). *"A nice, sharp sort, we've been pleased with him and he's done well since he came in so hopefully he'll be like most of the Kyllachy's and make a racehorse".*

815. LANGAVAT (IRE) ★★★

b.c. Bushranger – Bishop's Lake (Lake Coniston). February 21. Fifth foal. 50,000Y. Tattersalls October Book 1. Peter & Ross Doyle. Half-brother to the modest 6f (at 2 yrs) to 9f and hurdles winner Lakeman (by Tillerman), to the fair 9f winner Euphrasia (by Windsor Knot) and the modest 1m winner Strike The Deal (by Chineur). The dam, a quite useful dual 2-y-o 6f winner, was listed-placed and is a half-

sister to 6 winners including the useful 2-y-o 6f winner and Group 2 6f Gimcrack Stakes third Sir Reginald and to the smart 2-y-o 6f winner and Group 1 1m Racing Post Trophy third Henrik. The second dam, Clincher Club (by Polish Patriot), a fair 5f (at 2 yrs) and 7.5f winner, is a half-sister to 9 winners including the dual listed winner Paradise Isle. (Kennet Valley Thoroughbreds II). *"A big, strong horse for a 2-y-o, he's done one piece of work and did it very nicely. He appears to be a very sound, likeable colt and we should see a fair bit of him this year".*

816. LA TINTA BAY ★★★

b.f. Compton Place – Cumana Bay (Dansili). March 6. First foal. The dam, a quite useful 5f (at 2 yrs), 7f and 1m winner, is a half-sister to one winner. The second dam, Mayaro Bay (by Robellino), a very useful 6f (at 2 yrs) to 1m winner, is a half-sister to 4 winners including the Group 2 7f Rockfel Stakes winner Distant Valley. (J R Shannon). *"I quite like her, she looks as if she can go a bit and she'll be fairly early".*

817. LEGEND RISING (IRE) ★★★★

ch.c. Tamayuz – Encouragement (Royal Applause). April 19. Fourth foal. €80,000Y. Goffs Orby. Peter & Ross Doyle. Half-brother to the quite useful 6f (at 2 yrs) to 1m winner of 4 races Joe Eile (by Iffraaj) and to a winner in Hong Kong by Marju. The dam, a fair dual 6f placed 2-y-o here, was later placed in the USA. She is a sister to the winner and listed-placed Approval and a half-sister to 4 winners including the very useful Group 2 6f Moet and Chandon Rennen winner Sharp Prod and to the unraced dam of the Group 2 German 2,000 Guineas winner Royal Power. The second dam, Gentle Persuasion (by Bustino), a fairly useful 2-y-o 6f winner, was fourth in both the Princess Margaret Stakes and the Rockfel Stakes and is a half-sister to 11 winners. (Mr M S Al Shahi). *"A particularly nice horse, he's good-looking, has a good action and is one for six/seven furlongs. He's a sound horse that appears to go very well".*

818. LIGEIA ★★★★

b.f. Rail Link – Elegant Beauty (Olden Times). March 24. Third foal. 2,000Y. Tattersalls December. Not sold. Half-sister to the modest 2012 7f fourth placed 2-y-o Royal Guinevere (by Invincible Spirit). The dam is an unraced half-sister to 8 winners including the champion 2-y-o Grand Lodge and the listed winners La Persiana and Papabile. The second dam, La Papagena (by Habitat), is an unraced half-sister to 7 winners including the listed winners Lost Chord and Eagling. (The Pineapple Stud). *"She's got a pedigree as long as your arm and she's a nice filly that's done really well since she came in. She was very cheap, but I like her a lot and although on pedigree you'd think she'd want time she's showing plenty now. She's a big filly and ideally she'll benefit for another six weeks, but she'll definitely win".* TRAINERS' BARGAIN BUY

819. LILBOURNE LASS ★★★ ♠

ch.f. Pastoral Pursuits – Talampaya (Elusive Quality). January 15. Second foal. £16,000Y. Doncaster Premier. Peter & Ross Doyle. The dam is an unraced half-sister to 3 winners. The second dam, Argentina (by Storm Cat), a minor US 2-y-o winner, is a sister to a US stakes-placed winner and a half-sister to 5 winners. (Mrs S Ensor). *"She's a nice, sharp filly but bear in mind that there's a question mark over the temperament of a horse with a Pastoral Pursuits/Elusive Quality cross. But at the moment she seems to be very nice, she's in the Supersprint and you never know".*

820. LILBOURNE LEGACY ★★★

b.c. Kyllachy – Gold And Blue (Bluebird). February 14. Fourteenth foal. £60,000Y. Doncaster Premier. Peter & Ross Doyle. Half-brother to the quite useful 6f (at 2 yrs) to 9f winner of 7 races Blue Star, to the quite useful 2-y-o 5f and 6f winner Blue Reigns, the modest 7f winner Blue Mystique (all by Whittingham), the quite useful 5f (at 2 yrs) and 6f winner of 6 races Blue Kite (by Silver Kite), the quite useful triple 5f winner (including at 2 yrs) Westbrook Blue (by Kingsinger), the quite useful 5f winner of 8 races Jodeeka (by Fraam), the fair 6f winner of 6 races Bid For Gold (by Auction Ring) and the moderate 1m winner It's A Deal (by Indian Haven). The dam, a lightly-raced Irish maiden, was placed fourth once over 9f at 2 yrs and is a full or half-sister to 4 winners. The second dam, Golden Grundy (by Grundy), a winner at

2 yrs and second in the Pretty Polly Stakes, is a half-sister to 6 winners. (Mr A T J Russell). *"He's a nice horse but he's taking time to learn his job and he's gone backward. We thought he'd be sharp but he's quite lazy and he's taking some time to learn. There's a racehorse in there somewhere and I'm certain that the man that owns him will find it. He's a very lucky owner".*

821. LINDART (ITY) ★★★

ch.c. Dutch Art – Linda Surena (Southern Halo). May 4. Fifth foal. €57,000Y. Tattersalls Ireland September. Peter & Ross Doyle. Half-brother to a minor 3-y-o winner in Italy by Medicean. The dam is an unraced sister to the Argentine dual Group 2 winner and Group 1 placed The Lord. The second dam, Lourdes (by Ringaro), is an unraced sister to a Group 3 winner in Argentina. (Potensis Ltd & Mr Chris Giles). *"He's a real nice colt and I expect he'll be running early".*

822. LORD LEXINGTON ★★★

ch.c. Dutch Art – Spiralling (Pivotal). April 15. Third foal. 62,000Y. Tattersalls December. Peter & Ross Doyle. Closely related to the unplaced 2012 2-y-o Multi Fours (by Medicean). The dam is an unraced half-sister to 5 winners including Producer (Group 3 Supreme Stakes). The second dam, River Saint (by Irish River), is a placed half-sister to 5 winners including the multiple US Grade 1 winner Serena's Song (herself the dam of four Group winners including Group 1 Coronation Stakes winner Sophisticat). (Middleham Park Racing XXIII). *"Related to Producer, he's not as big and strong as he was but he's still a nice, big horse. Looks to have gears but he's only cantered so far".*

823. MAGNUS MAXIMUS ★★★ ♠

b.c. Holy Roman Emperor – Chanrossa (Galileo). March 23. First foal. Tattersalls October Book 1. 190,000Y. Amanda Skiffington. The dam, a modest 10f winner, is a sister to a winner and a half-sister to the very useful 1m and subsequent US Grade 3 9f winner Diamond Tycoon and to the useful listed 11f winner and Group 3 Lillie Langtry second Cassique Lady. The second dam, Palacoona (by Last Tycoon), a French listed 1m winner, was Group 3 placed and subsequently won in the USA and is a half-sister to 8 winners. *"A lovely big horse but he needs time and you won't see him until much later on".*

824. MAHLAH ★★★

b.f. *Acclamation – Somerset Falls (Red Ransom)*. February 3. Second foal. 190,000Y. Tattersalls October Book 2. Tony Nerses. Half-sister to Manzanita (by Barathea), unplaced in one start at 2 yrs in 2012. The dam, a modest maiden, was placed twice over 7f including at 2 yrs and is a half-sister to 5 winners including the Group 1 Prix Ganay winner Cutlass Bay, the Group 2 12f King Edward VII Stakes winner Boscobel and the useful 2-y-o 8.3f winner and subsequent US Grade 2 placed Crested. The second dam, Dunnes River (by Danzig), a quite useful 3-y-o 1m winner, is a sister to the one winner and a half-sister to 5 winners including the US Grade 3 winner and Grade 1 second Bayeaux. (Saleh Al Homaizi). *"A nice filly, she cost a lot of money and we haven't really done anything with her as yet, but I should imagine she'll be a five/six furlong 2-y-o".*

825. MALACHIM MIST (IRE) ★★★

gr.c. *Dark Angel – Sixfields Flyer (Desert Style)*. March 28. Third foal. £45,000Y. Doncaster Premier. Peter & Ross Doyle. Half-brother to the fair 2012 6f winner Rich Forever (by Camacho). The dam, a moderate 1m placed maiden, is a half-sister to 6 winners including Rich Ground (Group 3 July Stakes) and the Group 3 Princess Margaret Stakes third Bandanna. The second dam, Gratclo (by Belfort), a modest winner of 5 races from 2 to 4 yrs, is a half-sister to 3 winners. (Mr M Daniels). *"We thought he might run in the Brocklesbury but he went backwards. Now we're thinking he won't be ready until the six furlong races".*

826. MALORY TOWERS ★★★

b.f. *Giant's Causeway – Dalisay (Sadler's Wells)*. February 2. Fifth living foal. Half-sister to a minor 4-y-o winner in the USA by Seeking The Gold. The dam, a fair 10f and 12f placed maiden, is a half-sister to 5 winners including the Irish listed winner and Group 3 second Dabtiya. The second dam, Dabiliya (by Vayrann), is an unraced half-sister to 12 winners including the French Derby winner and high-class sire Darshaan, the Prix

Vermeille winner and top-class broodmare Darara and the dam of the Coronation Cup winner Daliapour. *"This is a nice filly. She has a good action, she's improved since she came in and she's big and tall. One for seven furlongs this year and she'll be OK".*

827. MANDERLEY (IRE) ★★★★

gr.f. *Clodovil – Three Days In May (Cadeaux Genereux)*. April 28. Fourth living foal. 150,000Y. Tattersalls October Book 1. Peter & Ross Doyle. Sister to the very smart 7f (including at 2 yrs) and 1m winner, Group 1 Prix Jean Prat second and Group 1 St James's Palace third Gregorian and to the fairly useful 2-y-o 6f winner Kalam Daleel. The dam, a fair 3-y-o 6f winner, is a half-sister to 8 winners including the very useful 6f winner and Cheveley Park Stakes, Queen Mary Stakes and Cherry Hinton Stakes placed Crazee Mental - herself dam of the multiple Group 2 winner Premio Loco. The second dam, Corn Futures (by Nomination), a fair 2-y-o 6f winner, is a half-sister to 7 winners. (Mrs Julie Wood). *"A nice, big filly, she could be anything and I like her a lot but she'll need a bit of time. One of the biggest 2-y-o's we've got".*

828. MANOR WAY (IRE) ★★★★

b.c. *Holy Roman Emperor – Cannikin (Lahib)*. February 26. Eighth living foal. 50,000Y. Tattersalls October Book 2. Peter & Ross Doyle. Half-brother to the fairly useful Irish dual 6f winner and listed-placed Moone Cross, to the fair 1m winner on her only start Star Lahib (both by Cape Cross), the Italian winner of 6 races (including over 9f at 2 yrs) Gioell (by In The Wings), the modest 6f (at 2 yrs) to 12f winner of 8 races Icannshift (by Night Shift) and a winner over hurdles by Alhaarth. The dam, a quite useful 2-y-o 6f winner, is a half-sister to 7 winners including the multiple listed winner Tout A Coup. The second dam, Coupe d'Hebe (by Ile de Bourbon), won at 2 yrs and is a half-sister to 6 winners. (Mrs A Williams). *"A big, good-looking colt with a good way of going, he'll be a very nice six furlong horse".*

829. MIDNIGHT RAMBLER (IRE) ★★★

ch.c. *Compton Place – Crowd Pleaser (Royal Applause)*. February 28. First foal. 62,000Y. Tattersalls October Book 2. Peter & Ross Doyle.

The dam is an unraced half-sister to 3 winners including the Irish listed winner and Group 3 third Truly Mine. The second dam, Truly Yours (by Barathea), a 2-y-o 1m winner in France, is a half-sister to 5 winners including Dream Peace (Group 2 Prix de la Nonette) and the French 2,000 Guineas second Catcher In The Rye. (M.A.C Buckley). *"A nice, big horse, he's typical of the sire and clean-winded which is always a worry with that stallion, but just like all of them he seems to have a lot of speed. Hopefully he'll turn into the nice, sharp 2-y-o he was bought for".*

830. MIDNITE ANGEL (IRE) ★★★
gr.f. Dark Angel – Two Sets To Love (Cadeaux Genereux). February 14. Fourth foal. £26,000Y. Doncaster Premier. Peter & Ross Doyle. Sister to the fair 7f and 1m winner Emman Bee and half-sister to the fair 6f (at 2 yrs) to 1m winner of 4 races Sabatini (by One Cool Cat) and a winner in Spain by Whipper. The second dam, Mirage (by Red Sunset), a dual listed winner in Germany, is a sister to the multiple listed winner Red Hero and a half-sister to 7 winners. (Elaine Chivers & Richard Kidner). *"She did a nice piece bit of work the other day, she has quite a high knee action and she's quite heavy, but she's learning quickly and if she continues to improve you'll see her soon. She ought to go close first time out".*

831. MIGHTY FORCE (IRE) ★★★
b.c. Acclamation – Ikan (Sri Pekan). April 21. Sixth foal. £40,000Y. Doncaster Premier. Peter & Ross Doyle. Half-brother to the fair 2012 7f placed 2-y-o Athman (by Sri Pekan), to the modest 5f winner Betty Brook (by Refuse To Bend) and the moderate 6f and 7f winner Exceedingly Good (by Exceed And Excel). The dam, a fairly useful winner over 5f and 6f (at 2 yrs) and listed-placed, is a half-sister to 7 winners including the listed-placed Valjarv and Qadar. The second dam, Iktidar (by Green Desert), a quite useful Irish 1m placed maiden, is a half-sister to 6 winners. (Mr M S Al Shahi). *"A little bit backward for an Acclamation, he hasn't kicked into gear yet so we're giving him a bit of time. A nice, strong sort, with a good action".*

832. MILDENHALL ★★★
ch.f. Compton Place – Night Kiss (Night Shift). February 14. Fourth foal. £24,000Y. Doncaster Premier. Not sold. Sister to the fairly useful 2-y-o 7f winner Minal and half-sister to the quite useful 5f (at 2 yrs) to 11f winner Avon River (by Avonbridge). The dam was a fair dual 7f winner at 2 and 3 yrs. The second dam, Roxy (by Rock City), is an unraced half-sister to 3 winners including the Irish 1,000 Guineas second Goodnight Kiss. (Barry Bull). *"A nice filly, she's a bit leggy and one for the middle of the season".*

833. MUHEED (IRE) ★★★★
b.c. Raven's Pass – Wolf Cleugh (Last Tycoon). January 31. Eleventh foal. 130,000Y. Tattersalls October Book 1. Mandore International. Half-brother to the Group 2 5f Prix du Gros-Chene and dual Group 3 5f winner Moss Vale (by Shinko Forest), to the fairly useful 6f winner and Group 3 6f third Alexander Youth, the modest 2-y-o 6f winner Spennymore (both by Exceed And Excel), the fairly useful 6f (including at 2 yrs) and 5f winner of 5 races Jarrow (by Shamardal), the fairly useful dual 1m winner Natural Force (by King's Best), the quite useful 6f winner of 6 races (including at 2 yrs) Cape Vale (by Cape Cross), the quite useful 10f winner of 3 races Street Life (by Dolphin Street) and the modest 7f winner Red Trump (by Red Clubs). The dam is an unplaced half-sister to 8 winners including the Irish listed 6f winner King's College. The second dam, Santa Roseanna (by Caracol), won the listed 9f The Minstrel Stakes, was second in the Group 2 6f Moyglare Stud Stakes and is a half-sister to 9 winners. (Sheikh J B H bin Khalifa Al Thani). *"This is a really nice horse. He's had a couple of niggling problems but he's a lovely, big horse by a stallion that's seriously going places. This fellow will help him do that and we'll take our time with him. One to look out for, even if it takes some time".*

834. MUMTAZA ★★★
b.f. Nayef – Natagora (Divine Light). March 31. Second foal. Sister to the quite useful 2012 2-y-o 6f winner Rayaheen. The dam, a champion 2-y-o filly and winner of the Group 1 Cheveley Park Stakes and the 1,000

Guineas, is a half-sister to 2 winners in France (including one over jumps). The second dam, Reinamixa (by Linamix), a minor French 11f winner, is a half-sister to 6 winners including the French listed winner Reinstate. (Hamdan Al Maktoum). *"She's a nice little filly out of a very good mare. Not as big as her half-sister Rayaheen but she looks like being a bit sharper".*

835. MUNFALLET (IRE) ★★★★ ♠

b.c. Royal Applause – Princess Mood (Muhtarram). February 26. Eighth foal. 220,000Y. Tattersalls October Book 1. Shadwell Estate Co. Half-brother to the very useful 6f and 7f listed winner and subsequent UAE Group 1 placed Kingsgate Prince (by Desert Sun), to the useful 2-y-o listed 7f winner of 6 races Captain Ramius (by Kheleyf), the fairly useful 6f and 7f winner Avenuesnalleyways (by Bertolini), the fair 2-y-o 6f winner Barolo Top (by Amadeus Wolf), the fair 8.5f winner Smugglers Bay (by Celtic Swing) and the modest 7f winner Old English (by Marju). The dam, placed over 1m in Germany, is a half-sister to 6 winners in Germany and Italy. The second dam, Princess Nana (by Bellypha), won the Group 2 German 1,000 Guineas and is a half-sister to 6 winners. (Hamdan Al Maktoum). *"A really nice colt and one of our nicest. He has a good action and I wish we had a few more like him. Six or seven furlongs will suit him this year".*

836. MUNJALLY ★★★★

b.c. Acclamation – Parabola (Galileo). March 15. First foal. £75,000Y. Doncaster Premier. Peter & Ross Doyle. The dam, a fair Irish 7f to 11f placed maiden, is a half-sister to 2 minor winners. The second dam, Zietory (by Zieten), a 2-y-o 6f and 3-y-o dual 1m listed winner, is a half-sister to 4 winners. (Hamdan Al Maktoum). *"We like him a lot, he's a typical Acclamation and he's showing up well. He looks a very nice colt and one that will be winning early, over five or six furlongs. He could be a Royal Ascot sort".*

837. MUSICAL COMEDY ★★★

b.c. Royal Applause – Spinning Top (Alzao). March 3. Half-brother to the fairly useful 7f and 1m winner of 4 races (including at 2 yrs)

Humdrum (by Dr Fong), to the fairly useful 7f (at 2 yrs) to 11f winner Full Toss (by Nayef) and the moderate triple 1m winner Life's A Whirl (by Machiavellian). The dam, a useful 10f winner, is a half-sister to numerous winners including the fairly useful 3-y-o 7f and subsequent US dual 9f winner Daytime. The second dam, Zenith (by Shirley Heights), was a fairly useful 2-y-o 8.5f winner. (The Queen). *"A really nice colt, I like him and he goes very well. He might be fairly early".*

838. MUSICORA ★★★ ♠

b.f. Acclamation – Belladera (Alzao). March 17. Ninth living foal. €115,000Y. Arqana Deauville August. Peter & Ross Doyle. Sister to the quite useful 6f and 7f winner and listed-placed Little Scotland and half-sister to the quite useful Irish 12f to 2m winner Mrs Gillow (by Danzero), to the Italian winner of 8 races from 2 to 5 yrs and listed-placed Sgiaff (by Spinning World), the fair 7f, 1m and subsequent Italian winner Satyricon (by Dr Fong) and the modest 2-y-o 5f winner Irrational (by Kyllachy). The dam won over 6f at 2 yrs and is a half-sister to 7 winners including the listed Woodcote Stakes winner Silca Blanka. The second dam, Reality (by Known Fact), won twice at 3 yrs and was third in the Group 3 Premio Royal Mares and is a half-sister to 6 winners including the Group 2 Champagne Stakes winner Unblest. (The Three Points Partnership). *"She goes really well and is a typical Acclamation. Six furlongs should suit her and she should be racing before Ascot".*

839. MUTAMAKKIN (IRE) ★★★★

b.c. Shamardal – Princess Speedfit (Desert Prince). March 20. Seventh foal. 245,000Y. Tattersalls October Book 2. Peter & Ross Doyle. Half-brother to the modest 2012 6f placed 2-y-o Speedfit Boy (by Red Clubs), to the useful 6f winner of 5 races (including a 2-y-o listed event) Imperial Guest (by Imperial Dancer), to the fairly useful 6f (at 2 yrs) and 7f winner Excellent Guest (by Exceed And Excel) and a winner abroad by Barathea Guest. The dam, a fair 8.3f winner at 3 yrs, is a half-sister to 5 winners including the French listed 12f winner and dual Group 2 placed Sibling Rival. The second dam, Perfect Sister (by Perrault), a minor French winner, is a sister to the US Grade 1 winner Frankly Perfect and a half-sister to the French listed winner and US Grade 1 placed Franc Argument. (Hamdan Al Maktoum). *"A nice colt of a great colour, he's a little bit plain of his head but he was a really nice yearling and he hasn't let us down. I'm very hopeful of him and he's quite a neat little horse too".*

840. MUTAWATHEA ★★★★
b.c. Exceed And Excel – Esteemed Lady (Mark Of Esteem). February 26. Fourth foal. Half-brother to the quite useful dual 6f (at 2 yrs) and 1m winner Edgewater (by Bahamian Bounty) and to the fair 5f and 6f winner of 7 races Sleepy Blue Ocean (by Oasis Dream). The dam, placed once over 6f at 2 yrs, is a half-sister to 4 winners including the 2-y-o Group 2 6f Richmond Stakes winner Revenue. The second dam, Bareilly (by Lyphard), is an unraced three-parts sister to the Group 3 1m Prix de la Grotte winner Baya and the Italian Group 2 winner Narrative. (Hamdan Al Maktoum). *"One for six furlongs, he's doing everything nicely, he's a good-sized colt and a real nice 2-y-o".*

841. NOS GALAN (IRE) ★★
b.c. Dylan Thomas – Chalice Wells (Sadler's Wells). March 27. Fifth foal. €20,000foal. Goffs November. Woodstock. Half-brother to the fair 10f and hurdles winner Jolly Roger (by Oratorio). The dam is an unraced sister to the Group 1 Coronation Cup and triple Group 1 Ascot Gold Cup winner Yeats and a half-sister to the Group 2 Royal Whip Stakes winner Solskjaer and the Japanese stakes winner and Grade 1 fourth Tsukuba Symphony. The second dam, Lyndonville (by Top Ville), a minor Irish 3-y-o 14f winner, is a half-sister to 4 winners including the Group 1 Fillies Mile winner Ivanka. (Mrs Julie Wood). *"A big, leggy horse he's going quite nicely and he's a very good mover, but he's quite backward".*

842. ORAYDA (IRE) ★★★★
ch.f. New Approach – Wadaat (Diktat). March 6. First foal. 400,000Y. Tattersalls October Book 1. Mandore International. The dam, a useful 1m winner and second in the Group 2 Italian Oaks, is a half-sister to 4 winners including the German 2-y-o winner and Italian Group

3 placed Mrs Snow. The second dam, Shining Vale (by Twilight Agenda), is an unraced half-sister to the German and Italian Group 2 winner Walzerkoenigin (herself dam of the Group 1 German Derby winner Wiener Walzer). (Sheikh J B H bin Khalifa Al Thani). *"This filly is a Queen! We'll take our time with her because she may be an Oaks filly. Really nice, very attractive, she'll want seven furlongs or a mile and she's a very classy filly".*

843. ORIEL ★★★ ♠
b.f. Fastnet Rock – Labisa (High Chaparral). February 21. First foal. 60,000Y. Tattersalls October Book 1. John Warren. The dam, a fair 3-y-o 7f winner, is a half-sister to 3 winners including the 6f (at 2 yrs) and Group 2 7f Challenge Stakes winner Stimulation. The second dam, Damiana (by Thatching), was placed 5 times in France at 2 and 3 yrs and is a half-sister to 4 winners including the listed Prix Coronation winner and US Grade 2 placed Dirca. (Highclere Thoroughbred Racing – Petrushka). *"She's shown signs of temperament but she's a sharp filly. The stallion is obviously going great in Australia and this filly won't let him down if she keeps her head together".*

844. OUR QUEENIE ★★★★
ch.f. Strategic Prince – Matibibi (Barathea). March 2. Third foal. £22,000Y. Doncaster Premier. Sackville/Donald. The dam, placed at 3 yrs in Italy, is a half-sister to 7 winners including the listed winner Orso and the dam of the Group 2 Prix Noailles winner Ruwi. The second dam, Palombella (by Groom Dancer), won 3 minor races at 3 yrs in France and is a half-sister to 11 winners including the Group 2 winner Passionaria and the dam of the Group 1 winners Lit De Justice and Commander Collins. (N Woodcock/R Hannon). *"A nice little filly, she's sharp and neat. A real 2-y-o type and we should see her out early".*

845. OXLIP ★★
b.f. Three Valleys – Age Of Chivalry (Invincible Spirit). February 17. Second foal. Half-sister to the fair 2012 7f placed 2-y-o Cash Is King (by Bahamian Bounty). The dam won twice over 5f (at 2 yrs) and the Group 3 6f Ballyogan Stakes and is a half-sister to Sebastian Flyte (a winner here and in the USA where he was Grade 1

placed). The second dam, Aravonian (by Night Shift), won once over 1m at 3 yrs. (Rockcliffe Stud). *"She'll take a bit of time because she's not quite ready yet. We'll start with her when she gets her act together".*

846. PRISCA ★★★

b.f. Holy Roman Emperor – Ainia (Alhaarth). January 23. First foal. 39,000foal. Tattersalls December. Woodstock. The dam, a fair 4-y-o 9f winner, is a half-sister to 8 winners including the useful 2-y-o 1m winner and Group 3 1m Autumn Stakes second Taameer, to the useful 6f and 6.5f (at 2 yrs) and dual listed 1m winner Expensive and the useful 6f (at 2 yrs) and 8.5f winner and US Grade 3 placed Sweet Prospect. The second dam, Vayavaig (by Damister) a fair 2-y-o 6f winner, is a half-sister to 6 winners including the Group 3 Palace House Stakes winner Vaigly Great and the July Cup second Vaigly Star (herself dam of the Group 3 winners Sahara Star and Yalaietanee). (Mrs Julie Wood). *"A nice filly and an early sort, she's well-built and typical of the sire".*

847. PRIZE ★★★

b.f. Exceed And Excel – Holamo (Montjeu). January 23. First foal. 135,000foal. Tattersalls December. Woodstock. The dam, a fair dual 1m placed 2-y-o, is a half-sister to 3 winners including the US Grade 2 San Felipe Stakes winner Preachinatthebar (by Silver Charm) and the French listed winner Royal Revival. The second dam, Holy Nola (by Silver Deputy), a stakes winner of 5 races in the USA, is a half-sister to 5 winners including the triple US Grade 3 winner Bare Necessities. (Mrs Julie Wood). *"When she came in she looked like a pony but she's done nothing but improve and I love her now. One for a bit later on".*

848. PUPIL (IRE) ★★★★

b.c. Mastercraftsman – Blue Iris (Petong). March 29. Twelfth foal. €130,000Y. Goffs Orby. Peter & Ross Doyle. Half-brother to the dual listed 5f winner (including at 2 yrs) Swiss Lake (by Indian Ridge and herself the dam of three stakes winners), to the fairly useful 5f (including at 2 yrs) and 6f winner and listed-placed Dubai Princess (by Dubai Destination), the fairly useful 6f and 7f winner of 6 races Hajoum (by Exceed And Excel) and

the fair Irish 2-y-o 5f winner Nero Emperor (by Holy Roman Emperor). The dam, a useful winner of 5 races over 5f and 6f including the Weatherbys Super Sprint and the Redcar Two-Year-Old Trophy, is a half-sister to 10 winners including the quite useful triple 6f winner Abbajabba. The second dam, Bo' Babbity (by Strong Gale), a fair 2-y-o 5f winner, is a half-sister to 6 winners including the high-class Group 3 5f King George Stakes winner Anita's Prince. (Mr W A Tinkler). *"A really nice horse of Andrew Tinkler's, he's from a good, fast family, he moves well and he'll be a six furlong type".*

849. RAAJIS (IRE) ★★

gr.f. Dark Angel – Rumline (Royal Applause). January 4. First foal. £75,000Y. Doncaster Premier. Peter & Ross Doyle. The dam is an unplaced half-sister to 4 winners including very useful 2-y-o Group 2 5.5f Prix Robert Papin winner Never A Doubt. The second dam, Waypoint (by Cadeaux Genereux), a fairly useful 6f and 7f winner, is a half-sister to 5 winners including the Group 2 6f Diadem Stakes winner and sire Acclamation. (Hamdan Al Maktoum). *"She's slightly plain of her head and slightly long backed, but she's a nice filly that hasn't done a lot yet".*

850. SAND DANCER (IRE) ★★★

b.f. Footstepsinthesand – Annacloy Pearl (Mull Of Kintyre). February 15. First foal. 40,000Y. Tattersalls December. Peter & Ross Doyle. The dam is an unraced half-sister to 5 winners including the dam of the Group 2 Gimcrack Stakes winner Shaweel and to the unraced dam of Samitar (Irish 1,000 Guineas and Grade 1 Garden City Stakes) and Nijoom Dubai (Group 3 Albany Stakes). The second dam, Joyful (by Green Desert), a fair 7f winner at 3 yrs, is a half-sister to 7 winners including the Group 1 1m Coronation Stakes winner Golden Opinion. (Michael Pescod & Justin Dowley). *"A really nice filly with a good pedigree, she's a little bit backward and nowhere near doing anything yet, but she'll make a nice filly at some point in the season. More than likely that will be in August or September".*

851. SEBASTIAN BEACH (IRE) ★★★

b.c. Yeats – Night Club (Mozart). April 22. Fourth foal. 58,000Y. Tattersalls October Book

2. Peter & Ross Doyle. Half-brother to the modest 2-y-o 5f and 6f winner Dunmore Boy (by Iffraaj) and to the fair dual 1m winner Opening Nite (by Azamour). The dam is an unplaced half-sister to 12 winners including the French 1,000 Guineas and Group 1 7f Prix de la Foret winner Danseuse du Soir (herself dam of the Group 1 Gran Criterium winner Scintillo), the smart 7f (at 2 yrs) to 12f winner Don Corleone and the very useful 1m to 12f winner Dana Springs. The second dam, Dance By Night (by Northfields), a quite useful 2-y-o dual 7f winner, is a half-sister to 3 winners. (Michael Pescod & Justin Dowley). *"He was a really nice yearling but just after Christmas he started to lose a bit of weight. So we eased off him and he's back cantering now, he's put the weight back on and we'll just go steady with him. A nice horse".*

852. SEBS SENSEI (IRE) ★★★★

ch.c. Art Connoisseur – Capetown Girl (Danzero). April 5. Fifth foal. £50,000Y. Doncaster Premier. Peter & Ross Doyle. Half-brother to the unplaced 2012 2-y-o Dark Eros (by Dark Angel), to the quite useful 6f (at 2 yrs) and 7f winner of 5 races No Poppy (by Chineur) and the French 6f and 7f winner Whip My Heart (by Whipper). The dam, a fair 6f winner, is a half-sister to 4 winners. The second dam, Cavernista (by Lion Cavern), is a placed half-sister to 11 winners including the Group 1 Prix du Cadran winner Give Notice and the listed winners Times Up and Sovinista. (Potensis Ltd, Chris Giles, J Palmer-Brown). *"A lovely horse, he's a big colt with a great way of going, we wouldn't be in any hurry with him but we know he's there".*

853. SELWAAN (IRE) ★★★★

b.c. Invincible Spirit – Lia (Desert King). March 17. Seventh foal. €110,000Y. Goffs Orby. Mandore International Agency. Half-brother to the French listed 10f winner Lake Palace (by Nayef) and to the French 2-y-o 1m winner Lui Seul (by Dubawi). The dam won 3 races including over 12f in France and was listed placed twice and is a half-sister to 5 winners. The second dam, Lisheba (by Alysheba), was placed in France at 3 yrs and is a half-sister to the dam of the Group 1 winners Lawman and Latice. (Sheikh J B H bin Khalifa Al Thani). *"A*

nice horse that goes well, he's done one piece of work and he did it very nicely. I'm looking forward to working him again".

854. SHAFRAH (IRE) ★★★

b.c. Acclamation – Rosy Dudley (Grand Lodge). April 5. Fifth living foal. 240,000Y. Tattersalls October Book 1. Shadwell Estate Co. Closely related to the quite useful 6f (at 2 yrs) and 7f winner Apostle (by Dark Angel) and half-brother to the quite useful 2-y-o 5f and 7f winner Grand Honour (by Verglas). The dam, a fair Irish 8.5f winner at 3 yrs, is a half-sister to 6 winners including the Group 2 Criterium des Ans winner Deadly Dudley and the listed winner Miss Nosey Parker. The second dam, Renzola (by Dragonara Palace), is an unraced half-sister to the dam of the Group 1 and Grade 1 winner Millkom. (Hamdan Al Maktoum). *"A colt that goes well, he hasn't done a lot yet but when we step up his work I'm sure he'll be ready to go. A nice colt".*

855. SHAMSHON (IRE) ★★★★

b.c. Invincible Spirit – Greenisland (Fasliyev). March 29. First foal. 420,000Y. Tattersalls October Book 1. Mandore International. The dam, a fairly useful 1m (at 2 yrs) and 7f winner, was listed-placed three times and is a half-sister to 2 winners including the listed winner Ithoughtitwasover. The second dam, Green Castle (by Indian Ridge), was placed once over 1m at 4 yrs in Ireland from only 2 starts and is a half-sister to 12 winners including the Group 2 placed Luchiroverte. (Sheikh J B H bin Khalifa Al Thani). *"A really nice horse that cost a lot of money, I haven't done much with him yet but he could be anything. Physically he's as nice a 2-y-o as you will ever see".*

856. SHOWPIECE ★★★★

b.c. Kyllachy – Striving (Danehill Dancer). February 12. Second foal. 50,000Y. Tattersalls October Book 1. Not sold. The dam, a modest 1m and 10f placed maiden, is a sister to 2 winners including the listed 1m winner Pirateer, closely related to the Group 1 6f Cheveley Park Stakes winner Wannabe Grand and a half-sister to 3 winners including the useful 2-y-o dual 1m winner and Group 3 second Wannabe Posh. The second dam, Wannabe (by Shirley Heights), a quite useful

1m and 10f winner, is a half-sister to 3 winners including the Group 1 Cheveley Park Stakes second Tanami. (Cheveley Park Stud). *"He's a nice colt, a good-looking horse of a great colour, hasn't done much yet but he's strong, really nice and could be early".*

857. SPEED THE PLOUGH ★★★

b.c. Kyllachy – Danceatdusk (Desert Prince). April 4. Third foal. 85,000Y. Tattersalls October Book 1. Peter & Ross Doyle. Half-brother to the quite useful 2-y-o 7f winner Ninita (by Storming Home) and to the modest 6f winner Ooi Long (by Echo Of Light). The dam is an unraced half-sister to 8 winners including the smart 1m (at 2 yrs) and listed 10f winner Island Sound and the smart 1m winner and Group 3 1m Joel Stakes third Fair Trade. The second dam, Ballet (by Sharrood), a moderate 5f and 6f placed maiden, is a half-sister to 10 winners including the May Hill Stakes winner Satinette. (M Hughes, M Kerr-Dineen). *"A nice, five/six furlong colt, he's ready to do a bit more now and he could be an early sort".*

858. STARS ALIGNED (IRE) ★★★

b.f. Sea The Stars – Senora Galilei (Galileo). March 19. Third foal. €300,000foal. Goffs November. Woodstock. The dam, a fairly useful Irish 10f winner, is a sister to 2 winners including the champion 2-y-o colt and Group 1 Dewhurst Stakes and Group 1 National Stakes winner Teofilo. The second dam, Speirbhean (by Danehill), an Irish listed 1m winner, is a half-sister to 6 winners including the Irish listed 9f winner Graduated. (Mrs Julie Wood). *"She's put on weight since she came in and she'll probably need a lot of time, but she's growing big time and that's making her look light. She'll be a nice filly one day".*

859. STEVENTON STAR ★★★★ ♠

b.c. Pastoral Pursuits – Premiere Dance (Loup Solitaire). April 11. Eighth foal. 55,000Y. Tattersalls October Book 2. Sackville/Donald. Half-brother to the useful 5f to 7f winner and listed-placed Prince Tamino (by Mozart), to the poor 4-y-o 7f and subsequent winner Bicksta (by Haafhd) and the minor French 1m winner Sing Silence (by Sakhee). The dam won once over 1m at 3 yrs in France and is a half-sister to 4 winners including the Group

1 7f Prix de la Foret winner Poplar Bluff. The second dam, Plume Bleu Pale (by El Gran Senor), a listed-placed 3-y-o winner in France, is a half-sister to 5 winners including the multiple US Grade 3 winner Premier Ministre. (Mr R W Tyrrell). *"This colt goes very well, he'll be sharp and early and he's a really likeable 2-y-o. Will be winning over five or six furlongs (hopefully both) early on".*

860. STORM RIDER (IRE) ★★★★ ♠

b.c. Fastnet Rock – On The Nile (Sadler's Wells). April 1. Eighth foal. €150,000Y. Goffs Orby. Amanda Skiffington. Closely related to the quite useful 2012 2-y-o 6f winner Pussycat Lips, to the winner of 3 winners abroad Emperors Pearl (both by Holy Roman Emperor) and the fairly useful 1m and 10f winner Tommy Toogood (by Danehill). The dam, an Irish 2-y-o listed 9f winner, is a sister to the Irish listed 1m winner In The Limelight, closely related to the Singapore Gold Cup and Gran Premio del Jockey Club winner Kutub and a half-sister to 3 winners. The second dam, Minnie Habit (by Habitat), an Irish 4-y-o 9f winner, is closely related to the dual sprint Group 3 winner Bermuda Classic (herself dam of the Coronation Stakes winner Shake The Yoke) and a half-sister to 6 winners. (Carmichael Humber). *"A lovely colt that could be anything. Everything about him is nice, he's a lovely mover and he'll go to the better tracks".*

861. SUITE (IRE) ★★★★

b.f. Invincible Spirit – Rakiza (Elnadim). February 21. Third foal. 62,000Y. Tattersalls October Book 2. Peter & Ross Doyle. Half-sister to the quite useful 2012 2-y-o 6f winner Exactement (by Speightstown). The dam, a French 7f (at 2 yrs) and 6f winner, was listed-placed and is a half-sister to 3 winners including the Group 2 1m Prix de Sandringham winner Baqah. The second dam, Filfilah (by Cadeaux Genereux), a useful 6f and 7f winner, is a full or half-sister to 6 winners including the Canadian Grade 2 winner Muntej. (Mrs Julie Wood). *"A nice, racey sort, she's probably going to start her career in April and she's a real trainer's horse. A sharp filly".* Stable jockey Richard Hughes was quick to point out that he likes this filly.

862. SWANWICK SHORE (IRE) ★★★

b.c. Tagula – Cinzia Vegas (Dr Fong). January 26. Third foal. £70,000Y. Doncaster Premier. Peter & Ross Doyle. Half-brother to the fair 10f winner Star Deal (by Tagula) and to the minor Italian 3-y-o winner Cross Fade (by Rakti). The dam, placed at 3 yrs in Italy, is a half-sister to 5 winners including the smart Group 1 1m Gran Criterium and US Grade 3 8.5f winner Hello. The second dam, Itqan (by Sadler's Wells), a fairly useful winner of 3 races from 12f to 14.8f and is a half-sister to 3 winners and to the dams of the Group 2 winners Atlantis Prince and Dano-Mast. (Mrs Julie Wood). "A nice horse, we won't be in a hurry with him because he's a mid-season type but he has a good attitude".

863. SYDNEY JAMES (IRE) ★★★

b.c. Thousand Words – Blue Bamboo (Green Desert). April 7. Third foal. 18,000Y. Tattersalls October Book 2. Peter & Ross Doyle. The dam, a modest 7f winner, is a half-sister to one winner. The second dam, Silver Bandana (by Silver Buck), a US stakes winner of 6 races at 3 to 5 yrs and Grade 3 placed twice, is a half-sister to 5 winners. (The Sydney Arms, Chelsea). "A real nice horse, he's done really well. He did a half-speed on the gallops yesterday and did it nicely. A mid-season type".

864. TABREEK (USA) ★★★

ch.c. Distorted Humor – Blushing (Maria's Mon). February 24. First foal. £340,000Y. Keeneland September. Shadwell Estate Co. The dam is an unraced sister to the US dual Grade 1 winner and champion 3-y-o filly Wait A While. The second dam, Flirtatious (by A P Indy), a winner of 4 minor races 2 or 3 yrs, is a half-sister to 4 winners. (Hamdan Al Maktoum). "A nice horse that has a touch of sore shins so we'll leave him alone for a bit. But he's a strong, athletic horse and worth his purchase price at the moment".

865. TANQEYA (IRE) ★★★

b.c. Intense Focus – Spinning Well (Pivotal). March 8. First foal. 70,000Y. Tattersalls October Book 2. Peter & Ross Doyle. The dam, a fair 12f winner, is a half-sister to 4 winners including the Group 3 winners Anam Allta and Fox Hunt. The second dam, Kiltubber (by

Sadler's Wells), an Italian listed 12f winner, is a half-sister to 3 winners. (Hamdan Al Maktoum). "A medium-sized horse for the middle of the season, he has a good way of going and a good attitude".

866. THE ALAMO (IRE) ★★★

b.c. High Chaparral – Inner Strength (Take Risks). April 27. Fourth foal. €46,000Y. Goffs Orby. Peter & Ross Doyle. Brother to a minor 3-y-o winner in Greece. The dam, a minor winner at 3 yrs in France, is a half-sister to 5 winners including the US Grade 3 Laurel Dash winner and Group 3 Prix Thomas Bryon second Mayoumbe and the useful Irish 10f and 12f listed winner Tipperary All Star. The second dam, Moucha (by Fabulous Dancer), a winner of 3 races in France and listed-placed, is a half-sister to 7 winners including the US Grade 3 winner Daloma. (Ivory, Woodcock, Bull, Hannon). "A lovely colt, he's a really good-moving sort for the middle to back-end of the season".

867. THUNDER STRIKE ★★★

ch.c. Sakhee's Secret – Trump Street (First Trump). February 16. Eighth foal. £40,000Y. Doncaster Premier. Peter & Ross Doyle. Half-brother to the fair 5f (including at 2 yrs) and 6f winner of 5 races Top Bid (by Auction House), to the fair 2-y-o 6f winner Street Cred (by Bold Edge), the modest 6f (at 2 yrs) and 1m winner Military Call (by Royal Applause), the moderate 5f winner Trumpita (by Bertolini) and a winner abroad by Kyllachy. The dam, a fair 6f winner at 4 yrs, is a half-sister to 4 winners. The second dam, Pepeke (by Mummy's Pet), a fair 3-y-o 7f winner, is a half-sister to 6 winners. (Mr M S Al Shahi). "I like him, he's nice and he looks sharp too. He'll be ready to roll soon".

868. TOORMORE (IRE) ★★★★ ♠

b.c. Arakan – Danetime Out (Danetime). March 19. Fourth foal. £36,000Y. Doncaster Premier. Peter & Ross Doyle. Half-brother to the quite useful 6f (at 2 yrs) and 7f winner Try The Chance (by Majestic Missile). The dam is an unraced half-sister to 7 winners including the Group 3 second Easaar. The second dam, Matila (by Persian Bold), a fairly useful 3-y-o 6f winner, is a half-sister to 6 winners.

(Middleham Park Racing). *"This is a serious horse. He's the best of the Arakan's we've had – including Trumpet Major and Dick Turpin. He'll be ready to go soon and he's a really lovely horse. Physically he's as good-looking a colt as you could come across. The spitting image of Dick Turpin, he's done really well and enjoys his work".*

869. TOUCH PAPER (IRE) ★★★★

b.f. Acclamation – Light It Up (Elusive City). March 1. First foal. The dam, a fair 5f and 6f placed maiden, is a half-sister to the dual 2-y-o 7f and subsequent South African Group 2 winner Purple Orchid. The second dam, Fabuco (by Mujadil), a modest 2-y-o 5f winner, is a sister to the useful 2-y-o 5f winner and Group 3 placed Connemara and to the fairly useful 2-y-o 5f winner and Cherry Hinton Stakes fourth Presentation and a half-sister to 3 winners. (Mrs Julie Wood). *"She's shown plenty but she just needs to come in her coat so the warmer weather will help. I like her a lot, whether she'd be a Queen Mary filly we'll have to wait and see, but she has a bit of an attitude, which is a good thing".*

870. ULTIMATE WARRIOR (IRE) ★★

ch.c. Winker Watson – Sakaka (Tobougg). February 24. Fourth foal. £22,000Y. Doncaster Premier. Peter & Ross Doyle. The dam is an unraced half-sister to 2 winners. The second dam, Cotton House (by Mujadil), a useful listed sprint winner of 5 races, is a half-sister to 3 winners. (Mr M S Al Shahi). *"A bit of a playboy, he looked quite nice early on but he lost his way a bit. I think he just needs a bit of time".*

871. UNDER MY WING (IRE) ★★★

ch.c. Raven's Pass – Ra Hydee (Rahy). March 12. Ninth foal. €60,000foal. Goffs November. Woodstock. Half-brother to the 1m winner and Group 2 UAE Derby second Jack Junior, to the fairly useful 2-y-o 5f winner and listed-placed Perfect Paula, the fair 2-y-o 7f winner Liturgical (all by Songandaprayer) and a minor US 4-y-o winner by Devil's Bag. The dam, a minor US 3-y-o winner, is a half-sister to 7 winners including the minor US stakes winners Jonowo and Stolie. The second dam, Youpickem (by Droll Role), a minor US 3-y-o

winner, is a half-sister to 6 winners including the US Grade 2 winner Terra Incognita. (Mrs Julie Wood). *"He's shown us a fair bit already, but he isn't really ready so we're going to lay off him for a bit. But we do know there's an engine there".*

872. VALUE ★★★

br.f. Clodovil – Shalev (Java Gold). March 9. €11,000foal. Goffs November. Woodstock. Half-sister to the moderate 6f (at 2 yrs) and 1m winner Lady Advocate (by Lawman). The dam is an unplaced half-sister to 7 winners including the fairly useful 2-y-o 9f winner Maid Of Killeen (herself dam of the Group 1 Cheveley Park Stakes winner Indian Ink). The second dam, Sovereign Touch (by Pennine Walk), is an unraced half-sister to 7 winners including the Group 2 winners Royal Touch and Foresee. (Mrs Julie Wood). *"She's nice and she'll win. She's smaller than the other Clodovil the owner has and I like her".*

873. VIRILE (IRE) ★★★★

ch.c. Exceed And Excel – Winding (Irish River). March 2. Sixth foal. €40,000foal. Goffs November. Woodstock. Half-brother to the fair 5f winner of 4 races, including at 2 yrs, Gin Twist (by Invincible Spirit) and to the modest 9f winner Twisted (by Selkirk). The dam is an unplaced half-sister to 4 winners including the Group 3 placed Silver Desert. The second dam, Silver Fling (by The Minstrel), won the Group 1 Prix de l'Abbaye and the Group 3 King George Stakes and was placed in the William Hill Sprint Championship at York and the Vernons Sprint Cup (twice). She is a sister to the high-class filly Silverdip, winner of the Salisbury 1,000 Guineas Trial, the Strensall Stakes and the Montrose Handicap and a half-sister to 2 other stakes winners. (Mrs Julie Wood). *"A lovely horse with a really good way of going, he went nicely on the gallops yesterday and he showed he's a real nice horse that goes very well".*

874. WAHAAB (IRE) ★★★

ch.c. Tamayuz – Indian Ink (Indian Ridge). February 18. First foal. The dam won the Group 1 6f Cheveley Park Stakes and the Group 1 1m Coronation Stakes and is a full or half-sister to 3 winners. The second dam, Maid

Of Killeen (by Darshaan), a fairly useful 2-y-o 9f winner, was listed-placed and is a half-sister to 6 winners. (Hamdan Al Maktoum). *"Not over-big, he came in late and will need a bit of time".*

875. WAR SPIRIT ★★★★ ♠
b.c. Exceed And Excel – Alybgood (Alydeed). April 30. Eighth foal. €75,000Y. Goffs Orby. Peter & Ross Doyle. Half-brother to 3 winners in the USA by Gone West, Grand Slam and Consolidator. The dam, a listed winner of 5 races in the USA at 2 and 4 yrs, is a half-sister to 10 winners including the German Oaks winner Que Belle. The second dam, Qui Bid (by Spectacular Bid), is an unraced sister to the US Grade 3 winner Sum and a half-sister to 9 winners including the Group 1 winner Bakharoff and the Group 2 winner Emperor Jones. (Mr M S Al Shahi). *"One of the nicest 2-y-o's we've got. Funnily enough he's got one grey leg! He showed up very early, we gave him one piece of work and he looked exceptional. Hopefully that will continue and you'll see him out soon".*

876. WASHAAR (IRE) ★★★
b.c. Kodiac – Dabtiyra (Dr Devious). April 5. Third foal. 75,000Y. Tattersalls October Book 2. Peter & Ross Doyle. The dam, placed third over 10f on her only start at 3 yrs in Ireland, is a half-sister to 3 winners. The second dam, Dabtiya (by Shirley Heights), won the listed Ballyroan Stakes, was second in the Group 3 Meld Stakes and is a half-sister to 4 winners. (Hamdan Al Maktoum). *"A nice horse, he's a very loose-shouldered, good-moving sort. Probably one for six or seven furlongs"*

877. WAYLAY (IRE) ★★
b.c. Bushranger – Wings Of Fame (Namid). February 16. First foal. €32,000foal. Goffs November. Woodstock. The dam is an unraced half-sister to 5 winners including the listed winners Sharpest Image, Tycoon's Hill, Tycoon's Dolce and Desert Drama, and is a half-sister to three other listed winners. The second dam, Tycoon's Drama (by Last Tycoon), won 3 races at 2 yrs in France and the USA including the Grade 3 8.5f Selima Stakes and is a full or half-sister to 4 winners including the dam of the US Grade 1 winner King's Drama.

(Mrs Julie Wood). *"A backward colt that came in late, he's just starting to grow and he's a good-moving horse but we won't be in a hurry with him".*

878. WEDGEWOOD (IRE) ★★★
br.c. Mastercraftsman – Vingt Et Une (Sadler's Wells). April 18. Eleventh foal. €120,000Y. Goffs Orby. Peter & Ross Doyle. Half-brother to the very useful 12f winners Sayadaw and Year Two Thousand (both by Darshaan), the fair 9f and 2m winner Gaselee (by Toccet) and 3 minor French winners by Numerous, Inchinor and Linamix. The dam, a minor French 3-y-o winner, is a sister to the very useful Group 1 10.5f Prix Lupin and US Grade 2 1m winner Johann Quatz and to the smart French 10.5f to 13.5f listed winner Walter Willy and a half-sister to the top-class middle-distance colt Hernando, winner of the Group 1 Prix du Jockey Club and Group 1 Prix Lupin. The second dam, Whakilyric (by Miswaki), won the Group 3 7f Prix du Calvados and was third in the Prix de la Salamandre and in the Prix de la Foret. *"He's a very dark, rich-looking grey. He hasn't done a lot yet but he's a nice sort".*

879. WINDSHEAR ★★★★ ♠
b.c. Hurricane Run – Portal (Hernando). February 14. Second foal. €95,000Y. Arqana Deauville August. Peter & Ross Doyle. Half-brother to the fair 12f to 2m winner Porcini (by Azamour). The dam, useful listed 10f winner, is a half-sister to 6 winners including the useful 1m and listed 10f winner Ice Palace and the dam of the dual Group 2 winner Spacious. The second dam, White Palace (by Shirley Heights), a quite useful 3-y-o 8.2f winner, is a half-brother to one winner abroad. (Mr M Daniels). *"This colt will take some time, but he's a hell of a nice horse. He's a smasher and certainly looks the part – but you won't see him before the July meeting at Newmarket".*

880. UNNAMED ★★★ ♠
ch.f. Exceed And Excel – Amazon Beauty (Wolfhound). March 19. Third living foal. 60,000Y. Tattersalls December. Anthony Stroud. Half-sister to Switcharooney (by Bahamian Bounty), unplaced in one start at 2 yrs in 2012. The dam won twice at 2 and 3 yrs in France, was third in the Group 3 Prix de

Seine-et-Oise and is a half-sister to 3 winners including the US stakes winner and Group 1 Prix Saint-Alary second Asti. The second dam, Astorg (by Lear Fan), won the listed 1m Prix de la Calonne and is a half-sister to 8 winners including the Group 3 winners Android and Article Rare. (Saeed Manana). *"A lovely-looking filly, she's tall and we'll take our time with her. One for seven furlongs and a mile later in the year".*

881. UNNAMED ★★★★

b.c. Cape Cross – Anna's Rock (Rock Of Gibraltar). March 22. Second foal. 145,000Y. Tattersalls October Book 1. Peter & Ross Doyle. Half-brother to Breton Rock (by Bahamian Bounty), winner of both his starts over 6f at 2 yrs in 2012. The dam, a useful Irish 7f (at 2 yrs) and listed 7.5f winner, is a half-sister to the useful 1m winner and listed-placed Sugar Mint. The second dam, Anna Karenina (by Atticus), is an unraced half-sister to 10 winners including the Group 3 Prix de Psyche winner and French 1,000 Guineas and French Oaks placed Agathe (herself dam of the Grade/Group 1 winners Artiste Royale and Aquarelliste), to the Breeders Cup Classic winner Arcangues and the dams of the Group/Grade 1 winners Cape Verdi and Angara. (S H Altayer). *"This is a very nice colt. He has a little wall-eye on his off-side but otherwise he's pretty much a perfect looking 2-y-o out of a great family. He's a great colour, we'll take our time with him and he's a seven furlong type for later on".*

882. UNNAMED ★★★

b.c. Kyllachy – Coming Home (Vettori). February 10. Fifth foal. 45,000Y. Tattersalls October Book 1. Rabbah Bloodstock. Half-brother to the very useful 2-y-o 7f and 1m winner and listed-placed Mantoba (by Noverre), to the fair 2-y-o 6f winner Via Mia (by Namid) and the minor winner of 3 races abroad Free House (by Sir Percy). The dam, a minor French middle-distance winner, is a half-sister to 4 winners. The second dam, Bonne Etoile (by Diesis), a fairly useful winner of 3 races at 3 yrs including a listed event over 10f, is a half-sister to 5 winners. (Sheikh Juma Al Dalmook Maktoum). *"A nice little horse but we'll take our time with him, he'll be a six/*

seven furlong horse in mid-season. A good-moving sort".

883. UNNAMED ★★★

ch.c. Major Cadeaux – Dayville (Dayjur). February 14. Thirteenth foal. £34,000Y. Doncaster Premier. Anthony Stroud. Half-brother to the 5f and 6f winner and listed-placed Day By Day (by Kyllachy), to the Irish 3-y-o 5f winner Alexander Ballet (by Mind Games and herself dam of the Group 1 Gran Criterium winner Hearts Of Fire), the 2-y-o 1m winner Musical Day (by Singspiel), the 10f and 12f winner My Daisychain (by Hector Protector) – all quite useful - and the fair 2-y-o 6f winner Tedsmore Dame (by Indesatchel). The dam, a quite useful triple 6f winner at 2 and 3 yrs, is a half-sister to 4 winners including the Grade 1 Yellow Ribbon Handicap winner Spanish Fern and to the unraced dams of the Group/Grade 1 winners Lord Shanakill and Heatseeker. The second dam, Chain Fern (by Blushing Groom), is an unraced sister to the Irish 1,000 Guineas and Coronation Stakes winner Al Bahathri (herself dam of the 2,000 Guineas and Champion Stakes winner Haafhd) and a half-sister to the US Grade 2 winner Geraldine's Store. (Mr M Sultan). *"This is a nice horse and he's very like his Daddy. He's got the same head, he's got a lovely attitude and you hardly know he's here. He could be early but we haven't done much with him yet".*

884. UNNAMED ★★★

b.f. Invincible Spirit – Dundel (Machiavellian). March 28. Eleventh foal. Sister to the unraced 2012 2-y-o Botteen and to the fair 1m winner Tina's Spirit and half-sister to the smart 2-y-o 6f and subsequent US stakes winner and Group 2 6f Coventry Stakes third Luck Money (by Indian Ridge), to the 2-y-o Group 3 7f Prix du Calvados winner Charlotte O'Fraise (by Beat Hollow), the modest 2m 1f and hurdles winner Lodgician (by Grand Lodge), the Irish 1m and hurdles winner River Nurey (by Fasliyev), the minor French 3-y-o winner Wing And Wing (by Singspiel) and a dual hurdles winner by Sadler's Wells. The dam, a quite useful 7f winner, is a half-sister to 6 winners including the Group 3 6f Prix de Seine-et-Oise winner Seltitude. The second dam, Dunoof (by Shirley Heights), a fairly useful 2-y-o 7f winner, is a sister to the Premio Roma, Park Hill Stakes and Ribblesdale Stakes winner High Hawk (the dam of In the Wings) and to the winning dams of the Derby winner High-Rise and the Grade 1 Rothmans International winner Infamy. (C F Harrington). *"A nice filly, but she's started to grow again and gone a little weak. She'll be one for the middle of the season over six or seven furlongs".*

885. UNNAMED ★★★★

ch.c. Dubawi – Forest Storm (Galileo). March 12. First foal. 32,000Y. Tattersalls October Book 1. Rabbah Bloodstock. The dam, a useful Irish 2-y-o 7f winner and second in the listed Flame Of Tara Stakes, is a half-sister to one winner. The second dam, Quiet Storm (by Desert Prince), a fairly useful 7f and 10f winner, was listed-placed twice and is a half-sister to 4 winners. (Saeed Manana). *"I like him and he'll be ready to go soon. He's nice, he's a good goer, travels really well and being a Dubawi he could be anything".*

886. UNNAMED ★★★★

b.f. Selkirk – Forgotten Dreams (Olden Times). March 12. First foal. 52,000Y. Tattersalls October Book 2. Rabbah Bloodstock. The dam ran unplaced twice and is a half-sister to 4 winners including the Group 1 Italian Oaks, the Group 2 Royal Whip Stakes and Group 2 Premio Lydia Tesio winner Zomaradah (herself the dam of Dubawi). The second dam, Jawaher (by Dancing Brave), was placed over 1m and 9f and is a half-sister to 9 winners including the Derby winner High Rise. (Saeed Manana). *"I like her, she's really nice and much sharper than the other Selkirk filly we have. She's small, well-made and really nice".*

887. UNNAMED ★★★

b.c. Acclamation – Maid To Order (Zafonic). March 10. Sixth foal. £52,000Y. Doncaster Premier. Peter & Ross Doyle. Brother to the fair 7f (at 2 yrs) and 1m winner Jibaal (by Acclamation) and half-brother to the modest 2-y-o 5f winner Rightcar Ellie (by Namid). The dam, a modest Irish 1m winner, is a half-sister to 10 winners including the useful Irish 2-y-o 6f winner and Group 1 Phoenix Stakes third Catch A Glimpse (herself the dam of a US Grade 3 winner). The second dam, Spring To Light (by Blushing Groom), a winner over 6f and 7f and second in the Group 3 C L Weld Park Stakes, is a half-sister to 7 winners. (Magnier/Tabor/Smith). *"Not an overly-big horse, but he's a typical Acclamation. He's very pleasing, goes about his job without a problem and although we haven't done much with him yet he looks a racey sort. You'll see him over five and six furlongs early in the season".*

888. UNNAMED ★★★

ch.c. Bertolini – Marannatha (Pursuit Of Love). February 1. Third foal. 25,000Y. Tattersalls October Book 2. Peter & Ross Doyle. Half-brother to a minor winner abroad by Dalakhani. The dam, a fair Irish 7f 2-y-o winner, is a half-sister to 6 winners including the Italian Group 3 winner Uruk and the listed Fred Archer Stakes winner All The Aces. The second dam, Lili Cup (by Fabulous Dancer), is an unraced half-sister to 11 winners including the Irish triple Group 3 winner Nysaean. *"A nice, liver-chestnut colt. For some reason he hasn't got any friends because we haven't sold him, but Canford Cliffs was the last 2-y-o we sold in his year. He's a nice little horse, there's nothing wrong with him, we'll get him out early and he might be a nice little 2-y-o".*

889. UNNAMED ★★★

b.c. Royal Applause – Mountain Law (Mountain Cat). March 13. Seventh foal. 45,000Y. Tattersalls October Book 2. Peter & Ross Doyle. Half-brother to the useful listed 7f Pipalong Stakes winner of 5 races and Group 3 Oak Tree Stakes third Law Of The Range (by Alhaarth), to the fairly useful Irish 7f and 1m winner and subsequent US Grade 2 placed High Court Drama (by Theatrical), the fair 1m to 12f winner Alshazah (by Haafhd) and to the fair 6f winner Pearl Of Manacor (by Danehill Dancer). The dam is an unraced half-sister to 7 winners including the smart Group 3 7f Hungerford Stakes winner With Reason and the useful Group 3 1m Curragh Futurity Stakes and 7f Sweet Solera Stakes winner Jural. The second dam, Just Cause (by Law Society), is an unraced half-sister to 5 winners out of the Group 1 Prix Saint-Alary winner Tootens. (Malih L Al Basti). *"He travels really well and he's a nice horse but with temperament issues. Quite a big horse, I'd say he wants six furlongs".*

890. UNNAMED ★★★★

b.c. Exceed And Excel – Mystery Ocean (Dr Fong). March 29. Third foal. 80,000Y. Tattersalls October Book 1. Rabbah Bloodstock. Half-brother to the fair 2-y-o 5f winner Ocean Myth (by Acclamation). The dam, a quite useful 2-y-o 5f winner, was third in the listed Masaka Stakes and is a half-sister to 5 winners including the useful Group 3 7f Dubai Duty Free (Fred Darling Stakes) and Irish 1,000 Guineas second Penkenna Princess. The second dam, Tiriana (by Common Grounds), is a placed half-sister to 6 winners including the 2-y-o listed 5.2f winner Head Over Heels. (S H Altayer). *"I think he could be anything and perhaps one that could be aimed for Royal Ascot. He's shown plenty and is one of the better ones. A lovely horse that looks the business".*

891. UNNAMED ★★★

b.c. Exceed And Excel – Pink Stone (Bigstone). April 28. Ninth foal. 50,000Y. Tattersalls October Book 1. Peter & Ross Doyle. Half-brother to the useful but ill-fated 2-y-o 7f winner Tiger Eye (by Danehill Dancer), to the quite useful 2-y-o 8.3f winner Alright My Son (by Pennekamp), the quite useful 12f and 2m winner Battleoftrafalgar (by Galileo) and a minor winner abroad by Agnes World. The dam was placed three times in France and stayed 10f and is a half-sister to 8 winners including the triple Group 3 winner Pink and the French listed winners Ring Pink and Lypink. The second dam, Pink Valley (by Never Bend), won the listed Prix d'Aumale and is a half-sister to 12 winners including the French 2,000 Guineas winner and sire Green Dancer. *"A nice little horse, he's grown so he hasn't done a lot and we'll have to wait until he's ready before stepping him up".*

892. UNNAMED ★★★★ ♠

b.c. Royal Applause – Rolexa (Pursuit Of Love). March 11. Third foal. 160,000Y. Tattersalls October Book 2. Amanda Skiffington. Brother to the fair 2012 2-y-o 6f winner Mayaasem and half-brother to the modest 5f and 6f winner Seventeen Seventy (by Byron). The dam, a fair dual 1m placed 3-y-o, is a half-sister to 9 winners including the smart Green Card, a winner from 1m to 10.3f and Group 3

placed three times. The second dam, Dunkellin (by Irish River), a minor 3-y-o winner in the USA, is a half-sister to 4 winners including the Group 1 Criterium des Pouliches winner Oak Hill. (Carmichael Humber). *"A lovely, big horse – in looks he's quite unlike most Royal Applause 2-y-o's. A strong colt, he has speed written all over him".*

893. UNNAMED ★★★

b.f. Royal Applause – Singitta (Singspiel). January 24. Fifth foal. 95,000Y. Tattersalls October Book 1. Peter & Ross Doyle. Half-sister to the useful 5f winner of 7 races (including four times at 2 yrs) and listed placed Singeur (by Chineur), to the modest 7f and 1m winner Samasana (by Redback) and a winner in the Czech Republic and Germany by Needwood Blade. The dam is an unplaced half-sister to 3 winners including the dam of the Group 3 July Stakes winner Nevisian Lad and to the dam of the listed winners Pyman's Theory and Forthefirstime. The second dam, Ferber's Follies (by Saratoga Six), a US 2-y-o winner and third in the Grade 2 Adirondack Stakes, is a half-sister to 11 winners including the Grade 2 Sorority Stakes winner Blue Jean Baby. (Sheikh R D Al Maktoum). *"She's quite tall but racey and as soon as the weather picks up we can start doing a bit with her. I imagine she'll show up quite nicely because she looks a nice filly".*

894. UNNAMED ★★★★

b.f. Bushranger – Undulation (Alhaarth). February 11. Third foal. €50,000Y. Goffs Orby. Peter & Ross Doyle. The dam is an unraced half-sister to 6 winners. The second dam, High And Low (by Rainbow Quest) won the Cheshire Oaks, was second in the Yorkshire Oaks and the St Leger and is a half-sister to the very useful 12f to 14.6f winner Corradini and to the unraced dam of the triple Group 1 winner American Post. (Abdulla Mansoori). *"A nice filly, you'd think she was a colt if you didn't know because she's very thick-set and very strong. She's showing the signs that she'll be quite early".*

895. UNNAMED ★★★

b.c. Acclamation – Venoge (Green Desert). April 28. Third foal. 140,000Y. Tattersalls

October Book 2. Demi O'Byrne. Half-brother to the modest 2012 5f and 6f placed 2-y-o Ayr Missile (by Cadeaux Genereux). The dam is an unraced half-sister to 3 winners here and abroad. The second dam, Horatia (by Machiavellian), won the Grade 3 Matchmaker Stakes in the USA and was third in the Grade 2 Long Island Handicap and is a half-sister to 6 winners including Opinion Poll (Group 2 Lonsdale Cup). (Magnier, Tabor, Smith). *"A nice horse, we're giving him some time but he seems to be doing his job OK, he's sound and hasn't had any issues at all. We'll look under the bonnet when his time comes".*

JESSICA HARRINGTON
896. BUTTERFLY DANCER (IRE) ★★
b.f. Teofilo – Azolla (Cadeaux Genereux).
February 20. Third foal. €20,000Y. Goffs Orby. Not sold. The dam, a Scandinavian 1m and 10f winner of 4 races, is a half-sister to 5 winners including the smart multiple listed winner (from 7f to 10f) Nashmiah and the useful 2-y-o 7f and listed 1m winner Streets Ahead. The second dam, Frond (by Alzao), a quite useful 2-y-o 7f winner, is a half-sister to 8 winners. (Hot to Trot Racing). *"She's just going through a backward stage at the moment but I'm hoping she'll be racing around June/July. She'll probably want seven furlongs".*

897. HOMERIC HYMN (FR) ★★★★
b.f. Acclamation – Mary Arnold (Hernando).
February 2. Second foal. €20,000Y. Arqana Deauville August. Not sold. Sister to the fair 2-y-o 7f winner Stateos. The dam ran once unplaced and is a half-sister to 5 winners including the Group 1 Criterium de Saint-Cloud winner Linda's Lad. The second dam, Colza (by Alleged), a quite useful 2-y-o 1m winner, is a half-sister to 10 winners including the Group 3 6f July Stakes winner Wharf and the top-class broodmare Docklands (dam of the Arc winner Rail Link). (Niarchos Family). *"A nice Acclamation filly, she's a good mover and I'm happy with her. She'll be racing by late May/early June, she's going nicely and six/seven furlongs will suit her. Possibly the classiest of my 2-y-o's at this stage".*

898. KABJOY (IRE) ★★★
b.f. Intikhab – Lunar Love (In The Wings).
March 25. First foal. €42,000Y. Goffs Sportsman's. BBA (Ire). The dam is an unraced half-sister to 3 winners including the UAE Group 1 Sheema Classic third Falstaff. The second dam, Dance Of Love (by Pursuit Of Love), a fairly useful 2-y-o 7f winner, was listed-placed and is a half-sister to 2 winners. (Favourites Racing Ltd). *"A lovely big filly with a great temperament, she's just starting her first bits of work and she'll probably be a six/seven furlong 2-y-o".*

899. PAR THREE (IRE) ★★
b.br.g. Azamour – Little Whisper (Be My Guest). May 5. Fifth foal. 20,000Y. Tattersalls October Book 2. BBA (Ire). Brother to the quite useful 10f and 12f winner Ex Oriente (by Azamour) and half-brother to the fair 2-y-o 7f winner If You Whisper (by Iffraaj) and the moderate 9f winner Lilli Palmer (by Bertolini). The dam, an Irish 2-y-o 6f and 7f winner and listed-placed, is a half-sister to 5 winners including the dual Group 3 winner Confuchias. The second dam, Schust Madame (by Second Set), won over 11f in Ireland and is a half-sister to 4 winners including the dual US Grade 2 winner Sweet Ludy and the Italian Group 3 winner Late Parade. (Peter Winkworth). *"A big, strong colt and looking at him we'll have to see how he goes on in the next couple of months. He could end up being one for the back-end of the season".*

900. PORT MERRION (IRE) ★★★
b.c. Intense Focus – Aminata (Glenstal). March 11. €11,000Y. Goffs Open. BBA (Ire). Half-brother to the very useful Group 3 1m Desmond Stakes winner Swift Gulliver (by Gulch), to the useful 2-y-o 6f and subsequent dual US stakes winner Abderian, the modest 1m winner Prince Minata (both by Machiavellian), the fairly useful 1m and 10f winner Requested Pleasure (by Rainbow Quest), the Irish 2-y-o 6f winner and listed-placed Minatonic (by Zafonic), the Irish 2-y-o 1m winner Musadaf (by Pennekamp), the quite useful staying winner Turquoise Sea (by Shirley Heights), the modest 6f winner Mint Whip (by Whipper), the Irish 3-y-o 6f winner Amandian (by Indian Ridge) and a winner in Japan by King's Best. The dam, a useful winner of the Group 3 5f Curragh Stakes and the

listed 6f Smurfit Italia Stakes, is a half-sister to 3 winners. The second dam, Belle Epoque (by Habitat), was a placed sister to the Group 1 Prix de l'Abbaye winner Double Form and a half-sister to the Lupe Stakes winner Scimitarra. (Mr John Harrington). *"A lovely colt, he's done a bit of work, does everything right and he'll be a seven furlong 2-y-o. He's good-looking and he moves well".* TRAINERS' BARGAIN BUY

901. UNNAMED ★★★
b.f. *Jeremy – Krynica (Danzig).* February 4. Third living foal. €19,000Y. Tattersalls Ireland September. BBA (Ire). Half-sister to the fair dual 1m winner Songburst (by Singspiel). The dam, a quite useful 2-y-o 5f winner, is a half-sister to 5 winners including the Group 3 9f Earl Of Sefton Stakes winner and multiple Group 1 second Phoenix Tower. The second dam, Bionic (by Zafonic), a very useful 2-y-o 7f winner, is a half-sister to the Group 3 7f Prestige Stakes winner Sense Of Joy (by Dansili) and the multiple Group 3 middle-distance winner and French Derby fourth Day Flight. *"She's a lovely big filly, but she's grown a lot so she'll take a bit of time. A good-moving filly for seven furlongs".*

902. UNNAMED ★★★
b.f. *Big Bad Bob – Little Miss Diva (Diktat).* April 16. Second foal. €600Y. Goresbridge October. Jessica Harrington. Half-sister to the unraced 2012 2-y-o Translucent (by Trans Island). The dam, a modest Irish 1m (at 2 yrs) and 9f placed maiden, is a half-sister to 8 winners and to the placed dam of the Group winners Sayif and Hunter Street. The second dam, Anchorage (by Slip Anchor), a quite useful dual 12f winner, is a half-sister to 6 winners including the Group 3 Ormonde Sakes winner Brunico. *"She's likely to be our first runner, she's sharp and typical of the sire – straightforward and tries her best".*

903. UNNAMED ★★★
b.c. *Big Bad Bob – Lamanka Lass (Woodman).* February 14. Seventh foal. €55,000foal. Goffs November. BBA (Ire). Half-brother to the 7f (at 2 yrs), 1m and subsequent US Grade 2 9f Oak Tree Derby winner Dark Islander (by Singspiel), to the quite useful 2-y-o 7f winner

Suffolk Punch (by Barathea), the fair dual 12f winner Crocolat (by Croco Rouge), the modest dual 1m winner Miss Mojito (by Lucky Story) and a winner in Spain by Desert Prince. The dam, a fair 3-y-o 1m winner, is a half-sister to 7 winners including the Group 3 Darley Stakes winner Far Lane. The second dam, Pattimech (by Nureyev), won at up to 7f in the USA and is a sister to the triple US Grade 1 winner Annoconnor and a half-sister to the Group 1 16f Grand Prix de Paris and Grade 1 Melbourne Cup winner At Talaq. *"A nice, medium-sized colt, he's good-looking and he'll be racing in May over six/seven furlongs".*

RON HARRIS
904. DANDEENA (IRE) ★★★★
b.f. *Dandy Man – Xena (Mull Of Kintyre).* February 19. Fourth foal. £25,000 2-y-o. Kempton Breeze-Up. Ron Harris. Half-sister to the 2-y-o listed 5f Roses Stakes winner New Planet and to the fair 5f and 6f winner Planetex (both by Majestic Missile). The dam is an unraced half-sister to one winner. The second dam, Trendy Indian (by Indian Ridge), ran once unplaced and is a half-sister to one winner. *"We really like her and she came with a good recommendation from a man who would know whether she was any good or not! She could be one of the most exciting two-year-old fillies I've had. It's early days but she's doing everything nicely, she's well-grown and sharp".* TRAINERS' BARGAIN BUY

905. DANETIMERANGER ★★★
b.f. *Bushranger – Brave Cat (Catrail).* February 27. 14,000Y. Tattersalls October Book 3. Ron Harris. Half-sister to the quite useful 5f (including at 2 yrs) and 6f winner of 12 races Italian Tom (by Le Vie Dei Colori), to the quite useful 2-y-o 5f winner Eileen's Violet (by Catcher In The Rye) and the Italian winner of 7 races from 5f to 1m from 2 to 4 yrs Revovegas (by Revoque). The dam is an unraced half-sister to 4 minor winners here and abroad. The second dam, Flimmering (by Dancing Brave), is an unraced half-sister to 7 winners. (Ridge House Stables Ltd). *"She's coming along nicely and I'm looking forward to running her. She would have been out earlier but I've only just found an owner for her. A really strong individual, not over-big, but she looks more like*

a colt than a filly and she'll definitely be a five furlong 2-y-o".

906. FANTASY JUSTIFIER (IRE) ★★★

b.c. *Arakan – Grandel (Owington).* April 20. Eighth foal. €20,000Y. Goffs Sportsman's. Ron Harris. Half-brother to the Group 2 5f Prix du Gros-Chene and triple Group 3 5f winner Tax Free (by Tagula), to the Group 3 5f Prix de Saint-Georges winner Inxile, the useful 5f (at 2 yrs) and 6f winner Green Beret (both by Fayruz) and the fairly useful 6f and 7f winner Xilerator (by Arakan). The dam is an unraced half-sister to 3 minor winners. The second dam, Fernlea (by Sir Ivor), was listed-placed in Ireland and is a half-sister to 3 winners. (Ridge House Stables Ltd). *"He has a very good pedigree and he's a lovely, scopey, strong type of horse. He'll probably go for his maiden and then we'll progress, because he looks like a sprinter that'll get better with a bit of time".*

907. GO GLAMOROUS (IRE) ★★★★

b.f. *Elnadim – Glamorous Air (Air Express).* May 22. €20,000Y. ITS September (Italy). Ridge House Stables. Half-sister to the fairly useful Group 3 5f Sapphire Stakes winner of 7 races (including at 2 yrs) Glamorous Spirit (by Invincible Spirit) and to the quite useful 2-y-o 5f and 6f winner of 4 races Glamorous Angel (by Dark Angel). The dam won 6 races at 2 and 3 yrs in Italy and is a half-sister to 3 minor winners here and abroad. The second dam, Glamorous Bride (by Baillamont), is a placed half-sister to 2 winners. (Robert and Nina Bailey). *"I was disappointed she finished second on both her two starts, but the first one looks as if it was quite a useful race and then maybe I ran her too quick, particularly as she was a late foal. She's growing quite a bit so I'll need to give her a break to let her level up and get over her two quick runs. She's got loads of speed and has a great future – I'm hoping she'll end up at Royal Ascot".*

908. MR DANDY MAN (IRE) ★★★

ch.c. *Dandy Man – Boudica (Alhaarth).* April 1. Seventh foal. €15,000Y. Goffs Sportsman's. Ron Harris. Half-brother to the quite useful dual 6f winner (including at 2 yrs) Sandrey (by Noverre), to the fair 5f winner Chivola (by Invincible Spirit), the moderate 1m winner Abu Dubai (by Kheleyf) and a minor winner abroad by Librettist. The dam is an unplaced half-sister to 9 winners including the useful 5f and 6f winner and Group 3 Cornwallis Stakes third Grand Lad. The second dam, Supportive (by Nashamaa), won four races over 5f at 2 and 3 yrs in Ireland and is a half-sister to 3 winners. (S & A Mares). *"I'm very pleased with him, he ran a good second on his debut and he's quite a big, scopey individual that's maturing all the time. He's changed dramatically in the last month, he's grown up and is very sensible about his job, so he'll probably win his maiden and we'll look to the future. Six furlongs would help him".*

909. M'SELLE (IRE) ★★★★

b.f. *Elnadim – Key Rose (Key Of Luck).* March 21. Second foal. €19,000Y. Goffs Sportsman's. Ron Harris. The dam, a fairly useful Irish 2-y-o 6f and subsequent dual US winner, was listed-placed and is a full or half-sister to 3 winners including the useful Irish 6f and 7f winner of 6 races Empirical Power. The second dam, Rumuz (by Marju), was placed 4 times at up to 10f and is a half-sister to 7 winners. (Robert and Nina Bailey). *"A total 2-y-o, she's all speed, strong and not over-big but powerful. She won on her debut in good style and she'll probably run again in April. I think she's just the type for Chester, so I'm excited about taking her there for the Lily Agnes in May".*

910. WALTA (IRE) ★★★

b.g. *Tagula – Hi Katriona (Second Empire).* February 4. Fifth foal. €12,000Y. Goffs Sportsman's. Ron Harris. Half-brother to the fairly useful 2012 Irish 2-y-o 7f winner and Group 3 Anglesey Stakes second Hard Yards (by Moss Vale), to the fairly useful 2-y-o dual 6f winner Beyleyf (by Kheleyf) and the fair 6f winner of 6 races (including at 2 yrs) Shostakovic (by Fasliyev). The dam, a modest 6f placed Irish 2-y-o, is a half-sister to 11 winners including the Group 2 Premio Melton winner Fred Bongusto. The second dam, Hi Bettina (by Henbit), a fairly useful Irish sprint winner, was second in the Group 3 Debutante Stakes in Ireland and is a half-sister to 5 winners including the Group 3 Norfolk Stakes winner Marouble and the Irish Oaks and Irish 1,000 Guineas second Kitza. (Robert and Nina

Bailey). *"A very nice horse for six furlongs in August. We've had to cut him because he was too colty to concentrate on his job. He's got some nice entries but he won't be as early as we expected him to be".*

911. UNNAMED ★★★

b.c. Hard Spun – Sindy Jacobson (More Than Ready). April 21. Third foal. £15,000 2-y-o. Kempton Breeze-Up. Ron Harris. Half-brother to the minor US dual 3-y-o winner Socio d'Oro (by Medaglia d'Oro). The dam, a US listed-placed 2-y-o winner, is a half-sister to 6 winners including the stakes winner and Grade 2 placed Changing Weather. The second dam, Behaving (by Rubiano), won 3 minor races in the USA and is a half-sister to 11 winners. *"He's ready to roll and once he's named he'll race straight away. Not over-big, but a typical 2-y-o and a five furlong type".*

912. UNNAMED ★★★

b.c. Iffraaj – Woodbury (Woodborough). March 12. Second foal. £10,000 2-y-o. Kempton Breeze-Up. Ron Harris. The dam, a fair winner of 6 races over 5f and 6f from 2 to 5 yrs, is a half-sister to 4 winners including the high-class dual Group 1 5f Nunthorpe Stakes winner Borderlescott. The second dam, Jeewan (Touching Wood), a fair 12f winner, is a sister to a listed winner in Austria. *"His page isn't over-exciting if you take Borderlescott out of it, but he's a very nice colt and ready to race now. He's probably more of a six furlong 2-y-o".*

CHARLES HILLS

I need to thank assistant trainer Kevin Mooney for discussing all the yard's two-year-olds with me. Whether it's Kevin or his boss Charlie, I always get a kind welcome and an enlightening interview here each spring.

913. ABATIS ★★★

b.br.f. Aptitude – Rouwaki (Miswaki). February 23. Sister to the smart 7f (at 2 yrs) and listed 1m winner Critical Moment and half-sister to the smart 2-y-o 6f and Group 3 7f Somerville Tattersall Stakes winner Rerouted (by Stormy Atlantic), the quite useful 1m winner Rattan (by Royal Anthem) and the fair dual 1m winner Cornish Castle (by Mizzen Mast). The

dam is an unplaced half-sister to the Grade 1 Kentucky Oaks winner Flute. The second dam, Rougeur (by Blushing Groom), won over 10f and 12f in the USA. (Khalid Abdulla). *"She came in from America and she's a nice filly that's just ticking over at the minute. She's a nice, good-moving filly that I can see being a seven furlong type in the second half of the season".*

914. A GREAT BEAUTY ★★

b.f. Acclamation – Regatta (Giant's Causeway). February 28. Second foal. €160,000Y. Goffs Orby. BBA (Ire). The dam is an unraced half-sister to 3 winners including the US Grade 2 winner and Grade 1 second Sightseeing. The second dam, Resort (by Pleasant Colony), a winner of four races in the USA at 2 and 3 yrs, was second in the Grade 1 CCA Oaks and is a half-sister to 6 winners including the Graded stakes winners Living Vicariously and With Distinction. *"This filly has gone through two different stages. She's grown, gone weak, filled out and then grown again. She looked a better yearling than she does now, but she's a nice filly but I'll have to withhold judgement for now".*

915. ALMUHALAB ★★★

br.c. Dansili – Ghanaati (Giant's Causeway). February 15. First foal. The dam, winner of the 1,000 Guineas and Coronation Stakes, is a half-sister to numerous winners including the Group 3 12f Cumberland Lodge Stakes winner and Group 1 Champion Stakes second Mawatheeq and the useful 1m (at 2 yrs) and listed 9f winner Rumoush. The second dam, Sarayir (by Mr Prospector), winner of a listed 1m event, is closely related to the Champion Stakes winner Nayef and a half-sister to Nashwan and Unfuwain. (Hamdan Al Maktoum). *"He didn't have the best start to his life because he had a serious problem as a foal and nearly died. But he's fine now and since he's been here he's grown into a great big horse. He has a lot of white about him, a lovely temperament and a lovely way of going. He'll take time and is probably one for the middle of the season onwards over seven furlongs. A lovely horse to deal with, he's nice but he isn't like his mother who won the Guineas for us".*

916. ALZAMMAAR ★★

b.c. Birdstone – Alma Mater (Sadler's Wells).
March 18. Second foal. 170,000Y. Tattersalls
October Book 1. Shadwell Estate Co. The dam,
a fairly useful French listed 12.5f winner, is
a half-sister to 7 winners including the dual
Champion Stakes winner Alborada, the triple
German Group 1 winner Albanova and the
fairly useful dual middle-distance winner and
useful broodmare Alakananda. The second
dam, Alouette (by Darshaan), a useful 1m (at
2 yrs) and listed 12f winner, is a sister to the
listed winner and Irish Oaks third Arrikala and
a half-sister to the dual Group 2 winner Last
Second (dam of the French 2,000 Guineas
winner Aussie Rules), the Doncaster Cup
winner Alleluia (dam of the Prix Royal-Oak
winner Allegretto) and the placed dam of the
Group 1 winners Yesterday and Quarter Moon.
(Hamdan Al Maktoum). *"A horse that's grown
a lot, he's a bit babyish at the minute but that's
probably because he's still going through the
growing stage. He definitely won't be pushed
but he does his work well. Probably more of a
3-y-o type".*

917. ARABLE ★★★

ch.c. Three Valleys – Cut Corn (King's Theatre).
March 8. Fourth foal. The dam won over 10f in
France. The second dam, Harvest (by Zafonic),
is a half-sister to the July Cup and Nunthorpe
Stakes winner Oasis Dream, the French 1,000
Guineas winner Zenda and the very useful
dual listed 1m winner Hopeful Light. (Khalid
Abdulla). *"A nice, big, flashy horse. You'll see
him coming up the track because he has a
big white face and four white socks. He's got a
touch of sore shins so he's on the back burner
at the minute but he's a nice, big, strong horse.
He will make a 2-y-o and looking at him I'd say
he'll be a sprinter".*

918. AURELIA COTTA (IRE) ★★★

b.f. Holy Roman Emperor – Art Work (Zafonic).
February 9. Third foal. £38,000Y. Doncaster
Premier. BBA (Ire). Half-sister to the fair
2-y-o 7f winner Napoleon's Muse (by Peintre
Celebre) and to the moderate 1m winner
Somerset Island (by Barathea). The dam, a
quite useful 1m winner, is a sister to the fairly
useful 7f winner Portland and a half-sister to
5 winners. The second dam, Bayswater (by

Caerleon), a fair 12.3f winner, is a sister to
3 winners including the high-class Group 1
1m Ciga Grand Criterium and Group 2 10.4f
Dante Stakes winner Tenby and a half-sister to
9 winners. *"Not very big but well-made, she's
got a good neck and backside on her. We'll be
getting on with her soon, she looks like she's
got a bit of speed and she's a nice filly".*

919. BAJAN BEAUTY (IRE) ★★★

b.f. Footstepsinthesand – Blue Crystal (Lure).
April 6. Ninth foal. €34,000Y. Goffs
Sportsman's. BBA (Ire). Half-sister to the quite
useful 1m (including at 2 yrs) and 9f winner
Aciano (by Kheleyf), to the Italian 2-y-o
winner and listed placed Golden Liberty (by
Statue Of Liberty) and the minor Italian winner
of 4 races at 3 yrs Guangico (by Grand Lodge).
The dam, a fair 10.5f winner in Ireland, is a
half-sister to 3 minor winners including the
dam of the Group 3 winners Above Average
and Sent From Heaven. The second dam,
Crystal Cross (by Roberto), a quite useful
winner of 4 races at up to 14f, is a half-sister
to 7 winners including the Group 1 Haydock
Park Sprint Cup winner Iktamal, the French
Group 2 winner First Magnitude, the Grade 2
Arkansas Derby winner Rockamundo and the
dam of the Group 2 Gimcrack Stakes winner
Conquest. *"She had a bit of a setback so she's
on the back burner for now, but she's the most
wonderful moving filly. A good goer and a nice
filly for seven furlongs and a mile".*

920. BEATABOUT THE BUSH (IRE) ★★★★

b.br.c. Bushranger – Queen Of Fibres (Scenic).
February 13. Seventh foal. £36,000Y.
Doncaster Premier. G Howson. Half-brother
to the fairly useful 5f to 7f winner of 9 races
(including at 2 yrs) Rocket Rob (by Danetime)
and to the moderate 7f to 9f winner of 4 races
Hi Spec (by Spectrum). The dam, a moderate
9f and 11f winner at 5 yrs in Ireland, is a half-
sister to 3 winners. The second dam, Lightning
Bug (by Prince Bee), won 5 races from 12f to
2m and over hurdles and is a half-sister to 8
winners. *"He'll be one of those we'll be cracking
on with. He shows plenty of speed and he's a
gutsy, tough horse. A nice horse, five furlongs
won't be a problem for him and he might be
our first 2-y-o winner".*

921. BROWN DIAMOND (IRE) ★★★

b.f. *Fastnet Rock – Adjalisa (Darshaan).* May 14. Closely related to the Turkish winner of 8 races Kurtaran (by Danehill) and to the modest 1m winner Music Maestro (by Oratorio) and half-brother to the South African and UAE Grade 2 12f winner Front House (by Sadler's Wells), to the listed Marble Hill Stakes and Group 1 Heinz 57 Phoenix Stakes second Access All Areas (by Approach The Bench), the fair 4-y-o 9f winner Golden Legend (by Last Tycoon) and a winner over hurdles by Desert Prince. The dam was placed once over 7f at 5 yrs and is a half-sister to 5 winners including the listed Leopardstown 2,000 Guineas Trial winner and Group 1 placed Adjareli. The second dam, Adjriyna (by Top Ville), won over 8.5f and is a half-sister to 5 winners. *"A lot of people are suggesting that Fastnet Rock is the sire of the future. This is a lovely filly with a good temperament and hasn't had a problem, but she was a late foal and she is backward. One for the second half of the season, she has a good action and although we haven't worked her yet I'd say she'll be a nice filly when her time comes".*

922. CABLE BAY ★★★★★

b.c. *Invincible Spirit – Rose De France (Diktat).* March 2. Second foal. €130,000Y. Goffs Orby. BBA (Ire). Brother to the fair 2013 3-y-o 5f winner Tanghan. The dam, placed four times at 3 yrs in France, is a half-sister to 4 winners including the Group 3 winner and French 2,000 Guineas third Bowman and the dam of the Group 1 winners Kirklees and Mastery. The second dam, Cherokee Rose (by Dancing Brave), won the Group 1 Haydock Park Sprint Cup and the Group 1 Prix Maurice de Gheest and is a half-sister to 4 winners. *"He may have been expensive, but as things stand I'd say he's our best two-year-old. He's grown and although sometimes horses by this sire can be a bit 'buzzy' this colt has a lovely attitude and a nice way of going. If you asked me to give you a rating out of ten I'd give him nine, right now. He takes me up the gallop beautifully and does everything right. A typical 2-y-o, he's well put-together and with the speed to start off at five furlongs in May. Everyone who rides him likes him and the way he goes you'd think he was a 3-y-o".*

923. CAPE KARLI (IRE) ★★

br.f. *Cape Cross – Karliysha (Kalanisi).* April 26. Third foal. €57,000Y. Goffs Orby. Jim & Susan Hill. Half-sister to the fair 7f and 10f winner Maude Adams (by Rock Of Gibraltar). The dam, a minor French 3-y-o winner, is a half-sister to 7 winners including Karasta (2-y-o Group 3 1m May Hill Stakes), Kasthari (Group 2 2m 2f Doncaster Cup in a dead-heat) and Kargali (Group 3 Gladness Stakes). The second dam, Karliyka (by Last Tycoon), a French 3-y-o winner of 4 races, was listed placed over 1m and 10f and is a half-sister to 4 winners. *"A very backward filly and a fairly late foal, she's growing and on the back burner at the moment, but her pedigree tells you she'll be a better 3-y-o".*

924. CAPTAIN BOB (IRE) ★★★★

b.c. *Dark Angel – Birthday Present (Cadeaux Genereux).* April 17. Seventh foal. €80,000Y. Goffs Orby. BBA (Ire). Half-brother to the quite useful 2-y-o 7f winner Red Presence (by Redback), to the 2-y-o 6f winner and Group 3 6f third May Day Queen (by Danetime) and the 2-y-o 7f and 1m winner Call It On (by Raise A Grand) – all quite useful. The dam is an unraced half-sister to 3 winners including the Group 1 Moyglare Stud Stakes third Supposition. The second dam, Topicality (by Topsider), won once at 3 yrs and is a sister to the Cherry Hinton and Fred Darling Stakes winner Top Socialite and a half-sister to the US Grade 1 winners Expelled and Exbourne. *"A strong horse, he's done really well, had a bit of time off for sore shins but he's back cantering now. I think he'll be alright and he'll definitely be a 2-y-o".*

925. CHRISELLIAM (IRE) ★★★★ ♠

b.f. *Iffraaj – Danielli (Danehill).* February 2. Fourth foal. 40,000Y. Tattersalls October Book 2. Sackville/Donald. Half-sister to the fair 2-y-o 7f winner and subsequent US Grade 3 9f third Janicellaine (by Beat Hollow) and to a hurdles winner by Soviet Star. The dam, placed four times at up to 13f in Ireland, is a sister to the Group 3 C L Weld Park Stakes winner Eva's Request and a half-sister to 7 winners including the Group 1 7f Moyglare Stud Stakes winner Priory Belle and the Group 3 7f Concorde Stakes winner Wild Bluebell.

The second dam, Ingabelle (by Taufan), won the Group 3 Phoenix Sprint Stakes and is a half-sister to 4 winners. *"A 2-y-o through-and-through, she's got loads of speed and is a nice filly. We won't be hanging about with her, she's tough enough to take it and she's built like a colt".*

926. COLUMBIAN ROULETTE (IRE) ★★

b.c. Bushranger – Rainbow Lyrics (Rainbow Quest). March 18. Seventh foal. £50,000Y. Doncaster Premier. BBA (Ire)/C Hills. Half-brother to the quite useful 12f winner Boucheron (by Galileo) and to a jumps winner by Montjeu. The dam is an unraced half-sister to 4 winners including the Irish listed winner of 10 races Free To Speak. The second dam, Love For Poetry (by Lord Gayle), won 3 races at 3 yrs and is a half-sister to 5 winners. *"A typical 2-y-o, we'll have to get on with him but he's not straightforward to ride – I think Bushranger was a bit like that. He's got a bit of speed, which must come from the sire looking at the pedigree. He's got to grow up mentally and go the right way".*

927. COMPUTER (USA) ★★★★

ch.c. Mizzen Mast – Tolerance (Seeking The Gold). February 27. The dam is a half-sister to the triple US Grade 1 winner Empire Maker and to the US Grade 1 winners Honest Lady (herself dam of the US Grade 1 winner First Defence), Chester House and Chiselling. The second dam, Toussaud (by El Gran Senor), a 6f and 7f winner here, subsequently won a Grade 1 stakes event in North America. (Khalid Abdulla). *"Quite a strong horse, he's done really well. We've taken our time with him but he's got plenty of bone and he'll make a 2-y-o. Definitely a nice horse, we haven't done anything with him yet but physically he's done well and he looks a sprinting type".*

928. CORAL MIST ★★★★

ch.f. Bahamian Bounty – Treasure Trove (The Minstrel). March 6. Thirteenth foal. €55,000Y. Goffs Orby. BBA (Ire). Closely related to the Group 1 7f Prix de la Foret and German Group 3 6.5f winner of 16 races Toylsome and to the fair dual 7f winner What A Treasure (both by Cadeaux Genereux) and half-sister to the useful 10f, 14f and hurdles winner Woolfall Treasure (by Daylami), the quite useful 6f (at 2 yrs) to 8.6f winner of 9 races Zhitomir (by Lion Cavern), the fair 1m winner Huntingfortreasure (by Pastoral Pursuits), the fair 9f winner Dutch Diamond (by Dutch Art), the French 2-y-o 1m winner Playwithmyheart (by Diktat). The dam, a modest 5f to 7f placed 2-y-o, is a half-sister to 4 winners including the US Grade 3 winner Ocean Queen and the Queen Mary Stakes and Fred Darling Stakes winner Dance Parade – subsequently a Grade 2 winner in the USA. The second dam, River Jig (by Irish River), a useful 2-y-o 9f winner here, also won over 12f in Italy and is a half-sister to 6 winners including the dam of the Australian Grade 1 winner Always Aloof. *"She looks like she's got plenty of speed. We haven't pressed any buttons with her yet, but she's one of those that's always going forward and has a good action. She'll make a 2-y-o and I like her".*

929. CULDAFF (IRE) ★★★

b.c. Aqlaam – Nenuphar (Night Shift). February 21. Tenth foal. €42,000Y. Goffs Orby. BBA (Ire). Half-brother to 5 winners in Germany and France including the champion German 2-y-o filly and Group 3 winner Night Lagoon (by Night Shift and herself dam of the Group 2 winner Nobellist) and the German Derby second Night Tango (as Acatenango). The dam, a winner of 3 races in Germany at 2 and 3 yrs including a listed event, is a half-sister to 11 winners. The second dam, Narola (by Nebos), won 3 minor races at 3 yrs in Germany and is a half-sister to 7 winners. *"Well put-together, he's a bit babyish but he's done nothing wrong and he's a good, strong-looking horse. He moves well and although he hasn't worked yet I'd definitely say he'll be a 2-y-o, probably setting off at six furlongs".*

930. DESPOT (IRE) ★★★

gr.c. Verglas – Ms Bossy Boots (Grand Slam). April 24. Fourth living foal. £46,000Y. Doncaster Premier. BBA (Ire)/C Hills. Half-brother to the minor US 4-y-o winner Carry Barry (by Cat Thief). The dam is an unraced half-sister to 3 winners including the Group 3 Irish 1,000 Guineas Trial and Group 3 C L Weld Park Stakes winner and triple Group 1 placed Arch Swing. The second dam, Gold Pattern (by Slew O'Gold), a minor US winner of 4 races, is a half-sister to 2 stakes winners in the USA and the dam of the US Grade 1 winner Archarcharch. *"He's had a touch of sore shins but he's grown and changed an awful lot, so he'll just take a bit of time. He's a nice horse that does his work well, so I wouldn't knock him".*

931. EMERALD BREEZE (IRE) ★★★

b.f. Tagula – Rebel Aclaim (Acclamation). February 4. First foal. £28,000Y. Doncaster Premier. BBA (Ire)/C Hills. The dam, a modest Irish 7f and 1m winner, is a half-sister to 6 winners including the Italian 1m listed winner Silent Tribute. The second dam, Tribal Rite (by Be My Native), a fairly useful Irish 2-y-o listed 6f and 3-y-o 10f winner, is a half-sister to the Middle Park Stakes winner Balla Cove, the US stakes winner Burning Issue and the Irish listed winner Blasted Heath. *"A nice filly, she's not over-big, has a nice way of going and always wants to please. She won't be very early but she'll make a 2-y-o alright and she'll be a six furlong filly I should think".*

932. FROSTY THE SNOWMAN (IRE) ★★

gr.c. Mastercraftsman – Sleeveless (Fusaichi Pegasus). March 23. Second foal. 80,000Y. Tattersalls October Book 1. BBA (Ire). The dam, a fair Irish 7f placed maiden, is a half-sister to 5 winners including the Group 3 Beresford Stakes winner and dual Group 1 second Castle Gandolfo. The second dam, Golden Oriole (by Northern Dancer), won at 3 yrs and is a sister to the champion 2-y-o's El Gran Senor and Try My Best and a half-sister to 4 winners. *"He's a nice, big horse that's lost a lot of time because of a setback, but he's still worth a mention in the book because he'll be alright a bit later on. He's actually down in the book as a chestnut but he's more like a grey/roan colt".*

933. GOWN (IRE) ★★★

b.f. Excellent Art – Chehalis Sunset (Danehill Dancer). January 20. Second foal. 10,000Y. Tattersalls October Book 2. BBA (Ire). The dam is an unraced half-sister to 5 winners including the US Grade 2 9f Honeymoon Handicap winner and Grade 1 placed Country Garden. The second dam, Totham (by Shernazar), a quite useful 12f winner, is a half-sister to 6 winners. *"She only cost ten grand and you*

wouldn't mind a few more like her for that sort of money. She's grown and she's in the middle of growing again at the moment so she's only ticking over for now, but she's a nice filly and I think she'll win at six furlongs".* TRAINERS' BARGAIN BUY

934. IFTAAR (IRE) ★★★★

b.c. Bushranger – Kheleyf's Silver (Kheleyf). February 21. First foal. £90,000Y. Doncaster Premier. Shadwell Estate Co. The dam, a fairly useful 2-y-o 5f winner, is a half-sister to 3 winners including the very useful Group 3 6f Norfolk Stakes winner of 6 races Masta Plasta. The second dam, Silver Arrow (by Shadeed), was placed once at 2 yrs and is a half-sister to 4 winners. (Hamdan Al Maktoum). *"A nice-looking horse, he's like a little tank and he's going to make a 2-y-o. Everyone likes him, he's forward-going and he's got a bit about him. I'd definitely give him the thumbs up and he'll go five furlongs without a problem".*

935. INTERJECT (USA) ★★★★

b.br.f. Empire Maker – Introducing (Deputy Minister). March 21. Half-sister to the moderate 11f to 14f and hurdles winner Short Supply (by Point Given). The dam, a quite useful 9f winner, is a half-sister to numerous winners including the US Grade 1 10f winner Midships, the multiple listed 10f winner Principal Role (by Empire Maker) and the very useful 10f and 12f winner and US Grade 1 placed Staging Post. The second dam, Interim (by Sadler's Wells), a very useful 1m and 10f winner, is a half-sister to the high-class Interval, a sprinting winner of four races from 5f to 1m including the Group 2 Prix Maurice de Gheest and to the unraced dam of the Hoover Fillies Mile winner Invited Guest. (Khalid Abdulla). *"This is a nice filly, quite well-made and a seven furlong type for the middle of the season. A quality filly".*

936. JAZZ (IRE) ★★★

b.c. Danehill Dancer – Jazz Baby (Fasliyev). March 11. Fourth foal. €40,000Y. Goffs Orby. BBA (Ire)/C Hills. The dam is an unraced half-sister to 10 winners including the Group 1 10.5f Prix de Diane winner Rafha (the dam of 4 stakes winners including Invincible Spirit) and the Group 3 Blandford Stakes winner

Chiang Mai (dam of the Group 1 Pretty Polly Stakes winner Chinese White). The second dam, Eljazzi (by Artaius), a fairly useful 2-y-o 7f winner, is a half-sister to 8 winners including the good miler Pitcairn. *"He's a bit of a playboy but he's one we'll be getting on with and he's done a few half-speeds upsides and does it nicely. He'll be racing soon and he's shown enough, so I think he'll go six furlongs and probably seven later on".*

937. KIYOSHI ★★★★ ♠

b.f. *Dubawi – Mocca (Sri Pekan)*. March 5. Fourth living foal. 80,000Y. Tattersalls October Book 2. David Redvers. Half-sister to the modest 2012 6f and 1m placed 2-y-o Miss Mocca (by Bahamian Bounty) and to the quite useful placed 2-y-o and hurdles winner Red Riverman (by Haafhd). The dam, a quite useful 1m (at 2 yrs) and 10f winner, was listed-placed in Germany is a half-sister to one winner. The second dam, Ewan (by Indian Ridge), is an unraced half-sister to one winner. (Qatar Racing Ltd). *"A lovely filly, Jamie Spencer has been down to ride her a couple of times for the owner and he thinks she's quite smart. A big, strong filly that'll make a 2-y-o, she's got plenty of 'poke' and she goes well. One to watch out for".*

938. LATE NIGHT MARK ★★

b.c. *Marju – Khatela (Shernazar)*. April 18. Tenth living foal. €80,000Y. Goffs Orby. Jim & Susan Hill. Brother to the 2-y-o 7.2f and listed 1m Heron Stakes winner and Group 3 9f Prix de Conde second Massive and half-brother to the modest 15f winner Khayar (by Refuse To Bend), the modest 2-y-o 9f winner Khandala (by Soviet Star), the French 11f winner Jimbeck and a winner over jumps in France (both by Night Shift). The dam won over 1m and 9f in Ireland and is a half-sister to 4 minor winners. The second dam, Khatima (by Relko), won at 3 yrs and is a half-sister to the French triple listed winner Kaldoun. *"A big, strong horse, he's done well since we've had him from the sales. He'll want seven furlongs in the second half of the year".*

939. LOVELOCKS (IRE) ★★★

b.f. *High Chaparral – Civility Cat (Tale Of The Cat)*. March 28. Fourth foal. €87,000Y. Goffs

Orby. BBA (Ire). Half-sister to the fair Irish 2-y-o 7f winner Rogue Element (by Holy Roman Emperor). The dam, a stakes-placed winner at 2 and 3 yrs USA, is a half-sister to 7 winners including the dam of the 2-y-o dual Group 2 winner Flashy Wings. The second dam, Civility (by Shirley Heights), a very useful 12f winner, is a half-sister to 4 winners including the smart 2-y-o Piney Ridge. *"A big filly, but a good mover and all the riders like her. She's going to want time but she's forward-going and is a nice filly for the middle to back-end".*

940. MAHAATA (IRE) ★★★

br.f. *Halling – Tafaani (Green Desert)*. January 29. Half-sister to the useful 2012 2-y-o 6f winner and Group 3 7f Sweet Solera Stakes third Reyaadah and to the quite useful 1m and 10f winner Kaafel (by Nayef). The dam is an unraced sister to one winner and a half-sister to numerous winners including the high-class 7.3f Hungerford Stakes and Tripleprint Celebration Mile winner and French 2,000 Guineas second Muhtathir. The second dam, Majmu (by Al Nasr), a useful winner of the Group 3 1m May Hill Stakes at 2 yrs, was third in a listed event over 10f at 3 yrs and is a half-sister to 5 minor winners. (Hamdan Al Maktoum). *"A nice, strong filly that's built like a colt with a big neck on her. She's only just arrived from Dubai and has had four days cantering with us, but she looks nice".*

941. MARINETTE ★★

b.br.f. *Mizzen Mast – Faraway Flower (Distant View)*. February 15. The dam was a useful 2-y-o 6f winner. The second dam, Silver Star (by Zafonic), won over 1m at 2 yrs in France, was listed-placed over 1m at 3 yrs and is a sister to the champion European 2-y-o Xaar (winner of the Group 1 Dewhurst Stakes and the Group 1 Prix de la Salamandre) and a half-sister to the Group 3 10.5f Prix Corrida winner Diese and the Group 3 1m Prix Quincey winner Masterclass. (Khalid Abdulla). *"She's huge. A nice filly that stands out, she'll be a back-end type because she's got a lot of strengthening up to do".*

942. MINNIE HAZEL (IRE) ★★

ch.f. *Excellent Art – Reprise (Darshaan)*. March 7. €15,000Y. Goffs Orby. BBA (Ire). Sister to the

7f (at 2 yrs) and Group 3 12f St Simon Stakes winner Hazel Lavery and half-sister to the useful 10f and 12f winner and Group 3 12f second Leo Gali and to the minor French 12f winner Orient Meissa (both by Galileo). The dam, placed fourth once over 10f, is a half-sister to 3 winners. The second dam, Rapid Repeat (by Exactly Sharp), a quite useful 2-y-o 7f winner, is a half-sister to 5 winners including the Irish Group 3 winner Artema. *"A small filly, she's a different model than her sister and she'll be one for the second half of the season".*

943. MY PAINTER (IRE) ★★

b.f. *Jeremy – Last Cry (Peintre Celebre).* February 9. Fourth foal. €28,000Y. Goffs Orby. Jim & Susan Hill. Half-sister to the fair 10f, 2m and hurdles winner Master Fong (by Dr Fong) and to the modest Irish 1m winner Madeira Girl (by Bachelor Duke). The dam, a 3-y-o 1m winner and listed-placed in France, is a half-sister to 5 winners. The second dam, Last Dream (by Alzao), won once at 3 yrs and is a half-sister to 6 winners including the French Group 1 winners Fijar Tango and Lost World. *"She'll want some time and seven furlongs, but she'll be a lovely filly one day".*

944. NATHR (USA) ★★★★

b.br.c. *Dixie Union – Sweet Rider (Seeking The Gold).* February 10. Second foal. $200,000Y. Keeneland September. Shadwell Estate Co. The dam is an unraced half-sister to 5 winners including the US Grade 2 winner and Grade 1 placed Sweet Catarina. The second dam, Purrfectly (by Storm Cat), a minor winner of 2 races at 3 yrs in the USA, is a half-sister to the French 1,000 Guineas winner Culture Vulture. (Hamdan Al Maktoum). *"A lovely horse. He's a typical 2-y-o, very natural and we'll be getting on with him. He'll have loads of speed".*

945. QAWAASEM (IRE) ★★★

b.f. *Shamardal – Misdaqeya (Red Ransom).* February 6. First foal. The dam, a useful 2-y-o 7f winner and second in the Group 3 Sweet Solera Stakes, is a half-sister to 2 winners. The second dam, Crystal Power (by Pleasant Colony), won once at 3 yrs in the USA and is a half-sister to 5 winners including the US Grade 1 Flower Bowl Invitational Handicap winner Chelsey Flower (herself dam of the French

Group 3 winner Kentucky Dynamite). *"A nice filly, she's likely to make a 2-y-o in June over seven furlongs".*

946. QUEEN CATRINE (IRE) ★★

b.f. *Acclamation – Kahira (King's Best).* May 16. Fifth foal. 55,000Y. Tattersalls October Book 2. BBA (Ire). Half-sister to the quite useful Irish dual 7f winner Vastitas (by Green Desert). The dam, a fair 2-y-o 7f placed maiden, is a half-sister to the Group 1 6f Haydock Park Sprint Cup winner Tamarisk. The second dam, Sine Labe (by Vaguely Noble), is an unplaced half-sister to the Group 1 Prix Saint-Alary winner Treble. *"She's grown, had a touch of sore shins and she's back cantering now. A fairly late foal, she's quite nice and she'll be alright".*

947. RANDWICK (IRE) ★★

b.c. *High Chaparral – Subito (Darshaan).* March 22. Ninth foal. 70,000Y. Tattersalls October Book 2. BBA (Ire). Half-brother to the quite useful Irish 9f winner Silk Mascara (by Barathea), to the 2012 7f and 1m placed 2-y-o Zipp, the moderate 12f winner Excellent News (both by Excellent Art), the modest 11f and 12f winner Onemoreandstay (by Dr Fong) and the minor US winner of 8 races Chasm (by Gulch). The dam, a fairly useful 2-y-o 7f winner, is a half-sister to 3 winners. The second dam, Rapid Repeat (by Exactly Sharp), a 2-y-o 7f winner, is a half-sister to 5 winners including the Group 3 Derrinstown Stud Derby Trial and US stakes winner Artema. *"This horse has had a few niggling issues but he's a lovely, good-moving horse. He's a bit too exuberant so we need to keep the lid on him a bit and he's only ticking over at the minute, but he's a nice horse".*

948. RIVER GODDESS (IRE) ★★★

b.f. *Marju – Talwin (Alhaarth).* February 19. Fourth foal. 50,000Y. Tattersalls October Book 2. BBA (Ire). The dam, a fairly useful Irish 7f (at 2 yrs), 9f and 10f winner, was listed-placed and is a half-sister to 7 winners including the useful 7f (at 2 yrs) to 12f winner Our Teddy. The second dam, Lady Windley (by Baillamont), an 11f winner of 3 races in France, is a half-sister to 6 winners and to the placed Lingerie (herself dam of the Oaks winner Light Shift, the Group 1 Tattersalls Gold Cup winner Shiva and the Group 2 Prix Jean du

Chaudenay winner Limnos). *"She's a nice filly and very much like the 2-y-o Rosehill Artist. If you put the two of them together you'd have a job knowing which is which. I can see her being alright, she'll make a 2-y-o, has a nice way of going and she'll win races".*

949. ROCK OF DREAMS (IRE) ★★

b.c. Rock Of Gibraltar – Manhattan Dream *(Statue Of Liberty).* February 21. Second foal. 32,000Y. Tattersalls October Book 1. BBA (Ire). Half-brother to the quite useful 2012 2-y-o 7f winner Muharrib (by Oasis Dream). The dam, a fair 7f and 1m winner at 3 yrs, is a half-sister to 3 winners including the Group 1 1m Coronation Stakes and winner and 1,000 Guineas second Maid's Causeway. The second dam, Vallee Des Reves (by Kingmambo) is an unraced half-sister to the Group 2 Prix du Muguet winner Vetheuil, the Group 3 Prix de l'Opera winner Verveine (herself dam of the Grade 1 winners Vallee Enchantee and Volga) and the dam of the Group 1 Grand Prix de Paris winner Vespone. *"He's grown, changed and wants a bit of time, so he'll just be ticking over for a while yet".*

950. ROSEHILL ARTIST (IRE) ★★★

b.f. Excellent Art – Conference *(Montjeu).* May 10. Second foal. 35,000Y. Tattersalls October Book 2. BBA (Ire). The dam is an unraced half-sister to 7 winners including the US stakes winner, Group 3 Chester Vase third and US Grade 3 third Distant Mirage and the listed-placed Roses In The Snow (dam of the US Grade 3 winner Snowdrops). The second dam, Desert Bluebell (by Kalaglow), is a placed half-sister to 10 winners including the Group 3 Solario Stakes winner Shining Waters (herself dam of the Group 1 Grand Criterium winner Tenby). *"She's done nothing wrong and she's grown into a nice filly. The lad who rides her all the time likes her and she's straightforward, but she was a May foal and she'll just take a bit of time".*

951. SCILLONIAN SUNSET (IRE) ★★

ch.f. Teofilo – Hundred Year Flood *(Giant's Causeway).* January 30. Fourth foal. 35,000Y. Tattersalls October Book 2. BBA (Ire). Sister to the quite useful dual 12f winner Castilo Del Diablo. The dam, a minor 2-y-o winner in the

USA, is a half-sister to 3 winners including the US Grade 3 winner and Grade 1 placed Sweet Hope. The second dam, High Heeled Hope (by Salt Lake), won two stakes events at 2 yrs in the USA, was Grade 1 placed twice and is a half-sister to 6 winners. *"A big filly, she was a lovely yearling but she's changed and grown quite a bit. She's had a few niggling issues and we won't see her racing until the second half of the season".*

952. SELLINGALLTHETIME (IRE) ★★

b.c. Lawman – Anthyllis (IRE) *(Night Shift).* March 12. Fifth foal. 20,000Y. Tattersalls December. Not sold. Half-brother to the French 7f winner and German triple listed-placed Topkapi Diamond (by Acclamation), to the fair 2-y-o 7f winner Red Alpha (by Red Clubs) and a minor winner at 3 yrs in the USA by Compton Place. The dam is an unraced sister to the US Grade 2 Sunset Handicap winner Plicck. The second dam, Anthis (by Ela-Mana-Mou), is a placed half-sister to 5 winners including the dam of the Group 2 Queen Anne Stakes winner Waajib. *"He's altered a lot and strengthened up having been very slight and 'buzzy' when he first came in. He'll be alright a bit later on".*

953. SOCIAL RISER (IRE) ★★

b.f. High Chaparral – Parvenue *(Ezzoud).* April 6. Eighth foal. €52,000Y. Goffs Orby. Jim & Susan Hill. Half-sister to the South African Group 2 and Group 3 winner Gorongosa, to the useful Irish 2-y-o 1m winner Vivaldi, the minor South African 4-y-o winner Monaco Dream (all by Montjeu), the fairly useful 2-y-o 1m winner Luxurious (by Galileo), the quite useful 2-y-o 6f winner Three Decades (by Invincible Spirit) and a winner at 2 yrs in Italy by Fasliyev. The dam, a quite useful 2-y-o 6f winner, is a half-sister to 5 winners including the useful 8.3f winner Pedrillo. The second dam, Patria (by Mr Prospector), a fair 2-y-o 7.6f winner, is a sister to Lycius (winner of the Group 1 6f Middle Park Stakes and placed in numerous Group 1 events) and to the Group 3 6f Prix de Cabourg winner Tereshkova and a half-sister to the US dual Grade 2 winner Akabir. *"A nice-actioned filly, she's by High Chaparral and so not bred to be a sharp 2-y-o and she's a bit weak at the moment. She'll want seven furlongs and a mile this year".*

954. SOLID JUSTICE (IRE) ★★★

b.c. Rock Of Gibraltar – Burnin' Memories (Lit de Justice). February 25. Fifth foal. €85,000Y. Goffs Orby. Jim & Susan Hill. Half-brother to the useful Irish 2-y-o 6f winner and Group 2 Railway Stakes second In Some Respect (by Indian Haven), to the quite useful 1m winner Glebe Queen (by Hawkeye) and the fair 7f and 1m winner Adorable Choice (by Choisir). The dam won 5 races at 2 to 5 yrs in the USA including a minor stakes event and is a half-sister to 7 winners. The second dam, Adorable Vice (by Vice Regent), a US stakes-placed winner of 3 races, is a half-sister to 4 winners including the Italian Group 1 winner Looking For and the Italian Group 2 winner Life On Mars. *"He's grown and lengthened, so he's not going to be early but he does his work nicely and he's a good mover. He's cantering away steadily and had no problems. If he can grow into his frame he'll be alright and he has a nice way of going".*

955. SOUND OF SUMMER (IRE) ★★★★

b.f. Excellent Art – Ibtikar (Private Account). March 9. Sixteenth foal. €65,000Y. Arqana Deauville August. BBA (Ire). Half-sister to 7 winners including the US stakes-placed Vegas Venture (by Gold Fever), the South African stakes-placed Brown Linnet (by King Of Kings), the quite useful 2-y-o 7f winner Just Name It (by Miswaki) and the fair 12f winner Sea Change. The dam, a poor 6f (at 2 yrs) and 2m placed maiden, is closely related to the Grade 1 Hollywood Gold Cup, Charles H. Strub Stakes and Californian Stakes winner Desert Wine and a half-sister to 6 winners including the dual Grade 1 winner Menifee and to the unraced dam of the dual Group 1 winner Fasliyev. The second dam, Anne Campbell (by Never Bend), won three races in the USA including a minor stakes event and is a half-sister to 4 winners including the French Group 3 winner Repercutionist. *"A filly bought in France, she's done well, strengthened up and I like her. She'll be racing in early summer and she's got a bit of speed".*

956. TAMALUK (USA) ★★

br.c. Discreet Cat – Mabaahej (Belong To Me). Third foal. Half-brother to the 2012 2-y-o 7f winner (on his only start) Kerbaaj (by Dixie Union). The dam, a 1m placed maiden, is a half-sister to the smart 2-y-o 6f winner and Group 1 6f Middle Park Stakes third Tajdeef and to the listed 7f winner Alyarf. The second dam, Tabheej (by Mujtahid), a useful 2-y-o 5f and 6f winner, was third in the Lowther Stakes and is a sister to the Group 3 5f Cornwallis Stakes winner Mubhij. (Hamdan Al Maktoum). *"He only arrived from Dubai the other day and has only had four days cantering with us. He's a good mover but he's got a bit of making-up to do because he's got the frame but he's quite narrow at the minute".*

957. TANZEEL (IRE) ★★★

b.c. Elusive City – Royal Fizz (Royal Academy). May 10. Twelfth foal. 100,000Y. Tattersalls October Book 2. Shadwell Estate Co. Half-brother to the Group 3 6f Greenlands Stakes and UAE Group 3 6f winner of 8 races (including at 2 yrs) Hitchens (by Acclamation), to the useful 2-y-o dual 7f winner and listed-placed Grand Marque (by Grand Lodge), the fair 10f winner Effervesce (by Galileo) and a winner in Belgium by Brief Truce. The dam won once over 6.5f at 2 yrs in France and is a half-sister to 7 winners here and abroad including the £1.4m Hong Kong earner Floral Pegasus. The second dam, Crown Crest (by Mill Reef), won once at 3 yrs and is a sister to the high-class middle-distance horses Glint Of Gold and Diamond Shoal. (Hamdan Al Maktoum). *"He's quite a nice horse that's strengthened up and he's doing well. His riders say he feels as if he's got a bit of speed, he hasn't done anything wrong and I'd say he'd make a 2-y-o alright, setting off at six furlongs".*

958. UNNAMED ★★

b.c. Royal Applause – Passing Hour (Red Ransom). April 2. Third foal. 55,000Y. Tattersalls October Book 2. BBA (Ire). Half-brother to the unraced 2012 2-y-o Sixty Minutes (by Compton Place). The dam, a fair 3-y-o 1m winner, is a sister to the Group 3 5f Queen Mary Stakes winner Shining Hour and to the Group 1 Prix Marcel Boussac second

Titian Time and a half-sister to 5 winners. The second dam, Timely (by Kings Lake), a useful 1m winner, was third in the Group 1 Moyglare Stud Stakes and is a half-sister to 3 winners including the dam of the Italian Group 1 winner Le Vie Dei Colori. *"He's a great, big horse by a stallion that's been disappointing for us. This colt doesn't ride like a sharp horse so he's been given some time to develop and we'll have to see how he goes on".*

JOHN HILLS

959. UNNAMED
b.c. High Chaparral – Cabo (Sagamix). March 15. Second foal. 35,000Y. Tattersalls October Book 2. Amanda Skiffington. The dam, a fair 10f and 2m winner, is a half-sister to 3 winners. The second dam, Debate (by High Line), won 3 minor races at 3 yrs in France and is a half-sister to 3 winners. (Prolinx Ltd).

960. UNNAMED
b.f. Excellent Art – Course de Diamante (Galileo). March 14. First foal. 24,000Y. Tattersalls October Book 2. Rae Guest. The dam, a modest maiden, was placed fourth once over 10f and is a half-sister to 7 winners including the Group 3 Chester Vase third and US listed stakes winner Distant Mirage and the dam of the US triple Grade 3 winner Snowdrops. The second dam, Desert Bluebell (by Kalaglow), is a placed half-sister to 10 winners including the Group 3 Solario Stakes winner Shining Waters (herself dam of the Group 1 Grand Criterium winner Tenby).

961. UNNAMED
b.c. Montjeu – Inkling (Seeking The Gold). April 25. Closely related to the Irish 2-y-o 1m winner (on his only start) Kingdom Of Naples (by Sadler's Wells) and half-brother to the fairly useful Irish 2010 2-y-o 6f winner and Group 3 6f second Emerald Ring (by Johannesburg) and to the fair Irish 12f winner Campeche Bay (by Giant's Causeway). The dam, a useful 2-y-o 6f winner on her only start, is closely related to the Group 1 Grand Criterium winner Jade Robbery and the US Grade 3 winners Chequer and Numerous and a half-sister to 5 winners. The second dam, Number (by Nijinsky), won the Grade 2 Firenze Handicap and the Grade 2 Hempstead

Handicap and is closely related to Nureyev and a half-sister to the dam of Sadler's Wells. (Mrs M Kingham).

962. UNNAMED
b.f. Sleeping Indian – Toffee Vodka (Danehill Dancer). March 3. Third living foal. £14,500Y. Doncaster Festival. Anthony Stroud. Half-sister to the unraced 2012 2-y-o Toffee Shot and to the fair 2-y-o 6f winner Toffee Tart (both by Dutch Art). The dam, a fair 6f (at 2 yrs) to 1m winner, is a half-sister to 6 minor winners. The second dam, Vieux Carre (by Pas de Seul), is an unplaced half-sister to 6 winners. (Gary and Linnet Woodward).

JO HUGHES

963. CALEDONIA LAIRD ★★★
b.c. Firebreak – Granuaile O'Malley (Mark Of Esteem). February 17. Brother to the very useful listed 5f (at 2 yrs) and Group 3 5f winner Caledonia Lady and half-sister to the fair 5f and 6f winner of 5 races from 2 to 5 yrs Caledonia Princess (by Kyllachy) and the fair 1m winner of 5 races Caledonia Prince (by Needwood Blade). The dam, a moderate 6f placed maiden, is a half-sister to several winners. The second dam, Dame Laura (by Royal Academy), a useful 5f (at 2 yrs) and 6f winner, was Group 3 placed over 5f and 1m. (Isla & Colin Cage). *"A home-bred that was sent to us, he's very much like his sister, the 4-y-o Caledonia Lady, in that he's not over-big but quite sharp. She got better as she got older and stronger. Having said that he'll start his career in mid-April and he looks a 2-y-o type".*

964. UNNAMED ★★★
ch.c. Manduro – Precious Citizen (Proud Citizen). February 7. First foal. £40,000 2-y-o. Kempton Breeze-Up. Jo Hughes. The dam, a moderate 9f and 10f placed maiden, is a half-sister to 3 winners. The second dam, Fasateen (by Alysheba), a winner over 1m at 2 yrs and a listed 12f event at 3 in France, is a half-sister to the 1,000 Guineas and Prix de l'Opera winner Hatoof and to the US Grade 1 winner Irish Prize. *"I like him a lot and I think he'll be a six/seven furlong 2-y-o. I'm hoping we'll get to the Chesham Stakes, he has a lovely action and I don't think he's just an out-and-out 2-y-o. I think he'll win as 2-y-o but he's got the scope*

to train on. I still have 50% of him for sale if anyone is interested".

965. UNNAMED ★★

b.f. *Bushranger – Tranquil Sky (Intikhab)*. April 9. Fifth foal. 6,200foal. Tattersalls December. Kilronan Stud. Half-sister to the fair 10f winner Diamond Vision (by Diamond Green). The dam, a quite useful 2-y-o 6f and 7f winner, is a half-sister to 7 winners. The second dam, Tranquillity (by Night Shift), a fair winner of one race over 1m at 3 yrs, is a half-sister to 3 winners. *"I bought her privately in Ireland. She has plenty of speed and will start off at five furlongs but she has the scope to see the season out as well. A nice type of filly and she's still for sale".*

966. UNNAMED ★★

b.c. *Multiplex – Vita Mia (Central Park)*. March 11. First foal. £5,000Y. Doncaster Premier. Jo Hughes. The dam, a modest 10f and 12f winner, is a half-sister to one winner. The second dam, Ma Vie (by Salse), a modest 4-y-o 10f winner, is a half-sister to 10 winners. *"I thought he was a nice type at the sales so I bought him. I'm a fan of Multiplex because I've done well with them. He's quite a big, scopey type that shows plenty of speed and I'll be able to start him off at five furlongs although I think he'll be better over six. He should be running in May and I like him".*

967. UNNAMED ★★★

b.c. *Bahri – Wana Doo (Grand Slam)*. March 18. Fifth foal. Half-brother to the 2012 2-y-o Group 2 7f Champagne Stakes and 2013 3-y-o Group 3 Craven Stakes winner Toronado (by High Chaparral) and to a winner over jumps in France by Tagula. The dam, a French 2-y-o 1m winner, is a half-sister to 4 winners including the 2-y-o Group 1 1m Racing Post Trophy and Group 2 1m Beresford Stakes winner Casamento and the very useful 6f (at 2 yrs) and 7f winner Inler. The second dam, Wedding Gift (by Always Fair), a French 2-y-o listed 1m winner, was Group 3 placed twice and is a half-sister to 7 winners. *"It's quite exciting to have a 2-y-o half-brother to Toronado in the yard! We saw how impressive Toronado was last year and had the opportunity to buy this colt privately so we got him quick! He's a very*

strong and tough colt, there's no rush with him at all and I would imagine he'd be a seven furlong type 2-y-o.

WILLIAM JARVIS

968. AMETRINE (IRE) ★★

b.f. *Fastnet Rock – Amethyst (Sadler's Wells)*. March 28. Tenth foal. €65,000Y. Goffs Orby. Ric Wylie. Closely related to the fairly useful 2-y-o 6f winner Sydney Harbour (by Danehill Dancer) and half-sister to the quite useful 11f, 12f and hurdles winner Audit (by Fusaichi Pegasus), the fair 6f winner Fifty (by Fasliyev) and a minor winner abroad by Kingmambo. The dam, winner of the Leopardstown 1,000 Guineas Trial, was second in the Irish 1,000 Guineas. She is a sister to the 2,000 Guineas and Group 1 National Stakes winner King Of Kings and the Group 3 Athasi Stakes winner Lucky and a half-sister to the Group 2 5.5f Prix Robert Papin winner General Monash. The second dam, Zummerudd (by Habitat), is an unplaced sister to the Irish Group 3 and US Grade 3 winner Ancestral. (Mr Kevin Hickman). *"The most expensive of the 2-y-o's we've got, but she's not a big filly and she's just on the weak side at the moment. The sire has an outstanding record in Australia and this is an attractive filly that just needs to grow an inch more".*

969. BEAKERS N HUM NUMS (IRE) ★★

b.c. *Iffraaj – Ivy League Star (Sadler's Wells)*. February 25. Fourth living foal. 10,000Y. Tattersalls October Book 2. Blandford Bloodstock. Half-brother to Carneades (by Exceed And Excel), unplaced on his only start at 2 yrs in 2012 and to the modest dual 9f winner Hard Road (by Cape Cross). The dam, a fair 12f winner, is a sister to the fillies Ivrea and Iviza, both 2-y-o 7f winners and second in the Ribblesdale Stakes and a half-sister to 5 winners including the very useful Ivyanna, a winner of two races over 1m (at 2 yrs) and the Group 1 12f Italian Oaks and to the dam of the Group 2 Goodwood Cup winner Distinction. The second dam, Ivy (by Sir Ivor), placed twice at 2 yrs in the USA, is a full or half-sister to 12 winners including the Graded stakes winners An Act, Din and Sarsar and the dam of the Grade 2 winner Herat. *"He'll make a 2-y-o by July or August, he's a nice horse that does everything well and he has a good temperament, but he will take a bit of time and apart from the sire it is more of a 3-y-o pedigree".*

970. BISHAN BEDI (IRE) ★★★

b.c. Intikhab – Knockatotaun (Spectrum). April 6. Sixth foal. 27,000Y. Tattersalls October Book 2. BBA (Ire). Brother to the fair Irish dual 1m winner Rassi Maguire and half-brother to the fairly useful Irish 2-y-o 6f winner of 4 races (including at 2 yrs) and Group 3 third Knock Stars (by Soviet Star), the fair 2-y-o 6f winner Sanad (by Red Clubs) and the moderate 6f winner Donard Lodge (by Elnadim). The dam, a moderate 12f and 13f winner, is a half-sister to 4 winners including the Irish dual listed 11f winner and multiple Group 3 placed Indiana Gal. The second dam, Genial Jenny (by Danehill), won 4 minor races over 9f in Ireland and is a half-sister to 7 other minor winners. *"He's very woolly in his coat at the moment so we haven't pressed the button yet, but he looks like being a summer 2-y-o. I like him and he looks OK. Six furlongs should do to start with".*

971. NEW ROW ★★★

b.f. Teofilo – Memo (Groom Dancer). February 4. Sixth foal. 16,000Y. Tattersalls October Book 2. William Jarvis. Half-sister to the fair 11f and 12f winner Tripitaka (by Sulamani). The dam is an unraced half-sister to 6 winners including the US stakes placed Front Row. The second dam, The Jotter (by Night Shift), a useful 2-y-o 5f and 6.5f winner, was second in three listed events and is closely related to the Group 1 Gran Criterium second Line Dancer. *"She's a pretty nice filly, strong, active and goes well. We like her and I think she's alright. Despite the dam's disappointing record there have been reasons, so I think there's every chance that this will be her second winning foal. Quite precocious, she could be racing by May or June".*

972. SILVER MOUNTAIN ★★★

gr.c. Sir Percy – Pearl Bright (Kaldoun). March 19. Seventh foal. 20,000Y. Tattersalls December. William Jarvis. Brother to the fair 2012 2-y-o 1m winner Gold Show and half-brother to the useful 6f (at 2 yrs) and 7f winner and Group 2 6f Mill Reef Stakes third

Berbice, the quite useful 6f and 7f winner Great Acclaim (both by Acclamation), the quite useful 10f and 12f winner Bebopalula (by Galileo) and a winner in Greece by Namid. The dam, a quite useful 2-y-o 7f winner, is a half-sister to 4 winners. The second dam, Coastal Jewel (by Kris), is an unraced half-sister to 5 winners. (Ms Wendy Dio). *"A typical Sir Percy, he's well put-together and a nice, strong horse. His pedigree suggests that he's probably going to need seven furlongs so he's just ticking over at the moment, but he goes nicely. I see no reason why he shouldn't win as a 2-y-o but it'll sometime from August onwards".*

973. UNNAMED ★★★

b.f. Dubawi – Bronwen (King's Best). May 10. Fifth foal. 35,000Y. Tattersalls October Book 2. William Knight. Half-sister to the 2012 Italian 2-y-o dual listed 1m winner Castello Aragonese (by Authorized), to the fair 10f winner Heatherbird (by Shamardal) and the modest 9f and 10f winner Painted Tail (by Mark Of Esteem). The dam, a fairly useful 9f to 15f winner, is a half-sister to 6 winners including the Group 1 Fillies' Mile and Group 3 May Hill Stakes winner Teggiano. The second dam, Tegwen (by Nijinsky), a quite useful 10f winner, is a half-sister to 4 winners. (Mr A S Belhab). *"From a family that we know quite well having had the half-sister Heatherbird who threatened to be very useful but just wasn't as good as we'd thought. Dubawi is obviously an outstanding stallion and this filly isn't over-big, she's very likeable and goes well. We like her and she'll be racing by June I would have thought".*

974. UNNAMED ★★★

b.c. Royal Applause – Sparkling Eyes (Lujain). April 23. Third foal. 25,000Y. Tattersalls October Book 2. Blandford Bloodstock. Half-brother to the quite useful 2-y-o 5f winner Pea Shooter (by Piccolo). The dam, a fairly useful dual 5f winner (including at 2 yrs), was fourth in the Group 2 5f Queen Mary Stakes, is a half-sister to 3 winners here and abroad. The second dam, Lady Georgia (by Arazi), a useful 3-y-o 7.8f winner, was fourth in the Group 3 7f Prestige Stakes at 2 yrs. *"I like him – and I'm the owner at the owner at the moment. But I'm quite happy about that because he's very* nice. A medium-sized colt who really points his toe, he's enthusiastic on the gallops and he has a 2-y-o pedigree. I think he's quite smart and he'll do a good job as a 2-y-o". TRAINERS' BARGAIN BUY

EVE JOHNSON HOUGHTON

975. AJIG ★★★
ch.f. Bahamian Bounty – Atwirl (Pivotal). February 27. Third foal. 9,000Y. Tattersalls October Book 3. Not sold. Half-sister to the 1m (at 2 yrs) to 11f winner Amistress (by Kalanisi). The dam, a moderate 7f winner, is a half-sister to 2 minor winners. The second dam, Amidst (by Midyan), a fair winner dual 6f (at 2 yrs) and 7f winner of 3 races, is a half-sister to one winner. (Eden Racing Club). *"A half-sister to Amistress who won four races for me. She's not very big but she's very racey. She's done quite a bit of growing so I don't think she'll be out until the end of May, but I'd like to think she's got a race or two in her as a 2-y-o. She should have plenty of pace".*

976. ALUTIQ (IRE) ★★★★
b.f. Kodiac – Marasem (Cadeaux Genereux). March 18. Sixth foal. €15,500Y. Tattersalls Ireland September. Eve Johnson-Houghton. Half-sister to the quite useful 7f winner Faleh (by Silver Hawk) and to the fair 2-y-o 9f winner Maraca (by Danehill Dancer). The dam, a quite useful 3-y-o 7f winner, is a half-sister to 6 winners including the very useful Group 2 7f Rockfel Stakes winner Sayedah (by Darshaan). The second dam, Balaabel (by Sadler's Wells), a quite useful 1m winner, is a half-sister to 6 winners including the US Grade 2 7f winner Kayrawan and the dam of the Group 2 winner and sire Haatef. *"An easy winner on her debut at Kempton, she's very speedy and isn't a one-race wonder – she'll progress and she'll get six furlongs. I'd like to think I could give her one more race and then go to Royal Ascot. She's also in the Sales race in Ireland and the Supersprint".*

977. CHARLIE WELLS (IRE) ★★★
b.c. High Chaparral – Numbers Game (Rainbow Quest). April 8. Third foal. 15,000Y. Tattersalls October Book 2. Eve Johnson Houghton. Brother to the winner Madam St Clair and half-brother to the 2012 2-y-o Good Game (by Excellent Art). The dam is an unraced half-sister to 5 winners. The second dam, Equity Princess (by Warning), a useful 1m (at 2 yrs) and 9.2f winner and listed-placed four times here, was Group 2 second in Germany and is a half-sister to 5 winners. *"He's grown a bit and I think he'll be a better 3-y-o but he's doing really well, going nicely and he'll be out by the end of May/beginning of June. He may start at six furlongs but I think he'll be better over seven".*

978. COOL BAHAMIAN (IRE) ★★★
b.c. Bahamian Bounty – Keritana (One Cool Cat). March 11. First foal. €18,000Y. Goffs Orby. Eve Johnson Houghton. The dam is an unplaced half-sister to 3 winners including Keraka (Group 3 Anglesey Stakes). The second dam, Kerita (by Formidable), winner of the Group 3 7f Supreme Stakes and second in the Group 2 Challenge Stakes, is a half-sister to 3 winners. *"He's been going really well just lately so he might be on the racecourse in May because he's thriving now. It's a real good family and my Dad trained all the mares from it. I'd like to think he's got the pace for six furlongs".*

979. MAPPA MUNDI ★★★★
b.c. Henrythenavigator – Princess Desire (Danehill). March 4. First foal. €48,000Y. Goffs Orby. Eve Johnson Houghton. The dam, a winner at 3 yrs in Japan, is a half-sister to 2 minor winners. The second dam, Dance Desire (by Caerleon), is an unraced half-sister to 9 winners including Intimate Guest (Group 3 May Hill Stakes) and the dams of the Group 1 winners Luas Line, Kingsfort and Prince Arch. (Anthony Pye-Jeary & Mel Smith). *"A lovely horse, has had sore shins but is a real 2-y-o. When we get him going I expect him to be pretty decent. A speedy-looking 2-y-o, he could be very nice".*

980. PEACEMAKER (IRE) ★★
b.f. High Chaparral – Sauterne (Rainbow Quest). April 17. Eighth foal. 8,000Y. Tattersalls October Book 2. Eve Johnson-Houghton. Half-sister to the modest 2012 7f placed 2-y-o Sweet Vintage (by Singspiel), to the useful 10f and 12f winner Senate (by Pivotal) and the fair 2-y-o 7f winner Determined Stand (by Elusive Quality). The dam, a listed winner

of 3 races from 7f to 10f, is a half-sister to 6 winners including the smart 2-y-o Group 2 6f Cherry Hinton Stakes winner Applaud. The second dam, Band (by Northern Dancer), is a placed half-sister to 5 winners including the US Grade 3 9f New Orleans Handicap winner Festive. (Mr R L Maynard & Mr B McNamee). *"Going nicely, she'll make a 2-y-o from July/ August onwards over seven furlongs. She wasn't expensive but she's nicely bred and was a bargain I think".*

981. PERSIAN BOLT (USA) ★★★★

b.f. U S Ranger – Silent Cat (Rahy). April 15. Eighth foal. €67,000Y. Arqana Deauville August. Lillingston/Marner. Half-sister to 4 winners including the listed stakes winner and smart broodmare Dynamic Cat (by Dynaformer), the minor French winner Private Dining (by Royal Academy) and the minor US winner Oh So Nice (by Smart Strike). The dam is an unraced half-sister to 5 winners including the US Grade 3 Saranac Stakes winner Crowd Pleaser. The second dam, Creaking Board (by Night Shift), won the Grade 1 Hollywood Starlet Stakes and is a sister to the dual Group 3 winner Dyhim Diamond and a half-sister to the Group 2 German 1,000 Guineas second Dakhla Oasis. (B Larizadeh/P Wollaston). *"A really nice filly, she's quite big but she's got plenty of speed which makes me think she'll be a six or seven furlong 2-y-o and I can see her being out around June or July time. A really nice, classy filly".*

982. PICANIGHT ★★★

b.f. Piccolo – Midnight Fling (Groom Dancer). April 27. Second foal. Half-sister to the quite useful 2012 2-y-o dual 5f winner Bridge Night (by Avonbridge). The dam, a fair 5f, 6f (both at 2 yrs) and 7f placed maiden, is a half-sister to the dual Group 3 winning sprinter winner Definightly. The second dam, Perfect Night (by Danzig Connection), a fair 6f and 7f winner, is a half-sister to one winner. *"A half-sister to a filly that won twice for me last year. She won't be as early as Bridge Night was but she's got as much pace as her. A six furlong type, she's got some filling out to do, looks a bit rangy and needs strengthening up but when she gets there she'll be nice".*

983. SPARKLING ICE (IRE) ★★

b.f. Verglas – Sand Crystal (Singspiel). March 8. Second foal. €10,500Y. Tattersalls Ireland September. Eve Johnson Houghton. The dam is an unraced half-sister to 2 minor winners. The second dam, Star Crystal (by Brief Truce), a fairly useful 12f and 14f winner, is a half-sister to the Group 1 Fillies' Mile winner Crystal Music and to the Group 3 winners Dubai Success, Solar Crystal and State Crystal. (Miss E A Johnson-Houghton). *"She'll be alright but having looked like she'd be sharp and early she's done a lot of growing. She's coming back to hand now, I think we'll start her off in late May or early June over six furlongs and then keep going up".*

984. STARLIT CANTATA ★★

b.f. Oratorio – Starlit Sky (Galileo). March 30. Third foal. 8,500foal. Tattersalls December. Not sold. Half-sister to the quite useful 10f winner Sky Khan (by Cape Cross) and to the modest 5f winner Green Warrior (by Green Desert). The dam is an unraced half-sister to 8 winners including the Group 2 13.5f Prix de Pomone winner Interlude and the dam of the stakes winners Barney McGrew, National Park and Film Script. The second dam, Starlet (by Teenoso), won 7 races from 7f (at 2 yrs) to 12f including a Group 2 event in Germany and is a half-sister to 8 winners including the US Grade 1 Arlington Handicap winner Unknown Quantity. (Mrs H B Raw). *"Bred on the same lines as a 3-y-o filly we have called Starlight Symphony, being by Oratorio out of a Galileo mare. She's really nice, she'll take a bit of time but she's got it all there. One for the mid-summer onwards I'd like to think".*

985. WHAT ABOUT CARLO (FR) ★★★★

b.c. Creachadoir – Boccatenera (Artan). March 1. First foal. 23,000Y. Tattersalls October Book 2. Eve Johnson Houghton. The dam won 2 minor races at 2 yrs in France and is a sister to the Group 2 Prix Robert Papin winner Boccassini and a half-sister to 2 winners. The second dam, Bella Monica (by Big Shuffle), a minor winner at 3 yrs in Germany, is a half-sister to 5 winners. (Anthony Pye-Jeary & Mel Smith). *"A lovely horse, he's big, rangy and won't be out early but he could be really nice. I think he'll win as a 2-y-o, he'll not be out before August/September 2-y-o but he's got plenty of pace and does everything so easily".*

986. UNNAMED ★★★
b.c. Tagula – Thelma Louise (Desert Style). April 10. Third foal. £15,000 2-y-o. Kempton Breeze-Up. Eve Johnson-Houghton. Half-brother to the modest 9f winner Cool Hand Luke (by Le Vie Dei Colori). The dam is an unraced half-sister to 4 winners. The second dam, Thelma (by Blakeney), is an unraced sister to the dual listed winner and useful broodmare Alys. *"I'm really happy with him, he's nice and I'm looking for an owner for him. He needed a bit of time after the sale but he's settled in now and going nicely. A nice, big, strong horse for six furlongs from mid-May onwards I should think".* TRAINERS' BARGAIN BUY

MARK JOHNSTON
987. ARABDA
br.f. Elnadim – Ghizlaan (Seeking The Gold). March 19. Second foal. Half-sister to Tallaay (by Cape Cross), unplaced in two starts at 2 yrs in 2012. The dam, unplaced in 3 starts, is a half-sister to the Grade 1 Belmont Stakes and Grade 1 Breeders Cup Classic winner Drosselmeyer and to the US stakes winner and Group 1 Ruffian Handicap third Stage Luck. The second dam, Golden Ballet (by Moscow Ballet), won 6 races including the Grade 1 Santa Anita Oaks and the Grade 1 Las Virgines Stakes and is a half-sister to 6 winners. (Hamdan Al Maktoum).

988. BAILEYS CELEBRATE
b.f. Royal Applause – Southern Psychic (Alwasmi). April 5. Twelfth foal. 30,000Y. Tattersalls October Book 3. Mark Johnston. Sister to the useful 7.2f (at 2 yrs) to 10f winner of 6 races Wing Commander and half-sister to the very useful 6f (at 2 yrs) and 1m winner Rumpold (by Mister Baileys), the fairly useful 15.4f winner Trew Style (by Desert King), the quite useful 2-y-o 7f winner Psychic Star (by Diktat), the minor French 11f winner Oskar The Winner (by Pivotal) and a minor 2-y-o winner in the USA by Alydeed. The dam, a sprint winner at 4 yrs in the USA, is closely related to the Canadian dual 6f stakes winner Sing And Swing and a half-sister to 8 winners

including the US 9f stakes winner Windansea and the dam of the Group 2 Gimcrack Stakes winner Chilly Billy. The second dam, Sun And Snow (by Hawaii), won the Grade 2 9f Kentucky Oaks and the Grade 3 8.5f Ashland Stakes and is a half-sister to 7 winners. (G R Bailey Ltd).

989. CROWDMANIA
ch.c. Shamardal – Riotous Applause (Royal Applause). January 30. Third foal. 115,000Y. Tattersalls October Book 1. Mark Johnston. Half-brother to the useful 2012 2-y-o listed 6f winner Invincible Warrior (by Invincible Spirit) and to the quite useful 7f winner Riot Of Colour (by Excellent Art). The dam, a fairly useful dual 6f winner (including at 2 yrs), was listed-placed and is a sister to one winner and a half-sister to 6 winners including the high-class 2-y-o Group 1 1m Racing Post Trophy winner Crowded House and to the placed dam of the US dual Grade 1 winner Ticker Tape. The second dam, Wiener Wald (Woodman), is an unplaced half-sister to 6 minor winners abroad. (Sheikh Majid bin Mohammed Al Maktoum).

990. IBECKE
b.f. Exceed And Excel – Granted (Cadeaux Genereux). April 21. Ninth foal. 60,000Y. Tattersalls October Book 1. Mark Johnston. Half-sister to the useful 7f (including at 2 yrs) and listed 1m winner of 5 races Perfect Star (by Act One), to the useful dual 1m winner and Group 3 third Rewarded (by Motivator), the quite useful 7f winner Commended (by Royal Applause), the quite useful 9f to 12f winner of 5 races Barodine (by Barathea) and the modest 1m and 9f winner Bestowed (by Kyllachy). The dam, a useful 1m and 8.3f winner, was listed placed at up to 9f and is a half-sister to 4 winners including the Italian listed winner and US Grade 2 second Lucky Chappy. The second dam, Germane (by Distant Relative), a useful winner of the Group 3 7f Rockfel Stakes and placed in two listed events, is a half-sister to 9 winners including the very useful German dual listed Fabriano. (J Abdullah).

991. INEVITABLE
b.c. Dubawi – Come What May (Selkirk).

February 8. Third foal. 90,000foal. Tattersalls December. John Ferguson. Half-brother to the quite useful 2012 2-y-o 6f winner Woodlandsway (by Oasis Dream). The dam, a the modest 5f winner, is a sister to the very smart 2-y-o Group 2 7f Champagne Stakes winner Etlaala and to the useful 7f and 1m winner and listed-placed Selective and a half-sister to 4 winners. The second dam, Portelet (by Night Shift), a fairly useful 5f winner of 4 races, is a half-sister to 4 winners. (Hamdan bin Mohammed Al Maktoum).

992. LANARK (IRE)

b.c. Cape Cross – Amenixa (Linamix). March 10. Tenth foal. 70,000Y. Tattersalls October Book 1. Darley Stud. Closely related to the quite useful 7f, 1m (both at 2 yrs) and subsequent UAE winner Palm Court (by Green Desert) and half-brother to the 2012 Irish 2-y-o 6f winner Forester (by Danehill Dancer), the 2-y-o Group 2 6f Criterium de Maisons-Laffitte and Group 3 Prix Eclipse winner Zinziberene (by Zieten and herself the dam of three stakes winners), the fairly useful French 9f winner Iron Age (by Pivotal) and the flat 13f and 14f winner Appeal (by Selkirk). The dam, a 4-y-o 10f winner, is a sister to the dual Group 1 Prix Royal-Oak winner Amilynx and the listed winner Amie De Mix and a half-sister to 5 winners including Amiwain (Group 2 Criterium de Maisons-Laffitte). The second dam, Amen (by Alydar), was a Grade 3 placed winner of 5 races in the USA and a half-sister to 4 winners. (Hamdan bin Mohammed Al Maktoum).

993. LYN VALLEY

b.c. Shamardal – Demisemiquaver (Singspiel). January 28. Second foal. 42,000Y. Tattersalls October Book 1. Mark Johnston. Half-brother to the quite useful 2012 2-y-o 7f winner Makafeh (by Elusive Quality). The dam, a dual winner at 3 yrs in the USA and stakes-placed, is a half-sister to 5 winners including the US Grade 3 Cardinal Handicap winner Miss Caerleona (herself dam of the Graded stakes winners Karen's Caper and Miss Coronado) and the dam of the Group 2 Windsor Forest Stakes winner Joviality. The second dam, Miss d'Ouilly (by Bikala), won a listed event over 9f in France and is a half-sister to 6 winners including the Prix Jacques le Marois winner

Miss Satamixa and the Group 3 placed Mrs Annie (the dam of four stakes winners). (Mr J A Barson).

994. MARINERS MOON (IRE)

ch.c. Mount Nelson – Dusty Moon (Dr Fong). February 19. First foal. 28,000Y. Tattersalls October Book 2. Newsells Park Stud. The dam, a quite useful 2-y-o 7f winner, is a sister to the listed 1m and subsequent US Grade 2 winner Spotlight and a half-sister to 3 winners including the dam of the Group 1 Phoenix Stakes winner Zoffany. The second dam, Dust Dancer (by Suave Dancer), won 4 races including the Group 3 10f Prix de la Nonette and is a half-sister to 6 winners including the Group 3 7.3f Fred Darling Stakes winner Bulaxie (herself dam of the Group 2 winner Claxon). (Newsells Park Stud Ltd).

995. MASTER OF FINANCE (IRE)

ch.c. Mastercraftsman – Cheal Rose (Dr Devious). March 13. Eighth foal. 30,000Y. Tattersalls October Book 2. Mark Johnston. Half-brother to the Irish listed 6f (at 2 yrs) and 1m winner and Group 1 7f National Stakes second Golden Arrow (by Danehill), to the Italian listed 11f winner Pretty Diamond (by Hurricane Run), the quite useful Irish 1m winner Perpetual Motion (by Spinning World), the modest 10f winner Nom De La Rosa (by Oratorio) and the Japanese winner Cosmo Jungle (by Montjeu). The dam was placed 8 times at up to 1m in Ireland and is a half-sister to 6 winners including the US Grade 3 winner Buffalo Berry (herself dam of the US Grade 3 winner and Grade 1 placed Chattahoochee War). The second dam, Palm Dove (by Storm Bird), is an unplaced half-sister to 6 winners including the very smart sprinter Nabeel Dancer. (Mr J D Abell & Mr M Graff).

996. MUTALABA

b.f. Aqlaam – Zaaqya (Nayef). January 26. First foal. The dam, a quite useful 7f, 1m (both at 2 yrs) and 12f winner, is a sister to one winner. The second dam, Classical Dancer (by Dr Fong), a fairly useful 8.3f winner, was listed-placed twice and is a half-sister to 5 winners including the Group 1 Premio Roma winner Imperial Dancer. (Hamdan Al Maktoum).

997. MUTEELA
b.f. Dansili – Nufoos (Zafonic). February 19.
Fifth foal. Half-sister to the 2-y-o Group 1 6f
Middle Park Stakes and Group 2 6f Mill Reef
Stakes winner Awzaan (by Alhaarth), to the
useful 1m to 10f winner of 4 races Hajras
(by Dubai Destination) and the fair 2-y-o 7f
winner Tasfeya (by Haafhd). The dam, a useful
5f, 6f (both at 2 yrs) and listed 7f winner, is a
half-sister to the 5 winners including the fairly
useful 2-y-o sprint winner of 3 races Valiant
Romeo. The second dam, Desert Lynx (by
Green Desert), a fair dual 6f winner, is a half-
sister to the very smart dual listed 5f winner
Watching. (Hamdan Al Maktoum).

998. PEMBROKESHIRE
b.c. Shamardal – Solva (Singspiel). February
2. Second foal. 130,000Y. Tattersalls October
Book 2. John Ferguson. Half-brother to the
modest 2012 5f to 7f placed 2-y-o Solvanna
(by Haafhd). The dam, a dual 10f and
subsequent US stakes winner, was second
in the Grade 2 Beverly Hills Handicap and is
a half-sister to 3 winners. The second dam,
Annapurna (by Brief Truce), a useful 2-y-o
7f winner, was listed placed over 9f and is a
half-sister to 5 winners including the 2-y-o
Group 3 7f Rockfel Stakes and listed 7f winner
Name Of Love. (Hamdan bin Mohammed Al
Maktoum).

999. PIGEON PIE ♠
b.f. Bahamian Bounty – Pixie Ring (Pivotal).
March 12. Second foal. The dam, a fair 2-y-o
dual 6f winner, is a half-sister to 3 winners. The
second dam, Ard Na Sighe (by Kenmare), is
an unraced half-sister to 9 winners including
the champion sprinter Marwell (herself dam of
the high-class Coronation Stakes and Sussex
Stakes winner Marling and of the good 5f
to 1m colt Caerwent) and the Group 2 Mill
Reef Stakes winner Lord Seymour. (Hot to
Trot Racing Club). A winner on her debut at
Newcastle in mid-April.

1000. QUICKASWECAN
b.c. Shamardal – Arctic Air (Polar Falcon). April
4. Ninth foal. 75,000Y. Tattersalls October
Book 1. Mark Johnston. Half-brother to the
triple listed winner and Group 2 6f Gimcrack
Stakes second Andronikos (by Dr Fong), to

the quite useful 6f (at 2 yrs) and 9f winner
Arctic Cape (by Cape Cross) and the moderate
7f winner Selkirk Sky (by Selkirk). The dam,
a quite useful 2-y-o 7f winner, is a sister to
the useful listed 7f winner Arctic Char and a
half-sister to 6 winners including the Group 2
winners Barrow Creek and Last Resort and the
dam of the Group 2 winner Trans Island. The
second dam, Breadcrumb (by Final Straw), a
very useful 6f and 7f winner, is a half-sister to
4 winners including the Group 2 Prix Maurice
de Gheest winner College Chapel. (Mark
Johnston Racing Ltd).

1001. SIR GUY PORTEOUS (IRE)
ch.c. Shamardal – Ermine And Velvet (Nayef).
February 2. First foal. 67,000Y. Tattersalls
October Book 1. Mark Johnston. The dam, a
quite useful 7f listed-placed maiden, is a sister
to 2 winners including the winner and Group
1 German Derby third Top Lock. The second
dam, Ermine (by Cadeaux Genereux), a quite
useful 3-y-o 1m winner, is a half-sister to 7
winners including the very smart 1m (at 2
yrs) and Group 3 10f Brigadier Gerard Stakes
winner and 2,000 Guineas and Derby third
Border Arrow. (Mr Paul Dean).

1002. SIR PAUL DEAN ♠
b.c. Byron – Hunter's Fortune (Charismatic).
February 25. Third foal,. 8,000Y. Tattersalls
October Book 2. M Johnston. Half-brother
to the 2012 2-y-o winner Miss Rosie (by
Librettist). The dam, a winner of 3 races in
the USA at 2 and 3 yrs, was stakes-placed
and is a half-sister to 5 winners. The second
dam, Salty Perfume (by Salt Lake), won the
Grade 2 Adirondack Stakes in the USA and is
a half-sister to 6 winners including the Group
1 Dewhurst Stakes second Green Perfume.
(Mark Johnston Racing Ltd).

1003. STETCHWORTH (IRE)
*ch.c. New Approach – Hallowed Park
(Barathea).* March 5. Second foal. Half-brother
to the fair dual 7f winner, including at 2 yrs,
Shamrocked (by Rock Of Gibraltar). The dam
is an unraced half-sister to 3 winners including
the Derby second Walk In The Park. The
second dam, Classic Park (by Robellino), won
3 races including the Irish 1,000 Guineas and
is a half-sister to 10 winners including the US

Grade 2 winner Rumpipumpy. (Hamdan bin Mohammed Al Maktoum).

1004. TAMAYUZ DREAM (IRE)

ch.c. Tamayuz – Cradle Brief (Brief Truce). April 4. Ninth foal. €35,000Y. Goffs Orby. Mark Johnston. Half-brother to the useful 2-y-o listed 6f winner and Group 2 6f Mill Reef Stakes second Sir Xaar (by Xaar), to the useful Irish 1m to 9.5f winner Fuerta Ventura (by Desert Sun), the quite useful 6f and 7f winner of 4 races Redvers (by Ishiguru) and the quite useful 13f and hurdles winner Mamlook (by Key Of Luck). The dam is an unraced half-sister to the Group 3 6f Greenlands Stakes winner Tiger Royal. The second dam, Lady Redford (by Bold Lad), ran once unplaced and is a half-sister to 5 winners. (Mr A Al Mansoori).

1005. TAMAYUZ MAGIC (IRE)

b.c. Tamayuz – Anne Tudor (Anabaa). February 21. Fourth foal. €30,000Y. Goffs Orby. Mark Johnston. Half-brother to the quite useful 5f (at 2 yrs), 1m and 10f winner and Group 2 Railway Stakes second Alhaban (by Verglas). The dam, a quite useful 3-y-o 7f winner, is a half-sister to 3 winners including the fairly useful triple 7f winner (including at 2 yrs) Silk Fan. The second dam, Alikhlas (by Lahib), a fair 3-y-o 1m winner, is a half-sister to 4 winners including the listed winner and Group 2 Lancashire Oaks second Sahool and to the dam of the dual Group 2 winner Maraahel. (Mr A Al Mansoori).

1006. TANSEEB

b.c. Royal Applause – Perfect Story (Desert Story). February 4. Third foal. 90,000Y. Tattersalls October Book 2. Shadwell Estate Co. Half-brother to the quite useful 7f and 1m winner Perfect Cracker (by Dubai Destination). The dam, a quite useful 6f and 7f winner of four races at 3 and 4 yrs and listed-placed, is a half-sister to 3 winners. The second dam, Shore Lark (by Storm Bird), is an unraced half-sister to 11 winners including the smart Group 2 5f Temple Stakes and Group 3 5f Norfolk Stakes winner Tipsy Creek, the Group 3 Ballycorus Stakes winner Abunawwas and the listed winners Wathik and Magic Cove. (Hamdan Al Maktoum).

1007. TESTING (FR)

gr.f. New Approach – Testama (Testa Rossa). March 23. First foal. €65,000Y. Arqana Deauville August. Mark Johnston. The dam, a listed 1m winner of 4 races in France, is a half-sister to 2 minor winners. The second dam, Maid Of Honor (by Highest Honor), a listed 12f winner in France, is a half-sister to 6 winners. (A D Spence).

1008. TIZLOVE REGARDLESS (USA)

b.c. Tiznow – Dianehill (Danehill). March 8. Seventh foal. $150,000Y. Keeneland September. Mark Johnston. Half-brother to the Group 3 Dubai 2,000 Guineas winner Splash Point (by Street Cry) and to two minor winners in the USA by A P Indy and Elusive Quality. The dam, a US stakes winner of 6 races and Grade 2 and Grade 3 placed, is a half-sister to 3 winners. The second dam, Very Subtle (by Hoist The Silver), won four races including the 6f Breeders Cup Sprint, the 1m Hollywood Starlet Stakes and the 8.5f Fantasy Stakes (all Grade 1 events) and is a half-sister to the stakes winner Schematic. (Crone Stud Farm Ltd).

1009. TORNADO CHALLENGE USA

b.c. War Chant – Princess Kris (Kris). April 30. Eleventh foal. €36,000Y. Goffs Orby. Mark Johnston. Brother to the 2-y-o Group 1 National Stakes winner Kingsfort and half-brother to the US Grade 1 11f winner Prince Arch, the minor US winner of 4 races Art Crafty (both by Arch) and a minor winner in the USA by Boundary. The dam, a quite useful 3-y-o 1m winner, is half-sister to 8 winners including the Group 3 May Hill Stakes winner Intimate Guest and the dam of the US Grade 1 winner Luas Line. The second dam, As You Desire Me (by Kalamoun), won 2 listed events in France over 7.5f and 1m and is a half-sister to 7 winners including the Group 2 King Edward VII Stakes winner Classic Example. (J Abdullah).

1010. UNNAMED

b.f. Three Valleys – Boa Estrela (Intikhab). February 24. Third living foal. 20,000Y. Tattersalls December. Mark Johnston. Half-sister to the Group 1 7f Prix de la Foret winner and Haydock Sprint Cup second Gordon Lord Byron (by Byron). The dam is an unraced half-sister to 5 winners including the smart Irish Group 3 7f and 1m winner Cheyenne Star. The second dam, Charita (by Lycius), a listed 1m winner in Ireland, is a half-sister to 4 winners including the Italian Group 2 winner Stanott. (Mark Johnston Racing Ltd).

1011. UNNAMED

b.c. Dubawi – Easy To Love (Diesis). March 27. Tenth foal. 40,000Y. Tattersalls October Book 2. Mark Johnston. Half-brother to the fairly useful 2-y-o 7f and 1m winner and listed-placed Easy Lover (by Pivotal), to the fair 2-y-o 7f winner Pezula Bay (by Oasis Dream) and the modest 13f winner Blinka Me (by Tiger Hill). The dam, a quite useful 4-y-o 11.5f winner, is a sister to the Oaks winner Love Divine (herself dam of the St Leger winner Sixties Icon) and a half-sister to 5 winners including the listed winners Floreeda and Dark Promise. The second dam, La Sky (by Law Society), a useful 10f winner and second in the Group 3 Lancashire Oaks, is closely related to the Champion Stakes winner Legal Case and a half-sister to 4 winners. (Hamdan bin Mohammed Al Maktoum).

SYLVESTER KIRK

1012. ASSOLUTA (IRE) ★★★★

ch.f. Danehill Dancer – A P Easy (A P Indy). March 20. Third foal. 20,000Y. Tattersalls October Book 1. Not sold. Half-sister to Codrington College (by Duke Of Marmalade), unplaced in one start at 2 yrs in 2012. The dam, a minor winner at 3 yrs in the USA, is a half-sister to 4 winners including the French 2,000 Guineas winner Astronomer Royal and the US Grade 2 Pan American Handicap winner Navesink River. The second dam, Sheepscot (by Easy Goes), a minor stakes winner of 5 races in the USA, is a half-sister to 8 winners including the dual US Grade 1 winner Vicar. (M Nicolson, G Doran, A Wilson). *"A cracking filly, she's doing really well, she's tall and leggy so we may have to give her more time, but mentally she's quite precocious. Tough and hardy, I really like her and if she won a maiden she'd be a bargain for what she cost considering she's out of a half-sister to a classic winner. Seven furlongs should be right for her this year, although she's probably quick enough to start over six".*

1013. ARISTOCRACTIC DUTY ★★

b.f. Zamindar – Duty Paid (Barathea). February 9. Sixth foal. Half-sister to the modest 7f and 1m winner Duty Doctor (by Dr Fong). The dam, a useful 2-y-o listed 6f winner, is a sister to the useful 1m winner and listed-placed Lady Miletrian and a half-sister to 3 winners. The second dam, Local Custom (by Be My Native), was placed at up to 7f at 2 yrs and is a sister to the listed winner Tribal Rite and a half-sister to the Middle Park Stakes winner Balla Cove. (J C Smith). *"A big, tall, leggy filly, first impressions tell me she'll stay a bit further than her relatives but you never know because as she strengthens up she could come a bit earlier. She has a smashing attitude, goes along really well and she's very straightforward".*

1014. BAKER MAN ★★★

b.c. Dandy Man – Anne Bonney (Jade Robbery). March 14. Second foal. 18,000Y. Tattersalls October Book 3. K A Kirk. The dam, a moderate 9f placed maiden, is a half-sister to 3 winners in Japan and one in France. The second dam, Sanchez (by Wolfhound), a fair 9f placed maiden, is a half-sister to the Group 1 winners Ballingarry, Aristotle and Starborough. (Mr R Hannon & Mr P Rogers). *"He's a big horse but surprisingly forward. He has a wonderful attitude, he's mentally precocious and he's doing everything easily, but physically you'd say seven furlongs would be right for him".*

1015. BELLETRISTE (FR) ★★★★

gr.f. Literato – Mulled Wine (Night Shift). March 5. Third foal. €32,000Y. Arqana Deauville August. J Brummitt. Half-sister to the 2013 French 3-y-o 1m Cassini (by Astronomer Royal) and to the minor French 2-y-o winner Yadira (by Archange d'Or). The dam is an unraced half-sister to 3 winners including the Group 1 Prix de l'Opera winner Lily Of The Valley. The second dam, Pennegale (by Pennekamp), is a placed half-sister to 5 winners. (The Hon. Mrs J M Corbett & Mr C Wright). *"A smashing filly with a wonderful temperament and I think the sire is doing quite well from limited opportunities. She's small and sharp, quick enough for six furlongs and she's laid-back. I really like her".*

1016. FOREST GLEN (IRE) ★★★

b.f. Camacho – Lisfannon (Bahamian Bounty).
April 16. Fourth foal. £16,000Y. Doncaster
Premier. Sylvester Kirk. Half-sister to the 2012
Irish 2-y-o 6f winner Mironica (by Excellent
Art) and to the quite useful 2-y-o 5f winner
Dress Up (by Noverre). The dam is a placed
half-sister to 4 winners including the listed 5f
winner of 5 races Dazed And Amazed. The
second dam, Amazed (by Clantime), a modest
5f placed 3-y-o, is a sister to the Group 3 Prix
du Petit Couvert winner Bishops Court and
a half-sister to 5 winners including the listed
winning sprinter Astonished. (Sapphire Racing
Partnership). *"A sharp, five/six furlong filly, she's
had a touch of sore shins and I've eased off her
a bit. She was coping with it all and she shows
a bit of speed".*

1017. INSPECTOR NORSE ★★

*b.c. Norse Dancer – Indiana Blues (Indian
Ridge).* February 22. Brother to the quite
useful dual 7f (including at 2 yrs) and 1m
winner Norse Blues and half-brother to the
fair 2012 7f placed 2-y-o Secret Rebel (by
Sakhee's Secret). The dam, a fair 6f winner, is
a half-sister to several winners including the
useful 2-y-o listed 5.2f winner and Group 2
Flying Childers Stakes third Speed Cop and
the fairly useful triple 5f winner (including
at 2 yrs) and listed-placed Siren's Gift. The
second dam, Blue Siren (by Bluebird), a very
useful winner of three races from 5f to 7f,
was disqualified from first place in two more,
notably the Group 1 5f Nunthorpe Stakes (the
winner on merit) and is a half-sister to several
winners including the quite useful 9f winner
Northern Habit. (Mr J C Smith). *"A smashing
horse, he's the same sort of horse as his brother
Norse Blues. He's straightforward, won't be
early but he's a big, scopey horse with a great
attitude. A back-end seven furlong maiden will
be his starting point".*

1018. LEAD A MERRY DANCE

*b.f. Bertolini – Green Supreme (Primo
Dominie).* April 9. Half-sister the Group 2
Diadem Stakes, Group 3 Duke Of York Stakes
and Group 3 Prix de Saint-Georges winner
Sampower Star, the Group 3 Molecomb Stakes
winner Strike Up the Band, the modest 6f
winner Sessay (all by Cyrano de Bergerac), the

Group 3 5f King George winner Fire Up The
Band (by Prince Sabo) and the fair 6f winner
Green Howard (by Bahamian Bounty), the
modest 6f winner Dash Of Lime (Bold Edge),
the modest 12f winner Kampai (by Sakhee)
and the moderate 7f winner Eliza Doolittle
(by Royal Applause). The dam is an unraced
half-sister to 6 winners. The second dam, Pea
Green (by Try My Best), was unplaced.

1019. LITTLE BIG MAN ★★★

*b.c. Sleeping Indian – Doris Souter (Desert
Story).* April 17. The dam, a fair dual 10f and
hurdles winner, is a half-sister to 8 other minor
winners. The second dam, Hope And Glory
(by Well Decorated), a 2-y-o 6f winner, is a
half-sister to 6 winners. (Mr P Merritt). *"He's a
sharp colt even though he wasn't an early foal,
he's going along well and you should certainly
put him in the book".*

1020. MAYMYO (IRE) ★★★★

*b.c. Invincible Spirit – Lady Windermere
(Lake Coniston).* May 5. Ninth foal. 50,000Y.
Tattersalls October Book 1. S Kirk. Half-brother
to the useful Irish listed 6f winner and Group 3
placed Absolutelyfabulous (by Mozart), to the
quite useful 1m winner Russian Jar (by Xaar)
and the fair 2-y-o 1m and hurdles winner
Mark Twain (by Rock Of Gibraltar). The dam is
an unraced half-sister to 5 winners including
the Group 1 Fillies' Mile winner Listen and the
Group 1 7f Moyglare Stud Stakes winner and
high-class broodmare Sequoyah (dam of the
multiple Group 1 winner Henrythenavigator).
The second dam, Brigid (by Irish River), a
minor French 3-y-o 1m winner, is a full or half-
sister to 7 winners including the listed 7f Prix
de l'Obelisque winner Or Vision (herself dam
of the Group/Grade 1 winners Dolphin Street,
Insight and Saffron Walden). (Mr H Balasuriya).
*"A horse with a lovely pedigree, he's doing
everything right and he shows a little bit of
speed. He was a bit weak at the sales otherwise
he'd have brought more than fifty grand. I
think he's a smart horse, he's developing well,
he's taking everything in his stride and he's
lovely. He looks a six furlong type to start with".*

1021. MISS SKYFALL (IRE) ★★★

ch.f. Tagula – Full Of Nature (Monsieur Bond).
January 28. First foal. The dam, a fair 2-y-o 6f

winner, is a half-sister to numerous winners including the fairly useful 5f (at 2 yrs) and 6f winner of 5 races Alben Star. The second dam, Secret Circle (by Magic Ring), is an unraced half-sister to 8 winners including the Group 1 1m St James's Palace Stakes winner Bijou d'Inde. *"A little, sharp, early filly, she'll probably be my first runner. Her dam won first time out and she's showing the same way so I'm hoping she'll be running in May".*

1022. NORSE STAR ★★

b.c. Norse Dancer – Spot Prize (Seattle Dancer). March 14. Half-brother to the fair 2012 2-y-o 7f winner Royal Prize (by Nayef), to the Group 2 15f Prix Kergorlay winner Gold Medallist (by Zilzal), the useful 7f (at 2 yrs) and listed 10f winner Premier Prize (by Selkirk), the fairly useful 12f winner Stage Right (by In The Wings), the quite useful 1m and 12f winner Western Prize (by High Chaparral), the quite useful 14f winner Prize Dancer (by Suave Dancer) and the modest 12f and hurdles winner Prize Ring (by Bering). The dam, a useful filly, won over 5f at 2 yrs and was fourth in the Oaks. The second dam, Lucky Break (by What Luck), won 4 races in the USA. (J C Smith). *"A bit stronger and a bit bigger than my other Norse Dancer 2-y-o but otherwise they're very similar. A lovely horse for the autumn, we can take our time with him".*

1023. SILVERCOMBE ★★

gr.c. Archipenko – Cherrycombe-Row (Classic Cliche). February 10. Fourth living foal. 11,000Y. Tattersalls October Book 2. S Kirk. Half-brother to the US Grade 2 Santa Maria Handicap winner and Grade 1 second St Trinians (by Piccolo). The dam, a fair 2-y-o 7f winner, is a half-sister to 5 winners abroad. The second dam, Key To The Ring (by Pyjama Hunt), is an unraced half-sister to 7 winners. (T K Pearson). *"He looks like a 2-y-o, he's a smashing, good-looking, correct horse and he was cheap considering the dam's already bred a Grade 2 winner. I thought he was going to be early but he got a touch of sore shins and I've backed off him a bit. He's a good mover with a good attitude".*

1024. SIMMA (IRE) ★★★

gr.f. Dark Angel – Staylily (Grand Lodge).

February 21. 12,500Y. Tattersalls October Book 3. Neil Simpson. Half-sister to the fairly useful dual 7f winner Candle Sahara (by Noverre), to the quite useful 6f winner of 5 races Kyle (by Kyllachy) and the fair 2-y-o dual 6f winner Speedfit Girl (by Kodiac). The dam is an unraced half-sister to 4 winners including the US stakes winner and Grade 1 placed She's Classy. The second dam, Stately Dance (by Stately Don), won twice in the USA and is a half-sister to the Coronation Cup winner Be My Native. (Mr N Simpson). *"A lovely filly and physically very like a nice Dark Angel filly I had called My Sharona who won 3 races. She's big and just needs to strengthen up into herself but when she does that I can see her racing by June or July. She's straightforward and doing everything right but I haven't asked her anything yet. Ideally I would have thought she'd start off at six furlongs".* TRAINERS' BARGAIN BUY

1025. UNNAMED ★★★

gr.c. Henrythenavigator – C'Est La Cat (Mountain Cat). January 28. Fourth foal. 30,000Y. Tattersalls December. Peter & Ross Doyle. Half-brother to two winners in the USA by Thunder Gulch including the stakes-placed Cody Peak. The dam, a minor 3-y-o winner in the USA, is a half-sister to 4 winners including the US Grade 2 winner C'Est L'Amour (herself dam of the Group 1 Criterium De Saint-Cloud winner Passion For Gold) and the stakes winner Passion Flower (dam of the US Grade 2 winner Maceo). The second dam, L'Amour Toujours (by Blushing Groom), won the listed Prix Charles Laffitte and is a half-sister to 5 winners. (Verano Quartet). *"A very mature, strong-topped colt, he's straightforward and going well. I'll just carry on with him and he gives me the impression of being a 2-y-o type for six furlongs".*

1026. UNNAMED ★★

b.c. Duke Of Marmalade – Green Room (FR) (In The Wings). February 22. Third foal. 15,000Y. Tattersalls October Book 2. S Kirk. The dam, a useful Italian listed 12f winner of 4 races, was placed in two other listed events here and is a half-sister to 4 winners. The second dam, Scarlet Plume (by Warning), won 2 races including the Group 3 1m Premio

Dormello and is a half-sister to 4 winners out of the Oaks winner Circus Plume. *"A smashing colt but he's backward and more of a 3-y-o type. I haven't sold him yet but he was cheap and he might turn out to be the best of them. He's on the back burner at the moment".*

1027. UNNAMED ★★

b.f. Tagula – Housa Dancer (Fabulous Dancer). May 16. Ninth foal. 20,000Y. Tattersalls December. Not sold. Half-sister to the Group 2 Prix Noailles winner Grand Vent (by Shirocco) and to the Group 3 Diomed Stakes winner and Group 2 York Stakes second Bushman (by Maria's Mon) and the quite useful 1m winner Dubawi Island (by Dubawi). The dam, a 2-y-o listed 9f winner in France, subsequently won two US stakes events and was Grade 1 placed in the USA and is a half-sister to the Group 2 Prix Niel winner Housamix. The second dam, Housatonic (by Riverman), won over 7f at 3 yrs and is a half-sister to 7 winners including the US Grade 2 and Grade 3 winner Globe. *"When I saw her at the sales she was backward and narrow, partly because she was a late foal, but she's improved so much in between and now she's a nice filly with a great attitude. She's strengthening up all the time and you'd be thinking of seven furlongs for her. With her pedigree you'd only have to win a little race and she'd be worth a fair bit".*

1028. UNNAMED ★★★

b.f. Footstepsinthesand – Inis Boffin (Danehill Dancer). April 14. First foal. The dam, a fair 9f winner, is a half-sister to several winners. The second dam, Windmill (by Ezzoud), a fair 13.8f winner, is a half-sister to 8 winners including the very smart Group 2 12f Ribblesdale Stakes winner Gull Nook (herself dam of the top-class colt Pentire), the equally smart Group 3 12f Princess Royal Stakes winner Banket and the useful Group 3 Ormonde Stakes winner Mr Pintips. (Ms C Cleary & Mr D O'Loughlin). *"A precocious filly, she's straightforward, just a tiny bit light all over so she'll take a bit longer, but she'll make a 2-y-o by May".*

1029 UNNAMED ★★

b.f. Archipenko – Mennetou (Entrepreneur). March 28. Sixth foal. 37,000Y. Tattersalls October Book 1. BBA (Ire). Half-sister to Zeva

(by Zamindar), placed third over 7f on her only start at 2 yrs in 2012 and to the Irish 3-y-o Group 3 9f winner Obama Rule (by Danehill Dancer). The dam is an unraced half-sister to 5 winners including the Prix de l'Arc de Triomphe winner Carnegie, the Group 2 10f Prix Guillaume d'Ornano winner Antisaar and the Group 3 St Simon Stakes winner Lake Erie. The second dam, Detroit (by Riverman), won the Prix de l'Arc de Triomphe and is a half-sister to 7 winners including the Cheveley Park Stakes winner Durtal. *"She's probably got the best pedigree of all mine considering there are two Arc winners in there. She was a cheap buy because she's a bit weak and backward and I wouldn't dare even think about getting her going yet. We won't be pushing her before the back-end of the season".*

1030. UNNAMED ★★★

b.c. Tagula – Notepad (King's Best). April 24. Second foal. €13,000Y. Goffs Sportsman's. Sylvester Kirk. The dam is an unplaced half-sister to 9 winners including the useful 2-y-o Group 3 7f C L Weld Park Stakes winner Rag Top and the dam of the listed winner Elhamri. The second dam, Petite Epaulette (by Night Shift), a fair 5f winner at 2 yrs, is a half-sister to 3 winners including the Group 1 1m Gran Criterium second Line Dancer. *"The family are small and he's just the same. A little bit backward but improving all the time, he just needs to strengthen up a little bit more but I see him as a six furlong 2-y-o before June. A nice little horse with a good attitude".*

1031. UNNAMED ★★

b.f. Mastercraftsman – Sheba Five (Five Star Day). April 17. First foal. 22,000Y. Tattersalls October Book 2. Not sold. The dam, placed fourth over 6f once at 2 yrs, is a half-sister to 4 winners including the stakes winners Arch Rebel and On My Dime. The second dam, Sheba's Step (by Alysheba), is an unraced half-sister to 8 winners including the dam of the US Grade 1 stakes winner Archcharch. *"A nice, big filly, she's won't be precocious but she has a nice action and a lovely attitude – you don't even know you have her. A nice seven furlong fillies' maiden at Newbury will do for starters. She goes along lovely".*

WILLIAM KNIGHT

1032. ALLERGIC REACTION (IRE) ★★

b.c. Kyllachy – Wood Chorus (Singspiel). March 12. Second foal. 35,000Y. Tattersalls October Book 2. Richard Knight. Half-brother to the moderate 2012 6f placed 2-y-o Duchess Of Dreams (by Royal Applause). The dam, a fairly useful 10f winner, was listed placed over 10f and is a half-sister to the very smart 7f (at 2 yrs), Group 2 Yorkshire Cup and Group 3 11.8f Lingfield Derby Trial winner Franklins Gardens and to the very smart Group 3 7f and Group 3 1m winner Polar Ben. The second dam, Woodbeck (by Terimon), a fairly useful 3-y-o dual 7f winner, is a half-sister to 8 winners. (Four Men & A Dream Partnership). *"A very nice-moving colt, with a good attitude, he's going to take a bit more time than I first thought and is probably a seven furlong/mile 2-y-o for July or August. I like him, but he seems to take after the dam's side of the family and it's looking like he'll be a ten furlong horse next year".*

1033. ALL YOURS (IRE) ★★★★

gr.f. Verglas – Totally Yours (Desert Sun). February 18. Fourth foal. 24,000Y. Tattersalls October Book 2. G Howson. Half-sister to the quite useful 2012 2-y-o 7f winner Salutation (by Iffraaj) and to the fairly useful 7f (at 2 yrs) and 1m winner and listed-placed Totally Ours (by Singspiel). The dam, a quite useful 2-y-o 6f winner, is a half-sister to 3 winners including the 2-y-o Group 1 7f Dewhurst Stakes winner Tout Seul (by Ali-Royal). The second dam, Total Aloof (Groom Dancer), a fair dual 5f winner at 3 yrs, is a half-sister to 3 winners in Japan. (Merton Place Stud). *"She's a nice, athletic filly, quite precocious and with a lot of quality about her. She's well made and I'm hoping she'll be ready by the end of May or early June over six furlongs. The pedigree backs up her appearance of a proper 2-y-o type".*

1034. BEACH BAR (IRE) ★★★

b.c. Azamour – Toasted Special (Johannesburg). March 1. First foal. 22,000Y. Tattersalls October Book 2. Tom Malone. The dam, a fair triple 6f winner, is a half-sister to 7 winners. The second dam, Sajjaya (by Blushing Groom), a useful 2-y-o 7f and 3-y-o 1m winner, was second in the Group 3

Matron Stakes and is a half-sister to 8 winners including the Group 1 1m Queen Elizabeth II Stakes winner Lahib. (Mr P Winkworth & Mrs Bex Seabrook). *"He's a very well-made colt, strong and mature-looking – especially for an Azamour. He's going to be ready when the seven furlong maidens start in mid-June. As long as he keeps his temperament intact he'll be alright, but he is a bit hot-headed. I think if he can channel his enthusiasm he'll be alright".*

1035. BLACK MARY ★★★

b.f. Bushranger – Corps de Ballet (Fasliyev). February 12. Fifth foal. 32,000Y. Tattersalls October Book 2. T G Roddick. Half-sister to the 2-y-o 6f and subsequent Hong Kong winner Georges Lane (by Diamond Green), to the quite useful 6f winner of 7 races (including at 2 yrs) Dark Lane (by Namid), the quite useful triple 7f winner Dance Company (by Aussie Rules) and the fair 7f winner Compton Park (by Compton Place). The dam, a fairly useful 5f (at 2 yrs) and 6f winner, is a half-sister to 7 winners including the prolific Hong Kong winner of 8 races and £750,000 Quick Action and the listed winners Doowaley and Misraah. The second dam, Dwell (by Habitat), a fairly useful 3-y-o 1m winner, was listed-placed and is a half-sister to the dams of the South African Grade 2 winner Gleaming Sky and the smart winner of the Cambridgeshire, Cap Juluca. (G Roddick). *"She's quite typical of the sire, small and compact. I've trained a couple out of the dam and they've all won and had ability. I think this filly will follow suit but she's had a setback which sets us back to mid-July, probably over six furlongs. I thought quite a lot of the Bushranger's at the sales looked plain, but she's got a lot of quality".*

1036. CAPMONDE (IRE) ★★★

b.f. Cape Cross – Esclarmonde (In The Wings). April 15. Third foal. €26,000Y. Arqana Deauville October. Richard Knight. The dam, a fair 12f placed maiden, is a sister to the Group 3 10f Prix Corrida and Group 3 10.5f Prix de Flore winner Trumbaka and a half-sister to the listed winners Arctic Hunt and Spirit Of Dubai. The second dam, Questina (by Rainbow Quest), won twice at 3 yrs in France and is a half-sister to 6 winners. (Mrs F Ashfield). *"She's on the small side but I like her, she's quite precocious and has a really nice action. She wants to please and looks like being out relatively early, so she might be speedy enough for six furlongs to start with, at the end of May/beginning of June".*

1037. CRAFTY EXIT ★★★★
gr.c. *Mastercraftsman – Demerger (Distant View).* January 31. Sixth foal. 48,000Y. Tattersalls October Book 1. Richard Knight. Half-brother to the Group 1 5f Nunthorpe Stakes and Group 2 Temple Stakes winner Sole Power (by Kyllachy), to the fairly useful 5f (including at 2 yrs) to 7f winner of 15 races and Group 3 Cornwallis Stakes second Cornus (by Inchinor) and the French 2-y-o 5f winner and listed-placed Sotka (by Dutch Art). The dam is an unraced half-sister to 5 winners. The second dam, Merida (by Warning), a 1m winner in France and the USA, is a full or half-sister to 8 winners including the dual US Grade 2 1m winner Tychonic. (Brooks, Cavanagh & Tracey). *"He's a nice-looking horse, solid and well-made with a good temperament. He moves well and has a bit of quality about him, so I like him".*

1038. EXALTED (IRE) ★★★
b.c. *Acclamation – Eman's Joy (Lion Cavern).* April 8. Seventh foal. €105,000Y. Goffs Orby. Richard Knight. Half-brother to the 2-y-o Group 3 1m Autumn Stakes winner Blitzkrieg, to the quite useful 1m and 10f winner Summer Gold (all by Barathea) and the fair 2-y-o 6f winner Toledo Gold (by Needwood Blade). The dam, a modest 3-y-o 6f winner, is a half-sister to 8 winners including the Group 3 Diomed Stakes winner Eton Lad. The second dam, Carolside (by Music Maestro), a very useful 2-y-o 5f winner, was second in the Cherry Hinton Stakes and is a half-sister to 6 winners. (The Old Brokers). *"A big, scopey son of Acclamation, he's going to need a bit of time. He's a lovely mover and has a bit of class about him, but I can't see him being out before July or August. So he's not one to rush, but he was my pick as a yearling when they came in".*

1039. GOODWOOD STORM ★★★
ch.f. *Shamardal – Artifice (Green Desert).* April 13. Seventh foal. 27,000Y. Tattersalls October Book 2. R Frisby. Half-sister to the

quite useful 7f (at 2 yrs) and 1m winner Subtefuge (by Observatory) and to the quite useful 7.5f winner Ramaad (by Dr Fong). The dam, a fair 3-y-o 6f winner, is a sister to 3 winners including the very useful Group 3 7f Jersey Stakes winner Ardkinglass and the useful dual 7f winner Darnaway and a half-sister to 5 winners. The second dam, Reuval (by Sharpen Up), a useful winner of 2 races over 1m at 3 yrs, is a half-sister to 6 winners and to the dams of the Group 2 winners Ozone Friendly, Reprimand and Wiorno. (Goodwood Racehorse Owners Group). *"A medium-sized, racey filly that looks quite precocious. She has a slightly hot temperament but if we can keep the lid on her she should be winning races as a 2-y-o for sure. Six/seven furlongs should suit her I should think".*

1040. HANDS UP (IRE) ★★★
b.c. *Bushranger – Christa Maria (Alhaarth).* March 25. Second foal. £33,000Y. Doncaster Premier. Peter & Ross Doyle. Half-brother to the French 3-y-o dual 10f winner Maria Crista (by Red Clubs). The dam is an unraced half-sister to 6 winners including the 7f, 1m and subsequent US Grade 1 placed stakes winner Tamweel. The second dam, Naazeq (by Nashwan), a quite useful 10.5f winner, is a full or half-sister to 10 winners. (Richoux Partnership). *"He should be one of my first 2-y-o runners. He's small, butty and goes along quite well. Hopefully he'll be out by the middle of May, probably over six furlongs, but he may have the speed for five".*

1041. HURRICANE HARRY ★★★★
b.c. *Royal Applause – Stormy Weather (Nashwan).* March 24. Sixth foal. 52,000Y. Tattersalls October Book 2. Richard Knight. Half-brother to the quite useful 2012 2-y-o 5f and 6f winner Ovett (by Exceed And Excel), to the very useful listed 1m winner Chigun (by Oasis Dream) and a hurdles winner by Hernando. The dam is an unraced half-sister to 8 winners including the Group 3 Prix d'Arenburg winner Starlit Sands and the smart broodmare Summer Night (the dam of four stakes winners). The second dam, Shimmering Sea (by Slip Anchor), a fairly useful Irish 2-y-o 5f and 7f winner and third in the Group 3 Silken Glider Stakes, is a half-

sister to 5 winners including the King George VI and Queen Elizabeth Stakes winner Petoski. (Brooks, Cavanagh & Tracey). *"A strong colt, quite typical of the sire and I like him. He's got a touch of quality and he'll start off in six or seven furlong maidens from early June time. A nice mover, he's just a nice, solid colt".*

1042. ONE PIXEL ★★★
b.f. Primo Valentino – Mays Dream (Josr Algarhoud). January 20. Third foal. £20,000Y. Doncaster Festival. Tom Malone. Half-sister to the quite useful 7f and 1m winner at 2 and 3yrs Fire Ship (by Firebreak). The dam ran once unplaced and is a half-sister to 8 winners Golden Nun (Group 3 6f Ballyogan Stakes) and the fairly useful 2-y-o 5f winner and Group 3 third Amber Valley. The second dam, Amber Mill (by Doulab), a useful winner over 5f (twice) and 6f, is a half-sister to 4 winners. (Hot to Trot Racing Club). *"A half-sister to Fire Ship, who we have in the yard, she's got lots of scope and a nice action. The stallion isn't fashionable but this filly looks like being OK. A seven furlongs/mile 2-y-o around August time".*

1043. PERCYBELLE ★★★
ch.f. Sir Percy – Chelsea (Miswaki). March 5. Eleventh foal. 11,000Y. Tattersalls October Book 3. Gill Richardson. Half-sister to the fair 7f winner Donna Giovanna (by Mozart), to the fair 6f (at 2 yrs) and 1m winner Cedar Rangers (by Anabaa) and a winner in Japan by Spinning World. The dam, a French 9f winner, is a half-sister to 7 winners including the US Grade 1 10f winner Super Staff and the French and US Grade 2 winner Public Purse and to the unplaced dam of Rob Roy (Group 2 Sandown Mile). The second dam, Prodigious (by Forli), won 4 races at 3 and 4 yrs in France and is a half-sister to 7 winners. (Jon & Julia Aisbitt). *"Quite racey and a good-moving filly, we'll aim her for the seven furlong maidens around July time. She goes along quite well for a cheap yearling".*

1044. UNNAMED ★★★
b.f. Duke Of Marmalade – Crinolette (Sadler's Wells). April 15. Twelfth foal. 18,000Y. Tattersalls October Book 2. Richard Knight. Half-sister to the useful 2-y-o 6f winner and

Group 2 6f Richmond Stakes third Cedarberg (by Cape Cross), to the fairly useful 2-y-o 5f and 7f winner of 3 races Cravat (by Dubai Destination) and the fair dual 7f winner Materialism (by Librettist) and to the placed dam of the Irish dual listed winner Lisvale. The dam, unplaced over 8.2f on her only start at 2 yrs, is a half-sister to 3 winners including the very smart Group 3 7f Tetrarch Stakes and Group 3 7f Ballycorus Stakes winner Desert Style. The second dam, Organza (by High Top), a useful 10f winner, is a half-sister to the Group 1 Prix de la Foret winner Brocade - herself the dam of Barathea and Gossamer. (Mr & Mrs N Welby). *"She's quite a nice, well-made filly and a good mover that should be out around July time. I quite like the sire – I have a nice 3-y-o by him and I think this filly will be alright. She's got a bit of quality about her and I think she'll make a 2-y-o over six/seven furlongs".* TRAINERS' BARGAIN BUY

DANIEL KUBLER
1045. BAILIWICK ★★★
b.c. Oratorio – Imperial Bailiwick (Imperial Frontier). April 27. Fifteenth foal. Half-brother to the fair 2-y-o 6f winner Eminently (by Exceed And Excel), to the high-class Haydock Park Sprint Cup and the Nunthorpe Stakes winner Reverence (by Mark Of Esteem), the very useful 2-y-o listed 7f Chesham Stakes and 5-y-o 1m winner and 1m Britannia Handicap second Helm Bank (by Wild Again), the quite useful 6f (at 2 yrs) and 5f winner of 5 races Impressible (by Oasis Dream), the fairly useful 5f (at 2 yrs) and 6f winner Quiet Elegance (by Fantastic Light), the modest 6f winner Fortress (by Generous), the fair 1m to 12f winner Sedgwick (by Nashwan) and a winner at up to 7.5f in Italy by Efisio. The dam, a useful winner of 3 races at around 5f including the Group 2 Flying Childers Stakes, was placed in the Molecomb Stakes and the Prix du Petit-Couvert and is a half-sister to 3 winners in France (all over 1m+). The second dam, Syndikos (by Nashua) was second 6 times in the USA and is a half-sister to 5 minor winners. (Mr & Mrs G Middlebrook). *"The last foal out of a very good mare, he's not very big but he is strong and he should be out in early June. He's bulking out now and he'll be a quick horse".*

1046. DISKO (IRE) ★★★

b.f. *Kodiac – Dissonance (Rossini)*. April 2. Third foal. £6,000Y. Doncaster Premier. Tark Bloodstock. Half-sister to the modest Irish 7f winner Consonance (by Chineur). The dam is an unraced sister to the 2-y-o Group 3 Firth Of Clyde Stakes winner Golden Legacy and a half-sister to a winner in Italy. The second dam, Dissidentia (by Dancing Dissident), won four races in Belgium and France and is a half-sister to 4 winners abroad. *"A sharp, speedy filly, she's an obvious 2-y-o and she should be running in May, but she'll train on to be a 3-y-o as well. She seems to be typical of the Invincible Spirit/Kodiac line in that she's not overly big but all there in proportion. There are two shares left in her, should anyone be interested"*. TRAINERS' BARGAIN BUY

1047. IL PAPARAZZI ★★

b.c. *Royal Applause – Birdie (Alhaarth)*. March 19. Sixth foal. 32,000Y. Tattersalls October Book 2. Kubler Racing. Half-brother to the French 12f winner Salvation (by Montjeu). The dam, a 1m and listed 11.5f winner, is a half-sister to 7 winners including the French middle-distance winner of 10 races (including four listed events) Faru and the listed winner Fickle (herself dam of the Group 3 winner Tarfah). The second dam, Fade (by Persepolis), is an unraced half-sister to Tom Seymour, a winner of five Group 3 events in Italy. (Capture The Moment). *"A big horse but surprisingly quite forward and he'll be racing this year over seven furlongs. It's a middle-distance family and he's just short of 16.1 already, so although I think he's finished growing he's probably more of a 3-y-o type"*.

1048. NORSE LEGEND ★★

b.c. *Norse Dancer – Methodical (Lujain)*. April 13. First foal. £1,000Y. Doncaster November. Woodhaven Stud. The dam, a winner over jumps, is a half-sister to one winner. The second dam, Simple Logic (by Aragon), a 2-y-o winner and listed placed, is a half-sister to 5 winners. (Woodhaven Racing Syndicate). *"A neat colt, he'll probably be earlier than you'd expect from the pedigree. Very straightforward, he has a nice attitude and he seems to love his work. A seven furlong type 2-y-o in the second half of the season"*.

1049. POETIC JUSTICE ★★

b.c. *Byron – Toleration (Petong)*. April 14. Fifth foal. £2,500Y. Doncaster November. Woodhaven Stud. Half-brother to Apaa (by Compton Place), a winner of 6 races in Spain (including over 5f at 2 yrs). The dam, a quite useful 2-y-o 6f winner, is a half-sister to 5 winners including the listed-placed Simple Logic. The second dam, Dancing Chimes (by Petong), was unraced. (Woodhaven Racing Syndicate). *"A sprinting type, but he's a big, strong horse that's going to need some time. One for the second half of the season"*.

1050. TRINITY RIVER ★★★

b.f. *Three Valleys – Blane Water (Lomond)*. February 1. Half-sister to the modest 9f and 10f winner Bracklinn (by Deploy) and to a winner in Hungary by Benny The Dip. The dam, a quite useful 2-y-o 6f winner, is a half-sister to 4 winners. The second dam, Triode (by Sharpen Up), a useful 1m winner, was third in the Group 3 Premio Bagutta and is a half-sister to 2 winners. (Mr P Whitten). *"A very sharp, very strong filly. If she hadn't had a little setback she'd have been racing in early April. She's like a bullet and although she's not the biggest she's all there – mentally and physically"*.

DAVID LANIGAN

1051. ALLEGATION (FR) ★★★

b.f. *Lawman – Anja (Indian Ridge)*. April 29. Seventh foal. €82,000Y. Arqana Deauville October. Charlie Gordon-Watson. Half-sister to the French 1m winner You Rock Me (by Gulch) and to the 3-y-o 7f winner (on her only start) Funky Lady (by El Corredor). The dam was placed in France and subsequently won a minor race in the USA and is a half-sister to numerous winners including the Group 1 12f Prix du Jockey Club winner Anabaa Blue, the very useful listed 10f winner Reunite and the fairly useful listed 10f winner Measured Tempo. The second dam, Allez Les Trois (by Riverman), a smart winner of 3 races in France including the Group 3 10.5f Prix de Flore, is a half-sister to 6 winners including the Prix de l'Arc de Triomphe winner Urban Sea (the dam of Galileo and Sea The Stars) and the 2,000 Guineas winner King's Best. *"A pretty straightforward, compact type and strong, she ought to make a 2-y-o around June time over six furlongs and she's a nice filly".*

1052. ALIGHIERI (IRE) ★★★
b.c. Sea The Stars – Ange Bleu (Alleged). April 19. Twelfth foal. Half-brother to the US Grade 1 Beverly D Stakes and Grade 1 Diana Stakes winner Angara, to the French listed 13f winner Arlesienne (both by Alzao), to the Group 2 11f Prix Corrida winner Actrice (by Danehill), the French 10f winner Altesse Imperiale (by Rock Of Gibraltar), the French 11f winner Artaban (by Peintre Celebre) and the 13f winner Ange Du Salut (by Dalakhani). The dam was placed at 3 yrs in France and is a half-sister to 10 winners including the Group 3 Prix de Psyche winner and French 1,000 Guineas and French Oaks placed Agathe (herself dam of the Grade/Group 1 winners Artiste Royale and Aquarelliste), to the Breeders Cup Classic winner Arcangues and the dam of the 1,000 Guineas winner Cape Verdi. The second dam, Albertine (by Irish River), a smart winner of 2 races at up to 10f, was placed in the Group 2 Prix de l'Opera and is a half-sister to 8 winners including the high-class middle-distance stayer Ashmore and the smart middle-distance filly Acoma. (B E Nielsen). *"A big horse that's strengthened up a lot over the last couple of weeks. He went through a weak period but he's actually going alright although I wouldn't think you'd see him until August or September. The ones I have by Sea The Stars all look like they'll take a bit of time. He'll want seven furlongs or a mile to start off with and we're pleased with him now".*

1053. BABUR (IRE) ★★★★
ch.c. Pivotal – Bright Morning (USA) (Storm Cat). April 6. First foal. 200,000Y. Tattersalls October Book 1. Charlie Gordon-Watson. The dam is an unraced half-sister to 8 winners including the top-class Group 1 1m Queen Elizabeth II Stakes and Group 1 9.3f Prix d'Ispahan winner Observatory and the Group 2 Prix de Malleret winner High Praise. The second dam, Stellaria (by Roberto), won from 5f to 8.5f including the listed 6f Rose Bowl Stakes and is a half-sister to 8 winners. *"A nice horse, he looks like he'll make a 2-y-o and hopefully he'll be out around May or June time. He's strong and compact, quite forward and a*

well put-together horse. We'll start him off at six or seven furlongs".

1054. BOLD LASS (IRE) ★★★★
b.f. Sea The Stars – My Branch (Distant Relative). April 9. Half-sister to the Group 1 6f Haydock Sprint Cup winner Tante Rose (by Barathea), to the useful 2-y-o listed 7f winner Bay Tree (by Daylami), the useful 1m winner and listed-placed Melodramatic (by Sadler's Wells), the 7f (at 2 yrs) and 6f winner Priceless Jewel, the 2-y-o 5.7f winner Rosie's Posy (by Suave Dancer) and the 3-y-o 7f winner Future Flight (by Polar Falcon) – all 3 quite useful. The dam, a very useful winner of the listed 6f Firth Of Clyde Stakes (at 2 yrs) and the listed 7f Sceptre Stakes, was fourth in the 1,000 Guineas and third in the Irish 1,000 Guineas. The second dam, Pay The Bank (by High Top), a quite useful 2-y-o 1m winner, stayed 10f. (B E Nielsen). *"A nice filly and we'd like to think that she'd be a bit more precocious than some of the Sea The Stars 2-y-o's. She goes nicely, she's very straightforward and hopefully she'll be one we could start off at six furlongs around June time. She's a nice model".*

1055. HIGHPLAINS DRIFTER (IRE) ★★
b.c. High Chaparral – Qhazeenah (Marju). May 9. Seventh foal. €155,000Y. Goffs Orby. J Brummitt. Half-brother to the US Grade 2 winner Girl Warrior (by Elusive Quality), to the French 3-y-o winner and listed 10.5f placed Londonintherain, the quite useful 10.5f and 11f winner Soul Mountain, the fair 1m winner Robens Rock (all by Rock Of Gibraltar) and the fairly useful 2-y-o 7f and 9f winner Roman Eagle (by Holy Roman Emperor). The dam, a useful 6.5f (at 2 yrs) to 7f winner, is a half-sister to 9 winners including the smart Group 2 14.6f Park Hill Stakes winner Ranin, the very useful 7f and 1m winner Ghalib and the useful 2-y-o 1m and listed 9f placed Wahchi. The second dam, Nafhaat (by Roberto), a fairly useful 12f winner, stayed 15f. *"He's a nice, big horse that'll take some time, especially as he's having a break at the moment, but he's a good-looking colt".*

1056. HOIST THE COLOURS (IRE) ★★★
b.c. Sea The Stars – Multicolour Wave (Rainbow Quest). March 14. Eighth foal.

475,000Y. Tattersalls October Book 1. Charlie Gordon-Watson. Half-brother to the Group 1 French 1,000 Guineas winner Elusive Wave (by Elusive City), to the Irish 2-y-o 7f winner and listed-placed Million Waves (by Mull Of Kintyre), the quite useful 7f (at 2 yrs) and 1m winner Million Spirits (by Invincible Spirit), the quite useful Irish 2-y-o 7f winner Wealdmore Wave (by Oratorio) and the minor French 9.5f winner Photophore (by Clodovil and herself the dam of a listed winner). The dam is a placed half-sister to 4 winners and to the unraced dam of the Group 2 Queen Mary Stakes winner Langs Lash. The second dam, Echoes (by Niniski), won the Group 3 Prix Corrida, was Group 2 placed and is a half-sister to 5 winners. (B E Nielsen). *"He's done well, strengthened and he's going in the right direction. He's very straightforward, a good mover and we've had no problems with him, but you won't see him until late summer".*

1057. PLACIDIA (IRE) ★★★

b.f. *Sea The Stars – Palmeraie (Lear Fan).* March 27. Half-sister to Tinghir (by Dansili), placed second over 1m on his only start at 2 yrs in 2012, to the multiple French Group 2 middle-distance winner Policy Maker (by Sadler's Wells), the very useful listed 11f winner Place Rouge (by Desert King), the useful 1m (at 2 yrs) and listed 2m winner Pushkin (by Caerleon), the quite useful 11f and 12f winner Planetoid (by Galileo), the French middle-distance winners Pinacotheque (by In The Wings) and Petrograd (by Peintre Celebre), the French 2-y-o 1m winner Palme Royale (by Red Ransom). The dam is a half-sister to the Grade 2 12f Long Island Handicap winner Peinture Bleue (herself dam of the Prix de l'Arc de Triomphe winner Peintre Celebre), to the US Grade 3 1m William P Kyne Handicap winner Provins, the Irish 2-y-o winner and Group 3 Gladness Stakes second Chateau Royal and the Group 3 11f Andre Baboin winner Parme. The second dam, Petroleuse (by Habitat), won the Group 3 8.5f Princess Elizabeth Stakes and the 6f Blue Seal Stakes and is a half-sister to Pawneese (winner of the King George VI and Queen Elizabeth Stakes, the Oaks and the Prix de Diane). (Mr B Nielsen). *"A very forward filly, so although she's bred to be a middle distance type she actually looks a lot more forward than anything else out of the mare. Hopefully she'll be a bit precocious than the others because she's smaller and stronger. At the moment she's pleasing me and she's a completely different model than the rest of the family".*

1058. PRETZEL (IRE) ★★★

ch.c. *New Approach – Foodbroker Fancy (Halling).* March 13. Half-brother to the smart 7f (at 2 yrs), listed 10f and subsequent US Grade 3 12f winner Dalvina (by Grand Lodge) and to the very useful 7f (at 2 yrs) and listed 10f winner Soft Centre (by Zafonic). The dam, a smart 6f (at 2 yrs) and dual listed 10f winner, is a half-sister to the useful listed 2-y-o 6f winner Femme Fatale. The second dam, Red Rita (by Kefaah), a fairly useful 4-y-o 6f winner, was second in the Group 3 6f Cherry Hinton Stakes and the Group 3 6f Princess Margaret Stakes at 2 yrs and is a half-sister to 3 minor winners. (Normandie Stud). *"Small and compact, the family aren't that big and although he's not been in long he's sharp and very straightforward. A nice sort, we'll start him off at six furlongs".*

1059. RAGGED ROBBIN (FR) ★★★

ch.c. *Speightstown – Ikat (Pivotal).* February 27. Third foal. Half-brother to the very smart Group 3 12f Derby Trial winner and Epsom Derby second Main Sequence (by Aldebaran). The dam, a French 2-y-o 7f winner, was second in the Group 3 1m Prix d'Aumale and is a half-sister to 2 winners. The second dam, Burning Sunset (by Caerleon), a useful 7f and listed 1m winner, is a half-sister to the Group 1 Oaks winner Light Shift, to the Group 2 10.5f Tattersalls Gold Cup and Group 3 10f Brigadier Gerard Stakes winner Shiva and the Group 2 12f Prix Jean de Chaudenay and Group 3 12f Prix Foy winner Limnos. *"A half-brother to a good colt of ours, Main Sequence, he's a very similar type and by a sire who gets them a bit more precocious. But he's still a big horse and you wouldn't imagine he'd be out any time before August over seven furlongs".*

1060. RAINBOW LOLLIPOP ★★★

b.f. *Dubawi – Cross Section (Cape Cross).* March 2. The dam, a modest 6f to 9f placed maiden, is a half-sister to 8 winners including the very smart colt Diffident, winner of the Group 3 6f Diadem Stakes, the Group 3 6f Prix de Ris-Orangis and the listed 7f European Free Handicap and to the dams of 4 stakes winners. The second dam, Shy Princess (by Irish River), a smart French 2-y-o 7f winner and second in the Group 1 Prix Morny, won over 6f as a 3-y-o and is a half-sister to 8 winners including the Breeders Cup Mile winner and Eclipse Stakes second Opening Verse and the US Grade 3 winner So She Sleeps. *"Not the most attractive filly to look at, but when it comes to Dubawi you shouldn't judge a book by it's cover. They can be a bit plain-looking. She was a very weak and backward foal but she's done well, she's cantering now and I can see her being out in June or July".*

1061. REMBRANDT VAN RIJN (IRE) ★★★
b.c. Peintre Celebre – Private Life (Bering). May 13. Half-brother to the unplaced 2012 2-y-o Plutocracy (by Dansili) and to the 7f (at 2 yrs) and dual German Group 3 10f winner Persian Storm (by Monsun). The dam won over 1m (at 2 yrs) and 12f and was listed-placed twice in France and is a half-sister to the French listed winners Pretty Tough and Parisienne. The second dam, Poughkeepsie (by Sadler's Wells), won once at 3 yrs in France and is a daughter of the King George and Oaks winner Pawneese. (B E Nielsen). *"A nice sort of horse, he goes very well and has strengthened up a lot. He's a horse I like and we'll start him over seven furlongs sometime from July onwards".*

1062. ST VINCENT (IRE) ★★★★
b.c. Danehill Dancer – Lace (Sadler's Wells). March 6. Second foal. 125,000Y. Tattersalls October Book 2. Charlie Gordon-Watson. Brother to the promising 2012 Irish 7f placed 2-y-o Davanti. The dam is an unraced half-sister to 4 winners including the Group 1 Coronation Stakes and Grade 1 Milady Handicap third Zarani Sidi Anna. The second dam, Emmaline (by Affirmed), won twice at up to 9f in the USA including a stakes event and is a half-sister to 8 winners including the Grade 1 winners Bates Motel and Hatim. *"A nice colt that we bought for a new owner, he's nice and a bit more compact than I thought he'd be at this stage. He's doing very well, so*

I'll start to step him up soon and he'll be one of the earlier ones, starting over six furlongs".

1063. WARRIOR OF LIGHT (IRE) ★★★
b.c. High Chaparral – Strawberry Fledge (Kingmambo). March 10. Second foal. 320,000Y. Tattersalls October Book 1. Course Investment Co. Half-brother to The Best Doctor (by Pivotal), unplaced in one start at 2 yrs in 2012. The dam, placed once at 2 yrs in France, is a sister to 2 winners including the Group 1 12f Oaks winner Light Shift and a half-sister to 7 winners including the Group 2 10.5f Tattersalls Gold Cup and Group 3 10f Brigadier Gerard Stakes winner Shiva and the Group 2 12f Prix Jean de Chaudenay and Group 3 12f Prix Foy winner Limnos. The second dam, Lingerie (by Shirley Heights), placed 6 times in France, is a half-sister to 7 winners and to the placed dam of two Grade 1 winners in Brazil. *"'A good-looking horse and a great walker, he has a lovely action but he's light and hasn't grown into his frame. He could probably do with some time off so we could bring him out at the back of the year, over seven furlongs at least. But he's a gorgeous looking horse and one of the nicest walkers I've ever had".*

GER LYONS
1064. ANGEL OF JOY (IRE) ★★★
gr.c. Dark Angel – Moy Joy (Orpen). March 23. Third foal. The dam, a fair Irish 9f winner, is a half-sister to one winner. The second dam, Berhala (by Doyoun), is an unraced half-sister to the Group 1 Prix Saint-Alary winner Behera. (Mr John Quinn). *"He's not as forward as he thinks he is, he's very light and we're trying to put weight on him now and teach him how to grow up. I trained the dam who was a lovely filly and border line black type but she got injured. Once he grows up he'll be a nice horse and straightforward. He gives the impression he likes to race and I do like the sire Dark Angel".*

1065. AZURITE (IRE) ★★
b.c. Azamour – High Lite (Observatory). April 8. Second foal. 12,000Y. Tattersalls December. BBA (Ire). Half-brother to the modest 2012 dual 5f placed 2-y-o Red Highlites (by Red Clubs). The dam is an unplaced half-sister to 6

winners including the 2-y-o Group 2 Gimcrack Stakes winner Bannister. The second dam, Shall We Run (by Hotfoot), is a placed full or half-sister to 8 winners including Dead Certain (Group 1 Cheveley Park Stakes). (Mr Sean Jones). *"He could be seen out around June time which would be soon enough for an Azamour. I'd like him to be a bit bigger than he is but he has a good temperament".*

1066. CRISTAL FASHION (IRE) ★★★

b.f. Jeremy – Mango Groove (Unfuwain). February 16. Third foal. €40,000Y. Goffs Orby. Jim McDonald. The dam is an unplaced half-sister to 4 winners including very useful 2-y-o 6f winner and Group 1 Racing Post Trophy third Feared In Flight. The second dam, Solar Crystal (Alzao), won the Group 3 1m May Hill Stakes, was third in the Group 1 1m Prix Marcel Boussac and is a half-sister to 6 winners including the Group 1 Fillies' Mile winner Crystal Spirit, the Group 3 winners State Crystal and Dubai Success, and the Irish Derby third Tchaikovsky. (Jim McDonald). *"I'd like to think she's a maiden winner at least because she's lovely – there's a lot of class about her, but you won't be seeing her before September. She's big, scopey and long-striding. Every bit a seven furlong filly, I think a lot of her".*

1067. EXOGENESIS (IRE) ★★★

b.c. Dark Angel – Secret Key (Key Of Luck). April 25. Second foal. £20,000Y. Doncaster Premier. BBA (Ire). The dam, a modest 7f winner at 4 yrs, is a half-sister to 3 winners. The second dam, Sky Lover (by Ela-Mana-Mou), won once at 2 yrs in Ireland and is a half-sister to 2 winners. (Mr Sean Jones). *"Our first 2-y-o runner, we like him and he's up to winning a country maiden. He's a nice horse without being exceptional, he's thrived and progressed well and he'll improve a lot for his first run. A typical Dark Angel, he's good and precocious".*

1068. FOG OF WAR ★★★★

b.c. Azamour – Cut Short (Diesis). April 18. Fifth foal. 120,000Y. Tattersalls October Book 1. David Redvers. Half-brother to the quite useful 2012 2-y-o 1m winner Concise (by Lemon Drop Kid), to the useful 2-y-o listed 6f

winner Brevity (by Street Cry), the fairly useful 9f winner Fluctuate (by Exchange Rate) and the fair 5f winner Special Quality (by Elusive Quality). The dam, a quite useful 1m winner here, subsequently won in the USA and is a sister to the smart Daggers Drawn (winner of the Group 2 6f Richmond Stakes and the Group 2 7f Champagne Stakes) and a half-sister to 3 winners including the very useful 2-y-o dual 6f winner Enemy Action (herself dam of the 1,000 Guineas third Super Sleuth). The second dam, Sun And Shade (by Ajdal), a useful 2-y-o 6f winner here and a stakes-placed winner in the USA, is a half-sister to the very smart dual Group 2 winner Madame Dubois (herself dam the Irish 2,000 Guineas winner Indian Haven and the Group 1 Gran Criterium winner Count Dubois). (Qatar Racing Ltd). *"He's a lovely horse, he'll take time but he holds some nice entries and he's a horse we like a lot. Very straightforward, being an Azamour he wouldn't be out until July onwards but he'll definitely be a 2-y-o – and a nice one".*

1069. HARLEM SHAKE (IRE) ★★★

b.g. Moss Vale – Ladylishandra (Mujadil). February 15. Seventh foal. £22,000Y. Doncaster Premier. Ger Lyons. Half-brother to the Group 3 7f Oak Tree and Group 3 7f Supreme Stakes winner of 6 races Tropical Paradise (by Verglas) and to the fair 9f and 10f winner Nicomedia (by Key Of Luck). The dam, an Irish 2-y-o 6f winner, is a half-sister to 7 winners including the fairly useful 2-y-o 6f winner Pigeon Point. The second dam, Mevlana (by Red Sunset), a French 11f and 12f winner, is a sister to 2 winners including the Group 3 10f Royal Whip Stakes winner Dancing Sunset and a half-sister to 3 winners. (Mr Sean Jones). *"Moss Vale might not encourage you but we've won with every one we've had. A good, honest, nursery type 2-y-o for six/seven furlongs and he's thriving at the moment since being castrated".*

1070. INFLATION RISK ★★★

b.g. Compton Place – Small Fortune (Anabaa). January 29. Third foal. 35,000Y. Tattersalls October Book 2. BBA (Ire). Half-brother to the quite useful 13f winner Bank Bonus (by Motivator). The dam, a fair 1m winner, is a half-sister to 3 winners including the useful dual 6f winner (including at 2 yrs) Instalment.

The second dam, New Assembly (by Machiavellian), a useful 9f and 10f winner, was stakes-placed in the USA and is a sister to the 7f (at 2 yrs) and Group 1 9f Dubai Duty Free Stakes winner Right Approach and a half-sister to 7 winners. (Mr Sean Jones). *"A big, scopey horse that's forward and precocious, I like him enough and he shows enough to suggest he's up to winning a race".*

1071. KAMINARI (IRE) ★★

b.f. Sea The Stars – Karmifira (Always Fair). March 30. Eighth foal. €280,000Y. Goffs Orby. David Redvers. Half-sister to the French 2-y-o 1m winner and Group 1 1m Prix Marcel Boussac second On Verra (by Smart Strike), to the French listed-placed winner Keladora (by Crafty Prospector) and a 2-y-o winner in Japan by Cozzene. The dam, winner of the listed Prix Finlande and second in the French 1,000 Guineas, is a half-sister to 5 winners including the listed 1m Prix Coronation winner Kart Star. The second dam, Karmiska (by Bikala), won the Group 3 10f Prix de la Nonette and is a full or half-sister to 6 winners including the French listed 12f winner Karmichah. (Qatar Racing Ltd). *"She's tiny, works well and has a really good heart and a good temperament, but there's a question mark over her size".*

1072. MANSURI ★★★

b.c. Piccolo – Antonia's Choice (Music Boy). February 14. Sixth foal. £26,000Y. Doncaster Premier. BBA (Ire). Half-brother to the moderate 3-y-o 5f winner Moonlight Applause (by Royal Applause), to the quite useful 2-y-o 5f winner and listed-placed Ivania (by First Trump). The dam, a quite useful 5f winner, is a full or half-sister to 5 sprint winners. The second dam, Mainly Sunset (by Red Sunset), was once-raced due to an injury but is a half-sister to 9 winners including the high-class sprinter Bolshoi. (Mr Sean Jones). *"He's done a lot of growing since Christmas and he's just starting work now. He's nice enough without saying any more than that, he's got a good temperament and is a good, honest horse that's thriving, but we won't see him out before June".*

1073. MISS MOUSEY (IRE) ★★★

ch.f. Camacho – Miss Orah (Unfuwain). April

6. €5,000Y. Tattersalls Ireland November. Muppets Syndicate. Half-sister to the fair 10f winner Why But Why (by Whywhywhy) and to the modest 11f, 12f and hurdles winner Parc De Princes (by Ten Most Wanted). The dam, a fairly useful 2-y-o 7f here, subsequently won at 4 yrs in the USA and is a half-sister to 9 winners including the Canadian Grade 2 and 7f listed winner of 7 races Vanderlin and the French 7.5f and 1m winner Monaiya (dam of the listed Pretty Polly Stakes winner Musetta). The second dam, Massorah (by Habitat), a very useful winner of the Group 3 5f Premio Omenoni and second in the Group 3 5f Prix du Gros-Chene, is a half-sister to 4 minor winners abroad. (Muppets Syndicate). *"She'll be running in late April and she'll win a little auction maiden. A lovely filly that was well-bought and she'll pay her way".* TRAINERS' BARGAIN BUY

1074. RELENTLESS PURSUIT (IRE) ★★★

b.c. Kodiac – Dancing Debut (Polar Falcon). May 12. Tenth foal. 26,000Y. Tattersalls December. BBA (Ire). Half-brother to the fair 2012 7f and 1m placed 2-y-o World Record (by Choisir), to the fairly useful listed 10f winner of 5 races Dance Partner, to the fair 10f and 12f winner of 5 races Prelude (both by Danzero), the quite useful 7f to 9f winner of 10 races and listed-placed Kindlelight Debut (by Groom Dancer), a hurdles winner by Bishop Of Cashel, a bumpers winner by Pyrus and to the unraced dam of the Grade 1 E P Taylor Stakes and Group 2 Rockfel Stakes winner Lahaleeb. The dam was placed twice over 10f and is a half-sister to 4 winners including Virtuous (dam of the Group 1 Lockinge Stakes winner Virtual and the Group 2 Coventry Stakes winner Iceman). The second dam, Exclusive Virtue (by Shadeed), a fairly useful 2-y-o 7f winner, stayed 12f and is a half-sister to 9 winners including the 2,000 Guineas winner Entrepreneur and the Coronation Stakes winner Exclusive (herself dam of the Group 1 winner Echelon). (Mr Vincent Gaul). *"He's getting there, I'm just stepping him up now and he'll be a typical Kodiac, capable of winning a seven furlong maiden in Dundalk in October – or hopefully before that. He thinks he's precocious, but he isn't".*

1075. ROHERYN (IRE) ★★★★
b.f. Galileo – La Chunga (More Than Ready).
February 23. Third foal. $400,000Y. Keeneland
September. David Redvers. The dam won the
Group 3 6f Albany Stakes (at 2 yrs) and the
Group 3 6f Summer Stakes and is a half-sister
to 3 winners. The second dam, Gypsy Monarch
(by Wavering Monarch), a minor winner in
the USA, is a half-sister to 4 winners including
the US Grade 3 6f winner Mint. (Qatar Racing
Ltd). *"A lovely, honest filly, she has a good
temperament and is very forward for a Galileo.
I'd like her to have a month or two of fine
weather now and let her grow up from that.
She'll be ready to run from May onwards, she
shows enough pace for six furlongs but being a
Galileo I'd prefer to wait for seven".*

1076. SNIPER ★★★★
b.c. Dubawi – Anayid (A P Indy). March 28.
Fifth foal. Brother to the very useful 2-y-o
listed 7f winner Titus Mills and half-brother
to the quite useful 2-y-o 7f winner Mirabella
(by Motivator) and the quite useful 7f (at 2
yrs in France) and 9f winner Sand Tiger (by
Indian Ridge). The dam is an unraced half-
sister to 3 winners. The second dam, Aqaarid
(by Nashwan), a smart winner of the Group 1
Fillies Mile and the Group 3 7.3f Fred Darling
Stakes, was second in the 1,000 Guineas and
is a half-sister to 2 winners. (Qatar Racing Ltd).
*"By a great sire, he's a lovely colt that's just
coming back after a small setback, but he was
very precocious up to that point. He has a lot
of good entries, so we'll be expecting him to
run in a real nice maiden and we'll see what
happens after that".*

1077. SNOWMANE (IRE) ★★★
b.c. Galileo – Tree Tops (Grand Lodge). May 3.
Sixth foal. 190,000Y. Tattersalls October Book
1. David Redvers. Brother to the French 1m (at
2 yrs) and 15f winner and listed-placed Martial
Law and half-brother to a winner in Spain by
Hawk Wing. The dam, a fair 1m to 10f placed
maiden, is a half-sister to 3 winners including
the US Grade 1 and multiple Grade 2 winner
Tuscan Evening and the listed winner Barbican.
The second dam, The Faraway Tree (by Suave
Dancer), a very useful 6f and 14f winner, was
second in the Group 3 Park Hill Stakes and is
a half-sister to 12 winners including the Prix

d'Ispahan winner Sasuru, the Challenge Stakes
and Jersey Stakes winner Sally Rous and the
dam of the French 1,000 Guineas winner Rose
Gypsy. (Qatar Racing Ltd). *"He's precocious for
a Galileo, but not as precocious as our other
Galileo 2-y-o. You'd like him, but he'll be better
from the middle of the season onwards".*

1078. SYSTEM OVERLOAD (IRE) ★★★
gr.g. Verglas – Candelabra (Grand Lodge).
April 21. Seventh foal. €33,000Y. Goffs Orby.
Ger Lyons. Half-brother to two winners abroad
by Cape Cross and to the fair 7f winner Steel
Free (by Danehill Dancer). The dam, a fairly
useful dual 7f winner, is a half-sister to 3
winners. The second dam, Chatterberry (by
Aragon), a modest 2-y-o 5f winner, is a sister
to the Group 3 Cornwallis Stakes and Group
3 King George Stakes winner Argentum and
a half-sister to 7 winners. (Mr Sean Jones). *"A
grand horse, he's big and had sore shins so we
gave him a break and I gelded him at the same
time. He did a nice piece of work this morning
and he'll be running in May over six furlongs
before we step him up to seven".*

1079. THIRD DIMENSION ★★★★
b.c. Dubawi – Round The Cape (Cape Cross).
May 5. Second foal. 38,000Y. Tattersalls
October Book 2. BBA (Ire). Half-brother to the
quite useful 2012 2-y-o 7f winner Heading
North (by Teofilo). The dam, a quite useful 1m
winner, is a half-sister to 4 winners including
the useful listed 1m winner and Group 2
Falmouth Stakes second Heavenly Whisper
and the listed winner Gipsy Moth (dam of
the Group 2 winner Illustrious Blue). The
second dam, Rock The Boat (by Slip Anchor),
a modest 6f (at 2 yrs) and 1m placed maiden,
is a half-sister to 9 winners including the smart
Cherry Hinton Stakes winner Kerrera and the
high-class colt Rock City. (Mr Sean Jones). *"A
lovely colt, we like him a lot and he's ready to
run now but he's a May foal so we'll wait a
bit. He's precocious and he might start at five
furlongs but he'll go seven later on and he has
some good entries".*

1080. TRINITY FORCE (IRE) ★★★
ch.c. Iffraaj – Nasharaat (Green Desert). March
28. Third foal. 30,000Y. Tattersalls October
Book 2. BBA (Ire). Half-brother to the modest

1m winner Wolf Spirit (by Amadeus Wolf). The dam, a minor Irish 7f winner, is a half-sister to 3 winners including the listed second Qalahari. The second dam, Daqtora (by Dr Devious), a minor Irish 11f winner, is a half-sister to 5 winners including the 2-y-o Group 1 1m National Stakes winner Mus-If and the very smart 1m (at 2 yrs) and 10f winner of three listed events Jammaal. (Mr Sean Jones). *"A big, strapping horse, he's had sore shins and as he's so big we're taking our time with him, so he's one for June/July".*

1081. UBIQUITOUS MANTLE (IRE) ★★★
b.f. Alhaarth – Za Aamah (Mr Prospector). February 26. Sister to the fairly useful 1m and 11f winner Dawla and half-sister to the Group 3 10f Ballysax Stakes winner Moiqen (by Red Ransom), the fairly useful 7f (at 2 yrs) and 14f winner and Group 2 1m Beresford Stakes second Rekaab (by In The Wings) and the fair dual 9.5f and 12f winner Desert Leader (by Green Desert) and the French 1m winner Tabreed (by Sakhee). The dam is an unraced sister to the listed Pretty Polly Stakes winner Siyadah and a half-sister to the Pretty Polly Stakes winner and Fillies Mile third Esloob. The second dam, Roseate Tern (by Blakeney), a very smart winner of the Group 1 12f Yorkshire Oaks and the Group 2 12f Jockey Club Stakes was second in the Epsom Oaks and third in the St Leger and is a half-sister to the high-class middle-distance stayer Ibn Bey. (Ennistown Stud). *"She'll be one of our earlier runners and we'd like to win with her for the sake of the pedigree for the owner-breeder. She's shown us enough to say she'll win a little maiden".*

GEORGE MARGARSON
1082. BOUNTIFUL SIN ★★
ch.c. Sinndar – Tropical Barth (Peintre Celebre). April 23. Seventh foal. 12,500Y. Tattersalls October Book 2. George Margarson. Half-brother to the French 11f winner and listed-placed Cashelgar (by Anabaa) and to the French 1m winner Mazayyen (by American Post). The dam, a minor winner at 3 yrs in France, is a half-sister to one winner. The second dam, Tropical Lass (by Ballad Rock), is a placed half-sister to 8 winners including the Group 3 5f and Group 3 6f winner Bermuda Classic (herself dam of the multiple Group 1

winner Shake The Yoke and the multiple Group 3 winner Tropical) and the dam of the triple Group 1 winner Kutub. (Maxwell Morrison). *"He's going to be a big, rangy type of horse suited by the seven furlong races this year. Quite an athletic, forward horse, he's never took a wrong step, he's just done upsides work but I haven't had to stop him and I can see him doing OK. He's not a big, weak 2-y-o so he'll be trained to start his career as a 2-y-o, but obviously everything with be geared towards next year. He does have a Derby entry!"*

1083. ELUSIVE GUEST (FR) ★★★
b.c. Elusive City – Mansoura (Kalanisi). April 3. Second foal. €190,000Y. Arqana Deauville August. G Margarson. The dam is an unraced half-sister to 5 winners including the US dual Grade 1 winner Manndar and the dam of the French triple Group 1 winner Mandesha. The second dam, Madiriya (by Diesis), won the listed Galtres Stakes and is a half-sister to 4 winners. (John Guest Racing). *"We paid plenty for him because there were a lot of people after him. He's a lovely type and although I originally bought him for his 3-y-o career he does look like he could make a 2-y-o. His sire gets plenty of those and he seems to get a 2-y-o winner every week, especially in France where he's based. He's making up into a nice type of horse and he's pleased me more than I'd hoped. Everything he does is easy, so the problem I've got with him is keeping the lid on him. He'll hopefully be racing this year from the mid-summer onwards if he's showing the right signs at the time".*

1084. JAY GEE SPEEDFIT (IRE) ★★★
b.c. Bushranger – Prodigal Daughter (Alhaarth). January 26. Fourth foal. 80,000Y. Tattersalls October Book 2. George Margarson. Half-brother to the very useful 2-y-o Group 3 7f Horris Hill Stakes winner Carnaby Street (by Le Vie Dei Colori) and to the Swedish winner at 2 and 3 yrs Kodiac King (by Kodiac). The dam is an unraced half-sister to one winner. The second dam, Shallow Ground (by Common Grounds), a listed-placed 6f winner in Ireland, is a half-sister to 6 winners including the US Grade 2 winner Shanawi and the dam of the Australian Group 1 winner Brazilian Pulse. (John Guest Racing).

"A cracking little horse, I've got on with him, he's got a racey 2-y-o pedigree and he looked a 2-y-o type at the sale. He's not over-big but he's grown since we got him, he's filling out and is a six/seven furlong type. Hopefully he'll be out in May and he's just starting to go through the gears now, he's a nice type and he ticks most of the boxes. Once I've galloped him I'll hopefully be able to say he ticks them all"!

1085. LUCKY KRISTALE ★★★
b.f. *Lucky Story – Pikaboo (Pivotal)*. March 6. Third foal. 22,000Y. Tattersalls October Book 2. George Margarson. Half-sister to the fair 2-y-o 6f winner Mon Visage (by Ishiguru) and to the fair dual 5f winner (including at 2 yrs) I See You (by Sleeping Indian). The dam is a placed half-sister to 7 winners including Arabian Gleam (Group 2 Challenge Stakes and Group 2 Park Stakes, twice). The second dam, Gleam Of Light (by Danehill), won over 7f and is a full or half-sister to 4 winners. (Graham Lodge Partnership). *"I'm very pleased with her, she's a half-sister to two 2-y-o winners and I trained one of them, I See You. This is a nicer type – a proper racey 2-y-o, a big strong filly and you could do what you like with her. She's still hanging on to her coat so as soon as we get some warm weather we'll get her started. Fast ground won't worry her, she's shown me a lot and she has a good temperament unlike her half-sister who was a bit of a livewire. I'll be looking at six furlongs with her".*

1086. SHYRON ★★
b.c. *Byron – Coconut Shy (Bahamian Bounty)*. April 21. First foal. The dam, a fair 2-y-o dual 6f winner, is a sister to one 2-y-o winner and a half-sister to another. The second dam, Lets Be Fair (by Efisio), a fairly useful 2-y-o dual 5f (from 3 starts) is a half-sister to 6 winners. (Mr & Mrs F Butler). *"A homebred out of a 2-y-o winner, he's quite an athletic horse but he was a late foal and he's still very immature. We'll be training him with nurseries in mind so we'll give him a bit of time because he does need to develop. A nice sort and very straightforward".*

ALAN M^CCABE
1087. CHAMBERLAIN ★★
b.c. *Indesatchel – Citron (Reel Buddy)*. March 7. Third foal. Doncaster Premier. 8,000Y. Keith

Stone. Brother to the moderate 3-y-o 5f winner Bitter Lemon and half-brother to the modest 2012 7f placed 2-y-o Loki's Strike (by Firebreak). The dam is an unraced half-sister to 8 winners including Golden Nun (Group 3 Ballyogan Stakes). The second dam, Amber Mill (by Doulab), a useful winner over 5f (twice) and 6f, is a half-sister to 4 winners. (Brian Morton). *"He'll be starting his career in mid-April, so he's precocious enough, although five furlongs might be a bit sharp for him".*

1088. CLEVER MISS ★★★
b.f. *Mount Nelson – Clever Millie (Cape Canaveral)*. March 3. Second foal. 12,000Y. Tattersalls October Book 3. Mark Crossman. Sister to the moderate 2013 3-y-o 9f winner Majeed. The dam, a fair Irish 7f winner at 4 yrs, is a half-sister to 6 winners including the US Grade 2 winner Points Of Grace and the smart listed 1m winner Fatefully (herself dam of the Group 1 Nassau Stakes winner Favourable Terms). The second dam, Fateful (by Topsider), a fairly useful 6f (at 2 yrs) and 7f winner, is a half-sister to 2 winners. (Mr K Dasmal). *"A very nice, compact filly, she's growing in the right direction rather than getting taller. I like her a lot, she's strong and I'm very pleased with her. She has enough speed for six furlongs but I could see her getting better over seven furlongs plus".*

1089. LOMA MOR ★★★
b.f. *Auction House – Dancing Loma (Danehill Dancer)*. April 10. Third foal. £5,200Y. Doncaster Festival. Tom Malone/Alan McCabe. Half-sister to Whatwehaveheld (by Avonbridge), unplaced on his only start at 2 yrs in 2012. The dam is an unraced half-sister to 9 minor winners. The second dam, Jabali (by Shirley Heights), is an unplaced half-sister to 4 winners including the French Group 2 winner Dadarissime and the French Group 3 winner Floripedes (the dam of Montjeu). (Lucky Heather). *"She got a bit upset in the stalls on her debut which was surprising because she's been very good at home. I do rate her, she goes very nicely and she's an out-and-out five furlong 2-y-o".*

1090. PACKET STATION ★★★
ch.f. *Compton Place – Jump Ship (Night Shift)*.

April 1. Third foal. Half-sister to the fair 10f winner Monopoli (by Cadeaux Genereux). The dam, a modest 12f winner from 3 starts, is a half-sister to 4 winners. The second dam, Flagship (by Rainbow Quest), a quite useful 10f winner, is a sister to the very useful 2-y-o Group 3 7f Rockfel Stakes winner and Lupe Stakes second Yawl and a half-sister to 6 winners. (Mr M Dixon). *"A nice home-bred that the owner kindly sent me, she's ready to run and I'd expect her to win a maiden. She's sharp enough for five furlongs, she's a bit 'on the leg' at the moment, but she goes well enough".*

1091. ROYAL WARRIOR ★★★

b.c. *Royal Applause – Tiana (Diktat)*. March 13. Third foal. 8,000Y. Tattersalls October Book 2. Not sold. The dam, a fairly useful 2-y-o 6f winner, was listed-placed over 7f and is a half-sister to 5 winners including the useful 2-y-o dual 5f winner and Group 3 Molecomb Stakes second Mary Read (by Bahamian Bounty). The second dam, Hill Welcome (by Most Welcome), was placed twice at 2 yrs and stayed 7f and is a half-sister to 5 winners including the Group 1 6f Middle Park Stakes winner Stalker. (Premspace Ltd). *"A very nice colt, we took him to Southwell first time out and he duly obliged, as we expected him to do. He'll improve for that and although Southwell isn't an easy track for 2-y-o's he came out of it well. We're in no hurry with him and he looks a horse that might get seven furlongs later on, especially as he has a very laid-back attitude and a good constitution".*

1092. SHANINA ★★★

ch.f. *Soviet Star – Why Now (Dansili)*. April 4. Fifth foal. £10,000Y. Doncaster Premier. Alan McCabe. Half-sister to the fair 2012 2-y-o winner Woodland Mill, to the quite useful 5f winner of 4 races (including at 2 yrs) Here Now And Why (both by Pastoral Pursuits), the quite useful 2-y-o 6f winner What About You (by Statue Of Liberty) and the fair 5f winner Al Freej (by Iffraaj). The dam, a fair 5f and 6f winner, is a half-sister to 4 winners. The second dam, Questionable (by Rainbow Quest), is an unraced sister to the Group 3 15f Prix Berteux winner Ecologist and a half-sister to 7 winners including the St James's Palace Stakes second Greensmith, the Group 3 winners Infrasonic

and Green Reef and the dam of the St Leger winner Toulon. (A Lot In Common Partnership). *"A nice big, strong filly, she's going the right way. We'll wait for the six furlong races with her and the lads who own her have had quite a bit of luck with us, so hopefully that'll continue".*

1093. SPIRIT O GOODCHILD ★★

b.c. *Sleeping Indian – Well Of Echoes (Diktat)*. First foal. The dam, a modest 9f winner of 3 races at 4 yrs, is a half-sister to 2 winners. The second dam, Seeker (by Rainbow Quest), a fair 12f winner, is a half-sister to the listed winner Cybinka. *"A compact little 2-y-o I bred myself. His mother won 3 races in 10 days for me. This colt is ready to race now and he's a small, compact 2-y-o type for five furlongs".*

1094. UNNAMED ★★★

ch.c. *Auction House – Vida (Wolfhound)*. April 25. Brother to the useful listed 5f winner of 3 races Fratellino, to the fair 6f (at 2 yrs) and 8.7f winner of 4 races Common Diva and 2 minor winners in Italy and Sweden. The dam is an unplaced half-sister to the dual 6f winner Maghaarb and the listed-placed Mudawin – both fairly useful. The second dam, Fida (by Persian Heights), is a half-sister to 7 winners including the Coronation Stakes, Irish 1,000 Guineas and Eclipse Stakes winner Kooyonga and the Irish listed winner and Group-placed Hatton Gardens – herself dam of the South African Grade 1 winner Kundalini. *"He came in late but he's a similar horse to his brother Fratellino in that he's not very big – I just hope he's as good as him. A fairly late foal, he'll probably be out in May or June and he's a five furlong type".*

ED McMAHON

1095. BROADCASTER (IRE) ★★★

b.c. *Jeremy – River Abouali (Bluebird)*. April 6. Ninth foal. £39,000Y. Doncaster Premier. John Fretwell. Half-brother to the fair 2-y-o 5f winner Maugwenna (by Danehill and herself dam of the Group 2 placed 2-y-o Bould Mover), to the fair 6f, 7f (both at 2 yrs) and 1m winner Vito Volterra (by Antonius Pius), the modest 6f winner Trouble Maker (by Green Desert), the moderate 5f winner Claretintheblood (by Elusive City) and two minor winners abroad by Bertolini and Diktat. The dam is an unraced half-sister to 5 winners including the Group 3 winner Psalm and the Irish listed winner Queen Titi (herself dam of the Group 1 Dewhurst Stakes winner Beethoven). The second dam, Litani River (by Irish River), was listed-placed in France and is a sister to the French 5.5f and 7f winner Or Vision (herself dam of the Group/ Grade 1 winners Dolphin Street, Insight and Saffron Walden) and a half-sister to 7 winners including the dam of the Group 1 winners Sequoyah and Listen. *"A nice, big horse, he's a little bit green mentally so I wouldn't say he's your 'first time out' type, but he's on the move now doing half-speeds and I think he'll be racing in May".*

1096. CAPITULATE ★★★

b.c. Avonbridge – Succumb (Pursuit Of Love). April 23. Seventh foal. £18,000Y. Doncaster Premier. John Fretwell. Half-brother to the fair 2-y-o 5f winner Rare Art (by Kyllachy) and to a winner in Greece by Pivotal. The dam is an unraced half-sister to 7 winners including the useful On Call, a listed winner of 7 races at up to 2m and herself dam of the US Grade 2 winner One Off. The second dam, Doctor Bid (by Spectacular Bid), is an unraced half-sister to 9 winners including the smart Group 3 Prix Thomas Bryon winner Glory Forever and the dam of the Group winners Verglas and Cassandra Go. *"Avonbridge was the sire of a good colt we had called Temple Meads, but he doesn't breed many as good as him. This colt is fairly straightforward, he's a nice-bodied type, a typical five furlong 2-y-o and he'll probably have run before the book is out".*

1097. CLUMBER STREET ★★★

ch.c. Compton Place – Tinnarinka (Observatory). March 22. Second foal. £42,000Y. Doncaster Premier. John Fretwell. Half-brother to the quite useful 2012 2-y-o 7f winner Mystical Moment (by Dutch Art). The dam, a modest 1m winner at 4 yrs, is a half-sister to 3 winners. The second dam, Dancing Fire (by Dayjur), is an unraced half-sister to 4 winners including Scintillo (Group 1 Gran Criterium) and the multiple Group 3 winner Jumbajukiba. *"A nice, big, colt, probably a bit 'on the leg' but he'll be out by the middle of May I should think. He's done a lot of growing and he could turn out to be a nice horse, but*

we'll have to wait and see. Not a typical five furlong type, he's got a bit of scope and size about him and he'll start at six furlongs I should think".

1098. EXPRESS HIMSELF (IRE) ★★

b.c. Dylan Thomas – Lightwood Lady (Anabaa). April 20. Fourth foal. 28,000Y. Tattersalls October Book 2. Ed McMahon. Half-brother to the quite useful 2-y-o 5f winner (on only start) Its Alright (by King's Best), to the fair 1m and subsequent US winner Totheendoftheearth (by Hurricane Run) and the minor French 3-y-o winner Halendale (by Elusive City). The dam, a fair Irish 6f winner, is a half-sister to 6 winners. The second dam, Lyrical Dance (by Lear Fan), a minor winner at 4 yrs in the USA, is a sister to the French listed 10.5f winner Shaal and a half-sister to the Group/Grade 1 winners Black Minnaloushe, Pennekamp and Nasr El Arab and the placed dam of the US dual Grade 1 winner Round Pond. (Milton Express Ltd). *"He's a nice, big sort and a good walker. Obviously he's going to take a bit of time but that's the type the owners were after. He's a nice stamp pf horse, only cantering at the moment and I'll only start to pick him up during the summer. His conformation is correct and he's filling into himself now".*

1099. INCITING INCIDENT (IRE) ★★★

b.c. Camacho – Halliwell House (Selkirk). April 20. Second foal. £14,000Y. Doncaster Premier. Not sold. Half-brother to the fair 2012 2-y-o 5f winner Dusty Storm (by Kyllachy). The dam ran once unplaced and is a half-sister to 3 winners including the Group 2 Italian Oaks second Counterclaim. The second dam, Dusty Answer (by Zafonic), a quite useful 2-y-o 7f winner, was listed placed over 1m and is a half-sister to 4 winners including the listed 1m and subsequent US Grade 2 winner Spotlight and the dam of the Group 1 Phoenix Stakes winner Zoffany. (The W.H.O Society). *"He was a cheap enough purchase from Doncaster, he's sharp, has a nice action and he'll start his career in April as long as the ground isn't too soft. A nice, compact sort and a typical 2-y-o, I train his half-sister Dusty Storm who is a little more 'buzzy' than he is".* TRAINERS' BARGAIN BUY

1100. RENAISSANCE RIO (IRE) ★★★★
b.f. Captain Rio – Danish Gem (Danehill).
March 21. Seventh foal. €46,000foal. Goffs
November. Jim McDonald. Half-sister to the
useful 2-y-o 5f and listed 6f winner Artistic
Jewel (by Excellent Art), to the fairly useful
5f and 6f (at 2 yrs) and listed 1m winner
Ponty Rossa (by Distant Music), the fair dual
6f winner Jimmy The Poacher (by Verglas),
the modest dual 9f winner Midnight Strider
(by Golan) and a winner in Greece by Marju.
The dam, a 1m winner at 3 yrs in France, is
a half-sister to 6 winners. The second dam,
Gemaasheh (by Habitat), is an unraced half-
sister to 5 winners. "A half-sister to a nice 4-y-o
we have, Artistic Jewel, she's a nice filly with
a good action. She was on the small side but
she's grown a bit and is continuing doing that,
so I'm not putting the gun to her head straight
away. A nice filly in the making, she'll want top
of the ground".

1101. WHERE THE BOYS ARE (IRE) ★★★
b.f. Dylan Thomas – Promise Of Love (Royal
Applause). March 29. Second foal. £13,000Y.
Doncaster Festival. Ed McMahon. Closely
related to the unplaced 2012 2-y-o Lady Of
Seville (by Duke Of Marmalade). The dam, a
fair 5f and 6f placed maiden, is a half-sister
to 3 winners including the 2-y-o Group 2 6f
Criterium de Maisons-Laffitte winner and sire
Captain Rio. The second dam, Beloved Visitor
(by Miswaki), won twice over 6f in Ireland at 2
yrs, was listed-placed and is a half-sister to 6
winners. (Mr P A Wilkins). "A nice stamp of filly,
she wasn't expensive but she's a nice strong
type and she'll be earlier than my other the
Dylan Thomas 2-y-o. She could be racing as
soon as the six furlong races start in the middle
of May".

1102. UNNAMED ★★★
b.c. Compton Place – Athboy Nights (Night
Shift). March 3. Fourth foal. £12,000Y.
Doncaster Premier. John Fretwell. Half-brother
to the Italian 2-y-o winner and listed 6f
second Poneifattu (by Footstepsinthesand)
and a minor winner abroad by High Chaparral.
The dam, a modest 5f and 6f placed 2-y-o, is
a half-sister to 4 minor winners. The second
dam, Missing Love (by Thatching),
won at 3 yrs and is a half-sister to 8 winners.

(Mr J Fretwell). "He's a nice, big horse and
reminds of one we used to train for the owner
called Iron Range. He's not as forward mentally
as you might expect for a Compton Place, but
he's a strong colt. A bit of cut in the ground
wouldn't go amiss, I'm not going to push him
and it may be mid-summer before we see him
out, probably over six furlongs".

1103. UNNAMED ★★★
b.f. Dark Angel – First Lady (Indian Ridge).
January 13. First foal. £13,000Y. Doncaster
Premier. John Fretwell. The dam is an unraced
half-sister to 7 winners including the Group
3 5f Premio Omenoni winner Kathy College.
The second dam, Katy Guest (by Be My Guest),
won at 2 and 3 yrs in Italy and is a half-sister
to 4 winners. (Mr J Fretwell). "She's a little bit
'warm' – has a bit of a temperament and as
she's a first foal she's not over-big. She had a
bit of a snotty nose and a cough for a while, so
I haven't been over anxious to get her going.
So I need to give her a bit of time and she'll
probably come to hand around May or June
time. A typical Dark Angel filly that looks like
being a sprinter".

1104. UNNAMED ★★★
ch.g. Kyllachy – Look Here's Carol (Safawan).
April 1. Fifth foal. Brother to the modest
2-y-o dual 5f winner Look Here's Lady and
half-brother to the quite useful 2012 2-y-o
5f and 6f winner Secret Look (by Sakhee's
Secret), the fair 2-y-o 5f winner Look Whos
Next (by Compton Place) and the modest
2-y-o 1m winner Imperial Look (by Royal
Applause). The dam, a fairly useful 6f and 7f
winner of 3 races, was listed-placed and is a
half-sister to 4 winners including the smart
listed 6f winner Now Look Here. The second
dam, Where's Carol (by Anfield), was a fair
2-y-o 6f winner of 4 races. (S L Edwards). "The
dam wasn't over-big and he's the same, he has
a little bit of a rounded action and is probably
on the weak side at the moment. Whether he'd
be as good as his mother I'm not sure. She
was our first winner – up at Haydock Park –
and unfortunately she died after foaling the
other day. He's a little bit fiery, as a lot of the
Kyllachy's are, and he'll be a sprinting type for
May/June time".

1105. UNNAMED ★★★

gr.c. Alhaarth – Look Here's Dee (Dansili). February 2. First foal. The dam is an unraced half-sister to 5 winners including the smart listed 6f winner Now Look Here and the fairly useful 6f and 7f winner of 3 races and listed-placed Look Here's Carol. The second dam, Where's Carol (by Anfield), was a fair 2-y-o 6f winner of 4 races. (S L Edwards). "As he's by Alhaarth I'm just cantering him at the moment, but he's grown, he has a nice action and he'll make a 2-y-o in June/July. More likely a seven furlong type than a sprinter".

1106. UNNAMED ★★★

br.c. Duke Of Marmalade – Winged Harriet (Hawk Wing). February 16. First foal. 30,000Y. Tattersalls October Book 1. Not sold. The dam, a quite useful 6f winner at 3 yrs, is a half-sister to 7 winners including the smart Group 3 7f Minstrel Stakes winner and Group 1 6f Phoenix Stakes second Air Chief Marshal, the listed winners and Group 3 placed Misu Bond and Slip Dance and the Group 1 Irish 2,000 Guineas second Foxtrot Romeo. The second dam, Hawala (by Warning), a useful 8.3f winner, is a half-sister to 4 winners including the French Group 3 winner Afaf. "He's not over-big but he's got a nice action and he could run over six furlongs because he's fairly sharp. I'd be looking at seven furlongs and a mile for him later in the season. He's settled down a lot after being a bit of a "Jack the Lad" when he came in".

BRIAN MEEHAN

1107. AHD (USA) ★★★

b.f. Elusive Quality – Abby Road (Danehill). The dam won the listed 5f St Hugh's Stakes at 2 yrs and is a sister to one winner. The second dam, Bells Are Ringing (by Sadler's Wells), a fairly useful Irish 2-y-o 7f winner, is a half-sister to the US dual Grade 1 winner Unbridled's Song. (Hamdan Al Maktoum).
"Her half-brother has just won the Wood Ditton, she only arrived here from Dubai a couple of weeks back and she'll probably need a bit of time. A very nice filly for six/seven furlongs".

1108. AUTOPILOT ★★★

b.c. Kyllachy – Khyber Knight (Night Shift). March 4. Third foal. 25,000Y. Tattersalls October Book 2. McKeever Bloodstock. Half-brother to Khyber Bridge (by Avonbridge), unplaced in two starts at 2 yrs in 2012 and to the Italian winner and 1m listed-placed Red Roof (by Statue Of Liberty). The dam, a moderate 1m and 10f placed maiden, is a half-sister to 7 winners. The second dam, Peshawar (by Persian Bold), is an unraced half-sister to 7 winners including the German 1,000 Guineas winner Princess Nana. "A five/six furlong 2-y-o, he'll be racing in May, he's sharp and well-forward".

1109. CABAAN (IRE) ★★★

b.c. Acclamation – Abington Angel (Machiavellian). March 31. Sixth foal. £40,000Y. Doncaster Premier. McKeever Bloodstock. Brother to Blazing Storm, unplaced in one start at 2 yrs in Ireland in 2012 and half-brother to a bumpers winner by Marju. The dam, a fair 12f winner, is a half-sister to 6 winners including the very useful Group 3 6f Cherry Hinton Stakes winner Applaud, the useful listed 10.2f winner Sauterne and the useful 10f winner and Group 3 placed Glam Rock. The second dam, Band (by Northern Dancer), is a placed half-sister to 5 winners including the US Grade 3 9f New Orleans Handicap winner Festive. "A lovely horse and a very easy mover. A six furlong type 2-y-o, he'll hopefully be racing in May".

1110. EMTINAAN (USA) ★★★★

ch.f. Tamayuz – Almass (Elnadim). March 3. Second foal. Sister to Fitrah, unplaced in two starts at 2 yrs in 2012. The dam, a smart listed 7f and listed 1m winner, is a half-sister to numerous winners including the very smart dual listed 10f winner and dual Group 1 placed Volochine and the listed winners Kahtan, Sakha and Ghataas. The second dam, Harmless Albatross (by Pas de Seul), won the Group 3 1m Prix des Chenes at 2 yrs and a 1m listed event at 3 yrs and is a half-sister to the Group 2 10f Prix d'Harcourt winner Fortune's Wheel. (Hamdan Al Maktoum). "A nice, sharp filly with lots of speed. She won't take long and I expect her to be racing in mid-May. A quality filly".

1111. GHASAQ (IRE) ★★★

b.c. Invincible Spirit – Manuka Magic (Key

Of Luck). March 1. Fifth foal. €90,000Y. Goffs Orby. Shadwell Estate Co. Half-brother to the smart 2-y-o Group 3 6f Firth Of Clyde Stakes winner and Group 1 6f Cheveley Park Stakes second Aspen Darlin (by Indian Haven) and to the quite useful 7f winner of 5 races Konstantin (by Balmont). The dam is an unraced full or half-sister to 4 winners. The second dam, Magic Garter (by Precocious), is an unraced half-sister to 7 winners and to the unraced dam of Grand Lodge. (Hamdan Al Maktoum). *"A sharp sort, he'll be racing in mid-May and would be better over six furlongs than five. A nice colt".*

1112. MADEED ★★★

b.c. Nayef – Danehill Dreamer (Danehill). March 5. Third foal. 40,000Y. Tattersalls October Book 2. Shadwell Estate Co. Brother to the fair 2012 1m placed 2-y-o Khudoua. The dam is an unraced half-sister to 8 winners including the Group 1 10f Coral Eclipse Stakes winner Compton Admiral, the Group 1 1m Queen Elizabeth II Stakes winner Summoner and the dam of the Group 1 Nassau Stakes winner The Fugue. The second dam, Sumoto (by Mtoto), a useful 6f (at 2 yrs) and 7f winner, is a half-sister to 5 winners including the dam of the Group/Graded stakes winners Adagio and Arvada. (Hamdan Al Maktoum). *"A lovely colt, he'll want plenty of time but he's very straightforward. One for seven furlongs or a mile from mid-to-late summer".*

1113. MAWFOOR (IRE) ★★★

b.c. Iffraaj – Miss Odlum (Mtoto). February 25. Seventh foal. £82,000Y. Doncaster Premier. Shadwell Estate Co. Brother to the modest 2-y-o 9f winner Let Your Love Flow and to the Italian 2-y-o winner Freetrack and half-brother to the fair 7f (including at 2 yrs) and 6f winner of 4 races Suhayl Star (by Trans Island) and the moderate 2-y-o 7f winner Annamay (by Invincible Spirit). The dam, a fair 10f winner in Ireland, is a half-sister to one winner. The second dam, Trexenta (by Green Desert), is a placed half-sister to 6 winners including the French Group 3 winner Caprarola and the French 1,000 Guineas second Cortona. (Hamdan Al Maktoum). *"He'll be out in May over six furlongs and he's the type to keep improving as the season goes on".*

1114. MISTY SPARKLER ★★★★

ch.f. Mount Nelson – Statua (Statoblest). April 2. Ninth foal. 40,000Y. Tattersalls October Book 2. Oliver St Lawrence. Sister to the 2012 2-y-o 1m winner, from one start, Ice Pie and half-sister to the dual listed 1m winner and Group 3 Diomed Stakes second St Moritz (by Medicean), the fairly useful 6f to 1m winner of 4 races Annemasse (by Anabaa), the fair 7f (at 2 yrs) and 2m winner Dream Mountain (by Mozart) and the fair 2-y-o 5f winner Dance Anthem (by Royal Academy). The dam was placed four times at 2 yrs including in the Group 3 Rockfel Stakes and subsequently won 3 minor races in the USA. She is a half-sister to 8 winners including the Group 3 Diomed Stakes and US Grade 3 winner Bluegrass Prince and the placed dam of the Group 1 winner Sumati. The second dam, Amata (by Nodouble), won 3 races in France and the USA over middle-distances, was Grade 3 placed and is a half-sister to the Group 3 Princess Royal Stakes winner Trillionaire. (Newsells Park Stud Ltd). *"A nice, sharp filly that'll be racing in May. I'm very pleased with her. A six/seven furlong type 2-y-o".*

1115. MOUNT CHEIRON (USA) ★★★★

b.c. Henrythenavigator – Chalamont (Kris). May 23. Eleventh living foal. 20,000Y. Tattersalls October Book 2. McKeever Bloodstock. Half-brother to the very useful 7f listed and 8.2f winner Secret Garden (dam of the 2-y-o Group 1 Criterium International and Irish 2,000 Guineas winner Roderic O'Connor), to the fairly useful 2-y-o 7f and subsequent US winner Texas Hill (both by Danehill), the useful 2-y-o 6f winner and Group 3 6f Sirenia Stakes third Lady Aquitaine (by El Prado) and minor US winners by Aragorn and Distorted Humor. The dam, a quite useful 2-y-o dual 6f winner, is a half-sister to 5 winners including the dual Ascot Gold Cup winner Gildoran. The second dam, Durtal (by Lyphard), won the Cheveley Park Stakes and the Fred Darling Stakes, was second in the French 1,000 Guineas and is a full or half-sister to 7 winners including the Prix de l'Arc de Triomphe winner Detroit (herself dam of the Arc winner Carnegie). (Sangster Family). *"For a late foal he's quite a sharp colt and has a lot of speed. He'll be racing from mid-May onwards over six furlongs".*

1116. PIPE DREAM ★★★

ch.c. Piccolo – Bold Love (Bold Edge).
April 15. Third foal. £20,000Y. Doncaster
Premier. McKeever Bloodstock. Half-brother
to the fair 7f (at 2 yrs) and 6f winner Love Tale
(by Lucky Story). The dam, a poor 3-y-o 7f
winner, is a half-sister to 5 winners including
the smart all-weather 5f and 6f winner J M W
Turner. The second dam, Noor El Houdah (by
Fayruz), a modest 5f to 7f winner of 6 races,
is a half-sister to 2 winners and a half-sister to 3
winners including the useful 2-y-o listed 6f
winner Smittenby. (Mr M Wilmshurst). *"He
goes well, he'll be a five/six furlongs 2-y-o and
will be racing in May".*

1117. RACING'S DREAM ★★★★

b.c. Iffraaj – There's Two (Ashkalani). March 26.
Fourth foal. 20,000Y. Tattersalls October Book
2. McKeever Bloodstock. Half-brother to the
fair 5f to 10f winner of 6 races Ken's Girl (by
Ishiguru), to the fair 10f to 2m 1f winner Sula
Two (by Sulamani) and the poor 6f winner My
Reflection (by Cape Cross). The dam, a fairly
useful 2-y-o 6f winner, is a half-sister to 5
winners. The second dam, Sudden Interest (by
Highest Honor), a minor dual 3-y-o winner in
France, is a half-sister to 4 winners including
Sudden Love (Grade 1 E P Taylor Stakes). *"A
nice colt that goes well, he's had a touch of sore
shins and we've backed off him. One for the
mid-summer and I like him a lot".*

1118. SAALIB (USA) ★★★

*b.c. War Front – Dixie Quest (Coronado's
Quest).* February 21. Fourth foal. 150,000Y.
Tattersalls October Book 1. Shadwell Estate
Co. Half-brother to the minor US dual 3-y-o
winner Financially Secure (by Grand Reward).
The dam, placed once at 3 yrs in the USA, is
a half-sister to 5 minor winners in the USA
and Canada. The second dam, Dixie Flag (by
Dixieland Band), won two Grade 2 and two
Grade 3 events in the USA and is a half-sister
to 7 minor winners. (Hamdan Al Maktoum).
*"A mid-season type over seven furlongs and a
mile, he's quite straightforward and does nice
work".*

1119. SEFAAT (IRE) ★★★★

br.f. Haatef – Thamara (Street Cry). February
9. Second foal. Half-sister to the quite useful
2012 2-y-o 7f winner Altharoos (by Sakhee).
The dam is an unraced half-sister to the smart
listed 1m winner Tazahum. The second dam,
Huja (by Alzao), a very useful 2-y-o 7f winner,
was third in the Group 3 7f Prestige Stakes, is a
sister to the high-class Group 2 12f Hardwicke
Stakes winner Maraahel and a half-sister to
numerous winners. (Hamdan Al Maktoum).
*"She's very forward and will be ready early. She
works like a nice filly".*

1120. STORMY PARADISE (IRE) ★★★★

*b.c. Excellent Art – Stormy Larissa (Royal
Applause).* March 26. Fifth foal. £20,000Y.
Doncaster Premier. McKeever Bloodstock.
Half-brother to 3 winners including the 2012
Italian 2-y-o winner Annistedda (by Oratorio)
and the fair 14f and 2m winner of 6 races
Storm Hawk (by Hawk Wing). The dam, a
modest 10f winner, is a half-sister to 3 winners
including the listed winner of 6 races Khibrah.
The second dam, Sabayik (by Unfuwain), a
fairly useful 3-y-o 1m winner, is a half-sister to
6 winners. (Decadent Racing). *"An early type,
I'd say he'd be racing any time from late April
and he goes really well. He has a good attitude,
he's sharp and five/six furlongs will suit him".*

1121. TAGHREEB (IRE) ★★★ ♠

b.c. Dubawi – Ghaneema (Forestry). March
25. First foal. The dam was second over 1m at
3 yrs on her only start and is a half-sister to
2 winners. The second dam, Unify (by Farma
Way), won over 1m in the USA and is a half-
sister to the Group/Graded stakes winners
Bernstein, Caress, Country Cat and Della
Francesca. (Hamdan Al Maktoum). *"A lovely,
big horse that goes really well. He'll want a
couple of months yet but I see him being ready
in mid-summer".*

1122. WINDFAST (IRE) ★★★★ ♠

b.c. Exceed And Excel – Fair Sailing (Docksider).
February 20. Second foal. 30,000Y. Tattersalls
October Book 2. McKeever Bloodstock. The
dam is an unplaced half-sister to 5 winners
including the Group 1 12f Italian Derby winner
and King George VI and Queen Elizabeth
Stakes second White Muzzle, the Group 2
German St Leger winner Fair Question and
the listed 10f winner Elfaslah (dam of the
Dubai World Cup winner Almutawakel). The

second dam, Fair of the Furze (by Ela-Mana-Mou), won the Group 2 10f Tattersalls Rogers Gold Cup and is a half-sister to four listed winners. *"A lovely colt, it won't be long before we see him on the track. He'll be grand over six furlongs and he'll get further. Very nice"*.

1123. ZORA SEAS (IRE) ★★★★

b.br.f. Marju – Urgele (Zafonic). March 23. Seventh foal. 140,000Y. Tattersalls October Book 1. Not sold. Half-sister to the very useful 2-y-o listed 6f winner Al Aasifh (by Invincible Spirit) and to the fairly useful 1m winner of 3 races Cordell (by Fasliyev). The dam, a listed winner of 4 races in France and third in the Group 3 Prix Miesque, is a half-sister to 7 winners. The second dam, Urmia (by Persian Bold), a listed-placed winner of 3 races in France, is a half-sister to 10 winners including the Group 2 Prix Noailles winner Gunboat Diplomacy. *"Shows a lot of speed, she's a nice filly we'll start off in late May. A six/seven furlongs 2-y-o"*.

1124. ZIEBAWI ★★★★

b.f. Dubawi – Zietory (Zieten). March 31. Sixth foal. 50,000Y. Tattersalls October Book 2. McCalmont Bloodstock. Half-sister to the quite useful 7f (including at 2 yrs) and 6f winner Ziefhd (by Haafhd) and to the fair triple 7f winner, including at 2 yrs, Zing Wing (by Hawk Wing). The dam, a 2-y-o 6f and 3-y-o dual 1m listed winner, is a half-sister to 4 winners. The second dam, Fairy Story (by Persian Bold), won 5 races over 7f (including at 2 yrs) and is a half-sister to 4 winners. *"A really sharp filly, she's just had a short break and she'll be racing in May. A five/six furlong 2-y-o and she's nice"*.

1126. UNNAMED ★★★

b.c. Holy Roman Emperor – Bankeress (Barathea). February 2. First foal. 65,000Y. Tattersalls October Book 2. McKeever Bloodstock. The dam, unraced due to an injury, is a half-sister to one minor winner. The second dam, Banco Suivi (by Nashwan), a fairly useful 12f winner, is a half-sister to 6 winners including the listed 6f and listed 7f winner and Group 1 Cheveley Park Stakes second My Branch (herself dam of the Group 1 Haydock Park Sprint Cup winner Tante

Rose). *"A very nice colt with a good attitude, he's one for six furlongs and I'm very happy with him"*.

1127. UNNAMED ★★★★

b.f. Footstepsinthesand – Canterbury Lace (Danehill). March 19. Sixth foal. $300,000foal. Keeneland November. Hugo Merry. Sister to the Group 1 1m Matron Stakes and Group 2 7f Lennox Stakes winner Chachamaidee and half-sister to the fair 7f (at 2 yrs) and 1m winner of 4 races Maybe I Will (by Hawk Wing). The dam is an unraced sister to the Group 3 Gallinule Stakes winner and Irish Derby second Alexander Of Hales and to the Irish 2-y-o 1m winner and Group 1 1m Criterium International second Chevalier and a half-sister to the 1,000 Guineas winner Virginia Waters. The second dam, Legend Maker (by Sadler's Wells), won the Group 3 10.5f Prix de Royaumont, was third in the Group 2 13.5 Prix de Pomone and is a half-sister to 7 winners including the Group 2 12f King Edward VII Stakes winner Amfortas. (Mr A Rosen). *"She should be racing in May, she's really nice and is working very well. A six/seven furlong 2-y-o"*.

1128. UNNAMED ★★★

b.c. Empire Maker – Deaconess Bonnie (Pulpit). February 17. Fifth foal. £250,000Y. Keeneland September. Reddam Racing. Half-brother to the minor US winner of 3 races at 3 and 4 yrs Swashbuckler (by Orientate). The dam is an unraced half-sister to 4 winners including the US Grade 2 and Grade 3 winner Diabolical. The second dam, Bonnie Byerly (by Dayjur), is a placed daughter of the US Grade 1 winner Plenty Of Grace. (Reddam Racing LLC). *"A lovely colt for when the seven furlong races start"*.

1129. UNNAMED ★★★ ♠

b.c. Archipenko – Diablerette (Green Desert). February 17. Fourth foal. 42,000Y. Tattersalls October Book 2. McKeever Bloodstock. Half-brother to the fair 1m winner Ecossaise (by Selkirk). The dam, a fair 2-y-o dual 6f winner, is a sister to one winner and a half-sister to 7 winners including the German Group 1 10f winner Lady Jane Digby, the very smart Group 3 7f and 9f winner and Group 1 placed Gateman and the smart 1m Royal Hunt Cup winner Surprise Encounter. The second dam, Scandalette (by Niniski), is an unraced half-sister to 9 winners including the Group 1 July Cup winner Polish Patriot and the Italian listed winner Grand Cayman. *"A nice colt for the late summer onwards. He'll want a mile as a 2-y-o".*

1130. UNNAMED ★★★

ch.f. Dutch Art – Felucca (Green Desert). April 14. Thirteenth foal. 48,000Y. Tattersalls October Book 2. McKeever Bloodstock. Half-sister to the 1m (at 2 yrs), Group 3 9f Prix Daphnis and listed 10.5f winner Lateen Sails, to the quite useful 1m winner Mainstay (both by Elmaamul), the minor Italian 3-y-o winner Burgee, a sprint winner in Scandinavia (both by Zafonic) and a minor winner abroad by Selkirk. The dam, a fairly useful 2-y-o 6f winner, is a half-sister to 5 winners including the Group 2 10f Prix Eugene Adam winner Radevore. The second dam, Bloudan (by Damascus), is an unraced half-sister to the Irish 1,000 Guineas and Coronation Stakes winner and top-class broodmare Al Bahathri (dam of the 2,000 Guineas and Champion Stakes winner Haafhd) and the US Grade 2 winner Geraldine's Store. *"A relatively early filly, she'll be racing in early May I should think. Six furlongs would be better for her than five and she's a nice filly".*

1131. UNNAMED ★★★★

b.c. Iffraaj – Graceful Air (Danzero). April 26. Sixth foal. 38,000Y. Tattersalls October Book 2. McKeever Bloodstock. Half-brother to the useful 2-y-o 5f and 6f winner Forjatt (by Iffraaj), to the quite useful 5f and 6f winner of 5 races (including at 2 yrs) Amenable (by Bertolini) and the fair 2-y-o 7f winner Brickfielder (by Jeremy). The dam, a fair 8.3f and 10f winner, is a half-sister to 3 winners including the very useful 2-y-o 5f winner and Group 2 6f Mill Reef Stakes second Mystical Land. The second dam, Samsung Spirit (by Statoblest), a fair dual 6f winner (including at 2 yrs), is a half-sister to 7 winners and to the placed dam of the Group 2 6f Mill Reef Stakes winner Indian Rocket. *"A big horse that'll need a bit of time but he's very nice. He's doing well and will want seven furlongs from mid-season".*

1132. UNNAMED ★★★★

ch.c. Smart Strike – L'ile Aux Loups (Rock Of Gibraltar). March 19. First foal. 55,000Y. Tattersalls October Book 2. Not sold. The dam, a 3-y-o 10f winner in France and listed-placed, is a sister to one winner and a half-sister to 4 winners including the Group 2 Prix d'Harcourt and US Grade 2 winner Loup Breton. The second dam, Louve (by Irish River), winner of the Group 3 10.5f Prix de Flore, is closely related to the very smart Group 1 Prix d'Ispahan winner Loup Sauvage and a half-sister to the Group 1 1m Grand Criterium winner and Group 1 10.5f Prix Lupin second Loup Solitaire. *"A lovely horse, I'm pleased with him and he'll be a seven furlongs 2-y-o around June/July time".*

1133. UNNAMED ★★★

b.c. Mastercraftsman – Rose Briar (Grand Lodge). April 11. Third foal. 55,000Y. Tattersalls October Book 2. McCalmont Bloodstock. The dam is an unplaced half-sister to 5 winners including the Group 1 6f Haydock Sprint Cup winner Tante Rose and the dual 2-y-o listed 7f winner Bay Tree. The second dam, My Branch (by Distant Relative), a very useful winner of the listed 6f Firth Of Clyde Stakes (at 2 yrs) and the listed 7f Sceptre Stakes, was second in the Group 1 Cheveley Park Stakes and third in the Irish 1,000 Guineas and is a half-sister to 6 winners including the dam of the dual Group 1 winner Dubawi Heights. *"He showed a bit of speed early on but he's just grown and he's one for the middle of the season onwards. He goes well and he's a nice horse".*

1134. UNNAMED ★★★

b.c. Clodovil – Salonga (Shinko Forest). April 19. Second foal. 35,000Y. Tattersalls October Book 1. McKeever Bloodstock. Half-brother to the fair 2012 2-y-o 6f winner Hardy Red (by Mujadil). The dam, a modest 9f winner, is a half-sister to 4 winners. The second dam, Alongside (by Slip Anchor), an Irish 4-y-o 9f winner, is a half-sister to 4 winners including the Group 2 Prix Eugene Adam and US Grade 2 winner Kirkwall and to the placed dam of the Group 1 Moyglare Stud Stakes winner Termagant. *"He looked like being quite early and then he grew. He's filled out a lot recently and he's a nice horse for late May".*

1135. UNNAMED ★★★
b.f. *Arch – Shoofha (Bluebird).* February 28. Ninth foal. $250,000Y. Keeneland September. David Redvers. Half-sister to 3 winners including the 2-y-o Group 3 7f Prix Miesque winner and Group 1 6f Prix Morny second Magic America and the US Grade 3 placed Psychic Income. The dam is an unplaced sister to the Group 3 and US Grade 3 winner Delilah and a half-sister to 4 winners. The second dam, Courtesane (by Majestic Light), is an unplaced half-sister to 4 winners including the Group 3 5f Greenlands Stakes winner Drama (dam of the US Grade 3 winner Tycoon's Drama). (Mr A Rosen). *"A nice filly, she's a typical Arch in that she won't be early, but I like her a lot and she'll be a seven furlong/mile 2-y-o".*

1136. UNNAMED ★★★
b.f. *Oasis Dream – So Silk (Rainbow Quest).* March 28. Third foal. 155,000Y. Tattersalls October Book 1. Hugo Merry. The dam is an unraced half-sister to 3 winners including the 2-y-o Group 1 Racing Post Trophy winner Ibn Khaldun. The second dam, Gossamer (by Sadler's Wells), won the Group 1 Fillies' Mile and the Group 1 Irish 1,000 Guineas and is a sister to the Breeders Cup Mile and Irish 2,000 Guineas winner Barathea and a half-sister to 6 winners including the Group 3 winners Zabar and Free At Last (herself dam of the US multiple Grade 2 winner Coretta). (Mr A Rosen). *"A nice filly with the speed to start over six furlongs in May, she'll get further".*

1137. UNNAMED ★★★★
gr.c. *Aussie Rules – Trois Graces (Alysheba).* May 3. Eleventh foal. 60,000Y. Tattersalls October Book 2. McKeever Bloodstock. Closely related to the 2-y-o listed 5f Prix Yacowlef winner and Group 3 Prix de Cabourg second Abbeyside (by Danehill Dancer) and half-brother to the smart 7f (at 2 yrs) and listed 1m winner Flat Spin (by Spinning World), the fairly useful 2-y-o 7f winner Goodness Gracious (by Green Desert) and the quite useful 10f and 12f winner Tartan Tie (by Grand Lodge). The dam won once over 1m at 3 yrs in France and is a

half-sister to 5 winners including Rami (Group 3 Concorde Stakes), Crack Regiment (Group 3 Prix Eclipse) and La Grand Epoque (second in the Group 1 Prix de l'Abbaye). The second dam, Ancient Regime (by Olden Times), won the Group 1 Prix Morny and is a full or half-sister to 5 winners including the Prix Maurice de Gheest winner Cricket Ball. *"He shows a lot of speed and should be racing in mid-May. A colt with a great attitude, he's done a lot of work, we'll start him at six furlongs and move him up to seven".*

1138. UNNAMED ★★★★
b.br.c. *Awesome Again – Unbridled Romance (Unbridled Time).* May 25. Second foal. $150,000Y. Keeneland September. Reddam Racing. The dam, a minor US stakes winner of 3 races at 2 and 3 yrs, is a half-sister to one winner. The second dam, Cabernet Queen (by Relaunch), is an unraced half-sister to the US dual Grade 1 winner River Special. (Reddam Racing LLC). *"Even though he's a late foal he's quite a sharp horse. He goes very well and he'll be racing in May over six furlongs".*

ROD MILLMAN
1139. BLUE ANCHOR BAY (IRE) ★★★
b.c. *Ad Valorem – New Foundation (College Chapel).* February 15. Fourth foal. €11,000Y. Tattersalls Ireland September. Rod Millman. Half-brother to the fair 2-y-o 5f winner Just A Dancer (by Choisir). The dam, a fairly useful 2-y-o 5f winner, is a half-sister to 3 winners including the Group 3 Queen Mary Stakes third Roundtree. The second dam, Island Desert (by Green Desert), is a placed half-sister to 9 winners. (Crowcombe Racing). *"He's a very attractive horse and there's some speed his dam's side but the sire is unfashionable now, otherwise he'd have been more expensive at the sales. He'll start his career in April, he works well and he's the sort that will improve with racing".*

1140. COTTON CLUB (IRE) ★★★
b.c. *Amadeus Wolf – Slow Jazz (Chief's Crown).* March 26. Fifteenth foal. £18,000Y. Doncaster Premier. G Howson. Half-brother to the fairly useful 2012 2-y-o 5f winner and listed-placed Zoola (by Iffraaj), to the useful Italian dual listed winner and Group 3 second Mister

Cavern (by Lion Cavern), the quite useful 6f (at 2 yrs) and 1m winner Satanic Beat (by Dark Angel), the quite useful 6f (at 2 yrs) and 1m winner Mellow Jazz (by Lycius), the modest 12f to 2m winner of 10 races Blue Hills (by Vettori), the fair 2-y-o 6f winner Magadar, the 6f and subsequent UAE 9f and 10f winner Storyville (both by Lujain), the quite useful 1m winner Ivory Jazz (by Dubai Destination) and a winner in Russia by E Dubai. The dam, a French 6f, 6.7f and 1m listed winner, is a three-parts sister to the smart Group 1 6f Middle Park Stakes and Group 2 7f Challenge Stakes winner Zieten and to the Group 1 6f Cheveley Park Stakes and Group 3 5f Queen Mary Stakes winner Blue Duster. The second dam, Blue Note (by Habitat), won 5 races from 5f to 7f in France including the Group 2 Prix Maurice de Gheest and the Group 3 Prix de le Porte Maillot. (The Links Partnership). *"His dam has bred lots of winners over all sorts of trips. Being by Amadeus Wolf I was hoping he'd be sharp and early, but he looks like he wants six furlongs plus, although I will start him over five just to sharpen him up. A good-looking horse, if he'd been by most other sires he would have cost a lot more because the sire is unfashionable".*

1141. DOVIL'S DUEL (IRE) ★★★

b.c. Clodovil – Duelling (Diesis). April 21. Fourth foal. £5,000Y. Doncaster Festival. G Howson. Half-brother to the fair 6f and 9f winner Slikback Jack (by Dr Fong). The dam, a quite useful 2-y-o 6f winner, is a half-sister to the useful 2-y-o listed 1m placed Super Sleuth. The second dam, Enemy Action (by Forty Niner), a very useful 2-y-o dual 6f winner, is a half-sister to 4 winners including the smart Daggers Drawn (Group 2 6f Richmond Stakes and Group 2 7f Laurent Perrier Rose Champagne Stakes). (Always Hopeful Partnership). *"He ran fifth in the Brocklesby at Doncaster. We were disappointed by that but the ground was really bad. He's a bit of a handful, but he's quite a strong 2-y-o, he's been ready to run for two months and came to hand very early. He works like a 3-y-o now and he'll run in one of the bonus races in mid-April. He's a big horse and maybe my other 2-y-o's will improve past him later in the season, but if he went to the breeze-ups now no horse would breeze better than him".*

1142. DYLAN CENTENARY ★★

b.c. Kyllachy – Sheka (Ishiguru). February 21. First foal. £25,000Y. Doncaster Premier. Rod Millman. The dam, a fair 2-y-o 5f winner, is a half-sister to a winner in Hong Kong. The second dam, Maid For Running (by Namaqualand), a quite useful 2-y-o 5f winner, is a half-sister to the useful winners Polar Kingdom and Goodwood Prince. (Seasons Holidays). *"He had a virus throughout the winter and he's only just shaken it off, so he's a bit behind the rest but he's a good-looking horse. He's a bit 'up behind' so the delay is helping to give him time to level up. I'd expect to get him out at the end of May".*

1143. GRAPHENE ★★★

b.c. Nayef – Annapurna (Brief Truce). February 10. Ninth foal. 22,000Y. Tattersalls October Book 2. Rod Millman. Half-brother to the quite useful dual 10f and subsequent US stakes winner and Grade 2 second Solva, to the modest 7f (at 2 yrs) and 10f winner History Repeating (both by Singspiel), the quite useful 2-y-o 7f winner Anthology (by Haafhd) and the fair (at 2 yrs) and 1m winner Aberdovey (by Mister Baileys). The dam, a useful 7f winner (at 2 yrs) and listed-placed twice, is a half-sister to 5 winners including the very useful 2-y-o Group 3 7f Rockfel Stakes winner Name Of Love. The second dam, National Ballet (by Shareef Dancer), is an unraced half-sister to 7 winners including the listed winners Broken Wave, Guarde Royale, Clifton Chapel and Saxon Maid. *"A very attractive colt, he's quite small for a Nayef but I don't think I'd start him before the six furlong races and he'll probably want seven to a mile. It's quite a good family, he's very forward, very athletic and a good mover".*

1144. KAIZEN FACTOR ★★★

b.c. Azamour – Best Side (King's Best). February 10. Fourth foal. 11,000Y. Tattersalls October Book 2. Rod Millman. Brother to the listed 7f (at 2 yrs), Group 3 Dee Stakes and Group 3 Sandown Classic Trial winner Azmeel and half-brother to the fair 11f and subsequent German listed 1m winner Baisse (by High Chaparral). The dam, an Irish 7f (at 2 yrs) and 1m winner, was listed-placed and is a half-sister to 7 winners including the Irish

Group 3 winner Grand Ducal and the useful 2-y-o 6f winner and listed-placed Hurricane Floyd. The second dam, Mood Swings (by Shirley Heights), a fair 2-y-o 6f winner, is a sister to the listed 2-y-o Sweet Solera Stakes winner Catwalk and a half-sister to 6 winners. (Mustajed Partnership). *"He was sold as one of the last lots of the day and I think I got good value. He might start off at six furlongs but I'd say seven furlongs or a mile was more his type of trip. He's very attractive, a little bit on the small side but he's a perfect specimen".*

1145. MASTER CARPENTER (IRE) ★★★★
b.f. *Mastercraftsman – Fringe (In The Wings).* February 27. Third foal. £25,000Y. Doncaster Premier. Not sold. Half-sister to the modest 2012 6f placed 2-y-o Curl (by Duke Of Marmalade) and to the modest 10f winner Chignon (by Dalakhani). The dam, a quite useful 10f winner at 4 yrs, is a half-sister to 4 winners including the listed winner Mount Elbrus. The second dam, El Jazirah (by Kris), is an unraced sister to the Group 1 Prix de Diane winner Rafha (herself the dam of four stakes winners including the Group 1 Haydock Park Sprint Cup winner Invincible Spirit) and a half-sister to 9 winners. (The Links Partnership). *"When we first got him we thought he's want six or seven, but I think he'll probably stay a mile now! A nice, quality horse, we gave him a run just to bring him on a bit and he won quite easily. He's in the Supersprint, he's from a good family and I thought he was one of the picks of the sale on appearance".*

1146. SEAHAM ★★★
b.c. *Myboycharlie – Be Decisive (Diesis).* March 25. Eighth living foal. £20,000Y. Doncaster Premier. G Howson. Half-sister to the quite useful 2-y-o 5f winner To The Point (by Refuse To Bend) and to the quite useful Irish 2-y-o 6f and subsequent German winner Be Fantastic (by Fantastic Light). The dam, a fair 1m winner, is a half-sister to 7 winners including the listed 7f winner Miss Ivanhoe. The second dam, Robellino Miss (by Robellino), won 7 races at up to 9f in the USA, was stakes-placed and is a half-sister to the listed winners Grangeville and Palana. *"A very nice horse, the sire is pretty hot because everyone liked his yearlings at the sales and his runners in Australia have*

done really well. He'll start in mid-April in one of the Bonus races, he's not over-big but he's a nice, athletic, early 2-y-o. He's well entered up, he's in the Sales race and the Supersprint, so hopefully he'll be a nice horse".* TRAINERS' BARGAIN BUY

1147. URBAN DREAMER ★★★
gr.c. *Intense Focus – Sioduil (Oasis Dream).* March 31. First foal. £20,000Y. Doncaster Premier. G Howson. The dam, a fairly useful Irish 5f winner, is a half-sister to 3 winners. The second dam, Indian Belle (by Indian Ridge), a fairly useful Irish 10f winner, is a half-sister to 3 winners including the dam of the Group 3 winner. (Mustajed Partnership). *"He was small in the autumn, but physically he's improved more than any of my 2-y-o's and he's now a very good-looking horse. He'll start off at Bath in mid-April, he's very sharp, tough and has good conformation. He's a bit cheeky at the moment but I think a few races will get that out of him".*

GARY MOORE

1148. DUTCHARTCOLLECTOR ★★
b.g. *Dutch Art – Censored (Pivotal).* February 24. Second foal. 50,000Y. Tattersalls October Book 2. G L Moore. The dam, a quite useful 1m winner, is a half-sister to 4 winners including the Group 3 7f (at 2 yrs) and Group 1 10.5f Prix de Diane winner Confidential Lady. The second dam, Confidante (by Dayjur), a fairly useful 3-y-o dual 7f winner, was listed-placed and is a half-sister to 7 winners including the US Grade 3 winner Drilling For Oil, the Group 3 7f Solario Stakes winner White Crown and the US Grade 1 placed Dr Caton. (Mr R A Green). *"He's quite backward so he won't be very early but he's very nice and he goes well. I haven't done much with him yet, he just needs plenty of time".*

1149. FINE ART FAIR ★★★
b.c. *Kodiac – Church Mice (Petardia).* April 28. Eighth foal. £43,000 2-y-o. Kempton Breeze-Up. G L Moore. Brother to the fair 6f and 7f winner of 4 races Strictly Pink and to a minor winner in Belgium and half-brother to the quite useful 2012 Irish 2-y-o 7f winner Angela's Dream (by Chineur), the fairly useful 6f (at 2 yrs) to 1m winner Red Rumour (by

Redback) and the fair 2-y-o 6f winner Dustry (by Chevalier). The dam, a quite useful 5f (at 2 yrs) and 6f winner, is a half-sister to 5 winners. The second dam, Negria (by Al Hareb), a German 2-y-o 6f winner, is a half-sister to 7 winners. *"I always give my horses a month off when they come from the breeze up's like this colt, but he's definitely a 2-y-o and he certainly looks a nice type. He wasn't an early foal so he'll develop even further over the coming weeks".*

1150. LADY MARL ★★★

b.f. Duke Of Marmalade – Empress Anna (Imperial Ballet). April 6. Fifth foal. 20,000Y. Tattersalls October Book 2. Not sold. Closely related to the fair 7f winner Poker Hospital (by Rock Of Gibraltar) and half-sister to the fair 7f winner Greenflash (by Green Desert) and a winner in Greece by Gulch. The dam, a minor winner at 3 yrs in the USA, is a half-sister to 5 winners including the Irish listed winner and Group 3 placed Clean Cut. The second dam, Cutlers Corner (by Sharpen Up), a very useful winner of the 5f Rous Stakes, was fourth in the Group 3 King George Stakes and is a half-sister to 6 winners. (Sir Eric Parker). *"She's a lovely filly and although she's quite big she'll come to hand earlier than the Dutch Art 2-y-o. She goes well, looks speedy enough for six furlongs to start with and we like her a lot".*

GEORGE MOORE

1151. LADY LIZ ★★★

b.f. Byron – Sister Rose (One Cool Cat). January 9. First foal. £5,000Y. Doncaster November. George Moore. The dam is an unraced daughter of the unraced Lady Of St Kilda (by Mark Of Esteem), herself a half-sister to 4 winners including the dual Group winner Alkaadhem. (Mrs Liz Ingham). *"She'll be early and I expect she'll be racing in late April/early May. She's quick enough for five furlongs but she might just stay a bit further as well. I do like her, she's very strong and there are no worries with her at all. There's plenty about her and she's done very well since the sales".*

1152. LADY YEATS ★★

b.f. Shirocco – Oblique (Giant's Causeway). February 13. Fifth foal. 8,000Y. Tattersalls October Book 2. C Thornton. Half-sister to

the quite useful Irish 7f (including at 2 yrs) and 1m winner Obligada (by Beat Hollow), to the modest 7f and 12f winner Rubi Dia (by Hernando) and a winner in Switzerland by Shirocco. The dam, a fairly useful 9f, 10f and listed 12f winner, is a half-sister to 5 winners including the useful 12f to 15.4f winner One Off. The second dam, On Call (by Alleged), a useful winner of 7 races at up to 2m, is a half-sister to 6 winners including the fairly useful 5.2f (at 2 yrs) and 6f winner Doctor's Glory (herself the dam of 5 stakes winners). (Mrs Liz Ingham). *"She'll take a bit of time but she's doing upsides work and enjoying what she's doing, so we're very happy with her. Despite being by Shirocco she might not take too long, but nevertheless she'll set off at seven furlongs in the second half of the season".*

1153. ROKEBY ★★★

b.c. Byron – Scarlet Royal (Red Ransom). April 7. Second foal. Half-brother to the fairly useful 2012 2-y-o 6f winner and Group 3 6f Firth Of Clyde Stakes third Momalorka (by Dutch Art). The dam is an unplaced half-sister to several winners. The dam is an unraced half-sister to 6 winners including the high-class Group 1 1m Queen Elizabeth II Stakes winner Where Or When and the smart 10f and 12f winner and Group 1 St Leger fourth All The Way. (Mrs Liz Ingham). *"He'll start his career in April, he's quick, he's sharp, he enjoys what he does and I do like him. He looks as if he's got a bit of ability and he just does what he needs to do – no matter what I work him with".*

STAN MOORE

1154. BONJOUR STEVE ★★★

b.c. Bahamian Bounty – Anthea (Tobougg). April 20. Third foal. 4,000Y. Tattersalls December. J S Moore. Half-sister to the unplaced 2012 2-y-o Sea And Be Seen (by Sakhee's Secret). The dam, a modest 7f (at 2 yrs) to 10f placed maiden, is a half-sister to 2 winners including the useful 1m (at 2 yrs) and subsequent US Grade 3 winner Genre. The second dam, Blue Indigo by Pistolet Bleu), was placed 5 times in France and is a half-sister to 6 winners. (Paul Mendoza & J S Moore). *"He shows good paces, he's a big horse and seems to be earlier than he should be for his size. He's definitely one to follow and is a very nice horse with the speed to win over five furlongs but he'll be better over six. He'll definitely win his races and I think he could be quite decent".*

1155. COCKNEY BOB ★★
b.g. Cockney Rebel – Wizby (Wizard King). April 19. Second foal. £500Y. Ascot November. Not sold. The dam, a modest winner of 3 of her 51 races over 5f, 6f (both at 2 yrs) and 1m, is a half-sister to one winner in Italy. The second dam, Diamond Vanessa (by Distinctly North), is an unplaced half-sister to 2 winners abroad. (Miss D L Wisbey & Mr R Viney). *"He'll definitely win his early season 2-y-o races so he's one to follow in the first half of the season. Six furlongs would probably be his optimum trip".*

1156. MY MY MY DILIZA ★★★
br.f. Sakhee's Secret – Diliza (Dilum). March 26. Sixth foal. 4,200Y. Tattersalls October Book 3. Stan Moore. Closely related to the 2-y-o 6f winner, from two starts, Major Dude (by Sakhee) and half-sister to the 2012 1m placed 2-y-o Misfer (by Byron). The dam, a moderate 1m winner, is a half-sister to one winner. The second dam, Little White Lies (by Runnett), is a placed half-sister to 5 winners. *"She's very nice, showing good paces and has quite a nice pedigree. A six/seven furlong 2-y-o, definitely one to follow and one of the nicest of our fillies".* TRAINERS' BARGAIN BUY

1157. OUTBACK LOVER ★★★
b.f. Bushranger – Lady Thyne (Mujadil). March 14. Fifth foal. £500Y. Ascot November. Not sold. The dam, a fair 6f winner at 3 yrs in Ireland, is a half-sister to 2 winners over hurdles. The second dam, Stairway To Heaven (by Godswalk), won 7 races from 6f to 1m and at 2 to 4 yrs and is a half-sister to 7 winners. *"I think she's very quick and she could go to the Lily Agnes at Chester. A five furlong speedster and although she was cheap she's out of a Mujadil mare who is out of a Godswalk mare, so there's plenty of speed there. She put up a good time when she won her race the other day".*

1158. SHEILA'S FOOTSTEPS ★★
b.g. Footstepsinthesand – Marmaga (Shernazar). April 19. Eighth foal. £5,000Y.

Doncaster Premier. J Gompertz. Half-brother to the Italian winner of 14 races Destination World (by Alzao), to the modest Irish 8.5f winner Misima Sunrise (by Tagula) and a minor winner abroad by Noverre. The dam is an unraced half-sister to 7 winners including the French dual Group 3 winner Masslama. The second dam, Marmana (by Blushing Groom), is a placed sister to the Group 3 Prix d'Hedouville winner Malakim and a half-sister to 6 winners. (Mr Ray Styles & J S Moore). *"He'll be very nice when the seven furlong and mile races start. He does everything nicely, has plenty of size and scope and will train on to be a decent 3-y-o".*

1159. SWEET ALIBI (IRE) ★★★
b.f. Lawman – Zingari (Groom Dancer). February 24. Fifth foal. €4,500Y. Tattersalls Ireland September. J S Moore. The dam, a quite useful 7f (including at 2 yrs) and 1m winner of 6 races, is a half-sister to 4 winners including the German listed-placed winner of 4 races Phantastic Wings. The second dam, Antigua (by Selkirk), is an unraced half-sister to 7 winners. (Mr G V March & J S Moore). *"The dam was as tough as nails and this filly will start at six furlongs but would be better at seven. One of our nicer fillies".*

1160. VODKA CHASER (IRE) ★★★
b.f. Baltic King – Suffer Her (Whipper). January 25. First foal. £6,500Y. Doncaster Premier. Stan Moore. The dam is an unraced half-sister to 3 winners including the useful 2-y-o dual 6f winner and listed-placed Campbeltown. The second dam, Jallaissine (by College Chapel), placed twice at 2 yrs in France, is a half-sister to the smart 12f listed winner Riyafa. (Mr N Attenborough, Mrs L Mann, J S Moore). *"She's sharp, an out-and-out 2-y-o, and I'd expect her to win a maiden auction and end up running in the nurseries. A thick-set, very well-built 2-y-o".*

1161. UNNAMED ★★
b.g. Elnadim – Endis (Distant Relative). February 8. Fifth foal. €5,000Y. Tattersalls Ireland September. J S Moore. Half-brother to the modest 2012 5f to 7f placed maiden Alhaarth Beauty (by Alhaarth). The dam, a minor dual winner at 3 yrs in Italy, is a sister to the US Grade 3 and Italian listed winner De

Puntillas and a half-sister to 6 winners. The second dam, Enola (by Ela-Mana-Mou), is an unraced half-sister to 8 winners. (Mr K Kirkup & J S Moore). *"He'll be a nice horse, he's grown a lot on me, he seems to have good paces and his main aim will be the Tattersalls Sales race in Ireland. He'll probably run just once or twice before then but he seems to be a horse with a lot about him. He didn't cost a lot but he's the best one I've had heading for the race since Southandwest who was second in it".*

HUGHIE MORRISON

1162. ARAB DAWN ★★★★

gr.c. *Dalakhani – Victoire Celebre (Stravinsky)*. April 25. Second foal. 62,000Y. Tattersalls October Book 1. Sackville/Donald. Half-brother to the modest 2012 7f placed 2-y-o Lionheart (by Zamindar). The dam ran twice unplaced and is a half-sister to the Group 2 Prix du Muguet winner Vetheuil, the Group 3 Prix de l'Opera winner Verveine (herself dam of the Grade 1 winners Vallee Enchantee and Volga) and the dams of the Group 1 Coronation Stakes winner Maid's Causeway and the Group 1 Grand Prix de Paris winner Vespone. The second dam, Venise (by Nureyev), is an unraced three-parts sister to the Mill Reef Stakes and Richmond Stakes winner Vacarme and a half-sister to the Prix Jacques le Marois winner Vin de France. (Eason, Kerr-Dineen, Hughes, Edward-Jones). *"He seems to find everything quite easy, he's quite mature, 'together' and strong, so he may be running in July if he goes the right way. He has speed, he's a lovely mover and is a quality horse that doesn't look expensive at the moment".*

1163. BACKSTAGE GOSSIP ★★★

b.f. *Sakhee's Secret – Theatre Royal (Royal Applause)*. February 4. Second foal. The dam, a moderate 10f winner, is a half-sister to one winner. The second dam, Rada's Daughter (by Robellino), a useful winner of 5 races at up to 12f, was second in the Group 3 Park Hill Stakes and is a half-sister to 8 winners. (Runs In The Family). *"A nice little filly, she's compact and it would help if she grew a bit but she seems honest and she could run in mid-summer. They tell me the dam showed a lot at two and then lost her way, so I'll be careful not to over cook*

this filly early on. She looks a sharp, sprinting type".

1164. BALTIC BRAVE (IRE) ★★★

b.c. *Baltic King – Negria (Al Hareb)*. March 30. Twelfth foal. €15,000Y. Goffs Sportsman's. H Morrison. Half-brother to the quite useful 5f (at 2 yrs) and 6f winner Church Mice (by Petardia), to the quite useful dual 5f winner Melrose Place (by Danetime), the fair 7f, 1m and hurdles winner Carlitos Spirit, the minor US and Canadian winner Kouloura (both by Redback), a winner in Greece by Indian Rocket and a hurdles winner by Chevalier. The dam, a German 2-y-o 6f winner, is a half-sister to 7 winners, two of them listed-placed. The second dam, June Goddess (by Junius), an Irish 7f winner at 3 yrs, is a half-sister to 4 winners including the Italian listed winner of 11 races Sir Lanca. (The Brave Partnership). *"A nice, straightforward Baltic King with a good temperament. I quite like his sire and this colt is a sprinting type that could be out by July. He should win as a 2-y-o but he's got enough scope for next year as well".*

1165. BLACK RODDED ★★★

ch.f. *Bahamian Bounty – Palace Affair (Pursuit Of Love)*. March 19. Sixth foal. 55,000Y. Tattersalls October Book 1. Sackville/Donald. Sister to the useful 2-y-o listed 6f winner Queen's Grace and half-sister to the fair 7f to 9f winner of 15 races April Fool (by Pivotal) and the modest 2-y-o 5f winner Dubai Affair (by Dubawi). The dam, a smart listed winner of 6 races from 5f to 7f, is a sister to one winner and a half-sister to 9 winners including the high-class Group 1 6f July Cup winner Sakhee's Secret. The second dam, Palace Street (by Secreto), a useful winner over 6f and 7f including the listed Cammidge Trophy, is a half-sister to 7 winners including the Extel Handicap winner Indian Trail. (Mr M Kerr-Dineen, Mr M Pallett, Mrs L Tullett). *"A full sister to Queen's Grace who won a listed race as a 2-y-o at the back-end and she's similar to her except that Queen's Grace was about three inches shorter. This one is a much leggier sort, more delicate looking and a beautiful mover. She floats across the ground and she could be a summer 2-y-o or we might wait – it depends how she comes on during May. She's a nice filly, the pedigree suggests six furlongs but actually she looks more like a seven furlong type".*

1166. CASCADING (FR) ★★★★

b.f. *Teofilo – Angel Falls (Kingmambo).* April 14. First foal. 60,000Y. Tattersalls October Book 1. Will Edmeades. The dam is an unraced half-sister to 6 winners including the Group 3 1m Prix de la Grotte winner and Irish 1,000 Guineas second Anna Salai and the listed winners Iguazu Falls and Advice. The second dam, Anna Palariva (by Caerleon), a smart winner of the 2-y-o Group 3 1m Prix d'Aumale, is a half-sister to 5 winners. (Thurloe Thoroughbreds). *"A very nice filly, she seems well-bought, has a decent pedigree, the French breeders premium and is very straightforward. She does everything you ask with no trouble at all and I think some of these Teofilo's are quite mature so she could make a July 2-y-o. A nice, strong sort with a good bit of size and depth".*

1167. CONCRETE MAC ★★

b.c. *Mastercraftsman – Merry Diva (Bahamian Bounty).* February 5. First foal. 25,000Y. Tattersalls October Book 2. Hughie Morrison. The dam, a fair 2-y-o 6f winner, is sister to the dual listed winner and Group 3 third Paradise Isle and a half-sister to 8 winners. The second dam, Merry Rous (by Rousillon), won once at 2 yrs and is a half-sister to 5 winners including the dual Group 3 winning sprinter Tina's Pet. (Adrian McAlpine & Partners). *"I thought most of the Mastercraftsman yearlings at the sales had slightly common heads. This one is small, so he'll need to be a 2-y-o, he's a bit nervy and I hope he'll be racing in May over five furlongs".*

1168. NISSAKI KASTA ★★★

ch.f. *Sakhee's Secret – Casterossa (Rossini).* March 4. Third foal. The dam, a modest 5.5f winner, is a half-sister to several minor winners. The second dam, First Musical (by First Trump), a fairly useful winner of 4 races from 5f to 6f at 2 yrs and second in the listed Firth Of Clyde Stakes and is a half-sister to 5 winners. (Mr D Barrie). *"She only arrived in February, we broke her in and she's coped surprisingly well with everything. The owners might have a bit of fun with her later in the year and I'll be surprised if she's not better than the dam.*

1169. SOUTHERN CROSS ★★★★

ch.f. *Mount Nelson – Bread Of Heaven (Machiavellian).* March 5. Fifth foal. 22,000Y. Tattersalls October Book 2. Hughie Morrison. Half-sister to a minor winner abroad by Cadeaux Genereux. The dam, a quite useful 2-y-o 6f winner, is a half-sister to 8 winners including the Group 2 1m Prix du Rond-Point and Group 3 8.5f Diomed Stakes winner Trans Island and the Italian Group 3 winner Welsh Diva. The second dam, Khubza (by Green Desert), a quite useful 3-y-o 7f winner, is a half-sister to 7 winners including the Group 2 winners Barrow Creek and Last Resort. (Major D Chappell, Mr R Lloyd & Partners). *"She's full of beans, very athletic, a good-moving filly and she's obviously got natural ability. She's nice and she's got an engine too, but she's quite full of herself and needs to relax a bit. A superb mover, she really covers the ground and the reason I bought her was because of the Selkirk influence in the pedigree – as well as the fact she was the most fabulous walker at the sales. She canters really well too, so she should be alright and she'd have the speed for six or seven furlongs".* TRAINERS' BARGAIN BUY

1170. SWEEPING UP ★★★

b.f. *Sea The Stars – Farfala (Linamix).* April 14. Half-sister to the 2-y-o listed 10f Zetland Stakes winner and Group 2 12f Lancashire Oaks second Under The Rainbow (by Fantastic Light), to the useful dual 12f winner and Group 2 Park Hill Stakes second Starfala (by Galileo), the quite useful 2-y-o 1m winner Swingland (by Pivotal), the quite useful 2-y-o 8.3f winner Speightstown (by Grand Lodge) and the moderate 5f winner Mujma (by Indian Ridge). The dam, a French listed 12f winner, is a sister to the Group 1 Grand Prix de Saint-Cloud winner Fragrant Mix and the Group 3 Prix d'Hedouville winner Fracassant. The second dam, Fragrant Hill (by Shirley Heights), was a useful winner of the listed 10f Lupe Stakes and is a half-sister to 8 winners. (Ben & Sir Martyn Arbib). *"A very attractive filly, she isn't one to hurry because she's bound to stay ten furlongs at least. A good mover and a quality filly, she's a nice size. We had her half-sibling by Montjeu and she's already got more scope than her and moves better. She has a charming head on her – I think Sea The*

Stars will get them with very nice personalities. Much more of a 3-y-o type, but hopefully she'll be competing in the autumn".

1171. TRIPLE STAR ★★★★

b.f. Royal Applause – Triple Sharp (Selkirk). April 1. Eighth foal. Sister to the French 2-y-o 7f winner Royal Sharp and half-sister to the useful 6f (including at 2 yrs) and 7f winner of 4 races and triple listed-placed Nasri (by Nayef), the useful 6f (at 2 yrs) to 11f winner and 2-y-o Group 2 7f Superlative Stakes third Ellmau (by Dr Fong), the listed-placed Laureldean Express (by Inchinor) and a winner in Spain by Vettori. The dam, a quite useful 10f and hurdles winner, is a half-sister to 5 winners including the US stakes winner and Grade 2 placed Pina Colada and to the unraced dam of the top-class miler Canford Cliffs. The second dam, Drei (by Lyphard), placed fourth over 1m at 3 yrs on her only outing, is a half-sister to 3 winners. (Lady Hardy). "She's a nice filly. The sire can get them with slightly dodgy temperaments but she's settled down well now having been a bit 'free' earlier on. She could be a July 2-y-o, six or seven furlongs should suit her and we like her".

1172. UNNAMED ★★★

gr.f. Verglas – Ive Gota Bad Liver (Mt Livermore). March 19. Seventh foal. €90,000Y. Goffs Orby. Hugo Lascelles. Half-sister to the quite useful 10f winner Longliner (by Dalakhani) and to the fair 9f winner Otelcaliforni (by Gulch). The dam, a US winner of 3 races and second in a Grade 3 stakes event, is a half-sister to 6 winners including the 1,000 Guineas, Coronation Stakes, Nassau Stakes and Lockinge Stakes winner Russian Rhythm and the Group 2 1m Royal Lodge Stakes winner Perfectperformance. The second dam, Balistroika (by Nijinsky), is an unraced half-sister to 8 winners including Park Appeal (winner of the Cheveley Park Stakes and the Moyglare Stud Stakes and the dam of Cape Cross), Alydaress (Irish Oaks) and Desirable (winner of the Cheveley Park Stakes and the dam of Shadayid). "She arrived here two weeks ago from pre-training. Everyone here says she feels weak but she doesn't look it. Our most expensive 2-y-o, she's quite strong looking, muscled-up, mature and a decent size for a 2-y-o. Hopefully I'll get her out in June and you'd hope that she'd have enough speed for seven furlongs".

1173. UNNAMED ★★★

b.f. Major Cadeaux – Miss Poppy (Averti). February 19. Second foal. £14,000Y. Doncaster Premier. H Morrison. The dam, a modest 6f placed maiden (including at 2 yrs), is a half-sister to 10 winners including the top-class Group 1 5f Nunthorpe Stakes winner Kyllachy and the fairly useful 2-y-o 5f winner Follow Flanders. The second dam, Pretty Poppy (by Song), a modest 2-y-o 5f winner, stayed 7.6f and is a half-sister to 4 winners. (A C Pickford). "A nice filly that's never stopped doing, she'll need a break for a few weeks now because of a small setback, but everyone really likes her. Based on her I'd be happy to buy another by the sire. She's very straightforward, she has a nice personality and moves well, so she could be alright later on".

WILLIE MUIR

1174. ARMOURER (IRE) ★★★

b.c. Azamour – Engraving (Sadler's Wells). April 30. Third foal. 30,000Y. Tattersalls October Book 1. Willie Muir. Half-brother to the 2012 Italian 2-y-o listed 1m winner Virtual Game (by Kheleyf) and to the fair 2-y-o 6f winner Ladykin (by Holy Roman Emperor). The dam is an unraced half-sister to 2 winners including the multiple French listed winner and Group 2 second Kocab. The second dam, Space Quest (by Rainbow Quest), won the listed Prix Joubert and is a half-sister to 7 winners including the French Group winners Dance Routine and Apsis. (D G Clarke & C L A Edginton). "I think he's a really nice individual. He's big, strong and good moving. Looking at him you'd say he'd be one for the back-end of the season but Azamour's can look like that sometimes. They're a little bit sharper than you think. Everyone that rides him doesn't think he's weak, so my impression is that he'll be a very nice horse from mid-summer onwards.

1175. BLACKE FOREST ★★★

b.f. Manduro – Welsh Cake (Fantastic Light). March 7. Second foal. 25,000Y. Tattersalls October Book 1. Not sold. Half-sister to the useful 2012 2-y-o 5f winner and Group 1

Cheveley Park Stakes fourth Upward Spiral (by Teofilo). The dam, a fair 7f winner, is a half-sister to 8 winners including the Group 2 1m Prix du Rond-Point and Group 3 8.5f Diomed Stakes winner Trans Island and the Italian Group 3 winner Welsh Diva. The second dam, Khubza (by Green Desert), a quite useful 3-y-o 7f winner, is a half-sister to 7 winners including the Group 2 winners Barrow Creek and Last Resort (herself dam of the US Grade 2 winner Rebellion) and the listed winners Arctic Char and Heard A Whisper. (M J Caddy). *"She's interesting because her half-sister last year was fourth in the Cheveley Park and the owner has told me he thinks this filly will win the Queen Mary, despite the fact she's by Manduro! She's not overly big and she looks sharp but I don't know whether her looks are deceiving me. She does everything well although I haven't pushed any buttons yet and there's no reason why she shouldn't be a good filly. I hesitate to agree with the owner about the Queen Mary though, simply because of her sire and damsire. I won't push her because she's been growing but she's got a good temperament and does everything fine".*

1176. CHILLY IN RIO (IRE) ★★★

gr.f. Verglas – Brazilian Spirit (Invincible Spirit). January 29. First foal. £10,000Y. Doncaster Premier. W Muir. The dam, a quite useful 2-y-o 5f and 7f winner, is a half-sister to 5 winners including the 2-y-o Group 3 6f winner Brazilian Bride and the very useful 2-y-o 7.5f winner and Group 3 7f second Brazilian Star. The second dam, Braziliz (by Kingmambo), is an unplaced half-sister to 8 winners including the 2-y-o winner Or Vision (dam of the Irish 2,000 Guineas winner Saffron Walden, the Grade 1 E P Taylor Stakes winner Insight and the Group 1 7f Prix de la Foret winner Dolphin Street). (Muir Racing Partnership – Manchester). *"She'll be my first 2-y-o runner, she's done some work and shown she's got speed and ability. A sharp filly, she's not overly-big and the mare was decent herself. She'll definitely win races".* TRAINERS' BARGAIN BUY

1177. DIVISION BELLE ★★

gr.f. Dalakhani – Multiplication (Marju). February 12. First foal. 65,000Y. Tattersalls

October Book 1. Willie Muir. The dam, a quite useful 11f winner, is a half-sister to 9 winners including the very smart 1m (at 2 yrs) and dual Group 3 middle-distance winner Blue Monday and the very useful 1m to 10f winner and Italian Derby third Lundy's Lane. The second dam, Lunda (by Soviet Star), is an unplaced half-sister to 6 winners including the high-class middle-distance horses Luso (winner of the Aral-Pokal, the Italian Derby and the Hong Kong International Vase) and Warrsan (Coronation Cup and Grosser Preis von Baden). (Foursome Thoroughbreds). *"I love her, I think she has a fantastic pedigree but she'll take her time this season because she's by Dalakhani. She's quite strongly built, she moves well and could be anything. One for the late summer onwards probably".*

1178. GULLAND ROCK ★★★★

b.c. Exceed And Excel – Sacre Coeur (Compton Place). April 26. Third foal. 60,000Y. Tattersalls October Book 1. Willie Muir. Half-brother to the fair 2012 2-y-o 5f winner Cross My Heart (by Sakhee's Secret) and to the 2-y-o listed 5f winner and Group 2 Prix du Gros-Chene second Stepper Point (by Kyllachy). The dam, a fair 2-y-o 6f winner, is a half-sister to 5 winners including the useful dual 10f winner and listed-placed Lonely Heart (herself dam of the Group 3 Tetrarch Stakes winner Leitrim House) and the useful 6f and 7f winner of 4 races Indian Trail. The second dam, Take Heart (by Electric), a quite useful 7f to 10f winner of 4 races, is a half-sister to 3 winners. (C L A Edginton & K Mercer). *"Mr Edginton owned Stepper Point, so he and Kevin Mercer decided to join forces to own this colt, his half-brother. He's a cracker, he's strong, does everything right, will be a 2-y-o and he'll be very good. I love him".*

1179. IMPROVISED ★★★

b.f. Authorized – Rhapsodize (Halling). March 16. Fourth foal. 13,000Y. Tattersalls October Book 2. Not sold. Half-sister to the fair 5f winner Nawarah (by Acclamation) and to the modest triple 5f winner (including at 2 yrs) Melodize (by Iceman). The dam is an unraced half-sister to 5 winners including the Group 1 Cheveley Park Stakes winner Hooray and the useful 2-y-o listed 8.3f winner Hypnotic. The second dam, Hypnotize (by Machiavellian), a useful 2-y-o listed 7f winner, is a closely related to 2 winners including Dazzle (Group 3 6f Cherry Hinton Stakes) and a half-sister to 6 winners including the useful 1m listed winner Fantasize and to the placed dam of the Group winners Danehurst and Humouresque. (Foursome Thoroughbreds). *"Probably because she's by Authorized she didn't attract too much attention at the sale but she goes very well and shows there's something about her already. Unlike a lot by the sire who take a lot of time she doesn't look that way. The dam is from a very fast family and maybe this filly has inherited some of it. I like her and she seems to be going the right way".*

1180. ORACLE BOY ★★★

b.c. Mount Nelson – Snow Princess (Ela-Mana-Mou). March 6. Tenth foal. 10,000Y. Tattersalls October Book 2. Willie Muir. Half-brother to the 2-y-o Group 2 1m Royal Lodge Stakes winner and 2,000 Guineas second Snow Ridge (by Indian Ridge), to the German listed winner Snow Gretel (by Green Desert), the French winner of 7 races White King, the quite useful Irish dual 12f winner White Queen (both by Spectrum) and the modest 9f winner Snowy Peak (by Pivotal). The dam, a smart winner of 6 races at up to 2m including the November Handicap and an Italian listed event, was second in the Group 1 Prix Royal-Oak and is a half-sister to 7 winners. The second dam, Karelia (by Sir Ivor), won over 1m and was third in the Group 3 12.5f Prix de Royallieu. *"I think he was a steal really. The mare was Group 1 placed and she's bred a Group 2 winning 2-y-o. Everyone seemed to have gone off the stallion at the sales thinking that everything he sires takes ages to mature, but I trained his 2-y-o Purr Along to win a Group 3. When I bought this colt he was very weak and gangly but everything's gone well and he's just continuing to mature".*

1181. STRAWBERRY MARTINI ★★★

ch.f. Mount Nelson – Strawberry Lolly (Lomitas). March 6. Third foal. 10,000Y. Tattersalls October Book 2. Willie Muir. Half-sister to the fair 2012 2-y-o 7f winner Kolonel Kirkup (by Dr Fong). The dam, a quite useful 9f and 10f winner, is a half-sister to 3

winners including the Group 2 1m Windsor Forest Stakes and Group 3 9f Dahlia Stakes winner Strawberrydaiquiri. The second dam, Strawberry Morn (by Travelling Victor), a triple Canadian stakes winner of 15 races, is a half-sister to 6 winners. *"She's a big, strong filly that'll take a wee bit of time like the other Mount Nelson we have. I loved her at the sales, she moves nicely and she's not small but she's scopey enough to do anything".*

1182. UNNAMED ★★★

b.f. Acclamation – Amistad (Winged Love). February 6. Sixth foal. 45,000Y. Tattersalls October Book 2. Willie Muir. Sister to the fair 2012 1m placed 2-y-o Wayfoong Express and to the quite useful 6f and 7f winner, including at 2 yrs, Amary and half-sister to the quite useful 6f and 7f winner Amazing Amoray (by Tagula). The dam won once at 2 yrs in Germany and is a half-sister to 7 winners including the German Derby third Acamani. The second dam, Adjani (by Surumu), was placed in Germany and is a half-sister to 6 winners. (M J Caddy). *"I really like her, she's a strong filly that I have a lot of time for. I trained her brother Wayfoong Express last year who was slow to learn but a lovely horse. He just got pipped in a Conditions race by a horse that ended up running in Dubai on World Cup night. This filly has scope and size, she's beautiful and I really like her. She'll be ready by mid-summer".*

1183. UNNAMED ★★★

b.c. Acclamation – Daqtora (Dr Devious). April 15. Seventh foal. 40,000Y. Tattersalls October Book 2. Willie Muir. Half-brother to the fairly useful 2-y-o 6f winner and listed-placed Qalahari (by Bahri), to the fair Irish 7f winner Nasharaat (by Green Desert), the fair 1m and 9f winner Mrs Dee Bee (by Barathea) and the fair Irish 2m and hurdles winner Almolahek (by Red Ransom). The dam, a minor Irish 11f winner, is a half-sister to 5 winners including the 2-y-o Group 1 1m National Stakes winner Mus-If and the very smart 1m (at 2 yrs) and listed 10f winner Jammaal. The second dam, Navajo Love Song (by Dancing Brave), placed once at 4 yrs, is a half-sister to 5 minor winners in France and Italy. *"He'll be quite sharp, he goes well, looks the part and does everything right. I'll be trying to get him out in May".*

1184. UNNAMED ★★★

gr.f. Mount Nelson – Lady Xara (Xaar).
February 4. Third foal. 14,000Y. Tattersalls October Book 2. Willie Muir. Half-sister to the poor 2012 2-y-o Miss Penny Arcade (by Royal Applause). The dam is an unraced half-sister to 5 winners including the Group 3 Meld Stakes winner Khalafiya (herself dam of the dual Group 2 winner Predappio). The second dam, Khalisiyn (by Shakapour), a fairly useful 7f and 1m winner at 3 yrs, is a half-sister to 5 winners including the US Grade 2 Dixie Handicap and listed Scottish Derby winner Kadial and the Group 2 placed Kalim. *"She goes well, she's quite big and strong and in the same mould as Purr Along, my Group 3 winning Mount Nelson filly from last year. She does everything nicely and I can see her being out any time from the middle of the season onwards. I couldn't knock her".*

1185. UNNAMED ★★★

gr.f. Dark Angel – Tintern (Diktat). February 18. Third foal. 17,000Y. Tattersalls October Book 3. Willie Muir. Half-sister to the fair 1m and 9f winner Siouxperhero (by Sleeping Indian). The dam is an unraced half-sister to 4 winners including the dual 10f and subsequent US stakes winner and Grade 2 placed Solva. The second dam, Annapurna (by Brief Truce), a useful 2-y-o 7f winner, was listed placed over 9f and 10f and is a half-sister to 5 winners including the 2-y-o Group 3 7f Rockfel Stakes and listed 7f winner Name Of Love. *"She'll be relatively early, she's done a bit of work, goes well and shows she's got ability, so I can see her being out in late April. Her brother Siouxperhero was a dream to train and he won me two races last year, but this filly is a lot stronger, she shows more than he did as a 2-y-o and I've no doubt she'll be a winner".*

1186. UNNAMED ★★

b.f. New Approach – Porthcawl (Singspiel).
January 29. Third foal. 35,000foal. Tattersalls December. Not sold. The dam, a fairly useful triple 1m winner here, subsequently won a stakes event in the USA and is a half-sister to the very smart 6f (at 2 yrs) and 7f winner and

Group 3 7f Hungerford Stakes second Tarjman and the smart 2-y-o 6f and 3-y-o listed 6f winner Nota Bene. The second dam, Dodo (by Alzao), a fairly useful 3-y-o 6f winner, is a half-sister to 8 winners. *"She hasn't been in the yard long because she got a bit of a knock at the sales, but she looks strong, the sire has been a great success and it's a very successful sprinting family. She certainly looks like a sprinter and although I've only cantered her so far she looks strong and a 2-y-o type. I don't want to rush her at this stage".*

1187. UNNAMED ★★

b.c. Manduro – Ornellaia (Mujadil). April 20. 15,000Y. Tattersalls October Book 2. Not sold. Half-brother to the modest 2012 2-y-o 5f winner Slipstream Angel, to the modest 7f and 1m winner Hi There (both by Dark Angel) and the fair 2-y-o 5f winner Super Tuscan (by Fath). The dam, placed fourth once over 6f at 2 yrs, is a half-sister to 4 winners including the useful 2-y-o 6f and listed 1m winner Henri Lebasque. The second dam, Almost A Lady (by Entitled), was placed over 7f and 1m at 2 yrs in Ireland and is a half-sister to 5 winners including Insatiable (Group 2 Prix Dollar and Group 3 Brigadier Gerard Stakes). *"I bought him privately after the sale, he's a Manduro so he'll take a bit of time but he shows he has ability and he'll be racing from the middle of the season. He's the one horse I haven't sold but he goes quite well and I do like him".*

JEREMY NOSEDA

1188. ANAKAYA ★★★

b.c. Pastoral Pursuits – Rhapsilian (Dansili).
March 19. First foal. £37,000Y. Doncaster Premier. Hugo Merry. The dam, a moderate 6f winner, is a sister to the dual listed winner Ripples Maid and a half-sister to 6 winners including the very smart 2-y-o Group 3 Horris Hill Stakes winner Peak To Creek. The second dam, Rivers Rhapsody (by Dominion), a useful winner of the listed 5f Scarborough Stakes and third in the Group 2 5f Temple Stakes, is a half-sister to the Group 3 5f Prix d'Arenberg winner Regal Scintilla. *"He should be a mid-season 2-y-o over six furlongs, he's a good mover but he's grown and lengthened so he just needs to strengthen up at this stage".*

1189. ANNA'S FANCY (IRE) ★★★

gr.f. Acclamation – Step Too Far (Cozzene). March 27. Third foal. 120,000Y. Tattersalls October Book 1. Sackville/Donald. Half-sister to the modest 7f and 1m winner Dashing Eddie (by Dubawi). The dam is an unraced half-sister to 3 minor winners in France and the USA. The second dam, Out Of Reach (by Warning), won the Grade 3 Brown Bess Handicap in the USA and is a full or half-sister to 7 winners including the dam of the Group 1 King's Stand Stakes winner Prohibit. "Quite a nice filly that moves well, she wasn't the most precocious at the sales and she looks a July type 2-y-o. A sprinting filly and the type to do a job as a 2-y-o".

1190. ANNA'S VISION (IRE) ★★★

b.f. Invincible Spirit – House In Wood (Woodman). April 30. Ninth foal. 130,000Y. Tattersalls October Book 1. Sackville/Donald. Closely related to the minor German 3-y-o winner Hideki Danon (by Oasis Dream) and half-sister to the US Grade 1 Garden City Stakes and Group 3 Irish 1,000 Guineas Trial winner Alexander Tango (by Danehill Dancer) and the fair 10f winner Highland Duke (by Dansili). The dam is an unraced half-sister to the Group 2 Prix Niel winner Housamix, to the French listed 2-y-o 9f winner and US Grade 1 placed Housa Dancer (herself the dam of the Group winners Bushman and Grand Vent). The second dam, Housatonic (by Riverman), won over 7f and is a half-sister to 7 winners including the US Grade 2 winner Globe. "Quite sharp, she's just had a little setback recently and was nearly ready to do her first piece of work, but she'll get over that soon. Hopefully she'll be racing in mid-May because although she's quite a late foal she's definitely a 2-y-o type – neat and fast".

1191. AUTUMNS BLUSH (IRE) ★★★★

b.f. Kheleyf – Park Romance (Dr Fong). April 10. Fifth foal. 65,000Y. Tattersalls October Book 2. Willie Browne. Half-sister to the unraced 2012 2-y-o Desert Skies (by Green Desert) and to the fair 2-y-o 6f winner Ihtiraam (by Teofilo). The dam, a fairly useful 2-y-o 6f winner, was third in the Group 3 Sweet Solera Stakes and is a half-sister to 6 winners including the 6f (at 2 yrs) and Group

3 7f Ballycorus Stakes winner Rum Charger (herself dam of the US multiple Grade 1 winner Winchester) and the dam of the Sweet Solera Stakes winner English Ballet. The second dam, Park Charger (by Tirol), a useful winner over 1m and 10f at 3 yrs in Ireland, was listed-placed four times and is a half-sister to 9 winners. "She's a sharp filly and she'll start off in mid-April at Newmarket's Craven meeting. Everything she's been asked to do she's done well and she'll definitely win her races. A filly with the speed for five furlongs but she'll get six and she's definitely sharp and early. With luck she'll end up at Royal Ascot but whether it's as a 5-1 shot or a 25-1 shot only time will tell!"

1192. BISHOPS AVENUE (IRE) ★★★★

b.c. Lawman – Shesasmartlady (Dolphin Street). April 7. Eighth foal. 360,000Y. Tattersalls October Book 1. Sackville/Donald. Half-brother to the smart Group 2 6f Criterium de Maisons-Laffitte winner and Group 1 Middle Park Stakes third Captain Marvelous (by Invincible Spirit), to the fairly useful 10f and 12f winner Hero Worship (by Kalanisi), the fair Irish 6f winner Smartest (by Exceed And Excel) and the minor US 4-y-o winner French Fern (by Royal Applause). The dam is an unplaced half-sister to 8 winners including the listed winners Dashing Colours and Dash Of Red. The second dam, Near The End (by Shirley Heights), is an unraced half-sister to 2 minor winners. "A good type, he's a strong, racey horse with a good attitude and he moves well. He's done everything right at this point and it's just a matter of deciding when I move with him. A well-balanced horse, he's one that I like and he might have a run at the end of May, but we'll have to see. He's a very good individual".

1193. DREAMING BEAUTY ★★★ ♠

b.f. Oasis Dream – Independence (Selkirk). March 16. Eighth foal. 200,000Y. Tattersalls October Book 1. Jeremy Noseda. Sister to the 1m (at 2 yrs) and Group 2 12f Great Voltigeur Stakes winner and St Leger third Monitor Closely, closely related to the modest 12f winner Apparel (by Cape Cross) and half-sister to the promising 2012 2-y-o 7f winner Singersongwriter (by Raven's Pass), the Group 1 1m Criterium International and Group

1 Eclipse Stakes winner Mount Nelson (by Rock Of Gibraltar), the fairly useful 1m and 10f winner Stone Of Scone (by Pivotal) and the quite useful 9.5f winner Off Message (by In The Wings). The dam won four races at 3 yrs from 7f to 1m including the Group 2 Sun Chariot Stakes and the Group 3 Matron Stakes and is a half-sister to one winner. The second dam, Yukon Hope (by Forty Niner), a fair maiden, was placed five times and is out of a half-sister to Reference Point. *"A good-moving filly, I like her but she'll take a bit of time and is one for August onwards. Whatever she's done so far I'm happy with and I do like her, but I haven't forced anything and she definitely looks more of a seven furlong/mile filly to me".*

1194. EXPECT ★★

b.f. Invincible Spirit – Expressive (Falbrav). March 13. First foal. The dam, a fair 9f winner, is a half-sister to several winners including the Group 1 1m Matron Stakes winner Echelon and the dual Group 2 1m winner Chic. The second dam, winner of the Group 1 1m Coronation Stakes, is a half-sister to the 2,000 Guineas winner and Derby fourth Entrepreneur, the smart Cheshire Oaks winner and Epsom Oaks second Dance a Dream, the very useful middle-distance listed winner Sadler's Image and the useful French 2-y-o listed 7f winner Irish Order. (Cheveley Park Stud). *"She's still at the stud because she had a little setback so I don't know enough about her, but they say she's quite a nice filly and she's about to come into the yard soon".*

1195. GONE WITH THE WIND (GER) ★★★

b.c. Dutch Art – Gallivant (Danehill). March 14. Seventh foal. 115,000Y. Tattersalls October Book 1. Hugo Merry. Closely related to the fair 6f winner Junket (by Medicean) and half-brother to the quite useful dual 6f winner Pumpkin and the poor 4-y-o 1m winner Gay Gallivanter (by Iceman). The dam, a quite useful 2-y-o 6f winner, is a closely related to the smart 2-y-o Group 2 6f Mill Reef Stakes winner Byron and a half-sister to 6 winners including the useful 1m and 10.3f winner Gallant Hero and the Group 3 placed Gallant. The second dam, Gay Gallanta (by Woodman), a very smart winner of the Group 1 6f Cheveley Park Stakes and the Group 3 5f

Queen Mary Stakes, was second in the Group 2 1m Falmouth Stakes and is a half-sister to 10 winners including the Group 2 10f Gallinule Stakes winner Sportsworld. *"A good, strong horse, he's quite lazy but he looks a 2-y-o type. We're just stepping up his work now and I'm hopeful he'll be running by the second half of May. The dam's been disappointing but Dutch Art is a solid stallion and this is a great-looking horse. He definitely looks like a sprinter".*

1196. HEAVENLY ★★★

b.f. Pivotal – Celeste (Green Desert). February 11. Second foal. The dam is an unraced half-sister to the US triple Grade 1 winner Megahertz and the dual Group 3 9f winner Heaven Sent. The second dam, Heavenly Ray (by Rahy), a fairly useful 7f and 1m winner, is a half-sister to 3 winners. (Cheveley Park Stud). *"A good-moving filly, it looks like she'll make a 2-y-o in the second half of the summer and she's a nice type. I haven't done a lot with her but she's athletic, she goes well and looks racey enough".*

1197. IAN'S MEMORY ★★★★

b.br.c. Smart Strike – Rite Moment (Vicar). February 23. Second foal. $235,000Y. Keeneland September. Sackville/Donald. The dam won 6 races in the USA including the Grade 2 Bed O'Roses Handicap and the Grade 2 Distaff Handicap. The second dam, Moments Of Joy (by Lost Code), won 3 minor races in the USA and is a half-sister to 10 winners. *"A bonny horse with strength and scope, I like him, he's a July type 2-y-o and he'll be suited by seven furlongs and a mile this year. A good type by a very good stallion".*

1198. KAGAMI ★★★

ch.c. Teofilo – Sky Wonder (Observatory). April 18. Third foal. 115,000Y. Tattersalls October Book 1. Hugo Merry. Half-brother to the 2012 French 2-y-o dual 1m winner Blissful Thinking (by Oasis Dream) and to the fair 6f (at 2 yrs) and 1m winner Sky Crossing (by Cape Cross). The dam is an unraced half-sister to 6 winners including the high-class Hong Kong horses Mensa and Firebolt and the good broodmare Pizzicato (dam of the Group winners Wunders Dream and Grecian Dancer). The second dam, Musianica (by Music Boy), was a fairly useful 2-y-o dual 6f winner. *"A very athletic, good-moving horse, he's a little bit weak and immature at present but he'll make a 2-y-o from August onwards. Quite a nice horse and as good a mover as I have amongst my 2-y-o's, I think he'll definitely win this year but probably towards the end of the season".*

1199. MARGARET'S MISSION (IRE) ★★★

b.f. Shamardal – Wimple (Kingmambo). February 27. Seventh foal. 310,000Y. Tattersalls October Book 1. Sackville/Donald. Sister to the fairly useful 2-y-o 6f winner and Group 3 Fred Darling Stakes second Sharnberry and half-sister to the fair 2012 2-y-o 7f winner New Falcon (by New Approach), the quite useful 6f (at 2 yrs) and 5f winner Master Rooney (by Cape Cross), the modest 6f winner Jamhara (by Authorized) and a winner in Russia by Daylami. The dam, a useful 5f and 6f winner at 2 yrs, was listed-placed and is a half-sister to 3 winners. The second dam, Tunicle (by Dixieland Band), won 4 minor races in the USA and is a full or half-sister to 5 winners. *"She's grown, changed and gone a bit weak and backward. But when she gets her strength back she has the make and shape to be a 2-y-o. A nice model, it's going to be the back-end of July at the earliest before we see her on the track. She'll want six/seven furlongs this year".*

1200. MERLETTA ★★★

b.f. Raven's Pass – Light Hearted (Green Desert). February 17. Second foal. The dam, a quite useful 6f winner, is a sister to 2 winners including the smart 2-y-o Group 2 6f Mill Reef Stakes winner Byron, closely related to the fairly useful 7f and 1m winner Resort and half-sister to 4 winners including the useful 1m and 10.3f winner Gallant Hero, the fairly useful 9f winner and US Grade 3 placed Gallant and the useful 10.4f listed-placed maiden Gay Heroine. The second dam, Gay Gallanta (by Woodman), a very smart winner of the Group 1 6f Cheveley Park Stakes and the Group 3 5f Queen Mary Stakes, was second in the Group 2 1m Falmouth Stakes and is a half-sister to 11 winners including the smart Group 2 10f Gallinule Stakes winner Sportsworld. (Cheveley Park Stud). *"Quite a racey, mid-summer type 2-y-o for six furlongs. He lacks a bit of action,*

but he's a 2-y-o type with a good mind and he wants to please".

1201. OUTBACK TRAVELLER (IRE) ★★★

b.c. Bushranger – Blue Holly (Blues Traveller). April 6. Seventh foal. 92,000Y. Tattersalls October Book 1. Jeremy Noseda. Half-brother to the quite useful 2012 2-y-o 6f winner Blue Bullet (by Red Clubs), to the 2-y-o Group 3 Molecomb Stakes and dual listed winner and Group 1 Golden Jubilee Stakes second Monsieur Chevalier, the quite useful 2-y-o 5f and subsequent US winner Mister Fips (both by Chevalier), the fair 2-y-o 7f winner Kyanight (by Kodiac) and the modest 2-y-o 5f seller winner Suzieblue (by Redback). The dam, a quite useful 5f (including at 2 yrs) and 6f winner of 5 races, is a half-sister to 5 winners including the listed winner Rockets 'N Rollers. The second dam, Holly Bird (Runnett), won over 12f in Ireland and was listed-placed. *"A strong, sharp, workmanlike 2-y-o type and definitely a sprinter".*

1202. RED VELOUR ★★★★ ♠

ch.f. Pivotal – Regal Velvet (Halling). February 18. Fourth foal. Sister to the 2012 7f placed 2-y-o (in one start) Regal Silk and half-sister to the quite useful 1m winner Robemaker (by Oasis Dream). The dam, a quite useful 10f winner, is a half-sister to 8 winners including the Group 1 6f Cheveley Park Stakes winner Regal Rose and the Japanese dual listed winner Generalist. The second dam, Ruthless Rose (by Conquistador Cielo), ran twice unplaced and is a half-sister to 9 winners including the high-class miler Shaadi. (Cheveley Park Stud). *"She's a nice filly and she should be racing by the back-end of July. A good mover, she's got a bit of quality and what I've seen so far makes me feel quite positive about her. I've got the 3-y-o Regal Silk who could be listed class, but this one is much nicer than her and in a different league".*

1203. SHAMA'S CROWN (IRE) ★★

ch.f. New Approach – Classic Park (Robellino). February 18. Tenth foal. €260,000Y. Goffs Orby. Charlie Gordon-Watson. Closely related to the useful 7f (at 2 yrs) and listed 1m winner Soon and half-sister to the French 2-y-o 1m winner, Group 1 1m Criterium International third and

Epsom Derby second Walk In The Park, to the quite useful dual 2m winner Regal Park (both by Montjeu), the smart 1m winner Secret World (by Spinning World) and the quite useful Irish 6f and 7f winner Mufradat (by Desert Prince). The dam won 3 races including the Irish 1,000 Guineas and is a half-sister to 10 winners including the US Grade 2 winner Rumpipumpy. The second dam, Wanton (by Kris), a useful 2-y-o 5f winner and third in the Group 2 Flying Childers Stakes, is a half-sister to 8 winners including the listed 5f St Hugh's Stakes winner and Group 2 5f Prix du Gros-Chene second Easy Option (herself dam of the dual Group 1 winner Court Masterpiece). *"A big-framed filly with size and scope and she moves well, but she's going to need time and patience".*

1204. THE SILVER KEBAYA (FR) ★★★

b.f. Rock Of Gibraltar – Music House (Singspiel). March 7. Second foal. 68,000Y. Tattersalls October Book 1. Badgers Bloodstock. Closely related to the 2012 French placed 2-y-o L'Empereur (by Holy Roman Emperor). The dam, a French listed-placed 12f winner, is a sister to the French 12f winner and Group 3 placed Crimson And Gold and a half-sister to 2 winners. The second dam, Rosia (by Mr Prospector), is an unplaced half-sister to the very useful listed 10f Predominate Stakes winner Roscius. *"I'm pleased with his filly, she's done well and she's a good mover. I'm tempted to give her a breeze sometime towards the end of April and yet I also want to mind her. If I decide to go with her then it'll be with a view to racing her in May to see if she's good enough for Royal Ascot. If I don't think that's reasonable then I'll take my time".*

1205. YOU'VE GOT IT ★★★

b.f. Sea The Stars – Song (Sadler's Wells). April 10. First foal. The dam is an unraced sister to the Irish 1,000 Guineas winner Yesterday, to the Group 1 7f Moyglare Stud Stakes winner and Irish 1,000 Guineas, Oaks and Irish Oaks placed Quarter Moon and the smart 10f winner and Oaks and Irish Oaks third All My Loving. The second dam, Jude (by Darshaan), a moderate 10f placed maiden, is a sister to the very useful Irish listed 14f winner and Irish Oaks third Arrikala and to the useful

Irish 12f listed winner Alouette (herself dam of the Champion Stakes winner Alborada and the German triple Group 1 winner Albanova) and a half-sister to the very smart Group 2 10f Nassau Stakes and Sun Chariot Stakes winner Last Second (dam of the Irish 2,000 Guineas winner Aussie Rules). *"A good-moving filly, she's going to need a bit of time and the plan is to give her a break in the spring. She'll definitely run this year but probably not before August because she's going to change a lot and improve. She's very athletic and she's a filly with a future, but one that needs time at this stage. I like her but I haven't pushed her hard yet".*

1206. ZESHOV (IRE) ★★★★

b.c. Acclamation – Fathoming (Gulch). February 16. Second foal. 120,000Y. Tattersalls October Book 1. Jeremy Noseda. Brother to the 2012 2-y-o 6f winner and listed-placed Mister Marc. The dam ran once unplaced and is a half-sister to 3 minor winners. The second dam, Ocean Ridge (by Storm Bird), winner of the Group 2 6f Prix Robert Papin and second in the Group 1 1m Coronation Stakes, is a half-sister to 6 winners including the Group 2 Gimcrack Stakes second Fokine. *"One of the 2-y-o's I've done a bit of work with, he's definitely a 2-y-o type and he'll definitely win races, I just need to decide whether to wait for six furlongs or start him at five. He goes nicely and has a good temperament but he's not a typical five furlong horse".*

1207. UNNAMED ★★

gr.c. Duke Of Marmalade – Exotic Mix (Linamix). April 10. Fourth foal. 95,000Y. Tattersalls October Book 1. Kerri Radcliffe. Closely related to the 2012 Group 3 6f Princess Margaret Stakes winner Maureen (by Holy Roman Emperor) and to the fair 7f and 9f winner of 4 races Roedean (by Oratorio) and half-brother to the modest 1m and 10f winner Glass Mountain (by Verglas). The dam, placed once at 3 yrs in France, is a sister to a listed-placed winner and a half-sister to 5 winners including the Group winners Spinola and Shot To Fame. The second dam, Exocet (by Deposit Ticket), won once at 3 yrs in the USA and is a half-sister to 5 winners. *"A good-moving horse with plenty of size and scope. He's a horse I really like but he's one for August onwards. He's light on his feet, more of a 3-y-o type, but he does have a future".*

1208. UNNAMED ★★★★

b.c. Bushranger – Polish Belle (Polish Precedent). March 27. Ninth foal. 220,000Y. Tattersalls October Book 1. Jeremy Noseda. Half-brother to the quite useful 2-y-o 6f winner Jairzihno (by Royal Applause), to the fairly useful 2-y-o dual 6f winner and dual listed-placed Misty Conquest (by Mujadil), the fair 1m and 9f winner Tijori (by Kyllachy) and a winner in Italy by Red Ransom. The dam is an unraced half-sister to 6 winners including the very smart sprinter Danehurst, winner of the Cornwallis Stakes (at 2 yrs), the Curragh Flying Five, the Prix de Seine-et-Oise and the Premio Umbria (all Group 3 events) and the smart Group 3 10.5f Prix Penelope winner Humouresque. The second dam, Miswaki Belle (by Miswaki), second over 7f on her only start, is a half-sister to 9 winners including the smart Group 3 6f Cherry Hinton Stakes winner and 1,000 Guineas third Dazzle. *"He's done his first bit of half-speed, he's a good mover, a very good-looking individual and a strong 'together' horse. He could be a Royal Ascot 2-y-o, he's got a great attitude and he's definitely more of a six furlong horse than five, but he could be running in the first half of May".*

1209. UNNAMED ★★★

b.c. Holy Roman Emperor – Taking Liberties (Royal Academy). March 19. Tenth foal. €80,000Y. Arqana Deauville August. Hugo Merry. Brother to the fair 2-y-o 7f winner Fistful Of Dollars, closely related to the listed 1m winner of 7 races here and in Hong Kong Troubadour, to the fair 2-y-o 6f winner Danapali (both by Danehill) and the fair 10f and 12f winner Mons Calpe (by Rock Of Gibraltar) and half-brother to the fair 1m to 10f winner Eccollo, the French 2-y-o winner and 5f listed-placed Agapimou (both by Spectrum), the quite useful 5-y-o dual 1m winner Saponi and the minor French dual winner Tosca's Impulse (both by Indian Ridge). The dam ran once unplaced and is a sister to the Irish 2-y-o Group 3 1m Futurity Stakes winner Equal Rights and a half-sister to 6 winners including the Australian Grade 3

winner Freedom Fields. The second dam, Lady Liberty (by Noble Bijou), won the Grade 1 12f South Australian Oaks and is a half-sister to 4 winners. *"He's just beginning to come to me now after a weak stage in the winter. He moves well and we need to decide sometime in April whether to kick on with him or not. He's a nice enough horse but temperamentally he gets a bit anxious, so I need him to relax a bit more".*

AIDAN O'BRIEN

1210. COACH HOUSE

b.c. Oasis Dream – Lesson In Humility (Mujadil). February 7. First foal. The dam, a winner of 6 races including the Group 3 6f Ballyogan Stakes, was third in the Group 1 Golden Jubilee Stakes and the Group 1 Prix Maurice de Gheest and is a half-sister to 4 winners including the listed 1m winner Boastful. The second dam, Vanity (by Thatching), is a placed half-sister to 5 winners including the listed winner and smart broodmare Ffestiniog. (Magnier/Tabor/Smith).

1211. CRAFTSMAN

b.c. Mastercraftsman – Weekend Fling (Forest Wildcat). February 17. Third foal. £185,000Y. Doncaster Premier. Eddie Fitzpatrick. The dam, a fair 6f winner at 3 yrs, is a half-sister to the US Grade 1 Arkansas Derby winner Archarcharch and to the US stakes winner Run Sally Run. The second dam, Woodman's Dancer (by Woodman), a winner of 5 races in the USA and Grade 2 placed, is a half-sister to 7 winners including two listed stakes winners.

1212. EXPEDITION (IRE)

b.c. Oasis Dream – Littlefeather (Indian Ridge). May 6. Eighth foal. €25,000Y. Goffs Orby. Demi O'Byrne. Closely related to the 6f winner of 4 races at 3 yrs and listed-placed Bee Eater (by Green Desert) and half-brother to the fair 2-y-o 5f winner Rock Dove (by Danehill), the quite useful dual 9f winner Rare Tern (by Pivotal) and a winner in Greece by Dalakhani. The dam, a very useful 5f (at 2 yrs) and 6f winner of 4 races, was third in the Group 1 7f Moyglare Stakes and is a half-sister to 7 winners including the Cheveley Park Stakes, Irish 1,000 Guineas, Coronation Stakes and Sussex Stakes winner Marling and the good 5f to 1m colt Caerwent, a winner of 4 races and placed in the Prix de l'Abbaye, Irish 2,000 Guineas, St James's Palace Stakes and Vernons Sprint Cup. The second dam, Marwell (by Habitat), was a champion sprinter and won 10 races, notably the July Cup, the Prix de l'Abbaye, the Kings Stand Stakes and the Cheveley Park Stakes.

1213. FOUNTAIN OF YOUTH (IRE)
b.c. Oasis Dream – Attraction (Efisio). April 10. Fifth foal. 420,000Y. Tattersalls October Book 1. Demi O'Byrne. Closely related to the fair 2-y-o 7f winner Elation (by Cape Cross) and half-brother to the quite useful 2012 dual 1m placed Cushion (by Galileo) and the quite useful 2-y-o 1m winner Devastation (by Montjeu). The dam, a high-class 1,000 Guineas, Irish 1,000 Guineas, Coronation Stakes, Matron Stakes and Sun Chariot Stakes winner, is a half-sister to 4 winners. The second dam, Flirtation (by Pursuit Of Love), ran unplaced and is a half-sister to 4 winners including the French listed 12f winner and Group 2 placed Carmita.

1214. FRIENDSHIP
ch.c. Galileo – Squeak (Selkirk). January 8. Half-brother to the moderate 5f winner Illustrious Lad (by Bertolini). The dam, winner of the Group 3 Lancashire Oaks and subsequently the Grade 1 Matriarch Stakes and Grade 1 Matriarch Stakes in the USA, is a half-sister to 7 winners. The second dam, Santa Linda (by Sir Ivor), is an unraced half-sister to 5 winners including the Group 1 Premio Roma winner Noble Saint. (Mrs J Magnier).

1215. GIOVANNI BOLDINI (USA)
b.c. War Front – Dancing Trieste (Old Trieste). February 25. Fourth foal. $675,000Y. Saratoga August. Demi O'Byrne. Half-brother to a minor winner in the USA by Open Forum. The dam is an unplaced half-sister to 3 winners. The second dam, La Promenade (by Southern Halo), a winner and Grade 1 placed in the Argentina, is a sister to two Grade 1 winners in Argentina and a half-sister to another.

1216. HOUSEHOLD CAVALRY
b.c. Oasis Dream – Masskana (Darshaan). March 10. Twelfth foal. 230,000foal. Tattersalls December. Charlie Gordon-Watson. Half-

brother to the very smart Group 1 10f Hong Kong Cup, Group 2 1m Beresford Stakes and Group 2 10f Royal Whip Stakes winner Eagle Mountain (by Rock Of Gibraltar), to the smart 2-y-o Group 1 1m Prix Marcel Boussac winner and Group 1 10f Nassau Stakes second Sulk (by Selkirk), the smart 1m listed winner Wallace (by Royal Academy), the quite useful 10f winner Anna Pallida (by Sadler's Wells) and the modest 9f winner Twilight World (by Night Shift). The dam, a minor 9f and 10f winner in France, is a half-sister to the US Grade 3 Arcadia Handicap winner Madjaristan and the Group 2 Gallinule Stakes winner Massyar. The second dam, Masarika (by Thatch), won the French 1,000 Guineas and the Prix Robert Papin and is a half-sister to 4 winners.

1217. HUMPHREY BOGART (IRE)
b.c. Galileo – Alexander Goldrun (Gold Away). January 28. First foal. 950,000Y. Tattersalls October Book 1. Demi O'Byrne. The dam, a top-class and multiple Group 1 winner of £1.9 million (Nassau Stakes, Pretty Polly Stakes etc), is a half-sister to 5 winners including Group 3 Prix de la Jonchere winner and Group 1 placed Medicis. The second dam, Renashaan (by Darshaan), a listed winner in France, was third in the Group 3 9f Prix Vanteaux and is a half-sister to 4 minor winners.

1218. JOHANN STRAUSS
b.c. High Chaparral – Inchmina (Cape Cross). February 7. First foal. 110,000Y. Tattersalls October Book 1. Demi O'Byrne. The dam is an unraced half-sister to one winner. The second dam, Incheni (by Nashwan), a useful 7f (at 2 yrs) and listed 10f winner, was second in the Group 3 Nell Gwyn Stakes and is a full or half-sister to 7 winners including the triple Group 3 7f winner and sire Inchinor.

1219. JOYA (IRE)
b.f. Galileo – Secrete Marina (Mujadil). April 16. Eighth foal. €280,000Y. Arqana Deauville August. Demi O'Byrne. Half-sister to 3 winners including the Group 2 Prix de Sandringham and triple Group 3 winner Joanna (by High Chaparral) and the Italian dual listed winner and Group 2 Italian Derby second Cazals (by Aussie Rules). The dam, a listed-placed winner of 6 races at 2 to 4 yrs

First crop 2YO's with all the top trainers...

Richard Hannon (x6)   Aidan O'Brien (x4)   Jean-Claude Rouget (x3)

Richard Fahey (x3)   Mark Johnston (x2)   Ed Dunlop (x2)   Mikael Delzangles (x2)

Michael Bell (x2)   David Wachman (x2)   Roger Varian (x2)   Marco Botti (x2)

MASTERCRAFTSMAN

THE BEST SON OF CHAMPION SIRE **DANEHILL DANCER**.

FIRST CROP YEARLINGS SOLD FOR...
€230K, €230K, €210K, €210K, €200K, €155K, €150K, €135K, €130K, €130K, €125K, €120K, €120K, €115K, €105K, €105K.

 COOLMORE   FEE: €12,500

THE LIVING LEGEND RACING PARTNERSHIP

For an inexpensive way to enjoy the benefits of being a racehorse owner, join us in 2013.

Call Steve Taplin on 07754 094204
or e-mail stevetaplin@blueyonder.co.uk

"Excellent app quick and easy to use and place bets."

★★★★★

RACING POST
MOBILE APP

The Racing Post App.
The five-star betting app.

★★★★★*7,714 REVIEWS

in Italy, is out of the unraced Marina Lady (by Riverman), herself a half-sister to 9 winners.

1220. KEYWORD
b.c. Myboycharlie – Time Will Show (Exit To Nowhere). March 22. Sixth foal. 160,000Y. Tattersalls October Book 2. Demi O'Byrne. Half-brother to the 6f, 7f (both at 2 yrs) and listed 1m winner Choose Your Moment (by Choisir), to the quite useful 10f and 12f winner and listed-placed Dragonera (by Doyen), the German 9f to 13f winner Cavan Gael (by Dansili), the German 2-y-o winner Lights On Me (by Kyllachy) and the modest 12f and hurdles winner Maximax (by Linamix). The dam, placed once at 3 yrs in France, is a half-sister to 4 winners including the listed winner Wedding Night. The second dam, Green Field Park (by Akarad), a dual 3-y-o winner in France, herself a half-sister to 8 winners including the Group 2 Prix du Conseil du Paris winner Majorien and the Group 2 Prix de Malleret winner America (herself dam of the Melbourne Cup winner Americain).

1221. MICHAELMAS (USA)
b.c. Elusive Quality – Christmas Kid (Lemon Drop Kid). February 24. First foal. $525,000foal. Keeneland November. T Hyde. The dam won 4 races including the Grade 1 Ashland Stakes and the Grade 2 Davona Dale Stakes and is a half-sister to the US stakes winner Elusive Gift. The second dam, Christmas Gift (by Green Desert), won two Grade 3 events in the USA and is a half-sister to 10 winners.

1222. OKLAHOMA CITY
b.c. Oasis Dream – Galaxy Highflyer (Galileo). April 8. Third foal. 675,000Y. Tattersalls October Book 1. Demi O'Byrne. The dam is an unraced half-sister to 7 winners including Opera House (King George VI and Queen Elizabeth Stakes, Eclipse Stakes, Coronation Cup), Kayf Tara (Ascot Gold Cup and Irish St Leger), Zee Zee Top (Prix de l'Opera and herself dam of the Group 1 winner Izzi Top) and the dam of the Group 1 Moyglare Stud Stakes winner Necklace. The second dam, Colorspin (by High Top), won 3 races notably the Irish Oaks and is a half-sister to 8 winners including the Irish Champion Stakes winner

Cezanne and the Group 2 Prix de l'Opera winner Bella Colora (herself the dam of four stakes winners including the high class colt Stagecraft).

1223. RULER OF FRANCE
b.c. Holy Roman Emperor – Syvilla (Nayef). February 15. First foal. 170,000Y. Tattersalls October Book 1. Demi O'Byrne. The dam, a fairly useful 12f winner, was listed placed over 10f and is a half-sister to 5 winners including the useful La Martina (a 7f winner at 2 yrs in Italy and subsequently a stakes winner in the USA). The second dam, Dance Steppe (by Rambo Dancer), showed no form but is a half-sister to 8 winners including the smart 12f winner Carlingford Rose.

1224. STUBBS (IRE)
b.c. Danehill Dancer – Moonstone (Dalakhani). February 23. Second foal. Closely related to the fairly useful 2012 2-y-o 1m winner Nevis (by Dansili). The dam, winner of the Group 1 Irish Oaks, is closely related to the Breeders Cup second L'Ancresse, to the Group 1 10f Prix Saint-Alary winner Cerulean Sky (herself dam of the Group 2 Doncaster Cup winner Honolulu) and the useful 10f winner and Group 3 placed Qaatef. The second dam, Solo de Lune (by Law Society), a French 11f winner, is a half-sister to 6 winners including the Grade 2 E P Taylor Stakes winner Truly A Dream and the French Group 2 winner Wareed.

1225. SUPPOSING (IRE)
b.f. Invincible Spirit – Landmark (Arch). February 22. Fourth foal. 525,000Y. Tattersalls October Book 1. Demi O'Byrne. Half-sister to the very useful 12f winner and Group 2 Ribblesdale Stakes second Field Of Miracles, to the very useful 9f, 10f and listed 12f winner Cameron Highland (both by Galileo) and the fairly useful dual 10f winner Sour Mash (by Danehill Dancer). The dam, a minor 2-y-o winner in the USA, is a sister to the Grade 1 E P Taylor Stakes and Grade 1 Del Mar Oaks winner Arravale. The second dam, Kalosca (by Kaldoun), won 3 races in France and the USA, was Grade 2 placed and is a half-sister to the listed winners Mykonos and Crillon.

1226. THE DRAUGHTSMAN

b.c. Danehill Dancer – Queen Cleopatra (Kingmambo). March 15. Third foal. Brother to the 2012 Irish 2-y-o 6f winner (from two starts) Francis Of Assisi and to the Irish 7f (at 2yrs) and listed 1m winner and Group 2 10f Blandford Stakes second Look At Me and half-brother to the quite useful 2011 Irish 2-y-o 5f winner Wave (by Dansili). The dam, winner of the Group 3 Irish 1,000 Guineas Trial, was third in the Irish 1,000 Guineas and the Prix de Diane and is a sister to the 2,000 Guineas, Irish 2,000 Guineas, St James's Palace Stakes and Sussex Stakes winner Henrythenavigator. The second dam, Sequoyah (by Sadler's Wells), winner of the Group 1 7f Moyglare Stud Stakes, is a sister to the 2-y-o Group 1 Fillies' Mile winner Listen and a half-sister to the Irish listed 5.6f winner and Group 3 7f placed Oyster Catcher.

1227. WILSHIRE BOULEVARD (IRE)

b.c. Holy Roman Emperor – Tyranny (Machiavellian). February 21. Sixth foal. €130,000Y. Goffs Orby. Demi O'Byrne. Half-brother to the 2-y-o Group 1 6f Phoenix Stakes and Group 3 7f Tyros Stakes winner Zoffany (by Dansili) and to the quite useful 6f winner Queen Of Mean (by Pivotal). The dam, a fairly useful dual 7f winner, is a half-sister to 4 winners including the listed 1m and subsequent US Grade 2 winner Spotlight. The second dam, Dust Dancer (by Suave Dancer), won 4 races including the Group 3 10f Prix de la Nonette and is a half-sister to 6 winners including the Group 3 7.3f Fred Darling Stakes winner Bulaxie (herself dam of the Group 2 winner Claxon) and the dual French listed winner Zimzalabim.

1228. UNNAMED

b.c. Galileo – Again (Danehill Dancer). March 9. First foal. The dam won the 2-y-o Group 1 Moyglare Stud Stakes and the Irish 1,000 Guineas and is closely related to 2 winners including the fairly useful 9f winner and Group 3 12f third Arkadina. The second dam, Cumbres (by Kahyasi), is an unraced half-sister to Montjeu. (Mssrs O'Flynn, Magnier & Tabor).

1229. UNNAMED

b.c. Galileo – Beauty Is Truth (Pivotal). February 11. Third foal. Brother to the Irish 2012 2-y-o 7f debut winner The United States and half-brother to the smart Group 3 6.3f Anglesey Stakes, Group 3 6f Ballyogan Stakes and Group 3 6f Phoenix Sprint Stakes winner and dual Group 1 placed Fire Lily (by Dansili). The dam, winner of the Group 2 5f Prix de Gros-Chene, is a half-sister to numerous winners including the French listed 9f winner Glorious Sight. The second dam, Zelda (by Caerleon), won once over 6.5f in France at 3 yrs, is closely related to the dam of the French 1,000 Guineas winner Valentine Waltz and a half-sister to the Breeders Cup Mile and William Hill Sprint Championship winner Last Tycoon and the Group winners Astronef and The Perfect Life. (Mssrs O'Flynn, Magnier & Tabor).

1230. UNNAMED

b.c. Montjeu – Birmanie (Aldebaran). March 2. First foal. €650,000Y. Arqana Deauville August. Demi O'Byrne. The dam was placed at 2 and 3 yrs and is a half-sister to 3 winners including the multiple US Grade 1 winner English Channel and the US Grade 2 placed Sedgefield. The second dam, Belva (by Theatrical), is an unraced sister to the US Grade 1 winner Pharma and a half-sister to the multiple US Grade 2 winner Hap.

1231. UNNAMED

ch.c. Galileo – Chintz (Danehill Dancer). February 8. First foal. The dam was a useful winner of the 2-y-o Group 3 7f C L Weld Park Stakes and is a half-sister to 3 winners. The second dam, Gold Dodger (by Slew O'Gold), a listed 10f winner of 2 races in France, is a half-sister to 9 winners including the French Group winners Prospect Wells and Prospect Park. (Derrick Smith).

1232. UNNAMED

b.c. Galileo – Dietrich (Storm Cat). April 9. Brother to the useful 2012 Irish 2-y-o 7f winner The Ferryman and to the useful 2-y-o 7f winner Eskimo and half-brother to the Irish 5f (at 2 yrs) and Group 3 6f winner Beauty Bright, the fair 7f winner Port Of Spain (both by Danehill), the Irish 2-y-o 7f winner and Group 3 6f second Marquesa, the fairly useful Irish 7f winner Greatwallofchina (both by

Kingmambo). The dam won the Group 3 5f King George Stakes and Group 3 5f Ballyogan Stakes. The second dam, Piquetnol (by Private Account), a French 3-y-o winner and second in the Group 1 Prix Marcel Boussac, is a sister to the dual Group 1 winner Chimes of Freedom (the dam of two Grade 1 winners) and a half-sister to the multiple US Grade 1 winner Denon and the dam of Spinning World. (Mrs J Magnier).

1233. UNNAMED
b.c. Galileo – Elletelle (Elnadim). February 19. First foal. The dam, a 2-y-o Group 2 5f Queen Mary Stakes winner and third in the Group 1 6f Phoenix Stakes, is a half-sister to the German listed 10f winner of 3 races Freedom. The second dam, Flamanda (Niniski), was placed over 9.5f here prior to winning 5 races at 4 yrs in Germany from 1m to 9f and is a half-sister to 8 winners. (Derrick Smith).

1235. UNNAMED
ch.c. Giant's Causeway – Galleon Of Gold (Gone West). March 19. Fourth foal. $210,000Y. Keeneland September. Demi O'Byrne. Half-brother to 2 winners including the US Grade 1 Princess Rooney Handicap and dual Grade 2 winner Game Face (by Menifee). The dam is an unraced half-sister to the US stakes winner and dual Grade 3 placed Holzmeister. The second dam, Harbour Club (by Danzig), a US stakes winner, was second in three Grade 1 stakes.

1236. UNNAMED
b.c. Montjeu – Helsinki (Machiavellian). February 18. Half-brother to the Dewhurst Stakes, French 2,000 Guineas, French Derby and St James's Palace Stakes winner Shamardal, to the fairly useful 10f and 12f winner Yorgunnabelucky (by Giant's Causeway) and the modest 7f winner Lushs Lad (by Wolfhound). The dam, listed placed over 10f at 3 yrs in France, is a sister to the Dubai World Cup and US Grade 1 winner Street Cry and a half-sister to 7 winners including the useful 8.3f to 11.6f winner Grecian Slipper (herself dam of the Group 3 winners Magna Graecia and Graikos). The second dam, Helen Street (by Troy), won 3 races including the Irish Oaks. (M Tabor).

1237. UNNAMED
b.c. Montjeu – Honorlina (Linamix). February 26. Second foal. 450,000Y. Tattersalls October Book 1. Demi O'Byrne. The dam, a French 2-y-o 1m winner, is a sister to the French 2,000 Guineas winner Vahorimix and to the French listed winner Vadalix and a half-sister to 4 winners. The second dam, Vadsa Honor (by Highest Honor), won the listed Prix de Thiberville and is a half-sister to 12 winners including the dam of the Breeders Cup Mile winner Val Royal.

1238. UNNAMED
b.c. Oasis Dream – I'm In Love (Zafonic). April 27. Second foal. 135,000Y. Tattersalls December. Demi O'Byrne. Half-brother to the US Grade 3 Miesque Stakes winner More Than Love (by More Than Ready). The dam, a quite useful 7f to 9f winner, subsequently won in the USA and was second in the Grade 3 Athenia Stakes and is a half-sister to 5 winners. The second dam, Bank On Her (by Rahy), a 7f winner at 3 yrs, is a half-sister to 7 winners including the listed winner and Group 2 placed Weldnaas.

1239. UNNAMED
b.c. Montjeu – Jewel In The Sand (Bluebird). April 4. Fourth foal. €500,000Y. Goffs Orby. Demi O'Byrne. Half-brother to the fair 2012 2-y-o 5f winner Dansili Dual (by Dansili) and to the fair 2-y-o winner The Rising (by Pivotal). The dam, a winner of 4 races including the Group 2 6f Cherry Hinton Stakes and the Albany Stakes, is a half-sister to 4 winners including the German 3-y-o listed 6f winner Davignon. The second dam, Dancing Drop (by Green Desert), a useful dual 2-y-o 6f winner, was listed-placed and is a half-sister to 9 winners.

1240. UNNAMED
b.c. Galileo – Khoruna (Lagunas). April 12. Twelfth foal. Half-brother to four winners including the 1,000 Guineas, Oaks and Flower Bowl Invitational winner Kazzia (by Zinaad and herself dam of the Group 1 Dubai Sheema Classic winner Eastern Anthem) and the German listed winner Kimbajar (by Royal Abjar). The dam won 2 minor races at 2 and 4 yrs in Germany and is a half-sister to one

winner. The second dam, Khora (by Corvaro), is an unraced half-sister to 6 winners including the Group 1 Puma Europa-Preis winner Kamiros II. (Mrs J Magnier).

1241. UNNAMED

b.c. Galileo – Looking Back (Stravinsky). January 4. Brother to A Star Is Born (unplaced in one start at 2 yrs in 2012) and to the Sussex Stakes, Queen Elizabeth II Stakes and Juddmonte International winner Rip Van Winkle and half-brother to the Italian Group 3 1m winner Le Vie Infinite (by La Vie Dei Colori). The dam, an Italian winner of 2 races at 2 and 3 yrs and listed-placed, is a half-sister to 2 winners. The second dam, Mustique Dream (by Don't Forget Me), a quite useful dual 1m winner, is a half-sister to 6 winners. (Derrick Smith).

1242. UNNAMED

b.c. Montjeu – Love Me True (Kingmambo). April 8. Closely related to the quite useful 2-y-o 7f winner So In Love With You (by Sadler's Wells) and half-brother to the multiple Group 1 10f to 12f winner Duke Of Marmalade (by Danehill), the US Group 3 placed Countess Lemonade and the quite useful 2-y-o 6f winner Looking Lovely (both by Storm Cat). The dam, an Irish 1m winner, was third in the Group 3 Killavullan Stakes and is a half-sister to the Grade 2 Sanford Stakes winner Bite The Bullet and the smart listed 10f winner Shuailaan. The second dam, Lassie's Lady (by Alydar), a stakes-placed winner in the USA, is a half-sister to 10 winners including the dual US Grade 3 winner Weekend Surprise, the high-class sprinter Wolfhound, the US stakes winner Spectacular Spy and the French Group 3 placed Foxhound.

1243. UNNAMED

b.c. Montjeu – Marquesa (Kingmambo). February 17. First foal. The dam, an Irish 2-y-o 7f winner and second in the Group 3 6f Swordlestown Stud Sprint Stakes, is a sister to the fairly useful Irish 7f winner Greatwallofchina and a half-sister to 4 winners including the Irish Group 3 6f Renaissance Stakes winner Beauty Bright. The second dam, Dietrich (by Storm Cat), won the Group 3 5f King George Stakes and Group 3 5f Ballyogan Stakes.

1244. UNNAMED

b.f. Invincible Spirit – Miss Dela (King's Best). February 15. Third foal. 300,000Y. Tattersalls October Book 1. Demi O'Byrne. The dam, a modest Irish 7f placed maiden, is a half-sister to 6 winners including the 2-y-o Group 3 7f Somerville Tattersall Stakes winner and Group 1 placed Governor Brown and the smart 2-y-o listed 1m and 3-y-o listed 10.4f winner Hataab. The second dam, Miss Mistletoes (by The Minstrel), a listed-placed winner of 2 races over 7f and 9f at 3 yrs in Ireland, is a half-sister to the Irish Group 3 Killavullen Stakes winner Lomond Blossom and to the dam of the Australian Group 1 winner Zagalia.

1245. UNNAMED

ch.c. Galileo – One Moment In Time (Danehill). February 20. The dam is an unraced sister to the Group 1 Fillies' Mile and Group 1 Falmouth Stakes winner Simply Perfect and closely related to one winner. The second dam, Hotelgenie Dot Com (by Selkirk), a 7f winner at 2 yrs, was second in the Group 1 7f Moyglare Stud Stakes and third in the Group 1 Fillies' Mile and is a half-sister to 4 winners including the Moyglare Stud Stakes and the Group 2 6f Lowther Stakes winner Bianca Nera. (Derrick Smith).

1246. UNNAMED

ch.c. Galileo – Ouija Board (Cape Cross). April 8. Fourth foal. 525,000Y. Tattersalls October Book 1. Demi O'Byrne. Half-brother to the quite useful 1m and 10f winner Voodoo Prince (by Kingmambo). The dam was a top-class winner of 10 races from 7f (at 2 yrs) to 12f including seven Group/Grade 1 races and is a half-sister to 6 winners. The second dam, Selection Board (by Welsh Pageant), was placed over 7f at 2 yrs and is a sister to the top-class Queen Elizabeth II Stakes and Budweiser Arlington Million winner Teleprompter and a half-sister to 5 winners. (Mssrs O'Flynn, Magnier & Tabor).

1247. UNNAMED

gr.c. Tapit – Que Belle (Seattle Dancer). May 5. Tenth foal. $500,000Y. Keeneland September. Demi O'Byrne. Half-brother to 4 winners including the US Grade 3 winner and Grade 2 placed Osidy (by Storm Cat) and the Group

3 Prix de Royaumont winner Quetsche (by Gone West). The dam, a winner of 4 races including the Group 2 German Oaks, was Group 1 placed three times and is a half-sister to 19 winners. The second dam, Qui Bid (by Spectacular Bid), is an unraced sister to the US Grade 3 winner Sum and a half-sister to 9 winners including the Group 1 winner and champion 2-y-o colt Bakharoff and the Group 2 winner Emperor Jones.

1248. UNNAMED

b.c. Galileo – Red Evie (Intikhab). February 18. Third foal. Brother to the 2012 Group 3 7f C L Weld Park Stakes winner Magical Dream. The dam won 9 races including the Group 1 1m Matron Stakes and the Group 1 1m Lockinge Stakes. The second dam, Malafemmena (by Nordico), winner of a listed event in Italy and third in the Group 3 Prix du Calvados, is a half-sister to 7 winners including the smart Group 3 5f Prix du Bois and Group 3 6f Prix de Ris-Orangis winner Export Price. (Derrick Smith).

1249. UNNAMED

b.c. Holy Roman Emperor – Rumored (Royal Academy). March 1. Seventh foal. €250,000Y. Arqana Deauville August. Demi O'Byrne. Half-brother to 4 winners including the Group 1 Prix Morny and Group 1 Prix Jean-Luc Lagardere winner Dabirsim (by Hat Trick) and the US stakes-placed winner Preferred Yield (by High Yield). The dam is a placed half-sister to 7 winners out of the Italian Oaks winner and Group 1 Moyglare Stud Stakes second Bright Generation (by Rainbow Quest).

1250. UNNAMED

b.f. Galileo – Shadow Song (Pennekamp). May 1. Fifth foal. 1,300,000Y. Tattersalls October Book 1. Demi O'Byrne. Sister to the 2-y-o Group 3 7f Silver Flash Stakes winner, multiple Group 1 placed and subsequent US Grade 1 9f winner Together and closely related to the promising 2012 2-y-o 7f winner Kingdom and to the 2-y-o Group 1 1m Criterium International winner and Irish Derby third Jan Vermeer (both by Montjeu). The dam won once at 3 yrs in France and is a half-sister to 7 winners including the Group 3 May Hill Stakes winner Midnight Air (herself dam of the Group 3 and subsequent US Grade 2 winner

Midnight Line) and to the placed dam of the Group 1 Prix de l'Abbaye winner Imperial Beauty. The second dam, Evening Air (by J O Tobin), is an unraced half-sister to 5 winners including the Irish Derby Trial second Ancient Times.

1251. UNNAMED

b.c. Galileo – Simply Perfect (Danehill). January 10. Brother to the fair 2-y-o 1m winner Really Lovely. The dam won the Group 1 Fillies' Mile and the Group 1 Falmouth Stakes. The second dam, Hotelgenie Dot Com (by Selkirk), a 7f winner at 2 yrs, was second in the Group 1 7f Moyglare Stud Stakes and third in the Group 1 Fillies' Mile and is a half-sister to 4 winners including the Moyglare Stud Stakes and the Group 2 6f Lowther Stakes winner Bianca Nera. (Mssrs O'Flynn, Magnier & Tabor).

1252. UNNAMED

b.c. Bernardini – Wilshewed (Carson City). February 22. Sixth foal. $1,550,000Y. Keeneland September. Demi O'Byrne. Half-brother to 4 winners by Stormy Atlantic including the Grade 1 Hollywood Futurity winner Stormello. The dam was placed at 3 yrs in the USA and is half-sister to 9 winners including four stakes winners. The second dam, So Cozy (by Lyphard), was a 2-y-o stakes winner in the USA.

1253. UNNAMED

b.c. Galileo – Withorwithoutyou (Danehill). April 4. Half-brother to the Group 1 6f Golden Jubilee Stakes and Group 2 6f Coventry Stakes winner and Group 1 6f Phoenix Stakes second Art Connoisseur (by Lucky Story). The dam, a quite useful 2-y-o 7f winner, is a half-sister to 2 winners. The second dam, Morningsurprice (by Future Storm), is an unraced half-sister to 5 winners including the high-class broodmare Morning Devotion (dam of the Oaks and Irish Derby winner Balanchine and the Group 2 winners Romanov and Red Slippers). (Mssrs O'Flynn, Magnier & Tabor).

JAMIE OSBORNE

1254. ALMOST FAMOUS (IRE) ★★★

b.c. Acclamation – Array Of Stars (Barathea). March 1. Third foal. €37,000Y. Tattersalls Ireland September. Half-brother to Cape Glory (by Cape Cross), placed fourth over 1m on his only start at 2 yrs in Ireland in 2012. The dam, a modest Irish 4-y-o 9f winner, is a half-sister to 3 winners including the Group 2 Beresford Stakes third Going Public. The second dam, Gifts Galore (by Darshaan), is a 1m placed half-sister to 7 winners. (M A C Buckley). *"A nice, quality colt with a bit of scope, he's doing little bits of work at the moment but I can't imagine he's going to be that early. Hopefully he'll be out by the end of May and he seems to go OK. He's an Acclamation, which can't be bad, but he was at the cheaper end of the sire's yearlings. A good-looking horse and quite typical of his sire".*

1255. FEISTY DRAGON (IRE) ★★

b.f. Camacho – Ejder (Indian Ridge). March 12. Sixth foal. €12,000Y. Tattersalls Ireland September. Jamie Osborne. Half-sister to the fair 5f and 6f winner Brazilian Brush (by Captain Rio). The dam is an unplaced half-sister to 6 winners including the Italian dual listed winner and Group 2 placed Nenna. The second dam, Eskaroon (by Artaius), is an unraced half-sister to 8 winners. (Cavendish Star Racing). *"A sharp, strong little filly, she should be early and she's straightforward. She goes OK and five or six furlongs will be fine for her".*

1256. HARDY BLACK (IRE) ★★★★

b.c. Pastoral Pursuits – Wondrous Story (Royal Academy). February 14. Fourth foal. 50,000Y. Tattersalls October Book 2. Anthony Stroud. Half-brother to the very useful 2-y-o listed 7f winner and Group 3 7f Greenham Stakes third Bronterre (by Oasis Dream). The dam, a quite useful 2-y-o 7f winner, is closely related to a winner in the USA by Caerleon and a half-sister to 5 winners including the very useful 6f Cherry Hinton Stakes, 7f Rockfel Stakes and 7.3f Fred Darling Stakes winner Musicale and the 2-y-o 1m winner and Group 2 12f King Edward VII Stakes third Theatre Script. The second dam, Gossiping (by Chati), a minor winner over 6f in the USA at 3 yrs, is a half-sister to 5 winners including the high-class sprinter and smart broodmare Committed (herself dam of the US Grade 1 winner Pharma). (Patrick Gage & Tony Taylor). *"A colt*

with a lot of quality, he does things very easily, he's got quite a bit of scope and doesn't have the physique of an early 2-y-o but he's taking what I can throw at him and doing it nicely. A very nice horse, he'd be my pick of the bunch at the moment. He cost quite a bit for a Pastoral Pursuits but the dam has already bred a good horse, this colt is exceptionally good-looking and his work so far would appear to be in line with that. He's showing enough speed to start at six furlongs, so hopefully I'll have him ready for when those races start".*

1257. HARDY PINK (IRE) ★★★

b.f. Clodovil – Secret Circle (Magic Ring). April 30. Tenth foal. 35,000Y. Tattersalls October Book 3. Anthony Stroud. Sister to the fairly useful 5f (at 2 yrs) and 6f winner of 5 races Alben Star and to the 2013 3-y-o 6f winner Two In The Pink and half-sister to the fairly useful 5f and 7f winner of 7 races Secret Place (by Compton Place), the quite useful 6f and 7f winner of 5 races Ektimaal (by Bahamian Bounty), the fair 6f (at 2 yrs) and 7f winner So Surreal (by Avonbridge), the fair dual 1m winner Ambrosiano (by Averti), the fair 2-y-o 6f winner Full Of Nature (by Monsieur Bond) and the winner of 10 minor races in France and Germany, Secret Affair (by Piccolo). The dam is an unraced half-sister to 8 winners including the Group 1 1m St James's Palace Stakes winner Bijou d'Inde. The second dam, Pushkar (by Northfields), is an unraced half-sister to the Group 3 1m Brownstown Stakes winner Red Chip. (Tony Taylor & Patrick Gage). *"A good-looking filly, she's a good mover from a good family. Probably not as precocious as I thought she'd be and is one for the second half of the season. When she does run she'll be quick, but she has a bit of scope too and she goes OK".*

1258. SUMMERSAULT (IRE) ★★

b.c. Footstepsinthesand – Sumingasefa (Danehill). May 4. Sixth living foal. €22,000Y. Tattersalls Ireland September. BBA (Ire). Half-brother to the quite useful 2-y-o dual 7f winner Famcred (by Inchinor) and to the Italian winner of 7 races at 3 to 5 yrs Fagutela (by Dr Fong). The dam, a listed-placed winner of 5 races in Italy, is a half-sister to 7 winners. The second dam, Svanzega (by Sharpen Up), winner of the Group 3 Premio Baggio, was third in the Group 2 Premio Lydia Tesio and is a half-sister to 8 winners. *"He's done a lot of growing so he'll be one for the second half of the season. He's just been cantering, he's going to be quite tall and he'll take a bit of time, so I'd say he'll be a seven furlong 2-y-o later in the season".*

1259. THEWANDAOFU (IRE) ★★★★

b.f. Clodovil – Sweet Times (Riverman). March 21. Eleventh foal. 16,000Y. Tattersalls October Book 3. Jamie Osborne. Half-sister to the 2-y-o Group 3 Killavullan Stakes winner Stonemason (by Nureyev), to the fair 9f to 11f winner Shakalaka (by Montjeu), the fair 6f (at 2 yrs) to 12f winner of 10 races Pelham Crescent (by Giant's Causeway) and the French 2m and jumps winner Saddler's Times (by Sadler's Wells). The dam, a moderate 6f placed 3-y-o, is a sister to the Group 3 7f Jersey Stakes winner and US Grade 2 placed River Deep and a half-sister to 5 winners including the US stakes winner Dreamer. The second dam, Affection Affirmed (by Affirmed), won 4 races in the USA and is a half-sister to 6 winners including the dam of the dual Group 1 winner Zoman. (From The Stables Partnership). *"She's sharp, she shows plenty of speed and for a filly with a pretty decent pedigree she was relatively cheap. She'll start her career in April and shows enough speed for five furlongs even though there are stamina influences there. One for five and six furlongs, she shows plenty of boot".* TRAINERS' BARGAIN BUY

1260. UNNAMED ★★★

b.c. Dandy Man – Bronze Queen (Invincible Spirit). May 4. Second foal. €28,000Y. Tattersalls Ireland September. Jamie Osborne. The dam is an unplaced half-sister to one winner. The second dam, Sheba (by Lycius), won twice at 2 yrs in France and is a half-sister to 4 winners including the Group 3 Prix Vanteaux winner and US Grade 1 third Campsie Fells. (Chris Watkins & David Reynolds). *"He's quite sharp and he looks very strong and forward. He's doing bits of work at the moment and he goes OK. So far so good, he was a May foal but he doesn't look it by any means".*

1261. UNNAMED ★★★★

b.f. Royal Applause – Child Bride (Coronado's Quest). April 7. Seventh foal. 25,000Y. Tattersalls October Book 2. Jamie Osborne. Half-sister to the US Grade 2 12f and 14f winner Juniper Pass (by Lemon Drop Kid), to two minor winners in the USA by Out Of Place and Holy Bull and a minor winner in Argentina by Theatrical. The dam is an unraced half-sister to 6 winners including the dam of the US Grade 2 winner Postponed and to the dam of the Group 1 Racing Post Trophy winner Crowded House. The second dam, Chapel Of Dreams (by Northern Dancer), won 7 races in the USA including two Grade 2 events and is a half-sister to 5 winners including the Grade 1 winner and top-class sire Storm Cat. *"She goes well, she's strong and forward and shows a fair bit of speed. Looking at the dam's side she's probably not bred to be a five furlong filly so I'll probably wait for the six furlong races and she'd have enough speed for that. She's all 2-y-o and she goes nicely".*

1262. UNNAMED ★★★

b.c. Lawman – Flaming Song (Darshaan). February 18. Eleventh foal. €26,000Y. Goffs Orby. Jamie Osborne. Half-brother to the very smart German 10f Group winners Fight Club (by Laverco) and Flambo (by Platini), the fairly useful dual 7f winner Bullwhip (by Whipper), the fair Irish 10f winner Slan Abhaile (by Montjeu) and two minor winners in Germany by Winged Love and Poliglote. The dam, a 2-y-o winner in France, is a half-sister to 2 other minor winners. The second dam, Pale Blue (by Kris), was listed-placed and is a half-sister to 7 winners. (Dean Margolis & J O'Connor). *"He's done very well since the sale. There's nothing in his pedigree to suggest he'd be a five furlong type so I won't be in too much of a rush with him, but he looks a 2-y-o. His breeder John O'Connor has kept half of him because he likes him and I like him as well".*

JOHN OXX

1263. AFFINISEA (IRE) ★★★

b.c. Sea The Stars – Affianced (Erins Isle). March 22. Eighth foal. €850,000foal. Goffs November. Sunderland Holding Inc. Half-brother to the 1m (at 2 yrs) and Group 1 Irish Derby, Group 1 Coronation Cup, Group 2 Prix

Niel and Group 2 Prix Noailles winner Soldier Of Fortune, to the smart 7f (at 2 yrs) and Group 3 10f Meld Stakes winner Heliostatic, the minor Irish 10f winner Singe The Turf (all by Galileo), the useful listed 10f winner Carraiglawn (by Rock Of Gibraltar) and the quite useful Irish dual 10f winner Ard Fheis (by Lil's Boy). The dam, a useful 7f listed (at 2 yrs) and 10f winner in Ireland, is a half-sister to the Group 1 1m Gran Criterium winner Sholokhov and to 4 other stakes horses. The second dam, La Meillure (by Lord Gayle), a listed winner and Group 3 placed in Ireland, is a half-sister to 8 winners. (Christopher Tsui). *"A very nice horse that cost a lot of money as a foal, he's fluent, has a lovely temperament and is a beautiful mover. Obviously he's bred to be a back-end 2-y-o and he had a little setback in January which held him up a bit. He's very promising, but we'd be happy if he just had the one run at end of the season".*

1264. ALYASAN (IRE) ★★★
ch.c. Sea The Stars – Alaya (Ela-Mana-Mou). April 1. Half-brother to the dual 7f (at 2 yrs) and Group 3 10f Mooresbridge Stakes winner Alayan (by Sri Pekan), to the very useful listed 12f winner and Grade 2 winning hurdler Alaivan (by Kalanisi), the useful 2-y-o 1m winner and Group 2 10f Royal Whip Stakes second Alarazi (by Spectrum) and the fair Irish 12f winner Alayir (by Azamour). The dam won over 12f in Ireland and is a half-sister to 4 winners including the Irish Derby and King George winner Alamshar. The second dam, Alaiyda (by Shahrastani), a minor Irish 3-y-o 10f winner, is a half-sister to the smart Group 3 1m Craven Stakes winner and Group 2 10.4f Dante Stakes second Desert Story (by Green Desert). (H H Aga Khan). *"Alaya has been a good mare and she's bred useful horses by all sorts of stallions. It's a family that tend not to do much until they're 3-y-o's and he's not the pick of my Sea The Stars 2-y-o's on looks, but he's alright and there's certainly nothing wrong with him. We like him and he'll be out in the autumn".*

1265. AWESOME STAR (IRE) ★★★
b.c. Sea The Stars – Always Awesome (Awesome Again). April 19. Fifth foal. Half-brother to the quite useful dual 10f and

subsequent French 9f winner and listed-placed Street Secret (by Street Cry). The dam, a stakes-placed winner in Canada, is a half-sister to 7 winners including the Group 1 Deuschland Preis winner Anzillero. The second dam, Anzille (by Plugged Nickle), is a placed half-sister to the Prix de l'Arc de Triomphe winner and outstanding broodmare Urban Sea and the 2,000 Guineas winner King's Best. (Mr C E Fipke). *"A well-bred horse, in fact he's in-bred to Allegretta who is the dam of Urban Sea. He's lighter and not as big and strong as the others I have by Sea The Stars but he has the same good temperament and the fluent action. He doesn't look like a backward horse, so hopefully he'll out just after mid-season".*

1266. AZAMA (IRE) ★★
b.f. Sea The Stars – Asmara (Lear Fan). February 5. Half-sister to the Group 1 St James's Palace Stakes and Group 1 Irish Champion Stakes winner Azamour (by Night Shift), to the 2-y-o Group 2 7f Futurity Stakes winner and Group 1 National Stakes third Arazan (by Anabaa), the useful 2-y-o 7f winner and Group 3 placed Surveyor, the Irish 2-y-o 7f winner Ahsanabad (both by Muhtarram), the fairly useful Irish 7f winner Ardistan (by Selkirk), the quite useful 7f winner Arawan (by Entrepreneur), the Irish 2-y-o dual 7f winner Arameen (by Halling) and the fair Irish 14f and hurdles winner Ardalan (by Sinndar). The dam, a useful winner in Ireland at up to 10f, is a half-sister to the high-class Prix Ganay and Prix d'Harcourt winner Astarabad. The second dam, Anaza (by Darshaan), only ran at 2 yrs when she was a useful 1m winner in France. (H H Aga Khan). *"A very nice filly, but she is quite backward and won't be out until the autumn. The mare can get 2-y-o's and we don't know what the sire is capable of doing yet, he may well get plenty of 2-y-o winners, but this filly has a backward look to her".*

1267. BALANSIYA (IRE) ★★★
b.f. Shamardal – Baliyana (Dalakhani). February 11. First foal. The dam won the Group 3 Irish 1,000 Guineas Trial and is a half-sister to numerous winners including the very smart Group 2 10f King Edward VII Stakes winner Balakheri. The second dam, Balanka (by Alzao), a French listed winner and third in

the Group 2 9.2f Prix de l'Opera, is a half-sister to 7 winners. (H H Aga Khan). *"A nice filly that could make a 2-y-o in July. She's a fluent mover and I like her".*

1268. DUNURE HARBOUR ★★★

ch.c. Dubawi – Hobby (Robellino). February 19. First foal. 85,000Y. Tattersalls October Book 1. BBA (Ire). The dam, a useful 2-y-o 7f winner on her debut, was third in the Group 2 12f Ribblesdale Stakes and is a half-sister to one winner abroad. The second dam, Wydah (by Suave Dancer), is an unraced half-sister to 5 winners including the Irish listed winner Golden Temple. (Mr T Barr). *"A very nice, correct, good-moving colt. He'll be a horse for the mid-season onwards, Dubawi can get winners at all sorts of distances and I'd expect this colt to get eight to ten furlongs eventually".*

1269. EBANORAN (IRE) ★★★

b.c. Oasis Dream – Ebadiyla (Sadler's Wells). March 13. Closely related to the useful 1m winner and Group 1 National Stakes third Eyshal (by Green Desert) and half-brother to the useful Irish 10f winner Ehsan (by Sinndar), the dual 12f and very smart hurdles winner Ebaziyan (by Daylami), the fairly useful 9f winner Ebashan (by King's Best) and the quite useful 12f winner Ebalista (by Selkirk). The dam won the Group 1 Irish Oaks and the Group 1 Prix Royal-Oak and is a half-sister to the smart Group 1 7f Moyglare Stud Stakes winner Edabiya and the high-class Ascot Gold Cup winner Enzeli. The second dam, Ebaziya (by Darshaan), won from 7f (at 2 yrs) to 12f including three listed races and was third in the Group 2 12f Blandford Stakes. (H H Aga Khan). *"It's a family that takes a bit of time but they can show a bit at two and he's a nice-looking horse that's done well since we broke him. I like him, he's a good sort and could be a mid-season 2-y-o. The three-parts brother Eyshal by Green Desert ended up a stakes winner in Hong Kong and the family could do with that bit of an injection of speed".*

1270. ERINIYA ★★★★

b.f. Acclamation – Erdiyna (Selkirk). February 24. First foal. The dam, a quite useful 9f and 12f winner, is a half-sister to one winner. The second dam, Ebareva (by Machiavellian) was

an unraced half-sister to the Group 1 winners Edabiya, Ebadiyla and Enzeli. (H H Aga Khan). *"A good-looking filly and quite correct, she could be one for July, she's straightforward to deal with and hopefully we can press on with her shortly. The mating of this filly is a good example of the project whereby a few of the Aga Khan mares have recently been bred to sires likely to inject speed and precocity into the pedigree".*

1271. FOREST OF SEAS (IRE) ★★★

b.br.f. Sea The Stars – Epping (Charnwood Forest). April 24. Eighth foal. Half-sister to the smart 10f winner and Group 1 St Leger second The Last Drop, to the useful Irish 2-y-o 7f winner and listed-placed Nebula Storm, the quite useful 12f, 2m and hurdles winner Ardlui (all by Galileo) and the minor French 3-y-o 1m winner Cherry Orchard (by King's Best). The dam, a quite useful 3-y-o 7f winner, is a half-sister to 5 winners including the French listed winner and multiple Group-placed Self Defense. The second dam, Dansara (by Dancing Brave), is an unraced half-sister to 10 winners including the Irish Oaks winner Princess Pati and the Great Voltigeur Stakes winner Seymour Hicks. (Christopher Tsui). *"A nice filly that's had a few minor setbacks so she won't be early, but she's very strong and very correct. A good sort for the second half of the year and she's a good-looker".*

1272. GENTRY (IRE) ★★★

ch.c. Nayef – Elegant Way (Cape Cross). April 19. First foal. The dam, a fair French 1m winner, is a half-sister to the very smart Group 3 5f Palace House Stakes winner Dandy Man. The second dam, Lady Alexander (by Night Shift), a very useful winner of the Group 3 6.3f Anglesey Stakes and the Group 3 5f Molecomb Stakes, is a half-sister to 2 winners. (Sheikh Mohammed). *"He's a nice-looking horse and a good mover with a relaxed temperament. I like him but those Nayef's are not early, so he's one for July or August onwards. Although there's some speed in the family my experience with Nayef is that he tends to dominate!"*

1273. HAZARABA (IRE) ★★★★

b.f. Oasis Dream – Hazariya (Xaar). February 19. Fourth foal. Half-sister to the 2012 2-y-o

Group 3 7f Silver Flash Stakes winner Harasiya (by Pivotal), to the useful dual 10f winner and Group 3 second Haziyna (by Halling) and the useful listed 12f winner Hazarafa (by Daylami). The dam, winner of the Group 3 7f Athasi Stakes and a listed event over 7f, is a half-sister to the Group 3 Blue Wind Stakes winner Hazarista and a half-sister to numerous minor winners. The second dam, Hazaradjat (by Darshaan), won twice at 2 and 3 yrs and is a half-sister to 10 winners including the Group 1 Flying Childers Stakes winner Hittite Glory. (H H Aga Khan). *"A lovely filly, she's having a break now having had a little setback but she's particularly nice, very promising and Hazariya is a good mare. One for the autumn and I'd have quite high hopes for her".*

1274. JUPITER AND MARS (IRE) ★★
b.c. *Sea The Stars – Hill Of Snow (Reference Point)*. June 3. Twelfth foal. 75,000Y. Tattersalls October Book 1. Rob Speers. Half-brother to the Group 3 Lingfield Derby Trial winner Kong, to the useful listed 14f winner Mount Kilimanjaro and the fair 12f and 13f winner Big Game Hunter (all by Sadler's Wells), to the smart 2-y-o Group 1 7f Moyglare Stud Stakes winner Preseli, the fair 10f winner Valley Of Song (both by Caerleon) and the smart 7f winner and 1,000 Guineas second Snowfire (by Machiavellian). The dam, an Irish 10f winner, is a half-sister to 5 winners including the smart Group 2 Prix de Pomone winner Whitehaven. The second dam, White Star Line (by Northern Dancer), won 3 Grade 1 events in the USA and is a half-sister to the Prix Morny winner Filiberto and to the dam of the Group/Grade 1 winners Northern Trick and On The Sly. (Miss Pinar Araci). *"He's a fine colt and one of the cheapest Sea The Stars at the sales for the simple reason that he was a very late foal. He was big to begin with so I think everyone thought he'd end up huge, but he hasn't grown much since the sales and he's still a fine-looking horse with a lovely temperament and he's a great galloper. Time will tell because he may start to grow in the summer, but we took a punt at the price and so far it looks like a gamble that might pay off".*

1275. KAREZAK (IRE) ★★★★
b.c. *Azamour – Karawana (King's Best)*. March

7. Fourth foal. Half-brother to the fairly useful 2012 Irish 2-y-o 6f winner Karamaya (by Invincible Spirit) and to the fairly useful 10f winner Karatash (by Halling). The dam, a fairly useful Irish 1m and 10f winner, is a half-sister to 2 winners. The second dam, Karaliyfa (by Kahyasi), a quite useful 9f winner, is a half-sister to 6 winners including the 2-y-o Group 3 1m May Hill Stakes winner Karasta and to the Group 2 2m 2f Doncaster Cup dead-heat winner Kasthari. (H H Aga Khan). *"A particularly nice colt, he's well-grown, strong, muscular and a good mover. I like him a lot, he's very nice and he'll be a 2-y-o for July onwards. The dam's made a decent enough start at stud".*

1276. KATILAN (IRE) ★★★
b.c. *Cape Cross – Katiyra (Peintre Celebre)*. February 5. First foal. The dam won the Group 2 Blandford Stakes winner and was third in the Oaks and is a half-sister to numerous winners. The second dam, Katiykha (by Darshaan), a smart Irish listed 12f and 14f winner, is a half-sister to 6 winners. (H H Aga Khan). *"He's a very nice colt but he's had a setback and needed some time off after treatment, so we won't see him until the autumn. A particularly nice colt out of a good racemare but he will take time".*

1277. KERKENI (IRE) ★★★★
b.c. *Manduro – Kerania (Daylami)*. February 27. Half-brother to the quite useful 2012 7f and 1m placed second Kerisa (by Azamour), to the useful Irish 2-y-o 7f winner and Group 3 9f Kilboy Estates Stakes second Kirinda (by Tiger Hill) and the fairly useful 7f (at 2 yrs) and listed 12f winner Karasiyra (by Alhaarth). The dam, unplaced in one start, is a half-sister to the useful Irish 12f winner and Group 2 placed and dual Australian Group 2 placed Kerdem. The second dam, Kermiyana (by Green Desert), won the listed 1m Brownstown Stakes at 3 yrs in Ireland. (H H Aga Khan). *"A very good-looking colt and a lovely, fluent mover. He's quite strong, well-built and precocious-looking. The pedigree wouldn't suggest precocity, but he should make a 2-y-o from July onwards. I like him – he's a very nice colt and a potential 2-y-o winner".*

1278. MARAKOUSH (IRE) ★★★★★

b.c. Danehill Dancer – Mouramara (Kahyasi).
March 12. Half-brother to the very smart
2-y-o listed 9f winner and Irish Derby third
Mourayan (by Alhaarth), to the very smart
listed 14f winner and Melbourne Cup third
Mourilyan (by Desert Prince) and the useful
12f, 13f and hurdles winner Mourad (by
Sinndar). The dam, winner of the Group
2 12.5f Prix de Royallieu, is a half-sister to
several winners in France and Germany. The
second dam, Mamoura (by Lomond), won
over 10f and 12f in Ireland and is a half-sister
to 5 winners including the Group 3 12f Meld
Stakes third Mirana (herself dam of the Group
3 Prix de Flore winner Miliana). (H H Aga
Khan). *"He's quite big and rangy but he's a
very nice colt and we like him a lot. A beautiful
mover and a quick learner, he doesn't look a
2-y-o type in particular but I'd say he'll be out
in mid-season over seven furlongs because he
seems to get on with the job and learns quickly.
He's a promising horse, the mare was a good
filly herself and she's bred some good horses".*

1279. MY TITANIA (IRE) ★★★★

*b.f. Sea The Stars – Fairy Of The Night
(Danehill).* March 12. Fourth foal. Half-sister
to the fairly useful 2-y-o 1m winner and
listed-placed Aneedah (by Invincible Spirit).
The dam, an Irish 7f listed and 9.5f winner,
is a sister to one winner and a half-sister to
2 winners including the US Grade 3 12f and
Irish listed 11f winner Dress Rehearsal. The
second dam, Sassenach (by Night Shift), a
winner over 13f at 4 yrs in Ireland, is a half-
sister to 5 winners including the Group 3 2m
2f Doncaster Cup winner Far Cry. (Christopher
Tsui). *"A very nice, very well-made, strong and
short-coupled filly. A 2-y-o type to look at, she's
done everything right and although we won't
be rushing her she's likely to be out in late June
or early July. We like her a lot".*

1280. NECTAR DE ROSE (FR) ★★★

*ch.f. Shamardal – Bal De La Rose (Cadeaux
Genereux).* April 11. Third foal. €200,000Y.
Arqana Deauville August. Mandore
International. Half-sister to the 2012 French
1m placed 2-y-o Askania Nova (by New
Approach). The dam won 4 races at 2 and
3 yrs in France including a Group 3 event in
Lyon and a listed race. She is a half-sister to 4
winners including the French 2,000 Guineas
and French Derby winner Loup de Vega. The
second dam, Lady Vettori (by Vettori), won the
Group 3 Prix du Calvados and is a half-sister
to 5 winners. (Christopher Tsui). *"She's growing
a lot at the moment so we can't just rush her
but she had a straightforward run through the
winter and was as forward as any of them.
She's a nice filly but needs a bit of time to level
off, so she won't be out until the second half of
the year".*

1281. PONFEIGH (IRE) ★★★

*gr.c. Teofilo – Water Fountain (Mark Of
Esteem).* April 23. Third foal. 150,000Y.
Tattersalls October Book 1. BBA (Ire). The
dam is an unraced sister to the Group 3 Prix
Cleopatre winner Spring Oak and a half-sister
to 8 winners including the 10f Lupe Stakes
winner Fragrant Hill (herself the dam of five
stakes winners including the French Group 1
winners Fragrant Mix and Alpine Rose). The
second dam, English Spring (by Grey Dawn
II), won 7 races from 1m to 10f including the
Group 2 Prince of Wales's Stakes and is a half-
sister to 4 winners including the US Grade 1
winner Dance of Life. (Mr T Barr). *"A nice horse,
a good looker and a good walker. He's a racey
sort, he should be out from July onwards and
there's a lot to like about him".*

1282. PRINCESS YOUMZAIN ★★★

b.f. Dalakhani – Wonder Why (Tiger Hill).
March 7. Third foal. Half-sister to the smart
Irish 7f (at 2 yrs) and listed 1m winner and
Group 2 1m Beresford Stakes second Akeed
Mofeed (by Dubawi) – subsequently winner of
the Group 1 10f Hong Kong Derby. The dam
is an unraced half-sister to 5 winners including
the German listed winners Whispered Secret
and Wells Present. The second dam, Wells
Whisper (by Sadler's Wells), was placed over
1m and 10f and is a sister to the very useful
Group 1 10.5f Prix Lupin and US Grade 2 1m
winner Johann Quatz and to the smart French
10.5f to 13.5f listed winner Walter Willy and
a half-sister to the top-class middle-distance
colt Hernando. (Jaber Abdullah). *"She's a nice,
big, rangy filly, a very fluent mover and an
autumn type 2-y-o. There's nothing wrong with
her, she's correct and very acceptable".*

1283. ROUSAYAN (IRE) ★★★★
b.c. Invincible Spirit – Rose Quartz (Lammtarra).
March 14. Half-brother to the French dual
Group 2 1m and dual Group 3 1m winner
Rajsaman, to the listed 1m winner Rosawa
(herself dam of the Group 1 Prix Marcel
Boussac winner Rosanara) and the French 12f
winner Radiyya (by Sinndar). The dam won
once over 13f at 3 yrs in Ireland and is a half-
sister to several winners out of Graphite (by
Mr Prospector). (H H Aga Khan). "A precocious
horse and typical of the sire who gets a lot of
good-looking 2-y-o types and this colt is no
exception. He's a very nice colt and might be
one of the first of ours to run. Six furlongs in
early June could be his starting point".

1284. SEA'S ARIA (IRE) ★★★★
b.c. Sea The Stars – Speed Song (Fasliyev).
April 12. Second foal. Half-brother to the
modest 2012 2-y-o 6f winner Winter Song
(by Pivotal). The dam, a quite useful dual
5f winner (including at 2 yrs), is a half-sister
to the very smart Group 3 5f Molecomb
Stakes and Group 3 5f King George Stakes
winner Enticing and the useful listed winner
Sentaril. The second dam, Superstar Leo (by
College Chapel), a very smart 2-y-o, won 5
races including the Group 2 5f Flying Childers
Stakes and the Weatherbys Super Sprint and is
a full or half-sister to 10 winners. (Christopher
Tsui). "A particularly nice colt, he's a big strong
fellow, quite heavy but beautiful looking. He's
really nice and typical of the sire with a lovely
action and a lovely temperament. This is a
speedy family but as he's a big colt we can't
rush him and we'll play it by ear. I'm sure he
could be a six furlong type though".

1285. SEAS OF WELLS (IRE) ★★★★
b.f. Dansili – Kiyra Wells (Sadler's Wells).
February 7. First foal. 310,000Y. Tattersalls
October Book 1. Sunderland Holding. The
dam, a quite useful 7f winner, is closely related
to 4 winners including the 2-y-o Group 1 6f
Phoenix Stakes and Group 2 5f Queen Mary
Stakes winner Damson (herself dam of the
2-y-o Group 2 winner Requinto) and the
2-y-o Group 3 7f Prestige Stakes winner and
Group 3 Musidora Stakes second Geminiani.
The second dam, Tadkiyra (by Darshaan),
won over 10f at 3 yrs in France and is a
half-sister to 8 winners including the Group 3

winners Tashtiya, Tassmoun and Tashkourgan.
(Christopher Tsui). "She's a sharp filly, not very
big, but this is a small family and she's typical
of it. By my standards she could be early - the
end of May perhaps and she's a nice, athletic
filly".

1286. SHE'S MINE (IRE) ★★★
b.f. Sea The Stars – Scribonia (Danehill).
May 17. Seventh foal. €800,000foal. Goffs
November. Mertoun Paddocks. Half-sister
to the smart Irish 2-y-o 7f winner and
Coronation Stakes second and 1,000 Guineas
third Gile Na Greine, to the smart 2-y-o
dual Group 3 6f winner and 1,000 Guineas
second Cuis Ghaire and the very useful Irish
1m winner and dual Group 3 placed Claiomh
Solais (all by Galileo). The dam is an unraced
half-sister to 6 winners including the very
useful 2-y-o listed 6f winner and dual Group
1 placed Luminata and the very useful dual 6f
winner (including at 2 yrs) and Group 3 placed
Aretha. The second dam, Smaoineamh (by
Tap On Wood), an Irish 6f winner at 2 yrs and
useful at up to 14f, is a half-sister to 6 winners
including the champion sprinter Double Form
and the Lupe Stakes winner Scimitarra. (Mr V I
Araci). "A beautiful filly, she cost a lot of money
as a foal and she's a cracking filly to look at.
Lovely in every way, she was a late foal so we
won't see her until the autumn".

1287. SINKAL (USA) ★★★★
b.c. Smart Strike – Sindirana (Kalanisi). May 9.
Third foal. Half-brother to Sinaniya (by More
Than Ready), a 7f winner on her only start at
2 yrs in 2012 and to the fairly useful 1m (at 2
yrs) and 10f winner Sindjara (by Include). The
dam won over 7f (at 2 yrs) and the listed 11f
Lingfield Oaks Trial and is a half-sister to 2
winners. The second dam, Sinndiya (by Pharly),
won over 13f and is a half-sister to Sinndar. (H
H Aga Khan). "A nice colt, he's very fluent and
good-looking. Having been to three American
stallions so far the mare has had a good start
and hopefully this promising colt will be out in
mid-season".

1288. STREETCAR TO STARS ★★★
b.c. Sea The Stars – Approach (Darshaan).
April 19. Sixth foal. 250,000Y. Tattersalls
October Book 1. Sunderland Holding Inc.

Closely related to the Group 2 Irish Derby Trial winner, Irish Derby second and St Leger second Midas Touch (by Galileo) and half-brother to a minor French 3-y-o winner of 4 races Arabescatta (by Monsun). The dam, a 7.5f (at 2 yrs) and listed 10f winner, was second in a US Grade 2 9.5f event and in the Group 3 May Hill Stakes and is a sister to the very useful 2-y-o 8.5f winner and Group 1 Prix Marcel Boussac fourth Intrigued and a half-sister to 6 winners including the French 2,000 Guineas and US Grade 1 winner Aussie Rules. The second dam, Last Second (by Alzao), winner of the Group 2 10f Nassau Stakes and the Group 2 10f Sun Chariot Stakes and second in the Group 1 Coronation Stakes, is a half-sister to 7 winners including the Moyglare Stud Stakes third Alouette (dam of the Group 1 winners Albanova and Alborada) and the Group 3 Doncaster Cup winner Alleluia (dam of the Group 1 Prix Royal-Oak winner Allegretto) and to the placed dam of the Group 1 winners Yesterday and Quarter Moon. (Christopher Tsui). *"A lovely colt, he's done very well since breaking and done everything right. It's a very good pedigree although not a precocious one, but he's a well-made horse, he's had a good winter and he'll be starting fast work soon".*

1289. UNNAMED ★★★
b.f. Cape Cross – Alaiyma (Refuse To Bend). February 4. First foal. The dam, a fairly useful 7f (at 2 yrs) and listed 1m winner, is closely related to the 7f (at 2 yrs) and listed 1m winner, Grade 1 E P Taylor Stakes second and 1,000 Guineas third Alasha and a half-sister to 6 winners. The second dam, Alasana (by Darshaan), won twice in France over 1m and 9f and is a half-sister to the Prix Maurice de Nieuil winner Altayan and the Grand Prix de Vichy winner Altashar. (H H Aga Khan). *"An autumn type 2-y-o, she's strong, good-looking, but growing quite a bit so she'll need a bit of time. She could be a nice filly at the end of the season".*

1290. UNNAMED ★★★★
b.f. Oasis Dream – Ebalista (Selkirk). March 1. The dam, a quite useful 12f winner, is a half-sister to 5 winners including the useful 1m winner and Group 1 National Stakes third Eyshal and the useful Irish 10f winner Ehsan. The second dam, Ebadiyla (by Sadler's Wells), won the Group 1 Irish Oaks and the Group 1 Prix Royal-Oak and is a half-sister to the smart Group 1 7f Moyglare Stud Stakes winner Edabiya and the high-class Ascot Gold Cup winner Enzeli. (H H Aga Khan). *"She had a small setback and is having a break at the moment but she'll be back in soon. A good-looking filly, correct and a good mover, the dam's side takes a bit of time but she's nice and I like her. Hopefully the sire has brought a bit of speed and precocity to the pedigree".*

1291. UNNAMED ★★★
gr.f. Mizzen Mast – Ebaza (Sinndar). April 28. Half-sister to the very useful Group 3 7f Athasi Stakes winner Emiyna (by Maria's Mon), to the fairly useful 10f winner Ebazan (by Lemon Drop Kid) and the quite useful 11f and 2m winner Emrani (by Rahy). The dam is an unplaced half-sister to the Group 1 winners Ebadiyla, Edabiya and Enzeli. The second dam, Ebaziya (by Darshaan), won from 7f (at 2 yrs) to 12f including three listed races and was third in the Group 2 12f Blandford Stakes. (H H Aga Khan). *"She's a very nice filly, very good-looking and a good mover. She's grown a fair bit though, so she'll take time and is one for the back-end of the season".*

1292. UNNAMED ★★★★
ch.c. Mr Greeley – Lidakiya (Kahyasi). February 18. Half-brother to the dual 7f (at 2 yrs) and Group 2 German 6f and Group 2 UAE 1m winner Linngari (by Indian Ridge), to the quite useful Irish 2-y-o 7f winner Lidana (by King's Best), the quite useful Irish 7f and 1m winner Lingapour (by Gulch) and the modest 12f winner Lilakiya (by Dr Fong). The dam, a useful 10f and 12f winner, is a half-sister to the fairly useful 10f winner Lishtar and to the Irish 9f winner of 3 races and listed placed Livadiya. The second dam, Lilissa (by Doyoun), a French 9f and 10.5f winner, is a half-sister to 5 winners including the Group 3 12f Prix Minerve winner Linnga. (H H Aga Khan). *"A lovely horse, a half-brother to Linngari and he's quite like him in looks. He's very fluent, good-tempered and a promising 2-y-o for July onwards".*

1293. UNNAMED ★★★
b.f. *Holy Roman Emperor – Sharesha (Ashkalani).* May 9. Seventh foal. Half-sister to the smart listed 1m and listed 10f winner Sharestan (by Shamardal), to the useful Irish Group 3 8.5f winner Shareen (by Bahri), the useful 6f (at 2 yrs) and 7f winner and listed-placed Sharleez (by Marju) and a hurdles winner by Kahyasi. The dam, a fairly useful Irish 10f winner, is a half-sister to 4 winners out of the 1m placed Sharemata (by Doyoun). (H H Aga Khan). *"She's had a setback and is at home at the moment but she's quite a nice, sharp-looking filly. I'd say she'll be back and make a 2-y-o in the second half of the year. The dam has done well for us and this filly is sharp-looking – just what you'd expect from the pedigree".*

HUGO PALMER

1294. CLOSE COMPANION ★★
b.f. *Azamour – Vittoria Vetra (Danehill Dancer).* April 11. First foal. The dam, a minor 1m winner in France, is a half-sister to 5 winners including Valley Chapel – a winner of five Group 3 events in Scandinavia from 9f to 12f. The second dam, Valley Springs (by Saratoga Springs), won twice and is a half-sister to 3 stakes winners abroad. (Mr V I Araci). *"She's all Danehill Dancer and still a bit weak but come July-time I think she'll be ready. A very pretty filly that's strengthening up all the time".*

1295. EXTREMITY (IRE) ★★★ ♠
ch.c. *Exceed And Excel – Chanterelle (Indian Ridge).* March 30. Fifth foal. 30,000Y. Tattersalls October Book 1. McKeever Bloodstock. Half-brother to the moderate 12f and hurdles winner Zelos Diktator (by Diktat) and to a minor winner 3-y-o abroad by Royal Applause. The dam, a fair 2-y-o 6f winner, is a half-sister to 5 winners. The second dam, Chantereine (by Trempolino), a minor winner at 3 yrs in France, is a half-sister to 2 winners including the dam of the Kentucky Derby and Belmont Stakes winner Thunder Gulch. (Kremlin Cottage II). *"For just 30 Grand I think we stole him because he's a big, strong, incredibly easy-going horse. For his size he's probably going to be earlier than you'd think and he's bred on the same cross as Excelebration. So if I've got a superstar hiding amongst these 2-y-o's I think*

it's possibly him. I do have two shares left in him, should anyone be interested".

1296. KNIFE POINT (GER) ★★
b.c. *High Chaparral – Knightsbridge (Yagli).* April 6. Third foal. €16,000Y. Baden-Baden. BBA (Ire). The dam, a Grade 2 winner in Brazil, is a half-sister to 4 other winners there. The second dam, All American (by Midnight Tiger), a listed-placed winner of 5 races in Brazil, is a half-sister to 6 winners. (Decadent Racing). *"Probably the strongest of all my 2-y-o's – he's a big, impressive horse and much more forward than his pedigree would suggest".*

1297. PHOTOGRAPHY (IRE) ★★★
b.c. *Haatef – Sierva (Darshaan).* April 1. Ninth foal. 20,000Y. Tattersalls October Book 2. Amanda Skiffington. Half-brother to the German winner and listed-placed Perseida, to the hurdles winner Tus Nua (both by Galileo), the fair 5f (including at 2 yrs) and 6f winner Overwing (by Fasliyev) and the minor French 3-y-o winner Sweet Whip (by Whipper). The dam, placed once at 2 yrs in Germany, is a half-sister to 8 winners including the German listed winning sprinter/miler and Group 3 placed Sommernacht (herself the dam of 3 stakes winners) and to the placed dam of the US Grade 1 winner Sanagas. The second dam, Shona (by Windwurf), a listed winner in Germany, is a half-sister to 3 winners. (Weybridge Mafia). *"Probably the earliest of my 2-y-o's. He's got a lot of zip, seems more of a six furlong horse rather than five and he's not big but he's sharp. Interestingly, looking at the mare, her good one was by Fasliyev who is a grandson of Northern Dancer out of a Mr Prospector mare, which is exactly what Haatef is".*

1298. PYJAMA DAY ★★★
b.f. *Royal Applause – Miss Otis (Danetime).* January 28. Third foal. 8,000Y. Tattersalls Book 2. Not sold. Half-sister to the minor Italian 3-y-o winner Danzig's Bone (by Bertolini). The dam, a fair 2-y-o 5f winner, is a half-sister to 2 winners including the sprint winner and Group 3 Palace House Stakes second Hoh Hoh Hoh. The second dam, Nesting (by Thatching), is an unplaced full or half-sister to 3 winners and to the dams of the Group 2 winners Tariq and

Wi Dud. (Anglia Bloodstock III). *"She'll be one of my first 2-y-o's to run. She's very nice, she's grown and she's 16 hands now. They all say she's like a colt to sit on, seems to have a lot of early speed and she's a very well-balanced individual. As a 2-y-o type I'd say she's the nicest of my fillies and I have a couple of shares left in her if anyone is interested".* TRAINERS' BARGAIN BUY

1299. TACTICAL STRIKE ★★

ch.c. Pivotal – Alvee (Key Of Luck). March 6. First foal. 150,000Y. Tattersalls October Book 1. Rob Speers. The dam, a modest 12f placed maiden, is a half-sister to 4 winners including the Group 1 Prix Royal Oak and multiple Group 2 winner Allegretto. The second dam, Alleluia (by Caerleon), winner of the Group 3 Doncaster Cup, is a half-sister to 7 winners including the dual Group 2 winner Last Second (dam of the French 2,000 Guineas winner Aussie Rules), the Moyglare Stud Stakes third Alouette (dam of the dual Champion Stakes winner Alborada and the triple German Group 1 winner Albanova) and to the placed dam of the Group 1 winners Yesterday and Quarter Moon. (Mr V I Araci). *"A gorgeous colt that's changing all the time. He's one of those that finds life a little bit easy but he's not that forward. So it's a tricky balance of finding him enough to do to keep him busy without doing too much. It's a staying family and I would have though he's one of those Pivotal horses that will be at his best over a mile next year. I would hope that he'll been racing this year in August. He has the looks and the pedigree of a good horse so if he shows he's got an engine as well we can plan accordingly".*

AMANDA PERRETT
1300. A LEGACY OF LOVE (IRE) ★★★★

b.f. Sea The Stars – Nashmiah (Elusive City). January 30. First foal. 200,000Y. Tattersalls October Book 1. Brenda Karn-Smith. The dam, a winner of four listed events at 3 yrs from 7f to 10f, is a half-sister to 5 winners including the useful 2-y-o 7f and listed 1m winner Streets Ahead. The second dam, Frond (by Alzao), a quite useful 2-y-o 7f winner, is a half-sister to 8 winners. (Mrs B A Karn-Smith). *"A January foal out of a very good racemare,*

she's a lovely filly, not over-big (about 15.1), light on her feet and shows a nice bit of speed. She wouldn't want the ground too soft because she has a quick action. All being well she'll be ready to have a run by the end of May because she's very forward".*

1301. APPROACHING (IRE) ★★★★

ch.c. New Approach – Dust Dancer (Suave Dancer). April 15. Twelfth foal. 95,000Y. Tattersalls October Book 1. Not sold. Half-brother to the listed 1m and subsequent US Grade 2 winner Spotlight, to the quite useful 2-y-o 7f winner Dusty Moon (both by Dr Fong), the fairly useful dual 7f winner Tyranny (by Machiavellian and herself dam of the Group 1 Phoenix Stakes winner Zoffany), the quite useful 2-y-o 7f winner and listed 1m placed Dusty Answer (by Zafonic), the fair 2-y-o 7f winner Dusty Moon (by Dr Fong) and a winner in Hungary by Dubai Destination. The dam won 4 races including the Group 3 10f Prix de la Nonette and is a half-sister to 6 winners including the Group 3 7.3f Fred Darling Stakes winner Bulaxie (herself dam of the Group 2 winner Claxon). The second dam, Galaxie Dust (by Blushing Groom), a quite useful 2-y-o 6f winner, is a half-sister to 2 minor winners. (Bluehills Racing Ltd). *"He's a nice, compact, well put-together colt, the sire had a great year with his three Royal Ascot winners and this horse goes quite nicely and sometime in late July we'll hopefully have him on the racetrack. I like him a lot, he'll start over seven furlongs I should imagine and it would be nice to think he could be coming up the Ascot straight at some stage".*

1302. ARTFUL ROGUE (IRE) ★★★

b.c. Excellent Art – Szabo (Anabaa). May 5. Seventh foal. 55,000Y. Tattersalls October Book 2. Peter & Ross Doyle. Half-brother to the fair 12f, 14f and hurdles winner Teak (by Barathea), to the modest 2-y-o 6f winner Sensational Love (by Cadeaux Genereux), the Italian 10f winner Fuente Apache (by Hawk Wing) and a winner in Russia by Marju. The dam, a fairly useful Irish 7f placed 2-y-o, is a half-sister to 5 winners including the listed winners Edinburgh Knight and Nightbird. The second dam, Pippas Song (by Reference Point), a fair 12f winner, is a half-sister to 8 winners including the Group 3 Prestige Stakes winner Glatisant (dam of the 2,000 Guineas winner and sire Footstepsinthesand) and the dam of the champion 2-y-o filly Superstar Leo. (Mr & Mrs F Cotton and Mr & Mrs P Conway). *"He's a May foal, a nice, big, strapping horse and there are a couple of nice stayers under the second dam. A big, powerful horse, I can see him starting off at seven furlongs from July time onwards".*

1303. ARTISTIC FLAME ★★

b.g. Archipenko – Umlilo (Mtoto). May 8. Fifth foal. 25,000Y. Tattersalls October Book 2. Amanda Perrett. Half-brother to Ike's Pond (by Royal Applause), unplaced in one start at 2 yrs in 2012, to the US Grade 2 9f winner Fantastic Pick (by Fantastic Light) and to a minor 3-y-o winner in Italy by Araafa. The dam is a placed half-sister to 9 winners including the Canadian Grade 2 winner and Grade 1 second Miss Keller and the dam of the Group 2 Superlative Stakes winner Hatta Fort. The second dam, Ingozi (by Warning), a fairly useful winner over 7f and 1m at 3 yrs including a listed event at Sandown Park, is a half-sister to 7 winners including the very smart and tough triple Group 3 7f winner Inchinor. (Coombelands Racing Syndicate). *"He's one for the mid-to-late season and he'll be a middle-distance horse next year. The dam has already proved she can produce a nice horse and with the sire's pedigree there's no reason why he can't do the same. A nice, long-striding horse, I should imagine you'll be seeing him in a Newbury seven furlong maiden later in the year. He's from the Woodcote Stud which produces lots of two-year-old winners".*

1304. ASTRONEREUS (IRE) ★★★★ ♠

ch.c. Sea The Stars – Marie Rheinberg (Surako). February 17. Fifth foal. 190,000Y. Tattersalls October Book 1. Not sold. Half-brother to the Group 1 French Derby winner and French 2,000 Guineas second Le Havre (by Noverre), to the minor French 11f winner Scarlet And Gold (by Peintre Celebre) and the minor French 1m winner Alamarie (by Acclamation). The dam is an unraced half-sister to 7 winners including the Group 1 Haydock Park Sprint Cup winner Polar Falcon. The second dam, Marie d'Argonne (by Jefferson), a US stakes winner, was Grade 2 placed and is a half-sister to the Group 2 Prix de Pomone winner Marie de Litz. (John Connolly & Odile Griffith). *"A half-brother to a French Derby winner, but there's plenty of speed under the second dam, notably Polar Falcon, and he's a nice horse. I should think seven furlongs from June onwards will be the plan for him. He's light on his feet and has more Polar Falcon about him than a twelve furlongs Sea The Stars at the moment. I should think he's well capable of winning over seven furlongs and he probably won't get further than a mile".*

1305. BEST KEPT ★★

ch.c. Sakhee's Secret – Ashlinn (Ashkalani). May 7. Fourth living foal. 30,000Y. Tattersalls October Book 2. Peter & Ross Doyle. Half-brother to the fair 6f winner of 4 races China Cherub (by Inchinor), to the modest 10f winner Sylas Ings (by Kyllachy) and the modest 6f winner Compton Ashdown (by Proclamation). The dam, a quite useful 2-y-o 7f winner, is a half-sister to 7 winners including Alloway (Group 3 Prix Cleopatre). The second dam, Always Far (by Alydar), is an unraced half-sister to 6 winners and to the placed dam of the triple Group 1 winner Desert Prince. (Coombelands Racing Syndicate 3). *"The dam has a 100% record of winners to foals so far. This colt was a May foal, he's big and wants a bit of time to mature but he's got a very willing attitude and a good action. There's a lot to like about him but he won't be seen out much before July I don't think".*

1306. BLACK SHADOW ★★★

b.c. New Approach – Shadow Dancing (Unfuwain). February 18. Fifth foal. 55,000Y. Tattersalls October Book 1. Amanda Perrett. Half-brother to the useful 2-y-o 1m winner and Group 3 10.3f Dee Stakes third Rasmy (by Red Ransom) and to the fair 2-y-o 1m winner Hazy Dancer (by Oasis Dream). The dam, winner of the listed Cheshire Oaks, was third in the Oaks and second in the Group 2 Ribblesdale Stakes and in the Group 2 Prix de Pomone and is a half-sister to 6 winners. The second dam, Salchow (by Niniski), won the listed Cheshire Oaks, was second in the Group 2 Park Hill Stakes and is a half-sister to 7 winners. (A D Spence). *"Bred by Willie and*

Elaine Carson, both the dam and the second dam won the Cheshire Oaks. He's a nice horse for when the seven furlong races start, I haven't done much with him at the moment but he's very straightforward. Hopefully he'll be up to starting off in a seven furlong maiden at Goodwood".

1307. DOUBLE CZECH (IRE) ★★★★

b.c. Bushranger – Night Of Joy (King's Best). February 23. Fourth foal. 55,000Y. Tattersalls October Book 2. Peter & Ross Doyle. Half-brother to the fairly useful 2012 2-y-o dual 7f winner Baltic Knight (by Baltic King). The dam, a fairly useful 2-y-o dual 1m winner, is a half-sister to 3 winners. The second dam, Gilah (by Saddlers' Hall), is an unraced half-sister to 7 winners including the very useful 10.2f winner Cocotte (the dam of six stakes winners including the top-class colt Pilsudski). (G D P Materna). *"He's got plenty of speed, looks all over a 2-y-o and is ready to go. He was bought to run in the six furlong races at Goodwood and hopefully we'll see him there in May".*

1308. DREAMING BRAVE ★★

b.c. Sleeping Indian – Beechnut (Mujadil). February 20. Fifth living foal. 35,000Y. Tattersalls October Book 2. Peter & Ross Doyle. Half-brother to the modest 6f and 1m placed maiden Age Of Bronze (by Byron), to the modest 1m and 9f winner Beach Babe (by Zafeen), the modest 2-y-o 1m winner Super Fourteen and the Scandinavian winner River Landing (both by Lucky Story). The dam is an unraced sister to the winner and Group 3 Molecomb Stakes placed Connemara and to the listed-placed winner Presentation and a half-sister to 4 winners. The second dam, Beechwood (by Blushing Groom), won over 10.8f in France and is a half-sister to 5 winners. (Coombelands Racing Syndicate 2). *"He's quite a big horse so although he's bred to be speedy I think he's going to take until mid-season. He'll probably start off at six furlongs".*

1309. EXCEDO PRAECEDO ★★★★

b.c. Exceed And Excel – Merle (Selkirk). February 3. Fifth foal. 150,000Y. Tattersalls October Book 2. Peter & Ross Doyle. Half-brother to the French 3-y-o winner and 12f listed-placed Ominous (by Oasis Dream) and

to a hurdles winner by Dr Fong. The dam is an unraced half-sister to 11 winners including the multiple Group 3 winner Solo Mio. The second dam, Marie de Flandre (by Crystal Palace), a French listed 10f winner, is a full or half-sister to 7 winners including the high-class Prix Morny winner Sakura Reiko. (John Connolly & Odile Griffith). *"Very much stamped like his Dad, he was an early foal, he looks a strong colt and he's been doing some nice work so I should think he'll be racing in the second half of May over six furlongs. We trained Solo Mio under the second dam so there's a bit of stamina there as well, but he's not short of speed at home – that's for sure".*

1310. FAINTLY (USA) ★★★★

b.c. Kitten's Joy – Tinge (Kingmambo). February 11. Third foal. The dam is an unraced half-sister to the triple US Grade 1 winner Empire Maker and the US Grade 1 winners Honest Lady (herself dam of the US Grade 1 winner First Defence), Chester House and Chiselling. The second dam, Toussaud (by El Gran Senor), a 6f and 7f winner here, subsequently won a Grade 1 in North America. (Khalid Abdulla). *"He'd be one of our most forward 2-y-o's, he's from a wonderful family and I can see him racing in May over six furlongs. A nice, compact horse, he's not big but he's all there, he's strong and ready to go".*

1311. FIELD FORCE ★★★

b.c. Champs Elysees – Fairy Steps (Rainbow Quest). April 19. Third foal. Half-brother to Online (by Rail Link), unplaced in two starts at 2 yrs in 2012. The dam won over 11f in France and is a half-sister to the French listed 1m (at 2 yrs) and listed 7f winner Nova Step. The second dam, Light Step (by Nureyev), a fairly useful 3-y-o listed 10f winner, is a half-sister to 8 winners including Eltish (Group 2 Royal Lodge Stakes) and Forest Gazelle (US Grade 3 winner). (Khalid Abdulla). *"He's a lovely horse, I really like what I see in the Champs Elysees horses. He's quite immature at the moment and I would think seven furlongs in September time would suit him. So there's plenty of time for him but he's a really nice individual, well put-together and I'm looking forward to him in the second half of the season".*

1312. HARWOODS VOLANTE (IRE) ★★★
ch.c. Kheleyf – Semiquaver (Mark Of Esteem).
February 11. Third foal. 45,000Y. Tattersalls
October Book 2. James Delahooke. Brother
to the fair triple 5f winner Heartsong and
half-brother to Elusive Joe (by Elusive City),
unplaced in one start at 2 yrs in 2012. The
dam is an unraced half-sister to one winner.
The second dam, Dal Segno (by Sadler's
Wells), won 2 minor races at 3 yrs in France
and is a half-sister to 4 winners from the
family of Darshaan. (Harwoods Racing Club
Ltd). *"A big, powerful horse, the Kheleyf – Mark
Of Esteem cross has a very good success rate
and we wanted something that was going to
be speedy and run as a 2-y-o for the racing
club. Although he's a big colt he's quite mature
and hopefully we'll see him in May over six
furlongs".*

1313. KALIFI (USA) ★★★
b.br.f. First Defence – Out Of Reach (Warning).
March 4. Half-sister to the French 3-y-o 7f
winner Reaching Ahead (by Mizzen Mast). The
dam, a very useful listed 1m and subsequent
US Grade 3 8.5f winner, is a sister to the useful
2-y-o 6f winner and Group 3 Cherry Hinton
Stakes third Well Warned (herself the dam
of three listed winners) and a half-sister to 4
winners. The second dam, Well Beyond (by
Don't Forget Me), a 2-y-o 5f and useful 3-y-o
listed 1m October Stakes winner, is a half-
sister to 3 winners. (Khalid Abdulla). *"A nice
filly, good-moving with a bit of size and scope,
she has a good, deep girth and there's a lot to
like about her. They say that the sire produces
fast horses and she's out of a Warning mare, so
why not? I would think she'd be a seven furlong
2-y-o from July onwards".*

1314. PACK LEADER (IRE) ★★★
*b.c. Hurricane Run – Bright Enough (Fantastic
Light).* February 2. First foal. 65,000Y.
Tattersalls October Book 1. Peter & Ross
Doyle. The dam, a fair 2-y-o 1m winner, is a
half-sister to 3 winners including the useful
7f (at 2 yrs) and listed 6f winner of 6 races
Oasis Dancer and the very useful 1m winner
of 4 races and subsequent Scandinavian listed
winner Smart Enough. The second dam, Good
Enough (by Mukaddamah), won once at 3 yrs
in the USA and was third in the Group 1 Prix

Saint-Alary and is a half-sister to 5 winners
including the Group 3 Molecomb Stakes
winner Classic Ruler. (G D P Materna). *"A neat
colt, he's done some swinging canter work and
although he's out of a Fantastic Light mare and
you'd think he'd need a trip there is some speed
in the family. I think he'll start in June over
seven furlongs".*

1315. TORRID ★★★
*ch.c. Three Valleys – Western Appeal (Gone
West).* February 18. Half-brother to the fairly
useful 2012 2-y-o 7f winner and listed 1m
second Desert Image (by Beat Hollow) and to
the quite useful French 1m winners Full Steam
(by Oasis Dream) and Calm (by Montjeu). The
dam, a 7f winner at 3 yrs in France, was third
in the listed 7f Prix de Saint-Cyr and is a sister
to the champion 2-y-o and 3-y-o Zafonic,
winner of the 2,000 Guineas, the Dewhurst
Stakes, the Prix de la Salamandre and the Prix
Morny and to the smart Zamindar – winner of
the Group 3 6f Prix de Cabourg and second
in the Prix Morny. The second dam, Zaizafon
(by The Minstrel), a dual 2-y-o 7f winner, was
placed in the Group 1 1m Queen Elizabeth
II Stakes and the Group 3 1m Child Stakes
and is a half-sister to the dam of the Eclipse
Stakes and Phoenix Champion Stakes winner
Elmaamul. (Khalid Abdulla). *"The 3-y-o half-
sister is doing well and this is a big horse, 16.1
already, doing nice swinging canters. Seven
furlongs around June time should be right for
him and I like him".*

TIM PITT
1316. MONET MONET MONET ★★
*b.c. Art Connoisseur – Paix Royale (Royal
Academy).* March 23. Tenth foal. 6,000Y.
Tattersalls October Book 3. Tim Pitt. Half-
brother to the fairly useful triple 7f winner
(including at 2 yrs) Go Dutch (by Dutch
Art), to the French listed 7f winner Peach
Pearl (by Invincible Spirit), the French 7f
and subsequent US stakes-placed winner
Peacefally (by Grand Lodge), the fair 6f (at 2
yrs) and 5f winner of 6 races Captain Royale
(by Captain Rio), the French 1m and 10f
winner Soul Of Love (by Desert Prince) and
two minor winners in France (by Trempolino)
and Italy (by Alzao). The dam won once at 2
yrs in France and was listed-placed and is a

half-sister to 6 winners including the French listed winners Playact and Play Around. The second dam, Play Or Pay (by Play Fellow), a French listed-placed winner, is a half-sister to 9 winners. (Only Fools Buy Horses). *"A cheap and cheerful horse bought for a lovely syndicate of lads, he goes quite sweetly at the moment and he'll be racing in late April or early May. He's an athletic looking colt rather than a sharp 2-y-o type, so although he'll probably start off over five furlongs he will get six and maybe even seven as the season goes on. Probably one to make his mark in the nurseries during the summer".*

1317. ONE CHANCE (IRE) ★★★★

b.f. Invincible Spirit – Towards (Fusaichi Pegasus). February 22. First foal. 120,000Y. Tattersalls October Book 1. Recycled Products Ltd. The dam is an unplaced half-sister to 3 winners including the multiple Grade 1 winner Spinning World and the French listed winner Visions Of Clarity (herself dam of the Group 1 National Stakes winner Pathfork). The second dam, Imperfect Circle (by Riverman), winner of the 2-y-o listed 6f Firth of Clyde Stakes and second in the Group 1 Cheveley Park Stakes, is a half-sister to the Group/Grade 1 winners Denon and Chimes of Freedom (herself the dam of 2 Grade 1 winners) and the dam of the German Group 1 winner Saddex. (Recycled Products Ltd). *"The owners are very good clients of mine and they wanted a filly that would hopefully become a nice broodmare for them one day. She has a really nice pedigree but she's a racehorse with it. She's going nicely, I'm hoping she'll be out in May, she looks like a 2-y-o and she was an early foal which will stand her in good stead this year. She isn't the biggest but she's very solid, she has a wonderful temperament and, touch wood, she hasn't missed a day".*

1318. UNNAMED ★★

ch.f. Selkirk – Rubies From Burma (Forty Niner). March 9. Ninth foal. 33,000Y. Tattersalls October Book 2. Ferrybank Properties. Half-sister to the useful 5f to 1m winner of 8 races Alo Pura (by Anabaa), to the useful 12f winner and listed 12f second Ivory Gala (by Galileo), the fair 6f winner of 4 races Hatta Stream, the fair 6f winner Dreaming Of Rubies (both

by Oasis Dream), the modest dual 7f winner Diamond Run (by Hurricane Run) and the placed Wyola (by Sadler's Wells and herself dam of the Group 2 Norfolk Stakes winner Approve). The dam, a winner of 3 races from 5f to 6f and listed placed over 5.5f in Ireland, is a half-sister to 9 winners including the French 1,000 Guineas, Fillies Mile and Prix Marcel Boussac winner Culture Vulture. The second dam, Perfect Example (by Far North), is an unraced half-sister to the dams of the Grade/Group 1 winners Awe Inspiring, Polish Precedent and Zilzal. (Ferrybank Properties Ltd). *"A lovely filly with a really nice pedigree. She's gone home for a bit of a break and realistically she's more of a 3-y-o type, but that's not because she's slow, she's just immature. She'll be back in during the summer and you would hope she'll be running over seven furlongs later in the season".*

JON PORTMAN

1319. BENOORDENHOUT ★★★

br.g. Footstepsinthesand – Tara Too (Danetime). April 21. Second foal. The dam, a quite useful 5f (at 2 yrs) to 7f winner, is out of the unplaced Gone With The Wind (by Common Grounds), herself a half-sister to numerous winners including the very useful listed Scarborough Stakes winner and Group 2 Kings Stand Stakes second Flanders. (Prof. C D Green). *"He looks like a seven furlong type for the second half of the year, so he'll start off at six or seven furlongs around July time. A nice physical specimen, I can see him turning out alright and I like him".*

1320. CONNAUGHT RIVER (IRE) ★★★

b.c. Aussie Rules – Chingford (Redback). March 26. Second foal. £5,000 2-y-o. Ascot February. Not sold. Half-brother to the modest 2-y-o 5f winner Courtland Avenue (by Kodiac). The dam, a modest 5f placed 2-y-o, is a half-sister to a fair 2-y-o winner. The second dam, Beverley Macca (by Piccolo), a fair 5f winner of 4 races including at 2 yrs, is a half-sister to 5 winners including the 2-y-o Group 1 Cheveley Park Stakes and dual Group 2 winner Airwave. (Prof. C D Green). *"He'll be reasonably early so he'll probably start off at five furlongs but will be better over six. A nice physical specimen, I trained the dam and her 2-y-o of last year*

Courtland Avenue. I would think that this colt would be marginally better than him".

1321. CUECA (FR) ★★

b.f. *Country Reel – Costa Packet (Hussonet).* March 14. €12,000Y. Arqana Deauville November. MAB Agency. Half-sister to the fairly useful 5f and 6f winner and listed-placed Joe Packet (by Joe Bear). The dam ran once unplaced and is a half-sister to a winner in Chile. The second dam, Costa Balena (by Great Regent), a winner in Chile, is a sister to one winner and a half-sister to 8 winners including Giulietta (Grade 1 winner in Chile). *"A half-sister to Joe Packet, a colt that's been good to us. She's not as early as I'd hoped and she needs a bit more time, but she's alright and she goes nicely. One for the late summer and hopefully she'll be a nice 3-y-o as well".*

1322. FENELLA FOGHORN ★★★

b.f. *Elnadim – Bundle Up (Miner's Mark).* April 24. Seventh foal. £17,000Y. Doncaster Premier. J Portman. Half-sister to the fair 6f (at 2 yrs), 10f, 12f and hurdles winner Cheshire Prince (by Desert Prince), to the fair 1m to 12 winner Bennelong (by Bahamian Bounty) and the French winner of 6 races and listed-placed Ut Majeur (by Brahms). The dam is an unplaced half-sister to 6 winners including the Group 2 Prix Robert Papin winner Balawaki. The second dam, Balakhna (by Tyrant), a French 5f to 1m winner, was third in the Group 3 5f Prix du Gros-Chene and is a half-sister to 5 winners including the top-class broodmare Blue Note (dam of the Group 1 winners Blue Duster and Zieten). (Mr D Redvers). *"Likely to be our first 2-y-o runner, in mid-March I thought she was going very well, but now she's just going quite well. So I'd say she'll be earlyish but will come on for her first run. She looks sharp but she's a late April foal, so we'll aim for the end of April over five furlongs and see how she goes. I think she'll be better over six".*

1323. FERNGROVE (USA) ★★★★

gr.c. *Rockport Harbor – Lucky Pipit (Key Of Luck).* February 26. Fifth living foal. 38,000Y. Tattersalls October Book 2. J Portman. Half-brother to 3 minor winners in North America by Mr Greeley (2) and Rahy. The dam, a useful 2-y-o 7f listed winner, is a half-sister to 5

winners. The second dam, Meadow Pipit (by Meadowlake), a smart winner of 4 races at 4 yrs from 7f to 10f including a listed event, is a half-sister to 9 winners. (Mr J T Habershon-Butcher). *"A very big horse, very strong with legs of timber and a very aloof attitude. At the moment he's looking like my nicest 2-y-o but he won't be rushed. I'll probably start him at six furlongs at the end of May and see how we get on. He does everything easily but I haven't done any fast work with him yet and hopefully he won't fall in a heap when I do. He's so big you wouldn't want to get into a fight with him, but thankfully his temperament is fine at the moment. If you looked at them all in the string you would pick him out".*

1324. HOLY WATER (IRE) ★★

b.c. *Holy Roman Emperor – Gambling Spirit (Mister Baileys).* May 3. Third foal. €12,000Y. Tattersalls Ireland September. J Portman. The dam was a fair 10f to 13f winner of 5 races. The second dam, Royal Roulette (by Risk Me), a modest 1m to 2m winner of 4 races, is a half-sister to 3 winners. (Port Or Brandy Syndicate). *"A tough colt and a June type 2-y-o over six furlongs. He goes OK but he's a late foal that was quite small as a yearling and he's growing now. He may not be top drawer, but he'll be OK".*

1325. MOLLASSES ★★★★

b.f. *Authorized – Muscovado (Mr Greeley).* April 13. Second foal. 24,000Y. Tattersalls October Book 2. Not sold. Half-sister to the fair 2012 7f and 9f placed 2-y-o Monsieur Rieussec (by Halling). The dam ran twice unplaced and is a half-sister to 4 minor winners here and abroad. The second dam, Only Royale (by Caerleon), won 9 races including the Group 1 Yorkshire Oaks (twice) and the Group 2 Jockey Club Stakes and is a half-sister to 5 winners. (Mrs J Wigan). *"A half-sister to my nice 3-y-o Monsieur Rieussec, she looks very nice and does everything very easily but her temperament is hot, probably because of her sire. Nevertheless I'd put her top of the list of my fillies and she won't be rushed. If her temperament holds together she looks to have some class. She'll want seven furlongs to begin with".*

1326. PETALE NOIR ★★★

b.f. *Mount Nelson – Apple Blossom (Danehill Dancer)*. February 24. First foal. £8,000Y. Ascot December. Not sold. The dam, a fair 7f winner, is a half-sister to one winner. The second dam, Silk (by Machiavellian), is an unraced daughter of the listed-placed winner Dances With Dreams (herself a half-sister to the dual Group 1 winner Dark Moondancer). (Dr Anne Gillespie). *"A home-bred for a new owner, she's very leggy, still growing a bit and is one for the second half of the season. She moves very nicely and at this stage I like her, but she's still up at the back".*

1327. POLAR EXPRESS ★★★

ch.g. *Sakhee's Secret – Polar Dawn (Polar Falcon)*. April 12. Third foal. €9,500Y. Tattersalls Ireland September. J Portman. Half-brother to the fair 2-y-o 5f winner Morgans Choice (by Namid). The dam, a modest 7f and 1m winner, is a half-sister to 3 minor winners. The second dam, Leave At Dawn (by Slip Anchor), is an unraced half-sister to 5 winners. (Whitcoombe Park Racing). *"I was very excited about him initially because he looked quite sharp. He goes very well but he's just had a small setback. I'd put him in the same category as my 2-y-o Verglas filly, a fun, nursery-type 2-y-o. I wouldn't be averse to running him over five furlongs but he'll come into his own over six or seven".*

1328. SUMMERLING ★★★

br.f. *Excellent Art – Sun Seasons (Salse)*. February 19. Fifth foal. 7,000Y. Tattersalls October Book 2. J Portman. Half-sister to the fair 6f winner El Djebena (by Invincible Spirit). The dam, a fairly useful Irish 2-y-o 7f winner, is a half-sister to 9 winners including the Group 2 11f Blandford Stakes and Grade 2 Orchid Handicap winner Lisieux Rose. The second dam, Epicure's Garden (by Affirmed), a useful Irish 7f (at 2 yrs) to 9f winner, was Group 3 placed three times and is a sister to the Irish 1,000 Guineas winner Trusted Partner (dam of the high-class filly Dress To Thrill) and a half-sister to the Group 2 winner Easy To Copy (the dam of 3 stakes winners). (A H Robinson). *"She's a big filly and does everything fairly easily. Ideally I'd like to start her off over six furlongs at the end of May. She's nice, I like her*

and although she's big she's pretty forward". TRAINERS' BARGAIN BUY

1329. UNNAMED ★★

b.f. *Azamour – Akarita (Akarad)*. March 22. Ninth foal. £6,000Y. Doncaster Premier. J Portman. Half-sister to the quite useful Irish 6f winner Scarsdale (by Polar Falcon), to the moderate 6f winner Tahitian Princess (by One Cool Cat) and the moderate Irish 7f winner Soviet Trooper (by Soviet Lad). The dam won over 7.5f at 3 yrs and was listed placed twice. She is a half-sister to 9 winners including the useful 2-y-o 5f winner and Group 3 third Safka (herself dam of the listed winner Speedfit Too), the Group 2 7f Lockinge Stakes winner Safawan and the dam of the Group 2 12f Prix Hocquart winner Sayarshan. The second dam, Safita (by Habitat), won the listed 1m Prix de la Calonne and was second in the French 1,000 Guineas and the Prix Saint-Alary. *"She's grown a lot so I've not done a lot with her, but I like her and I'd like to find an owner for her. She reminds me a lot of Annecdote this time last year, a lightly-raced 2-y-o who won two races including a Newmarket nursery. She needs to fill her frame so she just needs a bit of time and I could see her running by June or July".*

1330. UNNAMED ★★★

gr.f. *Verglas – Deira (Green Desert)*. February 21. Second foal. €10,500Y. Tattersalls Ireland September. J Portman. The dam, a fair dual 7f winner, is a half-sister to 4 winners. The second dam, New Sayyedati (by Shadeed), is an unraced sister to multiple Group 1 winner Sayyedati and a half-sister to the multiple Group 1 winner Golden Snake. *"We like her, she's not top drawer but she'll be running by the end of May over six furlongs. She might win a maiden but she's probably a nursery type. I can see her being a fun 2-y-o".*

1331. UNNAMED ★★

gr.f. *Mastercraftsman – Second Act (Sadler's Wells)*. March 1. Second foal. £8,000Y. Doncaster Premier. Not sold. Half-sister to Rock Act (by Rock Of Gibraltar), unplaced in one start at 2 yrs in 2012. The dam, placed once over a mile in France at 3 yrs, is a half-sister to 4 winners including the Group 2 Dante Stakes winner Tuning Fork. The second dam, Tuning (by Rainbow Quest), a smart winner of the 14f Ebor Handicap, is a sister to the fairly useful French 12f winner Raincloud and a half-sister to the useful Group 3 7f Rockfel Stakes second Clog Dance. *"She came in quite late and was a tiny, weak filly but she's just picked herself up nicely. Not a five furlong 2-y-o at all, but she'll be ready when the six furlong races start. Small but very tough and with a good action, I can just see her improving as she gets stronger".*

KEVIN PRENDERGAST

1332. ABUSHAMAH (IRE) ★★

b.c. Nayef – Adaala (Sahm). May 10. Fifth foal. Half-brother to Daymooma (by Pivotal), placed over 7f on both her starts at 2 yrs in 2012, to the useful 2-y-o 6f winner and Group 3 7f Killavullan Stakes third Aaraas (by Haafhd), the useful Irish 2-y-o 6f winner and Group 3 7f Silver Flash Stakes third Alshahbaa (by Alhaarth) and the fairly useful Irish 7f winner and listed placed Asheerah (by Shamardal). The dam, an Irish 7f (at 2 yrs) and listed 9f winner, is a half-sister to 2 winners. The second dam, Alshoowg (by Riverman), is an unraced half-sister to 4 winners. (Hamdan Al Maktoum). *"He only got here from Dubai about 10 days ago and they arrived in a bad environment considering the Dubai climate, but he seems to be a good mover and a fine, big horse. He was a late foal and is one for later in the season".*

1333. CRAFTY CODGER (IRE) ★★★

ch.c. Mastercraftsman – Rainbow Melody (Rainbows For Life). April 26. Seventh living foal. €20,000Y. Tattersalls Ireland September. Frank Barry. Half-brother to the quite useful dual 7f winner (including at 2 yrs) and US Grade 3 placed Musical Rain (by Val Royal) and to the fair 1m winner Sapphire Spray (by Viking Ruler). The dam, a quite useful dual 7f winner (including at 2 yrs), is a half-sister to 6 winners including the smart 3-y-o listed 5f winner Indian Prince. The second dam, Lingering Melody (by Nordico), was placed at up to 1m in Ireland and is a half-sister to 3 winners including the Group 2 Queen Anne Stakes and the Group 2 Sea World International Stakes winner Alflora. *"He's a nice horse, I bred him and he should be out in*

May. He seems to go well, he's not over-big but a nice, quality fella. Six/seven furlongs should suit him this year".

1334. GOT TO DREAM (IRE) ★★★

b.f. Duke Of Marmalade – Lady Of Everest (Montjeu). February 6. First foal. 50,000Y. Tattersalls October Book 2. F Barry. The dam is an unraced half-sister to 2 winners including the Irish listed winner and Group 1 Irish Oaks second Roses For The Lady. The second dam, Head In The Clouds (by Rainbow Quest), won the Group 3 12f Princess Royal Stakes and is a sister to the high-class St Leger, Chester Vase and Jockey Club Stakes winner Millenary and a half-sister to the very smart 1m (at 2 yrs) and 10f winner and Derby third Let The Lion Roar. *"A real nice filly out of a Montjeu mare, I'd say she'd want seven furlongs in July or August. A big, strong type but more of a 3-y-o really".*

1335. INVISIBLE FLASH ★★★

br.f. Invincible Spirit – Photo Flash (Bahamian Bounty). February 11. Eighth foal. 55,000Y. Tattersalls October Book 1. BBA (Ire). Half-sister to the moderate 2012 2-y-o winner Strasbourg Place, to the Group 2 6f Richmond Stakes winner Prolific (both by Compton Place) and the fairly useful 2-y-o 5f winner and subsequent US stakes winner Deal Breaker (by Night Shift). The dam, a fair 1m winner, is a half-sister to 8 winners including the smart 2-y-o Group 2 1m Royal Lodge Stakes winner Atlantis Prince. The second dam, Zoom Lens (by Caerleon), placed once over 7f at 2 yrs, is a half-sister to 4 winners. (Lady O'Reilly). *"She'll be racing in May, we like her a lot and she seems to go well. She's not a big filly but she looks an early type. Six furlongs would be better for her than five I would say".*

1336. J'AIME (IRE) ★★★

b.f. Amadeus Wolf – Jioconda (Rossini). February 22. Fourth foal. Half-sister to Interim (by Elusive City), unplaced in two starts at 2 yrs in 2012, to the 2-y-o Group 1 6f Cheveley Park Stakes and Group 3 6f Round Tower Stakes winner Lightening Pearl and to the 3-y-o 11f winner and 2-y-o Group 3 Tyros Stakes third Jolie Jioconde (both by Marju). The dam won the listed Silken Glider Stakes and was third in the Group 3 Killavullan Stakes.

The second dam, La Joconde (by Vettori), is an unraced half-sister to 4 winners. (Lady O'Reilly). *"She'll be racing in late April or early May and we'll start her off at five furlongs. She goes well, not very big but very well-made, she looks a runner and seems to have a good temperament".*

1337. MASKOON ★★★

ch.c. Aqlaam – Tamazug (Machiavellian). April 11. Fourth foal. The dam, a useful Irish 7f and 1m winner, was third in the Group 3 Derrinstown Stud 1,000 Guineas Trial and is a sister to the quite useful Irish 7f to 10f winner Mutadarek. The second dam, Nasheed (by Riverman), a useful 7f (at 2 yrs) and 10f winner, is a half-sister to the high-class Prix de l'Arc de Triomphe and Juddmonte International winner Sakhee. (Hamdan Al Maktoum). *"Of the three horses that arrived here from Dubai recently he looks the most forward. He's a nice, big horse that should make a 2-y-o by July over seven furlongs".*

1338. PIXIE HOLLOW ★★★

gr.f. Verglas – High Fun (Kahyasi). February 4. First foal. €19,000Y. Tattersalls Ireland September. Frank Barry. The dam is an unraced half-sister to 4 minor winners. The second dam, Silver Fun (by Saumarez), won the Group 2 Prix de Malleret and is a half-sister to 7 winners including 2 listed winners. (Lisa Kelly and Lady O'Reilly). *"We were hoping to run her early but she got a cough, but she should be racing around early May. She goes well and we'll start her at five furlongs I should think but I can see her getting seven later on. We had a useful Verglas filly last year that was very like her called Spinacre and she won a listed race. A nice, quality filly, she's not over-big but typical of the sire who unfortunately died last year".*

1339. RED BANDANA (IRE) ★★★★

ch.f. Raven's Pass – Mowazana (Galileo). February 9. Third foal. €60,000Y. Goffs Sportsman's. Skymarc Farm. Half-sister to the 1m (in Italy) and hurdles winner Crafty Roberto (by Intikhab). The dam, a fair 10.2f winner, is a half-brother to 6 winners including the useful 2-y-o 6f winner Shohrah and the useful 7f winner and 1m listed second Ma-Arif.

The second dam, Taqreem (by Nashwan), was second four times over middle-distances and is a half-sister to 7 winners including Ibn Bey (a winner of four Group 1 events including the Irish St Leger and second in the Breeders Cup Classic) and to the very smart Group 1 Yorkshire Oaks winner and smart broodmare Roseate Tern. (Lady O'Reilly). *"She's my star I think. She's out of a Galileo mare and she'll want six/seven furlongs this year. I like her a lot, she goes very well and she's a fine, big strong filly".*

1340. SAAKHEN (IRE) ★★★★

b.c. Invincible Spirit – Upperville (Selkirk). April 8. Fifth foal. €70,000Y. Goffs Orby. Shadwell Estate Co. Half-brother to the useful dual 7f winner Cannon Hill (by Holy Roman Emperor), to the quite useful Irish 9f to 12f winner Blue Ridge Lane (by Indian Ridge) and a winner over hurdles by Verglas. The dam, a fair Irish 12f winner, is a half-sister to 8 winners including the useful Irish listed 12f winner Mutakarrim and the very useful Irish listed 10f winner Nafisah. The second dam, Alyakkh (by Sadler's Wells), a fair 3-y-o 1m winner, is a half-sister to the Champion Stakes and 2,000 Guineas winner Haafhd, the Group 2 Challenge Stakes winner Munir and the 1m listed stakes winner and Group 1 Coronation Stakes second Hasbah. (Hamdan Al Maktoum). *"He ran well on his debut at the Curragh and was perhaps unlucky not to win. He's come out of the race well and he looks a nice horse. He's not big, but he's a nice, quality colt for five and six furlongs".*

1341. SAKHRA ★★★ ♠

b.c. Nayef – Noble Desert (Green Desert). March 5. Fifth foal. 38,000Y. Tattersalls October Book 2. F Barry. Half-brother to the quite useful 2012 triple 6f placed 2-y-o Star Of Rohm (by Exceed And Excel), to the quite useful 5f (including at 2 yrs) and 6f winner Mr Optimistic (by Kyllachy), the fair 6f (including at 2 yrs) and 7f winner The Human League (by Tobougg) and the modest 2-y-o 1m winner Noble Dictator (by Diktat). The dam is an unplaced half-sister to 9 winners. The second dam, Sporades (by Vaguely Noble), won 3 races in France including the Group 3 10.5f Prix de Flore and is a half-sister to 9 winners including the high-class colts Mill Native (Grade 1 10f Arlington Million) and the Group 3 winners French Stress and American Stress. (Hamdan Al Maktoum). *"A very nice, very good-actioned horse but because of his pedigree he'll take a bit of time. Very much like his sire, he's a big, easy-moving horse and I could see him being out around July time".*

1342. TAALUF (IRE) ★★★

b.f. *Nayef – Walayef (Danzig).* April 17. Sixth foal. Half-sister to the fairly useful Irish 2-y-o 6f and 7f winner and 3-y-o listed-placed Jamaayel (by Shamardal), to the quite useful Irish 1m winner Estithmaar (by Pivotal) and the quite useful Irish 2-y-o 7f winner Reyaada (by Daylami). The dam, a listed 6f (at 2 yrs) and Group 3 7f Athasi Stakes winner, is a sister to the smart 2-y-o 6f winner Haatef, to the listed 6f winner and Group 1 Moyglare Stud Stakes second Shimah and the Irish dual listed 6f winner Ulfah. The second dam, Sayedat Alhadh (by Mr Prospector), a US 7f winner, is a sister to the US Grade 2 7f winner Kayrawan and a half-sister to the useful winners Amaniy, Elsaamri and Mathkurh. (Hamdan Al Maktoum). *"She'll be racing in late May or early June over six furlongs and would have been out even earlier but for a touch of sore shins. She's nice, we like her, she's not a great big filly but very well-made and looks a runner".*

1343. TAANIF ★★★

b.c. *Aqlaam – Firebelly (Nicolotte).* April 4. Fifth foal. 125,000Y. Tattersalls October Book 1. Shadwell Estate Co. Half-brother to the useful 6f and 7f winner and Group 3 6f Hackwood Stakes second Firebeam (by Cadeaux Genereux) and to the fair dual 1m winner (including at 2 yrs) Bombina (by Lomitas). The dam, a fairly useful 2-y-o dual 6f and Italian listed 1m winner, is a half-sister to 3 winners including the South African listed winner L'Passionata. The second dam, Desert Delight (by Green Desert), is an unraced half-sister to 9 winners including the Group 3 May Hill Stakes winner Intimate Guest and the dams of the Grade 1 winners Luas Line, Kingsfort and Prince Arch. (Hamdan Al Maktoum). *"He goes well, he'll want six and maybe even seven furlongs, he's nice and we like him a lot. He*

seems to have a good temperament and he'll be racing in May".

1344. TAQARROB (IRE) ★★★★

b.c. *Bushranger – Lucky Date (Halling).* April 12. Fifth foal. 100,000Y. Tattersalls October Book 2. Shadwell Estate Co. Half-brother to the fair 9f winner Highkingofireland (by Danehill Dancer), to the fair dual 12f and hurdles winner and the French 1m (at 2 yrs) to 10f winner of 5 races Rava (by Nayef). The dam, a fairly useful 2-y-o 7f winner, was second in the listed 1m Masaka Stakes and is a half-sister to 4 winners. The second dam, Hesperia (by Slip Anchor), a winner over 11f and 12f including a listed event in Italy, is a half-sister to the French listed winners Wavey and Rebuff. (Hamdan Al Maktoum). *"A nice horse that wants six furlongs and firm ground. We like him, he's very good-looking and he'll be a winner hopefully. A very taking horse, he cost a lot for a first season sire".*

1345. THE ORGAN GRINDER (IRE) ★★★★

b.c. *Footstepsinthesand – Glebe Queen (Hawkeye).* January 28. First foal. €26,000Y. Goffs Sportsman's. Kevin Ross. The dam, a quite useful 1m winner, is a half-sister to 2 winners including the useful Irish 2-y-o 6f winner and Group 2 Railway Stakes second In Some Respect. The second dam, Burnin' Memories (by Lit de Justice), won 5 races at 2 to 5 yrs in the USA including a minor stakes event and is a half-sister to 7 winners. (On Target Syndicate). *"He'll be racing in late April or early May, preferably over six furlongs but five wouldn't be any trouble to him. I trained his dam who was quite useful, she gave us a fair bit of trouble with various issues she had, but she was a very good-looker. This is a nice horse, he was a first foal but he doesn't look that way at all – he's a good size. Could be a stakes horse".* TRAINERS' BARGAIN BUY

1346. TRIKALA (IRE) ★★★

b.f. *High Chaparral – Thiella (Kingmambo).* March 21. Second foal. Half-sister to the very smart 2012 2-y-o Group 2 6f Mill Reef Stakes winner Moohaajim (by Cape Cross). The dam, a fairly useful Irish 2-y-o 7f and subsequent US winner, is a half-sister to the US Grade 3 12f winner Niagara Causeway. The second dam, Theoretically (by Theatrical), won 2 races including the Group 3 7f C L Weld Park Stakes, was Grade 1 placed twice in the USA and is a half-sister to 8 winners including the Group 1 Prix Lupin winner Cudas. (Lady O'Reilly). *"Goes very well, she got slightly sore shins so we've had to ease off her, but we like her. A nice, quality filly, not over-big, and I see her wanting six furlongs plus this year".*

1347. ZAKHM (IRE) ★★★

b.c. Marju – Aadaat (Dixie Union). January 30. First foal. The dam, placed second over 7f at 2 yrs on her only start, is a half-sister to numerous winners including the smart 2-y-o Group 2 1m Royal Lodge Stakes winner Al Jadeed. The second dam, Aljawza (by Riverman), an Irish 2-y-o 6f winner, is a half-sister to 11 winners including the smart Group 2 10f Gallinule Stakes winner Sportsworld, the smart Group 1 6f Cheveley Park Stakes winner Gay Gallanta, the useful 10.4f John Smiths Cup winner Porto Foricos and the useful 6f (at 2 yrs) and 7f winner Sundance Kid. (Hamdan Al Maktoum). *"A nice enough horse, he's coming along nicely but he'll take a bit of time and will want six furlongs plus this year".*

SIR MARK PRESCOTT

1348. ALBA VERDE ★★★

gr.f. Verglas – Algarade (Green Desert). February 3. First foal. The dam, a quite useful 1m (at 2 yrs) and 10f winner, is a half-sister to numerous winners including the fairly useful 12f to 14f winner of 6 races and listed-placed Alambic. The second dam, Alexandrine (by Nashwan), a fair 10f to 13f winner of 4 races, is a half-sister to 7 winners including the Nassau Stakes and Sun Chariot Stakes winner Last Second (dam of the French 2,000 Guineas winner Aussie Rules), the Doncaster Cup winner Alleluia (dam of the Prix Royal-Oak winner Allegretto) and the Moyglare Stud Stakes third Alouette (herself dam of the dual Champion Stakes winner Alborada and the triple German Group 1 winner Albanova) and to the placed dam of the Group 1 winners Yesterday and Quarter Moon. (Miss K Rausing). *"A good sort, but she's big and backward. She's having a break at the moment and I see her as a seven furlong/mile filly in the autumn".*

1349. ANJIN (IRE) ★★★

b.c. Danehill Dancer – Twyla Tharp (Sadler's Wells). March 18. Fourth foal. 110,000Y. Tattersalls October Book 1. Highflyer Bloodstock. Closely related to the 2-y-o 7f, Group 1 10f Nassau Stakes and Group 3 10.4f Musidora Stakes winner and Group 1 Oaks third The Fugue (by Dansili) and half-brother to the fair 14f and 2m winner Susan Stroman (by Monsun). The dam, a useful 9f winner and second in the Group 2 12f Ribblesdale Stakes, is a half-sister to 7 winners including the Group 1 10f Coral Eclipse Stakes winner Compton Admiral and the Group 1 1m Queen Elizabeth II Stakes winner Summoner. The second dam, Sumoto (by Mtoto), a useful 6f (at 2 yrs) and 7f winner, is a half-sister to 5 winners including the good mare Lalindi (dam of the US Grade 2 winner Arvada and the Group 3 Craven Stakes winner Adagio). (Syndicate 2012). *"A big, strong colt for the middle of the season. I wouldn't know what sort of trip he'd want yet, but his three-parts sister The Fugue won her only 2-y-o start over seven furlongs in the autumn".*

1350. BEWITCHMENT ★★★★

b.f. Pivotal – Hypnotize (Machiavellian). April 6. Ninth foal. Sister to the quite useful 2-y-o 6f winner Hip and half-sister to the 2-y-o Group 1 6f Cheveley Park Stakes and Group 2 6f Lowther Stakes winner Hooray (by Invincible Spirit), the useful 2-y-o listed 8.3f winner of 7 races Hypnotic (by Lomitas), the fairly useful 2-y-o 1m winner Notorize (by Hernando) and the quite useful dual 7f winner Macedon (by Dansili). The dam, a useful 2-y-o dual 7f winner, is closely related to 2 winners including the Group 3 6f Cherry Hinton Stakes winner Dazzle and a half-sister to 5 winners including the useful 7f (at 2 yrs) and 1m listed winner Fantasize and to the placed dam of the Group 2 winning sprinter Danehurst. The second dam, Belle et Deluree (by The Minstrel), won over 1m (at 2 yrs) and 10f in France and is a half-sister to the very useful 6f and 1m winner and Cheveley Park Stakes second Dancing Tribute (herself dam of the Group/Grade 2 winners Souvenir Copy and Dance Sequence). (Cheveley Park Stud). *"She looks a 2-y-o type, we'll work her in late May and then see how she went. The dam breeds*

2-y-o winners and they seem to be either good or disappointing".

1351. CANNES MOUGINS ★★
b.c. Galileo – Miss Riviera Golf (Hernando). February 7. Closely related to the fairly useful 1m (at 2 yrs) and 14f winner Gassin Golf (by Montjeu) and half-brother to the fairly useful 2-y-o 1m winner Mont Agel (by Danehill Dancer), to the fairly useful listed 7f winner Hotel Du Cap, the fairly useful 10f and 12f winner The Carlton Cannes (both by Grand Lodge) and the fair 7f and 1m winner Gassin (by Selkirk). The dam won a listed event over 1m in France at 3 yrs and is a half-sister to several winners including the useful 2-y-o 6f winner and listed-placed Miss Riviera. The second dam, Miss Beaulieu (by Northfields), was a useful 6f and 10f winner. (J L C Pearce). "A backward colt, he won't run until the autumn, probably over a mile".

1352. CHINESE JADE ★★★
gr.c. Cape Cross – Chinese White (Dalakhani). March 25. First foal. 68,000Y. Tattersalls October Book 1. Not sold. The dam, a winner of 7 races including the Group 1 Pretty Polly Stakes and the Group 2 Blandford Stakes, is a half-sister to one winner. The second dam, Chiang Mai (by Sadler's Wells), won the Group 3 12f Blandford Stakes and is a half-sister to 9 winners including the very smart Group 1 10.5f Prix de Diane winner Rafha (the dam four stakes winners including Invincible Spirit). (Lady O'Reilly). "She'll make a 2-y-o by mid-season. The dam was good and this is her first foal. I'll probably wait for seven furlongs with him".

1353. CLARICE ★★★
b.f. Cape Cross – Phillipina (Medicean). April 15. First foal. The dam, a useful 10f winner, was listed-placed over 11f and is a half-sister to one winner. The second dam, Discerning (by Darshaan), a quite useful 11f winner, is a half-sister to 6 winners on the flat including the Group 2 Summer Mile winner Cesare and the Group 3 12f Prix la Force winner and French Derby second Nowhere To Exit and to the Grade 2 winning hurdler Trenchant. (Cheveley Park Stud). "Unlike most of the Cheveley park horses I haven't trained anything from this particular family before. She's not very big, but she canters well and she'll make a 2-y-o in mid-season, probably over seven furlongs".

1354. FLORA MEDICI ★★★
b.f. Sir Percy – Florentia (Medicean). March 13. First foal. The dam, a modest 1m and 10f winner, is a half-sister to 9 winners including the useful 6f and 7f winner of 4 races Flying Officer. The second dam, Area Girl (by Jareer), a fair 2-y-o 5f winner, is a half-sister to 3 minor winners. (W N Greig). "The dam was the last foal of a prolific winner-producing mare. I think I trained every one and they all won. This filly is only small but she canters very well and she looks a nice, mid-season 2-y-o type".

1355. HOT REPLY ★★★
br.f. Notnowcato – Cool Question (Polar Falcon). April 3. Seventh foal. Half-brother to the very smart Group 1 6f Golden Shaheen winner of 8 races Krypton Factor (by Kyllachy), to the quite useful dual 5f winner (including at 2 yrs) Fairfield Princess (by Inchinor), the quite useful 2-y-o dual 6f winner Haven't A Clue (by Red Ransom) and a winner in Sweden by Diktat. The dam, a useful 2-y-o 5f and listed 6f winner, is a half-sister to 4 winners. The second dam, Quiz Time (Efisio), a fairly useful 2-y-o 5f winner, was second in the listed St Hugh's Stakes and is a half-sister to 6 winners including the Group 3 Premio Dormello winner Brockette. (Lady Fairhaven & the Hon. C & H Broughton). "Not as sharp as some out of the mare, she gets 2-y-o's but this one will need a bit more time and is likely to run in the second half of the season".

1356. LADY BINGO (IRE) ★★★
b.f. Galileo – Sharp Lisa (Dixieland Band). May 3. Fourth foal. $250,000Y. Keeneland September. David Redvers. Half-sister to the quite useful Irish 3-y-o 7f and 1m winner Unanimous (by Dansili). The dam won the Grade 1 1m Las Virgines Stakes and two Grade 2 stakes in the USA and is a half-sister to the US Grade 1 9f Donn Handicap winner Spring At Last and the US Grade 2 9f Lake Placid Stakes winner Sharp Susan. The second dam, Winter's Gone (by Dynaformer), is an unplaced half-sister to 9 winners including the multiple US Grade 1 winner Bien Bien. (Qatar

Racing Ltd). *"An August type 2-y-o, she's not very big but she's big enough and beautifully bred. She has a very nice personality".*

1357. LEGAL SHARK (IRE) ★★★
b.c. Lawman – Sea Searcher (Theatrical). April 28. Second foal. 68,000Y. Tattersalls October Book 2. Amanda Skiffington. Half-brother to Admiral Quest (by Kheleyf), a 2012 2-y-o winner abroad. The dam is an unraced half-sister to 5 winners including the Canadian listed winner Atlantic Fury. The second dam, Search The Sea (by Seeking The Gold), a listed winner in Canada, is a half-sister to 10 winners including the Canadian Grade 2 winner Desert Waves. (Tim Bunting – Osborne House II). *"A big, strong horse that we almost sent away for a break, but we decided against it on the basis that he'd run at some point this year. One for the second half of the season".*

1358. MISS VERDOYANTE ★★
b.f. Montjeu – Miss Provence (Hernando). February 23. Fourth foal. Half-sister to the fairly useful 2012 2-y-o 7f winner and listed-placed Oasis Cannes (by Oasis Dream) and to the quite useful 10f to 12f winner of 3 races Miss Aix (by Selkirk). The dam, a quite useful 9f winner, is a sister to 2 winners including the 7f (at 2 yrs) and listed 10f winner Miss Corniche and a half-sister to 5 winners. The second dam, Miss Beaulieu (by Northfields), was a useful 6f and 10f winner. (J L C Pierce). *"A big, backward filly, being by Montjeu she won't run until September-time but I haven't turned her out so she'll hopefully do something this year".*

1359. MOUNTAIN KINGDOM (IRE) ★★★
b.c. Montjeu – Althea Rose (Green Desert). February 28. First foal. 95,000Y. Tattersalls October Book 1. Amanda Skiffington. The dam ran once unplaced and is a half-sister to 9 winners including the top-class National Stakes, Irish 2,000 Guineas and Irish Derby winner Desert King and the Group 3 Mooresbridge Stakes winner Cairdeas. The second dam, Sabaah (by Nureyev), a modest 8.2f placed maiden, is a full or half-sister to 8 winners including the Group 1 1m Queen Elizabeth II Stakes winner Maroof and to the placed dam of the Canadian Grade 2 winner

Callwood Dancer. (Tim Bunting – Osborne House). *"He should see the racecourse in August over seven furlongs. The first foal of the dam, he's not over-big but he's big enough".*

1360. NAMELY (IRE) ★★★
b.f. Rock Of Gibraltar – Viz (Darshaan). February 14. Fourth foal. €60,000Y. Goffs Orby. Not sold. Half-sister to the smart 2012 2-y-o listed 6f winner Viztoria (by Oratorio). The dam, a useful Italian listed 12f winner, is a half-sister to 6 winners including the smart 1m (at 2 yrs) to 10f winner and Group 3 placed Forbearing. The second dam, For Example (by Northern Baby), an Irish 10f placed maiden, is a half-sister to 5 winners and to the dams of the Group/Grade 1 winners Awe Inspiring, Culture Vulture, Polish Precedent and Zilzal. (Mrs Sonia Rogers). *"A good-looking filly, she'll be running in June/July. She didn't reach her reserve at the sale which surprised me as she was rather an attractive filly. Tall and leggy, she'll make a 2-y-o but she'll be better next year".*

1361. REAL JAZZ (IRE) ★★★
b.f. Marju – Sedna (Priolo). March 21. Second foal. 55,000Y. Tattersalls October Book 1. J R Collins. The dam, a quite useful Irish 6f and 7f winner at 5 yrs, is a half-sister to 4 winners including the dual Group 3 winning sprinter Captain Gerrard and the Hong Kong stakes winner Saturn. The second dam, Delphinus (by Soviet Star), won once at 3 yrs in France and is a half-sister to 3 minor winners. (T J Rooney). *"She'll be doing some work in May to see when she could run. She might want seven furlongs later on but she might have the pace to start at five".*

1362. RED PASSIFLORA ★★★
b.f. Danehill Dancer – Red Peony (Montjeu). April 25. Fourth foal. Half-sister to the 2012 7f placed 2-y-o Veronica Falls (by Medicean) and to the modest 2-y-o 7f winner Red Oleander (by Pivotal). The dam, a useful 7f (at 2 yrs) and 12f winner and Group 3 7f Prestige Stakes third, is a half-sister to 3 winners. The second dam, Red Azalea (by Shirley Heights), a fairly useful 7f (at 2 yrs) and 10f winner, is a half-sister to 4 winners including the Group 3 Prestige Stakes winner and French 1,000

Guineas third Red Camellia (herself dam of the Fillies Mile winner Red Bloom). (Cheveley Park Stud). *"A nice sort, she's having a break now but she'll make a 2-y-o in late September and will be a better 3-y-o".*

1363. ROHESIA ★★★

b.f. *High Chaparral – Common Knowledge (Rainbow Quest).* March 7. Closely related to the quite useful triple 12f winner Coin Of The Realm (by Galileo) and half-sister to the 2-y-o Group 3 7f C L Weld Park Stakes winner Coral Wave (by Rock Of Gibraltar) and to the smart dual Group 3 5f winner Astrophysical Jet (by Dubawi). The dam is an unraced half-sister to 6 winners including the Group 2 12f Jockey Club Stakes and dual US Grade 2 winner Blueprint and the listed 10f winner Fairy Godmother. The second dam, Highbrow (by Shirley Heights), a very useful 2-y-o 1m winner, was second in the Group 2 12f Ribblesdale Stakes, is closely related to the good middle-distance colt Milford and a half-sister to the Princess of Wales's Stakes winner Height of Fashion – herself the dam of Nashwan, Nayef and Unfuwain. (Qatar Racing Ltd). *"A nice, big filly, she'll be ready in August I should think. She's strong, quite athletic and a nice scopey filly".*

1364. SANCUS ★★★

ch.c. *Compton Place – Blue Echo (Kyllachy).* April 16. Third foal. 37,000Y. Tattersalls October Book 2. Sir Mark Prescott. Half-brother to the unplaced 2012 2-y-o Sword Of The Lord (by Kheleyf). The dam won 3 races including two listed events over 6f is a half-sister to 7 winners including the smart dual 2-y-o 6f winner and subsequent US Grade 2 9f winner Sapphire Ring and the smart dual listed winner Putra Pekan. The second dam, Mazarine Blue (by Bellypha), a modest sprint winner at 3 yrs, is a half-sister to 7 winners including Rich Charlie (Group 2 6f Richmond Stakes). (William Charnley & Richard Pegum). *"He's small and should make a 2-y-o at some point. He's been quite backward to come to hand in the spring but he's got to be a 2-y-o because of his size".*

1365. SARPECH (IRE) ★★★

b.c. *Sea The Stars – Sadima (Sadler's Wells).* March 6. Eighth foal. 430,000Y. Tattersalls

October Book 1. David Redvers. Half-brother to the high-class Group 1 12f Grand Prix de Saint-Cloud and Group 1 12f Preis von Europa winner Youmzain, to the minor Irish 12f winner Spontaneous (both by Sinndar), the Group 1 1m Lockinge Stakes and triple Group 3 winner Creachadoir, the fair 12f winner Savida (both by King's Best), the Irish Group 3 9.5f winner Shreyas and the Irish 2-y-o 1m winner Sagacious (both by Dalakhani). The dam, a fairly useful Irish 10f winner, is a half-sister to 6 winners abroad. The second dam, Anima (by Ajdal), was placed once at 3 yrs and is a half-sister to 8 winners including the multiple Group 1 winner Pilsudski. (Qatar Racing Ltd). *"A grand, big horse with plenty of size, scope and pedigree. The question with all those big ones is "will he be a nice jumper, or a nice stayer, a middleweight hunter-class animal or a top-class racehorse?! He's a gorgeous looking horse with a nice temperament and good limbs, but we haven't done anything with him yet obviously".*

1366. SECRET KEEPER ★★

ch.f. *New Approach – Confidante (Dayjur).* April 23. Eleventh foal. Half-sister to the Group 3 7f (at 2 yrs) and Group 1 10.5f Prix de Diane winner Confidential Lady (by Singspiel), to the fairly useful 7f winner Crown Counsel, the fair 5f and 7f winner Registrar (both by Machiavellian), the quite useful 11f and 12f winner Between Us (by Galileo), the quite useful 1m winner Censored (by Pivotal) and the moderate 1m and 10f winner Confide In Me (by Medicean). The dam, a fairly useful 3-y-o dual 7f winner, was listed-placed and is a half-sister to 6 winners including the US Grade 3 winner Drilling For Oil, the Group 3 7f Solario Stakes winner White Crown and the US listed winner and Grade 1 second Dr Caton. The second dam, Won't She Tell (by Banner Sport), a minor stakes winner of 9 races in the USA at up to 9f, is a half-sister to 9 winners notably the American Triple Crown winner Affirmed. (Cheveley Park Stud). *"The dam has bred one really good one but nothing much else. This filly is backward and we won't see her until the back-end of the season".*

1367. SHAFT OF LIGHT ★★★

b.c. *Exceed And Excel – Injaaz (Sheikh*

Albadou). March 11. Fourth foal. 42,000Y. Tattersalls October Book 2. Sir Mark Prescott. Brother to the fairly useful 2012 dual 5f placed 2-y-o Top Boy and half-brother to the fair 2-y-o 6f winners Fardyieh (by King's Best) and Classic Fortune (by Royal Applause). The dam, a quite useful 6f winner, was listed-placed and is a sister to the fairly useful 6f winner of 3 races Corndavon (herself dam of the smart 2-y-o Nevisian Lad) and a half-sister to the placed dam of the listed winners Pyman's Theory and Forthefirstime. The second dam, Ferber's Follies (by Saratoga Six), a winning 2-y-o sprinter, was third in the Grade 2 6f Adirondack Stakes and is a half-sister to 11 winners including the US 2-y-o Grade 2 6f winner Blue Jean Baby. (Mr B Haggas). *"He's what I'd call an 'un-Heath House type of horse' because he has a pedigree that's devoid of stamina! He owner said he wanted something quicker, so this is what we bought. He'll be out in mid-season and he's a nice, good-looking horse with the scope to make a 3-y-o as well".*

1368. SOIREE D'ETE ★★★

b.f. Selkirk – Souvenance (Hernando). February 20. Third foal. Half-sister to Sorcellerie (by Sir Percy), unplaced in two starts at 2 yrs in 2012 and to the fair 12f winner Nice Rose (by Teofilo). The dam, a fairly useful 2-y-o 7.2f winner, subsequently won a listed event in Germany, was third in the Group 1 Italian Oaks and is a sister to the 2-y-o Group 3 1m Prix des Reservoirs winner Songerie and a half-sister to 4 winners including the useful listed winners Soft Morning and Sourire. The second dam, Summer Night (by Nashwan), a fairly useful 3-y-o 6f winner, is a half-sister to 7 winners including the Group 3 Prix d'Arenburg winner Starlit Sands. (Miss K Rausing). *"She's a good-looking filly. The family normally produces seven furlong/mile 2-y-o types that win towards the end of the season. She looks like that".*

1369. SUNSET SHORE ★★★★ ♠

b.f. Oasis Dream – Summer Night (Nashwan). February 23. Tenth foal. Half-sister to the 2-y-o Group 3 1m Prix des Reservoirs winner Songerie, to the fairly useful 2-y-o 7.2f winner and Group 3 1m Prix des Reservoirs third Souvenance (both by Hernando), the useful listed 9.5f winner of 3 races Soft Morning

(by Pivotal), the fairly useful 7f (at 2 yrs) and Scandinavian listed 8.5f winner Sourire (by Domedriver), the fair triple 10f winner Aestival (by Falbrav) and a minor winner of 6 races in Italy by Selkirk. The dam, a fairly useful 3-y-o 6f winner, is a half-sister to 7 winners including the Group 3 Prix d'Arenburg winner Starlit Sands and the listed 6f winner Sea Dane. The second dam, Shimmering Sea (by Slip Anchor), a fairly useful Irish 2-y-o 5f and 7f winner and third in the Group 3 Silken Glider Stakes, is a half-sister to 5 winners including the King George VI and Queen Elizabeth Stakes winner Petoski. (Miss K Rausing). *"The dam is a half-sister to the fastest filly I've ever trained called Starlit Sands who was second in the Queen Mary and won the Prix d'Arenburg. She was by Oasis Dream, like this filly. She's a similar type, small, stocky and enormously strong. I haven't worked her yet".*

1370. THREETIMESALADY ★★★

b.f. Royal Applause – Triple Joy (Most Welcome). April 27. Twelfth foal. 37,000Y. Tattersalls October Book 3. Not sold. Half-sister to the French 1m (at 2 yrs) and listed 10.5f winner Trinity Joy (by Vettori and herself dam of the French dual listed winner Vaniloquio), to the very useful 6f (at 2 yrs) and 1m winner Triple Dash (by Nashwan), the fairly useful 2-y-o dual 6f winner and listed-placed Asaawir (by Royal Applause), the quite useful 6f and 7f winner of 4 races Triple Charm (by Pivotal), the fair 5f and 6f winner of 9 races Triple Dream (by Vision Of Night), the fair 7f and 1m winner of 5 races Tre Colline (by Efisio) and the Italian winner of 10 races Joy Of Norway (by Halling). The dam, a useful 6f and 7f winner and second in the listed Abernant Stakes, is a half-sister to 7 winners including the Sun Chariot Stakes winner Talented (dam of the Group 2 Dante Stakes winner Carlton House. The second dam, Triple Reef (by Mill Reef), is an unraced half-sister to 13 winners including the 1,000 Guineas and Oaks placed Maysoon and the Ribblesdale Stakes winner Third Watch. (Bluehills Racing Ltd). *"The last foal of an elderly mare who has done us well although she hasn't produced us anything as good as herself. A nice, straightforward filly and she'll run in mid-season".*

1371. TIMELY ★★★

gr.f. *Pivotal – Last Second (Alzao)*. March 17. Twelfth living foal. Half-sister to the French 2,000 Guineas and US Grade 1 winner Aussie Rules (by Danehill), to the useful 7.5f (at 2 yrs) and listed 10f winner and US Grade 2 second Approach, the very useful 2-y-o 8.5f winner and Group 1 Prix Marcel Boussac fourth Intrigued (both by Darshaan), the fairly useful 2-y-o 7f winner and Group 3 second Gooseberry Fool (by Danehill Dancer), the fairly useful 9f winner Fork Lightning (by Storm Bird), the fairly useful 10f winner Timeline (by Elusive Quality), the quite useful 10f winner Bold Glance and the minor US 2-y-o winner Pampered King (both by Kingmambo). The dam, winner of the Group 2 10f Nassau Stakes and the Group 2 10f Sun Chariot Stakes, is a half-sister to 7 winners including the Moyglare Stud Stakes third Alouette (herself dam of the Group 1 winners Albanova and Alborada) and the Group 2 Doncaster Cup winner Alleluia (dam of the Group 1 winner Allegretto) and to the placed dam of the Group 1 winners Yesterday and Quarter Moon. The second dam, Alruccaba (by Crystal Palace), a quite useful 2-y-o 6f winner, is out of a half-sister to the dams of Aliysa and Nishapour. (Denford Stud). *"A beautiful looking filly but she's grown a lot and I've got her turned out now. She'll run in September or October. I trained the sire and dam together and although Pivotal didn't show much at this stage of his life, Last Second showed plenty".*

1372. UPSHOT ★★★

b.f. *Pivotal – Soar (Danzero)*. Sister to the quite useful 6f and 1m winner Levitate and to the fair 6f winner Uprise and half-sister to the 2012 6f placed 2-y-o Hornboy and the quite useful 2-y-o 6f winner Racy (by Medicean). The dam, winner of the Group 2 6f Lowther Stakes and the Group 3 Princess Margaret Stakes at 2 yrs, is a half-sister to 5 winners including the very smart 6f and 7f winner of 7 races Feet So Fast. The second dam, Splice (by Sharpo), a smart winner of the listed 6f Abernant Stakes, is a full or half-sister to 7 winners. (Cheveley Park Stud). *"She's grown a lot but she's quite nice and will be an autumn sprinting filly I should think".*

1373. WINDSHIELD ★★

b.f. *Montjeu – Westerly Air (Gone West)*. March 26. Fifth foal. Half-sister to the fair 7f winner (on her only start at 2 yrs) Floodlit (by Fantastic Light) and to the fair 11f winner Weathervane (by Red Ransom). The dam, a fair 9.3f winner, is a sister to one winner and a half-sister to 4 winners including the Grade 2 Long Island Handicap, the Group 3 May Hill Stakes and Group 3 Prestige Stakes winner Midnight Line. The second dam, Midnight Air (by Green Dancer), won the Group 3 1m May Hill Stakes at 2 yrs and is a half-sister to 5 minor winners and to the dam of the Group 1 5f Prix de l'Abbaye winner Imperial Beauty. (Cheveley Park Stud). *"She's having a break at the moment and won't run until the back-end, probably over a mile".*

NOEL QUINLAN

1374. BELLE STAR ★★★

b.f. *Royal Applause – Dixie Belle (Diktat)*. April 12. Third foal. Half-sister to the fairly useful listed 6f winner Blanche Dubawi (by Dubawi) and to the fair 7f winner Diamond Belle (by Rock Of Gibraltar). The dam, a Group 3 5f and listed 6f winner, is a half-sister to one winner. The second dam, Inspiring (by Anabaa), is an unraced half-sister to 5 winners. *"We've trained all the dam's foals so far – the listed winner Blanche Dubois and the big, leggy filly Diamond Belle. This filly is leggy too, I won't rush her and I'll let her come to herself a bit more, but the dam has a 100% record so far and there's no reason why this filly shouldn't continue in the same vein".*

1375. GOLDEN SPEAR ★★★★

ch.c. *Kyllachy – Penmayne (Inchinor)*. April 20. Tenth foal. 130,000Y. Tattersalls October Book 2. BBA (Ire). Brother to the useful 2-y-o 5f and 6f winner and dual Group 3 placed Kylayne and the fairly useful 2-y-o 5f winner and Group 2 5f Norfolk Stakes third Tawaabb and half-brother to the Swedish winner of 4 races at 4 and 5 yrs Global Guardian (by Dr Fong) and the fair 1m winner Penzena (by Tobougg). The dam, a fairly useful 2-y-o 7f winner, was listed-placed and is a half-sister to 7 winners including the listed 1m winner Salamanca. The second dam, Salanka (by Persian Heights), a fair 3-y-o 10f winner, is a half-sister to one winner. *"A colt with a great attitude, he's full of energy and a real speed horse. A five/six furlong 2-y-o".*

1376. PAY THE GREEK ★★★

b.c. *Sleeping Indian – To Grace (Barathea).* February 18. Third foal. £8,000Y. Doncaster Festival. N Quinlan. Half-brother to a minor winner at 3 yrs in Italy by Jeremy. The dam, a minor French 3-y-o 1m winner, is a half-sister to 7 winners including US listed stakes winner Aliena and the US Grade 2 placed Brianda and Bedmar. The second dam, Gracious Line (by Fabulous Dancer), a minor French 3-y-o winner, is a half-sister to 6 winners including the Group 3 winners Gay Minstrel and Greenway and the dam of the Group 1 Prix de la Salamandre winner Oczy Czarnie. *"This little horse goes really well. We had a nice horse called Lewisham by Sleeping Indian last year so we know the sire can get a good one. At only £8k he's definitely the bargain buy for us and he's a nice, workmanlike 2-y-o that does everything easily".* TRAINERS' BARGAIN BUY

1377. SPEED FIEND ★★★★

b.c. *Bahamian Bounty – Vive Les Rouges (Acclamation).* February 21. First foal. 40,000Y. Tattersalls December. BBA (Ire). The dam, a fairly useful 2-y-o 6f winner, was second in the listed Dick Poole Stakes and is a half-sister to 3 winners including the useful dual listed 6f winner of 6 races (including at 2 yrs) Bounty Box. The second dam, Bible Box (by Bin Ajwaad), was a quite useful 7f to 9f winner of 3 races from 3 to 5 yrs. *"He was bred by Julia Scott and I'd seen the colt on the stud and loved him. There's plenty of Acclamation about him and I thought he was well bought for what he cost. A rangy colt, he's a six-furlong type 2-y-o and he could well start off in May. He goes so well that he might not even gallop at home and I like him a lot".*

1378. UNNAMED ★★★

b.f. *Green Desert – Steam Cuisine (Mark Of Esteem).* February 7. Second foal. 30,000Y. Tattersalls October Book 2. BBA (Ire). The dam, a fairly useful 7f and 1m winner of 4 races including at 2 yrs, was listed-placed twice. The second dam, Sauce Tartar (by Salse), a fairly useful 7f winner of 3 races (including

at 2 yrs), is a half-sister to one winner. *"There are eleven Green Desert 2-y-o's this year and it's his last crop. Nine of them are owned by Sheikh Hamdan, so this filly is something of a rarity. A really nice filly, she's like her mother in that she's a big, gross filly but surprisingly she'll come to hand around May or June time. She's very laid-back, like all my 2-y-o's this year".*

1379. UNNAMED ★★★

b.f. *Acclamation – Wildsplash (Deputy Minister).* February 19. Fifth foal. 100,000Y. Tattersalls October Book 1. Not sold. Sister to the fairly useful 2012 2-y-o 6f and 1m winner Janoub Nibras and half-sister to the fairly useful 2-y-o 6f winner Princess Severus, to the modest 1m to 11f winner of 3 races East Of Tara (both by Barathea) and the fair 7f to 9f winner of 9 races Just Five (by Olmodavor). The dam is an unraced half-sister to 4 winners including the French listed winner Royal God. The second dam, Gold Splash (by Blushing Groom), won the Group 1 Prix Marcel Boussac and the Group 1 Coronation Stakes and is a half-sister to the dam of the outstanding filly and Goldikova and the Group 1 winner Galikova. *"A nice filly that'll take a bit of time, although having said that her half-brother won twice as a 2-y-o and I expect she'll be racing by mid-summer. There's not a lot of Acclamation about her on looks, but the dam has had four winners from four foals and this filly can be another one".*

KEVIN RYAN

1380. ALASKAN NIGHT (IRE)

b.c. *Kodiac – Fingal Nights (Night Shift).* April 27. Fifth foal. £36,000Y. Doncaster Premier. Hillen & Ryan. Brother to the fair 2-y-o dual 5f winner Profile Star and half-brother to the fairly useful 2-y-o 6f winner and listed-placed Moonlit Garden (by Exceed And Excel). The dam, a fair 6f and 7f winner at 2 and 3 yrs, is out of the unplaced Advantageous (by Top Ville), herself a half-sister to 3 winners including the smart German Group 3 winner and 8.5f Diomed Stakes second Luzum. (Michael Beaumont & Brian Dunn).

1381. COMINO (IRE)

b.c. *Tagula – Malta (Gone West).* February 17. First foal. £31,000Y. Doncaster St Leger. Hillen & Ryan. The dam ran once unplaced and is a half-sister to 3 winners. The second dam, Kithira (by Danehill), a listed winner in France and the USA and was Group 3 placed twice and is a half-sister to 3 winners including the French Group 3 winner Tenuous. (D W Barker).

1382. LOCKY TAYLOR (IRE)
b.c. Bushranger – Hawk Eyed Lady (Hawk Wing). April 18. First foal. £27,000Y. Doncaster Premier. Hillen & Ryan. The dam, a modest 6f winner at 3 yrs, is a half-sister to 4 winners including Whitbarrow (13 wins including Group 3 Molecomb Stakes). The second dam, Danccini (by Dancing Dissident), won at 2 yrs and is a half-sister to 4 winners. (Kenneth MacPherson).

1383. MINDBLOWING
b.c. Mind Games – Musical Day (Singspiel). February 17. Fourth foal. £25,000Y. Doncaster Premier. Hillen & Ryan. Half-brother to the unplaced 2012 2-y-o Hit The Note (by Indesatchel). The dam, a quite useful 2-y-o 1m winner, is a half-sister to 4 winners including the 5f and 6f winner and listed-placed Day By Day and the Irish 3-y-o 5f winner Alexander Ballet (herself dam of the Group 1 Gran Criterium winner Hearts Of Fire). The second dam, Dayville (Dayjur), a quite useful triple 6f winner, is a half-sister to 4 winners including the Grade 1 Yellow Ribbon Handicap winner Spanish Fern and to the unraced dams of the Group/Grade 1 winners Lord Shanakill and Heatseeker. (Mr & Mrs Holdcroft & Mr K MacPherson).

1384. NELSON'S PRIDE
b.f. Mount Nelson – Bandanna (Bandmaster). February 2. Seventh foal. £22,000Y. Doncaster Premier. Hillen & Ryan. Half-sister to the fairly useful 2012 Group 3 6f placed 2-y-o Slope (by Acclamation), to the fairly useful 2-y-o 5.5f and subsequent Hong Kong winner Art Sale, the fair dual 5f winner Mandy's Hero (both by Compton Place), the fairly useful 2-y-o 7f winner Markazzi (by Dansili) and the quite useful 2-y-o 5f winner Rowayton (by Lujain). The dam, a fairly useful 5f and 6f winner of 6 races (including at 2 yrs), was third in the Group 2 Princess Margaret Stakes and is a half-sister to 5 winners including the Group 3 July Stakes winner Rich Ground. The second

dam, Gratclo (by Belfort), a modest winner of 5 races from 2 to 4 yrs, is a half-sister to 3 winners. (Hambleton Racing Ltd).

1385. ONLINE ALEXANDER (IRE)
b.f. Acclamation – Dance Club (Fasliyev). February 21. First foal. 100,000foal. Tattersalls December. BBA (Ire). The dam, a modest 7f winner, is a half-sister to the Group 1 Haydock Park Sprint Cup, Group 2 6f Coventry Stakes and Group 2 Diadem Stakes winner Red Clubs. The second dam, Two Clubs (by First Trump), won 5 races over 6f including the listed Doncaster Stakes and the listed Prix Contessina and is a half-sister to 7 winners including the 5f Windsor Castle Stakes winner and Group 1 Phoenix Stakes third Gipsy Fiddler. (Mr N I O'Callaghan).

1386. PROCLAMATIONOFWAR
b.c. Proclamation – Rockburst (Xaar). March 3. Second foal. £32,000Y. Doncaster Premier. Hillen & Ryan. Brother to the fairly useful 2012 2-y-o dual 5f winner and listed-placed Annunciation. The dam, a fair 2-y-o dual 6f winner, is a half-sister to 4 winners. The second dam, Topwinder (by Topsider), is an unplaced half-sister to 5 winners. (Mr M Beaumont).

1387. SOUL INSTINCT
b.c. Myboycharlie – However (Hector Protector). February 21. Fifth foal. £30,000Y. Doncaster Premier. Hillen & Ryan. Half-brother to the 5f winner of 4 races, including at 2 yrs, Mullglen (by Mull Of Kintyre). The dam is an unraced half-sister to 7 winners. The second dam, Evocatrice (by Persepolis), a winner at 2 yrs in France and listed-placed, is a half-sister to 6 winners and to the placed dam of the Group 1 winners Light Shift and Shiva. (Mr D Cork).

1388. UNNAMED
b.c. Exceed And Excel – Awwal Malika (Kingmambo). March 29. Third foal. 54,000Y. Tattersalls October Book 2. Rabbah Bloodstock. The dam, a fair 3-y-o 6f winner, is a half-sister to 2 winners in Japan. The second dam, First Night (by Sadler's Wells), a useful 1m winner and 10f listed-placed 3-y-o, subsequently won a minor event at 4 yrs in the USA. She is closely related to the Oaks

and Irish Derby winner Balanchine, to the Group 3 10f Rose Of Lancaster Stakes winner and Derby third Romanov and the Group 2 10f Sun Chariot Stakes winner Red Slippers (herself dam of the Group 1 Prix de Diane winner West Wind). (Saeed Manana).

1389. UNNAMED
b.c. Bahamian Bounty – Xtrasensory (Royal Applause). February 4. Fifth foal. £70,000Y. Doncaster Premier. Hillen & Ryan. Half-brother to quite useful the 2012 2-y-o 5f and 6f winner Tassel, to the quite useful 2-y-o 5f and 6f winner Tishtar (both by Kyllachy), the quite useful 2-y-o 6f winner Responsive (by Dutch Art), the fair 7f (at 2 yrs) and 1m winner Redsensor (by Redback) and the fair 6f winner Fenella Rose (by Compton Place). The dam, a fairly useful 2-y-o 6f winner, is a half-sister to 8 winners. The second dam, Song Of Hope (by Chief Singer), a useful 2-y-o 5f winner and second in the listed Firth of Clyde Stakes, is a half-sister to 10 minor winners. (Matt & Lauren Morgan).

DEREK SHAW
1390. BENS BOY (IRE) ★★★
b.c. Holy Roman Emperor – Final Opinion (King's Theatre). February 12. Fourth foal. £62,000Y. Doncaster Premier. Derek Shaw. Brother to the fair 1m winner Juvenal and half-brother to the French 2-y-o 1m winner and Group 3 1m second Footsteppy (by Footstepsinthesand) and the fair Irish 10f and 12f winner Fammi Sognare (by Bertolini). The dam, a quite useful Irish 10f and dual 13f winner, is a half-sister to 5 winners including the Group 3 6f Greenlands Stakes winner Final Exam and the 2-y-o Group 2 6f Lowther Stakes third Stuff Of Chester. The second dam, She Takes Two (by Alzao), is an unplaced half-sister to 2 minor winners. (Mr B Johnson). "He's quite forward, Martin Dwyer's ridden him and says he's very professional and ready for a run. He's a proper 2-y-o and has a good attitude".

1391. CAESAR'S GIFT (IRE) ★★★
b.c. Holy Roman Emperor – Jazz Up (Cadeaux Genereux). March 20. Eighth foal. 38,000Y. Tattersalls October Book 2. Derek Shaw. Half-brother to the smart 2-y-o Group 3 7f C L Weld Park Stakes and Group 3 7f Athasi

Stakes winner Jazz Princess (by Bahhare), to the useful 6f winner Sholaan (by Invincible Spirit) and the fair 8.5f winner Rudry Dragon (by Princely Heir). The dam is an unraced half-sister to 9 winners including the dual Italian listed winner Mister Cavern. The second dam, Slow Jazz (by Chief's Crown), a French 6f, 6.7f and listed 1m winner, is a three-parts sister to the smart Group 1 6f Middle Park Stakes winner Zieten and the Group 1 6f Cheveley Park Stakes winner Blue Duster and a half-sister to 8 winners. (Mr B Johnson). "Not as forward as my other Holy Roman 2-y-o, but he goes about his job nicely, he looks a proper 2-y-o and I'll probably start in April. He has a good temperament, he's quite laid-back and he might need a run to sharpen him up".

1392. DYNAMO WALT (IRE) ★★★
b.c. Acclamation – Cambara (Dancing Brave). April 14. Fourteenth foal. 50,000Y. Tattersalls October Book 2. Derek Shaw. Half-brother to the useful 7f (at 2 yrs) and 1m winner and Group 3 7f Horris Hill Stakes second Samhari (by Indian Ridge), to the fairly useful 2-y-o 7f and 10f winner Dubai On (by Daylami), the quite useful 4-y-o 1m winner Habshan (by Swain), the fair 2-y-o 6f winner Wohaida (by Kheleyf), the modest 10f winner Mrs Neat (by Refuse To Bend) and the UAE 6f winner Afreet (by Kris). The dam was a useful winner of three 1m events at 3 yrs and is a half-sister to 7 winners including the good French 6f to 1m triple Group 3 winner Pluralisme, the very useful German Group 3 and 10f Virginia Stakes winner Singletta, the Group 3 winner and Group 1 placed Only and the dam of the high-class miler Markofdistinction. The second dam, Cambretta (by Roberto), won over 9f in Ireland and is a sister to the high-class middle-distance colt Critique. (Mr B Johnson). "A lovely moving horse, he was going great but he's got a skin infection at the moment. He'll be ready to run by the middle of May, he's got a good attitude, a real gentleman to deal with and he's going the right way. He's very professional, a definite 2-y-o type on looks but with the size and scope to train on".

1393. JOHN LEA (IRE) ★★★
b.c. Bahamian Bounty – Eastern Appeal (Shinko Forest). March 2. Second foal. 30,000Y.

Tattersalls October Book 2. Derek Shaw. The dam, a dual Group 3 7f winner in Ireland, is a half-sister to 4 winners. The second dam, Haut Volee (by Top Ville), a German 2-y-o 6f and 1m winner, is a half-sister to 9 winners. (Mr B Johnson). *"He probably wants six furlongs, he's going OK and he seems to be going the right way. He seems sharp enough, he's certainly not slow and he's just starting to bloom. A professional, he goes about his job and once he's had a run I think he'll sharpen up".*

1394. KINGSWAY LAD (IRE) ★★★★

b.c. New Approach – Obsessive (Seeking The Gold). March 3. Twelfth foal. 42,000Y. Tattersalls December. Derek Shaw. Half-brother to the Group 1 St James's Palace Stakes and Group 2 Mill Reef Stakes winner and Grade 1 Breeders Cup Mile second Excellent Art (by Pivotal), to the smart 7f (at 2 yrs), 12f and 2m 4f Ascot Stakes winner Double Obsession (by Sadler's Wells), the fairly useful 1m winner Medallist (by Danehill), the quite useful 2-y-o 6f winner Spy Master (by Green Desert), the fair 2-y-o 8.6f winner Possessed (by Desert Prince) and a winner in Japan by Falbrav. The dam, a useful 2-y-o 6f winner and third in the Group 3 10.4f Musidora Stakes, is a half-sister to 7 winners. The second dam, Secret Obsession (by Secretariat), a fairly useful 10f winner, is a half-sister to 7 winners including the Group 2 12f King Edward VII Stakes winner Beyton. (Mr B Johnson). *"He has a bit of an attitude, but he goes about his job nicely and shows me plenty. I've just backed off him a bit because he was just getting a bit too keen and doing a bit too much too soon. He's quite tall, covers quite a bit of ground and he's a really willing horse that wants to please. He'll be out when the six furlong races start".*

1395. PHOENIX ANGEL ★★★

b.c. Footstepsinthesand – Ruthie (Pursuit Of Love). February 6. Fourth foal. 15,000Y. Tattersalls October Book 2. Derek Shaw. Half-brother to the quite useful 7f and 1m winner Dellbuoy (by Acclamation) and to the moderate 1m winner of 4 races Ermyntrude (by Rock Of Gibraltar). The dam, a fair 2-y-o 7.5f winner, is a half-sister to 6 winners the fairly useful 2-y-o listed 7f Sweet Solera Stakes winner Catwalk and the dam of the Group

3 Gallinule Stakes winner Grand Ducal. The second dam, Moogie (by Young Generation), a useful 2-y-o listed 5f winner, was fourth in the Group 1 Coronation Stakes and is a half-sister to 6 winners including the French listed winner Dazzling Heights. (Mr B Johnson). *"A nice, very 'buzzy' and sharp sort, he has a lot of natural speed and is probably a bit too keen for his own good. He's got an engine, but there's no rush with him because he doesn't look like an early 2-y-o and yet he does it all himself. I think he's alright and he's got plenty of speed even though he doesn't look a five furlong horse. He's got natural speed and I'm just trying to settle him down a bit".* TRAINERS' BARGAIN BUY

1396. PRIVADO ★★★

b.c. Excellent Art – Amaryllis (Sadler's Wells). January 28. Twelfth foal. £16,000Y. Doncaster Premier. Derek Shaw. Closely related to the fairly useful 2-y-o 7f winner and listed-placed Pipette (by Pivotal) and half-brother to the French 10f and 12f winner and Group 2 10.5f Prix Greffuhle second Day Or Night (by Daylami) and the French 12f and 14f winner According (by Dalakhani). The dam, a fair 7f winner at 2 yrs, is closely related to the smart French/US 1m/9f winner Corrazona and a half-sister to the Breeders Cup Classic third Thirty Six Red. The second dam, Heartbreak (by Stage Door Johnny), won at up to 9f in the USA. (Mr B Johnson). *"He's a nice 2-y-o that probably wouldn't want fast ground. He's showing a bit, but he's quite a heavy-topped horse and he's got sore shins at the moment. As soon as that's all cleared up he'll be ready to run, he's quite straightforward and he seems to be a six/seven furlong type".*

1397. UNNAMED ★★★

b.f. Dandy Man – Colourpoint (Forest Wildcat). March 29. First foal. 6,000Y. Tattersalls October Book 3. Derek Shaw. The dam, a 2-y-o listed 5f placed maiden, is a half-sister to 4 minor winners. The second dam, Farrfesheena (by Rahy), a fairly useful 1m placed maiden, is a sister to 2 winners and a half-sister 2 winners. *"She'll make a 2-y-o and I've entered her for the Supersprint. I didn't break her in until late on but she's got a lot of natural speed. She's not small – she's got a fair bit of size to her, but*

I've not really got going with her yet. She looks a proper sprinter".

1398. UNNAMED ★★★
gr.c. Elnadim – The Manx Touch (Petardia). May 1. Seventh foal. 40,000Y. Tattersalls October Book 2. Derek Shaw. Half-brother to the fairly useful 5f (at 2 yrs) and listed 6f winner of 8 races and Group 2 Criterium de Maisons-Laffitte second Baby Strange, to the modest 7f, 1m and hurdles winner Mambo Sun (both by Superior Premium), the 2012 7f placed 2-y-o Daring Dragon, the fairly useful 2-y-o dual 7f winner Frog Hollow, the fair triple 7f winner and listed-placed Moone's My Name (all by Intikhab) and the modest triple 6f winner Ride A White Swan (by Baryshnikov). The dam, a moderate 7f and 1m winner at 3 yrs, is a half-sister to 2 winners. The second dam, Chapter And Verse (by Dancer's Image), is an unraced half-sister to 4 winners out of the 1,000 Guineas and Oaks winner Altesse Royale. (Mr B Johnson). *"Just doing canter work at the moment, he has a good attitude and he's a lovely moving horse. I think I'll start him at six furlongs and he's doing everything asked of him without a problem. He's a lovely horse and he's got the scope to train on as a 3-y-o. The family make decent sprint handicappers and I've still got Baby Strange here".*

DAVID SIMCOCK
1399. ANYA'S ANGEL ★★★
b.f. Holy Roman Emperor – Someone's Angel (Runaway Groom). March 9. Fifth foal. £14,000Y. Doncaster Premier. Blandford Bloodstock. Half-sister to the fair 5f, 6f (including at 2 yrs) and 7f winner Ghostwing (by Kheleyf) and to the quite useful Irish 9f winner That Boy David (by Kodiac). The dam is an unplaced half-sister to 6 minor winners. The second dam, Yazeanhaa (by Zilzal), fourth over 6f at 2 yrs on her only outing, is closely related to the useful 2-y-o triple 6f winner Anjiz and a half-sister to the Group 2 5f Prix du Gros-Chene winner and Group 1 Prix de l'Abbaye third Nabeel Dancer. *"As a bunch my fillies are slightly more precocious than my colts. This filly is one of the more forward types and she's a good type. Quite strong, the sire gets them tough and she's just the same,*

so I'd expect to see her starting in a six furlong maiden in May".

1400. BARYE ★★ ♠
b.c. Archipenko – Oblige (Robellino). March 18. Second living foal. €57,000Y. Goffs Orby. Blandford Bloodstock. Half-brother to the French 2-y-o 10f winner Herrbuga (by Hernando). The dam, a useful 2-y-o dual 7f winner, was listed-placed twice and is a half-sister to 4 winners. The second dam, Acquiesce (by Generous), is an unraced half-sister to 4 winners including the Group 1 Prix Morny second Endless Summer. *"He doesn't go badly at all, but he's not an obvious 2-y-o so he won't see the racecourse until later in the season".*

1401. BORISOCRACY (IRE) ★★★
b.c. Acclamation – River Mountain (Reset). March 5. First foal. €190,000Y. Goffs Orby. Hugo Merry. The dam is an unraced half-sister to 7 winners including the useful 1m Britannia Stakes winner Analyser and the fairly useful 7f winner and listed 10f Lupe Stakes second Musical Treat (herself dam of the champion 2-y-o filly Finsceal Beo). The second dam, Mountain Ash (by Dominion), a winner over 7f twice at 2 yrs, was subsequently a very useful Italian Group 3 and listed winner over 7f and 1m. She is a half-sister to 7 winners including the 2,000 Guineas Trial winner Lidhame. *"A strong, mature type, he came in with a bit of a reputation as a playboy but he's settled down now, he's got into a good routine now and I'm happy with he's doing. A horse with plenty of size and scope, I think he's one of those later-maturing six furlong horses".*

1402. BRETON COMMANDER ★★★
b.c. Zamindar – Lady Donatella (Last Tycoon). April 1. Tenth foal. 30,000Y. Tattersalls October Book 2. Blandford Bloodstock. Brother to the useful 7f (at 2 yrs) and listed 1m winner Lord Zenith and half-brother to the quite useful 2-y-o 7f winner Maxwil (by Storming Home) and the modest 6f and 7.6f winner Dark Moon (by Observatory). The dam, a modest 12f placed maiden, is a half-sister to 7 winners including the very useful Group 3 Earl of Sefton Stakes winner Right Wing. The second dam, Nekhbet (by Artaius), a fair 5f to

7f placed 2-y-o, is a half-sister to 7 winners including the Irish St Leger winner M-Lolshan. *"Probably the type for later on in the season, he does everything in a nice way and he's a horse with a good outlook".*

1403. BREUGHEL (GER) ★★★
b.c. *Dutch Art – Bezzaaf (Machiavellian).* February 27. Eighth foal. €120,000Y. Goffs Orby. Tom Malone. Half-brother to the fairly useful 6f, 1m (both at 2 yrs) and 10f winner and listed-placed Zaskar (by Anabaa), to the useful 6f (at 2 yrs) and subsequent listed 7f Abu Dhabi winner Ans Bach (by Green Desert), the modest 7f (at 2 yrs) to 2m and hurdles winner Zefooha (by Lomitas) and two winners abroad by Bachir and Singspiel. The dam, a fairly useful 3-y-o 10f winner, is a half-sister to 5 winners. The second dam, Maid Of Kashmir (by Dancing Brave), a fairly useful Irish 10f winner and third in the listed Oaks Trial, is a half-sister to 7 winners. *"He's nicely related and the stallion is doing well. I don't think he's massively precocious and he's more of a seven furlong type but he has a nice way of going".*

1404. DIEGO VELASQUEZ (IRE) ★★★
b.c. *Duke Of Marmalade – Blessing (USA) (Pulpit).* February 8. The dam, a fair 10f placed maiden, is a half-sister to numerous winners in the USA including the Grade 3 placed Kris's Prayer. The second dam, My Prayer (by Hero's Honor), a US 6f winner, is a half-sister to the US Grade 2 winner Talakeno. *"I don't know a lot about the family but this colt goes well and I expect him to be an early seven-furlong type of 2-y-o. He has really nice outlook and he's a very mature horse – quite likeable".*

1405. DOCTOR SARDONICUS ★★★
ch.c. *Medicean – Never A Doubt (Night Shift).* March 5. Sixth foal. €120,000Y. Goffs Orby. Tom Malone/David Simcock. Half-brother to the useful 5f (at 2 yrs) and listed 7f winner and Group 2 7f Rockfel Stakes third Royal Confidence (by Royal Applause) and to the quite useful 1m winner Rougette (by Red Ransom). The dam, a very useful 2-y-o winner of the Group 2 5.5f Prix Robert Papin, is a half-sister to 3 winners. The second dam, Waypoint (by Cadeaux Genereux), a fairly useful 6f and 7f winner, is a half-sister to 5 winners including

the Group 2 6f Diadem Stakes winner and sire Acclamation. *"A colt from a fast family, but he's by Medicean and he won't be massively early I do feel that six furlongs will be his trip. He's likeable".*

1406. ERRONEUS (IRE) ★★★
br.c. *Footstepsinthesand – Atir Love (Green Dancer).* February 10. Fifth foal. £42,000Y. Doncaster Premier. Hugo Merry. Half-brother to 3 winners in Italy by Bachelor Duke (2) and Statue Of Liberty. The dam won 11 races in Italy and is a half-sister to 3 winners. The second dam, Really Nifty (by Prowess Prince), is an unplaced half-sister to 5 winners including Tropicaro (Group 1 Prix Marcel Boussac). *"He's forward enough and I'd like to think he'll out in May over six furlongs. He does everything easily but I wouldn't like to say how good he is just yet".*

1407. GREAT WAVE (IRE) ★★
b.f. *Duke Of Marmalade – Rosamixa (Linamix).* April 11. Third foal. Closely related to the listed 1m winner and Group 2 Superlative Stakes fourth Pearl Mix (by Oratorio). The dam, a winner at 2 yrs in France and fourth in the Group 3 Prix du Calvados, is a sister to the Group 3 Prix de Fontainebleau winner Rajsaman and the French listed winner Rosara (herself dam of the Group 1 Prix Marcel Boussac winner Rosanara). The second dam, Rose Quartz (by Lammtarra), won once over 13f at 3 yrs in Ireland. *"Not the prettiest to look at but she has a very natural way of going. One for the second half of the season I would imagine, she skips along and the sire hasn't had too bad a start".*

1408. HI LA MAI ★★★
b.c. *New Approach – Dance Lively (Kingmambo).* February 12. Sixth foal. 78,000Y. Tattersalls October Book 1. A & A. Half-brother to the Japanese 1m stakes winner Live Concert (by Singspiel), to the fairly useful 1m (at 2 yrs) and listed 13f winner Charleston Lady (by Hurricane Run), the fair 1m winner Tap Dance Way (by Azamour) and a winner in Greece by High Chaparral. The dam is an unraced half-sister to 7 winners including 3 stakes winners in the USA. The second dam, Tivli (by Mt Livermore), a US stakes winner of 7 races,

is a half-sister to a stakes winner. *"A nice, big horse, he's one for seven furlongs later on in the season. He has a good way of going and he's a good type".*

1409. MOMENTUS (IRE) ★★

b.f. Montjeu – Race For The Stars (Fusaichi Pegasus). April 6. Fourth foal. €82,000Y. Goffs Orby. Blandford Bloodstock. Half-sister to the quite useful Irish 2-y-o 1m winner Tibet (by Dansili). The dam, winner of the listed 7f Oh So Sharp Stakes (at 2 yrs) and the Group 3 9.5f Denny Cordell Fillies' Stakes, is a sister to the Irish 10f winner and Group 2 placed Zulu Chief, closely related to the National Stakes, Eclipse Stakes and Lockinge Stakes winner Hawk Wing and the minor Canadian stakes winner Alexandrina and a half-sister to numerous winners including the US dual Grade 3 placed Dr Sardonica. The second dam, La Lorgnette (by Val De L'Orne), was a champion 3-y-o filly in Canada. *"A big, scopey filly, she's still a bit on the weak side but she's doing everything right in her own way".*

1410. NO EASY DAY ★★★

b.c. Kheleyf – Komena (Komaite). April 29. Second foal. £29,000Y. Doncaster Festival. A & A. Brother to the fairly useful 5f (at 2 yrs) and 7f winner and Group 2 Norfolk Stakes second Reignier. The dam, a quite useful 2-y-o 6f winner, is a half-sister to 2 winners. The second dam, Mena (by Blakeney), is a placed half-sister to 3 winners. *"A forward 2-y-o, he has a few quirks about him which is very typical of the stallion but he does everything easily. A six furlong type for May".*

1411. SULTANTY ★★★

b.f. Shamardal – Caught On Camera (Red Ransom). February 10. First foal. 50,000Y. Tattersalls October Book 2. Blandford Bloodstock. The dam, a moderate 10f placed maiden, is a half-sister to 7 winners including the 2-y-o 5f and 7f Italian listed winner and Group 2 1m Falmouth Stakes second Croeso Cariad, the Irish listed 12f winner and Coronation Stakes and Irish Oaks third Mona Lisa and the Irish 2-y-o listed 7f winner Photogenic. The second dam, Colorsnap (by Shirley Heights), is an unraced half-sister to 9 winners including Colorspin (winner of the

Irish Oaks and dam of the Group 1 winners Opera House, Kayf Tara and Zee Zee Top), Bella Colora (winner of the Prix de l'Opera and dam of the very smart colt Stagecraft) and the Irish Champion Stakes winner Cezanne. *"A nippy filly and a real 2-y-o type, we won't be waiting too long to get her out".*

1412. SWAN LAKES (IRE) ★★★★

gr.f. Dalakhani – Rock Salt (Selkirk). April 14. Fifth foal. 280,000Y. Tattersalls October Book 1. Blandford Bloodstock. Half-sister to the Group 1 7f Moyglare Stud Stakes winner Termagant (by Powerscourt), to the fairly useful 1m (at 2 yrs) to 10f winner of 7 races and listed-placed Splinter Cell (by Johannesburg) and the quite useful 2-y-o 6f winner Planet Waves (by Red Ransom). The dam, placed twice at 3 yrs in France, is a sister to the very smart Group 2 10f Prix Eugene Adam and Group 3 9f Prix de Guiche winner Kirkwall and a half-sister to 4 winners. The second dam, Kamkova (by Northern Dancer), a placed middle-distance stayer, is a half-sister to 10 winners including the top-class US middle-distance colt Vanlandingham and the dams of the Group/ Grade 1 winners Distant Music and Funny Moon. *"Probably the most attractive filly we've got here. Even though she's by Dalakhani there's not a lot backward about her and she's very forward in everything she does. A nice-actioned filly with a lot of quality, she'll want seven furlongs to start with".*

1413. TOO FRISKY (IRE) ★★★★

b.g. Rock Of Gibraltar – Delisha (Salse). April 26. Eleventh foal. 25,000Y. Tattersalls October Book 2. Stephen Hillen. Half-brother to the very smart Group 3 6f Phoenix Sprint Stakes winner Al Qasi (by Elnadim), to the quite useful 10f winner of 5 races Ivan Vasilevich (by Ivan Denisovich), the modest 12f, 2m and hurdles winner Frameit (by Antonius Pius), the moderate 1m and 9f winner Margot Mine (by Choisir) and two multiple winners in Italy by Be My Guest and Victory Note. The dam won once at 3 yrs in Germany and is a half-sister to 6 winners including the Group 1 Hong Kong Mile winner Ecclesiastical. The second dam, Rachael Tennessee (by Matsadoon), was placed once in the USA and is a half-sister to 7 winners including the top-class miler Lear Fan.

"He's surprised me slightly. He's very natural and skips up the canter very well, he's a good-actioned horse and I would say the six/seven furlong maidens come May or June would be right up his street. I'm very pleased with him".

1414. ULTRAVIOLET (IRE) ★★★

b.f. *Tamayuz – Aphorism (Halling)*. April 9. Third foal. 68,000foal. Tattersalls December. Blandford Bloodstock. Half-sister to the fair 2012 2-y-o dual 5f winner Danz Choice (by Kheleyf). The dam, a fair 12f to 2m 2f winner, is a half-sister to 10 winners including the Group 2 12f Princess Of Wales's Stakes winner Craigsteel and the Group 1 20f Prix du Cadran winner and Ascot Gold Cup second Invermark. The dam, a smart winner of 3 races from 10f to 13.3f and placed in the Park Hill Stakes and the Princess Royal Stakes, is a half-sister to 6 winners including Coigach (Group 3 Park Hill Stakes). *"She showed up very well early on and I'd like to think she'll be one of the earlier 2-y-o runners. A filly with a nice way of going, she has a good action and is a filly I like".*

1415. VIGOR (IRE) ★★★

b.c. *Iffraaj – Miss Gibraltar (Rock Of Gibraltar)*. January 28. Second foal. £90,000Y. Doncaster Premier. Blandford Bloodstock. The dam ran once unplaced and is a half-sister to 3 winners. The second dam, Photogenic (by Midyan), a fairly useful 6f and listed 7f winner at 2 yrs, is a half-sister to 6 winners including the listed winner and Group 1 placed Mona Lisa and the very useful 2-y-o 5f and 7f Italian listed winner and Group 2 1m Falmouth Stakes second Croeso Cariad. *"One of the more forward 2-y-o's, I expect he'll start at six furlongs some time in May. He's done plenty and shows a good attitude".*

1416. WHISPERING STAR (USA) ★★★

b.br.f. *War Front – Eclisse (Ski Chief)*. April 26. First foal. $42,000Y. Keeneland September. Blandford Bloodstock. The dam, a winner of 3 races in France, subsequently won a stakes event in the USA and was second in the Grade 3 All Along Stakes and is a half-sister to 3 winners. The second dam, La Tzingara (by Crystal Glitters), won 3 minor races at 3 and 4 yrs in France and is a half-sister to a French listed winner. *"The sire's done fantastically*

well and we bought this filly relatively cheaply, probably because she was a bit small for the Americans. She's grown a bit since then, has a good, natural way of going and a bit of speed, so she's likeable".*

1417. UNNAMED ★★★

b.c. *High Chaparral – Clincher Club (Polish Patriot)*. March 15. Eleventh foal. 72,000Y. Tattersalls October Book 1. Blandford Bloodstock. Half-brother to the useful 2-y-o 6f winner and Group 2 6f Gimcrack Stakes third Sir Reginald (by Compton Place), to the smart 2 y o 6f winner and Group 1 1m Racing Post Trophy third Henrik (by Primo Dominie), the fairly useful 6f and listed 7f winner Intense Pink (by Pivotal), the quite useful 2-y-o 6f winners Bishop's Lake (by Lake Coniston) and Spritzeria (by Bigstone), the quite useful dual 7f winner Sard (by Bahamian Bounty) and a minor winner abroad by Soviet Star. The dam, a fair 5f (at 2 yrs) and 7.5f winner, is a half-sister to 9 winners. The second dam, Merry Rous (by Rousillon), won once at 2 yrs and is a half-sister to 5 winners including the dual Group 3 winning sprinter Tina's Pet. *"A good-sized horse, he's typical of the sire and will be better as the season goes on. A good type with a nice way of going and a good action".*

1418. UNNAMED ★★★

b.f. *High Chaparral – English Ballet (Danehill Dancer)*. April 3. Second foal. 30,000Y. Tattersalls October Book 2. Blandford Bloodstock. The dam, a 2-y-o Group 3 7f Sweet Solera Stakes winner, was third in the Group 1 Fillies' Mile and is a half-sister to 2 winners. The second dam, Stage Presence (by Selkirk), a 7f and 1m winner, is a half-sister to 6 winners including the 6f (at 2 yrs) and Group 3 7f Ballycorus Stakes winner Rum Charger (herself dam of the dual US Grade 1 winner Winchester). *"I'm surprised how forward she is and I would imagine she'll start off at seven furlongs in mid-season. A really good-goer, she's an attractive filly and although not the biggest she's plenty big enough".*

1419. UNNAMED ★★★

b.f. *Dutch Art – Greenfly (Green Desert)*. February 1. Sixth foal. 35,000Y. Tattersalls October Book 2. Blandford Bloodstock. Closely related to the fair 7f winner Desert Bump (by Medicean) and half-sister to the fair 2012 5f to 7f placed 2-y-o The Black Jacobin (by Piccolo) and a winner in Greece by Vettori. The dam, a modest 7f winner, is a half-sister to 2 winners. The second dam, Exact Replica (by Darshaan), is an unraced sister to the Group 2 winner and dual Group 1 placed Darnay. *"She was a bit sick earlier on in the year but she's caught up with the others now. A real 2-y-o type, she's not the biggest but she's very strong and mature so I'll be kicking on with her. Six furlongs in May should be her starting point".*

1420. UNNAMED ★★★
b.c. Thewayyouare – Luck Be A Lady (Alhaarth). February 13. The dam, placed fourth once over 7f at 3 yrs from 2 starts, is a half-sister to several winners including the smart Group 3 6f Phoenix Sprint Stakes winner of 10 races Bonus, to the very useful Irish listed 7f winner and Group 3 placed Georgebernardshaw and the useful 7f to 9f listed winner of 7 races Third Set. The second dam, Khamseh (by Thatching), a quite useful 7f winner at 3 yrs, is a half-sister to the high-class Group 2 12f Hardwicke Stakes and Group 2 12f Blandford Stakes winner Predappio. *"By a first season sire out of a mare that wasn't very good herself but she's closely related to a few nice ones. This is a big horse with a big stride and a very likeable way of going. One for the middle of the season over seven furlongs because although he's big he is very natural with it".*

1421. UNNAMED ★★★
ch.c. Street Cry – Modesty Blaise (A P Indy). March 9. Third foal. $100,000Y. Keeneland September. Blandford Bloodstock. Half-brother to the French listed 9f winner and Group 3 11f Prix Cleopatre second Poupee Flash (by Elusive Quality). The dam, placed at 2 yrs in France, is a sister to the stakes winner Tomisue's Indy and a half-sister to the triple US Grade 1 winner (over 7f and 1m) Aldebaran, the Canadian Grade 1 Atto Mile winner Good Journey and the US Grade 3 winner Sea Of Showers. The second dam, Chimes Of Freedom (by Private Account), won the Group 1 6f Moyglare Stud Stakes and the Group 3 6f Cherry Hinton Stakes at 2 yrs, prior to winning

the Group 1 1m Coronation Stakes and the Group 2 1m Child Stakes in her second season. She is a half-sister to the Grade 1 winner Denon and to the 2-y-o listed 6f winner and Cheveley Park Stakes second Imperfect Circle (herself dam of the top-class miler Spinning World). *"A colt from a lovely family, he's grown and grown since the sales but has a very likeable way of going. He's got half a chance and is one for the mid-to-late season".*

1422. UNNAMED ★★★
ch.c. Mastercraftsman – Mohican Princess (Shirley Heights). May 9. Ninth foal. €42,000Y. Goffs Orby. Blandford Bloodstock. Half-brother to the useful 2012 2-y-o 1m winner and Group 3 1m Autumn Stakes third Eye Of The Storm, to the fairly useful triple 12f winner Livia Galilei, the modest Irish 12f winner (on only start) Miss Coco (all by Galileo), the smart Group 3 6f Sirenia Stakes (at 2 yrs) and Group 3 1m Joel Stakes winner Satchem (by Inchinor), the useful Irish 2-y-o 6f winner and Group 2 7f Debutante Stakes second Oui Say Oui (by Royal Applause) and the quite useful 6f (at 2 yrs) to 9f winner Prince Golan (by Golan). The dam ran once when fourth over 10f at 3 yrs and is a half-sister to 5 winners. The second dam, Mohican Girl (by Dancing Brave), a dual listed 10f winner, is a half-sister to the good fillies Untold, Sally Brown (both winners of the Yorkshire Oaks) and Shoot Clear (Waterford Candelabra Stakes winner). *"A lovely, big, scopey horse with a lovely way of going, he has a good action and is a very likeable colt for later in the season".*

1423. UNNAMED ★★★
b.c. Hernando – Oval Office (Pursuit Of Love). May 2. Fourth foal. €75,000Y. Goffs Sportsman's. Stephen Hillen. Half-brother to the smart 2012 2-y-o Group 3 6f Sirenia Stakes winner Glass Office (by Verglas). The dam, a fairly useful 3-y-o dual 1m winner, is a half-sister to 12 winners including the smart 6f (at 2 yrs) and Nell Gwyn Stakes winner Myself and the smart 2-y-o 6f Princess Margaret Stakes and 3-y-o 6f Prix de Seine et Oise winner Bluebook. The second dam, Pushy (by Sharpen Up), a very useful 2-y-o winner of 4 races including the Queen Mary Stakes, is a half-sister to 10 winners including the good

winners Precocious and Jupiter Island. *"This is a horse I like. We trained his half-brother Glass Office last year and this is a much bigger type of horse. He should stay a mile without a problem, he has a very laid-back outlook on life and does everything right".*

1424. UNNAMED ★★★★

b.c. Halling – Preceder (Polish Precedent). March 15. Sixth foal. 52,000Y. Tattersalls October Book 2. Blandford Bloodstock. Half-brother to the 2012 7f placed 2-y-o (on her only start) Precinct (by Refuse To Bend) and to the Group 3 Craven Stakes winner and Group 2 third Metropolitan Man (by Dr Fong). The dam is an unraced half-sister to 10 winners including the US stakes winner Way Of The World and the very useful 6f and 1m winner and Group 3 second Hoy. The second dam, Fairy Tern (by Mill Reef), winner of the listed Strensall Stakes, is a full or half-sister to 8 winners including the Group 2 Tattersalls Rogers Gold Cup winner Elegant Air. *"I know the family quite well because I had his half-brother Metropolitan Man and he showed enough early doors, a bit like this fellow. A very natural horse that does everything very easily, he has a good action and wants to get on with it. He's very pleasing and one for the early seven furlong races. A horse with a real chance".*

1425. UNNAMED ★★★★

b.f. Giant's Causeway – Swan Nebula (Seeking The Gold). February 22. Third foal. $310,000Y. Keeneland September. Hugo Lascelles. Sister to the 2012 Irish 2-y-o 5f winner Vinson Massif. The dam, a fairly useful 2-y-o 6f and 6.5f winner, is a sister to the Japanese $3.5 million earner Gold Tiara and a half-sister to the Group 1 1m Queen Elizabeth II Stakes, Group 2 1m Celebration Mile and 2-y-o Group 2 7f Champagne Stakes winner Poet's Voice and the minor US stakes winner Queen's Park. The second dam, Bright Tiara (by Chief's Crown), a minor 2-y-o winner in the USA, is a sister to the Grade 1 Brooklyn Handicap winner Chief Honcho and a half-sister to 10 winners including the dam of the US dual Grade 2 winner American Chance. *"Quite classy, she's a good-sized filly with a good way of going. She's not going to be early but she*

has quality, finds everything very easy and never gets tired. A filly I have a lot of time for".*

1426. UNNAMED ★★★★

b.f. Fastnet Rock – Uriah (Acatenango). March 25. Fifth foal. 42,000Y. Tattersalls October Book 1. Blandford Bloodstock. Closely related to the 2-y-o 6f and subsequent Hong Kong 9f stakes winner Uramazin (by Danehill Dancer) and to the fair 10f winner City Vaults Girl (by Oratorio) and half-sister to the useful 10f and 12f winner and listed-placed Unleashed (by Storming Home). The dam won 5 races at 3 yrs from 10f to 12f in Germany and the USA including the Grade 2 Long Island Handicap and is a full or half-sister to 8 winners. The second dam, Ulanowa (by Kamiros II), won twice at 2 yrs in Germany and is a half-sister to 3 other German winners. *"A real hardy filly, she gives plenty and we'll push on with her. A strong, mature type with a great attitude to life, I'm pretty sure she'll have the speed for six furlongs but she'll get seven in time".*

1427. UNNAMED ★★★

b.c. Galileo – Walklikeanegyptian (by Danehill). January 23. The dam, a fair 2-y-o 5f and subsequent US winner, was Grade 3 placed and is closely related to numerous winners including the Canadian Grade 2 Nassau Stakes winner Callwood Dancer and the Group 2 Italian Oaks winner Contredanse. The second dam, Ahdaab (by Rahy), placed once over 10f, is a half-sister to 8 winners including the Group 1 1m Queen Elizabeth II Stakes winner Maroof and to the placed dam of the Irish Derby winner Desert King. *"A colt with a great outlook on life, he's a good-actioned horse, quite forward and you'd expect to see him around June/July time over seven furlongs".*

TOMMY STACK

1428. AIN'T NO SURPRISE (IRE) ★★★

b.f. Kheleyf – Harmonist (Hennessy). April 16. Sixth foal. £33,000Y. Doncaster Premier. C McCormack. Half-sister to the modest dual 9f winner Theother Haaf (by Alhaarth) and to a minor winner in Italy by Barathea. The dam won twice at 3 yrs in the USA and is a half-sister to 4 winners including the US Grade 2 placed Country Store. The second dam, Geraldine's Store (by Exclusive Native), won

13 races including the Grade 2 Diana Handicap and is a half-sister to the Irish 1,000 Guineas and Coronation Stakes winner Al Bahathri (herself dam of the 2,000 Guineas and Champion Stakes winner Haafhd). *"She was all set to run but had a minor setback. If all goes according to plan she'll be out in late April over five furlongs. She should get six, but she'll want very fast ground".*

1429. AMARIDIAN (IRE) ★★★

b.f. *Cape Cross – Idilic Calm (Indian Ridge).* March 30. Eighth foal. €100,000Y. Goffs Orby. Form Bloodstock. Half-sister to the UAE Group 2 Godolphin Mile and listed King Charles II Stakes winner Calming Influence (by King's Best), to the Irish listed and subsequent Canadian Grade 2 Nearctic Handicap winner Steel Light (by Stravinsky), the fairly useful 2-y-o 7f winner Dark Humour (by Bahri) and the fair 6f winner Marajel (by Marju). The dam, a fair Irish 7f winner, is a half-sister to 3 winners. The second dam, Miracle Drug (by Seattle Slew), ran unplaced twice and is a half-sister to 9 winners including the US Grade 1 winner Twilight Agenda and the dams of the Group 1 winners Go And Go, Refuse To Bend and Media Puzzle. *"She seems to go nicely but she's a bit backward because of the cold weather we've had. What we've seen of her so far we like".*

1430. ASHTAROTH ★★★

b.f. *Royal Applause – Asheyana (Soviet Star).* March 3. Fourth foal. 32,000Y. Tattersalls December. Cormac McCormack. Closely related to Cottrell (by Acclamation), placed fourth over 1m from two starts at 2 yrs in 2012 and half-sister to the quite useful 2-y-o dual 7f winner Dubarshi (by Dubawi) and to the modest 1m and 10f winner Ashkalara (by Footstepsinthesand). The dam is an unraced sister to the high-class miler Ashkalani, winner of the Group 1 Prix du Moulin and the Group 1 French 2,000 Guineas and a half-sister to 2 winners. The second dam, Ashtarka (by Dalsaan), won over 1m in France and is a half-sister to 4 winners including Shafaraz (Group 1 Prix du Cadran) and Ajarann (Group 1 Premio Roma second). *"A big, raw filly, she'll take a little bit of time – maybe until the mid-summer – but she's a good mover".*

1431. DASH (IRE) ★★★

ch.f. *Danehill Dancer – Challow Hills (Woodman).* January 31. First foal. 82,000Y. Tattersalls October Book 1. Cormac McCormack. The dam, a modest 1m winner, is a half-sister to 4 winners including the US stakes winner and Grade 3 placed Teide. The second dam, Cascassi (by Nijinsky), a fair 10f winner here, also won at 4 yrs in France and is a half-sister to 5 winners including Diminuendo (Epsom, Irish and Yorkshire Oaks winner) and the Oaks second Pricket. *"A good, strong filly that goes nicely. We'll hopefully have her out in May and although she'll get seven furlongs later on I wouldn't be afraid to set her off at six".*

1432. FERRARI SAFARI ★★★★

b.c. *Danehill Dancer – Mowaadah (Alzao).* May 6. Sixth foal. €100,000Y. Arqana Deauville August. Form Bloodstock. Brother to the fair 2-y-o 6f winner Biba Diva and half-brother to the fair 1m winner Balloura (by Swain). The dam won 3 races over 1m including a listed event and is a half-sister to 5 winners including the Eclipse Stakes and Irish Champion Stakes winner Oratorio and the English and US winner and US Grade 1 second Fahim. The second dam, Mahrah (by Vaguely Noble), a fairly useful 3-y-o 1m winner, is a half-sister to 6 winners including the very useful Group 2 12f Blandford Stakes winner Andros Bay. *"A fine, big, strong horse out of a half-sister to Oratorio. He's a good moving horse that I like. I would imagine seven furlongs to a mile would be his trip this year".*

1433. FINE CUT (IRE) ★★★

b.c. *Dark Angel – Non Dimenticar Me (Don't Forget Me).* May 14. Thirteenth foal. €27,000Y. Tattersalls Ireland September. John O'Byrne. Half-brother to the useful 1m (including at 2 yrs) and listed 6f winner and Irish 1,000 Guineas second Dimenticata (by Danetime), to the useful listed 6f winner Master Fay, the fair 2-y-o 5f winner Louvolite (both by Fayruz), the useful 7f winner and listed-placed Zarin (by Inzar), the quite useful triple 6f winner Didn't We and the German winner at up to 11f Sambucan Daze (both by Mujadil). The dam, a modest 3-y-o 5f winner, stayed 7f and is a half-sister to 7 winners. The second dam,

Amboselli (by Raga Navarro), was a fair 5f placed 2-y-o and a half-sister to 9 winners. *"He ran OK on his debut and he'll have his next outing at the end of April in an auction race. There's not much of him but he should be able to win a race like that and he's a five/six furlong 2-y-o".*

1434. MAIN STRAITS ★★★

b.c. Rock Of Gibraltar – Moojeh (King's Best). April 17. First foal. 45,000Y. Tattersalls October Book 2. De Burgh Equine. The dam, a fair dual 7f winner, is a half-sister to one winner. The second dam, Bahareeya (by Riverman), is an unraced sister to the Group 1 1m St James's Palace Stakes and Group 1 1m Queen Elizabeth II Stakes winner Bahri and a half-sister to 5 winners including the high-class 2-y-o Group 2 7f Laurent Perrier Champagne Stakes Bahhare. *"A good-moving horse, he should be racing by mid-May but he's probably more of a seven furlong type, or maybe even a mile".*

1435. ONENIGHTIDREAMED (IRE) ★★★

ch.c. Footstepsinthesand – Pivotalia (Pivotal). February 24. Second foal. 24,000Y. Tattersalls October Book 2. De Burgh Equine. Half-brother to the 2012 3-y-o Eesti Poiss (by Oratorio). The dam, a modest 9.5f winner, is a half-sister to 3 winners. The second dam, Viscaria (by Barathea), an Irish 1m (at 2 yrs) and 10f winner, was listed-placed in France and is closely related to the UAE Group 3 winner Stagelight and a half-sister to 7 winners including the 1,000 Guineas third Hathrah, the smart Group 2 12f Premio Ellington winner Ivan Luis and the French/German listed winners Amathia and Zero Problemo. The second dam, Zivania (by Shernazar), a useful Irish winner of 4 races from 1m to 9.5f, is a half-sister to 4 stakes winners. *"A big, strong horse that moves well, he'll probably want six or seven furlongs and he seems to go well, so we're happy with him".*

1436. ROBIN'S CHOICE (IRE) ★★★

b.f. Bushranger – Creekhaven (Definite Article). April 14. Fourth foal. €70,000Y. Goffs Orby. C McCormack Bloodstock. Half-sister to the quite useful Irish 6f winner and listed-placed Lechevelier Choisi (by Choisir). The dam, a

poor 7f to 9f placed maiden, is a sister to the 2-y-o listed 1m winner and Group 3 Prix Saint-Roman second La Vita E Bella and a half-sister to 4 winners including the useful 2-y-o dual listed 5f winner and Group 2 third Bella Tusa. The second dam, Coolrain Lady (by Common Grounds), was placed 12 times in Ireland from 1m to 10f and is a half-sister to 4 winners. *"A big, scopey filly, she'll make a 2-y-o by June/July time, she's a good-mover and there's plenty of strength to go with it".*

1437. SEA ADVENTURE (IRE) ★★★

b.f. Royal Applause – Miss Smilla (Red Ransom). February 13. First foal. £70,000Y. Doncaster Premier. John O'Byrne. The dam, a fair 2-y-o 6f winner, is a half-sister to 4 winners including the Group 2 and dual Group 3 sprint winner The Trader. The second dam, Snowing (by Tate Gallery), a quite useful dual 5f winner at 3 yrs, is a half-sister to 2 minor winners. *"She looks sharp, she'll be out in late April or early May and she'll want fast ground. I don't see her getting further than six furlongs".*

1438. TREADSTONE ★★★★

b.c. Myboycharlie – Lilli Marlane (Sri Pekan). February 17. Fifth foal. £52,000Y. Doncaster Premier. C McCormack. Half-brother to the fair 6f (at 2 yrs) and 7f winner Pearl Rebel (by Cockney Rebel) and to the moderate 7f winner Philmack Dot Com (by Traditionally). The dam, a fair and 1m and 10f winner, is a half-sister to 5 winners including Medici Code (by Medicean), a quite useful 1m and 9f winner here and subsequently winner of the Grade 2 Del Mar Derby in the USA. The second dam, Fiveofive (by Fairy King), a modest 5f (at 2 yrs) and 1m winner, is a half-sister to 4 winners. *"He seems to go nicely, he's a real uncomplicated horse and should be racing in mid-April. A bonny colt, he's not over-big but he's a real, early 2-y-o that'll start at five furlongs but should get six".*

1439. UNNAMED ★★★

b.f. Mastercraftsman – Amazing Krisken (Kris S). April 18. Sixth foal. 9,500Y. Tattersalls December. Not sold. Half-sister to the Group 3 12f Prix de Royaumont winner Sub Rose (by Galileo), to the minor French 10f winner Loch Etive (by Rock Of Gibraltar) and the minor Italian winner, at 2 and 4 yrs, Hell In A Cell (by Act One). The dam is an unraced half-sister to 4 winners including the US Grade 1 third Truckle Feature. The second dam, Magic Gleam (by Danzig), won the Group 2 Child Stakes and was placed in the Group 1 Coronation Stakes and the Group 1 Prix Jacques le Marois and is a half-sister to 4 winners including the South African Group 1 winner Flying Snowdrop. *"A nice, good-moving filly, she's strengthened up well. We haven't put a gun to her head yet but she looks like a seven furlong/mile type in the mid-summer".*

1440. UNNAMED ★★★★

b.f. Sea The Stars – Blas Ceoil (Mr Greeley). May 1. Second foal. Half-sister to the fair 2012 6f to 1m placed 2-y-o Rapid Approach (by New Approach). The dam, a useful Irish 2-y-o 5f and 6f winner, is a half-sister to the Irish dual Group 3 winner Radharcnafarraige out of Extraterrestral (by Storm Bird). *"A good-moving filly, she's developing well and she'll come to hand quick enough, so she'll be racing in May over six or seven furlongs I should think".*

1441. UNNAMED ★★★

b.f. Oratorio – Chantarella (Royal Academy). April 28. Half-sister to the fairy useful 2-y-o 5f winner, listed-placed and Group 2 6f Railway Stakes fourth Another Express, to the fairly useful triple 5f winner (including at 2 yrs) Celerina (both by Choisir) and the moderate Irish 6f winner Candy Kiss (by Mull Of Kintyre). The dam is an unplaced half-sister to several winners including the listed 5f Rous Stakes winner My-O-My. The second dam, Maimiti (by Goldhill), is an unplaced half-sister to the useful Irish sprinter Title Roll, winner of the Group 3 King George Stakes and to the listed sprint winner Northern Express. *"She goes nicely and we've been lucky with the family. She probably needs a bit of ease in the ground and at the moment she looks like a six furlong filly".*

1442. UNNAMED ★★★

gr.f. Mastercraftsman – Fand (Kingmambo). February 21. First foal. The dam is an unplaced sister to the listed 1m winner Mambo Light and a half-sister to the Group 3 5f King George Stakes and Group 3 5f Ballyogan

Stakes winner Dietrich. The second dam, Piquetnol (by Private Account), a French 3-y-o winner and second in the Group 1 Prix Marcel Boussac, is a sister to the dual Group 1 winner Chimes of Freedom (the dam of two Grade 1 winners) and a half-sister to the multiple US Grade 1 winner Denon and the dam of Spinning World. *"A nice filly and a good mover, she's taking a bit of time to come to hand with the cold spring that we've had. She looks a sprinting type and when the weather warms up she'll hopefully come to hand fairly quickly".*

1443. UNNAMED ★★

b.f. Fastnet Rock – Mer de Corail (Sadler's Wells). April 14. €180,000Y. Arqana Deauville August. Form Bloodstock. Half-sister to the quite useful 2-y-o 1m winner Hot Bed (by Dashing Blade) and to the useful 1m, 9f and listed 10f winner Alsace Lorraine (by Giant's Causeway). The dam, winner of the listed 10f Prix d'Automne, is a sister to the winner and listed-placed Maximum Security. The second dam, Miss Tahiti (by Tirol), won the Group 1 1m Prix Marcel Boussac at 2 yrs and was placed in the Prix de Diane, the Prix Vermeille and the Prix Saint-Alary. *"A nice filly and a good mover, she's probably one for the second half of the season and she's got a bit of size and scope".*

1444. UNNAMED ★★★

gr.f. Myboycharlie – Misty Eyed (Paris House). February 16. Fourth foal. 65,000Y. Tattersalls October Book 2. Cormac McCormack. Half-sister to the quite useful 5f and 6f winner Mister Musicmaster (by Amadeus Wolf). The dam, a smart 2-y-o winner of 4 races including the Group 3 5f Molecomb Stakes, was Group 2 placed twice and is a half-sister to 3 minor winners. The second dam, Bold As Love (by Lomond), is an unraced half-sister to 3 winners abroad. *"A big filly with plenty of size and scope, she's a good mover. She's not going to be early but hopefully she'll be a nice filly around June time".*

1445. UNNAMED ★★

b.f. Danehill Dancer – Simadartha (Gone West). May 13. Tenth foal. 70,000Y. Tattersalls October Book 1. Not sold. Sister to the useful Irish 2-y-o 6f and 7f winner and Group 3

Leopardstown 2,000 Guineas Trial third Vault and half-sister to the fairly useful 7f winner Top Class (by Storm Cat). The dam, a minor winner at 3 yrs in France, is a half-sister to 4 winners including the Group 1 Grand Criterium winner Way Of Light. The second dam, Salchow (by Nijinsky), is an unraced three-parts sister to the smart miler Hydro Calido and a half-sister to the Group 1 winners Coup de Genie, Machiavellian and Exit To Nowhere. *"She's a big, fine filly that'll take a bit of time. Definitely one for the second half of the season, but she's a nice-moving 2-y-o".*

1446. UNNAMED ★★★
b.f. Royal Applause – Starry Sky (Oasis Dream). March 11. Second foal. 13,500Y. Tattersalls December. C McCormack. Half-sister to the unplaced 2012 2-y-o Don't Tell (by Sakhee's Secret). The dam, a fair 2-y-o 7f winner, is a half-sister to one winner. The second dam, Succinct (by Hector Protector), a useful listed 10f winner, is a half-sister to 3 winners including the German listed winner Succession. *"A five/six furlong 2-y-o that moves well, I don't know a lot about her except that we like what we've seen so far and she should be racing sometime in the first half of the year".* TRAINERS' BARGAIN BUY

OLLY STEVENS
1447. EXTORTIONIST (IRE) ★★★★
b.c. Dandy Man – Dream Date (Oasis Dream). February 4. First foal. £30,000Y. Doncaster Premier. David Redvers (private sale). The dam, a quite useful dual 7f winner, is a half-sister to 3 winners. The second dam, Femme Fatale (by Fairy King), a useful dual 6f winner of 2 races (including a listed event at 2 yrs), is a half-sister to 3 winners including the dual listed 10f winner and smart broodmare Foodbroker Fancy. (Sheikh S A K H Al Thani). *"We're quite excited about this horse, he'll start in mid-April over five furlongs and he might get an easy six later on but no further than that. A muscular colt, he's built like a quarter horse and I wouldn't want to run him on a downhill track because he's such a heavy-topped horse. We'll point him towards the Coventry at Royal Ascot and hope he proves good enough to take his place".*

1448. FOXTROT PEARL ★★★
b.f. Bahamian Bounty – Nina Blini (Bertolini). March 2. First foal. 15,000Y. Tattersalls October Book 2. David Redvers. The dam, a 2-y-o 5f winner and third in the Group 2 Queen Mary Stakes, is a half-sister to one winner in the USA. The second dam, Film Buff (by Midyan), is a placed half-sister to 5 winners including the Irish listed 1m winner and Irish 1,000 Guineas third Starbourne. (Foxtrot Racing). *"She's fine, although she was a bit weaker than some of the others during the winter so she's not as forward as her breeding might suggest, but she's not big and she isn't going to take long to get ready. She's pretty sharp and she throws everything at it, but I don't she'll be going to the Queen Mary like her mother did, simply because we won't have enough time".*

1449. FRACKING (IRE) ★★★
ch.c. Intikhab – Carson Dancer (Carson City). March 30. Eighth foal. £26,000Y. Doncaster Premier. David Redvers. Half-brother to the quite useful Irish 2-y-o dual 7f winner Mistress Bailey (by Mister Baileys), to the fair 2-y-o 7f and 1m winner Digger Derek (by Key Of Luck) and the French 2-y-o 6.5f winner Irish Heart (by Efisio). The dam is an unplaced half-sister to 8 winners including the Japan Cup winner Tap Dance City. The second dam, All Dance (by Northern Dancer), a minor French 3-y-o winner, is a half-sister to 8 winners including the Kentucky Derby winner Winning Colors. (Peter Winkworth). *"He'll easily get seven furlongs I should think, but he's a bit hot headed and we're looking after him at the moment. He's shown us enough to persevere with and we'll start him off at six furlongs I should think".*

1450. G MAN (IRE) ★★★
b.g. Intense Focus – Saoodah (Green Desert). April 19. Third foal. €10,500Y. Tattersalls Ireland September. David Redvers. The dam, unplaced in 3 starts at 3 yrs, is a sister to the 2-y-o winner and Group 3 third Dallaah. The second dam, Saeedah (by Bustino), was placed twice at 2 yrs and is a sister to the Group 3 Fred Darling Stakes winner Bulaxie (herself dam of the Group 2 winner Claxon) and a half-sister to 5 winners including the French Group 3 winner Dust Dancer (dam of the US Grade

2 winner Spotlight). (Robins Farm Racing Syndicate/Pearl Bloodstock Ltd). *"I thought he'd be running in the Brocklesbury but he was pretty much unsafe to be around at first and we had to geld him. He puts everything into his work and recently he's grown and started to look a bit scopier and classier, so we've backed off him. I think he's going to go six furlongs and possibly seven. He's still a little bit of a wildman but he's just got a great attitude and throws everything in".*

1451. GREEN DOOR ★★★★ ♠
b.c. *Camacho – Inourhearts (Pips Pride).* May 10. Sixth foal. £19,000Y. Doncaster Premier. David Redvers. Half-brother to the fairly useful Irish 2-y-o 6f winner Briland (by Namid), to the quite useful Irish 2-y-o 5f winner Inourthoughts (by Desert Style) and the fair 6f winner Wandering Heart (by Iffraaj). The dam won 4 races in Ireland including the listed 5f Rockingham Handicap in Ireland and is a half-sister to 2 winners. The second dam, Secret Heart (by Vision), is a placed half-sister to 4 minor winners here and abroad. (David Redvers). *"He was a late May foal but he'll be running in mid-April. He's done nothing wrong at all, he's improving all the time and when Jamie Spencer sat on him before Christmas he really liked him and said he'd probably pick up a bad five furlong race but that he'd be better over six. A really athletic horse, I really like him and hopefully he'll prove good enough to go to Royal Ascot".*

1452. HOKU (IRE) ★★★
b.f. *Holy Roman Emperor – Scylla Cadeaux (Cadeaux Genereux).* February 19. Second foal. £14,000Y. Doncaster Premier. David Redvers. The dam, a modest 1m placed 3-y-o, is a half-sister to 4 minor winners. The second dam, She's Classy (by Boundary), a 2-y-o listed stakes winner in the USA, was Grade 1 placed twice and is a half-sister to 5 winners in Japan and the USA. (Sheikh S A K H Al Thani). *"I think a lot of her, but we do have to be cautious because her temperament is questionable. I don't want to rush her unnecessarily and I think she'll get better as the season progresses and make a nice 3-y-o. Having said that, I do think she'll win as a 2-y-o and if that happens in the first half of the season we'll probably run*

her in a pattern race". TRAINERS' BARGAIN BUY

1453. OVERPOWER ★★
b.c. *Hurricane Run – Trick (Shirley Heights).* February 14. Twelfth foal. 28,000Y. Tattersalls October Book 2. David Redvers. Half-brother to 9 winners including the fairly useful 2-y-o 6f winner and listed-placed White Rabbit (by Zilzal), the fairly useful 6f (at 2 yrs) to 12f winner Cap Ferrat (by Robellino), the fair 14f winner Onyergo (by Polish Precedent), the modest 2-y-o 6f winner Shinner (by Charnwood Forest), the modest 11f and 12f winner Attraction Ticket (by Selkirk), the German winner of 4 races Practical Joke (by Alhaarth) and a winner in the UAE by Dr Fong. The dam, a fair 10f winner, is a full or half-sister to 6 winners. The second dam, Hocus (by High Top), a fair 10f winner, is a half-sister to 10 winners including Hittite Glory (Group 1 6f Middle Park Stakes). (Pearl Bloodstock Ltd). *"He's got very long in his back and his legs need to grow a bit, so he needs time and we're sitting tight with him. He could be nice but we've not asked him enough questions to find out".*

1454. QUEEN OF THE TARTS ★★★
b.f. *Royal Applause – Tart And A Half (Distant Relative).* February 26. Seventh foal. £32,000Y. Doncaster Premier. David Redvers. Half-sister to the Group 2 Duke Of York Stakes winner Assertive (by Bold Edge) and to the multiple listed 5f winner Boogie Street (by Compton Place). The dam, a quite useful 2-y-o 5f winner, is a half-sister to 3 minor winners here and abroad. The second dam, Vaigrant Wind (by Vaigly Great), a quite useful 2-y-o 6f winner, is a half-sister to 3 winners. (Peter Winkworth). *"She's very small and she's about as wide as she is tall. I was disappointed with her debut because we lost the race at the start. She's sharp and if she wins her maiden we'll probably go for a Conditions race next but she's limited by her size so the next six months will be her time".*

1455. UNNAMED ★★
ch.c. *Dandy Man – First Bank (Anabaa).* March 13. Fourth foal. €22,000Y. Tattersalls Ireland September. David Redvers. Half-brother to

a 2-y-o winner in Poland by Hurricane Run. The dam, a minor French 3-y-o winner, is a half-sister to 3 minor winners and to the dams of three listed winners. The second dam, Fabulous Account (by Private Account), is a placed half-sister to 9 winners including the US Grade 1 winner Joyeux Danseur and the Group 3 placed Danseur Fabuleux (dam of the outstanding 2-y-o Arazi and the Sussex Stakes winner Noverre). (Pearl Bloodstock Ltd). *"A big, rangy colt and very different to our other Dandy Man 2-y-o. I don't think he'll go further than six furlongs but he'll take some time to come to hand – maybe as long as the autumn. Big and gorgeous, he's a really good-looking horse and he's shown himself to be athletic, but he is immature".*

1456. UNNAMED ★★★

b.f. Bushranger – Lilakiya (Dr Fong). February 10. Third foal. €32,000Y. Tattersalls Ireland September. David Redvers. Half-sister to the very useful 2-y-o 6f winner and Group 2 7f Champagne Stakes fourth Karam Albaari (by King's Best) and to the fair 7f winner Minstrels Gallery (by Refuse To Bend). The dam, a modest 12f winner, is a half-sister to 3 winners including the dual 7f (at 2 yrs) and subsequent German and Italian Group 1 winner Linngari. The second dam, Lidakiya (by Kahyasi), a useful 10f and 12f winner, is a half-sister to 7 winners including the triple listed winner Livadiya. (Pearl Bloodstock Ltd). *"She's fine, she was going along really nicely but we decided to give some of the fillies a break because they've been on the go over the winter and the weather has been tough. She'll make a 2-y-o by June or July over five or six furlongs".*

1457. UNNAMED ★★★

b.f. Bushranger – Nightbird (Night Shift). February 7. Eighth foal. £16,000Y. Doncaster Premier. Paul Hickey. Half-sister to the fairly useful 10f winner Silent Hawk (by Halling), to the fair 1m winner of 4 races Border Owl (by Selkirk), the German winner of 6 races at 4 and 5 yrs Crossbill (by Cape Cross) and a 2-y-o winner in Sweden by Cadeaux Genereux. The dam was very useful winner of 5 races from 5f to 7f including two listed events at Newmarket and York and is a half-sister to 4 winners. The second dam, Pippa's Song (by Reference

Point), a fair 12f winner, is a half-sister to 8 winners including the Group 3 Prestige Stakes winner Glatisant (herself dam of the 2,000 Guineas winner Footstepsinthesand). (Pearl Bloodstock Ltd). *"She's as hard as nails and right from the beginning I thought she'd be the one the would run early, but she's had a small setback. By the time she's ready it'll be the back-end of the season I should think, but at least the five furlong maidens will be weaker by then. She'll be a hard, sprinting filly that'll be able to run plenty once we get her right".*

1458. UNNAMED ★★★

b.f. Intikhab – Saramacca (Kahyasi). April 14. Ninth foal. €20,000Y. Tattersalls Ireland September. David Redvers. Half-sister to the fairly useful 7f and subsequent US winner and Group 3 Oh So Sharp Stakes third Hasty, to the modest 7f winner Invincible Miss, a minor winner in Greece (all by Invincible Spirit), the fairly useful 12f to 15f and hurdles winner Rajeh and a minor winner abroad (both by Key Of Luck). The dam, a 12f winner at 4 yrs, is a half-sister to 6 winners. The second dam, Herila (by Bold Lad), won at 3 yrs in France and is a half-sister to 8 winners including the dam of the Group 1 Italian Derby winner Houmayoun. (Pearl Bloodstock Ltd). *"I'm very quietly in love with her! She's not the most forward and we won't be running her until the late summer, but she's just got a lovely way of going and looks to have a bit of quality. That said, running her from six to eight furlongs from late summer will mean she'll have some tough company. She's having a break now to stop me from doing too much with her because time and distance will be her two best friends, but she is really attractive".*

1459. UNNAMED ★★

b.c. Captain Gerrard – Seren Teg (Timeless Times). February 26. Sixth foal. £12,000Y. Doncaster Premier. David Redvers. Half-brother to the quite useful winner of 10 races over 5f (including at 2 yrs) Triskaidekaphobia (by Bertolini), to the modest dual 6f winner (including at 2 yrs) Atephobia and a minor winner abroad (both by Auction House). The dam, a fair dual 6f (at 2 yrs) and 5f winner, is a half-sister to 5 minor winners here and abroad. The second dam, Hill Of Fare (by

Brigadier Gerard), is an unplaced half-sister to 3 winners. (Robins Farm Racing Syndicate/Pearl Bloodstock Ltd). *"He would have been an early runner but for a setback in the winter, but he's got the most fantastic attitude. I don't know what level his ability is but I should think he'll be an absolute pleasure to train - he's just one of those horses that makes you smile every day you see him".*

SIR MICHAEL STOUTE

1460. ARBAAB

br.c. Dynaformer – Kaseema (Storm Cat). February 26. The dam, a fairly useful 2-y-o 6f winner, is a half-sister to 3 winners including the US dual Grade 1 and dual Grade 2 winner Aragorn. The second dam, Onaga (by Mr Prospector), is a placed sister to the US Grade 2 All Along Stakes winner Sha Tha (herself dam of Group 2 10f Prix Dollar winner State Shinto) and a half-sister to the Group 3 Henry II Stakes winner Briar Creek and the dam of the Group 1 Phoenix Stakes and Group 1 National Stakes winner One Cool Cat. (Hamdan Al Maktoum).

1461. CANNOCK CHASE (USA) ♠

b.c. Lemon Drop Kid – Lynnwood Chase (Horse Chestnut). March 20. Fourth foal. 310,000Y. Tattersalls October Book 1. Charlie Gordon-Watson. Brother to the very smart Group 2 10f Prix Eugene Adam and Group 3 10f Tercentenary Stakes winner Pisco Sour and to the jumps winner Ultravox. The dam is a placed half-sister to 3 winners including the UAE Group 2 and Irish Group 3 Ballycorus Stakes winner Lord Admiral. The second dam, Lady Ilsley (by Trempolino), a winner in France and listed-placed twice, is a sister to the winner and Grade 2 second Najecam (herself dam of the Grade 1 Breeders Cup Juvenile winner Action This Day) and a half-sister to 5 winners.

1462. DIANORA

b.f. New Approach – Nannina (Medicean). May 8. Third foal. Half-sister to the fairly useful dual 6f winner (including at 2 yrs) Duke Of Firenze (by Pivotal). The dam, winner of the Group 1 Fillies' Mile and the Group 1 1m Coronation Stakes, is a half-sister to 5 winners. The second dam, Hill Hopper (by Danehill), a useful winner

of 4 races including the Group 3 7f Criterion Stakes, is a half-sister to 5 winners including the Australian Grade 1 winner Water Boatman. (Cheveley Park Stud).

1463. FITNAH (IRE)

br.f. Sea The Stars – Ecoutila (Rahy). February 5. 450,000foal. Tattersalls December. Shadwell Estate Co. Half-sister to the Group 3 7f Prix Djebel winner and Group 1 Prix de la Foret third Surfrider (by Dansili), to the listed 1m (at 2 yrs) and listed 10f winner and Group 3 Musidora Stakes third Enticement (by Montjeu), the fairly useful 1m to 10f winner of 8 races and listed-placed Loyalty (by Medicean) and the minor French 2-y-o winner Betilla (by Bering). The dam is an unraced half-sister to the US winner and Grade 2 placed Listen Indy. The second dam, Ecoute (by Manila), a winner of two listed events in France and the USA and third in the Group 1 Prix Saint-Alary, is a half-sister to 6 winners including the Group 1 winners Pas de Reponse and Green Tune. (Hamdan Al Maktoum).

1464. GOTHIC

b.c. Danehill Dancer – Riberac (Efisio). February 16. Eighth foal. 135,000Y. Tattersalls October Book 1. John Warren. Half-brother to the very useful 9f (at 2 yrs), Turkish Group 10f, Group 3 11.5f Lingfield Derby Trial and listed 9f winner Dordogne, to the quite useful 1m winner of 3 races and listed-placed Montrachet (both by Singspiel), the quite useful 14f and hurdles winner Cotillion (by Sadler's Wells), the fair 1m and 9f winner Epernay (by Tiger Hill) and the modest 12f winner Emilion (by Fantastic Light). The dam, a smart winner of 10 races from 5f to 1m including three listed events, was third in the Group 2 Sun Chariot Stakes and is a full or half-sister to 4 winners. The second dam, Ciboure (by Norwick), a fair 6f (at 2 yrs) and 1m winner, is a half-sister to 4 winners. (Highclere Thoroughbred Racing – The Petrushka).

1465. HIGH STAND

b.c. Kyllachy – Maugwenna (Danehill). April 27. Sixth foal. 150,000Y. Tattersalls October Book 2. Charlie Gordon-Watson. Brother to the useful 2-y-o dual 5f winner and Group 2

5f Flying Childers second Bould Mover and half-brother to the unplaced 2012 2-y-o Everreadyneddy (by Ad Valorem) and the modest 5f and 6f winner of 6 races including sellers at 2 yrs and a race in Norway, Mac Dalia (by Namid). The dam, a fair 2-y-o 5f winner, is a half-sister to 5 minor winners. The second dam, River Abouali (by Bluebird), is an unraced half-sister to 3 winners including the Irish Group 3 winner Psalm.

1466. PIVOTAL BRIDE

ch.f. Dubawi – Brazilian Bride (Pivotal). April 14. Fourth foal. €220,000Y. Goffs Orby. Charlie Gordon-Watson. Half-sister to the quite useful 2012 2-y-o 6f winner Rivellino and to the fair Irish 5f winner Brazilian Breeze (both by Invincible Spirit). The dam won the Group 3 6f Swordlestown Stakes at 2 yrs and is a half-sister to 5 winners including the 2-y-o 7.5f winner and Group 3 7f second Brazilian Star. The second dam, Braziliz (by Kingmambo), placed fourth once over 5f at 2 yrs, is a half-sister to 8 winners including Or Vision (dam of the Group 1 winners Saffron Walden, Insight and Dolphin Street).

1467. QAFFAAL (USA)

b.c. Street Cry – Wasseema (Danzig). February 8. The dam, a dual 1m listed winner, was third in the Group 2 Park Stakes and is a sister to the US stakes winner and Grade 3 placed Pitamakan and a half-sister to 2 winners. The second dam, Vantive (by Mr Prospector), a minor French 3-y-o winner, is a half-sister to 3 stakes winners including the US Grade 2 winner Seattle Dawn. (Hamdan Al Maktoum).

1468. RADIATOR

b.f. Dubawi – Heat Haze (Green Desert). May 23. The dam, winner of the Grade 1 Matriarch Stakes and the Grade 1 Beverly D Stakes, is closely related to the Coronation Stakes, Prix Jacques Le Marois and Breeders Cup Filly & Mare Turf winner Banks Hill, to the Grade 1 Matriarch Stakes winner Intercontinental, the US dual Grade 1 winner Cacique, the North American triple Group 1 winner Champs Elysees and the Group 2 winner and high-class sire Dansili. The second dam, Hasili (by Kahyasi), won over 5f at 2 yrs and stayed a mile. (Khalid Abdulla).

1469. ROYAL SEAL ♠

b.f. Dansili – Queen's Best (King's Best). March 3. Second foal. Half-sister to the unplaced 2012 2-y-o Cape's Best (by Cape Cross). The dam, a smart winner of the Group 3 10f Winter Hill Stakes and the listed 12f Chalice Stakes, was second in the Group 2 Blandford Stakes and is a half-sister to 4 winners including the French 12f winner and Group 3 Prix de Royaumont third Reverie Solitaire. The second dam, Cloud Castle (by In The Wings), won the Group 3 Nell Gwyn Stakes and was placed in the Group 1 Yorkshire Oaks and the Group 1 Prix Vermeille. She is a half-sister to 5 winners including the high-class middle-distance horses and multiple Group 1 winners Warrsan and Luso, and the dam of the Group 3 winners Tastahil, Hattan, Blue Monday and Laaheb. (Cheveley Park Stud).

1470. SHINGLE

b.c. Oasis Dream – Orford Ness (Selkirk). March 7. Brother to the smart dual Group 3 7f John Of Gaunt Stakes winner Main Aim and half-brother to the Group 2 10f Prix Dollar winner Weightless (by In The Wings), the smart 7f (at 2 yrs) and listed 8.3f winner Home Affairs (by Dansili), the useful 7f (at 2 yrs) to 12f winner of 4 races Verdant (by Singspiel) and the French 10.5f winner Castle Rising (by Indian Ridge). The dam won twice including the Group 3 1m Prix de Sandringham and is a half-sister to the French 10f winner and Group 2 10f Prix Eugene Adam second Aware. The second dam, Nesaah (by Topsider) is a half-sister to the very useful Group 2 12f Prix de Malleret winner Privity and the Group 3 9f Prix Saint Roman winner Zindari. (Khalid Abdulla).

1471. STAMPEDE (IRE) ♠

b.c. High Chaparral – Summerhill Parkes (Zafonic). April 16. Fifth foal. 100,000Y. Tattersalls October Book 2. John Warren. Half-brother to the fair 7f winner Lucky Meadows (by Noverre), to the fair 8.5f and subsequent minor Italian winner Seleet (by Sakhee) and a winner over hurdles by Haafhd. The dam, a useful 3-y-o listed 6f winner, is a half-sister to 7 winners including the useful 2-y-o 5f and 6f winner Ace Of Parkes, the useful dual 5f winner and Moyglare, Lowther and Queen Mary Stakes placed My Melody Parkes and the useful winner of 17 races over 5f Lucky Parkes. The second dam, Summerhill Spruce (by Windjammer), a fair 3-y-o 6f seller winner, is a half-sister to 6 winners including the German Group 2 winner Jimmy Barnie. (Highclere Thoroughbred Racing – The Ashes).

1472. SURSINGLE (USA)

b.f. Empire Maker – Promising Lead (Danehill). March 16. Second foal. Sister to Vital Evidence, unplaced in one start at 2 yrs in 2012. The dam, a very smart Group 1 10f Pretty Polly Stakes winner, is a half-sister to the very smart Group 3 6f Princess Margaret Stakes and Group 3 7f Oak Tree Stakes winner Visit. The second dam, Arrive (by Kahyasi), a very useful 10f (at 2 yrs) and listed 13.8f winner, is a half-sister to the 2-y-o 5f winner (stayed 1m) Hasili (herself dam of the top-class performers Banks Hill, Heat Haze, Cacique, Intercontinental, Champs Elysees and Dansili). (Khalid Abdulla).

1473. TALL SHIP (IRE)

b.c. Sea The Stars – Magical Romance (Barathea). March 30. Fourth foal. Half-brother to the 2012 2-y-o 7f winner, on her only start, Love Magic, to the quite useful 10f winner Dean Swift (both by Dansili) and the quite useful 6f winner Modern Tutor (by Selkirk). The dam, a 2-y-o Group 1 6f Cheveley Park Stakes winner, is a sister to the fairly useful 2-y-o 7f winner and subsequent Canadian Grade 3 placed Saree and closely related to the Oaks, Irish Oaks and Yorkshire Oaks winner Alexandrova and the smart listed 2-y-o 1m winner and Group 2 1m Beresford Stakes third Masterofthehorse. The second dam, Shouk (by Shirley Heights), a quite useful 10.5f winner, is closely related to the listed winner and Group 3 Park Hill Stakes third Puce and a half-sister to 6 winners.

1474. ZULEMA

b.f. Shamardal – Eva Luna (Alleged). February 26. Closely related to the Group 1 Racing Post Trophy and Group 1 St Leger winner Brian Boru, to the Irish listed 1m winner Kitty O'Shea, the Irish 12f winner and Group 3 Noblesse Stakes second Kushnarenkovo (all by Sadler's Wells), the Group 2 Great Voltigeur Stakes and Group 2 12f Hardwicke Stakes

winner Sea Moon (by Beat Hollow) and the Group 2 12.5f Prix de Royallieu winner Moon Search (by Rainbow Quest). The dam, winner of the Group 3 14.6f Park Hill Stakes, is out of the Oaks runner-up Media Luna (by Star Appeal). (Khalid Abdulla).

1475. UNNAMED

b.c. Montjeu – Festoso (Diesis). February 24. First foal. The dam, a useful 1m (at 2 yrs) and listed 6f winner, was third in the Group 1 Cheveley Park Stakes and is a half-sister to numerous times including the Group 1 9f Prix Jean Prat winner Olden Times. The second dam, Garah (by Ajdal), was a very useful winner of 4 races over 6f, was second in the Group 3 5f Duke Of York Stakes and is a half-sister to 3 winners.

KRISTIN STUBBS

1476. DANFAZI (IRE) ★★★

ch.c. Dandy Man – Distant Shore (Jareer). April 6. Ninth living foal. 12,000Y. Tattersalls October Book 3. R W Stubbs. Half-brother to the fairly useful 5f (at 2 yrs) and 7f winner and listed Doncaster Stakes second Donegal Man (by Jareer) and to a winner in Denmark by Mujadil. The dam, placed fourth over 7f on her only start, is a half-sister to 8 winners including the Group 3 Greenlands Stakes winner Nautilus Pet. The second dam, Sea Mistress (by Habitat), is an unraced half-sister to 2 winners. (Facts & Figures). *"A really compact 2-y-o type, he starts his career in mid-April, he'll come on for the run and I do like him. He's very laid-back and very professional so he may get six furlongs later on, but he's very much a sprinter and he has an entry in the Supersprint".*

1477. IDAMANTE ★★★

b.c. Amadeus Wolf – Gower Valentine (Primo Valentino). April 14. First foal. 10,000Y. Tattersalls October Book 3. R W Stubbs. The dam, a quite useful 2-y-o 6f winner, is a half-sister to 3 winners. The second dam, Mania (by Danehill), is an unraced half-sister to 7 winners including the dam of the Group 1 winners Youmzain and Creachadoir. (O J Williams & P G Shorrock). *"A nice colt, a bit leggy and he's grown a bit and filled out. He'll be racing in April, I expect he'll come on a lot for his first run and he'll be better suited by six furlongs and maybe even seven".*

1478. RIO YUMA (ITA) ★★
b.f. Gold Sphinx – Selsey (Selkirk). March 20. Second foal. 2,500Y. Tattersalls October Book 3. R W Stubbs. The dam, a fair 1m placed maiden, is a half-sister to 6 winners including the Group 1 Gran Premio di Milano winner Leadership and the Group 3 Oh So Sharp Stakes winner Havant. The second dam, Louella (by El Gran Senor), is a placed half-sister to 7 minor winners in Europe and the USA. *"She's doing everything nicely and we'll probably give her a run over six furlongs before stepping her up to seven. She's a bit quirky but once she gets on with her work she does everything she should do".*

1479. TOO ELUSIVE ★★
b.c. Major Cadeaux – Elusive Kitty (Elusive Quality). February 4. Sixth foal. 14,000Y. Tattersalls October Book 3. R W Stubbs. Half-brother to the moderate 6f (including at 2 yrs) and 5f winner of 4 races Elusive Ronnie (by One Cool Cat). The dam, a modest 1m and 9f placed maiden, is a half-sister to the 2-y-o 5f and 7f and subsequent US Grade 3 8.5f winner Southern Africa. The second dam, Al Fahdi (by Be My Chief), a fairly useful 6f (at 2 yrs) to 1m winner, was third in the Group 3 Prestige Stakes and is a half-sister to 9 winners. (Paul & Linda Dixon). *"A nice horse for later in the season, he's growing a lot but he's doing everything nicely and I do like him".*

JAMES TATE
1480. AILEEN'S ICON ★★★
b.c. Sixties Icon – Aileen's Gift (Rainbow Quest). April 3. Eighth foal. 65,000Y. Tattersalls October Book 1. Rabbah Bloodstock. Half-brother to the Group 1 Irish 1,000 Guineas winner Samitar (by Rock Of Gibraltar), to the 2-y-o Group 3 Albany Stakes winner Nijoom Dubai (by Noverre), the fair 7f winner of 6 races La Gifted (by Fraam) and a winner in Greece by Xaar. The dam is an unraced half-sister to 5 winners including the fairly useful listed-placed Roker Park and the dam of the Group 2 Gimcrack Stakes winner Shameel. The second dam, Joyful (by Green Desert), a fair 7f winner at 3 yrs, is a half-sister to 7

winners including the Group 1 1m Coronation Stakes winner Golden Opinion. (S Ali). *"He's a small horse but he's grand. He's done a lot of galloping and he goes nicely but I don't see him running until the six furlong races start. A likeable, racey colt".*

1481. BLACK VALE (IRE) ★★★
b.c. Moss Vale – Limit (Barathea). April 10. Fifth foal. 30,000Y. Tattersalls October Book 3. Rabbah Bloodstock. Half-brother to the useful 2012 2-y-o 6f winner and Group 3 5f Cornwallis Stakes third El Manati (by Iffraaj), to the fairly useful triple 6f winner Kellys Eye (by Noverre) and the modest 12f winner of 4 races Sky High Diver (by Celtic Swing). The dam, a modest 2-y-o 7f winner, is a half-sister to 2 winners. The second dam, Orlena (by Gone West), a minor 2-y-o 7f winner in France, is a half-sister to 7 winners including the listed winner and 1,000 Guineas third Vista Bella. (Sheikh R D Al Maktoum). *"A half-brother to one of our best 2-y-o's from last year, El Manati. He's a nice horse that shows plenty, but he's probably not one of my very early types. One for the mid-summer though and certainly worth putting in the book".*

1482. BLHADAWA (IRE) ★★★★
b.f. Iffraaj – Trois Heures Apres (Soviet Star). February 6. Eleventh foal. 37,000Y. Tattersalls October Book 2. Rabbah Bloodstock. Half-sister to the quite useful 2-y-o 6f and 7f winner and 1m listed placed Laurentina (by Cadeaux Genereux), to the French 9m to 10f winner of 9 races and listed placed Rising Talent (by Bering), the fairly useful 10f winner Feaat (by Unfuwain), the fair 6f winner Timeless Stride (by Kyllachy), the fair 1m to 2m and hurdles winner Groomsman (by Groom Dancer), a minor winner in Italy by King's Theatre and a hurdles winner by Medicean. The dam is an unraced half-sister to 4 winners including the very useful 7f (at 2 yrs) and 10f listed winner and Oaks third Mezzogiorno (herself dam of the Group 2 Blandford Stakes winner Monturani). The second dam, Aigue (by High Top), a fairly useful 4-y-o dual 1m winner, is a sister to the listed middle-distance winner Torchon. (Sheikh Juma Al Dalmook Maktoum). *"She'll probably make her debut at the Craven meeting here in Newmarket*

and she goes very nicely. Her owner had a few horses with me last year, they were his first in Britain and I think we had a winner and three placed. This is a strong, muscular, attractive filly that shows loads of speed. The dream with all of the earlier types is that they win their maiden and then we see if they're good enough for Royal Ascot. The name means 'try to be calm' in Arabic".

1483. BLOCKADE ★★★★
br.f. Kheleyf – Barracade (Barathea). March 4. Second foal. £12,000Y. Doncaster Premier. Rabbah Bloodstock. Half-sister to the modest 2012 5f placed 2-y-o Black Rider (by Elnadim). The dam, a modest 10f placed 3-y-o in Ireland, is a half-sister to the US stakes winner and triple Group 2 placed Spider Power. The second dam, America Calling (by Quiet American), a fair 6f winner at 3 yrs, is a half-sister to 8 winners. (Saeed Manana). "A small, fast 2-y-o filly, she'll be racing in April and she goes well. I'd be shocked if she hasn't won by mid-May". TRAINERS' BARGAIN BUY

1484. DESERT RANGER (IRE) ★★★★
b.c. Bushranger – Maleha (Cape Cross). March 21. Second foal. 25,000Y. Tattersalls October Book 3. Rabbah Bloodstock. Half-brother to the fairly useful 2012 2-y-o 6f winner Malilla (by Red Clubs). The dam is an unraced half-sister to the useful listed 1m winner of 7 races Yamal and to the quite useful 2-y-o 6f winner Trailblazing. The second dam Pioneer Bride (by Gone West), is an unplaced half-sister to 7 winners including Group 2 10f Prince of Wales's Stakes winner Faithful Son, the very smart Coventry Stakes and Prix Quincey winner Always Fair and to the placed dams of the Irish Oaks winner Lailani and the dual Group 3 winner Naheef. (Sheikh Juma Al Dalmook Maktoum). "A beautiful, big colt from the first crop of Bushranger that everyone seemed to go mad for at the Sales. He's a lovely, long-striding horse that shows plenty and although he won't start at five furlongs I might be tempted to run him over six because he goes so well. Definitely very nice".

1485. EXCEL BEST ★★★
b.c. Exceed And Excel – Hannah's Dream

(King's Best). March 17. Third foal. 30,000Y. Tattersalls October Book 2. Rabbah Bloodstock. The dam, a winner of 3 minor races abroad, is a half-sister to 2 winners. The second dam, Meritxell (by Thatching), won once at 3 yrs in France and is a half-sister to 10 winners including the Group 2 winner Almushtarak. (Sheikh Juma Al Dalmook Maktoum). "A very muscular, big, strong attractive son of Exceed And Excel. He has a lovely big stride on him, we'll start him off at six furlongs and he's very nice".

1486. EXCEL'S BEAUTY ★★★
b.f. Exceed And Excel – Continua (Elusive Quality). January 30. First foal. 56,000Y. Tattersalls December. Rabbah Bloodstock. The dam is an unraced sister to the 2-y-o winner and Group 1 Middle Park Stakes third Huntdown and a half-sister to 2 winners. The second dam, Infinite Spirit (by Maria's Mon), a fairly useful 6f (at 2 yrs) and UAE 1,000 Guineas winner, is a sister to the Irish listed winner Moquette and a half-sister to 4 winners. (Sheikh Juma Al Dalmook Maktoum). "She may start off at five furlongs because she galloped really well last week. She's a decent-sized, strong filly and I like her".

1487. MERSAD (IRE) ★★
ch.c. Shamardal – Fortress (Generous). April 10. Second foal. £38,000Y. Doncaster Premier. Rabbah Bloodstock. Half-brother to the moderate 2012 6f placed 2-y-o Tonality (by Amadeus Wolf). The dam, a modest 6f winner, is a half-sister to 7 winners including the high-class sprinter Reverence, winner of the Haydock Park Sprint Cup and the Nunthorpe Stakes and the very useful 2-y-o listed 6f Chesham Stakes winner Helm Bank. The second dam, Imperial Bailiwick (by Imperial Frontier), was a useful winner of 3 races at around 5f including the Group 2 Flying Childers Stakes, was Group 3 placed twice and is a half-sister to 3 winners in France. (S Ali). "He goes nicely enough and he's got plenty of speed in the pedigree, but he's a bit babyish at present and probably one for the middle of the season onwards".

1488. OCEAN STORM (IRE) ★★★★
b.c. Royal Applause – Cedar Sea (Persian Bold).

February 17. Seventh foal. £80,000Y. Doncaster Premier. Rabbah Bloodstock. Half-brother to the quite useful 2-y-o 7f winner Holy Roman Warrior (by Holy Roman Emperor) and to the smart 1m (at 2 yrs) and Group 3 13f winner and St Leger third Corsica (by Cape Cross). The dam, a French 1m winner and second in the listed Prix Yacowlef, is a half-sister to 3 winners including the Group 3 6f Coventry Stakes winner CD Europe. The second dam, Woodland Orchid (by Woodman), is an unplaced half-sister to the Group 3 Derrinstown Stud Derby Trial winner Truth Or Dare, the UAE Group 3 winner D'Anjou and the listed winner Sandstone. (Saeed Manana). *"He's working nicely, he's small, very strong and shows plenty. Should be running in April or early May. One to watch out for".*

1489. SORRY SAEED ★★★

b.f. Raven's Pass – Clear Impression (Danehill). February 19. Fourth foal. 65,000Y. Tattersalls October Book 1. Rabbah Bloodstock. Half-sister to the modest dual 6f winner Pettochside (by Refuse To Bend) and to two minor winners abroad by Dubawi and Dubai Destination. The dam, a fairly useful 3-y-o 6f winner, was listed-placed 3 times and is a half-sister to one winner. The second dam, Shining Hour (by Red Ransom), won the Group 3 5f Queen Mary Stakes and is a full or half-sister to 7 winners. (S Ali). *"She's a small, strong Raven's Pass filly and she's likely to be an early type".*

1490. UMNEYATI ★★★

b.f. Iffraaj – Honky Tonk Sally (Dansili). March 28. Second foal. 30,000Y. Tattersalls October Book 2. Rabbah Bloodstock. The dam, a quite useful 2-y-o 7f winner, is a half-sister to 7 winners including the very useful Group 3 1m Prix Saint-Roman winner Eco Friendly. The second dam, Flower Girl (by Pharly), a very useful winner of 5 races including the Group 3 6f Goldene Peitsche and the listed 6f Sandy Lane Stakes, is a sister to the useful listed 9.4f winner Farmost and a half-sister to 3 winners. (Sheikh R D Al Maktoum). *"She's very nice but she struggled during the late winter with a cough and other little niggles. She's going nicely now but I haven't been able to do enough to assess her as yet".*

1491. YAJAMILA ★★★ ♠

b.f. Royal Applause – Yatir (Red Ransom). March 6. Second foal. £40,000Y. Doncaster Premier. Rabbah Bloodstock. The dam is an unplaced half-sister to 2 winners. The second dam, Tycoon's Dolce (by Rainbows For Life), won the listed Prix de Lieurey and was Group 3 placed three times and is a half-sister to three listed winners in France and Italy. (Sheikh R D Al Maktoum). *"She goes nicely, she does nothing wrong and she looks like she'll be one for the mid-summer onwards".*

1492. ZALZILAH ★★★★

b.c. Kheleyf – Tarneem (Zilzal). March 23. Twelfth foal. Doncaster Premier. £45,000Y. Rabbah Bloodstock. Half-brother to the smart 7f (at 2 yrs) and Group 3 9f Darley Stakes winner and Group 1 Coronation Cup third Enforcer, to the quite useful 2-y-o dual 5f winner Lord Of The Inn, the modest 1m winner Uncle Brit (all by Efisio), the fair dual 10f winner and subsequent US listed-placed Canaveral (by Cape Cross), the fair 5.7f winner Innstyle (by Daggers Drawn) and the Italian winner of 9 races at up to 13.5f Kris's Bank (by Inchinor). The dam, a quite useful 3-y-o 1m winner, is a half-sister to 4 minor winners abroad. The second dam, Willowy Mood (by Will Win), won 14 races including two Grade 3 events in the USA and is a half-sister to 9 winners. (Sheikh Juma Al Dalmook Maktoum). *"He goes nicely, he's a strong, attractive, muscular colt and he's done plenty of work. He'll be one of our first 2-y-o runners, so he wants to be in the book for sure".*

1493. UNNAMED ★★

b.c. Authorized – Circle Of Love (Sakhee). March 4. Third foal. 20,000Y. Tattersalls October Book 2. Rabbah Bloodstock. The dam, a quite useful 10f winner, is a half-sister to the useful 7f (at 2 yrs) and listed Lingfield Oaks Trial and US Grade 3 winner and Group 1 Nassau Stakes second Cassydora and to the listed winner Classic Remark. The second dam, Claxon (by Caerleon), a very useful 1m (at 2 yrs) and Group 2 10f Premio Lydia Tesio winner, is a half-sister to 3 winners. (Saeed Manana). *"He's nice but you'll have to wait a while before you see him on the racecourse. A lovely, big, long-striding colt, he isn't a backward type by any means, so he may well be running in mid-summer".*

1494. UNNAMED ★★

b.f. *Royal Applause – Clinet (Docksider)*. April 20. Third foal. 24,000Y. Tattersalls October Book 2. Rabbah Bloodstock. The dam won 5 races at 2 to 4 yrs and from 7f to 9f, including a listed event in the UAE, was Grade 2 placed in the USA and is a half-sister to 3 winners. The second dam, Oiche Mhaith (by Night Shift), won once at 3 yrs and is a half-sister to 7 winners. (Saeed Manana). *"She's had the odd little problem so I don't know a lot about her yet, but she goes OK. A medium-sized filly and a beautiful mover that's cantering nicely".*

1495. UNNAMED ★★★★ ♠

b.f. *Cape Cross – Deveron (Cozzene)*. April 3. Fourth foal. 40,000Y. Tattersalls October Book 1. Oliver St Lawrence. Half-sister to the modest 2012 2-y-o 1m winner Open Letter (by New Approach) and to the quite useful 2-y-o 7f winner Dffar (by Shamardal). The dam, a very useful 2-y-o 7f winner, was third in the Group 1 1m Prix Marcel Boussac and is a sister to the Canadian dual Grade 2 winner Windward Islands and a half-sister to 5 winners including the minor US stakes winner Hunter Cruise. The second dam, Cruisie (by Assert), won 3 minor races at 3 yrs in the USA and is a half-sister to 4 stakes winners including the dam of the US Grade 1 winner Capote Belle. (S Ali). *"A big 'tank' of a filly who goes very nicely. On pedigree we should wait for the seven furlong races but she shows plenty and we'll work her when the six furlong races start and then decide if we go six or seven. She's huge but she's very well-balanced and cruises all over everything".*

1496. UNNAMED ★★

b.f. *Dutch Art – Ellway Queen (Bahri)*. March 17. Sixth foal. £44,000Y. Doncaster Premier. Rabbah Bloodstock. Half-sister to the quite useful 2-y-o 7f and subsequent US winner and Grade 2 fourth Ghetto, to the fair 2-y-o 6f winner Hythe Bay and the fair 2-y-o 5f winner Patteresa Girl (all by Auction House). The dam, a fair 3-y-o 1m winner, is a half-sister to one winner. The second dam, Queen Linear (by Polish Navy), won once at 3 yrs

and is a half-sister to 6 winners including the Group winners Castle Green and Hardgreen. (S Ali). *"She's had one or two minor niggles so I haven't been able to press any buttons yet. She canters nicely but I don't know much more than that".*

1497. UNNAMED ★★★

b.f. *Tobougg – Happy Lady (Cadeaux Genereux)*. April 16. Seventh living foal. £31,000Y. Doncaster Premier. Rabbah Bloodstock. Sister to the Group 2 German 1,000 Guineas and listed Bosra Sham Stakes winner and Group 2 6f Lowther Stakes second Penny's Gift and half-sister to the quite useful 2012 2-y-o 5f winner Rhamnus (by Sakhee's Secret), the modest 6f (at 2 yrs) and 7f winner Chorus Beauty and the moderate 1m winner Homme Dangereux (both by Royal Applause). The dam, a fair 1m placed maiden, is a half-sister to 4 winners including the smart middle-distance stayer and Group 2 Yorkshire Cup second Rainbow Ways. The second dam, Siwaayib (by Green Desert), a fairly useful winner of 3 races over 6f, is a half-sister to 8 winners here and abroad. (S Ali). *"A lovely, big, long-striding filly. She's just going through a growing spurt but she's one to look forward to when the six furlong races start".*

1498. UNNAMED ★★ ♠

ch.c. *Sir Percy – Hermanita (Hernando)*. February 8. Third foal. 26,000Y. Tattersalls October Book 2. Rabbah Bloodstock. The dam, a modest 12f winner, is a half-sister to 5 winners and to the unplaced dam of the Australian Group 2 winner Just Mambo. The second dam, Subjective (by Secretariat), a US listed-stakes winner of 5 races, is a full or half-sister to 13 winners including Molesnes (Group 1 Prix du Cadran). (Saeed Manana). *"He won't be racing until the seven furlong races start, but he goes nicely and is one of the those in the middle of the pack at the moment".*

1499. UNNAMED ★★★

ch.f. *Sakhee's Secret – Jasmick (Definite Article)*. January 22. Fifth foal. 22,000Y. Tattersalls October Book 2. Rabbah Bloodstock. Half-sister to the useful 7f (at 2 yrs) and 1m winner and dual Group 3 placed

Sagramor and to the modest 12f and 13f winner Jasmeno (by Catcher In The Rye). The dam, a quite useful 10f and 14f winner, is a half-sister to 2 winners. The second dam, Glass Minnow (by Alzao), was placed three times from 5f to 9f and is a half-sister to 4 minor winners. (Saeed Manana). *"She shows plenty of speed despite the stamina in her pedigree. A small, muscular filly, I'll wait until the six furlong races start".*

1500. UNNAMED ★★★

gr.f. Verglas – Katimont (Montjeu). January 29. Second foal. 25,000Y. Tattersalls October Book 2. Rabbah Bloodstock. The dam, a fair 8.5f winner, is a half-sister to 6 winners including the listed winner Katiykha (dam of the Group 2 winner and Oaks second Katiyra). The second dam, Katiyfa (by Auction Ring), won the listed 1m Prix de la Calonne and is a half-sister to 3 winners. (Saeed Manana). *"A beautiful filly, she probably won't run until the seven furlong races because she's tall and long. A strong filly and a good mover".*

1501. UNNAMED ★★★

b.c. Dandy Man – Lucky Flirt (Gulch). April 7. Fourth foal. 25,000Y. Tattersalls October Book 2. Rabbah Bloodstock. Half-brother to the fair 2012 Irish 2-y-o 1m winner Lucked Out (by Ramonti) and to a minor winner abroad at 2 and 3 yrs by Marju. The dam, unplaced in the USA at 2 yrs, is half-sister to 9 winners including a stakes winner. The second dam, Bashful Charmer (by Capote), a minor US 2-y-o stakes winner, is a half-sister to 5 winners in the USA. (Saeed Manana). *"A big, strong, masculine colt. He's a bit of a playboy but he's already shown ability and he'll be running in May".*

1502. UNNAMED ★★★

ch.f. Shamardal – Miss Hepburn (Gone West). March 13. Fourth foal. 11,000Y. Tattersalls October Book 2. Rabbah Bloodstock. Half-sister to the fair 2-y-o 1m winner Tamarrud (by Authorized). The dam is an unplaced half-sister to 2 winners. The second dam, Circle Of Gold (by Royal Academy), winner of the Group 3 7f Prestige Stakes at 2 yrs, was third in the Grade 2 Mrs Revere Stakes in the USA and is

a sister to the listed winner Crystal Crossing (dam of the St Leger winner Rule Of Law) and a half-sister to 4 winners. (Saeed Manana). *"In February I thought this would be the first of our 2-y-o fillies to run, but she's just gone a bit weak on me. She's been galloping, but she's now in a growing spurt and in the middle of the pack. So I don't know when she'll be ready for faster work again".*

1503. UNNAMED ★★

b.f. Shamardal – State Secret (Green Desert). March 13. Seventh foal. 26,000Y. Tattersalls October Book 2. Not sold. Half-sister to the quite useful dual 1m winner and listed Masaka Stakes second Song Of Silence (by Unbridled's Song), to the quite useful 1m and 9f winner Nahab (by Selkirk) and the moderate 10f winner Aiaam Al Wafa (by Authorized). The dam, a winner over 6.5f at 2 yrs in France, was fourth in the Group 3 1m Prix d'Aumale and is a half-sister to 8 winners including the 2-y-o Group 2 Criterium de Maisons-Laffitte winner Bitooh and the dams of the Group/Grade 1 winners Storming Home, Music Note and Musical Chimes. The second dam, It's In The Air (by Mr Prospector), a joint-champion 2-y-o filly in the USA, won 16 races from 6f to 10f. (S Ali). *"A filly with plenty of fire about her, she goes nicely. Probably won't run until the seven furlong races start but she's quite nice".*

1504. UNNAMED ★★★

gr.f. Authorized – Swift Dispersal (Shareef Dancer). February 14. Fifth foal. 22,000Y. Tattersalls October Book 1. Rabbah Bloodstock. Half-sister to the fair 11f and 12f winner Snow Hill (by Halling), to the fair 2-y-o 7f winner Swift Image (by Act One) and a winner in Germany by Fantastic Light. The dam, a quite useful 6f and 7f winner, was listed-placed over 1m and is a half-sister to 4 winners. The second dam, Minsden's Image (by Dancer's Image), won once at 3 yrs and is a half-sister to 5 winners. (S Ali). *"She's not a big filly but she's an easy mover and everything comes easy to her. On pedigree alone you'd want to wait for the seven furlong races but she shows plenty of speed and I'm looking forward to running her. She'll definitely make a 2-y-o".*

MARK TOMPKINS

1505. ASTROCAT ★★★

b.f. Zamindar – Mega (Petardia). February
27. Half-sister to the fair 2-y-o 7f winner, on
her only start, Mystic Winds (by Shirocco), to
the fair 7f (at 2 yrs) to 10f winner of 5 races
Marvo (by Bahamian Bounty), the fair 9f (at
2 yrs) and 1m winner of 4 races Astrodonna
(by Carnival Dancer) and the fair 1m and 9f
winner Mercoliano (by Medicean). The dam is
an unplaced half-sister to 7 winners including
the listed winners Bolino Star and Don Fayruz.
The second dam, Gobolino (by Don), won
over 7f in Ireland at 2 yrs and is a half-sister
to 4 winners. (Mystic Meg Ltd). *"She's lovely
and all this family have done alright. Her half-
brother Mercoliano is still winning regularly
in Saudi Arabia. This filly looks like being OK,
she'll make a mid-season 2-y-o and we really
like her. She goes well, she's nice natured and
looks to have everything in the right place.
I've always loved her ever since she was born.
Seven furlongs or a mile later in the season will
suit her".*

1506. ASTROWOLF ★★★

b.c. Halling – Optimistic (Reprimand). February
18. Eighth foal. Brother to the fair 2-y-o 7f
winner Rayvin Black and half-brother to the
quite useful 2-y-o 7f winner Such Optimism,
to the moderate dual 10f and hurdles winner
Astrolibra (both by Sakhee), the quite useful
2-y-o 7f winner Astrobella (by Medicean)
and the modest 2m 2f and hurdles winner
Rajayoga (by Kris). The dam, a fairly useful
2-y-o dual 7f winner, is a half-sister to several
winners including the fairly useful 3-y-o dual
7f winner Woodbeck (dam of the Group 2
Yorkshire Cup winner Franklins Gardens) and
the fairly useful 7f (at 2 yrs) and 10f winner
Carburton. The second dam, Arminda (by
Blakeney), is an unraced half-sister to the
Group 1 Prix de Diane winner Madam Gay.
(Mystic Meg Ltd). *"His full-brother won as
a 2-y-o and we thought he was going to be
really good but he had a few setbacks. The
mare won twice as a 2-y-o and she's had a few
2-y-o winners. This colt looks pretty strong, he's
going well at the moment so I'm optimistic that
he'll have enough speed to start at six furlongs.
He'll need further later on, but he's capable of
winning this year".*

1507. BE MY LITTLE FRIEND ★★★★

ch.c. Pastoral Pursuits – Sosumi (Be My Chief).
March 10. Eighth foal. Half-brother to the
quite useful 7f and 1m winner of 6 races
Tevez (by Sakhee), to the modest 2-y-o 1m
seller winner Benayoun (by Inchinor) and the
modest 11f winner Edward Whymper (by
Bahamian Bounty). The dam, a useful 2-y-o
dual 5f winner, was fourth in the Group 3 Prix
du Calvados. The second dam, Princess Deya
(by Be My Guest), ran twice unplaced and
is a half-sister to the Eclipse Stakes winner
Compton Admiral and the Group 1 1m Queen
Elizabeth II Stakes winner Summoner. (Sakal
Family). *"He's the first one out of the mare
that really looks like being a 2-y-o. He's small,
strong and compact, by a sire I like and he
goes well, so he'll be racing in April or May, he's
tough and he'll be sharp enough. The dam was
a good filly and her foals tend to win without
necessarily being that good, but they're all
alright. We'll start this colt off at five furlongs
and we'll progress to six. A real 2-y-o type, I'll
put him as my "Trainer's Pick" for this year".*

1508. BLUE BOUNTY ★★★

ch.c. Bahamian Bounty – Laheen (Bluebird).
April 18. Fourth foal. Half-brother to Lebresem
(by Elusive City), unplaced in one start at 2
yrs in 2012. The dam is an unplaced half-
sister to 2 winners including the listed-placed
New Design. The second dam, Ashirah (by
Housebuster), is an unraced half-sister to the
US dual Grade 3 winner Mustanfar and the
dual listed winner Tadris. (Raceworld). *"By
Bahamian Bounty, a sire I've always done
well with, this is a very nice colt of a good size
and he's a real 2-y-o type. He looks a lot like
a horse that did well for me a few years ago
called Babodana. I'm happy with him and he'll
be racing towards the end of April or early
May".*

1509. LITTLE TINKA ★★

b.f. Three Valleys – Tenpence (Bob Back).
March 5. Half-sister to the quite useful dual
1m winner Barwick (by Beat Hollow), to
the modest dual 10f winner Zenarinda (by
Zamindar) and the moderate 12f winner Like
Clockwork (by Rail Link). The dam, unplaced
in two starts, is a sister to the 2-y-o 1m winner
and Group 3 Prix Saint-Roman second Ten

Bob II and a half-sister to one winner. The second dam, Tiempo (by King Of Spain), was unplaced. (Dullingham Park). *"I like her, she's strong and forward enough to make a 2-y-o. The sire's been disappointing so we'll have to wait and see, but she goes well. She'll be a miler eventually".*

1510. SEE ME SOMETIME ★★★
ch.c. Observatory – Nice Time (Tagula). March 12. First foal. The dam, a fair 2-y-o 1m winner, is a half-sister to several winners including the useful 2-y-o 7f winner Prose, subsequently a winner in the USA. The second dam, Nicea (by Dominion), a fairly useful Irish 2-y-o 7f winner from 2 starts, is a half-sister to 2 winners. *"A colt from a nice family, he'll be an early 2-y-o, he's cheeky, not very big and although I'm not saying how good he'll be he'll definitely win a race. A very tough beggar, nothing bothers him and once we get him racing he'll love it".*

1511. TOPALING ★★★
ch.f. Halling – Topatori (Topanoora). April 29. Half-sister to the modest 2012 2-y-o 1m winner Topamichi (by Beat Hollow), to the Group 3 10.3f Middleton Stakes winner Topatoo (by Bahamian Bounty), the quite useful 1m to 14f winner Toparudi (by Rudimentary), the fair dual 1m winner Top Shot (by College Chapel) and the fair 1m winner Top Tiger (by Mtoto). The dam, a quite useful 7f to 11f winner of 4 races, is a half-sister to one winner. The second dam, Partygoer (by Cadeaux Genereux), was unplaced. (M P Bowring). *"She's lovely and as nice a foal as we've had out of the mare who's done really well for us. She's well-grown, a great mover and shows that little bit of quirkiness that I like in a filly, so I'm hoping she'll be above average. She'll want seven furlongs and a mile this year and I'm hoping she'll show a bit of quality".*

1512. UNNAMED ★★★
b.f. Beat Hollow – Missouri (Charnwood Forest). April 19. Half-sister to the quite useful Irish 2-y-o 7f winner Captain Cullen (by Strategic Prince), to the fair 1m (at 2 yrs) and 12f winner Battery Power (by Royal Applause), the modest 9f (at 2 yrs) to 12f and hurdles winner Dee Cee Elle (by Groom Dancer), the

modest 10f winner Bella Medici (by Medicean) and the moderate 12f winner Mekong Miss (by Mark Of Esteem). The dam, a quite useful 15f winner, is a half-sister to several winners. The second dam, Medway (by Shernazar), a modest 12f winner at 3 yrs, is a half-sister to 8 winners including the high-class Hong Kong horse Indigenous and the Cesarewitch winner Old Red. *"She's as nice a foal as the mare's had and we're very happy with her. They seem to have given up on the sire but I've done well with him. This is a strong, attractive, good-moving filly and she'll want seven furlongs this year which is typical of my 2-y-o's".*

MARCUS TREGONING

1513. AYERS ROCK (IRE) ★★★★
b.c. Bushranger – Red Fuschia (Polish Precedent). April 20. Fifth foal. £77,000Y. Doncaster Premier. Peter & Ross Doyle. Half-brother to the smart 7f (at 2 yrs) and Group 3 10f Select Stakes winner Red Badge (by Captain Rio), to the fairly useful 2-y-o 5f winner and listed-placed On The Dark Side (by Kheleyf) and the quite useful 2-y-o 7f winner Sister Red (by Diamond Green). The dam is an unraced half-sister to 4 winners including the Group 3 placed Red Peony. The second dam, Red Azalea (by Shirley Heights), a fairly useful 7f (at 2 yrs) and 10f winner, is a half-sister to 4 winners including the smart Group 3 Prestige Stakes winner and French 1,000 Guineas third Red Camellia (herself dam of the Fillies Mile winner Red Bloom). (Lady Tennant). *"We've done well with the ones we've bought with Peter Doyle. This colt is in full work and the sire has lots of 2-y-o's so he seems sure to do really well in terms of number of winners. This colt is from a good family and he looks a proper 2-y-o. A good mover, he's straightforward and he'll be out fairly soon".*

1514. BETWEEN WICKETS ★★★
b.c. Compton Place – Intermission (Royal Applause). February 10. Second foal. 26,000Y. Tattersalls October Book 3. M Tregoning. Half-brother to the modest 2012 2-y-o 7f winner Secret Symphony (by Sakhee's Secret). The dam is an unraced half-sister to the US Grade 1 Citation Handicap and dual Grade 2 winner Ashkal Way. The second dam, Golden Way (by Cadeaux Genereux), a fairly useful 10.5f

winner, is a half-sister to 8 winners including the useful Polish Spring (a winner here and a dual US stakes winner) and the French listed 11f winner and Group 3 placed Go Boldly. (Mr Rupert Villers). *"A lovely-looking horse. I don't think the Compton Place horses are necessarily the most precocious, but he gets you lots of winners. There's speed on both sides of this pedigree and he should be a 2-y-o winner. A very good-looking horse, he's stunning to look at and he stands out in the string. I've got a feeling he'll be one for June or July".* TRAINERS' BARGAIN BUY

1515. BOWSERS BOLD ★★★

gr.c. Firebreak – Cristal Clear (Clodovil). February 8. Second foal. £36,000Y. Doncaster Premier. Marcus Tregoning. Half-brother to the moderate 2012 5f placed 2-y-o Crystal Cove (by Dubawi). The dam, a quite useful 2-y-o 5f and 6f winner, was listed-placed and is a half-sister to 10 winners including the useful Irish 2-y-o 6f winner and Group 1 Phoenix Stakes third Catch A Glimpse (by Gulch and herself dam of the US Grade 3 winner Successful Outlook). The second dam, Spring To Light (by Blushing Groom), a winner over 6f and 7f in Ireland, was Group 3 placed and is a half-sister to 7 winners. (Mrs Simon Aldridge). *"He's a nice colt and we like him. I think the sire is underestimated. This colt will definitely make a 2-y-o, six furlongs is probably his trip and he's a big, strong horse. He's in full work and very tough-looking".*

1516. CASTLE COMBE (IRE) ★★★

b.c. Dylan Thomas – Mundus Novus (Unbridled's Song). February 9. Third foal. 16,000Y. Tattersalls October Book 2. M Tregoning. Half-brother to the quite useful 2012 2-y-o 6f and 7f winner Steer By The Stars (by Pivotal) and to the fair 9f winner Grey Seal (by Cape Cross). The dam, a French 1m winner, is closely related to the US Grade 2 Dahlia Handicap winner Surya (herself dam of the US Grade 2 winner Aruna) and a half-sister to 6 winners. The second dam, Wild Planet (by Nureyev), won at 2 yrs here and the listed Prix Coronation in France, was third in the Group 3 Prestige Stakes and is a half-sister to 6 winners. *"I have to say he's a lovely horse. Dylan Thomas gets late-maturing*

types of course and this is a big horse, but he's in full work and if we have to give him some time off he'll get that later on. The people who ride him think he's quite nice and interestingly the damsire Unbridled's Song gives you a bit of speed. I'm hopeful for this horse, he's a nice type, a little bit upright like a lot of American horses, but a beautiful mover for a bit later on".*

1517. EMPEROR FERDINAND ★★★

b.c. Holy Roman Emperor – Moon Flower (Sadler's Wells). February 14. Eleventh foal. 40,000Y. Tattersalls October Book 2. M Tregoning. Closely related to the French 10f and 11f winner Around The Moon and to the modest 10f winner Moonlight Rhapsody (by Danehill Dancer) and half-brother to the Australian Grade 2 winner Fantastic Love (by Peintre Celebre), the French winner and 2-y-o listed 5f placed Around Me (by Johannesburg), the French 2-y-o 5.5f winner Enchanting Muse (by Fusaichi Pegasus), the moderate 4-y-o 5f winner Silk Gallery (by Kingmambo) and a winner of 3 races in Japan by Spectrum. The dam, a winner over 1m (at 2 yrs) and 10f in Ireland, is a sister to the listed winners Side Of Paradise (dam of the Group 1 winner Immortal Verse) and Flowerdrum and a half-sister to the triple Grade 1 winner Last Tycoon, the Group 2 6f Premio Melton winner Astronef and the dam of the Group 1 winners Valentine Waltz, Tie Black and Sense Of Style. The second dam, Mill Princess (by Mill Reef), won over 10f at 2 yrs in France and is a half-sister to the Irish Sweeps Derby winner Irish Ball and to the top-class broodmare Irish Bird (dam of the classic winners Assert, Bikala and Eurobird). (Lady Tennant/Marcus Tregoning). *"I'm very keen on the sire, I'd always be prepared to buy one because they always seem to be tough and they win. He's not the most exuberant of movers but he looks as if he wants to be a 2-y-o and we ought to be getting on with him. He's very laid-back and goes alright".*

1518. HESBAAN (IRE) ★★★

b.c. Acclamation – Celestial Dream (Oasis Dream). March 2. First foal. 87,000Y. Tattersalls October Book 2. Shadwell Estate Co. The dam, a fair 5f winner, is a half-sister to 3 winners here and abroad. The second dam, Lochangel (by Night Shift), a very smart winner of the

Group 1 5f Nunthorpe Stakes, is a half-sister to the champion sprinter Lochsong. (Hamdan Al Maktoum). *"We liked him early on but he's got rather roundish joints – probably because he's got a biggish action and he's been overstretching a bit. But he's from a decent-enough family and he'll be a 2-y-o in mid-season".*

1519. LADY VIOLA ★★

b.f. Sir Percy – String Quartet (Sadler's Wells). March 19. Ninth foal. Sister to the fairly useful 2012 2-y-o 7f winner and listed-placed Mirsaale and half-sister to the Group 2 Park Hill Stakes and Group 3 Lillie Langtry Stakes winner Meeznah (by Dynaformer), to the smart 1m winner (at 2 yrs) and Group 2 12f Princess Of Wales's Stakes second Shahin (by Kingmambo), the fair 10f to 14f winner Lady Rosamunde (by Maria's Mon), the moderate 7f winner Lyric Art (by Red Ransom) and a minor winner abroad by Fantastic Light. The dam, a 12.5f listed winner in France and third in the Group 3 Lancashire Oaks, is a sister to the Irish listed 10f winner Casey Tibbs and a half-sister to 4 winners. The second dam, Fleur Royale (by Mill Reef), won the Group 2 Pretty Polly Stakes, was second in the Group 1 Irish Oaks and is a half-sister to 4 winners. (Mr & Mrs A E Pakenham). *"I've had a lot from this family and this is a filly for the back-end of the season. She's tallish, a good-mover, spirited and there's something very nice about her. As long as we don't rush her she'll cope mentally. They are quite 'fizzy' this family".*

1520. MABDHOOL (IRE) ★★★

b.c. Mount Nelson – Berry Baby (Rainbow Quest). February 22. Second foal. 50,000Y. Tattersalls October Book 2. Shadwell Estate Co. The dam, a modest 14f winner, is a half-sister to the very useful 2-y-o dual 7f winner and multiple Group 3 placed Measuring Time. The second dam, Inchberry (by Barathea), was placed 7 times including when second in a listed event over 1m at 2 yrs and fourth in the Oaks and is a half-sister to 3 winners including the very useful 12f listed winner Inchiri (herself dam of the South African Grade 3 winner Hawk's Eye). (Hamdan Al Maktoum). *"More of a backward type 2-y-o so he won't be early but he's a good mover, very nice-looking*

and one of the nicest types I've seen by this stallion. He's a solid horse, he's in work but the likelihood is that he's one for later on but I'd be disappointed if he didn't win this year".*

1521. MAJOR BOBBY ★★

b.c. Exceed And Excel – Dominica (Alhaarth). April 9. Sixth foal. Half-brother to the quite useful 7f winner of 4 races Jungle Bay, to the quite useful 5f winner Lulla (both by Oasis Dream) and the modest 5f and 6f winner of 3 races Todber (by Cape Cross). The dam, winner of the Group 2 5f Kings Stand Stakes and the Group 3 Cornwallis Stakes, is a half-sister to 3 winners including the listed-placed sprinter Bowness. The second dam, Dominio (by Dominion), a 2-y-o listed 5f winner, was second in the Group 2 5f Temple Stakes and is a half-sister to 6 winners including the very smart Group 1 5f Nunthorpe Stakes winner Ya Malak. (Mrs R B Kennard). *"The dam was very small and we didn't start training her until the second half of the season. This colt is tiny as well, so we wouldn't expect much from him until later on this season but let's hope he's as good as she was. The sire can get them a bit hot, but this colt has a very good temperament".*

1522. MAKRUMA ★★★

b.f. Dubawi – Qelaan (Dynaformer). March 11. First foal. The dam, a quite useful 11f and 12f winner, is a half-sister to one winner. The second dam, Irtahal (by Swain), a fairly useful 1m winner, was third in the Group 3 Musidora Stakes and is a half-sister to several winners. (Hamdan Al Maktoum). *"We broke her in before we moved yards, she's a nice type and you wouldn't cast out anything by Dubawi. She's absolutely fine and I'm looking forward to her arriving".*

1523. MUSHTAMMEL (IRE) ★★

b.c. Intikhab – Merayaat (Darshaan). March 17. Fifth foal. Half-brother to the smart 1m (at 2 yrs) and Group 3 12f Cumberland Lodge Stakes winner Hawaafez (by Nayef). The dam was a quite useful 14f winner. The second dam, Maddelina (by Sadler's Wells), is an unplaced half-sister to 2 winners. (Hamdan Al Maktoum). *"The dam stayed really well but the sire is a miler, so this colt could be anything as* far as his optimum trip is concerned. The half-sister Hawaafez was enormous and I think we did well to get her to win as a 2-y-o. This colt is likely to take a bit of time, so I'd say he's one for the second half of the season".

1524. NAWL (IRE) ★★★★

b.c. Bushranger – Crystalline Stream (Polish Precedent). March 18. Third foal. 40,000Y. Tattersalls October Book 2. Shadwell Estate Co. Half-brother to the fair 1m (at 2 yrs) to 11f and hurdles winner Unknown Rebel (by Night Shift). The dam, placed twice at 3 yrs in France, is a half-sister to 3 winners including the listed winner Mundybash and the Group 3 5f Prix du Bois third Sister Moonshine. The second dam, Cootamundra (by Double Bed), a winner at 2 and 3 yrs in France, is a half-sister to 9 winners including the triple Group 3 winner Big John and the dam of the Group 1 Prix du Cadran winner Bannaby. (Hamdan Al Maktoum). "I like this horse and he could prove to be a bargain. My most experienced riders like him, so we're quite hopeful of him being a 2-y-o winner. He shows enough pace, he's solid, very straightforward and he'll be racing in May".

1525. PURPLE SPOT ★★★

br.f. Kyllachy – Regal Gallery (Royal Academy). March 16. Half-sister to the fair 10f winner Suntrap (by Desert Sun). The dam, a modest 10f and 12f winner of 4 races, is a half-sister to several winners. The second dam, Polistatic (by Free State), was a moderate 11f and 12f winner. (Mrs Barbara Sumner). "A nice type, we did a little bit with her and she showed us some nice speed. She's not over-big and she'll be a 2-y-o alright".

1526. SERENA GRAE ★★★

gr.f. Arakan – Success Story (Sharrood). April 1. Half-sister to the useful 10f and 12f listed winner Film Script (by Unfuwain), to the fairly useful 6f and 7f and subsequent US stakes winner National Park (by Common Grounds), the useful Group 3 6f Chipchase Stakes winner of 7 races Barney McGrew (by Mark Of Esteem) and the fair 8.5f and 10f winner Champagne (by Efisio) and the modest 12f winner Fisadara (by Nayef). The dam, a modest 10f winner, is a half-sister to 7

winners including the Group 2 13.5f Prix de Pomone winner Interlude. The second dam, Starlet, a smart 10f and 12f performer, won a Group 2 event in Germany and is a half-sister to 8 winners including the US Grade 1 winner Unknown Quantity. (Heather Raw). "I like this filly, she's nice, sound and scopey. I'm pleased with her, she's well put-together and a six/seven furlong type 2-y-o that hasn't done a thing wrong yet".

1527. SIR PERCY BLAKENEY ★★

b.c. Sir Percy – Sulitelma (The Minstrel). March 22. Fifteenth foal. €12,000Y. Tattersalls Ireland September. M Tregoning. Half-brother to the quite useful 2-y-o 5f winner Ice Mountain (by Kyllachy), to the quite useful 10f to 12f winner Tromp, the fair 7f and 1m winner Robinzal (both by Zilzal), the fair 2-y-o 1m winner Min Mirri, the modest 6f and 1m winner Border Glen (both by Selkirk), the fair Irish 5f winner Neeze (by Cadeaux Genereux), the fair 2-y-o 7f winner Song Of The Siren (by With Approval), the modest 2-y-o 6f winner Seta Pura (by Domedriver) and the modest 9.4f winner Semiramis (by Darshaan). The dam, a modest 2-y-o 5f all-weather winner, is a half-sister to 3 winners including the German listed winner El Supremo. The second dam, Sharmila (by Blakeney), ran once unplaced and is a half-sister to the King George VI and Queen Elizabeth Diamond Stakes winner Petoski. "This colt was a cheap yearling, but he's butty, short-coupled and a 2-y-o type. Hopefully one for when the six furlong races start".

1528. STEVE ROGERS (IRE) ★★★

b.c. Montjeu – Three Owls (Warning). March 23. Ninth foal. 78,000foal. Tattersalls December. Charlie Gordon-Watson. Brother to the useful 10f winner and listed Pretty Polly Stakes second Three Moons, to the modest 11f winner Fire In Babylon and half-brother to the useful 2-y-o 5f winner and listed-placed Black Velvet (by Inchinor) and the quite useful 10f and 12f winner Hong Kong Island (by Alhaarth). The dam, a fair 1m winner, is a half-sister to 7 winners including the listed winners Thames and Three Wrens. The second dam, Three Terns (by Arctic Tern), won over 9f in France and is a half-sister to 3 winners including Three Angels (Group 3 1m Prix des

Reservoirs). (Nurlan Bizakov). *"Steve Rogers was the alter ego of "Captain America" in the old Marvel comic books – not that I'm old enough to remember him! This colt is quite nice and I have to say that the half-brother I trained, Black Velvet, was quite decent but he had temperament issues and should have been gelded earlier than he actually was. This horse is by Montjeu but nevertheless he shows speed, he could well start at six furlongs and I think he could be alright. I quite like him, he's not too big or backward and he'll certainly be running this year. I'm just a bit wary that we had to geld his half-brother because it can sometimes run in families".*

1529. STILLA AFTON ★★
b.br.f. Nayef – Sourire (Domedriver). February 22. Second foal. The dam, a dual 2-y-o 7f winner, later won a listed event over 1m in Sweden and is a half-sister to 5 winners including the 2-y-o Group 3 1m Prix des Reservoirs winner Songerie, the German listed winner and Group 1 Italian Oaks third Souvenance and the French listed winner and Group 3 placed Soft Morning. The second dam, Summer Night (by Nashwan), a fairly useful 3-y-o 6f winner, is a half-sister to 7 winners including the Group 3 Prix d'Arenburg winner Starlit Sands. (Miss K Rausing). *"The dam did really well, winning as a 2-y-o and a listed event at 3. This filly isn't the best looking in the world but she's very active and hasn't done anything wrong. She's not the biggest so she'll have to run as a 2-y-o, probably over seven furlongs".*

1530. SWEET P ★★
b.f. Sir Percy – Desert Run (Desert Prince). March 1. First foal. 13,000Y. Tattersalls October Book 3. M Tregoning. The dam is an unraced half-sister to numerous winners including the 2-y-o Group 3 Prix du Calvados winner Purr Along and the fairly useful 9f and subsequent US winner and dual listed-placed Lady Francesca. The second dam, Purring (by Mountain Cat), a quite useful 7f winner, is a half-sister to the Group 2 1m Falmouth Stakes and Group 3 1m Prix de Sandringham winner Ronda (herself dam of a Group 3 winner) and to the smart 1m (at 2 yrs) and listed 2m winner Silver Gilt. (Mr & Mrs A E Pakenham/M

Tregoning). *"I took a keen interest in her at the sales, partly because she's by Sir Percy but also because of the dam's half-sisters Purr Along and Lady Francesca – two of Willie Muir's best fillies. I don't think this filly will be particularly early but she's very good-looking, on the small side but not a bad type".*

1531. UNNAMED ★★★
gr.c. Verglas – Briery (Salse). May 5. Eighth foal. €16,000Y. Tattersalls Ireland September. M Tregoning. Half-brother to the quite useful 6f and 7f winner of 6 races Great Charm (by Orpen), to the quite useful 7f to 15f winner of 5 races Fregate Island, the fair 10f, 11f and hurdles winner Pearl (both by Daylami) and the Swiss 2-y-o winner Story Of Dubai (by Dubai Destination). The dam, a modest 3-y-o 7f winner, is out of the unraced Wedgewood (by Woodman), herself a half-sister to 10 minor winners. *"I'm pleased with this colt, he's a good-looking, big, strong horse and a beautiful mover. One for later in the season, but there's plenty to work on. His pedigree suggests he might prefer a bit of cut in the ground but we'll have to see about that. He could be nice".*

ROGER VARIAN

1532. ALJAAZIAH ★★★
b.br.f. Medaglia D'Oro – Eswarah (Unfuwain). February 23. Fourth foal. Half-sister to the 2012 2-y-o Qawaafy (by Street Cry), placed fourth once over 1m from 2 starts and to the useful 2-y-o 6f winner and Group 1 Fillies' Mile third Firdaws (by Mr Greeley). The dam won 3 races including the Group 1 Epsom Oaks and is a half-sister to 9 winners including the Group 3 12f Princess Royal Stakes winner Itnab, the very useful 6f winner of 4 races Haafiz and the useful 7f and 1m winner and Irish 1,000 Guineas third Umniyatee. The second dam, Midway Lady (by Alleged), won the Prix Marcel Boussac, the 1,000 Guineas and the Oaks and is a half-sister to 5 winners including the very useful 11.8f listed winner Capias. (Hamdan Al Maktoum). *"She's an attractive filly, she'll take time to reach full maturity and she'll be a second half of the season 2-y-o over seven furlongs or a mile. I've haven't done too much with her yet but there's no reason to dislike her at the moment".*

1533. ALMASHOOQA (USA) ★★★

b.br.f. Dubawi – Almoutezah (Storm Cat).
February 7. The dam was unplaced in two
starts and is a half-sister to 3 winners including
the US Grade 1 Personal Ensign Stakes winner
Summer Colony. The second dam, Probable
Colony (by Pleasant Colony), is an unraced
half-sister to the US dual Grade 3 winner With
Ability. (Hamdan Al Maktoum). *"She's in Dubai
and hasn't arrived here yet, but I've seen her
and she's a good, strong type. Big and scopey,
she's much bigger than a lot of Dubawi fillies
and they tell me she has a nice action".*

1534. ANDY IS ON THE RUN (IRE) ★★★

*b.c. Captain Rio – Harvest Joy (Daggers
Drawn).* February 7. First foal. £34,000Y.
Doncaster Premier. Armando Duarte. The
dam, a fairly useful 6f (at 2 yrs) and 10f winner
and listed-placed, is a half-sister to 2 winners.
The second dam, Windomen (by Forest Wind),
is an unraced half-sister to 3 winners. (Mr K J P
Gundlach). *"A 2-y-o type for May or June and
he has a nice action. He's done nothing wrong
so far and although I'm not sure what level
he'll pop in at he's a likeable little horse".*

1535. AYRAD (IRE) ★★★

*ch.c. Dalakhani – Sweet Firebird (Sadler's
Wells).* April 9. Fifth foal. 70,000Y. Tattersalls
October Book 1. Tony Nerses. Half-brother to
the modest 6f and 7f winner But Beautiful (by
Pivotal) and to the fair 6f winner Alsium (by
Invincible Spirit). The dam, a useful Irish 10f
winner and third in the Group 3 10f Blue Wind
Stakes, is a sister to the 2-y-o 7.5f winner
and Group 2 1m Royal Lodge Stakes second
Moscow Ballet and a half-sister to 6 winners
including the top-class Group 1 July Cup and
Group 1 Nunthorpe Stakes winner Stravinsky.
The second dam, Fire The Groom (by Blushing
Groom), a smart winner of 5 races here at
around 1m, subsequently won the Grade 1
9.5f Beverly D Stakes and the Grade 2 Wilshire
Handicap and is a half-sister to the Group 1 6f
Vernons Sprint Cup winner Dowsing. (Saleh Al
Homaizi & Imad Al Sagar). *"A nice type, he's a
very attractive colt that's forward-going and a
good mover. He'll be one for the late summer
over seven furlongs. His pedigree doesn't
scream 2-y-o at you but he's more forward
than you'd imagine".*

1536. CERTIFICATE ★★★

ch.c. Pivotal – Graduation (Lomitas). March
5. Second living foal. 100,000Y. Tattersalls
October Book 1. Oliver St Lawrence. The dam,
a fairly useful 1m winner, was listed-placed.
The second dam, Ceremonial (by Lion Cavern),
a fair 1m winner, is a half-sister to 6 winners
including the Group 2 Great Voltigeur Stakes
and Group 2 Prix Jean de Chaudenay winner
Sacrament. (Cheveley Park Stud). *"A nice type,
he's more of a later-maturing horse but he's
attractive and has a good action. He'll make an
autumn 2-y-o".*

1537. DORRAAR (IRE) ★★★

b.f. Shamardal – Dorrati (Dubai Millennium).
April 10. Fifth foal. Half-sister to the fair 2013
3-y-o 7f winner Kabbaas, to the fair 7f winner
Shaleek (both by Pivotal) and the quite useful
2-y-o 6f winner Dahakaa (by Bertolini). The
dam is an unraced half-sister to 4 winners
including the 7f (at 2 yrs) and dual listed 1m
winner Baharah and the fairly useful 2-y-o
winners In Dubai and Naaddey. The second
dam, Bahr (Generous), winner of the listed 7f
Washington Singer Stakes (at 2 yrs), the Group
3 12f Ribblesdale Stakes and the Group 3 10.4f
Musidora Stakes, is a half-sister to numerous
winners. (Sheikh Ahmed Al Maktoum). *"She's
a nice type and to my eyes the best the mare's
thrown so far. She's had three winners without
having had a black-type animal yet but, as
I say, this is a nice type of filly and hopefully
she'll step up to the plate for the mare".*

1538. DOUBLE UP ★★★

*b.c. Exceed And Excel – My Love Thomas
(Cadeaux Genereux).* April 20. Second foal.
90,000Y. Tattersalls October Book 1. Roger
Varian. Half-brother to the fair 5f (at 2 yrs) to
1m winner Full Support (by Acclamation). The
dam, a fair 2-y-o 6f winner, is a half-sister to
6 winners including the US Grade 3 Miesque
Stakes winner Louvain. The second dam,
Flanders (by Common Grounds), a very useful
sprint winner of 6 races including the listed
Scarborough Stakes, was second in the Group
2 Kings Stand Stakes and is a half-sister to 8
winners. (A D Spence). *"He's a good-moving
horse, he won't be early but he could be a mid-
summer 2-y-o. He doesn't have a bad action at*

all and we'll be able to move on with him quite soon, especially as it's quite a speedy pedigree".

1539. EJADAH (IRE) ★★★
b.f. *Clodovil – Bintalreef (Diesis).* April 20. Eighth foal. 170,000Y. Tattersalls October Book 2. Shadwell Estate Co. Sister to the fair 1m winner Epic Encounter and half-sister to the very smart 2012 Group 2 7f Futurity Stakes winner First Cornerstone (by Hurricane Run) and the useful 4-y-o triple 12f winner and Group 3 2m third Buxted (by Dynaformer). The dam, a useful French 2-y-o 7f winner, is a half-sister to 5 winners including the US stakes winner and Grade 3 1m placed Solar Bound. The second dam, Solar Star (by Lear Fan), a fairly useful 2-y-o 6f winner, is a half-sister to 7 winners including the US triple Grade 3 winner Gold Land. (Hamdan Al Maktoum). *"She could be a mid-summer filly, she's athletic and quite correct. It's a bit early to know what sort of ability she has but we don't dislike her. As you'd expect from her price tag she's not a bad type".*

1540. EL NAJMM (IRE) ★★★
ch.c. *Sea The Stars – My Dubai (Dubai Millennium).* May 6. Half-brother to the fair 2012 6f placed Mishaal (by Kheleyf), to the quite useful dual 7f winner Mizwaaj (by Invincible Spirit) and to the fair 7f and 9f winner Naddwah (by Pivotal). The dam, placed over 7f on her only start, is a half-sister to 7 winners including the very smart triple Group 2 7f winner Iffraaj, the useful 2-y-o Group 3 7f Prix du Calvados winner Kareymah and the useful dual 1m winner Jathaabeh. The second dam, Pastorale (by Nureyev), a fairly useful 3-y-o 7f winner, ran only twice more including in a walk-over. (Sheikh Ahmed Al Maktoum). *"A smaller Sea The Stars but he's a neat horse and I quite like him. Quite athletic and a good goer, he could be a late summer 2-y-o and he's not a bad type".*

1541. ELSHAADIN ★★★
gr.f. *Dalakhani – Distinctive Look (Danehill).* February 7. Third foal. 550,000Y. Tattersalls October Book 1. Shadwell Estate Co. Half-sister to the quite useful 12f winner Royal Peculiar (by Galileo). The dam, a quite useful 9f winner, is a half-sister to 9 winners including Nathaniel (King George VI and Queen Elizabeth Stakes and Eclipse Stakes), Playful Act (Group 1 Fillies' Mile), Great Heavens (Group 1 Irish Oaks), Percussionist (Group 2 Yorkshire Cup winner), Echoes In Eternity (Group 2 Sun Chariot Stakes and Group 2 Park Hill Stakes) and Changing Skies (US dual Grade 3 winner). The second dam, Magnificient Style (by Silver Hawk), won the Group 3 10.5f Musidora Stakes and is a half-sister to 5 winners including Siberian Summer (Grade 1 10f Charles H Strub Stakes). (Hamdan Al Maktoum). *"She hasn't been here long but she's a nice type with a good action. I quite like what I see of her at the moment and she's likely to make 2-y-o in the second part of the season. She was bought for her pedigree really and if we can get her to do anything on the track it'll be a bonus".*

1542. FENNANN ★★
b.g. *Dutch Art – Embraced (Pursuit Of Love).* May 4. Ninth foal. 60,000Y. Tattersalls October Book 2. Shadwell Estate Co. Half-brother to the fairly useful 7f to 9f winner of 5 races Tartan Gunna (by Anabaa), to the quite useful dual 1m winner Fondled, the quite useful 7f and 1m winner Paramour, the fair 12f winner Croftamie (all by Selkirk), the quite useful 7.5f and 1m winner of 3 races Caressed (by Medicean) and the fair 9f winner Abraccio (by Pivotal). The dam, a useful listed 1m winner, is a half-sister to 6 winners on the flat including the Group 2 Summer Mile winner Cesare and the Group 3 12f Prix la Force winner and French Derby second Nowhere To Exit and to the Grade 2 winning hurdler Trenchant. The second dam, Tromond (by Lomond), a fairly useful 9f winner, was second in the listed 10f Ballymacoll Stud Stakes at Newbury and is a half-sister to 6 winners including Mont Etoile (Group 2 Ribblesdale Stakes). (Sheikh Ahmed Al Maktoum). *"He's just been gelded and he's grown since the sales. Physically he's done well, but he's not an early type and could be one the mid-to-late summer".*

1543. FERAYHA (IRE) ★★★
b.f. *Cape Cross – Albahja (Sinndar).* April 13. Fifth foal. Half-sister to the quite useful 2-y-o 7f winner Jaaryah (by Halling) and to the fair 10f winner Kronful (by Singspiel). The dam, a useful 12f winner, was second in the Group 3 10f Golden Daffodil Stakes and in the listed

12f Galtres Stakes and is a half-sister to the fair 11f to 14f winner of 4 races Efrhina. The second dam, Eshq Albahr (by Riverman), is an unraced half-sister to the useful 1m to 10f winner Dayflower. (Sheikh Ahmed Al Maktoum). *"She's a nice type and when she came in I thought she was the most attractive the mare's thrown. She went a bit weak so we've given her a little break to develop. A second half of the season runner".*

1544. GO SAKHEE ★★★

br.c. Sakhee's Secret – Bling Bling (Indian Ridge). April 16. Fifth foal. 32,000Y. Tattersalls October Book 2. Roger Varian. Half-brother to the fairly useful 2012 6f placed 2-y-o New Rich (by Bahamian Bounty), to the fairly useful 2-y-o dual 6f winner Bling King (by Haafhd) and to the quite useful 2-y-o 7f winner Male Model (by Iffraaj). The dam, a fair fourth over 1m and 10f, is a sister to the very smart dual listed 5f winner Watching and a half-sister to 4 winners. The second dam, Sweeping (by Indian King), a useful 2-y-o 6f winner, was listed placed and is a half-sister to 10 winners. (Allen, Moss, Marchant & Jarvis). *"A nice type and a good, natural-moving horse. He's quite tall and could be ready by mid-summer. I quite like him and he's bred to be quick".*

1545. HADAATHA (IRE) ★★

gr.f. Sea The Stars – Hathrah (Linamix). April 24. Fourth foal. Half-sister to the fairly useful dual 10f and 2m winner Itlaak (by Alhaarth). The dam, winner of the listed 1m Masaka Stakes and third in the 1,000 Guineas, is a half-sister to 5 winners including the smart Group 2 12f Premio Ellington winner Ivan Luis and the French/German listed winners Amathia and Zero Problemo. The second dam, Zivania (by Shernazar), a useful Irish winner of 4 races from 1m to 9.5f, is a half-sister to the Group 3 Prix Gontaut Biron winner Muroto. (Hamdan Al Maktoum). *"She only arrived this morning because she was a little immature and broken late, but she has an eye-catching pedigree and it's obviously nice to have her in the yard".*

1546. HERBAH ★★★

b.f. Dansili – Khulood (Storm Cat). February 15. Sixth foal. Half-sister to the quite useful dual 7f winner Imaam (by Pivotal) and to the quite

useful 2-y-o 5f winner Kashoof (by Green Desert). The dam, a useful listed 7f (at 2 yrs) and Group 3 7f Nell Gwyn Stakes winner, is a half-sister to numerous winners including the Irish 1,000 Guineas winner Mehthaaf and the July Cup winner Elnadim. The second dam, Elle Seule (by Exclusive Native), a very smart winner of the Group 3 1m Prix d'Astarte, also won over 10.5f and is a half-sister to the Group/Grade 1 winners Fort Wood, Hamas and Timber Country and to the Group winners Northern Aspen, Colorado Dancer and Mazzacano. (Hamdan Al Maktoum). *"She lacks a bit of scope but she's a neat, correct filly. An early foal, she could be a summer 2-y-o I think and she skips along OK. It's about time the dam threw a decent one, so we'll have to see".*

1547. HIGH ACCOLADE ★★★★

ch.f. Medicean – Hightime Heroine (Danetime). February 13. First foal. 26,000Y. Tattersalls December. Hugo Merry. The dam, a fair 6f winner, is a half-sister to 3 winners including the listed 1m Heron Stakes winner and Group 1 1m Criterium International third Redolent and the useful 2-y-o 6f winner and Group 3 6f Albany Stakes third Illaunglass. The second dam, Esterlina (by Highest Honor), won over 1m at 3 yrs in Ireland and is a half-sister to 3 minor winners in France. (Cheveley Park Stud). *"Quite a forward filly, she's going nicely at the moment and she's in good work although she hasn't done fast work yet. I expect she'll be sharp enough to race over five and six furlongs in early summer. A filly with a likeable way of going".* TRAINERS' BARGAIN BUY

1548. HUMOUR (IRE) ★★★★ ♠

b.c. Invincible Spirit – Hucking Hot (Desert Prince). April 26. Second foal. 100,000Y. Tattersalls October Book 1. John Warren. Half-brother to the fair 2012 2-y-o 7f winner El Mirage (by Elusive Quality). The dam, a fair 2-y-o 5f winner and listed-placed here, subsequently won a 1m stakes event in the USA and was Grade 1 placed. The second dam, True Love (by Robellino), is an unraced half-sister to 9 winners including the Group 2 6f Coventry Stakes winner Hellvelyn. (Highclere Thoroughbred Racing – Heritage). *"He's a good-looking horse with a good action and the physique to be a 2-y-o from June onwards. I quite like what I've seen so far and he looks a six furlong type".*

1549. KEEPER'S RING (USA) ★★

b.f. Street Cry – Liffey Dancer (Sadler's Wells). January 31. First foal. 210,000Y. Tattersalls October Book 1. Not sold. The dam is an unraced sister to 4 winners including the Group 1 7f Moyglare Stud Stakes winner Sequoyah (herself dam of the multiple Group 1 winner Henrythenavigator) and the 2-y-o Group 1 Fillies' Mile winner Listen and a half-sister to the Irish listed 5.6f winner and Group 3 7f placed Oyster Catcher (by Bluebird). The second dam, Brigid (by Irish River), a minor French 3-y-o 1m winner, is a sister to 2 winners including the French listed 7f winner Or Vision (herself dam of the Group/Grade 1 winners Dolphin Street, Insight and Saffron Walden) and a half-sister to 5 winners. (Merry Fox Stud Ltd). *"She needed to strengthen up so she's just gone out for some spring grass. We've had her here bobbing along throughout the winter and it's a smart pedigree but she's not an early type".*

1550. LABJAAR ★★★

ch.c. Dutch Art – Interlace (Pivotal). March 16. First foal. 65,000Y. Tattersalls October Book 2. Shadwell Estate Co. The dam, a quite useful 2-y-o 6f winner, is a sister to 2 winners including the very smart 6f and 7f winner of 7 races Feet So Fast and a half-sister to 3 winners including the smart Group 2 6f Lowther Stakes and Group 3 Princess Margaret Stakes winner Soar. The second dam, Splice (by Sharpo), a smart winner of the listed 6f Abernant Stakes, is a full or half-sister to 7 winners. (Sheikh Ahmed Al Maktoum). *"A big horse, he had a little setback but he's quite strong and he could make into a summer 2-y-o".*

1551. LADY SPARKLER (IRE) ★★★

b.f. Tamayuz – Capote West (Capote). April 28. Third foal. 42,000Y. Tattersalls October Book 2. Blandford Bloodstock. Half-sister to the 2012 fourth-placed 2-y-o Sister Slew (by Kheleyf) and to the Irish 2-y-o 1m winner, on her only start, Capeslew (by Cape Cross). The dam, a minor dual winner at 3 yrs in the USA, is a half-sister to the 2-y-o listed Dragon Stakes winner Western Art. The second dam, Madam West (by Gone West), a minor US 3-y-o winner, is a half-sister to 6 winners, including two US stakes winners. (S Hassiakos & M Manasseh). *"She could be an early summer 2-y-o because she's quite forward in her work, she has a good action and a nice attitude. It's a bit early to know how good she is but I quite like what I've seen of her".*

1552. LAFTAH (IRE) ★★★

b.f. Invincible Spirit – Liscune (King's Best). April 18. Fourth foal. Sister to the smart dual 7f (at 2 yrs) and 10f winner and Group 2 Dante Stakes second Ektihaam. The dam, a fair 1m and 12f winner in Ireland, is a half-sister to 4 winners including the Group 3 Prix du Lys winner Lycitus and to the placed dam of the Group 1 Premio Roma winner Sunstrach. The second dam, Royal Lorna (by Val de l'Orne), won the Group 3 Premio Bagutta and is a half-sister to 7 winners including the Group 1 Yorkshire Oaks winner Awaasif (dam of the Oaks winner Snow Bride) and the 1,000 Guineas second Konafa (the dam of three Group winners). (Hamdan Al Maktoum). *"She's got quite a lot of scope for an Invincible Spirit so she won't be an early type, but she's a very attractive filly and a nice type".*

1553. MAHAABA (IRE) ★★

b.f. Oasis Dream – Masaafat (Act One). March 8. Half-sister to Hasheem (by New Approach), placed fourth over 1m in one start at 2 yrs in 2012. The dam is an unraced half-sister to the very useful 2-y-o listed 6f winner and Group 1 6f Cheveley Park Stakes second Suez. The second dam, Repeat Warning (by Warning), a fair 8.3f placed 3-y-o, is a half-sister to 9 winners including the Group 2 9.2f Prix de l'Opera winner Bella Colora (dam of the Prince Of Wales's Stakes winner Stagecraft), the Irish Oaks winner Colorspin (dam of the Group 1 winners Zee Zee Top, Opera House and Kayf Tara) and the Irish Champion Stakes winner Cezanne. (Hamdan Al Maktoum). *"She only arrived this morning because she was a bit immature and was broken in late. I haven't seen her yet, but I like her 3-y-o half-brother and as she's by Oasis Dream you'd have to be hopeful".*

1554. MASTER OF ALKMAAR ★★★★
ch.c. Dutch Art – Lalina (Trempolino). April
1. Fourth foal. £50,000Y. Doncaster Premier.
Hugo Merry. Half-brother to the modest 2-y-o
7f winner Wotsthehurry (by Proclamation).
The dam, a minor winner at 3 yrs in Germany,
is a half-sister to the German winner and
Group 3 second Lancetto. The second dam,
Lanciana (by Acatenango), a minor winner
of 2 races in France and Germany, was
listed-placed and is a half-sister to 3 winners
including the German Group 2 winner
Lanciano. (Mr F H Hay). *"I like this little horse,
he has a good action and skips along. He could
be an early summer horse over six furlongs on
fast ground".*

1555. MUHAWALAH (IRE) ★★★
ch.f. Nayef – Al Ishq (Nureyev). March 5. Sister
to the Group 1 Prix Jean Prat and Group 1
Prix Jacques le Marois winner Tamayuz and
half-sister to the fairly useful French 2-y-o
7f winner and Group 3 Prix Miesque second
Nuqoosh (by Machiavellian), the useful 10f
and 11f winner Ashaaq, the French 2-y-o 6f
winner Thamarat (both by Anabaa) and the
French 6f winner Naahedh (by Medicean).
The dam, a 3-y-o 8.3f winner in France, is a
half-sister to the Group 1 12f Prix du Jockey
Club winner Anabaa Blue (by Anabaa). The
second dam, Allez les Trois (by Riverman), a
smart winner of 3 races in France including
the Group 3 10.5f Prix de Flore, is a half-sister
to 6 winners including the Prix de l'Arc de
Triomphe winner Urban Sea and the 2,000
Guineas winner King's Best. (Hamdan Al
Maktoum). *"A filly for the second half of the
season. She's in the same category as a lot of
these Sheikh Hamdan fillies because they're
nice types with exceptional pedigrees and
hopefully a few of them will be above average.
This filly has a nice way of going but she's
having a break at the moment to pick at some
spring grass and let her develop. She'll be an
autumn 2-y-o I should think".*

1556. MUNATAS ★★★
b.c. Sea The Stars – Dashing (Sadler's Wells).
February 21. Second foal. The dam is an
unraced half-sister to numerous winners
including the top-class multiple Group 1
winner Alexander Goldrun and the Group 3

Prix de la Jonchere winner and Group 1 placed
Medicis. The second dam, Renashaan (by
Darshaan), a listed winner in France, was third
in the Group 3 9f Prix Vanteaux and is a half-
sister to 4 minor winners. (Saleh Al Homaizi &
Imad Al Sagar). *"This is a nice type of colt – he
has everything in the right place. He's a bit
immature at the moment but he's a nice one
for the future".*

1557. MUSHIR ★★★
b.c. Oasis Dream – Shimah (Storm Cat). March
24. First foal. The dam, a listed 6f winner and
second in the Group 1 Moyglare Stud Stakes,
is a half-sister to the listed 6f (at 2 yrs) and
Group 3 7f Athasi Stakes winner Walayef, the
Group 2 6f Diomed Stakes winner Haatef
and the Irish dual listed 6f winner Ulfah.
The second dam, Sayedat Alhadh (by Mr
Prospector), a US 7f winner, is a sister to the
US Grade 2 7f winner Kayrawan and a half-
sister to the useful winners Amaniy, Elsaamri
and Mathkurh. (Hamdan Al Maktoum). *"A
handy little colt, he lacks a bit of scope but he's
strong and he's one for the early summer over
six furlongs. The dam was very good but not
very big, so perhaps I shouldn't worry about
his size".*

1558. MUSTAJJID ★★
b.c. Byron – Skara Brae (Inchinor). March
27. Fifth foal. £75,000Y. Doncaster Premier.
Shadwell Estate Co. Half-brother to the useful
6f and 7f winner of 5 races Bonnie Brae (by
Mujahid), to the moderate 7f and 1m winner
Vogarth (by Arkadian Hero) and a minor 2-y-o
winner abroad by Josr Algarhoud. The dam is
an unraced half-sister to 5 minor winners. The
second dam, Tahilla (by Moorestyle), won 7
races at 2 and 3 yrs including two listed events
and is a half-sister to 8 winners including the
Group 1 Nunthorpe Stakes winner Piccolo.
(Hamdan Al Maktoum). *"I bought him to be
an early type but he's grown, developed and
lengthened, so he's more likely to make a mid-
summer 2-y-o. A nice, athletic horse, he could
be alright but it's a bit early to tell".*

1559. POPPING CANDY ★★★
*br.f. Oasis Dream – Blessing (Dubai
Millennium).* March 31. Fourth foal. Half-sister
to the fairly useful 2-y-o 6f winner and dual

listed 7f placed Sweetie Time (by Invincible Spirit). The dam is an unraced half-sister to 3 winners including the French listed 7f winner Esperero. The second dam, Hydro Calido (by Nureyev), a very useful filly and winner of the Group 2 1m Prix d'Astarte, was second in the French 1,000 Guineas and is a half-sister to the champion European 2-y-o and 2,000 Guineas second Machiavellian, to the smart Group 1 Prix Morny and Group 1 Prix de la Salamandre winner and 1,000 Guineas third Coup de Genie and the very smart Group 1 Prix Jacques le Marois winner Exit to Nowhere (by Irish River). (Lordship Stud). *"She was here throughout the winter but she needs to strengthen up so she's just gone out for a break. She moves OK and she could be alright one day".*

1560. PRINCESS NOOR (IRE) ★★★★

b.f. Holy Roman Emperor – Gentle Night (Zafonic). January 29. Seventh foal. £120,000Y. Doncaster Premier. Tony Nerses. Half-sister to the quite useful 7f (at 2 yrs) and dual 1m winner Oratory, to the quite useful Irish 7f winner Rockymountainhigh (both by Danehill Dancer) and the 4-y-o UAE triple 7f winner Knight Of Dance (by Singspiel). The dam ran once unplaced and is a half-sister to 6 winners including the Group 2 Flying Childers Stakes winner Land Of Dreams (dam of the multiple Group 1 winner Dream Ahead). The second dam, Sahara Star (by Green Desert), won the Group 3 Molecomb Stakes and is a half-sister to 6 winners including the Group 3 Greenham Stakes winner Yalaietanee. (Saleh Al Homaizi & Imad Al Sagar). *"A sharp sort of 2-y-o for five and six furlongs and she could be racing in May. A January foal, she's quite mature for her age and I quite like how she goes".*

1561. QUASQAZAH ★★★★

ch.c. Bahamian Bounty – Rock Lily (Rock Of Gibraltar). April 11. Third foal. 150,000Y. Tattersalls October Book 2. Shadwell Estate Co. Half-brother to the fairly useful 2012 2-y-o 5f winner and dual listed-placed Botanic Garden (by Royal Applause) and to the modest 7f winner Rockme Cockney (by Cockney Rebel). The dam, a quite useful Irish 2-y-o 1m winner, is a half-sister to 8 winners including the Group 2 6f Cherry Hinton Stakes winner

Please Sing, the very useful 7f (at 2 yrs) to 10f winner and Group 1 National Stakes third Mountain Song and the fairly useful 2-y-o 6f winner and Group 3 6f Princess Margaret Stakes third Raindancing. The second dam, Persian Song (by Persian Bold), is an unplaced sister to the Solario Stakes winner Bold Arrangement (placed in seven Group/Grade 1 races including the Kentucky Derby). (Hamdan Al Maktoum). *"He's a nice type that moves well and he's quite mature for his age so he could be an early summer horse. It's a fast pedigree so he'll be one for six furlongs in late May/early June I would think".*

1562. RAPID ADVANCE ★★★★ ♠

b.c. Medicean – Snow Gretel (Green Desert). February 25. Third foal. 100,000Y. Tattersalls October Book 2. Charlie Gordon-Watson. Half-brother to the minor French 3-y-o winner La Noe (by Nayef). The dam, a German listed 1m winner, is a half-sister to 4 winners including the 2-y-o Group 2 1m Royal Lodge Stakes winner and 2,000 Guineas second Snow Ridge. The second dam, Snow Princess (by Ela-Mana-Mou), a smart winner of 6 races at up to 2m including the November Handicap and an Italian listed event, was second in the Group 1 Prix Royal-Oak and is a half-sister to 7 winners. (S Suhail). *"He's a nice type, he's done well since the sales and he's a good-actioned horse. A horse with a nice way of moving, he'll be a seven furlong horse in July or August and I quite like him".*

1563. SHERIFF'S STAR (IRE) ★★★ ♠

gr.c. Lawman – Silver Bandana (Silver Buck). April 17. Eighth foal. 50,000Y. Tattersalls October Book 2. Charlie Gordon-Watson. Brother to the modest 2012 9f placed 2-y-o Lucky Black Star and half-brother to the quite useful triple 7f winner (including at 2 yrs) Silver Dip (by Gulch) and to the modest 7f winner Blue Bamboo (by Green Desert). The dam, a US stakes winner of 6 races at 3 to 5 yrs and Grade 3 placed twice, is a half-sister to 5 winners. The second dam, Datum Line (by High Line), is an unraced sister to the Group 2 winners Ancholia and Quay Line and to the dam of the Group 1 Lockinge Stakes winner Soviet Line. (S Suhail). *"He's a good-looking horse that's done well since the sales and he's grown a bit. I thought he was going to be an early 2-y-o but he went through a growing stage and went a bit more backward. So now I'd say he'll be one for the mid-to-late summer. A nice-actioned horse".*

1564. STAR JET (IRE) ★★

gr.f. *Teofilo – Silver Shoon (Fasliyev).* March 9. First foal. €58,000Y. Goffs Orby. Chris & May Mullen. The dam, a fairly useful 7f winner, was second in the Group 3 6f Round Tower Stakes and is a sister to the useful 2-y-o 5f winner and Group 2 5f Flying Childers Stakes second China Eyes and a half-sister to 10 winners including the Group 1 6f Haydock Park Sprint Cup and Group 3 5f Palace House Stakes winner Pipalong. The second dam, Limpopo (by Green Desert), a poor 5f placed 2-y-o, is a half-sister to 7 winners here and abroad. (Mr C Mullin). *"She's not with me yet but she's a nice, attractive filly that's still in pre-training".*

1565. SYNERGISE ★★★

ch.c. *Danehill Dancer – Splashdown (Falbrav).* February 17. First foal. 100,000Y. Tattersalls October Book 1. Armando Duarte. The dam, a listed 10f winner and listed-placed another four times, is a half-sister to 4 winners including listed 10f winner Cosmodrome and the US triple turf winner at around 1m and 9f and Grade 3 placed Tadreeb. The second dam, Space Time (by Bering) was placed over 7f at 2 yrs in France and is a half-sister to 4 minor winners. (Mr K H P Gundlach). *"Quite a nice type, I like him and he's a good mover with a bit of strength to him. He could be an early to mid-summer horse and he's done well. I see him as a six/seven furlong 2-y-o".*

1566. TAKREYM (IRE) ★★★

b.c. *Clodovil – Somoushe (Black Minnaloushe).* April 9. Fifth foal. 150,000Y. Tattersalls October Book 2. Shadwell Estate Co. Half-brother to the useful 2012 2-y-o 7f winner and listed-placed One More Road (by Thousand Words), to the useful 5f winner of 4 races and Group 3 Molecomb Stakes third Archers Road (by Titus Livius), the minor French 2-y-o 1m winner Somalian (by Tiger Hill) and a minor 3-y-o winner in Italy by Clodovil. The dam is an unraced half-sister to 9 winners including the 1m 2-y-o and subsequent German Group

1 10f winner Ransom O'War. The second dam, Sombreffe (by Polish Precedent), a fair 7f winner, is closely related to the Group 2 Mill Reef Stakes winner Russian Bond and the Group 2 Temple Stakes winner Snaadee and a half-sister to 9 winners including the Group 3 Prix de Conde winner Cristofori. (Sheikh Ahmed Al Maktoum). *"A good, forward horse who would have been an early type but for a setback. I like him and I think he's got ability but we'll have to be patient with him now. Hopefully he'll be a mid-season 2-y-o".*

1567. TALMADA (USA) ★★

b.f. *Cape Cross – Aryaamm (Galileo).* Fourth foal. Sister to the fairly useful 2012 2-y-o 7f and 1m winner Yarroom and half-sister to the 2-y-o Group 2 7f Champagne Stakes winner Saamidd (by Street Cry). The dam, a quite useful 10f winner, is a half-sister to the French 6f (at 2 yrs) and 7.5f winner and Group 2 1m third Mathematician. The second dam, Zibilene (by Rainbow Quest), a useful 12f winner and listed-placed over 10f, is a half-sister to 7 winners including the Breeders Cup Mile, Irish 2,000 Guineas and Queen Anne Stakes winner Barathea and the Fillies Mile and Irish 1,000 Guineas winner Gossamer. (Sheikh Ahmed Al Maktoum). *"Although she's a half-sister to a couple of 2-y-o winners she has a weaker physique so she'll take more time. She's still a nice type and the pedigree is very nice, but one for later on".*

1568. TAWEYLA (IRE) ★★★

b.f. *Teofilo – Qasirah (Machiavellian).* April 27. Sixth foal. Sister to the modest 12f winner Attwaal and half-sister to the quite useful 2012 2-y-o 6f winner Tantshi, the very useful 2-y-o listed 7f winner Toolain, to the fair 7f winner Kammaan (both by Diktat) and the modest 14f and hurdles winner Harry Hunt (by Bertolini). The dam, a useful 2-y-o 6f winner, was third in the Group 3 8.5f Princess Margaret Stakes is out of the useful 10.5f and 12f winner Altaweelah (by Fairy King), herself a half-sister to 7 winners including the useful 10f to 14f winner Lost Soldier Three. (Sheikh Ahmed Al Maktoum). *"A nice type and a good model, but she was terribly weak in the winter so we sent her away for some time at grass to develop. She'll be ready to do something in the second half of the season. A good-looking filly".*

1569. TEARS OF THE SUN ★★★

b.f. *Mastercraftsman – Perfect Star (Act One)*. February 9. First foal. 120,000Y. Tattersalls October Book 1. David Redvers. The dam, a useful 7f (including at 2 yrs) and listed 1m winner of 5 races, is a half-sister to 4 winners. The second dam, Granted (by Cadeaux Genereux), a useful 1m and 8.3f winner, was listed placed at up to 9f and is a half-sister to 4 winners. (Qatar Racing Ltd). *"She's having a break at the moment because she needs to develop, but she's quite athletic and isn't a bad type. She just needs to grow in stature a little bit".*

1570. THURAYAAT ★★★

b.f. *Tamayuz – Ghaidaa (Cape Cross)*. March 8. Second foal. Half-sister to the modest 2012 1m placed 2-y-o Tajheez (by Raven's Pass). The dam, a useful listed placed 10f winner, is closely related to the Group 3 12f Princess Royal Stakes winner Itnab, the very useful 6f winner of 4 races Haafiz and the useful 7f and 1m winner and Irish 1,000 Guineas third Umniyatee and a half-sister to numerous winners including the Group 1 Epsom Oaks winner Eswarah. The second dam, Midway Lady (by Alleged), won the Prix Marcel Boussac, the 1,000 Guineas and the Oaks and is a half-sister to 5 winners including the very useful 11.8f listed winner Capias. (Hamdan Al Maktoum). *"A good-moving filly out of a daughter of Midway Lady. She's doesn't do anything wrong and could make a 2-y-o come July I should think".*

1571. TOOFI (FR) ★★★★

b.c. *Henrythenavigator – Silver Bark (Royal Applause)*. February 15. Third foal. 220,000Y. Tattersalls October Book 1. Tony Nerses. Half-brother to the minor US winner at 2 and 3 yrs Ribat (by Officer). The dam, a modest 7f winner, is a sister to the 2-y-o 6.5f and 7f and subsequent US Grade 1 9f and 10f winner Ticker Tape and a half-sister to 3 winners including the dam of the 2-y-o dual Group 2 winner Reckless Abandon. The second dam, Argent du Bois (by Silver Hawk), was placed five times at 2 and 3 yrs in France, stayed 1m

and is a half-sister to 8 winners including the 2-y-o Group 1 Racing Post Trophy winner Crowded House. (Saleh Al Homaizi & Imad Al Sagar). *"He's a good-moving horse, quite mature and he could be racing by the end of May or early June. A nice type, I quite like him and he goes well. A horse with a fast ground action".*

1572. TWILIGHT SKY ★★ ♠

b.f. *Authorized – La Sky (Law Society)*. April 16. Half-sister to the Group 1 12f Oaks winner Love Divine (herself dam of the St Leger winner Sixties Icon), to the quite useful 11.5f winner Easy To Love (both by Diesis), the useful listed 12f winner Floreeda (by Linamix), the useful listed 1m winner Dark Promise (by Shamardal), the useful 12f winner and listed 14f third Solar Sky (by Galileo), the French 12f winner Laurentine and the US winner and Grade 1 fourth Security Code (both by Private Account). The dam, a useful 10f winner and second in the Lancashire Oaks, is closely related to the Champion Stakes winner Legal Case and a half-sister to 4 winners. The second dam, Maryinsky (by Northern Dancer), won twice at up to 9f in the USA and is a half-sister to the US Grade 3 winners Bold Place and Card Table. (Lordship Stud). *"She's just gone for a spell out to grass but I've had her throughout the winter. A nice-moving filly, I should think she'll be a racehorse one day but we'll just have to be patient with her".*

1573. YAGHEER (IRE) ★★★

b.c. *Lawman – Dawn Raid (Docksider)*. March 1. Fourth foal. 70,000Y. Tattersalls October Book 2. Shadwell Estate Co. Half-brother to the quite useful 10f and 11f winner Ansaab (by Cape Cross), to the quite useful 7f (including at 2 yrs) and 1m winner Solar Deity (by Exceed And Excel) and the quite useful Irish 7f winner Dance Hall Girl (by Dansili). The dam, a quite useful Irish 3-y-o 7f winner, is a half-sister to 8 winners including the French and Irish 2,000 Guineas and Richmond Stakes winner Bachir, to the smart 7f (at 2 yrs) to 10f and hurdles winner Albuhera and the useful 2-y-o listed 7f winner Elliots World. The second dam, Morning Welcome (by Be My Guest), placed once over 12f at 3 yrs in Ireland, is a half-sister to 9 winners including the Irish listed Debutante Stakes and subsequent US Grade 3 winner Down Again. (Sheikh Ahmed Al Maktoum). *"A likeable horse with a good action, he could be out in mid-summer and although he hasn't quite stepped into faster work yet we quite like how he goes".*

1574. UNNAMED ★★★★
b.f. Invincible Spirit – Alsace (King's Best). April 7. Second foal. 80,000Y. Tattersalls October Book 1. Rabbah Bloodstock. The dam, the French 7f (at 2 yrs) and 1m winner, was listed-placed and is a half-sister to 2 winners. The second dam, Annex (by Anabaa), a 7f winner at 3 yrs in Deauville, is a half-sister to 4 winners including the US Grade 2 1m and Group 3 1m Prix Quincey winner Bon Point. (Sheikh Juma Al Dalmook Maktoum). *"Yes, she's a nice filly actually and she's looking quite strong at the moment. She goes well, I can see her being out in May and I like what I've seen of her so far".*

1575. UNNAMED ★★★
gr.c. Mastercraftsman – Audacieuse (Rainbow Quest). January 15. Fifth foal. 70,000Y. Tattersalls October Book 2. Charlie Gordon-Watson. Half-brother to the fairly useful 1m (at 2 yrs) to 12f winner Ramona Chase (by High Chaparral) and to the unraced dam of the Group 2 Coventry Stakes third St Barths. The dam won 4 races including the Group 3 Prix de Flore and is a half-sister to 5 winners including the Group 3 Acomb Stakes winner Waiter's Dream and the Irish listed 14f winner Lord Jim. The second dam, Sarah Georgina (by Persian Bold), a quite useful 2-y-o 6f winner, is a half-sister to 11 winners including the French 1,000 Guineas winner Danseuse du Soir. (Mr P D Smith). *"He goes well and he'll be a July/August 2-y-o. He has a good action and he's quite likeable. I have two by the first season sire Mastercraftsman and they're both athletic horses".*

1576. UNNAMED ★★★ ♣
b.c. Exceed And Excel – Gower Song (Singspiel). March 20. Second foal. 200,000Y. Tattersalls October Book 1. Charlie Gordon-Watson. The dam, a very useful listed 10f winner here, subsequently won a Group 3 12f event in Dubai and is a half-sister to 7 winners

including the Group 2 and Group 3 placed Prince Of Denial and the dam of the listed winner and Oaks second Something Exciting. The second dam, Gleaming Water (by Kalaglow), a quite useful 2-y-o 6f winner, is a sister to the Group 3 Solario Stakes winner Shining Water (herself dam of the Group 1 Grand Criterium winner Tenby) and a half-sister to 8 winners. (HRH Sultan Ahmad Shah). *"He'll make a 2-y-o by mid-summer, he goes nicely and he'll be alright".*

1577. UNNAMED ★★★
ch.c. Compton Place – Highly Liquid (Entrepreneur). March 7. Sixth foal. £40,000Y. Doncaster Premier. Hugo Merry. Brother to the moderate 7f winner Fungible and half-brother to the fair 7f (at 2 yrs) and 10f winner No Compromise (by Avonbridge). The dam, a fair 6f (at 2 yrs) and 1m placed maiden, is a half-sister to 6 winners including the Italian Group 3 winner She Bat. The second dam, Premiere Cuvee (by Formidable), won the Group 3 Goldene Peitsche and is a half-sister to 4 winners. (Mrs F H Hay). *"He's only just arrived because of a setback in pre-training, but he's a strong type and he looks a 2-y-o. We'll have to see, because I haven't had much time with him yet".*

1578. UNNAMED ★★★
b.c. Dubawi – Idonea (Swain). April 4. First foal. 70,000Y. Tattersalls October Book 1. Rabbah Bloodstock. The dam won twice at 2 yrs in Germany. The second dam, Ivastar (by Alwasmi), a winner of 4 races in Canada and Group 3 placed, is a half-sister to 8 winners. (Sheikh Juma Al Dalmook Maktoum). *"He had a setback in January which kept him out of training but he's due to come back to me next week and he could be a summer 2-y-o I think".*

1579. UNNAMED ★★★
b.c. Montjeu – Madame Cerito (Diesis). April 4. Seventh foal. 125,000Y. Tattersalls October Book 1. Roger Varian. Half-brother to the fair 10f winner Sondeduro (by Manduro), to the modest 12f winner Ramora (by Monsun) and a winner in France by Aragorn. The dam, an Irish 3-y-o 1m winner and listed-placed 2-y-o, is a half-sister to 8 winners including the 1m 2-y-o and subsequent German Group 1 10f winner

Ransom O'War. The second dam, Sombreffe (by Polish Precedent), a fair 7f winner, is closely related to the Group 2 Mill Reef Stakes winner Russian Bond and the Group 2 Temple Stakes winner Snaadee and a half-sister to 9 winners including the Group 3 Prix de Conde winner Cristofori. (A D Spence). *"He's only just arrived in training, but he's a nice type and could be a late summer/early autumn 2-y-o because he's not that backward. A likeable colt with a good action".*

1580. UNNAMED ★★★

b.c. *Shamardal – Mazaaya (Cozzene)*. March 5. Second foal. 60,000Y. Tattersalls October Book 2. Stephen Hillen. The dam, a quite useful 7f (at 2 yrs) and 10f winner, is a sister to the useful 10f winner and dual listed-placed Cozy Maria (herself dam of the Group 2 Flying Childers winner Zebedee) and a half-sister to 6 winners in the North America and Argentina. The second dam, Mariamme (by Verbatim), won twice at 3 yrs in the USA and is a half-sister to 7 winners including the Grade 1 Breeders Cup Turf winner Miss Alleged. (S Ali). *"He's a bit plain, but I think that's the sire. Not a bad type, he's quite well-built, could be one for the late summer and he moves fine. Not very eye catching because he's a bit plain, but he could be alright".*

1581. UNNAMED ★★★

b.f. *Cape Cross – Miss Champagne (Bering)*. May 11. Fifth foal. 90,000Y. Tattersalls October Book 1. Rabbah Bloodstock. Half-sister to the Irish 2-y-o 6f winner (on her only start) Play Misty For Me (by Danehill Dancer and herself dam of the dual Group 3 winner Quest For Peace), to the fairly useful 2-y-o 7f winner and Group 3 7f Sweet Solera Stakes third Minor Vamp (by Hawk Wing) and the quite useful 1m and 10f winner Beaumont's Party (by High Chaparral). The dam is an unraced sister to the Group 3 Prix Eclipse winner Stella Berine and a half-sister to 4 winners. The second dam, Beaujolaise (by Thatching), won the Group 3 Prix Eclipse and is a half-sister to 6 winners. (Sheikh R D Al Maktoum). *"She's a little immature and one for later in the season really, but she's a good size and correct".*

1582. UNNAMED ★★

ch.c. *Exchange Rate – Miss Delta Dawn (Thirty Six Red)*. May 1. Tenth foal. 100,000Y. Tattersalls October Book 2. Stephen Hillen. Half-brother to the US listed stakes winner Langston (by Pine Bluff), to the US 2-y-o winner and stakes-placed Mississippi Madam (by Smoke Glacken) and two minor winners in the USA by Flower Alley and Tale Of The Cat. The dam is an unraced half-sister to 7 winners including Dyreen (Group 2 Premio Dormello). The second dam, Carol's Dawn (by Grey Dawn II), placed once at 2 yrs in the USA, is a half-sister to 3 winners. (Miss F H Hay). *"He went a bit narrow after the sale and he's only just picking up now, but he has a good, fast ground action. It's too early to tell on ability, but he's not a bad type".*

1583. UNNAMED ★★★

ch.c. *New Approach – Rafting (Darshaan)*. February 17. Seventh living foal. 80,000Y. Tattersalls October Book 2. Hugo Merry. Half-brother to the fairly useful dual 1m winner Colorado Rapid (by Barathea), to the fair 2-y-o 7f winner Broxbourne (by Refuse To Bend), the modest 9f and hurdles winner Herschel (by Dr Fong) and the German 3-y-o winner Ruffian Reef (by Singspiel). The dam, a quite useful 12f winner of 4 races, is a half-sister to 4 winners including the very useful Italian Group 3 1m winner Lear White. The second dam, White Water (by Pharly), won 10 races in France from 6.5f to 11.5f including a listed event and is a half-sister to 6 winners. (Mrs F H Hay). *"A nice-moving horse, he's well-balanced and is an August/September type 2-y-o, but it's too early to say what ability he has".*

1584. UNNAMED ★★★

b.c. *Cape Cross – Whatizzit (Galileo)*. March 10. Second foal. 40,000Y. Tattersalls October Book 2. Rabbah Bloodstock. Closely related to the fair 9f winner Dream Scape (by Oasis Dream). The dam, a fair 2-y-o 9f winner, is a half-sister to 5 winners including the useful 7f (at 2 yrs), listed 1m and Italian Group 3 1m winner Whazzis and the listed Chesham Stakes winner Whazzat. The second dam, Wosaita (by Generous), a fair 12.3f placed maiden, is a half-sister to 10 winners including the very smart Group 1 10.5f Prix de Diane winner Rafha (herself the dam of four stakes winners including the Haydock Sprint Cup winner Invincible Spirit) and the Group 3 12f Blandford Stakes winner Chiang Mai (dam of the Group 1 winner Chinese White). (Sheikh Juma Al Dalmook Maktoum). *"He's not a bad type and he looked quite precocious early on, but he's gone through a growing spurt and is a little more backward now. So he's probably one we'll get out by the mid to back-end of the summer. A good-moving colt".*

ED VAUGHAN

1585. COSTA FILEY ★★★

b.c. Pastoral Pursuits – Cosmic Destiny (Soviet Star). February 10. First foal. The dam, a modest but tough winner of 6 races over 5f and from 3 to 6yrs, is a half-sister to 3 winners. The second dam, Cruelle (by Irish River), was placed at up to 7.5f in France at 2 and 3 yrs and is a half-sister to 5 winners. (Alan Pickering). *"He'll be a rock n roll 2-y-o and he looks OK. I trained the dam who was very quick and I can promise you that the softest thing about her was her tooth enamel! She was the toughest filly you could ever come across and was always flat to the boards on the gallops because she was so keen you couldn't hold her. I hope this colt gets five furlongs because she barely made it! He'll probably be our first 2-y-o runner and he's definitely a sharp, five furlong type".*

1586. GENUINE QUALITY (USA) ★★★

b.f. Elusive Quality – Genuine Devotion (Rock Of Gibraltar). January 25. First foal. $140,000Y. Keeneland September. David Redvers. The dam won 5 races in the USA including the Grade 3 Locust Grove Handicap and is closely related to the Group 1 Phoenix Stakes, National Stakes and Irish 2,000 Guineas winner Mastercraftsman and to the Irish 2-y-o 7f winner and Group 1 7f Moyglare Stud Stakes second Famous. The second dam, Starlight Dreams (by Black Tie Affair), won twice at 3 yrs in the USA and is a half-sister to 5 winners including the listed Zetland Stakes winner Matahif and the dams of the dual Group 1 winner Pressing and the Group 3 Princess Royal Stakes winner Mazuna. (Qatar Racing Ltd). *"She's a very nice type of filly, small but well-grown and mature. It's a good*

pedigree, she's got a great constitution, has done one piece of work on the grass and I liked what she did. She won't take that long to get ready for the track, but whether she'd be quick enough for five furlongs I don't know".*

1587. QUAINTRELLE (IRE) ★★★

b.f. Dandy Man – Extravagance (King's Best). April 30. Third foal. 10,000Y. Tattersalls October Book 3. Ed Vaughan. Half-sister to the modest 2012 2-y-o 5f winner Chloe's Dream (by Clodovil) and to the quite useful 2-y-o dual 5f winner Signifer (by Titus Livius). The dam, a fair 6f (at 2 yrs) and 7f placed maiden, is a half-sister to 3 winners. The second dam, Meritxell (by Thatching), won once at 3 yrs in France and is a half-sister to 10 winners including the Group 2 Sandown Mile winner Almushtarak. *"A nice big filly, she's was quite a late foal and she's done nothing but grow since I bought her. She has a good action and she's a tough type of filly with the constitution of a colt. She's got a great attitude and I couldn't be happier with her development. I should imagine we'll wait until the six furlong races with her and I like her a lot. I haven't sold her but I don't mind that because I'm happy to keep her myself if necessary".* TRAINERS' BARGAIN BUY

1588. SI SENOR (IRE) ★★★

b.c. Dansili – Kotsi (Nayef). April 23. Second foal. 28,000Y. Tattersalls October Book 2. Not sold. Half-brother to the fair 2012 dual 5f placed 2-y-o Emirates Echo (by Pivotal). The dam, a smart 2-y-o 7f winner, was second in the Group 2 1m May Hill Stakes and is a half-sister to 8 winners including the Canadian Grade 2 winner Miss Keller, the very useful listed placed Tissifer and the useful dual Group 3 placed Sir George Turner and to the dams of the Group 2 winners Fantastic Pick and Hatta Fort. The second dam, Ingozi (by Warning), a fairly useful winner over 7f and 1m at 3 yrs including a listed event at Sandown Park, is a half-sister to 7 winners including the very smart and tough triple Group 3 7f winner Inchinor. *"He hasn't arrived here yet, but when I saw him at the pre-training yard I couldn't believe how much he'd improved from the sale where he was very immature. He stands over a lot of ground like his dam who was arguably unlucky in the May Hill. He's a 2-y-o type and quite a lot of the family do well as 2-y-o's as well".*

1589. UNNAMED ★★★
gr.c. Dalakhani – Adventure (Unbridled's Song). February 22. Fourth foal. 85,000Y. Tattersalls October Book 1. Oliver St Lawrence. Half-brother to the Group 2 Debutante Stakes winner and dual Group 1 placed Laughing Lashes (by Mr Greeley) and to the quite useful 1m winner Captain Ellis (by Five Star Day). The dam won 2 minor races in the USA at 3 yrs and is a half-sister to 5 winners including the Group 1 Racing Post Trophy winner Palace Episode. The second dam, Palace Weekend (by Seattle Dancer), is an unraced half-sister to US Grade 2 winners More Royal and Tejano Run. (Mr S Rashid). *"A very nice colt, he's quite forward-going so I need to be a bit careful with him but he's active in the mornings, takes a bit of a hold on the gallops and he's the type that'll get himself ready regardless because he's a hard worker. He was small and set at the sales but he's grown a lot and I'm delighted about that because I don't like small stayers. He's bred to race over ten furlongs plus and we'll start him off at seven furlongs this year. A lovely horse and very athletic".*

1590. UNNAMED ★★★
b.c. Royal Applause – Alhufoof (Dayjur). April 7. Tenth foal. 45,000Y. Tattersalls October Book 1. Oliver St Lawrence. Brother to the modest 2012 5f placed 2-y-o Sand And Deliver, to the Group 2 7f Lennox Stakes and 2-y-o Group 3 5f Molecomb Stakes winner Finjaan and the fair 7f winner Fustaan and half-brother to the fair 5f winner Sandfrankskipsgo (by Piccolo). The dam, a fairly useful 2-y-o 6f winner, was fourth in the Group 3 7f Nell Gwyn Stakes and is a half-sister to 6 winners including the dam of the 1,000 Guineas winner Lahan. The second dam, Cheval Volant (by Kris S), won 5 races from 5.5f to 8.5f in the USA including the Hollywood Starlet Stakes and the Las Virgines Stakes (both Grade 1 1m events) and is a half-sister to 4 winners including the US Grade 3 winner Chaldea. (Mr S Rashid). *"He didn't have a particularly good winter but I gave him some time and he's started to do really well now. For a horse that's bred to be*

precocious he's one of those horses that still looks on the weak side, but he's got a lovely attitude and he's improving every day. He'll tell us when he's ready but hopefully that'll be towards the end of May".

1591. UNNAMED ★★
b.f. Kheleyf – Caldy Dancer (Soviet Star). February 12. Fifth foal. 30,000Y. Tattersalls October Book 2. Oliver St Lawrence. Half-sister to On With The Dance (by Byron), unplaced in one start at 2 yrs in 2012 and to the smart 7f to 9f winner of 5 races and dual Group 3 placed Dance And Dance (by Royal Applause). The dam, a useful 2-y-o dual 5f winner and second in the Group 3 7f Debutante Stakes, is a half-sister to 4 winners. The second dam, Smile Awhile (by Woodman), ran once unplaced and is a full or half-sister to 3 winners. *"A small, 2-y-o type, she had a setback early on so I don't think we'll see her until mid-summer now".*

1592. UNNAMED ★★
ch.c. Mount Nelson – Lacework (Pivotal). March 31. Third foal. 41,000Y. Tattersalls October Book 2. Oliver St Lawrence. Brother to the fair 2012 2-y-o 1m winner Romantic Settings and half-brother to the useful 2-y-o listed 5f winner of 3 races and 3-y-o Group 3 6f Firth of Clyde Stakes second Miss Work Of Art (by Dutch Art). The dam, a fairly useful 7f (at 2 yrs) to 10f winner, is a sister to the multiple Scandinavian listed winner Entangle and a half-sister to 4 winners. The second dam, Entwine (by Primo Dominie), a quite useful 2-y-o dual 5f winner, is a half-sister to 5 winners including the Group 2 Lowther Stakes winner Soar and the very smart 6f and 7f winner Feet So Fast. (Mr S Rashid). *"This is a nice, big horse, but he's very immature mentally and the type that's going to improve with time. He'll start off at seven furlongs".*

1593. UNNAMED ★★★
ch.c. Pivotal – Quiet Protest (Kingmambo). February 15. First foal. 100,000Y. Tattersalls October Book 1. Paul Moroney. The dam, a minor winner in the USA at 3 yrs, is a half-sister to a minor winner in France. The second dam, Rosa Parks (by Sadler's Wells), a very useful 10.5f winner, was second in the

listed Galtres Stakes and is a sister to the dual Irish listed winner (including at 2 yrs) Mikado and a half-sister to 4 winners including the multiple US Grade 2 winner Coretta. (The Ballymore Down Under Syndicate). *"A nice, big, strong colt. He came into the yard in January and I thought he was too weak so we put him out to grass. He's been back now for three weeks and I can't believe how well he's done. I imagine I'll be kicking on with him soon because he has a mature look to him now. Possibly the type that could be running by early June, he doesn't look slow on the gallops and he's got a great hip on him, so I'd say we could start him at six furlongs".*

1594. UNNAMED ★★★★
b.c. Speightstown – Reboot (Rubiano). February 7. Tenth foal. 120,000Y. Tattersalls December. Oliver St Lawrence. Half-brother to the very smart 2-y-o 6f winner, Group 1 Middle Park Stakes second and Group 2 Mill Reef Stakes third Rebuttal, to the quite useful 1m winner Net Whizz (both by Mr Greeley), to the US stakes winner Summer Cruise (by Vicar), minor US winners by Bluegrass Cat, Carson City, French Deputy and Strong Hope and a winner in Trinidad by El Corredor. The dam, a minor winner of 4 races in the USA at 3 and 4 yrs, is a half-sister to 2 other minor winners. The second dam, Launch Light Tek (by Relaunch), a stakes winner in the USA and second in a Grade 3 event, is a sister to another minor US stakes winner. (Mr S Rashid). *"A lovely colt and a half-brother to the Middle Park second Rebuttal. I absolutely love the stallion because they seem to go on everything – dirt, synthetic, grass, the lot. This colt looks quick enough, he's done a bit of growing and he's like his Dad in that he's quite high behind. He was just a little bit headstrong so we've eased off him but hopefully he'll be out in May. He's a very natural, very fast-learning type of horse so I'm looking forward to him – I like him a lot and he has a real 2-y-o look about him".*

1595. UNNAMED ★★
b.c. Rock Hard Ten – To The Brim (Ascot Knight). March 20. Second foal. 60,000Y. Tattersalls October Book 1. Paul Moroney. The dam, a winner and stakes-placed in Canada at 3 yrs, is a half-sister to 4 minor winners in the USA. The second dam, Capacity (by Capote), is an unraced half-sister to 7 winners including the US Grade 2 winner Street Sounds. (The Ballymore Down Under Syndicate). *"A very big, scopey horse with a lovely fast ground action. He's big and gangly but very athletic and has a lovely attitude. He'll tell us when he's ready and I would imagine we'll be starting him at seven furlongs".*

ED WALKER
1596. ADORA (IRE) ★★★
gr.f. Mastercraftsman – Amathia (Darshaan). April 7. Fourth foal. 160,000Y. Tattersalls October Book 1. Blandford Bloodstock. Half-sister to the Group 3 10f Winter Hill Stakes winner and Group 2 Prix Dollar third Distant Memories (by Falbrav) and to the listed 12f winner Mohedian Lady (by Hurricane Run). The dam, a listed 9f winner in France and Group 3 placed twice, is a half-sister to 8 winners including the 1,000 Guineas third Hathrah, the smart Group 2 12f Premio Ellington winner Ivan Luis, the UAE Group 3 winner Stagelight and the German listed winner Zero Problemo. The second dam, Zivania (by Shernazar), a useful Irish winner of 4 races from 1m to 9.5f, is a half-sister to 7 winners including the Group 3 Prix Gontaut Biron winner Muroto. (Chasemore Stud). *"An extremely well-bred filly and very good-looking, I really like her. There's quite a lot of stamina on the dam's side so we won't get her out until the seven furlong maidens, but she's one of the best-bred 2-y-o's we've got and physically she reflects that".*

1597. AYA'S GIFT ★★★
ch.c. Compton Place – Ringarooma (Erhaab). February 2. Third foal. 40,000Y. Tattersalls October Book 2. Mark Crossman. Half-brother to a minor 4-y-o winner abroad by Kyllachy. The dam, a moderate 4-y-o 10f winner, is a half-sister to 2 winners and to the dams of the Group 2 winners Wi Dud and Tariq. The second dam, Tatouma (by The Minstrel), a quite useful 2-y-o 5f and 6f winner, is a half-sister to 4 winners. (K A Dasmal). *"A flashy-looking colt with a flaxen mane and tail, he's a really, strong, athletic type and a typical sprinter. Having said that he probably looks*

stronger than he really is at this early stage. One for late May or early June I'd say, he's a nice horse and an exciting type".

1598. BUSHCRAFT (IRE) ★★★

b.c. Bushranger – Lady Lucia (Royal Applause). March 15. Fifth foal. 60,000Y. Tattersalls October Book 2. Sackville/Donald. Half-brother to the useful 2-y-o 5f winner and listed-placed Mullionmileanhour (by Mull Of Kintyre), the fair 1m winner Bareback (by Redback) and the modest 2-y-o 5f winner Lady Lube Rye (by Catcher In The Rye). The dam, a moderate maiden, was placed fourth twice over 5f and 7f at 2 yrs and is a half-sister to 3 winners. The second dam, Inventive (by Sheikh Albadou), a quite useful 2-y-o dual 5f winner, is a half-sister to 3 minor winners in France. (Mr L Bellman). *"A compact, strong, good-looking little racehorse. He's very impressive to look at and although I haven't asked him any questions yet he is bred to be quick. Hopefully we'll get him out in May and he could be a nice 2-y-o".*

1599. FRESH AND FRESH ★★★★

b.c. Medicean – Red Blossom (Green Desert). March 5. Third foal. 40,000Y. Tattersalls October Book 2. Sackville/Donald. Half-brother to the 2012 2-y-o Grapes Hill (by Kingsalsa), unplaced in one start. The dam, a fair 9f winner, is a half-sister to the smart Group 1 Fillies' Mile and Group 2 10f Blandford Stakes winner Red Bloom and to the smart 10f, 12f and listed 13f winner Red Gala. The second dam, Red Camellia (by Polar Falcon), winner of the Group 3 7f Prestige Stakes and third in the French 1,000 Guineas, is a half-sister to 4 winners including the German middle-distance winner Red Bouquet. (Mr W T Cheng). *"A real nice 2-y-o by a stallion I love. I've had a bit of luck with Medicean's and this colt is from a good Cheveley Park family. He's doing everything right at the moment and I think he could be earlier than some by the sire as they can take a bit of time. He's very athletic, has a great attitude and I see him being a 2-y-o in June/July. We'll start him off at six furlongs because I think he'll have lots of speed. One of the most likeable of my 2-y-o's, he's very racey".*

1600. FRESH KINGDOM (IRE) ★★★

ch.c. Dubawi – Polyquest (Poliglote). April 17. Third foal. 75,000Y. Tattersalls October Book 2. Sackville/Donald. The dam, a modest 10f and 12f winner of 3 races, is a half-sister to 6 winners including the smart Group 3 11.5f Lingfield Derby Trial winner Saddler's Quest and the useful French listed 12.5f winner Seren Hill. The second dam, Seren Quest (by Rainbow Quest), was a fairly useful 10f winner. (Mr W T Cheng). *"Quite typical of his sire in that he's quite close-coupled and dumpy. They're quite hard to fall in love with, visually, as yearlings. But he's doing well now, he's an athletic sort and he's grown quite a bit since the sales. I don't envisage him running until July or August".*

1601. FULL MOON FEVER (IRE) ★★ ♠

b.f. Azamour – Hasaiyda (Hector Protector). March 8. Fifth foal. €12,000Y. Tattersalls Ireland September. Sackville/Donald. Sister to Glorious Protector (unplaced over 1m on her only start at 2 yrs in 2012) and half-sister to a 5-y-o winner in Germany by Dr Fong. The dam, a fair 9f and 10f winner, is a half-sister to 5 winners including the dual Irish listed winner and Group 3 placed Hasanka. The second dam, Hasainiya (by Top Ville), a listed 10f winner in Ireland, is a half-sister to 7 winners. (Bellman, Donald, Walker & Walker). *"She wasn't expensive but she's a really nice sort and a full-sister to an exciting 3-y-o prospect of ours called Glorious Prospector. She's not an early type and I don't think she'd be out until the back-end. She has loads of athleticism but she'll take a while to develop".*

1602. GLORIOUS EMPIRE (IRE) ★★ ♠

br.c. Holy Roman Emperor – Humble And Proud (Pivotal). February 5. First foal. 90,000Y. Tattersalls October Book 2. Sackville/Donald. The dam is an unraced half-sister to 4 winners including the listed 10f winner and Group 2 King Edward VII Stakes second Delsarte and the 7f and 12f winner and Group 3 Jockey Club Cup third Veenwouden. The second dam, Delauncy (by Machiavellian), a winner at 2 yrs in France and listed-placed over 1m and 10f, is a half-sister to 8 winners including the Japanese stakes winner Tenzan Seiza. (Ms A A Yap). *"By far the biggest colt I've seen by the* sire, which is very surprising considering he's a first foal as well. It's a good family, the dam was unraced and he's a really nice sort. He won't be early because of his size, but he has a lovely attitude and he moves very well. One for next year really, and if he runs this year it'll be towards the back-end".

1603. GLORIOUS SUN ★★★

b.c. Medicean – Sweet Cando (Royal Applause). April 11. Sixth foal. 50,000Y. Tattersalls October Book 2. Sackville/Donald. Half-brother to the 9f Hong Kong stakes winner of 6 races Jacobee (by Mark Of Esteem), to the US winner and Grade 2 third Hameildaeme (by Storming Home) and the minor US winner Candy's Girl (by Bertolini). The dam, a modest 2-y-o 5f winner, is a half-sister to 2 winners. The second dam, Fizzygig (by Efisio), a moderate 7f winner, is a half-sister to 6 winners. (Ms A A Yap). *"A lovely horse and a half-brother to a decent horse Michael Bell trained that went to Hong Kong. This colt has a cracking temperament and he's a very good mover, but he's going to take time. One we'll get out around September time, because he needs to fill his frame".*

1604. GRACEFILLY ★★★

b.f. Invincible Spirit – Marula (Sadler's Wells). April 27. Fourth foal. 60,000Y. Tattersalls October Book 2. Sackville/Donald. Sister to the Russian dual 3-y-o winner Majestic Spirit and half-sister to the minor Australian winner of 3 races at 4 yrs Aneel (by Danehill Dancer). The dam is an unraced sister to the Irish 2-y-o listed 9f winner On The Nile and the Irish listed 1m winner In The Limelight, closely related to the Singapore Gold Cup and Gran Premio del Jockey Club winner Kutub and a half-sister to 3 winners. The second dam, Minnie Habit (by Habitat), an Irish 4-y-o 9f winner, is closely related to the 5f Curragh Stakes and 6f Railway Stakes winner Bermuda Classic (herself dam of the Coronation Stakes winner Shake The Yoke and the dual Group 3 winner Tropical) and a half-sister to 6 winners. (Mr L Bellman). *"I thought she was very good value when we bought her, given her pedigree. We bought her on spec and Mr Bellman put his colours to her. She's really nice, very athletic and quite typical of Invincible Spirit. She's going*

to take a bit more time than most but she'll make a 2-y-o around August time".

1605. HOPEFILLY ★★★

b.f. Compton Place – Kondakova (Soviet Star). March 25. Third foal. 10,000Y. Doncaster Premier. Not sold. Half-sister to the modest 2012 2-y-o 6f winner Buy Art (by Acclamation) and to the moderate 7f seller winner Tooley Woods (by Cape Cross). The dam, a fair dual 6f winner (including at 2 yrs), was listed-placed and is a half-sister to 5 winners including the US stakes winner and Grade 3 1m placed Solar Bound. The second dam, Solar Star (by Lear Fan), a useful 2-y-o dual 6f winner, is a half-sister to 7 winners including the US triple Grade 3 winner Gold Land. (Mr L Bellman). *"She was a cheapie from Doncaster but I don't see why because she's a really nice sort and doesn't have a bad page at all. She does everything very nicely but she's actually grown quite a bit and won't be quite as early as we first thought. She's the type I'd like to give a run before Ascot and then see if she's good enough to go there".*

1606. INCREDIBLE FRESH (IRE) ★★★

b.c. Bushranger – Red Fox (Spectrum). April 12. Fifth foal. 70,000Y. Tattersalls October Book 2. Sackville/Donald. Half-brother to the fair 7f and 1m winner Regimental (by Refuse To Bend) and to the Italian winner of 3 races at 2 and 3 yrs Ziba (by King Charlemagne). The dam, a minor winner at 3 yrs, is out of the French listed winner Cunning Vixen (by Machiavellian), herself a half-sister to 4 winners. (Mr W T Cheng). *"He'll probably be my first runner, although the owners might decide to send him straight to Hong Kong. If he is allowed to run here he'll be early. He's by Bushranger who was a very popular first-season sire at the sales, deservedly in my opinion because they were good looking yearlings that looked like racehorses. This colt is very athletic, very switched on and a racey 2-y-o. He has got the scope to go on, but he's definitely an out-and-out 2-y-o".*

1607. INVINCIBLE FRESH (IRE) ★★★ ♠

b.c. Footstepsinthesand – Princess Serena (Unbridled's Song). February 23. Fifth foal. 80,000Y. Tattersalls October Book 2. Sackville/

Donald. Closely related to the Australian Group 3 13f winner Puissance de Lune (by Shamardal) and half-brother to the fair 7f winner of 4 races (including at 2 yrs) Serene Oasis (by Oratorio), to the quite useful 2-y-o 7f winner Serena's Storm (by Statue Of Liberty). The dam, a minor US 4-y-o winner, is a half-sister to 4 winners including the US Grade 2 American Turf Stakes winner Doubles Partner and the minor US stakes winner Stormy Venus. The second dam, Serena's Sister (Rahy), is an unplaced sister to the outstanding US winner of eleven Grade 1 events Serena's Song (herself dam of the Coronation Stakes winner Sophisticat and the US Grade 2 winners Harlington and Grand Reward) and a half-sister to the US Grade 3 Golden Rod Stakes winner Vivid Imagination. (Mr W T Cheng). *"He's a gorgeous colt and by far and away the most eye-catching and athletic two-year-old I've got, but he's all about next year and onwards. I expect him to run at the back-end but whatever he does this year will be a bonus".*

1608. MOUTAI ★★★ ♠

b.c. *Royal Applause – Naizak (Medicean).* February 16. First foal. 55,000Y. Tattersalls October Book 2. Sackville/Donald. The dam, placed twice at 3 yrs, is a half-sister to 8 winners including the useful 6f (at 2 yrs) and subsequent Swedish listed winner Warming Trends. The second dam, Sunny Davis (by Alydar), was a fair 2-y-o 7f winner. (Mr Brandon Lui). *"A lovely horse, on looks alone he'd be far too expensive for us to buy, but he doesn't have much of a pedigree. He does everything easily, has a wonderful temperament and for a first foal he's quite a good-sized horse. We should see him on the track in June or July".*

1609. OUTLAWED ★★★ ♠

b.c. *Kyllachy – Regent's Park (Green Desert).* February 24. Fourth foal. 52,000Y. Tattersalls October Book 2. Sackville/Donald. The dam, a quite useful 10f winner, is a half-sister to 3 winners including the useful dual 6f winner (including at 2 yrs) Instalment. The second dam, New Assembly (by Machiavellian), a useful 9f and 10f winner, is a sister to the 7f (at 2 yrs) and Group 1 9f Dubai Duty Free Stakes

winner Right Approach and a half-sister to 7 winners. (Mr L Bellman). *"A lovely, big horse out of a mare I knew well from my days at Roger Charlton's. He already weighs 512kgs so he's a big 2-y-o, but he does everything easily and well. He won't be out until later in the year but I do think he'll have a 2-y-o career. He's done all his growing and he just needs to fill his frame now. He's very athletic and light on his feet for a big horse, so I don't think he's that backward, just big. A very likeable sort and we'll plan to start him off at six furlongs and see how he goes".*

1610. TWENTY ROSES (IRE) ★★★★

b.f. *Mastercraftsman – Stunning Rose (Sadler's Wells).* February 5. Third foal. €135,000Y. Goffs Orby. Anthony Stroud. Half-sister to the useful 2012 2-y-o 7f winner and dual Group 3 placed Well Acquainted (by Orientate). The dam, a dual winner at 4 yrs in Canada, is a half-sister to 7 winners including the very useful Irish 2-y-o listed 6f winner Chanting and the US stakes winner Cherokee Reef. The second dam, Golden Reef (by Mr Prospector), winner of the Grade 2 Schuylerville Stakes and second in the Grade 1 Matron Stakes and the Grade 1 6f Spinaway Stakes, is a half-sister to 7 winners including the US Grade 3 winner Virginia Carnival. (Highland Yard LLC). *"She's a half-sister to a good 2-y-o in Well Acquainted and I expect her to be a 2-y-o as well. She's from the first crop of her sire who was a good 2-y-o and this is an extremely athletic, good-looking and very well-made filly. Out of a Sadler's Wells mare, I think she's a really exciting filly for later in the year and for next year as well. I would imagine she'd be a mid-to-late summer 2-y-o".*

1611. UNRAVELLED (IRE) ★★★

b.c. *Tamayuz – Beat The Rain (Beat Hollow).* March 9. Second foal. £24,000Y. Doncaster Premier. Sackville/Donald. Half-brother to Hail Shower (by Red Clubs), placed fourth once over 6f at 2 yrs in 2012. The dam won once at 3 yrs in France and is a half-sister to 4 winners including the listed winner Quenched. The second dam, Love The Rain (by Rainbow Quest), a winner over 11f in France, is a sister to the Group 2 winner Bonash (dam of the Group 1 winner Nebraska Tornado) and a half-sister to 5 winners including the Group 2 winner Media Nox. (De La Warr Racing). *"Not over-big but very athletic and very strong, unfortunately he's thrown a couple of splints so I don't know much about him as yet except he looks like a 2-y-o, but not an early one".*

1612. URBAN SANCTUARY ★★★

ch.c. Mount Nelson – White Dress (Pivotal). February 16. First foal. 40,000Y. Tattersalls October Book 2. Sackville/Donald. The dam is an unraced half-sister to 3 winners including the 2-y-o Group 1 Prix Marcel Boussac third Rainbow Springs. The second dam, Pearl Dance (by Nureyev), a useful 2-y-o 6f winner and third in the Group 1 Moyglare Stud Stakes, is a half-sister to 7 winners including the German listed winner Ocean Sea and the US winner and Grade 3 third Dixie Splash (herself dam of the Melbourne Cup winner Delta Blues). (John Nicholls Trading Ltd). *"Quite a lot more forward than most Mount Nelson's. We bought him thinking we'd give him time and bringing him on more as a 3-y-o, but he's doing well at the moment. A really nice horse and very athletic, I think the stallion has a good future. If this colt doesn't go through a growth spurt I imagine he'll be a July/August 2-y-o".*

1613. VEYA (USA) ★★★★

ch.c. Giant's Causeway – Gossamer (Seattle Slew). February 17. Eleventh foal. €160,000Y. Goffs Orby. Marc Keller. Half-brother to the Irish 2,000 Guineas winner Bachelor Duke (by Miswaki), to the German listed 12f winner Translucid (by Woodman), the useful Irish 11f winner and Group 3 10f Gallinule Stakes third Smartcity (by Smarty Jones) and two minor US 4-y-o winners by Storm Cat and Spinning World and to the placed dams of the listed winners Limonar and Gemstone. The dam, a winner of 2 races in the USA at up to 9f, is a half-sister to 5 winners including the German Group 3 winner Miss Tobacco. The second dam, Lisaleen (by Northern Dancer), won twice at 3 yrs, was third in the Group 3 1m Gilltown Stud Stakes and is a full or half-sister to 5 winners including the Group 1 National Stakes winner Fatherland. (Marc Keller). *"A really nice 2-y-o and a half-brother to a classic winner. He's very professional, has a huge amount of class, isn't overly-big but very*

athletic and he's one I'd like to get out before Royal Ascot to see how good he is. He hasn't put a foot wrong yet".*

1614. XANTHOS ★★★

ch.g. Medicean – My Girl Jode (Haafhd). March 12. First foal. £20,000Y. Doncaster Premier. Sackville/Donald. The dam, a modest 10f winner, is a half-sister to 5 winners including the French listed-placed Craft Fair. The second dam, Brush Strokes (by Cadeaux Genereux), is an unraced full or half-sister to 8 including the Group 1 Racing Post Trophy second Mudeer. (Mr M J Cottis). *"A really athletic little horse, he just had a few behavioural issues so we gelded him and he's fine now. He won't be that early – probably a second half of the year 2-y-o, but he could be anything because he's got a lot of changing and growing to do".*

1615. UNNAMED ★★★

b.c. Notnowcato – Blaenavon (Cadeaux Genereux). February 3. Fourth foal. 34,000Y. Tattersalls October Book 2. Rabbah Bloodstock. Half-brother to the unplaced 2012 2-y-o Valley Dreamer (by Sleeping Indian) and to the quite useful dual 10f and hurdles winner Discoteca (by Nayef). The dam is an unplaced half-sister to 3 winners. The second dam, One Of The Family (by Alzao), a fair 1m placed 4-y-o, is a sister to the Rockfel Stakes winner Relatively Special and a half-sister to 8 winners including the Dante Stakes and Craven Stakes winner Alnasr Alwasheek and to the Juddmonte International Stakes winner One So Wonderful. (Sheikh Juma Al Dalmook Maktoum). *"A nice horse, he's quite big but I don't think he'll take too long to come to hand. He's very strong and athletic and up to now he's done everything extremely well. I think the sire did surprisingly well with his 2-y-o's last year and I really like this horse. He'll be a second half of the season 2-y-o".*

1616. UNNAMED ★★★ ♠

b.f. Bahamian Bounty – Loveleaves (Polar Falcon). March 18. Seventh foal. 24,000Y. Tattersalls October Book 2. Sackville/Donald. Half-sister to the fair 2012 2-y-o 6f and 7f winner Tussie Mussie, to the very smart Group 2 1m Oettingen Rennen and Group 3 7f Supreme Stakes winner of 9 races Lovelace (both by Royal Applause), the quite useful 12f winner Greyfriars Drummer (by Where Or When), the fair 6f (at 2 yrs) to 1m winner of 7 races Avonrose (by Avonbridge) and a bumpers winner by Observatory. The dam, a fairly useful 8.3f winner, is closely related to the South African Group 3 winner Headstrong and a half-sister to 5 winners. The second dam, Rash (by Pursuit Of Love), is an unraced half-sister to 6 winners including the useful 2-y-o dual 6f winner Maid For The Hills and the useful 2-y-o 5f and 6f winner Maid For Walking (herself dam of the US Grade 1 winner Stroll) and to the placed High Savannah (the dam of three Group winners). (Mr Brandon Lui). *"She was cheap, all things considered. Her conformation isn't perfect and she was very leggy as a yearling but she's filled out, done really well and strengthened. Extremely athletic and with a wonderful attitude, she's quite tall but I think she'll definitely make a 2-y-o".* TRAINERS' BARGAIN BUY

1617. UNNAMED ★★★

b.c. Myboycharlie – Madam President (Royal Applause). March 4. First foal. 42,000Y. Tattersalls October Book 2. Rabbah Bloodstock. The dam, a fair 10f winner, is a half-sister to 4 winners including the 7f winner and Group 2 12f Ribblesdale Stakes second Eldalil. The second dam, White House (by Pursuit Of Love), a quite useful 10f winner, is a half-sister to 11 winners including the middle-distance Group winners Little Rock, Short Skirt and Whitewater Affair (herself dam of the Japanese champion 3-y-o colt Victoire Pisa). (Saeed Manana). *"A nice horse that's changed a lot since the sales. He's lengthened and just needs to grow now, so he's not going to be early. I really like him and he has a very good attitude and a lot of athleticism. By a first season sire in Myboycharlie, I saw quite a few of his 2-y-o's at the sales and I liked them so I was quite keen to get my hands on one. A good-sized horse for a first foal, he's really pleased me and I see him starting off in a six furlong maiden later in the summer".*

1618. UNNAMED ★★★

b.f. Invincible Spirit – Madura (Dashing Blade). February 6. Third foal. 50,000Y. Tattersalls

October Book 2. Rabbah Bloodstock. The dam, a minor winner at 3 yrs in Germany, is a half-sister to 5 winners including the triple Group 1 winner and sire Manduro. The second dam, Mandellicht (by Be My Guest), a winner and listed-placed in Germany, is a half-sister to 6 winners. (Saeed Manana). *"A nice filly by a very good stallion, she may need some cut in the ground because she has a high knee action. A mid-to-late summer type 2-y-o, she's very athletic and typical of the stallion – a good-looking, racey sort. The family is a good one but quite stout".*

1619. UNNAMED ★★★ ♠

b.c. Selkirk – Starlit Sands (Oasis Dream). April 12. First foal. 70,000Y. Tattersalls October Book 1. Rabbah Bloodstock. The dam, winner of the Group 3 6f Prix d'Arenburg and Group 2 placed twice, is a half-sister to 7 winners. The second dam, Shimmering Sea (by Slip Anchor), a fairly useful Irish 2-y-o 5f and 7f winner and third in the Group 3 Silken Glider Stakes, is a half-sister to 5 winners including the King George VI and Queen Elizabeth Stakes winner Petoski. (Saif Ali). *"He's an interesting and exciting 2-y-o, bred to be fast. I think Sir Mark Prescott said that the dam was the fastest he'd ever trained over four furlongs! He's a first foal and he looks a bit that way, a bit feminine, but he just needs to put on some weight. When he does I think he'll be a sharp-looking 2-y-o".*

CHRIS WALL
1620. BURMESE BREEZE ★★

b.g. Shirocco – Crimson Topaz (Hernando). April 2. Fourth foal. 30,000Y. Tattersalls October Book 2. C F Wall. Half-brother to the unplaced 2012 2-y-o Noosa Sound (by Halling). The dam, a quite useful 11f winner from two starts, is a half-sister to 11 winners including the Group 3 1m Premio Sergio Cumani winner Snow Goose, the listed Dee Stakes winner Merry Merlin and the Group 2 Doncaster Cup second Dusky Warbler. The second dam, Bronzewing (by Beldale Flutter), a useful 6f and 1m winner, was listed-placed and is a half-sister to 6 winners. (Mr Des Thurlby). *"A staying type of horse, but he's a nice type. He's doing a bit of growing at the moment and he's not a desperately backward 2-y-o and he's actually quite a nice, neat horse* so I would imagine he'll be one for the latter part of the season over seven furlongs and a mile. He has a nice attitude to life, so we'll see how we get on with him".

1621. ELEUSIS ★★★★
b.f. Elnadim – Demeter (Diesis). April 20. Sixth foal. 32,000foal. Tattersalls December. R Frisby. Half-sister to the quite useful 2012 2-y-o 6f winner Burning Blaze, to the quite useful 2-y-o 5f winner Farmer Giles (both by Danroad), the useful 6f (at 2 yrs) and Group 3 7f Chartwell Fillies' Stakes winner of 4 races Pyrrha (by Pyrus) and the quite useful 12f winner Alrafidain (by Monsun). The dam, placed over 1m at 2 yrs on her only start, is a half-sister to 3 winners. The second dam, Nicer (by Pennine Walk), won the Irish 1,000 Guineas and is a half-sister to 9 winners. (Lady Juliet Tadgell). "We trained her full sister Pyrrha who was a good filly. Sadly she had an unfortunate end because she fractured a pelvis at Goodwood. She was the apple of Lady Tadgell's eye and she was able to buy this filly as a foal. She's very nice, doing a bit of growing at the moment, but she looks like being a summer 2-y-o over six/seven furlongs, like her sister. A 2-y-o type but with the scope to do well next year as well".

1622. JOHARA (IRE) ★★★
b.f. Iffraaj – Hurricane Irene (Green Desert). April 11. Fourth foal. 22,000Y. Tattersalls October Book 1. C F Wall. Sister to the fair 2012 7f placed 2-y-o Hazzaat and half-sister to the French 2-y-o winner Nova Zarga (by Dubawi). The dam is an unraced sister to the quite useful 6f (at 2 yrs) to 10f winner of 4 races and listed-placed Mister Green and a half-sister to the Group 1 Prix Saint-Alary winner Wavering and the Group 1 Grand Prix de Saint-Cloud winner Mandaean. The second dam, Summertime Legacy (by Darshaan), winner of the Group 3 1m Prix des Reservoirs at 2 yrs and third in the Group 1 Prix Saint-Alary, is a half-sister to 6 winners. (Mrs Claude Lilley). "We picked her up quite cheaply out of Book 1, which was a bit of a surprise given what the sire has achieved, so maybe it's because he wasn't quite as popular as the previous year. This is a nice, sharpish filly that should be a summer 2-y-o. Although

we haven't done much with our 2-y-o's yet this filly is strong enough and forward enough. Six and seven furlongs ought to be her bag I would think and she has a good temperament". TRAINERS' BARGAIN BUY

1623. QUEEN OF THE NILE ★★
b.f. Sakhee – Vanishing Point (Caller I D). May 4. Ninth foal. Sister to the useful Group 3 6f winner of 8 races Royal Rock and half-sister to the quite useful 6f to 1m winner of 4 races Gold Express (by Observatory) and the fair triple 7f winner Aleqa (by Oasis Dream). The dam, a US 2-y-o and sprint winner of 3 races, is a half-sister to 3 winners including the US stakes winner and Grade 2 second The Way It's Binn (herself the dam of a US Grade 3 winner). The second dam, Last Chanz To Danz (by Dynastic), is an unraced half-sister to 4 winners. (Ms Aida Fustoq). "A full sister to Royal Rock who I trained, this is a smaller model and slightly finer, but she's strong. Royal Rock didn't show his form until he was a 3-y-o, so this filly won't be an early sort but she's doing nothing wrong and everything's OK with her".

1624. SYRIAN PEARL ★★★
gr.f. Clodovil – Syrian Queen (Slip Anchor). March 29. Tenth foal. 15,000Y. Tattersalls October Book 2. R Frisby. Half-sister to the fairly useful triple 6f winner (including at 2 yrs) Dark Mischief (by Namid), to the quite useful 2-y-o 6f winner Glee (by Bahamian Bounty), the modest 9f winner Sham Sharif (by Be My Chief), the modest 11f and 12f winner Damascus Symphony (by Pastoral Pursuits) and two minor French winners by Oscar and Croco Rouge. The dam, a quite useful 10f winner, is a half-sister to 8 winners including the Cherry Hinton Stakes winner and 1,000 Guineas second Kerrera and the Coventry, July, Gimcrack, Greenham and Criterion Stakes winner Rock City. The second dam, Rimosa's Pet (by Petingo), won the Group 3 8.5f Princess Elizabeth Stakes (at 2 yrs) and the Group 3 10.5f Musidora Stakes and is a half-sister to 5 winners. (The Clodhoppers). "A relatively cheap filly, she's quite sharp and I'd expect her to be racing in May over five furlongs although she's got the scope to stay six. She's out of a Slip Anchor mare which normally means stamina, but actually not

many in this family have stayed that far. She's not very big, so we'll crack on with her and get her out fairly early".

1625. THE NEW PHAROAH (IRE) ★★★

b.c. Montjeu – Out West (Gone West). March 8. Brother to the Derby, Racing Post Trophy and Dante Stakes winner Motivator and to the Group 2 12f Hardwicke Stakes winner Macarthur (both by Montjeu) and half-brother to the smart listed 10f winner Imperial Star (by Fantastic Light) and a minor 4-y-o winner in the USA (by Polish Precedent). The dam, a useful 7.5f (at 2 yrs) and listed 1m winner, is a half-sister to 3 winners including the US Grade 3 placed Auggies Here. The second dam, Chellingoua (by Sharpen Up), was placed over 1m and is half-sister to 5 winners including the dual Grade 1 winner Wavering Monarch. (Ms Aida Fustoq). "A full brother to the Derby winner Motivator, he's a slightly different type in that he's quite rangy, narrow and leggy, so he's more of a staying type. But if he's got any ability at all he should show something as a 2-y-o in the second half of the year. A colt with plenty of scope, he covers the ground well, but I've had two half-sisters that weren't any good. Hopefully this will be third time lucky, he looks a nice horse but he just needs to grow up a bit".

1626. UNNAMED ★★★

b.c. Teofilo – Kalagold (Magical Strike). April 17. Eighth foal. 38,000Y. Tattersalls October Book 2. C F Wall. Half-brother to the smart 2-y-o dual Group 3 7f winner and Group 1 6f Cheveley Park Stakes second Wake Up Maggie (by Xaar). The dam, a quite useful 2-y-o 1m winner, is a half-sister to 6 winners. The second dam, Showing Style (by Pas de Seul), is an unraced half-sister to 5 winners. (Mr D S Lee). "I trained the dam's only good foal, Wake Up Maggie, but I've seen quite a few of the others and they've been big and slow, to be honest, but the dam had visited a few dual purpose stallions so that would explain it to some extent. This colt is the first one I've seen that's small and sharp like Wake Up Maggie was. He seems to be going along OK but he's growing a bit at the minute so we're going a bit more slowly with him for now. He probably isn't quite as sharp as his sister was, so I can't see us getting him out before July. But he ought to be

a 2-y-o over seven furlongs and a mile because he has a bit more scope than she had".

DERMOT WELD

1627. AFTERNOON SUNLIGHT (IRE) ★★★★

ch.f. Sea The Stars – Lady Luck (Kris). April 10. Half-sister to the very smart 7f (at 2 yrs) and Group 2 10f Leopardstown Derby Trial winner and dual Derby placed Casual Conquest (by Hernando), to the Irish 2-y-o listed 7f winner Elusive Double (by Grand Lodge), the Irish 7f winners A Word Apart (by Desert Style) and Moving Heart (by Anabaa) and the quite useful Irish 9f winner Media Asset (by Polish Precedent). The dam won over 1m in Ireland and is a half-sister to several winners including the Irish Group 3 Boland Stakes winner Social Harmony. The second dam, Latest Chapter (by Ahonoora), is an unraced half-sister to the Grade 1 Belmont Stakes winner Go And Go. (Moyglare Stud Farm). "A very nice, medium-sized filly – she's all quality. I like her and she'll make a 2-y-o anytime from July onwards over seven furlongs. Very likeable".

1628. ALKASSER (IRE) ★★★★

b.c. Shamardal – Alexander Queen (King's Best). April 7. Fourth foal. €260,000Y. Goffs Orby. Shadwell Estate Co. Half-brother to the quite useful 5f (including at 2 yrs) and 6f winner of 4 races Bogini (by Holy Roman Emperor) and to the quite useful 2-y-o 6f winner Asraab (by Oasis Dream). The dam, a fairly useful 2-y-o 5f winner, is a half-sister to 4 winners including the Group 3 Palace House Stakes winner and Group 1 placed Dandy Man. The second dam, Lady Alexander (by Night Shift), won the Group 3 6.3f Anglesey Stakes and Group 3 5f Molecomb Stakes and is a half-sister to 2 winners. (Hamdan Al Maktoum). "A fine, big colt. He'll be nice in the second part of the year and he's very likeable, probably a seven furlong 2-y-o".

1629. ANTIQUE PLATINUM (IRE) ★★★

b.f. Holy Roman Emperor – Summer Trysting (Alleged). May 17. Sister to the smart 2012 2-y-o 7f winner and Group 1 National Stakes second Designs On Rome, closely related to the Irish 2-y-o 7f listed and subsequent US Grade 2 9.5f Arlington Derby winner Simple Exchange (by Danehill) and half-sister to the

Irish 7f (at 2 yrs), Group 3 Brigadier Gerard Stakes and Group 3 Newbury Dubai Duty Free 'Arc' Trial winner Sights On Gold, the fairly useful Irish 8.5f winner Romantic Venture (both by Indian Ridge), the fairly useful Irish 9f winner Beat The Heat (by Salse), the fair Irish 12f winner Tempting Paradise (by Grand Lodge), the fair 10f, 11f and hurdles winner Sublime Talent (by Sadler's Wells) and the modest 10f and hurdles winner Minsky Mine (by Montjeu). The dam was placed at up to 12f in Ireland and is a half-sister to the smart performer at up to 10f Smooth Performance. The second dam, Seasonal Pickup (by The Minstrel), won four listed races in Ireland and is a half-sister to the dam of Grey Swallow. (Moyglare Stud Farm). *"She'll take a bit of time because she's slightly backward, but she's a quality filly. She should be a 2-y-o in the second part of the year over seven furlongs".*

1630. BROOCH (USA) ★★★

b.f. Empire Maker – Daring Diva (Dansili). March 4. Half-sister to the listed 10f winner and Group 2 10f Blandford Stakes second Caponata (by Selkirk). The dam, a French 2-y-o listed 5f winner, is a sister to the Group 1 1m Matron Stakes and multiple Group 3 winner Emulous and a half-sister to the fairly useful 2-y-o 6f winner Striking Spirit. The second dam, Aspiring Diva (by Distant View), was placed at up to 1m in France and is a half-sister to numerous winners including the useful 10.2f winner Private Song. (Khalid Abdulla). *"She's a lovely, big, lengthy filly and she'll run in September or October over seven furlongs to a mile".*

1631. BUSHFIGHTER (IRE) ★★

b.g. Bushranger – Lady Meagan (Val Royal). March 22. First foal. £65,000Y. Doncaster Premier. Bobby O'Ryan. The dam, a fair Irish 2-y-o 6f winner, is a half-sister to 8 winners. The second dam, Born To Glamour (by Ajdal), a winner over 6f in Ireland at 2 yrs, is a half-sister to 9 winners including the French listed winner North Haneena. (Dr Ronan Lambe). *"I've gelded him, he's a medium-sized fellow I see running around June time".*

1632. BUSH PILOT (IRE) ★★★★

br.c. Bushranger – Dame Noir (Alzao). April

27. Fourth foal. 42,000Y. Tattersalls October Book 2. Bobby O'Ryan. Half-brother to the fair Irish 2-y-o 7f winner Dan Noir (by Spartacus). The dam, a moderate 7f and 1m winner of 4 races at 5 yrs, is a half-sister to a winner in Turkey. The second dam, Dame Rose (by Machiavellian), was placed once at 3 yrs in France and is a half-sister to one winner. (Dr Ronan Lambe). *"He's a colt I like a lot. I can see him running by the end of May because he's very forward. A nice horse for six and seven furlongs".*

1633. COUMLARA (IRE) ★★★

b.f. High Chaparral – Perfect Touch (Miswaki). April 7. Sixth foal. Half-sister to Breden (by Shamardal), placed third over 7f from 2 starts at 2 yrs in 2012, to the useful 2-y-o 5f winner and Group 3 Jersey Stakes third Rock Jock (by Rock Of Gibraltar) and the fairly useful 2-y-o 6f winner Shining Armour (by Green Desert). The dam won 3 races including the Group 3 Brownstown Stakes and is a half-sister to 7 winners including the Italian Group 2 and Irish Group 3 winner King Jock and the dam of the triple US Grade 2 winner Katdogawn. The second dam, Glen Kate (by Glenstal), won three Grade 3 events in the USA and is a half-sister to 3 winners. (Mrs C L Weld). *"A filly with a lot of quality, she's a fine big filly for September/October. A typical High Chaparral".*

1634. CROWN DIAMOND (IRE) ★★★

ch.g. Dandy Man – Cecilia's Pearl (Woodman). March 1. Fifth foal. €67,000Y. Goffs Sportsman's. Bobby O'Ryan. The dam was placed twice at 4 yrs in the USA and is a half-sister to 3 winners including the dual 7f winner (including at 2 yrs) and listed winner Newgate Lodge. The second dam, Oh'cecilia (by Scenic), won 3 races over 7f and 1m at 2 yrs, was second in the Group 3 C L Weld Park Stakes and subsequently won a race in the USA and is a full or half-sister to 6 winners. (Dr Ronan Lambe). *"We've gelded him but he's likeable and he'll be racing in May over six furlongs".*

1635. CRYSTAL SNOWFLAKE (IRE) ★★★

b.f. Danehill Dancer – Snowy Day In LA (Sadler's Wells). March 21. Third foal. €62,000Y. Goffs Orby. Dermot Weld. Sister to the fair

2012 2-y-o 5f winner Snow Angel and closely related to the fairly useful 2-y-o 5f winner and dual listed-placed Snowflake Dancer (by Dylan Thomas). The dam is an unplaced sister to a listed-placed winner in France and a half-sister to 4 winners including Kistena (Group 1 Prix de l'Abbaye). The second dam, Mabrova (by Prince Mab), a French 2-y-o 7f winner, is a half-sister to 6 winners. (Dr Ronan Lambe). *"Out of a Sadler's Wells mare, she'll be a nice seven furlong type for September and October".*

1636. ENTERPRISING ★★★
b.f. *Dansili – Indication (Sadler's Wells).* March 11. Sister to the very useful listed 9f winner and dual Group 3 placed Stipulation. The dam, a fair 9.5f winner, is a half-sister to 4 winners including the Group 3 7f Supreme Stakes winner Stronghold and the listed winner Take The Hint. The second dam, Insinuate (by Mr Prospector), a useful listed 1m winner, is a half-sister to numerous winners including the useful 6f and 7f winner and listed-placed Imroz. (Khalid Abdulla). *"A medium-sized, reasonable filly that goes nicely. One for seven furlongs in late summer to start off".*

1637. ENTIQAAM (IRE) ★★
br.c. *Sea The Stars – Cuis Ghaire (Galileo).* February 11. First foal. The dam, a smart 2-y-o dual Group 3 6f winner and second in the 1,000 Guineas, is a sister to the Irish 2-y-o 7f winner and Coronation Stakes second Gile Na Greine and to the very useful Irish 1m winner and dual Group 3 placed Claiomh Solais. The second dam, Scribonia (by Danehill), is an unraced half-sister to 6 winners including the very useful 2-y-o listed 6f winner and dual Group 1 placed Luminata and the very useful dual 6f winner (including at 2 yrs) and Group 3 placed Aretha. (Hamdan Al Maktoum). *"A big, backward fellow. I could see him making his debut in October over a mile".*

1638. FIRST SITTING ★★★
b.c. *Dansili – Aspiring Diva (Distant View).* April 18. Brother to the Group 1 1m Matron Stakes and multiple Group 3 winner Emulous and to the listed 5f winner Daring Diva and half-brother to the fairly useful triple 6f

winner (including at 2 yrs) Striking Spirit (by Oasis Dream). The dam, placed at up to 1m in France, is a half-sister to numerous winners including the useful 10.2f winner Private Song. The second dam, Queen Of Song (by His Majesty), won 14 races in the USA including the Grade 2 8.5f Shuvee Handicap and the Grade 3 8.5f Sixty Sails Handicap (twice), was Grade 1 placed and is a sister to the Grade 1 Jersey Derby winner Cormorant. (Khalid Abdulla). *"I've trained some of the family and this is a nice colt that'll just take a bit of time. I see him running around September time over seven furlongs to a mile".*

1639. FLYING JIB ★★★★
gr.f. *Oasis Dream – Jibboom (Mizzen Mast).* March 29. Second foal. The dam, a US Grade 2 7f and dual Grade 3 winner over 7f and 1m, was second in the Grade 1 Santa Monica Handicap and is a half-sister to 2 winners. The second dam, Palisade (by Gone West), a quite useful 2-y-o 7f winner, is a half-sister to the useful 3-y-o 1m winner Emplane and to the useful 2-y-o 1m winner Boatman. (Khalid Abdulla). *"Yes, there's lot of quality about her and she's quite forward. I can see her running in June or July over six/seven furlongs".*

1640. FREE EAGLE (IRE) ★★★★
b.c. *High Chaparral – Polished Gem (Danehill).* May 4. Fourth foal. Half-brother to the Group 2 12f British Champions Fillies' and Mares Stakes and dual Group 3 winner Sapphire (by Medicean) and to the useful 7f winner of 4 races Custom Cut (by Notnowcato). The dam, an Irish 2-y-o 7f winner, is a sister to 2 winners including the Grade 1 9f Matriarch Stakes and Group 2 1m Sun Chariot Stakes winner Dress To Thrill and a half-sister to 7 winners. The second dam, Trusted Partner (by Affirmed), was a very useful winner of the Group 3 7f C.L. Weld Park Stakes (at 2 yrs) and the Irish 1,000 Guineas and is a sister to the useful middle distance performers Easy to Copy and Epicure's Garden and to the useful Irish 7f listed and US Grade 3 winner Low Key Affair. (Moyglare Stud Farms Ltd). *"A lovely colt, he's all quality and will be a lovely horse going seven furlongs or a mile in August or September".*

1641. GLORY BOY (IRE) ★★★★
br.c. Myboycharlie – Spring Glory (Dr Fong).
March 22. Third foal. €145,000Y. Goffs Orby.
Bobby O'Ryan. Half-brother to the fair 2012
2-y-o 6f winner Ronaldhino (by Jeremy).
The dam, a fair 12f winner, is a half-sister to
6 winners including the useful winner of 7
races at up to 2m On Call (herself dam of the
US Grade 2 winner One Off) and the smart
broodmare Doctor's Glory (the dam of five
stakes winners). The second dam, Doctor Bid
(by Spectacular Bid), is an unraced half-sister
to 9 winners including the smart Group 3
Prix Thomas Bryon winner Glory Forever and
the dam of the Group winners Verglas and
Cassandra Go. (Dr Ronan Lambe). *"He had his
first run at Leopardstown and he was a shade
unlucky not to win. He'll be out again in mid-
May and he's one to watch out for I'd say".*

1642. GO FOR GOAL (IRE) ★★★
gr.c. Verglas – Triple Try (Sadler's Wells).
April 25. Half-brother to the useful 1m (at 2
yrs) and 10f winner and Group 3 10f Ballysax
Stakes third Unwritten Rule (by Dalakhani), to
the fairly useful dual 7f winner (including at
2 yrs) Offbeat Fashion (by Rock Of Gibraltar)
and the quite useful dual 10f and hurdles
winner Absinthe (by King's Best). The dam, a
quite useful Irish dual 10f winner, is a sister to
the Irish Oaks and Tattersalls Gold Cup winner
Dance Design. The second dam, Elegance
In Design (by Habitat), a useful Irish listed 6f
winner, is a sister to the high-class Coronation
Stakes winner Chalon (herself dam of the Prix
Ganay winner Creator). (Moyglare Stud Farms
Ltd). *"He's a nice colt, a little bit backward so
he's going to take a bit of time, but he'll be
alright in the second part of the year".*

1643. GOOD TRADITION (IRE) ★★★
b.c. Pivotal – Token Gesture (Alzao). April 1.
Twelfth foal. Brother to the quite useful 2-y-o
1m winner Hit The Jackpot and half-brother
to the 7f (at 2 yrs in Ireland) and Grade
1 Canadian International winner Relaxed
Gesture, the useful 10f winner and Group
3 10f Gallinule Stakes third Central Station
(both by Indian Ridge), the Irish 1m and
subsequent US Grade 2 9.5f American Derby
winner Evolving Tactics (by Machiavellian),
the fairly useful 7f (at 2 yrs) to 13f winner

Braveheart Move (by Cape Cross) and the Irish
1m, 12f and hurdles winner Turn Of Phrase
(by Cadeaux Genereux). The dam, a smart
winner of the Group 3 7f C L Weld Park Stakes,
is a half-sister to the US Grade 2 9f winner
Wait Till Monday, to the useful Irish 10f to
12.3f winner Blazing Spectacle and the useful
Irish middle-distance stayer and Triumph
Hurdle winner Rare Holiday. The second dam,
Temporary Lull (by Super Concorde), is an
unraced sister to the Nell Gwyn Stakes winner
Martha Stevens. (Moyglare Stud Farm). *"A nice
colt and a good, strong horse but he'd more
of a second part of the year 2-y-o. The mare
tends to get them to stay well, for example the
3-y-o half-sister by Danehill Dancer only made
her debut a few days ago over ten furlongs.
This will be a nice colt going seven furlongs in
September".*

1644. HIGHLAND FALCON (IRE) ★★★
b.c. Kyllachy – Gloved Hand (Royal Applause).
April 26. Fourth foal. €72,000Y. Goffs Orby.
Bobby O'Ryan. Half-brother to the modest
2013 3-y-o 9f winner Hidden Link (by Rail
Link) and to the fairly useful 7f and 1m
winner of 4 races Emilio Largo (by Cadeaux
Genereux). The dam, a useful 5f (at 2 yrs) to
7f winner of 4 races and second in the Group
3 Summer Stakes, is a half-sister to 5 winners.
The second dam, Fudge (by Polar Falcon), is
an unraced half-sister to 7 winners including
the dam of the Group winners Definite Article,
Salford City and Salford Express. (Dr Ronan
Lambe). *"He started his career in early April
and he's a smart little fellow that should win in
the coming weeks".*

1645. I'M YOURS ★★★
b.f. Invincible Spirit – Rebelline (Robellino).
April 21. Seventh foal. €420,000Y. Goffs Orby.
Moyglare Stud Farm. Sister to the winner
Redoubtable and closely related to the smart
Group 3 Irish 2,000 Guineas Trial and listed 1m
winner and Group 1 10.5f Tattersalls Rogers
Cup second Recharge (by Cape Cross) and to
the fair Irish 1m winner Regalline (by Green
Desert). The dam won 6 races from 7f to
10.5f including the Group 1 10.5f Tattersalls
Gold Cup and the Group 2 10f Pretty Polly
Stakes and is a sister to the Group 2 Blandford
Stakes winner Quws and a half-sister to 5

winners. The second dam, Fleeting Rainbow (by Rainbow Quest), a modest 10f placed 3-y-o, is a half-sister to 3 winners. (Moyglare Stud Farm). *"She's very much a quality filly but going through a growing stage at the moment. I'll look forward to her in the second half of the year".*

1646. KATIMAVIK (IRE) ★★
b.c. Invincible Spirit – Nunavik (Indian Ridge). February 3. First foal. The dam is an unraced sister to the useful Irish 1m winner Legal Jousting and a half-sister to the Group 2 12f Ribblesdale Stakes winner Irresistible Jewel and the listed 12f winner Diamond Trim. The second dam, In Anticipation (by Sadler's Wells), won over 12f and 14f in Ireland. (Moyglare Stud Farm). *"An attractive, big horse and I see him as one for the second part of the year. A big guy".*

1647. KEYBOARD MELODY (IRE) ★★★
gr.c. Verglas – Wrong Key (Key Of Luck). March 25. Fifth living foal. €140,000Y. Goffs Orby. Bobby O'Ryan. Brother to the useful 2-y-o listed 5f Marble Hill Stakes winner Wrong Answer and half-brother to the useful dual 1m winner and UAE Group 2 second Albaasil (by Dansili) and the quite useful Irish 2-y-o 1m winner Wrong Number (by King's Best). The dam, an Irish 7f (at 2 yrs) and listed 1m winner, was placed in the Group 2 1m Goffs International Stakes and the Group 2 10f Pretty Polly Stakes and is a sister to the 7f (at 2 yrs) and Group 3 10f and 12f winner Right Key and a half-sister to 3 winners. The second dam, Sarifa (by Kahyasi), is an unraced half-sister to the Group 3 Prix du Palais Royal winner Saratan. (Dr Ronan Lambe). *"A good, strong colt. Being by Verglas he'll probably want some ease in the ground and I could see him racing in the second part of the year, from July onwards. More of a staying type than his sister Wrong Answer".*

1648. LANYARD (USA) ★★
gr.f. Mizzen Mast – Geographic (Empire Maker). February 5. Second foal. Sister to the fair 2012 7f placed 2-y-o (from two starts) Market Town. The dam is an unraced half-sister to the Grade 1 9f Hollywood Oaks winner Sleep Easy and to the dual US Grade 1

winner Aptitude. The second dam, Dokki (by Northern Dancer), is an unraced half-sister to the champion US colt Slew O'Gold and the Belmont Stakes winner Coastal. (Khalid Abdulla). *"A strong filly, she'll be racing in August or September over seven furlongs".*

1649. LEAFCUTTER (IRE) ★★★
b.c. Shamardal – Bee Eater (Green Desert). April 14. Third foal. €220,000Y. Goffs Orby. John Ferguson. Half-brother to the minor French 3-y-o winner Picking Up Pieces (by Montjeu). The dam, a 6f winner of 4 races and listed-placed, is a half-sister to 3 winners. The second dam, Littlefeather (by Indian Ridge), a very useful 5f (at 2 yrs) and 6f winner of 4 races, was third in the Group 1 7f Moyglare Stakes and is a half-sister to 7 winners including the Cheveley Park Stakes, Irish 1,000 Guineas, Coronation Stakes and Sussex Stakes winner Marling and the Prix de l'Abbaye, Irish 2,000 Guineas, St James's Palace Stakes and Vernons Sprint Cup placed Caerwent. (Sheikh Mohammed). *"A very nice colt, he's reasonably forward and I can see him appearing in mid-summer".*

1650. LORD OF THE NILE (IRE) ★★★
ch.c. Galileo – Magic Carpet (Danehill). February 2. Second foal. Brother to the 2012 7f and 1m placed 2-y-o Signature Dish. The dam, a useful Irish 7f winner, was listed-placed twice and is a sister to one winner. The second dam, Paper Moon (by Lake Coniston), a minor Irish 3-y-o 1m winner, is a half-sister to 8 winners including the very useful Group 1 1m Prix Marcel Boussac winner Mary Linoa and the French listed winner and Group 3 placed Ming Dynasty. (Sir Robert Ogden). *"Forward and strong, he's a nice colt I see running in mid-summer".*

1651. MADAKHEEL (USA) ★★★
b.f. Mr Greeley – Manaal (Bahri). March 15. Third foal. The dam, a quite useful 7f and 1m winner, is a half-sister to one winner. The second dam, Muwakleh (by Machiavellian), winner of the UAE 1,000 Guineas and second in the Newmarket 1,000 Guineas, is a sister to the high-class Dubai World Cup and Prix Jean Prat winner Almutawakel and to the useful 10f winner Elmustanser and a half-sister to

numerous winners including the smart 10f winner Inaaq. (Hamdan Al Maktoum). *"She's a quality filly, very likeable and a fine big filly for the second part of the year".*

1652. MAHON FALLS ★★★★

ch.f. Dandy Man – Saphire (College Chapel). April 29. Sixth foal. 52,000Y. Tattersalls October Book 2. Bobby O'Ryan. Half-sister to the fairly useful 2-y-o 5f winner and Group 3 5f Cornwallis Stakes second Waffle (by Kheleyf), to the quite useful 7f and 1m winner and subsequent US stakes-placed Byrony (by Byron) and the modest Irish 1m winner King's Road (by King's Best). The dam, a fairly useful 2-y-o 5f and 6f winner, was listed-placed twice and is a half-sister to 4 minor winners. The second dam, Emerald Eagle (by Sandy Creek), a fair 6f to 1m winner of 5 races, is a half-sister to 4 winners. (Mrs C L Weld). *"A sharp filly belonging to my mother, hopefully she'll be running and winning from mid to late May. A five/six furlong 2-y-o".*

1653. MAWRED (IRE) ★★★

b.c. Tamayuz – Roscoff (Daylami). February 6. Second foal. €85,000Y. Goffs Orby. Shadwell Estate Co. The dam, a French listed-placed 7.5f winner, is a half-sister to 2 winners. The second dam, Traou Mad (by Barathea), a French listed 2-y-o winner, was Group 3 placed four times and is a half-sister to 7 winners including the Group 2 6f Gimcrack Stakes and dual Group 3 winner Josr Algharoud and the dual Group 2 5f Prix du Gros-Chene winner Saint Marine. (Hamdan Al Maktoum). *"He's a horse that I like. I would see him as a mid-summer 2-y-o over six/seven furlongs".*

1654. MUSTAJEEB ★★★★

ch.c. Nayef – Rifqah (Elusive Quality). March 18. Second foal. Half-brother to the useful 2012 2-y-o 7f winner Muaanid (by Kheleyf). The dam is an unraced half-sister to 2 winners. The second dam, Anja (by Indian Ridge), a minor winner in the USA, is a half-sister to 4 winners including the Group 1 12f Prix du Jockey Club winner Anabaa Blue. (Hamdan Al Maktoum). *"A very nice colt, he's forward for a Nayef so I guess Elusive Quality has added a touch of precocity. I could see him running in June over seven furlongs. He goes well".*

1655. NEXT BEND (IRE) ★★

b.c. Azamour – Polite Reply (Be My Guest). April 21. Half-brother to the fair 2012 6f and 1m placed 2-y-o Cool Metallic (by Medicean), to the fairly useful 2-y-o dual 5f winner Hidden Charm (by Big Shuffle) and the quite useful dual 7f winners In A Rush (by Hernando) and Flic Flac (by Bahamian Bounty). The dam, a quite useful 7f and 1m winner, is closely related to the Irish winner and listed-placed Dance Pass and a half-sister to 3 winners including the Group 3 Ballyroan Stakes winner Sense Of Purpose. The second dam, Super Gift (by Darshaan), won twice over 1m at 2 yrs and was second in the Group 3 7f C.L. Weld Park Stakes. (Moyglare Stud Farm). *"A big, backward sort of horse, but he's strong and powerful. I see him being out in September".*

1656. NIDHAAM (IRE) ★★★★

ch.f. Nayef – Malakaat (Danzig). February 18. First foal. The dam is an unraced half-sister to the useful UAE Group 3 1m winner of 5 races Snaafy. The second dam, Nafisah (by Lahib), a very useful 7f (at 2 yrs), 9f and listed 10f winner, is a half-sister to 6 winners including the Irish 12f listed and hurdles winner Mutakarrim. (Hamdan Al Maktoum). *"A quality filly, she's very nice. A big, powerful, lengthy 2-y-o for seven furlongs around September/October".*

1657. NONCHALANT ★★★

gr.c. Oasis Dream – Comeback Queen (Nayef). March 19. Second foal. 130,000Y. Tattersalls October Book 1. Juddmonte Farms. Half-brother to the modest 2012 6f and 7f placed Something Magic (by Proud Citizen). The dam, a fairly useful 2-y-o 1m winner, was second in the listed Masaka Stakes and is a half-sister to 5 winners including the US Grade 2 and Grade 3 winner Worldly and the 2-y-o Breeders Cup Juvenile Turf winner Donativum. The second dam, Miss Universe (by Warning), a useful 2-y-o 6f winner and third in the Group 3 Solario Stakes, is a half-sister to 5 winners. (Khalid Abdulla). *"A nice grey colt, he'll be a mid-summer horse and will be suited by seven furlongs to a mile this year".*

1658. PIRITA (IRE) ★★★★

b.f. Invincible Spirit – Spinamix (Spinning World). March 28. Eighth foal. €330,000Y. Goffs Orby. Moyglare Stud Farm. Half-sister to the French listed 10f winner and subsequent Group 1 Hong Kong Derby second Some World (by Hawk Wing), to the smart dual listed 5f winner Spin Cycle (by Exceed And Excel), the useful Group 3 7f winner of 3 races San Sicharia (by Daggers Drawn), the fairly useful 2-y-o 6f winner and subsequent US Grade 3 placed Codeword (by Dansili) and a minor 3-y-o winner in France by Dutch Art. The dam was placed at 2 yrs in France and is a half-sister to 4 winners. The second dam, Vadsagreya (by Linamix), a French 7f (at 2 yrs) and 1m winner, was listed-placed and is a half-sister to 12 winners including the dams of the French 1,000 Guineas winner Vahorimix and the Breeders Cup Mile winner Val Royal. (Moyglare Stud Farm). "A very nice filly, she's sharp and will be running in May. She goes well".

1659. RENOWN ★★★

ch.c. Champs Elysees – Fame At Last (Quest For Fame). May 23. Closely related to the very promising 2012 2-y-o Group 3 7f Killavullan Stakes winner Big Break and to the high-class Famous Name (by Dansili), a winner of 18 races including the Group 2 Royal Whip Stakes and twelve Group 3 events in Ireland from 1m to 10f and half-brother to the Irish listed 10f winner Zaminast, the quite useful Irish 1m winner Photo Opportunity, the fair French 1m winner Everlasting Fame (all by Zamindar), the quite useful 6f winner Anchor Date (by Zafonic) and the fair 1m winner Final Esteem (by Lomitas). The dam, a fairly useful 2-y-o 7f winner, is a half-sister to one winner. The second dam, Ranales (by Majestic Light), a minor 2-y-o 1m winner in the USA, is a half-sister to 9 winners including the listed 10f Virginia Stakes winner Rambushka and the Group 2 7f Laurent Perrier Champagne Stakes second Arokat. (Khalid Abdulla). "A three-parts brother to Famous Name, a winner of 21 races including 20 stakes races. He's a very nice colt, obviously a different sort, but I would see him racing over seven furlongs to a mile in September/October".

1660. RHYTHM OF THE SEA (IRE) ★★★

b.f. Bushranger – Chamela Bay (Sadler's Wells). February 1. Sixth foal. €60,000Y. Goffs Orby. Bobby O'Ryan. Half-sister to the fair 1m (at 2 yrs) and 2m 2f winner Ragamuffin Man (by Dalakhani). The dam, an Irish 12f winner, is a sister to the Group 3 12f Blandford Stakes winner Chiang Mai and a half-sister to 8 winners including the very smart Group 1 10.5f Prix de Diane winner and good broodmare Rafha. The second dam, Eljazzi (by Artaius), a fairly useful 2-y-o 7f winner, is a half-sister to the high-class miler Pitcairn, to the Blandford Stakes winner Valley Forge and the dam of the high-class stayer Assessor. (Dr Ronan Lambe). "A nice filly out of a Sadler's Wells mare and I see her running around July or August. It's a very good family".

1661. SCHOLARLY ★★★

b.f. Authorized – Historian (Pennekamp). March 12. Half-sister to the quite useful 2011 2-y-o 7f winner Master Of Ages (by Exceed And Excel), to the French 10f and 11f winner and listed placed Antiquities (by Kaldounevees), the quite useful 2-y-o 9f winner Book Of Facts (by Machiavellian) and the French 10f and hurdles winner Patterning (by Pivotal). The dam, a French listed 10.5f winner, is a sister to one winner and a half-sister to numerous winners including the Dubai World Cup winner Street Cry. The second dam, Helen Street (by Troy), won 3 races including the Irish Oaks. (Sheikh Mohammed). "I have a lot of big 2-y-o's this year and this is one of them. She's a lovely, scopey filly with a lot of quality. She'll be lovely come September/October time over a mile".

1662. SILVER GAUNTLET (IRE) ★★

gr.c. Verglas – Katch Me Katie (Danehill). March 21. Seventh foal. €40,000Y. Goffs Orby. Bobby O'Ryan. Half-brother to the listed 12f winner Pale Mimosa, to the fairly useful 12f and 2m winner and listed-placed Suailce (both by Singspiel) and the modest 14f winner Passion Planet (by Medicean. The dam, a fair 9f winner, is a half-sister to 4 winners including the Grade 2 E P Taylor Stakes winner and Grade 1 Gamely Handicap and Group 2 Sun Chariot Stakes second Kool Kat Katie and the smart 8.3f (at 2yrs) and Group 3 10.4f

Musidora Stakes winner, Epsom Oaks second and Grade 1 Beverley Hills Handicap third Kalypso Katie. The second dam, Miss Toot (by Ardross), a fair 10f and 15f winner on her only starts, is a half-sister to one winner. (Dr Ronan Lambe). *"A nice colt, I can see him running in mid-summer"*.

1663. STARLET (IRE) ★★★
b.f. Sea The Stars – Treasure The Lady (Indian Ridge). April 8. Sixth foal. Closely related to the quite useful Irish 1m winner Treasure The Cross (by Cape Cross) and half-sister to the quite useful 2012 1m placed 2-y-o Magnolia Ridge (by Galileo). The dam won once in Ireland at 2 yrs over 7f and was listed-placed and is a half-sister to 7 winners including the Derby winner High Chaparral and the Dante Stakes winner Black Bear Island. The second dam, Kasora (by Darshaan), is an unraced full or half-sister to 8 winners. (Mrs C L Weld). *"A quality filly, she's a very nice mover but a bit immature so I would see her running in September"*.

1664. TAHAANY (IRE) ★★★
b.f. Raven's Pass – Photophore (Clodovil). February 9. Second foal. €240,000Y. Goffs Orby. Shadwell Estate Co. The dam, a minor French 9.5f winner, is a half-sister to 4 winners including the Group 1 French 1,000 Guineas winner Elusive Wave. The second dam, Multicolour Wave (by Rainbow Quest), is a placed half-sister to 4 winners and to the unraced dam of the Group 2 Queen Mary Stakes winner Langs Lash. (Hamdan Al Maktoum). *"She's a sweet filly, medium-sized and she'll make a 2-y-o around June or July over seven furlongs"*.

1665. TARFASHA (IRE) ★★★★
ch.f. Teofilo – Grecian Bride (Groom Dancer). April 26. Closely related to the fairly useful 2012 2-y-o 1m winner Galileo Rock (by Galileo) and half-sister to the very smart Group 2 Doncaster Cup and Group 2 Goodwood Cup winner Saddler's Rock, to the fairly useful 10f winner Crowfoot (both by Sadler's Wells), the 7f, 1m (both at 2 yrs) and listed 10f and 12f winner and triple Group 3 placed Allexina, the useful 1m winner and Group 3 second Athenian Way (both by

Barathea) and the modest 7f to 9f winner of 6 races Champain Sands (by Green Desert). The dam is an unraced sister to the useful 7f (at 2 yrs) and listed 10f winner Athens Belle and a half-sister to the Group 1 Grand Prix de Saint-Cloud winner Gamut and the Group 2 13.3f Geoffrey Freer Stakes winner Multicolored. The second dam, the French 10f and 12f winner Greektown (by Ela-Mana-Mou) is a half-sister to the high-class stayer Sought Out (dam of the Derby winner North Light) and to Scots Lass (dam of the Group 2 Great Voltigeur Stakes winner Bonny Scot). (Hamdan Al Maktoum). *"Although there's a lot of stamina in the pedigree she doesn't look like a staying filly. I see her running around July over seven furlongs. She's a nice filly and all quality"*.

1666. TESTED ★★
b.f. Selkirk – Prove (Danehill). February 2. Half-sister to the fairly useful 10f and 14f winner and listed-placed Track Record (by Montjeu) and to the fair French 1m winner Trajectory (by Dubai Destination). The dam, a winner of 4 races including the Group 3 9f Prix Chloe, is a sister to the smart Group 3 12f Prix de Minerve and dual 10f listed winner Danefair and the smart multiple 7f to 8.5f winner Vortex and a half-sister to the listed 12f Prix Joubert winner Erudite. The second dam, Roupala (by Vaguely Noble), a fair 3-y-o 1m winner, is a half-sister to 4 winners including the useful 6f and 7f winner Ajuga (dam of the German Group 2 winner Bad Bertrich Again and the Group 3 Scottish Classic winner Prolix) and to the unraced Tikanova (dam of the US Grade 2 winner Daros). (Khalid Abdulla). *"Another nice filly, she's medium-sized and I see her running in July or August"*.

1667. TIGER LILLY (IRE) ★★★
b.f. Galileo – Banquise (Last Tycoon). April 1. Eleventh foal. Sister to the 7f (at 2 yrs) and 10f winner and Group 2 Blandford Stakes third Robin Hood, closely related to the minor Irish 10f winner Snow Lord (by Sadler's Wells) and half-sister to the fairly useful Irish dual 9f and subsequent US stakes winner Cold Cold Woman (by Machiavellian), the fair 1m to 10f winner Kelly Nicole and the moderate dual 1m winner Rivera Red (both by Rainbow Quest). The dam won over 2m in France and

is a half-sister to 8 winners including the high-class Group 2 10.5f Grand Prix de Chaudenay and Group 2 13.5f Grand Prix de Deauville winner Modhish, the smart Group 2 12.5f Prix de Royallieu winner and Irish Oaks second Russian Snows and the very useful French 2-y-o and 3-y-o 10.5f Prix de Royaumont winner Truly Special. The second dam, Arctique Royale (by Royal And Regal), won the Irish 1,000 Guineas and the Moyglare Stud Stakes and is a half-sister to the dam of the top-class middle-distance stayer Ardross. (Sir Robert Ogden). *"She's a medium-sized filly with a lot of quality but I don't think we'll see her before September or October".*

1668. WATEED (IRE) ★★★★

b.c. Iffraaj – Miss Adelaide (Alzao). February 1. Fifth foal. 68,000Y. Tattersalls October Book 2. Shadwell Estate Co. Half-brother to the quite useful 2-y-o 5f winner Rebecca de Winter (by Kyllachy). The dam, a fair dual 5f winner at 3 yrs, is a half-sister to 5 minor winners. The second dam, Sweet Adelaide (by The Minstrel), a dual winner at 2 yrs and third in the Group 1 National Stakes, subsequently won in South Africa and is a full or half-sister to 10 winners including the listed winner and dual Group 3 placed Soiree. (Hamdan Al Maktoum). *"A big, strong, strapping colt. There's a lot to like about him and he goes well. Although he's a big horse he appears to be precocious, but I'll take my time with him a little bit. I could see him running towards the end of June".*

1669. WELD ARAB (IRE) ★★★★

b.c. Shamardal – Itqaan (Danzig). January 29. Fourth foal. The dam, a fair 1m winner, is a sister to the very smart Group 3 12f winner and Group 1 Champion Stakes second Mawatheeq and a half-sister to 5 winners including the 1,000 Guineas and Coronation Stakes winner Ghanaati and the Oaks second Rumoush. The second dam, Sarayir (by Mr Prospector), winner of a 1m listed event, is closely related to the top-class Champion Stakes winner Nayef and a half-sister to numerous winners including the Two Thousand Guineas, Eclipse, Derby and King George winner Nashwan and the high-class middle distance colt Unfuwain. (Hamdan Al

Maktoum). *"A nice colt, he was an early foal and he's big, strong and powerful. He'll be an August/September 2-y-o and I like him".*

1670. WHITEY O'GWAUN (IRE) ★★★

gr.c. Dalakhani – Angel Of The Gwaun (Sadler's Wells). February 15. Seventh foal. 110,000Y. Tattersalls October Book 1. John Ferguson. Half-brother to the 7f (at 2 yrs) and Group 3 10f Blue Wind Stakes winner Beauty O'Gwaun (by Rainbow Quest), to the Japanese Grade 3 2m winner Cosmo Meadow, the fairly useful 2-y-o 7f winner Angelonmyshoulder and the fair Irish 12f winner Missy O'Gwaun (all by King's Best). The dam is an unraced sister to 3 winners including the Derby third Let The Lion Roar and a half-sister to the St Leger winner Millenary and the Group 3 Princess Royal Stakes winner Head In The Clouds. The second dam, Ballerina (by Dancing Brave), a quite useful 2-y-o 7f winner, is a half-sister to the Group 3 12f Princess Royal Stakes winner Dancing Bloom and the good French 2-y-o 5f winner and 1,000 Guineas third River Dancer (herself dam of the Champion Stakes winner Spectrum). (Sheikh Mohammed). *"There's a lot of stamina in the pedigree but he's very nicely put-together and he's going to be a 2-y-o in July or August over seven furlongs to a mile".*

1671. UNNAMED ★★

b.g. Amadeus Wolf – Fully Fashioned (Brief Truce). April 4. Fifth foal. €30,000Y. Goffs Sportsman's. Bobby O'Ryan. Half-brother to the smart Irish Group 3 5f and dual listed sprint winner of 9 races Invincible Ash (by Invincible Spirit) and to the fair 7f, 10f and 11f winner Prince Of Fashion (by Desert Prince). The dam won once over 9f at 3 yrs in Ireland and is a half-sister to 6 winners. The second dam, Insider's View (by Caerleon), won 3 races from 6f (at 2 yrs) to 1m and is a half-sister to 5 winners. (Mr Glen Devlin). *"He's a gelding now and he'll be running in May over six and seven furlongs".*

1672. UNNAMED ★★★

b.f. First Defence – Hasardeuse (Distant View). March 15. Half-sister to the useful Irish 2-y-o 7f winner Thunder Bridge (by Bernstein). The dam is an unraced daughter of the US Grade

3 7f winner Harpia (by Danzig), herself a sister to Danehill. (Khalid Abdulla). *"A lovely, big filly, she'll be nice for Aug/Sept over seven furlongs".*

1673. UNNAMED ★★★

b.f. Galileo – Sophisticat (Storm Cat). April 6. Closely related to the useful 1m winner Encompassing (by Montjeu) and half-sister to the Irish 2-y-o 6f winner and Group 1 6f Cheveley Park Stakes third Pursuit Of Glory (by Fusaichi Pegasus) and to the French listed 1m winner Sefroua (by Kingmambo). The dam, a very smart Group 1 1m Coronation Stakes winner, is a sister to the US Grade 2 9f winner Grand Reward and a half-sister to the US Grade 2 winner Harlington (by Unbridled) and the US listed winner Serena's Tune. The second dam, Serena's Song (by Rahy), was an outstanding US winner of eleven Grade 1 events and is a half-sister to the US Grade 3 Golden Rod Stakes winner Vivid Imagination. (Mrs J Magnier). *"She's very much a quality filly for August/September over seven furlongs".*

1674. UNNAMED ★★★★

b.br.c. Empire Maker – Supposition (Dansili). February 16. The dam, a useful Irish 2-y-o 7f winner, was third in the Group 1 7f Moyglare Stud Stakes. The second dam, Topicality (by Topsider), won once at 3 yrs and is a sister to the Cherry Hinton and Fred Darling Stakes winner Top Socialite and a half-sister to the US Grade 1 winners Expelled and Exbourne. (Khalid Abdulla). *"A big, strong horse, he's really nice and I trained the dam who was a good racemare. I would say seven furlongs about September would be right for this colt".*

Sires Reference

This section deals with those sires represented by three or more two-year-olds in the book. Amongst the stallions listed are top sires like Acclamation, Cape Cross, Dalakhani, Danehill Dancer, Dansili, Dubawi, Exceed And Excel, Galileo, Invincible Spirit, Montjeu, Oasis Dream, Pivotal and Selkirk. In addition, you should look out for successful two-year-old sires like Bahamian Bounty, Dark Angel, Dutch Art, Holy Roman Emperor, Kheleyf, Kyllachy, Royal Applause, Sakhee's Secret, Teofilo and Verglas.

You will also see some of the best sires standing in America, like Distorted Humor, Dynaformer, Elusive Quality, Empire Maker, Giant's Causeway, Medaglia d'Oro, Smart Strike, Street Cry and War Front.

Please note that the reference numbers given with each sire correspond with their two-year-olds in the book.

ACCLAMATION (2000)
Royal Applause – Princess Athena (Ahonoora). Racing record: Won 6 times, including Diadem Stakes. Also placed in King's Stand and Nunthorpe. Stud record: First crop now seven-year-olds, he was an instant hit with his first crop in 2007, notably with his Group 1 winner Dark Angel. His other Group winners to date are Equiano (G1 King's Stand Stakes), Harbour Watch (G2 Richmond Stakes), Lilbourne Lad (G2 Railway Stakes), Ponty Acclaim (G3 Cornwallis Stakes), Alsindi (G3 Oh So Sharp Stakes), Hitchens (G3 Greenlands Stakes) and Talwar (G3 Solario Stakes). He also has ten listed winners to his name. Standing at Rathbarry Stud, Ireland. 2013 fee: €35,000.

AMADEUS WOLF (2003)
Mozart – Rachelle (Mark of Esteem). Racing record: Won 4 races including the Gimcrack Stakes, the Middle Park Stakes and the Duke of York Stakes. Stud record: Only one stakes winner to date - Caledonian Spring. Standing at Haras de Saint Vincent. 2013 fee: €3,000.

AQLAAM (2005)
Oasis Dream – Bourbonella (Rainbow Quest).

Racing record: Won the Group 1 Prix de Moulin and the Group 2 Jersey Stakes. First Two-Year-Olds in 2013. Standing at Nunnery Stud. 2013 fee: £7,000.

ARAKAN (2000)
Nureyev – Far Across (Common Grounds). Racing record: Won 6 races including the Group 3 Criterion Stakes, the Group 3 Supreme Stakes (both 7f), the listed Abernant Stakes and the City Of York Stakes (both 6f). Stud record: Best winners to date are the Group 2 Richmond Stakes and Tattersalls Ireland Sales Race winner Dick Turpin and the Group 2 Champagne Stakes and Group 3 Craven Stakes winner Trumpet Major. Standing at Ballyhane Stud. 2013 fee: €3,500.

ARCH (1995)
Kris S – Aurora (Danzig). Racing Record: 5 wins including Super Derby and Fayette Stakes. Stud record: Best winners so far include Arravale (Grade 1 Del Mar Oaks), Archarcharch (Grade 1 Arkansas Derby), Hymn Book (Grade 1 Donn Handicap), Blame (three US Grade 1 wins), Les Arcs (Golden Jubilee Stakes and July Cup), Love Theway Youare (Grade 1 Vanity Handicap), Overarching (South African dual Group 1 winner), Pine Island (dual US Grade 1 winner), Prince Arch (US Grade 1 winner) and Montgomery's Arch (Group 2 Richmond Stakes), Waterway Run (Group 3 Oh So Sharp Stakes). Standing at Claiborne Farm, Kentucky. 2013 fee: $40,000.

ARCHIPENKO (2004)
Kingmambo – Bound (Nijinsky). Racing record: Won the Group 1 10f Audemars Piguet Queen Elizabeth ll Cup at Sha Tin and four other Group races including the Group 2 Summer Mile. First two Year Olds 2013. Standing at Lanwades Stud, Newmarket. 2013 fee: £6,000.

ART CONNOISSEUR (2006)
Lucky Story – Withorwithoutyou (Danehill). Racing record: Won the Group 1 6f Golden Jubilee Stakes and the Group 2 6f Coventry Stakes. First Two-Year-Olds appear in 2013.

Standing at the Irish National Stud. 2013 fee: €4,500.

ASTRONOMER ROYAL (2004)

Danzig – Sheepscot (Easy Goer). Racing record: Won the Group 1 1m French 2,000 Guineas and the Group 3 Greenland Stakes and placed in the St James's Palace Stakes and July Cup. Stud record: His first two year olds appeared in 2012 and to date he's had 4 individual winners, two of them listed-placed. Standing at Haras de la Reboursiere & De Montaigu. 2013 Fee: €5,000.

AUSSIE RULES (2003)

Danehill – Last Second (Alzao). Racing Record: Won four races including the US Grade 1 Shadwell Turf Mile and the Group 1 French 2,000 Guineas. Stud record: Among his winners to date are Djumame (two Group 3 wins in Germany), Duck Feet (Group 3 Premio Guido Berardelli) and the listed winners Cazals, Chinese Wall and Dinkum Diamond. Standing at Lanwades Stud. 2013 fee: £5,000.

AUTHORIZED (2004)

Montjeu – Funsie (Saumarez). Racing Record: Won four races including the Group 1 Racing Post Trophy, Epsom Derby, Juddmonte International (all Group 1 events). Stud record: Five listed winners to date – Ambivalent, Castello Anagonese, Sugar Boy, Tenenbaum and Toruk Macto. Standing at Dalham Hall Stud. 2013 fee: £7,000.

AZAMOUR (2001)

Night Shift – Azmara (Lear Fan). Racing record: Won the St James's Palace Stakes, Irish Champion Stakes, Prince of Wales's Stakes and King George VI and Queen Elizabeth Diamond Stakes. Stud record: First runners in 2009. Best winners to date include Valyra (Group 1 Prix de Diane), the Group 2 winners Eleonora Duse, Shankardeh and Wade Giles and six Group 3 winners including Azmeel, Native Khan and Colombian. Standing at Gilltown Stud, Ireland. 2013 fee: €10,000.

BAHAMIAN BOUNTY (1994)

Cadeaux Genereux – Clarentia (Ballad Rock). Racing Record: Winner of 3 races at 2 yrs, notably the Prix Morny and the Middle

Park Stakes. Stud record: Sire of the Group 1 winners Pastoral Pursuits (July Cup) and Goodricke (Sprint Cup), the US Grade 2 winner Mister Napper Tandy, the Group 2 Cherry Hinton Stakes winner Sendmylovetorose and the Group 3 winners Cay Verde, Life's A Bounty, Naahy and Topatoo. Standing at the National Stud, Newmarket. 2013 fee: £10,000.

BALTIC KING (2000)

Danetime – Lindfield Belle (Fairy King). Racing record : Won 8 races including two listed events and the Wokingham Handicap. Stud record: His first runners appeared in 2011. Sire of the winners of 39 races to date, two of them listed-placed. Standing at Tally Ho Stud. 2013 fee: €3,000.

BERTOLINI (1996)

Danzig – Aquilega (Alydar). Racing record: Won 2 races, including July Stakes at 2 yrs, and placed in July Cup, Sprint Cup and Nunthorpe Stakes. Stud record: First runners in 2005. Sire of the Group 1 Cheveley Park Stakes winner Donna Blini, the New Zealand Group 1 winner Juice, the Group 2 winners Prime Defender and Puttanesca and the dual Group 3 winning sprinter Moorhouse Lad. Standing at Haras Des Faunes. 2013 fee: €3,000.

BUSHRANGER (2006)

Danetime – Danz Danz (Efisio). Race record: Won the Group 1 Prix Morny and the Group 1 Middle Park Stakes, both at 2 yrs. Stud record: His first two-year-olds appear in 2013. Standing at Tally Ho Stud, Ireland. 2013 fee: €7,500.

BYRON (2001)

Green Desert – Gay Gallanta (Woodman). Racing Record: Won 3 races including the Group 2 6f Mill Reef Stakes (at 2 yrs) and the Group 2 7f Betfair Cup (Lennox Stakes). Stud record: His first runners appeared in 2010. His best winners to date are Gordon Lord Byron (Group 1 Prix de la Foret) and the useful triple 5f winner Ahtoug. Standing at Woodlands Stud, Ireland. 2013 fee €2,500.

CAMACHO (2002)

Danehill – Arabesque (Zafonic). Racing record: Won a listed race over 6f and was second in the Group 3 7f Jersey Stakes. Stud record: His best winners to date include the Group 3 Fred Darling Stakes winner Puff and the listed winners Humidor, Arctic Feeling, Star Rover and Winning Express. Standing at Mickley Stud. 2013 fee: £2,750.

CAPE CROSS (1994)

Green Desert – Park Appeal (Ahonoora). Racing record: Won 4 races including the Lockinge Stakes, Queen Anne Stakes and Celebration Mile. Stud record: First runners in 2003. Sire of the outstanding colt Sea The Stars (2,000 Guineas, Derby, Prix de l'Arc de Triomphe etc,), top-class Ouija Board (7 Group 1 wins including the Oaks & the Breeders' Cup Filly and Mare Turf), Hong Kong Group 1 winner Able One, Behkabad (Group 1 Grand Prix de Paris), Nayarra (Group 1 Gran Criterium), the New Zealand Group 1 winners Gaze, Kindacross and Mikki Street and numerous smart performers including Borthwick Girl, Cape Dollar, Cape Fear, Castleton, Charlie Farnsbarns, Crossing The Line, Crosspeace, Crystal Capella, Halicarnassus, Hatta Fort, Hazyview, Joviality, Mac Love, Madrid, Mazuna, Moohaajim, Musicanna, Privy Seal and Russian Cross. Standing at Kildangan Stud, Ireland. 2013 Fee: €35,000.

CAPTAIN GERRARD (2005)

Oasis Dream – Delphinus (Soviet Star). Racing record: Won the Group 3 5f Cornwallis Stakes at 2 yrs. Stud Record: His first Two-Year-Olds appear in 2013. Standing at Mickley Stud, Shropshire. 2013 fee: £3,500.

CAPTAIN RIO (2000)

Pivotal – Beloved Visitor (Miswaki). Racing record: Won 4 times including the Criterium de Maisons-Laffitte at 2 yrs. Stud record: His best progeny to date include the New Zealand Group 1 winner Il Quello Veloce, the Australian Group 1 winner Brazilian Pulse, the New Zealand Group 2 winner Riomoral and the Group 3 winners Art Beat, Capt Chaos Philario and Red Badge. Standing at Ballyhane Stud, Ireland. 2013 fee: €3,500.

CHAMPS ELYSEES (2000)

Danehill – Hasili (Kahyasi). Race record: Won

the Canadian International, the Hollywood Turf Cup and the Northern Dancer Turf Stakes (all Grade 1). Stud record: His first two-year-olds appear in 2013. Standing at Banstead Manor Stud, Newmarket. 2013 fee: £5,000.

CLODOVIL (2001)

Danehill – Clodora (Linamix). Racing record: Won 5 races, including Poule d'Essai des Poulains. Stud record: His first crop were two-year-olds in 2007 and his best winners to date are Nahoodh (Group 1 Falmouth Stakes), the dual Group 3 winner Beacon Lodge, Laugh Out Loud (Prix de Sandringham), the listed winners Boastful, Coupe de Ville, Rock My Soul, Sorella Bella and Tuttipaesi, and the Group 1 placed Gregorian and Secret Asset. Standing at Rathasker Stud, Ireland. 2013 fee: €7,500.

COMPTON PLACE (1994)

Indian Ridge – Nosey (Nebbiolo). Racing record: Won 3 races, notably the July Cup. Stud record: First runners in 2002. Sire of the Group 1 Nunthorpe Stakes winner Borderlescott, the Group 2 and multiple Group 3 winner Deacon Blues, the smart Boogie Street and Intrepid Jack, US Grade 2 winner Passified, the Group 2 winners Godfrey Street and Prolific, the Italian Group 3 winners Pleasure Place, Champion Place and Shifting Place, and numerous useful performers including Angus News, Compton's Eleven, If Paradise, Judd Street, Hunter Street, Master Of War, Pacific Pride and Pearl Secret. Standing at Whitsbury Manor Stud, Hampshire. 2013 fee: £6,500.

DALAKHANI (2001)

Darshaan – Daltawa (Miswaki). Racing record: Won 8 of his 9 starts, including the Prix du Jockey Club and the Arc. Stud record: First crop were two-year-olds in 2007. Stud record: Best winners to date are Conduit (St Leger, Breeders Cup Turf (twice), King George VI & Queen Elizabeth Stakes), Moonstone (Irish Oaks), Chinese White (Pretty Polly Stakes), Reliable Man (Prix du Jockey Club), Duncan (Irish St Leger), the Group 2 winners Centennial, Armure, Vadamar and Democratie, and 9 Group 3 winners. Standing at Gilltown Stud, Ireland. 2013 fee: €25,000.

DANDY MAN (2003)

Mozart – Lady Alexander (Night Shift). Racing record: Won 6 races including the Group 3 5f Palace House Stakes and two listed events. Stud record: His first two-year-olds appear in 2013. Standing at Ballyhane Stud. 2013 fee: €4,000.

DANEHILL DANCER (1993)

Danehill – Mira Adonde (Sharpen Up). Racing Record: Winner of 4 races, including the Phoenix Stakes and National Stakes at 2 yrs and the Greenham at 3. Stud record: First runners in 2001. Sire of 16 Group 1 winners including Again, Alexander Tango, Choisir, Dancing Rain, Lillie Langtry, Mastercraftsman, Private Steer, Speciosa and Where Or When. Standing at Coolmore Stud, Ireland. 2013 fee: €40,000.

DANSILI (1996)

Danehill – Hasili (Kahyasi). Racing record: Won 5 races in France and placed in six Group/Grade 1 events including Sussex Stakes and Breeders' Cup Mile. Stud record: First runners in 2004. Sire of 46 Group winners including the Group 1 winners Rail Link (Arc, Grand Prix de Paris), Harbinger (King George VI), Emulous (Matron Stakes), Giofra (Falmouth Stakes), Passage of Time (Criterium de Saint-Cloud), The Fugue (Nassau Stakes), Zoffany (Phoenix Stakes), Zambezi Sun (Grand Prix de Paris) and the US Grade 1 winners Price Tag and Proviso. Standing at Banstead Manor Stud, Newmarket. 2013 fee: £80,000.

DARK ANGEL (2005)

Acclamation – Midnight Angel (Machiavellian). Racing record: Won four races at 2 yrs including the Group 1 Middle Park Stakes. Stud Record: First runners 2011. His best winners to date are Lethal Force (Group 2 Hungerford Stakes), Alhebayeb (Group 2 July Stakes) and the listed winners Lily's Angel and Boomshackerlacker. Stands at Morristown Lattin Stud, Ireland. 2013 fee: €12,500.

DISTORTED HUMOR (1993)

Forty Niner – Danzig's Beauty (Danzig). Racing record: Won 11 races in the USA including the Champagne Stakes, Futurity Stakes, Haskell Invitational and Travers Stakes (all Grade 1).

Champion 2-y-o. Stud record: Sire of twelve Grade 1 winners – Aesop's Fables, Any Given Saturday, Awesome Humor, Bit Of Whimsy, Commentator, Drosselmeyer, Flower Alley, Fourty Niner's Son, Funny Cide, Hysericalady, Pathfork and Rinky Dink. Standing at Win Star Farm, Kentucky. 2013 fee: $100,000.

DUBAWI (2002)

Dubai Millennium – Zomaradah (Deploy). Racing record: Won the National Stakes at 2 and the Irish 2,000 Guineas and Prix Jacques le Marois at 3. Third in the Derby. Stud record: Sire of 28 Group winners including the 9 Group 1 scorers Dubawi Heights (Gamely Stakes, Yellow Ribbon Stakes), Happy Archer (two Group 1's in Australia), Hunters Light (Premio Roma), Luck Or Design (Hong Kong Sprint), Makfi (2,000 Guineas, Prix Jacques le Marois), Monterosso (Dubai World Cup), Poet's Voice (Queen Elizabeth II Stakes), Secret Admirer (two Group 1's in Australia) and Waldpark (German Derby). Standing at Dalham Hall Stud, Newmarket. 2012 fee: €75,000.

DUKE OF MARMALADE (2004)

Danehill – Love Me True (Kingmambo). Racing record: Won 6 races including the Juddmonte International Stakes, King George VI and Queen Elizabeth Stakes, Prince of Wales's Stakes, Tattersalls Gold Cup and Prix Ganay. Stud record: His first two year olds appeared in 2012 and he had five winners in the UK and Ireland, plus another 7 winners abroad. Standing at Coolmore Stud, Ire. Fee: €12,500.

DUTCH ART (2004)

Medicean – Halland Park Lass (Spectrum). Race Record: Won four races at 2 yrs including the Group 1 Prix Morny and the Group 1 Middle Park Stakes. Stud record: Leading first crop sire in 2011, his best winners to date are Caspar Netscher (Group 2 Mill Reef Stakes and Group 2 Gimcrack Stakes), Van Der Neer (Group 1 Racing Post Trophy second), Producer (Group 3 Supreme Stakes) and 6 listed winners including Miss Work Of Art. Standing at Cheveley Park Stud. 2013 fee: £18,000.

DYLAN THOMAS (2003)
Danehill – Lagrion (Diesis). Racing record: Won 10 races including the Prix de L'Arc de Triomphe & Irish Champion Stakes. Stud record: First runners appeared in 2011. His best to date include the Irish Group 3 winners Furner's Green and Tannery. Standing at Coolmore Stud. 2013 fee: €10,000.

DYNAFORMER (1985)
Roberto – Andover Way (His Majesty). Racing record: 7 wins in USA including Grade 2 Florida Derby and Grade 2 Discovery Handicap. Stud record: Best winners include the Group 1 winner Lucarno, the Group 1 Fillies' Mile winner Rainbow View, Group 2 Ribblesdale winner Michita, the very smart Beat All and (in USA) Grade 1 winners Barbaro, Brilliant Speed, Dynaforce, Film Maker, Perfect Drift, Star Billing and Starrer, Melbourne Cup winner Americain and numerous smart performers including Dynever, Ocean Silk, Point of Entry, Sharp Susan, Spanish John and White Moonstone. Died in 2012.

ELNADIM (1994)
Danzig – Elle Seule (Exclusive Native). Racing record: Won 5 races, notably the July Cup and the Diadem Stakes. Stud record: Sire of the New Zealand Group 1 winner Culminate, the smart performers Al Qasi (Group 3 Phoenix Stakes), Caldra (Group 3 Autumn Stakes), Culminate (New Zealand Group 1), Elletelle (Group 2 Queen Mary Stakes), Elnawin (Group 3 Sirenia Stakes), Wi Dud (Group 2 Flying Childers Stakes), Soraaya (Group 3 Princess Margaret Stakes), New Zealand Group 3 winners Accardo, Elblitzem and Pendragon, the US Grade 3 winner Pasar Silbano and the dual listed winner Almass. Standing at Derrinstown Stud, Ireland. 2013 fee: €5,000.

ELUSIVE QUALITY (1993)
Gone West – Touch of Greatness (Hero's Honor). Racing record: Won 9 races in USA including Grade 3 events at 7f/1m. Stud record: Sire of top-class Kentucky Derby/ Preakness Stakes winner Smarty Jones, Breeders Cup Classic and Queen Elizabeth II Stakes winner Raven's Pass, Prix Morny winner Elusive City, dual Group 1 winner Elusive Kate, Australian multiple Group 1 winner Sepoy, the US Grade 1 winners Quality Road and Maryfield, the Group winning two-year-olds Certify, Elusive Pimpernel and Evasive, numerous US graded stakes winners including Chimichurri, Elusive Diva, Girl Warrior, Omega Code, Royal Michele and True Quality, and the smart dual listed winner Baharah. Standing at Jonabell Farm, Kentucky. 2013 fee: $50,000.

EMPIRE MAKER (2000)
Unbridled – Toussaud (El Gran Senor). Racing record: Won the Belmont Stakes, Florida Derby, Wood Memorial Stakes and Jim Dandy Stakes. Stud record: Sire of the US Grade 1 winners Acoma, Battle Plan, Bodemeister, Country Star, Grace Hall, Mushka, Icon Project, Royal Delta and Pioneerofthe Nile. Standing in Japan. Fee Private.

EXCEED AND EXCEL (2000)
Danehill – Patrona (Lomond). Racing record: Champion sprinter in Australia, won 7 races including the Grade 1 Newmarket H'cap, the Grade 1 Dubai Racing Club Cup and the Grade 2 Todman Stakes. Stud record: First northern hemisphere runners in 2008. His best winners include Excelebration (Queen Elizabeth II Stakes, Prix du Moulin, Prix Jacques le Marois), Margot Did (Nunthorpe Stakes), the Group 2 winners Fulbright, Heavy Metal, Best Terms and Infamous Angel and the 2-y-o Group 3 winner Bungleinthejungle. His Australasian winners include the Group 1 winners Helmet and Reward For Effort, Group 2 winner Wilander and the Group 3 winners Exceedingly Good, Sugar Babe and Believe 'n' Succeed. Standing at Dalham Hall Stud, Newmarket. 2013 fee: £35,000.

EXCELLENT ART (2004)
Pivotal – Obsessive (Seeking The Gold). Racing record: Won 4 races including the Group 1 St James's Palace Stakes and the Group 2 Mill Reef Stakes. Stud record: First runners 2011. Winners include Experience (Group 3 Grangecon Stud Stakes) Hazel Lavery (Group 3 St Simon Stakes) and the listed winners Sparkling Portrait, Tropaios, Artistic Jewel and Nimohe. Standing at Coolmore Stud. 2013 fee: €10,000.

FASTNET ROCK (2001)

Danehill – Piccadilly Circus (Royal Academy). Racing record: Raced in Australia and won two Grade 1's, two Grade 2's and two Grade 3 events over 5f and 6f. Stud Record: Having stood in Australia he has produced 11 Group 1 winners including Foxwedge, Mosheen and Sea Siren. Now standing at Coolmore Stud in Ireland. 2013 fee: Private.

FIREBREAK (1999)

Charnwood Forest – Breakaway (Song). Racing record: Won the Godolphin Mile in Dubai (twice), Challenge Stakes and Hong Kong Mile. Stud record: With four crops racing he is the sire of the winners of 40 races, the best to date being Hearts Of Fire (Group 1 Gran Criterium), Caledonia Lady (Group 3 Sandown Sprint Stakes and listed Harry Rosebery Stakes) and the listed Radley Stakes winner Electric Feel. Standing at Bearstone Stud. 2013 fee: £3,500.

FIRST DEFENCE (2004)

Unbridled's Song – Honest Lady (Seattle Slew). Racing record: Won the Grade 1 7f Forego Handicap and the Grade 3 6f Jaipur Stakes. Stud record: His first crop in 2012 included Dundonnell, winner of the Group 3 Acomb Stakes at York and fourth in the Grade 1 Breeders Cup Juvenile Turf. Standing at Juddmonte Farms, Kentucky. 2013 fee: $7,500.

FOOTSTEPSINTHESAND (2002)

Giant's Causeway – Glatisant (Rainbow Quest). Racing record: Won all 3 of his starts, notably the 2,000 Guineas. Stud record: His best winners include the Chachamaidee (Group 1 Matron Stakes), the Group 2 winners Barefoot Lady, Formosina, Shamalgan and (in Argentina) Infiltrada and Sagitariana and five Group 3 winners. Standing at Coolmore Stud, Ireland. 2013 fee: €10,000.

GALILEO (1998)

Sadler's Wells – Urban Sea (Miswaki). Racing record: Won 6 races including the Derby, Irish Derby and King George VI and Queen Elizabeth Stakes. Stud record: First runners in 2005. Sire of 31 Group 1 winners, notably the outstanding colt Frankel, champion 2-y-o's Teofilo, Frankel (also champion 3-y-o) and New Approach (subsequent Derby, Champion Stakes and Irish Champion Stakes winner), the triple Group 1 winner Rip Van Winkle, Sixties Icon (St Leger), Red Rocks (Breeders' Cup Turf), Allegretto (Prix Royal-Oak), Lush Lashes (three Group 1 wins), Soldier Of Fortune (Irish Derby & Coronation Cup) and Nightime (Irish 1000 Guineas), Roderic O'Connor (Criterium International, Irish 2,000 Guineas), Cape Blanco (five Group 1 wins), Nathaniel (King George VI & Queen Elizabeth Stakes), Treasure Beach (Irish Derby, Secretariat Stakes), Golden Lilac (French 1,000 Guineas and Prix de Diane), Was (Oaks), Misty For Me (four Group 1 wins), Maybe (Moyglare Stud Stakes) and Galikova (Prix Vermeille). Standing at Coolmore Stud, Ireland. 2012 fee: Private (was €150,000).

GIANT'S CAUSEWAY (1997)

Storm Cat – Mariah's Storm (Rahy). Racing record: Won 9 races, 6 of them Group 1 events, including the Prix de la Salamandre, Juddmonte International and Sussex Stakes. Stud record: First runners in 2004. Sire of the high-class Shamardal (Dewhurst Stakes, St James's Palace Stakes and Prix du Jockey Club) and a number of other very smart performers including Footstepsinthesand (2,000 Guineas), Ghanaati (1,000 Guineas and Coronation Stakes), Aragorn (dual US Grade winner), Heatseeker (Santa Anita Handicap), Maids Causeway (Coronation Stakes), Intense Focus (Dewhurst Stakes), Eskendereya, First Samurai, My Typhoon, Swift Temper (US Grade 1 winners), Await The Dawn (Hardwicke Stakes), Dalkala (Prix Cleopatre and Prix de Royallieu) and Rite of Passage (Ascot Gold Cup). Standing at Ashford Stud, Kentucky. 2013 fee: $85,000.

GREEN DESERT (1983)

Danzig – Foreign Courier (Sir Ivor). Racing record: 5 wins including July Cup, Vernons Sprint Cup and Flying Childers Stakes. Stud record: Stud record: High-class sire. Best winners (all very smart or better) include Alkaadhem, Cape Cross (Lockinge Stakes), Desert Lord (Prix de l'Abbaye), Desert Prince (Irish 2000 Guineas, Prix du Moulin, Queen Elizabeth Stakes), Desert Style, Desert Sun, Gabr, Invincible Spirit (Haydock Sprint Cup),

Markab (Sprint Cup), Oasis Dream (Middle Park, July Cup, Nunthorpe Stakes), Owington (July Cup), Sheikh Albadou (Nunthorpe Stakes/Haydock Sprint Cup) and Tamarisk (Haydock Sprint Cup). Retired from stud.

HAATEF (2004)

Danzig – Sayedat Alhadh (Mr Prospector). Racing record: Won four races including the Group 2 6f Diadem Stakes. Stud record: His first two year olds appeared in 2012 and he is the sire of 10 individual winners to date. Standing at Derrinstown Stud, Ireland. 2013 fee: €3,000.

HALLING (1991)

Diesis – Dance Machine (Green Dancer). Racing record: Won 12 races including Coral-Eclipse Stakes (twice), Juddmonte International (twice) and Prix d'Ispahan. Stud record: First runners in 2000. Sire of the Group 1 Grand Prix de Paris winner Cavalryman, the high-class Norse Dancer, Group 1 Prix Ganay winner Cutlass Bay, Group 2 winners Boscobel, Opinion Poll, Coastal Path, Dandoun, Eastern Aria, Fisich, Franklins Gardens, Giovani Imperatore, Harland, Nordhal, Pinson and Vanderlin, plus numerous other smart performers including Bauer, Chancellor, Foodbroker Fancy, Hala Bek, Hattan, Hero's Journey, Mkuzi, Parasol and The Geezer. Standing at Dalham Hall Stud, Newmarket. 2013 fee: £10,000.

HENRYTHENAVIGATOR (2005)

Kingmambo – Sequoyah (Sadler's Wells) Racing record: Won the Sussex Stakes, St James's Palace Stakes, 2000 Guineas and Irish 2,000 Guineas. Stud record: His first two year olds appeared in 2012 and they included the good winners George Vancouver (Grade 1 Breeders Cup Juvenile Turf), Pedro The Great (Group 1 Phoenix Stakes) and the dual Group 2 placed Cristoforo Colombo. Standing at: Coolmore Stud. 2013 fee: €30,000.

HERNANDO (1990)

Niniski – Whakilyric (Miswaki). Racing record: Won 7 races including the Prix Lupin and Prix du Jockey Club. Stud record: His Group/Grade 1 winners are Look Here (Oaks), Holding Court (Prix du Jockey Club), Sulamani (Prix du Jockey Club, Arlington Million, Turf Classic Invitational, Juddmonte International), Casual Conquest (Tattersalls Gold Cup) and Gitano Hernando (US Goodwood Stakes). Also responsible for the US Grade 2 winners Arvada, Atlando and Herboriste, the multiple German Group winner Alianthus and the very smart performers Asian Heights, Foreign Affairs, Harris Tweed, Mr Combustible, Samando, Songerie and Tau Ceti. Standing at Lanwades Stud, Newmarket. 2013 fee: Private.

HIGH CHAPARRAL (2000)

Sadler's Wells – Kasora (Darshaan). Racing record: Won 10 races, including the Derby, Irish Champion Stakes and Breeders' Cup Turf (twice). Stud record: First crop were two-year-olds in 2007. Best performers to date include the multiple Group 1 winner So You Think, Australian Group 1 winners Descarado, Dundeal, Monaco Consul and Shoot Out, Grade 1 Northern Dancer Turf Stakes winners Redwood and Wigmore Hall, Grade 1 Breeders Cup Turf winner Wrote, Group 2 Champagne Stakes winner Toronado, Group 2 Park Hill Stakes winner The Miniver Rose, Group 2 Prix de Sandringham winner Joanna and 12 Group 3 winners. Standing at Coolmore Stud, Ireland. 2013 fee: €25,000.

HOLY ROMAN EMPEROR (2004)

Danehill – L'On Vite (Secretariat). Racing Record: Won 4 races at 2 yrs including the Group 1 7f Prix Jean-Luc Lagardere, the Group 1 6f Waterford Phoenix Stakes and Group 2 6f Railway Stakes. Stud record: His best winners so far include Homecoming Queen (1,000 Guineas), Morandi (Group 1 Criterium de Saint Cloud), Australian Group 1 winner Rollout The Carpet, Banimpire, (5 Group wins including Group 2 Royal Whip Stakes and Group 2 Ribblesdale Stakes) and the Group 3 winners Ishvana, Sandslash, Leitir Mor, Maureen and Sunday Times. Standing at Coolmore Stud, Ireland. 2013 fee: €20,000.

HURRICANE RUN (2002)

Montjeu – Hold On (Surumu). Racing Record: Won 8 races including the Group 1 12f King George VI & Queen Elizabeth Diamond Stakes, Group 1 10.5f Tattersalls Gold Cup and

Group 1 12f Prix de l'Arc de Triomphe. Stud record: Had his first runners in 2010 and his best to date are First Cornerstone (Group 2 Futurity Stakes), the Group 3 Desmond Stakes winners Future Generation and Freedom, Kreem (Prix du Lys), Don't Hurry Me (Group 3 Prix Penelope), Memphis Tennessee (Group 3 Ormonde Stakes) and 8 listed winners including Arizona Run, Barbican, Charleston Lady, Mohedian Lady and Racemate. Standing at Gestut Ammerland, Germany. 2013 fee: €9,000.

IFFRAAJ (2001)

Zafonic – Pastorale (Nureyev). Racing Record: Won 7 races including the Group 2 7f Park Stakes (twice), the Group 2 7f Betfair Cup (Lennox St) and the 6f Wokingham Stakes. Stud record: First runners came in 2010 when he had more winners (38) than any first-crop European sire ever. His best to date are Wootton Bassett (Group 1 Prix Jean-Luc Lagardere), the New Zealand Group 2 winner Fix, the Group 3 winners Espirita and Stay Alive and 6 listed winners abroad. Standing at Kildangan Stud, Ireland. 2013 fee €10,000.

INTENSE FOCUS (2006)

Giant's Causeway – Daneleta (Danehill). Racing record: Won the 2-y-o Group 1 7f Dewhurst Stakes. Stud record: First runners appear in 2013. Standing at Ballylinch Stud, Ireland. 2013 fee: €5,500.

INTIKHAB (1994)

Red Ransom – Crafty Example (Crafty Prospector). Racing record: 8 wins including the Diomed Stakes and the Queen Anne Stakes. Stud record: Sire of Snow Fairy (Queen Elizabeth II Cup in Japan (twice), Oaks, Irish Oaks, Cathay Pacific Hong Kong Cup), Red Evie (Group 1 Lockinge Stakes & Group 1 Matron Stakes), Paita (Group 1 Criterium de Saint-Cloud), the Group 3 winners Ascertain, Glen's Diamond, Hoh Mike, Moon Unit, Toupie and Tell Dad, plus 11 listed performers including Indiana Gal, Les Fazzani and Without A Prayer. Standing at Derrinstown Stud, Ireland. 2013 fee: €5,500.

INVINCIBLE SPIRIT (1997)

Green Desert – Rafha (Kris). Racing record:

7 wins, notably the Group 1 Sprint Cup at 5 yrs. Stud record: First runners in 2006. High-class sire of the dual Group 1 winner Lawman (French Derby & Prix Jean Prat), Fleeting Spirit (July Cup, Temple Stakes, Flying Childers Stakes and Molecomb Stakes), Grade 1 Breeders Cup Juvenile winner Vale Of York, Moonlight Cloud (Group 1 Prix Maurice de Gheest & Prix du Moulin), Yosai (three Group 1 wins in Australia), Mayson (Group 1 July Cup), Hooray & Rosdhu Queen (both Group 1 Cheveley Park Stakes), Lawman (Group 1 Prix Jean Prat), and the following eight Group 2 winners - Conquest, Our Jonathan, Madame Trop Vite, Zebedee, Allied Powers, Campfire Glow, Captain Marvelous and Spirit Song. Standing at the Irish National Stud. 2013 fee: €65,000.

JEREMY (2003)

Danehill Dancer – Glint in Her Eye (Arazi). Racing record: Won 4 races including the Group 2 Betfred Mile at Sandown and the Group 3 7f Jersey Stakes. Stud record: First runners 2011. Sire of the winners of 64 races to date including Yellow Rosebud (Group 3 Concorde Stakes and Group 3 1,000 Guineas Trial) and the Irish 1,000 Guineas third Princess Sinead. Standing at Garryrichard Stud, Ireland. 2013 fee: €3,000.

KHELEYF (2001)

Green Desert – Society Lady (Mr Prospector). Racing record: Won 3 races including the Group 3 Jersey Stakes. Stud record: An excellent source of two-year-old winners, his best so far are Sayif (Group 2 Diadem Stakes), Penny's Picnic (Group 2 Criterium de Maisons Laffitte), Percolator (Group 3 Prix du Bois) and 10 listed winners including Captain Ramius, Playfellow (third in the Group 2 Champagne Stakes) and Vladimir (third in the Group 1 Prix Morny). Standing at Dalham Hall Stud, Newmarket. 2013 fee: £6,000.

KODIAC (2001)

Danehill – Rafha (Kris). Racing Record: Won 4 races here and in the UAE over 6f and 7f including the Datel Trophy and Group 3 placed. Stud record: His first runners appeared in 2010 and he's had over 50 individual 2-y-o winners in 3 seasons. To date he has 6 listed winners to his name – Bathwick (Ripon Champion Two Year old Trophy), Kohala (St Hugh's Stakes), Sweet Cecily (Bosra Sham Stakes), Indigo River (Sweet Life Stakes in the USA), Star Kodiac and Ileny Princess (both in Italy) and the Group 3 placed Stone Of Folca and Eastern Sun. Standing at Tally Ho Stud, Ireland. 2013 fee: €7,500.

KYLLACHY (1998)

Pivotal – Pretty Poppy (Song). Racing record: Winner of 6 races including the Group 1 Nunthorpe Stakes at 4 yrs. Stud record: First runners in 2006. Sire of the Group 1 Nunthorpe Stakes and Group 2 Temple Stakes winner Sole Power, the Group 1 6f Golden Shaheen winner Krypton Factor, Hong Kong Group 1 winner Dim Sum, the Group 2 winners Arabian Gleam, Penitent and Tariq and numerous smart performers including Awinnersgame, Befortyfour, Mood Music, Dragon Plus, Gracia Directa and Noble Hachy. Standing at Cheveley Park Stud, Newmarket. 2013 fee: £12,500.

LAWMAN (2004)

Invincible Spirit – Laramie (Gulch). Racing Record: Won four races including the Group 1 Prix du Jockey Club and the Group Prix Jean Prat. Stud record: First runners 2011. Has had a good start at stud with winners such as Most Improved (Group 1 St James's Palace Stakes), Law Enforcement (Group 1 Premio Gran Criterium), Just The Judge (Group 2 Rockfel Stakes), Loi (Group 3 Prix de Conde), Forces of Darkness (Prix Minerve), Lady Wingshot (Group 3 Fairy Bridge Stakes) and US Law (Group 3 Prix Thomas Bryon). Ballylinch Stud, Ireland. 2013 fee: €20,000.

LEMON DROP KID (1996)

Kingmambo – Charming Lassie (Seattle Slew). Racing record: Won the Belmont Stakes, Whitney Handicap and Woodward Stakes (all Grade 1 events). Stud record: Best performers to date include the US Grade 1 winners Richard's Kid, Santa Teresita, Christmas Kid, Cittronade and Lemon's Forever and eight Group/Grade 2 winners (Bronze Cannon, Balance The Books, Bear's Kid, Charitable Man, Dreamy Kid, Juniper Pass, Pisco Sour

and Wilkinson). Standing at Lane's End Farm, Kentucky. 2013 fee: $35,000.

LUCKY STORY (2001)

Kris S – Spring Flight (Miswaki). Racing record: Won 4 races including the Group 2 Champagne Stakes and Group 2 Vintage Stakes. Stud record: His best winners include the high-class Group 1 Golden Jubilee and Group 2 Coventry Stakes winner Art Connoisseur, the listed Redcar Two-Year-Old Trophy winner Lucky Like, the listed winner Royal Rascal, the Group-placed Lucky Rave and the triple listed-placed Hartley. Died 2010.

MAJOR CADEAUX (2004)

Cadeaux Genereux – Maine Lobster (Woodman). Racing record: Won 4 races including the Group 2 Sandown Mile, the Group 2 7f John of Gaunt Stakes and the Group 3 7f Greenham Stakes. Stud record: His first two-year-olds appear in 2013. Standing at Bearstone Stud. 2013 fee: £3,500.

MANDURO (2002)

Monsun – Mandellicht (Be My Guest). Racing Record: Won the Group 1 1m Prix Jacques Le Marois, the Group 1 10f Prince of Wales's Stakes and Group 1 10f Prix d'Ispahan. Stud record: His first runners appeared in 2011. To date his best runners are Mandaean (Group 1 Criterium de Saint Cloud), Bonfire (Group 2 Dante Stakes), Fractional (Group 3 Prix Quincey) and Trois Lunes (Group 3 Prix Vanteaux). Standing at Haras du Logis, France. 2013 fee: €10,000.

MARJU (1988)

Last Tycoon – Flame of Tara (Artaius). Racing record: 3 wins including the St James's Palace Stakes and runner-up in the Derby. Stud record: Sire of the high-class Soviet Song (5 Group 1 wins including the Sussex Stakes), the multiple Hong Kong Group 1 winner Viva Pataca, the US Grade 1 and Group 1 Singapore Airlines International Gold Cup winner Chinchon, My Emma Group 1 Prix Vermeille), Sil Sila (Prix de Diane), Marju Snip (Group 1 Australasian Oaks) and numerous smart performers including Asset, Brunel, Green Destiny, Mufaarh, Munjiz, Naheef, Saturn and Watar. Retired 2011.

MASTERCRAFTSMAN (2006)

Danehill Dancer – Starlight Dreams (Black Tie Affair). Racing record: Won 7 races, notably the Phoenix Stakes, National Stakes, St James's Palace Stakes and Irish 2,000 Guineas (all Group 1 races). Stud record: His first two Year Olds race in 2013. Standing at Coolmore Stud, Ireland. 2013 fee: €12,500.

MEDAGLIA D'ORO (1999)

El Prado – Cappucino Bay (Bailjumper). Racing record: Won the Travers Stakes, Jim Dandy Stakes and San Felipe Stakes. Stud record: Best winners include the US champion Rachel Alexandra (five Grade 1 wins) and the Group/Grade 1 winners C. S. Silk, Champagne d'Oro, Gabby's Golden Gal, Passion For Gold, Marketing Mix, Plum Pretty, Violence and Warrior's Reward. Standing at Jonabell Farm, Kentucky. 2013 fee: $100,000.

MEDICEAN (1997)

Machiavellian – Mystic Goddess (Storm Bird). Racing record: 6 wins including the Lockinge Stakes and Eclipse. Stud record: First runners in 2005. Sire of very smart Dutch Art (Prix Morny, Middle Park), the smart performer Nannina (Fillies' Mile, Coronation Stakes), Capponi and Al Shemali (both Dubai Group 1 winners), the very smart miler Bankable (Dubai Group 2 and Group 3 winners), Siyouma (Group 1 Sun Chariot Stakes and Group 1 E P Taylor Stakes), Almerita (Group 1 German Oaks), Chevron (Group 1 Raffles International Cup), Bayrir (Grade 1 Secretariat Stakes), Hong Kong Group 1 winner Mr Medici and the Group 2 British Champions Fillies and Mares Stakes Sapphire. Standing at Cheveley Park Stud. 2013 fee: £10,000.

MIZZEN MAST (1998)

Cozzene – Kinema (Graustark). Racing record: Won the Grade 1 Malibu Stakes and the Grade 2 Strub Stakes. Stud record: His best to date include the Grade 1 winners Midships (Charles Whittingham Stakes), Mast Track (Hollywood Gold Cup), Ultimate Eagle (Hollywood Derby), Flotilla (Breeders Cup Juvenile Fillies), Mizdirection (Breeders Cup Turf Sprint) and the Grade 2 winners Jibboom and Madeo. Standing at Juddmonte Farms, Kentucky. 2013 fee: $15,000.

MONTJEU (1996)

Sadler's Wells – Floripedes (Top Ville). Racing record: Won 11 races including the Prix de l'Arc de Triomphe and King George VI and Queen Elizabeth Diamond Stakes. Stud record: First runners in 2004. A top-class stallion son of Sadler's Wells. Sire of the top-class Hurricane Run (Irish Derby, Prix de l'Arc de Triomphe, Tattersalls Gold Cup and King George), Authorized (Racing Post Trophy, Derby & Juddmonte International), Motivator (Racing Post Trophy and Derby), Camelot (four Group 1's including the 2,000 Guineas and Derby), Pour Moi (Derby) and Fame And Glory (Racing Post Trophy, Irish Derby, Ascot Gold Cup), St Nicholas Abbey (four Group 1 wins), Masked Marvel (St Leger) and the high-class Alessandro Volta, Frozen Fire, Honolulu, Jan Vermeer Corre Caminos, Jukebox Jury, Macarthur, Montmartre, Papal Bull and Scorpion. Died in 2012.

MOSS VALE (2001)

Shinko Forest – Wolf Cleugh (Last Tycoon). Racing record: Won 8 races including the Group 2 5f Prix Gros Chene, the Group 3 6f Phoenix Sprint Stakes and the Group 3 6f Greenlands Stakes. Stud record: First runners 2011. A modest start at stud with over 20 winners. Standing at Haras de la Rousseliere. 2013 fee: €2,500.

MOUNT NELSON (2004)

Rock of Gibraltar – Independence (Selkirk). Racing record: Won the Group 1 1m Criterium International at 2 yrs and the Group 1 10f Eclipse Stakes. Stud Record: His first two-year-olds ran in 2012. Sire of the winners of 24 races including Purr Along (Group 3 Prix du Calvados). Standing at Newsells Park Stud, Herts. 2013 fee: £6,000.

MR GREELEY (1992)

Gone West – Long Legend (Reviewer). Racing record: Triple Grade 3 winner in USA and runner-up in the Grade 1 Breeders' Cup Sprint. Stud record: Sire of Crusade (2011 2-y-o Group 1 6f Middle Park Stakes), Finsceal Beo (English & Irish 1,000 Guineas), Saoirse Abu (Phoenix Stakes, Moyglare Stud Stakes), Reel Buddy (Sussex Stakes), US Grade 1 winners Aruna, El Corredor, Celtic Melody, Nonsuch

Bay, Western Aristocrat and Whywhywhy, the Australian Group 1 winner Miss Kournikova and numerous other Group/Graded stakes winners. Died 2010.

MYBOYCHARLIE (2005)

Danetime – Dulceata (Rousillon). Racing record: Won the Group 1 6f Prix Morny and the Group 3 6f Anglesey Stakes, both at 2 yrs. Stud record: First two-year-olds 2013. Standing at Haras de Mezeray. 2013 fee: €6,500.

NAYEF (1999)

Gulch – Height of Fashion (Bustino). Racing record: Won 9 races including the Champion Stakes and the Juddmonte International Stakes. Stud record: His first crop were two-year-olds in 2007 and his best winners so far are Tamayuz (dual Group 1 winner in France), Lady Marian (Group 1 Prix de l'Opera), Spacious (dual Group 2 winner and 1,000 Guineas second), Tabassum (Group 3 7f Oh So Sharp Stakes), the very smart Confront (Group 3 1m Joel Stakes), Hawaafez (Group 3 Cumberland Lodge Stakes), Tasaday (Group 3 Prix des Reservoirs) and the Italian listed winner and Group 1 second Rosa Eglanteria. Standing at Nunnery Stud, Norfolk. 2013 fee: £9,000.

NEW APPROACH (2005)

Galileo – Park Express (Ahonoora). Racing record: Won five Group 1 events including the Derby, the Champion Stakes and the Irish Champion Stakes. Stud record: First two year olds appeared in 2012. Sire of the champion 2-y-o Dawn Approach (Group 1 Dewhurst Stakes, Group 1 National Stakes, Group 2 Coventry Stakes), New Fangled (Group 3 Albany Stakes) and Tha'ir (listed Chesham Stakes). Standing at: Dalham Hall Stud, Newmarket. 2013 stud fee: £50,000.

NORSE DANCER (2000)

Halling – River Patrol (Rousillon). Racing record: Won 4 races including the Group 3 Earl of Sefton Stakes and the Group 3 Sovereign Stakes and placed in numerous Group 1 events. Stud record: His first crop appeared in 2010 and the listed 10f winner Dorcas Lane (also placed in the Lancashire Oaks and the Ribblesdale Stakes) is comfortably the best of his runners to date. Standing at Littleton Stud. 2013 fee: £2,500.

NOTNOWCATO (2002)

Inchinor – Rambling Rose (Cadeaux Genereux). Racing record: Won 7 races including the Group 1 10f Eclipse Stakes, the Group 1 10.5f Tattersalls Gold Cup and the Group 1 Juddmonte International. Stud record: First runners 2010. Sire of the winners of 43 races including the listed winner Chil The Kite and the US dual Grade 3 placed Miss Cato. Standing at Stanley House Stud, Newmarket. 2013 fee: £5,000.

OASIS DREAM (2001)

Green Desert – Hop (Dancing Brave). Racing record: Won 4 races, including the Middle Park Stakes, July Cup and Nunthorpe Stakes (all Group 1 events). Stud record: His first crop were two-year-olds in 2007 and he's built himself an outstanding reputation already with the Group 1 winners Aqlaam (Prix du Moulin), Arcano (Prix Morny), Lady Jane Digby (in Germany), Midday (Nassau Stakes, Breeders Cup Filly & Mare Turf), Naaqoos (Prix Jean-Luc Lagardere), Power (National Stakes & Irish 2,000 Guineas), Prohibit (King's Stand Stakes), Querari (in Italy) and Tuscan Evening (US Gamely Handicap), along with over 9 Group 2 scorers including Approve, Misheer, Monitor Closely, Showcasing and Sri Putra. Standing at Banstead Manor Stud, Newmarket. 2013 fee: £80,000.

ORATORIO (2002)

Danehill – Mahrah (Vaguely Noble). Racing record: Won the Prix Jean-Luc Lagardere (at 2 yrs), the Eclipse Stakes and Irish Champion Stakes. Stud record: His first crop were two-year-olds in 2009 and his best winners so far include the Group 1 Dewhurst Stakes winner Beethoven the New Zealand Group 1 winning 2-y-o Banchee, Australian Group 1 winner Manawanui, Australian Group 2 winner Torio's Quest, the Group 2 Vintage Stakes winner King Torus and the Group 2 Windsor Forest Stakes winner Lolly For Dolly. Now standing at Avontuur Stud in South Africa.

PASTORAL PURSUITS (2001)

Bahamian Bounty – Star (Most Welcome).
Racing record: Won 6 races including the
Group 1 6f July Cup, Group 2 7f Park Stakes
and Group 3 6f Sirenia Stakes. Stud record:
His first crop were runners in 2009 and his
winners to date are Pastoral Player (Group 3
John of Gaunt Stakes), Rose Blossom (Group
3 Summer Stakes), the listed winners Angel's
Pursuit and Marine Commando and the triple
Group 3 placed Sagramor. Standing at the
National Stud. 2013 fee: £5,500.

PICCOLO (1991)

Warning – Woodwind (Whistling Wind).
Racing record: 4 wins including Nunthorpe
Stakes and Kings Stand Stakes. Stud record:
Sire of the Group 1 Nunthorpe Stakes winner
La Cucaracha, the Australian Group 1 winners
Picaday and Temple Of Boom, the Group
2 winners Ajigolo, Express Air, St Trinians,
Tiddliwinks, Winker Watson and Flying Blue
(in Hong Kong), plus numerous other smart
performers including Aegean Dancer, Bond
Boy (Steward's Cup winner), Hoh Hoh Hoh,
Hunting Lion, Lipocco, Pan Jammer, Pearl Flute
and Pickle. Standing at Throckmorton Court
Stud. 2012 fee: £3,000.

PIVOTAL (1993)

Polar Falcon – Fearless Revival (Cozzene).
Racing record: 4 wins including the Nunthorpe
Stakes and King's Stand Stakes. Stud record:
First runners in 2000. An outstanding sire
whose best winners include the high-class
Excellent Art (St James's Palace Stakes), Falco
(French 2,000 Guineas), Halfway To Heaven
(Irish 1,00 Guineas, Nassau Stakes and Sun
Chariot Stakes), Kyllachy (Nunthorpe Stakes),
Sariska (Oaks and Irish Oaks), Immortal Verse
(dual Group 1 winning miler) and Somnus
(Sprint Cup, Prix de la Foret, Prix Maurice de
Gheest), the very smart Beauty Is Truth (Group
2 Prix du Gros-Chene), Captain Rio (Group 2
Criterium des Maisons-Laffitte), Chorist (Pretty
Polly Stakes), Golden Apples (triple US Grade
1 winner), Leo (Group 2 Royal Lodge Stakes),
Peeress (Lockinge Stakes, Sun Chariot Stakes),
Pivotal Point (Group 2 Diadem Stakes) and
Virtual (Lockinge Stakes) and numerous very
smart performers including Falco (French
2,000 Guineas), Izzi Top (Prix Jean Romanet

and Pretty Polly Stakes) Megahertz (2 US
Grade 1 events), Regal Parade (Haydock Sprint
Cup), Silvester Lady (German Oaks), Siyouni
(2009 2-y-o Group 1 Prix Jean-Luc Lagardere)
and Saoire (Irish 1000 Guineas). Standing at
Cheveley Park Stud, Newmarket. 2013 fee:
£45,000.

RAIL LINK (2003)

Dansili – Docklands (Theatrical).
Racing record: Ran 7, won 5. Prix de L'Arc de
Triomphe, Prix Niel, Grand Prix de
Paris, Prix du Lys. Stud record: First runners
2011. Sire of the winners of 61 races including
Bugie d'Amor (Group 3 Premio Dormello),
Sediciosa (Group 3 Prix de Royaumont),
the listed winner and Group 2 Italian Derby
second Wild Wolf and the French Group 1
placed Last Train. Standing at Banstead Manor
Stud, Newmarket. 2013 fee: £5,000.

RAVEN'S PASS (2005)

Elusive Quality – Ascutney (Lord At War).
Racing record: Won 6 races, notably the Group
1 1m Queen Elizabeth II Stakes and the Grade
1 10f Breeders Cup Classic. Stud record: His
first crop of two-year-olds in 2012 included
Steeler (Group 2 Royal Lodge Stakes winner
and Group 1 Racing Post Trophy second), the
listed Chesham Stakes third and subsequent
listed UAE 1,000 Guineas winner Lovely Pass.
Standing at Kildangan Stud, Ireland. 2013 fee:
€10,000.

ROCK OF GIBRALTAR (1999)

Danehill – Offshore Boom (Be My Guest).
Racing record: Won seven Group 1 races
including the Dewhurst Stakes, 2,000 Guineas,
St James's Palace Stakes and Sussex Stakes.
Stud record: The sire of 9 Group 1 winners
including the US dual Grade 1 winner
Diamondrella, Eagle Mountain, Mount Nelson
(Eclipse and Criterium International), Samitar
(Irish 1,000 Guineas and Garden City Stakes),
dual Group 1 winning sprinter Society Rock
and Varenar (Prix de la Foret) as well as close
on 40 other Group winners. Standing at
Coolmore Stud, Ireland. 2013 fee: €17,500.

ROYAL APPLAUSE (1993)

Waajib – Flying Melody (Auction Ring).
Racing record: Winner of 9 races, including

Middle Park at 2 yrs and the Haydock Park Sprint Cup at 4 yrs (both Group 1). Stud record: First runners in 2001. Sire of the US dual Grade 1 winner Ticker Tape, the Group/Grade 2 winners Acclamation, Battle Of Hastings, Finjaan, Lovelace, Mister Cosmi, Nevisian Lad, Please Sing and Whatsthescript and numerous other very smart performers including Crime Scene, triple Group 3 winner Majestic Missile, Peak To Creek and Prince Siegfried. Standing at The Royal Studs, Norfolk. 2013 fee: £9,000.

SAKHEE'S SECRET (2004)
Sakhee – Palace Street (Secreto).
Racing record: July Cup. Stud record: Sire of 24 individual first-cop winners in 2012, but no stakes performers. Standing at Whitsbury Manor Stud. 2013 fee: £5,500.

SEA THE STARS (2006)
Cape Cross – Urban Sea (Miswaki).
Racing record: Won 9 races including the Derby, 2,000 Guineas, Prix de L'Arc de Triomphe, Irish Champion Stakes, Juddmonte International Stakes, Eclipse Stakes. Stud record: First two-year-olds appear in 2013. Standing at Gilltown Stud, Ireland. Stud fee: €85,000.

SELKIRK (1988)
Sharpen Up – Annie Edge (Nebbiolo).
Racing record: 6 wins including Queen Elizabeth II Stakes, Lockinge Stakes, Beefeater Gin Celebration Mile and Challenge Stakes. Stud record: A leading British-based stallion, he has sired 15 individual Group 1 winners. His best performers include Cityscape (Dubai Duty Free), Leadership (Gran Premio d'Italia), the Premio Presidente Repubblica winners Altieri and Selmis, Border Arrow, Etlaala, Favourable Terms (Nassau Stakes), Field of Hope (Prix de la Foret), Highest, Kastoria (Irish St Leger), Nahrain (Prix de l'Opera & Flower Bowl Handicap), Pipedreamer, Prince Kirk (Prix d'Ispahan), Red Bloom (Fillies' Mile), Scott's View, Squeak (Beverly Hills Handicap), Sulk (Prix Marcel Boussac), Tam Lin, The Trader, Tranquil Tiger, Trans Island, Wince (1000 Guineas) and Wordly. Stood at Lanwades Stud until his death in 2013.

SHAMARDAL (2002)
Giant's Causeway – Helsinki (Machiavellian).
Racing record: Won Dewhurst Stakes, French 2,000 Guineas, French Derby and St James's Palace Stakes. Stud record: His first European runners appeared in 2009 and he's already sired 8 Group 1 winners including Casamento (Racing Post Trophy), Lope De Vega (French 2,000 Guineas and French Derby), Sagawara (Prix Saint-Alary) and the Italian winners Amaron, Crackerjack King and Zazou. Standing at Kildangan Stud, Ireland. 2013 fee: €50,000.

SHIROCCO (2001)
Monsun – So Sedulous (The Minstrel).
Racing Record: Won 7 races including the German Derby, French Derby, Breeders Cup Turf and Coronation Cup (all Group 1, 12f events). Stud record: First runners in 2010 and he has four Group winners to his name so far - Grand Vent (Group 2 Prix Noailles), Arrigo (Group 2 Oppenheim Union Rennen), Wild Coco (Group 2 Park Hill Stakes) and Hartani (Curragh Cup) and four listed winners including the St Leger second Brown Panther. Standing at Dalham Hall Stud. 2013 fee: £7,000.

SINNDAR (1997)
Grand Lodge – Sinntara (Lashkari).
Racing record: Won 7 races, notably the Derby and the Prix de l'Arc de Triomphe. Stud record: First runners in 2004. Sire of the top-class colt and multiple Group 1 winner Youmzain, the 2-y-o Group 1 Prix Marcel Boussac winner Rosanara, Shawanda (Irish Oaks and Prix Vermeille), Shareta (Prix Vermeille and Yorkshire Oaks) and the Group 2/3 winners Aqaleem, Four Sins, Gertrude Bell, Louvain, Moonlight Dance, Pictavia and Visindar. Standing at Haras de Bonneval, France. 2013 fee: €6,000.

SIR PERCY (2003)
Mark of Esteem – Percy's Lass (Blakeney).
Racing Record: Won the Derby and the Dewhurst Stakes. Stud record: First runners 2011. Sire of the winners of 80 races including Alla Speranza (Group 3 Kilternan Stakes) and the listed winners Bomar and Coquet. Standing at Lanwades Stud, Newmarket. 2013 fee: £7,000.

SIXTIES ICON (2003)
Galileo – Love Divine (Diesis).
Racing record: Won 8 races including the Group 1 St Leger, the Group 2 Jockey Club Cup and four Group events. Stud Record: His first two year olds appeared in 2012 and he's had a good start, with winners like Chilworth Icon (Group 3 Premio Primi Passi & listed Woodcote Stakes), Cruck Realta and Effie B (both listed-placed winners). Standing at Norman Court Stud, Wiltshire. 2013 stud fee: £8,500.

SLEEPING INDIAN (2001)
Indian Ridge – Las Flores (Sadler's Wells).
Racing record: Won 6 races including the Group 2 7f Challenge Stakes, the Group 3 7f Hungerford Stakes and three listed events. Stud record: First runners 2010. Sire of Hototo (listed Windsor Castle Stakes), Melbourne Memories (listed Bosra Sham Stakes), Night Carnation (Group 3 Sandown sprint winner and Grade 1 placed in Canada), Indian Jade (third in the Group 1 Prix Jean-Luc Lagardere) and Lewisham (second in the Group 2 July Stakes). Standing at Beechwood Grange Stud. 2013 fee: £3,000.

SMART STRIKE (1992)
Mr Prospector – Classy 'n Smart (Smarten).
Racing record: Won 8 races in the USA including the Grade 2 8.5f Philip H Iselin Handicap and the Grade 3 Salvator Mile. Stud record: Best winners include the top-class colt Curlin (Preakness Stakes, Dubai World Cup, Breeders Cup Classic), the US Grade 1 winners English Channel, Fabulous Strike, Furthest Land, Lookin At Lucky, My Miss Aurelia, Never Retreat, Shadow Cast, Soaring Free and Square Eddie, the Japan Cup winner Fleetstreet Dancer and 14 Group 2 winners including Air Support (Bowling Green Handicap & Virginia Derby), Centre Court (Mrs Revere Stakes & Lake George Stakes), and Dominus (Bernard Baruch Stakes and Dwyer Stakes). Standing at Lane's End Farm, Kentucky. 2013 fee: €85,000.

STREET CRY (1998)
Machiavellian – Helen Street (Troy).
Racing record: 5 wins including the Group 1 10f Dubai World Cup and the 9f Stephen Foster Handicap (Grade 1 in the USA).

Stud record: First runners in 2006. Sire of the outstanding multiple Grade 1 winning racemare Zenyatta and the Group/Grade 1 winners Street Sense (Breeders' Cup Juvenile, Kentucky Derby, Travers Stakes), Cry And Catch Me (Oak Leaf Stakes), Majestic Roi (Sun Chariot Stakes), Street Boss (Triple Bend Invitational, Bing Crosby Handicap), Seventh Street (Go For Wand Handicap, Apple Blossom Handicap), Street Hero (Norfolk Stakes), Here Comes Ben (Forego Handicap), Victor's Cry (Shoemaker Mile Handicap), Street Hero (Norfolk Stakes), Zaidan (Hong Kong Classic Cup) and the Australian Group 1 winners Shocking (Melbourne Cup) and Whobegotyou (Caulfield Guineas and Yalumba Stakes), the Group 2 Dante Stakes winner Carlton House, the Ribblesdale Stakes winner Princess Highway and Group 2 Champagne Stakes winner Saamidd. Standing at Jonabell Stud Farm, Kentucky. 2013 fee: $100,000.

TAGULA (1993)
Taufan – Twin Island (Standaan).
Racing record: Won 4 races including the Group 1 6f Prix Morny (at 2 yrs) and the Group 3 7f Supreme Stakes. Stud record: Sires plenty of winners, amongst the best being the high-class 2-y-o and miler Canford Cliffs, the Group 2 Prix du Gros-Chene winner Tax Free, the Group 2 Royal Lodge Stakes winner Atlantis Prince, the German Group 2 winner Tagshira, the smart Group 2 placed Beaver Patrol and the listed winners Bakewell Tart, Double Vie, Drawnfromthepast, King Orchisios, Macaroon, Pure Poetry and Red Millennium. Standing at the Rathbarry Stud in Ireland. 2013 fee: €4,000.

TAMAYUZ (2005)
Nayef – Al Ishq (Nureyev).
Racing Record: Won the Group 1 1m Prix Jacques Le Marois and the Group 1 Prix Jean Prat. Stud Record: His first two year olds appeared in 2012 and he had a very good start. His winners included Sir Prancealot (Group 2 Flying Childers Stakes), the Japanese Group 3 winner Meiner Eternel and the Group-placed Taayel and Reyaadah. Standing at Derrinstown Stud in Ireland. 2013 fee: €15,000.

TEOFILO (2004)

Galileo – Speirbhhean (Danehill). Racing Record: Won 5 races at 2 yrs including the Group 1 Dewhurst Stakes and the Group 1 National Stakes. Stud record: First runners 2011. His best runners to date are Parish Hall (Group 1 Dewhurst Stakes), Loch Garman (Group 1 Criterium International), Light Heavy (Group 2 Derrinstown Stud Derby Trial, US Grade 2 winner Amira's Prince, the Group 3 winners Havana Gold, Remember Alexander and Trading Leather, and the listed winning filly and Group 1 Fillies' Mile second Roz. Standing at Kildangan Stud, Ireland. 2013 fee: €35,000.

THREE VALLEYS (2001)

Diesis – Skiable (Niniski). Racing Record: Won 5 races including the 2-y-o Group 3 Coventry Stakes and, in America, the Grade 2 1m Del Mar Breeders Cup Handicap and the Grade 3 8.5f Oceanport Stakes. Stud record. His first runners appeared in 2011 and his bets to date are the Italian Group 2 second Saint Bernard and the listed-placed The Nile – both useful. Standing at Banstead Manor Stud, Newmarket. 2013 fee: £5,000.

VERGLAS (1994)

Highest Honor – Rahaam (Secreto). Racing record: Won 3 races including the Group 3 6f Coventry Stakes. Stud record: Sire of the Group 1 French 2,000 Guineas winner Silver Frost, the Group 1 Prix Jean Prat winner Stormy River, the Australian Group 1 Mackinnon Stakes winner Glass Harmonium, the US dual Grade 2 winners Blackdoun and Grandeur, the Group 3 winners Love Lockdown, Ozone Bere, Spirited One, Tropical Paradise and Wilside, as well as numerous listed winners. Died 2011.

WAR FRONT (2003)

Danzig – Starry Dreamer (Rubiano). Race record: Won four races at 3 and 4 yrs including the Grade 2 6f Alfred G Vanderbilt Breeders Cup Handicap at Saratoga. Stud record: Has had an excellent start at stud. In his first two crops he has sired three US Grade 1 winners – Data Link, Summer Soiree and The Factor, along with the Grade 2 winners Soldat and State Of Play and the Grade 3 winners Declaration Of War and Summer Front. Standing at Claiborne Farm, Kentucky. 2013 fee: $80,000.

WHIPPER (2001)

Miesque's Son – Myth To Reality (Sadler's Wells). Racing record: Won 6 races including the 6f Prix Morny, the 6.5 Prix Maurice de Gheest and the 1m Prix Jacques le Marois (all Group 1 events). Stud record: His first runners appeared on the track in 2009 and to date the best of them have been Wizz Kid (Group 1 Prix de L'Abbaye and Group 2 Prix Gros Chene), the Group 2 Prix Daniel Wildenstein winner Royal Bench, the Group 3 winners Dolled Up, Malagenia and Topeka, and eight listed winners including the Group 1 second Willie The Whipper. Standing at Haras du Mezeray. 2013 fee: €8,000.

WINKER WATSON (2005)

Piccolo – Bonica (Rousillon). Racing record: Unbeaten as a 2-y-o, won 3 races including the Group 2 Norfolk Stakes and the Group 2 July Stakes. Stud record: First runners appear in 2013. Standing at Norman Court Stud. 2013 fee: £2,500.

ZAMINDAR (1994)

Gone West – Zaizafon (The Minstrel). Racing record: Won the Group 3 6f Prix de Cabourg at 2 yrs and was placed in the Prix Morny and the Prix de la Salamandre. Stud record: A full-brother to the champion Zafonic. He has sired a number of very good fillies, notably the outstanding Zarkava (five Group 1 wins including the Prix de l'Arc de Triomphe), Darjina (three Group 1 wins), the Group 1 Prix Saint-Alary winner Coquerelle, the Group 1 Falmouth Stakes winner Timepiece and the Group 1 French 1,000 Guineas winner Zenda. He also has the Group 2 winners Crossharbour and Modern Look, as well as the Group 3 winners Jubilation, So Beautiful, Starboard and Zantenda. Standing at Banstead Manor Stud, Newmarket. 2013 fee: £10,000.

Sires index

1128, 1472, 1630, 1674
English Channel 292
Exceed And Excel 39, 80, 97, 99, 159, 270, 306, 327, 403, 421, 470, 685, 735, 772, 780, 782, 795, 796, 840, 847, 873, 875, 880, 890, 891, 990, 1122, 1178, 1295, 1309, 1367, 1388, 1485, 1486, 1521, 1538, 1576
Excellent Art 14, 56, 69, 429, 700, 745, 762, 933, 942, 950, 955, 960, 1120, 1302, 1328, 1396
Exchange Rate 367, 1582

Fastnet Rock 41, 119, 214, 266, 340, 619, 622, 843, 860, 921, 968, 1426, 1443
Firebreak 6, 59, 195, 435, 963, 1515
First Defence 307, 315, 319, 1313, 1672
Footstepsinthesand 61, 247, 261, 390, 515, 528, 529, 534, 850, 919, 1028, 1127, 1158, 1258, 1319, 1345, 1395, 1406, 1435, 1607

Galileo 30, 91, 98, 141, 150, 216, 222, 224, 271, 289, 321, 369, 370, 449, 461, 463, 465, 549, 617, 637, 718, 750, 1075, 1077, 1214, 1217, 1219, 1228, 1229, 1231, 1232, 1233, 1240, 1241, 1245, 1246, 1248, 1250, 1251, 1253, 1351, 1356, 1427, 1650, 1667, 1673
Giant's Causeway 661, 826, 1235, 1425, 1613
Gold Sphinx 1478
Grand Slam 235
Green Desert 183, 409, 1378

Haatef 260, 414, 1119, 1297
Halling 19, 281, 591, 687, 940, 1424, 1506, 1511
Hard Spun 178, 911
Heliostatic 382
Henny Hughes 349
Henrythenavigator 157, 460, 979, 1025, 1115, 1571
Hernando 348, 1423
High Chaparral 10, 90, 179, 296, 377, 394, 411, 468,

491, 612, 659, 666, 689, 730, 776, 866, 939, 947, 953, 959, 977, 980, 1055, 1063, 1218, 1296, 1346, 1363, 1417, 1418, 1471, 1633, 1640
Holy Roman Emperor 102, 243, 287, 297, 401, 765, 784, 793, 823, 828, 846, 918, 1126, 1209, 1223, 1227, 1249, 1293, 1324, 1391, 1399, 1452, 1517, 1560, 1602, 1629
Hurricane Run 47, 775, 879, 1314, 1453

Iffraaj 167, 244, 336, 339, 342, 384, 424, 707, 746, 779, 912, 925, 969, 1080, 1113, 1117, 1131, 1415, 1482, 1490, 1622, 1668
Indesatchel 1087
Intense Focus 138, 140, 142, 144, 145, 152, 393, 428, 513, 754, 865, 900, 1147, 1450
Intikhab 67, 81, 665, 725, 898, 970, 1449, 1458, 1523
Invincible Spirit 36, 77, 105, 176, 223, 225, 240, 245, 363, 364, 379, 415, 417, 457, 505, 521, 527, 613, 632, 638, 657, 658, 664, 696, 715, 717, 726, 731, 732, 771, 785, 790, 792, 800, 853, 855, 861, 884, 922, 1020, 1111, 1190, 1194, 1225, 1244, 1283, 1317, 1335, 1340, 1548, 1552, 1574, 1604, 1618, 1645, 1646, 1658

Jeremy 58, 156, 238, 268, 430, 438, 808, 901, 943, 1066, 1095

Kheleyf 12, 15, 45, 53, 115, 162, 265, 320, 333, 448, 642, 811, 1191, 1312, 1410, 1428, 1483, 1492, 1591
Kirkwall 497
Kitten's Joy 1310
Kodiac 106, 127, 331, 398, 404, 426, 484, 548, 704, 758, 786, 876, 976, 1046, 1074, 1149, 1380
Kyllachy 68, 248, 350, 532,

728, 757, 783, 814, 820, 856, 857, 882, 1032, 1104, 1108, 1142, 1375, 1465, 1525, 1609, 1644

Langfuhr 352
Lawman 54, 407, 542, 595, 701, 738, 952, 1051, 1159, 1192, 1262, 1357, 1563, 1573
Le Havre 547
Lemon Drop Kid 317, 347, 1461
Literato 1015
Lucky Story 117, 440, 1085

Major Cadeaux 166, 171, 329, 467, 883, 1173, 1479
Manduro 120, 232, 964, 1175, 1187, 1277
Marju 690, 938, 948, 1123, 1347, 1361
Mastercraftsman 22, 116, 123, 181, 434, 481, 506, 541, 756, 777, 797, 848, 878, 932, 995, 1031, 1037, 1133, 1145, 1167, 1211, 1331, 1333, 1422, 1439, 1442, 1569, 1575, 1610, 1596
Medaglia d'Oro 584, 794, 1532
Medicean 37, 51, 309, 397, 498, 510, 623, 1405, 1547, 1562, 1599, 1603, 1614
Mind Games 1383
Mizzen Mast 927, 941, 1291, 1648
Monsieur Bond 185
Monsun 48, 571
Montjeu 26, 442, 618, 667, 961, 1230, 1234, 1236, 1237, 1239, 1242, 1243, 1358, 1359, 1373, 1409, 1475, 1528, 1579, 1625
Moss Vale 345, 1069, 1481
Mount Nelson 18, 135, 194, 539, 994, 1088, 1114, 1169, 1180, 1181, 1184, 1326, 1384, 1520, 1592, 1612
Mr Greeley 158, 1292, 1651
Multiplex 966
Myboycharlie 131, 188, 354, 395, 436, 456, 518, 674, 676, 709, 1146, 1220, 1387, 1438, 1444, 1617, 1641
Naaqoos 423

Racing Trends

The following tables focus on those two-year-old races that seem to produce winners that improve the following year as three-year-olds. This type of analysis can enable us to select some of the best of this year's classic generation.

In the tables, the figure in the third column indicates the number of wins recorded as a three-year-old, with GW signifying a Group race winner at that age.

The horses listed below are the winners of the featured races in 2012. Anyone looking for horses to follow in the Group and Classic events of this season might well want to bear them in mind. I feel that those in bold text are particularly worthy of close scrutiny

Battle of Marengo	**Big Break**
Certify	**Dawn Approach**
Dundonnell	**Ghurair**
Havana Gold	**Just The Judge**
Kingsbarns	**Olympic Glory**
Restraint of Trade	Rosdhu Queen
Sir Patrick Moore	Steeler
Wentworth	

Lowther Stakes
York, 6 furlongs, August.

2000	Enthused	0
2001	Queen's Logic	1 GW
2002	Russian Rhythm	3 GW
2003	Carry On Katie	0
2004	Soar	0
2005	Flashy Wings	0
2006	Silk Blossom	0
2007	Nahoodh	1 GW
2008	Infamous Angel	0
2009	Lady of the Desert	1 GW
2010	Hooray	1
2011	Best Terms	0
2012	Rosdhu Queen	

One has to look back to Russian Rhythm for a filly that had a real impact on the following season's Group 1 events, but it remains of race of some importance. Rosdhu Queen isn't expected to stay the trip in the 1,000 Guineas, but she can surely win another Group race over sprint distances.

Dewhurst Stakes
Newmarket, 7 furlongs, October.

2000	Tobougg	0
2001	Rock Of Gibraltar	5 GW
2002	Tout Seul	0
2003	Milk It Mick	0
2004	Shamardal	3 GW
2005	Sir Percy	1 GW
2006	Teofilo	NR
2007	New Approach	3 GW
2008	Intense Focus	0
2009	Beethoven	1 GW
2010	Frankel	5GW
2011	Parish Hall	0
2012	Dawn Approach	

The Dewhurst Stakes remains our premier race for two-year-old colts. Frankel proved himself a real champion of course and Rock of Gibraltar was a real star in his year too. The other outstanding colts to win this in the last twenty years are Shamardal, Zafonic, Dr Devious, Grand Lodge, Sir Percy and New Approach. The latter's son, Dawn Approach, is strongly fancied to further enhance his reputation in the early classics and it will be interesting to see if he enters the Derby picture. .

Zetland Stakes
Newmarket, 10 furlongs, October/November.

2000	Worthily	0
2001	Alexandra Three D	2 GW
2002	Forest Magic	NR
2003	Fun And Games	NR
2004	Ayam Zaman	0
2005	Under The Rainbow	0
2006	Empire Day	NR
2007	Twice Over	2 GW
2008	Heliodor	1
2009	Take It To The Max	0
2010	Indigo Way	NR
2011	Mojave	0
2012	Restraint of Trade	

Previous winners include the St Leger and Coronation Cup winner Silver Patriarch, the good four-year-olds Double Eclipse and Rock Hopper, Bob's Return (also a St Leger hero), the Ascot Gold Cup winner Double Trigger and of course Twice Over who won four Group 1's during his career with Henry Cecil including as a 6-y-o in 2011. So there's clearly an emphasis on winners of the Zetland improving with age. Last year this was just a three-runner affair. The Godolphin owned Restraint Of Trade is by Authorized and should be suited by twelve furlongs this year. He can win again.

This race can often provide us with Group race or Classic pointers and in that regard the 90's winners Lammtarra and Rodrigo de Triano were outstanding and Haafhd won the 2,000 Guineas and the Champion Stakes. Azmeel trained on to win the Sandown Classic Trial and the Dee Stakes, but the race needs a pick-me-up. Just The Judge can do that by winning a Group 1 over a mile this season.

Cheveley Park Stakes
Newmarket, 6 furlongs, October.

2001	Queen's Logic	1 GW
2002	Airwave	1 GW
2003	Carry On Katie	0
2004	Magical Romance	0
2005	Donna Blini	1
2006	Indian Ink	1 GW
2007	Natagora	2 GW
2008	Serious Attitude	1 GW
2009	Special Duty	2GW
2010	Hooray	1
2011	Lightening Pearl	0
2012	Rosdhu Queen	

A number of these fillies have gone on to further Group race success. Indian Ink saved her best day for Royal Ascot, Natagora and Special Duty both went on to win the 1,000 Guineas and Serious Attitude returned to sprinting for another Group race success and the following year she won a Grade 1 sprint in Canada. Rosdhu Queen should follow suit and win more races at distances less than a mile.

Washington Singer Stakes
Newbury, 7 furlongs, August.

2000	Prizeman	0
2001	Funfair Wane	1
2002	Muqbil	1 GW
2003	Haafhd	3 GW
2004	Kings Quay	0
2005	Innocent Air	1
2006	Dubai's Touch	2
2007	Sharp Nephew	1
2008	Cry of Freedom	0
2009	Azmeel	2 GW
2010	Janood	0
2011	Fencing	0
2012	Just The Judge	

Veuve Clicquot Vintage Stakes
Goodwood, 7 furlongs, July.

2000	No Excuse Needed	1 GW
2001	Naheef	1 GW
2002	Dublin	1
2003	Lucky Story	0
2004	Shamardal	3 GW
2005	Sir Percy	1 GW
2006	Strategic Prince	0
2007	Rio De La Plata	0
2008	Orizaba	0
2009	Xtension	0
2010	King Torus	2
2011	Chandlery	0
2012	Olympic Glory	

All in all this race is very informative in terms of sorting out future stars, with the classic winners Sir Percy, Shamardal, Don't Forget Me, Dr Devious and Mister Baileys and the King George winner Petoski being the standouts of the past twenty years. It's been 8 years since Sir Percy won the Derby, but Olympic Glory has at least started the season well, winning the Group 3 Greenham Stakes. He'll win again this year at distances around a mile.

National Stakes, Curragh, 7f, September.

2000	Beckett	1
2001	Hawk Wing	1 GW
2002	Refuse To Bend	3 GW
2003	One Cool Cat	1 GW
2004	Dubawi	2 GW
2005	George Washington	2 GW
2006	Teofilo	NR
2007	New Approach	3 GW
2008	Mastercraftsman	3 GW
2009	Kingsfort	1
2010	Pathfork	0
2011	Power	1 GW
2012	Dawn Approach	

As one can see by the list of recent winners, this race is as important as any for figuring out the following year's top performers. For instance New Approach was outstanding when winning the Derby, the Champion Stakes and the Irish Champion, Mastercraftsman managed a couple of Group One wins at 3 yrs and last year Power won the Irish 2,000 Gns. Dawn Approach looks sure to enhance his reputation (and that of his sire) by winning further races in Group 1 company this year.

Racing Post Trophy Doncaster, 8 furlongs, October.		
2000	Dilshaan	1 GW
2001	High Chapparal	5 GW
2002	Brian Boru	1 GW
2003	American Post	3 GW
2004	Motivator	2 GW
2005	Palace Episode	0
2006	Authorized	3 GW
2007	Ibn Khaldun	0
2008	Crowded House	0
2009	St Nicholas Abbey	0
2010	Casamento	1 GW
2011	Camelot	3 GW
2012	Kingsbarns	

Some notable performers have won this race, including the outstanding colt High Chaparral, the Derby heroes Motivator and Authorized (both by Montjeu – also the sire of St Nicholas Abbey) and of course last year's 2,000 Guineas and Derby hero Camelot. Kingsbarns looks likely to win another Group 1 event this season at up to a mile and a half.

Haynes, Hanson and Clark Stakes Newbury, 8 furlongs, September.		
2000	Nayef	4 GW
2001	Fight Your Corner	1 GW
2002	Saturn	0
2003	Elshadi	0
2004	Merchant	NR
2005	Winged Cupid	NR
2006	Teslin	2
2007	Centennial	2 GW
2008	Taameer	0
2009	Ameer	0
2010	Moriarty	0
2011	Cavaleiro	0
2012	Wentworth	

The high-class horses Rainbow Quest, Unfuwain, King's Theatre and Nayef have all won this race and indeed Shergar won it in 1980, but it's been a while since those glory days although Centennial did manage two Group race wins in 2008. Wentworth will win more races in 2013 – quite possibly at Group level.

Fillies' Mile Ascot, 8 furlongs, September.		
2000	Crystal Music	0
2001	Gossamer	1 GW
2002	Soviet Song	0
2003	Red Bloom	1 GW
2004	Playful Act	1 GW
2005	Nannina	1 GW
2006	Simply Perfect	1 GW
2007	Listen	0
2008	Rainbow View	1 GW
2009	Hibaayeb	2 GW
2010	White Moonstone	NR
2011	Lyric of Light	0
2012	Certify	

A very strong race in terms of seeking out future Group winners. Gossamer and Soviet Song are the standouts here, although the latter had to wait until after her 4-y-o career before reaching her full potential. Hibaayib won the Ribblesdale Stakes and then crossed the Atlantic to win the Grade 1 Yellow Ribbon. Certify has a tough task ahead of her if she's to remain unbeaten by winning the Guineas, but she's very smart and can give a good account of herself in more Group 1 events at around a mile.

Somerville Tattersall Stakes Newmarket, 7 furlongs, September/October.		
2000	King Charlemagne	3 GW
2001	Where Or When	2 GW
2002	Governor Brown	NR
2003	Milk It Mick	0
2004	Diktatorial	0
2005	Aussie Rules	2 GW
2006	Thousand Words	0
2007	River Proud	1
2008	Ashram	2
2009	Sir Parky	0
2010	Rerouted	0
2011	Crius	0
2012	Havana Gold	

The Group winners speak for themselves but Milk It Mick also went on to win a Grade 1 in America as a five-year-old. Aussie Rules took the French 2,000 Guineas and also won a Grade 1 event in the America. Both River Proud and Ashram won listed races in their 3-y-o season. Havana Gold has already proved he stays a mile and he can win again at distances around that trip.

Killavullan Stakes.
Leopardstown, 7 furlongs October.

2000	Perigee Moon	0
2001	Stonemason	0
2002	New South Wales	1
2003	Grey Swallow	2 GW
2004	Footstepsinthesand	1 GW
2005	Frost Giant	1 GW
2006	Confuchias	1 GW
2007	Jupiter Pluvius	0
2008	Rayeni	1
2009	Free Judgement	1 GW
2010	Dubai Prince	1
2011	Nephrite	0
2012	Big Break	

The most notable performers here are the Irish Derby winner Grey Swallow and the English 2,000 Guineas winner Footstepsinthesand. Big Break is a very smart filly and I feel she can win further Group races up to ten furlongs this year.

Rockfel Stakes, 7 furlongs, Newmarket.

2000	Sayedah	0
2001	Distant Valley	0
2002	Luvah Girl	1 in USA
2003	Cairns	0
2004	Maids Causeway	1 GW
2005	Speciosa	1 GW
2006	Finsceal Beo	2 GW
2007	Kitty Matcham	0
2008	Lahaleeb	2 GW
2009	Music Show	2 GW
2010	Cape Dollar	0
2011	Wading	0
2012	Just The Judge	

Three Newmarket 1,000 Guineas winners have hailed from the winners of this race since 1999 – Lahan, Speciosa and Finsceal Beo. For good measure Maids Causeway won the Coronation Stakes and Hula Angel won the Irish 1,000

Guineas (a race Finsceal Beo also added to her tally). The Mick Channon trained pair Lahaleeb and Music Show both went on to record Group 1 successes. Expect Just The Judge to do the same.

Beresford Stakes, Curragh, 1m.

2000	Turnberry Isle	0
2001	Castle Gandolfo	1
2002	Alamshar	3 GW
2003	Azamour	2 GW
2004	Albert Hall	0
2005	Septimus	1 GW
2006	Eagle Mountain	1 GW
2007	Curtain Call	1
2008	Sea The Stars	6 GW
2009	St Nicholas Abbey	0
2010	Casamento	1 GW
2011	David Livingston	0
2012	Battle of Marengo	

John Oxx must be very fond of this race because he's trained Sea The Stars, Alamshar and Azamour to win it and they've all subsequently hit the headlines as three-year-olds. Among the others, Eagle Mountain also went on to win as a 4-y-o in a Group 1 event (in Hong Kong) and Curtain Call won a Group 3 event at that age. Battle Of Marengo looks to have the Derby in his sights and given the stable's record at Epsom he'll be a tough nut to crack should he turn up.

Acomb Stakes, York, 7 furlongs, August.

2000	Hemingway	NR
2001	Comfy	NR
2002	Bourbonnais	0
2003	Rule Of Law	2 GW
2004	Elliots World	1
2005	Palace Episode	0
2006	Big Timer	0
2007	Fast Company	0
2008	ABANDONED	
2009	Elusive Pimpernel	1 GW
2010	Waiter's Dream	NR
2011	Entifaadha	0
2012	Dundonnell	

There have been a few disappointing seasons since the victories in the 90's of King's Best (2,000 Guineas) and Bijou d'Inde (St James's Palace Stakes), but Rule Of Law turned things around in 2004 with his St Leger victory and Elusive Pimpernel was successful in the Group 3 Craven Stakes. After winning this Dundonnell ran well to finish fourth in the Breeders Cup Juvenile and I expect him to win further Group races, quite possibly a Group 1, this season.

Two-Year-Old Maiden for Colts & Geldings Newbury Lockinge Meeting, 6 furlongs, May.		
2000	Patsy's Double	1
2001	Amour Sans Fin	0
2002	Cap Ferrat	2
2003	Grand Reward	1
2004	Iceman	0
2005	Championship Point	1
	To Sender	0
2006	Major Cadeaux	1 GW
2007	Coasting	NR
2008	Instalment	1
	Orizaba	0
2009	Canford Cliffs	3 GW
	Meglio Ancora	0
2010	Memen (Div 1)	0
	Strong Suit (Div 11)	3 GW
2011	Wise Venture	0
2012	Sir Patrick Moore	

One of the season's first six furlong 2-y-o maidens, it regularly attracts a high quality field with plenty of winners going on to future success. Richard Hannon trained winners have regularly gone on to Group success and Canford Cliffs in particular is a standout here. Sir Patrick Moore can win again, possibly at listed or Group 3 level.

7 furlong 2-y-o maiden at Newmarket's July Meeting (formerly the Strutt & Parker Maiden).		
2001	Dubai Destination	0
2002	Tycoon Hall	0
2003	Josephus	0
2004	Belenus	2 GW
2005	Gin Jockey	0
2006	Kalgoorlie	0
2007	Rio De La Plata	0
2008	Soul City	0
2009	Elusive Pimpernel	1 GW
2010	Native Khan	1 GW

2011	Rougemont	0
2012	Ghurair	

Although the statistics don't look that encouraging it should be noted that six out of the last ten winners went on to group success as older horses. Most notably, Dubai Destination took the Group 1 Queen Anne as a 4-y-o and Rio De La Plata was five before he won a pair of Group One's in Italy. Ghurair is a promising colt and he can win more races for champion trainer John Gosden.

Superlative Stakes Newmarket, 7 furlongs, July.		
2000	Vacamonte	NR
2001	Redback	1 GW
2002	Surbiton	NR
2003	Kings Point	0
2004	Dubawi	2 GW
2005	Horatio Nelson	0
2006	Halicarnasus	3 GW
2007	Hatta Fort	2 GW (in USA)
2008	Ole Ole	NR
2009	Silver Grecian	0
2010	King Torus	2
2011	Red Duke	0
2012	Olympic Glory	

This race was raised to Group 2 from Group 3 in 2006. The statistics are somewhat impacted by the winner being regularly sold to go abroad, but there are some very decent winners in this list, notably Dubawi of course. Olympic Glory, winner of the Greenham Stakes, will contest the French 2,000 Gns next and he's likely to go close.

Trundle Maiden, Glorious Goodwood, 7 furlongs.		
2000		
2001	Sweet Band	0
2002	Wahsheeq	0
2003	Psychiatrist	0
2004	Jonquil	0
2005	Opera Cape	0
2006	Kilburn	0
2007	Latin Lad	0
2008	Jukebox Jury	3 GW

2009	Stags Leap	1
2010	Pausanias	1 Listed
2011	Nawwaar	0
2012	Steeler	

This was once a reliable maiden where numerous quality horses made their debuts in 70's, 80's and early 90's. Results from 2001 show that the quality of winner has declined markedly, but there have been signs of an up turn recently. Steeler is well named and his battling qualities will help him win more races.

Horse Index

Miyachiku 452
Mizzou 370
Mocacha 713
Mollasses 1325
Momentus 1409
Mon Cigar 332
Monet Monet Monet 1316
Monsieur Blanc 333
Montaigne 80
Moonspring 344
Moontime 567
Morning Watch 210
Mount Cheiron 1115
Mount Logan 371
Mountain Fighter 600
Mountain Kingdom 1359
Moutai 1608
Mr Dandy Man 908
Mr Smith 637
Mr Wickfield 126
Much Promise 638
Muhawalah 1555
Muheed 833
Muir Lodge 39
Mumtaza 834
Munatas 1556
Munfallet 835
Munjally 836
Musalaha 453
Mushir 1557
Mushtammel 1523
Musical Comedy 837
Musicora 838
Muspelheim 435
Mustajeeb 1654
Mustajjid 1558
Mutakayyef 714
Mutalaba 996
Mutamakkin 839
Mutawathea 840
Muteela 997
My My My Diliza 1156
My Painter 943
My Titania 1279

Naadirr 160
Nabatean 40
Namely 1360
Nancy From Nairobi 257
Narborough 258
Nathr 944
Nectar De Rose 1280

Neighbother 521
Nelson's Pride 1384
Nevada Blue 356
Neveroddoreven 81
New Row 971
New Street 522
Next Bend 1655
Nictate 211
Nidhaam 1656
Night Party 601
Night Song 639
Nimble Kimble 497
Nissaki Kasta 1168
No Easy Day 1410
Noble Metal 294
Nonchalant 1657
Norse Legend 1048
Norse Star 1022
Nos Galan 841
Notebook 715
Novel Approach 147

Oasis Fantasy 454
Observational 321
Obsidian 640
Obstinate 41
Ocean Storm 1488
Oh Star 641
Oklahoma City 1222
Old Guard 322
Olymnia 486
On Demand 42
One Chance 1317
One Pixel 1042
Onenightidreamed 1435
Online Alexander 1385
Oracle Boy 1180
Orayda 842
Oriel 843
Orkney Island 568
Orton Park 345
Our Queenie 844
Outback Lover 1157
Outback Traveller 1201
Outlawed 1609
Overdrive 523
Overpower 1453
Oxlip 845
Oxsana 716

Pack Leader 1314
Packet Station 1090
Pageant Belle 323

Pantoloni 569
Paparima 673
Par Three 899
Parbold 524
Party Ruler 401
Passionate Affair 402
Patisserie 436
Patterned 372
Pay The Greek 1376
Peacemaker 980
Pearl Spectre 43
Pembrokeshire 998
Penhill 135
Peniaphobia 525
Penny Drops 717
Penny Sixpence 642
Percybelle 1043
Perfect Light 718
Peril 212
Persian Bolt 981
Personal Opinion 570
Petale Noir 1326
Petite Madame 437
Phoenix Angel 1395
Photography 1297
Piazon 109
Picanight 982
Piccadilly Jim 526
Pick Pocket 373
Pigeon Pie 999
Pink Dance 295
Pinzolo 571
Pipe Dream 1116
Pirita 1658
Pit Stop 746
Pivotal Bride 1466
Pixie Hollow 1338
Placidia 1057
Poetic Justice 1049
Polar Express 1327
Polish Ballet 342
Political Policy 747
Ponfeigh 1281
Pool House 44
Popping Candy 1559
Port Merrion 900
Posset 213
Postal Order 498
Postponed 374
Prairie Prize 491
Premium Pressure 62
Pretzel 1058
Primitorio 82
Prince Of Stars 643
Princess Hanane 334
Princess Noor 1560

Princess Rose 719
Princess Youmzain 1282
Printha 148
Prisca 846
Privado 1396
Prize 847
Proclamationofwar 1386
Prophet's Thumb 214
Prudent Approach 149
Psiloveyou 644
Pupil 848
Purple Spot 1525
Pushkar 215
Pyjama Day 1298

Qaffaal 1467
Qawaasem 945
Quaintrelle 1587
Quantum Dot 403
Quasqazah 1561
Quatuor 404
Queen Catrine 946
Queen Of The Nile 1623
Queen Of The Tarts 1454
Queenie's Home 543
Quickaswecan 1000

Raajis 849
Race Hunter 63
Racing's Dream 1117
Radiator 1468
Ragged Robbin 1059
Raging Bob 83
Rainbow Lollipop 1060
Randwick 947
Rapid Advance 1562
Rapunzal 194
Ravenous 84
Real Jazz 1361
Red Bandana 1339
Red Oasis 487
Red Passiflora 1362
Red Velour 1202
Redkirk 720
Redlorryyellowlorry 13
Regardez 85
Rehanaat 455
Relentless Pursuit 1074

Dams index